# READING,

# THINKING,

# AND WRITING

# WITH SOURCES

# READING,

# THINKING,

# AND WRITING

# WITH SOURCES

## Patrick J. Slattery
University of Arkansas at Fayetteville

## Susan R. Carlton
University of Michigan at Ann Arbor

MACMILLAN PUBLISHING COMPANY
New York

Editor: Barbara A. Heinssen
Production Supervisor: Ann-Marie WongSam
Production Manager: Nicholas Sklitsis
Text Designer: Linda M. Robertson
Cover Designer: Tom Mack
Cover Illustration: Tom Vitou

This book was set in Plantin and Helvetica by Publication Services, Inc.
and was printed and bound by R.R. Donnelley & Sons Company.
The cover was printed by Phoenix Color Corp.

Acknowledgments appear on pages 392–394, which constitute a continuation of
the copyright page.

Copyright ©1993 by Macmillan Publishing Company,
a division of Macmillan, Inc.

Printed in the United States of America

Macmillan Publishing Company
866 Third Avenue, New York, New York 10022

Macmillan Publishing Company is part of
the Maxwell Communication Group of Companies.

Maxwell Macmillan Canada, Inc.
1200 Eglinton Avenue East
Suite 200
Don Mills, Ontario M3C 3N1

Library of Congress Cataloging-in-Publication Data

Slattery, Patrick J., 1959–
    Reading, thinking, and writing with Sources / Patrick J. Slattery,
Susan R. Carlton.
        p.   cm.
    Includes index.
    ISBN 0-02-411561-4
    1. English language—Rhetoric.   2. Critical thinking.   3. College
readers.   I. Carlton, Susan R.   II. Title.
    PE1408.S565   1993
    808'.042—dc20         92-16974
                        CIP

Printing: 1 2 3 4 5 6 7     Year: 3 4 5 6 7 8 9

W e wrote *Reading, Thinking, and Writing with Sources* to aid college students with the reading, thinking, and writing processes associated with academic discourse. Because teachers across the curriculum often assign papers on complex topics, undergraduates are required to use multiple, and sometimes contradictory, sources of written information. College instructors typically expect their students to summarize, quote, paraphrase, and document sources correctly; to synthesize, analyze, and evaluate several authors' ideas reflectively; and to justify an original argument persuasively. A college composition course that uses *Reading, Thinking, and Writing with Sources* can help students successfully tackle these challenging writing tasks. The textbook is designed specifically for freshman and sophomore composition courses on writing from sources, academic writing, research writing, and writing across the curriculum but could also work well in argumentative writing classes.

The book's important features include:

- an emphasis on reading empathetically and analytically, so students learn how to understand the feelings and ideas that motivate an author's argument as well as how to evaluate it critically

- a case-study approach allowing students to follow the development of one student's writing process from prewriting through editing and documenting of an argumentative, multiple-source paper

- process-oriented instruction in drafting and revising that moves students from essay-level concerns to the paragraph, sentence, and word levels of their prose

- cross-disciplinary readings that reflect a variety of viewpoints on current, provocative topics

- a research chapter designed to teach students how to use tools such as computer databases, subject indexes, and interviews, how to document sources according to MLA and APA styles, and how to avoid plagiarism

- questions and exercises for both individual and collaborative learning situations.

## The Importance of Reading for Empathy and Analysis

Although college writing assignments often call for an argumentative response to sources, *Reading, Thinking, and Writing with Sources* instructs students first to read empathetically—that is, receptively and even sympathetically—because people need to appreciate the feelings and ideas that motivate an author's viewpoint before they can evaluate it effectively. The textbook, for example, teaches paraphrasing, quoting, and summarizing as methods for integrating information into essays but also as opportunities for reading with empathy. We believe empathetic reading can help students understand writers' views more fully and represent them more accurately.

However, students will have difficulty succeeding in college unless they are also taught how to make sound judgments about the competing positions found in sources. Therefore, we also focus much of the text on how to evaluate conflicting ideas, emphasizing comparison and synthesis—thinking processes that can help students analyze competing points of view. For example, our section on evidence and reasoning presents and explains a series of questions that students can ask themselves to determine which authors' arguments are more rational or more fully supported. But we also discuss strategies that will help students acknowledge the limitations of their own arguments, believing that reflective judgments are always contingent upon reevaluation.

## A Case-Study Approach

To illustrate the reading, thinking, and writing processes explained throughout the textbook, we offer an extended case study, closely following one student, Jane, as she completes several typical, college-level assignments: a formal summary, a summary-response essay, a synthesis paper, and an argumentative essay based on several sources. In addition to these student papers, the case study includes Jane's writing log entries—which illustrate processes for reading and thinking, and her rough drafts—which illustrate strategies for writing and revising.

Furthermore, all the sources Jane consults are provided within the text, so students can see exactly how she uses them to develop her paper. Writing about surrogate motherhood—a topic through which many disciplines intersect—Jane draws from articles that take biological, psychological, legal, ethical, sociological, and feminist approaches. As she reads these sources, makes her log entries, and completes the paper assignments, Jane moves from a dogmatic position on surrogate motherhood to a more informed and reflective perspective on the topic, offering students an excellent vantage point from which to observe the relationship of reading, thinking, and writing.

## An Emphasis on Writing as Process

*Reading, Thinking, and Writing with Sources* explains analysis and evaluation as it instructs students in drafting and revising: When students consider the audience of a paper they can begin to work out the details and implications of their arguments, slightly modifying or even drastically changing their theses. Our material on drafting an argumentative paper offers advice on considering audience and then on formulating a thesis statement, integrating information from sources, and organizing a rough draft. In the section on revising, students move from these essay-level concerns to the paragraph, sentence, and word levels of their prose, focusing on introductions, conclusions, topic sentences, transition sentences, strong verbs, and nonsexist language.

## Readings on Topics from Across the Disciplines

We also include additional readings that provide opportunities for students to read, think, and write about a topic in business (advertising), in natural science (waste management), and in social science (sports culture). Chosen to discourage the absolutist, right–wrong thinking that pro/con articles can elicit, the essays in this textbook reflect divergent points of view on complex topics. The selections on waste management, for example, invite students to analyze several proposed options for handling the solid waste crisis—landfills, incinerators, recycling programs, and waste reduction—and present case studies of New York City and Seattle.

## A Focus on Research

To help students find their own sources, we begin with how to use the research process to identify and brainstorm topics. *Reading, Thinking, and Writing with Sources* also guides students in how to use card catalogs, computer databases, discipline-specific indexes, and interviews. Furthermore, the text thoroughly covers plagiarism and the use of MLA and APA documentation styles. Reflecting our concern with empathy, the information on interviewing instructs students to create a safe environment in which the people being interviewed do not fear disapproval, and all the research strategies and documentation conventions are illustrated by detailed examples.

## Questions and Exercises

Following the case-study student's log entries and drafts are exercises that invite students to apply the tactics she illustrates. For example, after studying the marginal annotations that Jane makes on one of the articles she uses, students are encouraged to annotate one of the other essays included in the textbook. The readings on surrogate motherhood and advertising are followed by questions for reading, synthesizing, and analyzing the multiple perspectives on these topics. And because the group projects that college teachers assign in upper-level courses often require students to work closely as well as independently, many of our research exercises stress collaboration.

## ACKNOWLEDGMENTS

As our textbook progressed from its first rough draft to its published form, we benefitted from the thoughtful responses of several reviewers: Larry Beason, Eastern Washington University; Lance Bertelsen, University of Texas at Austin; Jeanne Cutler, University of Nebraska at Kearney; Carol Klimick Cyganowski, De Paul University; Albert C. DeCiccio, Merrimack College; Joyce R. Durham, University of Dayton; Philip H. Kelly, Gannon University; Mary Lynch Kennedy, State University of New York at Cortland; Phoebe A. Mainster, Wayne State University; Helen C. Othow, St. Augustine's College; Mary Rosner, University of Louisville; David E. Schwalm, Arizona State University; Mary Trachsel, University of Iowa; and Linda Woodson, University of Texas at San Antonio. At the University of Michigan Library, Bob Diaz and Lynn Westbrook provided helpful information on accessing library sources.

Barbara A. Heinssen, Senior English Editor, encouraged the book initially and made intelligent suggestions throughout our writing process; Ellie Eisenstat, Assistant Editor, saw the project through to closure. We thank them, Ann-Marie WongSam, Production Supervisor, and Linda Robertson, Book Designer, for making our association with Macmillan congenial and productive.

We also owe thanks to the scholars whose articles and books inform *Reading, Thinking, and Writing with Sources*. We draw from Barry M. Kroll's work on conceptual orientation and composition and, as we explain in the introductory chapter, from Mary Belenky, Blythe Clinchy, Nancy Goldberger, and Jill Tarule's exploration of women's ways of knowing; Peter Elbow's ideas about the believing and doubting games; Linda Flower and John Hayes's theory of problem solving; Mary Lynch Kennedy's research on writing from sources; and Nancy Sommers's case study of revision strategies.

Finally, we thank our students, whose struggles and successes with academic discourse played the most important role in shaping *Reading, Thinking, and Writing with Sources.* To our students we dedicate this book.

Patrick J. Slattery
University of Arkansas at Fayetteville

Susan R. Carlton
University of Michigan at Ann Arbor

# CONTENTS

## Chapter Eight
## READING FOR FURTHER ANALYSIS    303

# Chapter One

# UNDERSTANDING

# COLLEGE WRITING

*No man is an island, entire of itself; every man is a piece of the continent, a part of the main.*

*John Donne*

"No man is an island," wrote John Donne in the seventeenth century, and what was true then is even more true for men and women in contemporary society. Today, we rely extensively on collective wisdom because we are able to retrieve and expand the information that others have stored in libraries and on computer systems. The solitary writer, hunched over a plumed stylus in a garret, spinning out ideas with the originality and creativity of a god, is a mythical figure. Although some writers have worked alone, no writer has ever thought alone: The language and thought of each individual reflect an accumulation of received knowledge, a collection of voices. No writer has ever been an island.

## ■ ■ ■ ■ ■ THE SOCIAL DIMENSION OF COLLEGE WRITING

We have designed this textbook to help you with the social dimension of college writing. Typically, college-level writing assignments require you to base papers not only on personal or individual experiences but also on the ideas of others found in sources such as textbooks, library books, journal articles, lecture notes, and even interviews and films. By analyzing the ideas in sources, you can reflectively form your own beliefs and justify them

1

to an audience, adding your informed viewpoint to the many voices that surround you.

Most teachers know that one generation does not simply hand down information to the next one, and therefore they expect students not only to summarize but also to analyze and evaluate what they read. In an English class, for example, a teacher may ask you to read several published interpretations of Robert Frost's poem, "Stopping by Woods on a Snowy Evening," and to evaluate these multiple interpretations in light of your own understanding of the poem. In fulfilling such an assignment, you will probably discover that literary critics seldom agree on any single reading of a poem but offer a variety of insights and arguments to support their differing interpretations. Similarly, an assignment for a history class may require you to find and read several newspaper articles that offer varying reasons for the Allied ground attack in the Persian Gulf War. Your history professor may ask you to write a paper that analyzes the journalists' various arguments and defends one of their positions or a paper that offers your own position. For a psychology course, an instructor may have you read textbook chapters on Sigmund Freud's and Erik Erickson's theories of psychological development and write an essay that compares and evaluates their theories. Or, in an anthropology course, a writing task may require you to read several articles about the gift-giving customs in various cultures, to observe firsthand the customs in your own culture, and to write a paper that compares your observations to the arguments in your readings.

Furthermore, at the urging of your teachers or on your own initiative, you may write college papers that cut across disciplines. For example, while taking a history course about the Holocaust, you may find that the books and articles you read about Hitler and his regime give you new insights into George Orwell's *1984,* a fictional creation of a totalitarian state that you are reading for an English class. Interdisciplinary writing often draws from various kinds of sources, making interesting and creative connections. As you can see from these examples, college writing assignments are not merely perfunctory tasks that you must fulfill to earn a passing grade. Because these assignments provide you with an opportunity to read about important issues and encourage you to decide what you think about them, college writing is a dynamic process of learning and discovery.

DISCUSSION QUESTION
Even though you usually compose college papers alone in your room or the library, writing academic essays is still a social act. Explain what makes multiple-source writing social.

■ ■ ■ ■ ■ PRIMARY AND SECONDARY SOURCES

In reading and writing for any of the various disciplines in college, you can use primary and secondary sources, but definitions of "primary" and "secondary" differ according to discipline. Generally, *primary sources* are events or objects that researchers contemplate directly. In the natural and physical sciences, researchers usually conduct empirical studies, relying on controlled laboratory experiments; the observations and data from such research are primary sources. Researchers in the social sciences rely on empirical studies, too, but their primary sources can include statistical data and personal interviews as well as direct observations of experiments. For example, a sociologist studying the causes of suicide in New York City may gather statistics on the frequency of suicide in different age groups, sexes, races, or neighborhoods and also interview family members of suicide victims or survivors of suicide attempts. In the humanities, methods of inquiry are much less empirical, and primary sources are usually products of human thought, such as philosophical texts, paintings, musical scores, historical documents, or works of literature.

Generally, *secondary sources*, which also differ according to discipline, are *about* some object of study. In English, secondary sources include published critical interpretations of a work of literature; for example, a journal article about Robert Frost's "Stopping by Woods on a Snowy Evening" is a secondary source about a primary source, a poem. In historical research, a film, even a documentary about the Persian Gulf War or the Holocaust, is a secondary source because the producers have studied and interpreted an event, offering an argument or point of view about it. Alain Resnais's film about the Holocaust, *Night and Fog,* which combines scenes of deserted concentration camps and footage of actual victims living in the camps, is a secondary source about a historical event. In most studies, especially in the natural and physical sciences, researchers consult secondary sources before focusing on primary ones. For example, before botanists or sociologists begin their primary research, they read broadly in secondary sources to know what other scientists have written and to build on past knowledge. The distinction between primary and secondary sources, however, is not always clear. You might use the work of a historian as a primary rather than a secondary source if you are studying the methods and theories that Thomas Macaulay used to write *History of England from the Accession of James the Second* in the nineteenth century.

Academic writing assignments can call for using primary or secondary sources. Professors will sometimes ask you to compare primary sources, such as two short stories or two campaign speeches. More often, however, college writing involves secondary sources such as articles and books about an event or a primary object of study. Whether you use primary sources, secondary sources, or a combination of the two, academic writing is a social process because it reveals a community of thinkers who have addressed the same question from different perspectives and it allows you, the student, to join this community.

**DISCUSSION QUESTION**     What is the distinction between primary and secondary sources? Is Thomas Macaulay's *History of England* primary, secondary, or both? Explain your answer.

The social act of writing from sources involves two broad types of thinking processes—those that help you to understand the divergent viewpoints of other writers and those that help you to analyze and evaluate these different perspectives. College writing also involves two general types of writing processes—those that help you to compose rough drafts and those that help you to revise them. The rest of this introductory chapter gives an overview of these processes and the primary objectives of this textbook, briefly referring to some of the composition research and theory on which they are based.

## ■ ■ ■ ■ ■  THINKING PROCESSES

Peter Elbow, a well-known and highly respected expert on the teaching of writing, believes that colleges and universities teach students to read critically but not receptively. And it is our experience, too, that college teachers and textbooks encourage students mainly to test authors' beliefs and to challenge their arguments. As Elbow explains in *Writing Without Teachers*, the tradition of Western rationalism encourages students to play the "doubting game" instead of the "believing game." The doubting game, writes Elbow, "has gained a monopoly on legitimacy in our culture" (150). In fact, the mathematician and philosopher René Descartes, whom many people herald for ushering in the modern age of Western European philosophy, based an entire theory of knowledge on systematic doubting. Descartes wondered what he could know for certain if he proceeded to doubt everything, and he concluded that the only thing he could know absolutely was "I think, therefore I am." Belief in God, in the reality of the world, in everything except his own existence, fell under the scythe of his systematic doubt. Despite this tendency in Western thought to play the doubting game, Elbow urges college writers to get "inside the head of someone" whose argument they do not believe (149). According to Elbow, "Your belief in Y will become more trustworthy only if you can get *yourself* to really believe X. If you can really do that and come back to Y and find Y better again, then at least you have attained leverage. Your knowledge of Y is at least much more trustworthy" (164). In other words, to evaluate someone's argument legitimately and effectively, you must first explore, understand, even believe it.

In a sociopsychological study entitled *Women's Ways of Knowing*, Mary Belenky, Blythe Clinchy, Nancy Goldberger, and Jill Tarule distinguish between "separate" and "connected" ways of knowing, which at least in some ways resemble Elbow's notions of doubting and believing. According to Belenky, Clinchy, Goldberger, and Tarule, when separate knowers confront an argumentative proposition, they "immediately look for something wrong—a loophole, a factual error, a logical contradiction, the omission of contrary evidence" (104). In contrast, connected knowers "develop procedures for gaining access to other people's knowledge," trying to understand and share the experiences that have led them to their beliefs (113). Separate knowers, who are tough-minded and adversarial, judge people immediately; connected knowers, who are empathetic, first exercise care. Much like Elbow, who argues that schools emphasize doubting over believing, Belenky, Clinchy, Goldberger, and Tarule believe that colleges and universities typically privilege separate ways of knowing. The authors of *Women's Ways of Knowing* also suggest, however, that women tend to develop their sense of self in terms of relationships with other people—their children, parents, and friends—and therefore to develop connected ways of knowing. Because separate knowing monopolizes academic institutions, Belenky, Clinchy, Goldberger, and Tarule further argue that college women can become alienated from school and in turn experience a loss of voice. In this textbook, we try to help you balance connected and separate ways of knowing, to play the believing game before playing the doubting game.

## Reading with Empathy

Whether you are writing a history, sociology, or economics paper, you will find it helpful to play the believing game when reading sources for the first time. Try to enter imaginatively into the authors' frames of reference, appreciating the feelings and insights that motivate writers to argue as they do. Try to read so that your own biases and personal experiences do not interfere with your ability to understand a different point of view. This is reading with empathy. As Carl Rogers, a well-known psychotherapist, has observed, when people hear arguments that threaten their own values or beliefs, they tend to block some information out, understanding only part of what is said. A kind of defense mechanism, this blocking reduces a listener's, or a reader's, level of anxiety. Rogers found that patients in group therapy who could demonstrate that they understood another person's point of view, even when that view threatened their own, were far more likely to influence the thoughts and actions of other patients. To understand divergent points of view is especially important when you write argumentative papers based on sources; simply reading a source by no means guarantees that you will understand the points an author tries to make. Readers' prejudices and personal experiences act as filtering devices, influencing their interpretation of a text. If you read sources to find support for your own opinions rather than to explore different perspectives, you may cling to written passages that confirm your assumptions and miss ideas that challenge your point of view. If your biases lead you to assume that an author's point of view is "wrong" before you have read and thought about it empathetically, you can tend to focus on what you perceive to be the source's faults and risk misinterpreting and ultimately misrepresenting what the author is actually trying to say.

Because of its social dimension, academic writing demands that you try to understand divergent perspectives on a topic before reaching your own decisions about it—that you read with empathy. In Chapter Two, we explain and illustrate several specific strategies that can help you read with empathy: probing your own assumptions and biases, annotating a text, paraphrasing sources, and summarizing sources.

## Analyzing Different Points of View

If you read with empathy, trying to understand and appreciate authors' perspectives, then you will find it much easier to analyze varying points of view. Even after reading sources empathetically, however, you will probably find it challenging to evaluate the viewpoints reflected. In fact, empathetic reading can cause you to assume that all experts' views are equally valid, an assumption that can make analyzing and evaluating them nearly impossible. However, you can initially read sources to understand the authors' perspectives and ultimately to compare and evaluate them.

College writing often requires you to reflectively reach and persuasively justify your own decisions—to balance the need to explore with the need to judge sources. In Chapter Three, we explain and illustrate several specific strategies that will help you analyze different points of view: synthesizing and comparing multiple perspectives; evaluating authors' evidence, reasoning, and credentials; and recognizing the limitations of your argument. Too many college writers do not spend enough time thinking about the various views expressed in their sources. Rather, they jump immediately into writing their papers.

DISCUSSION
QUESTIONS

What are the "believing" and "doubting" games? How can you play them to understand and evaluate sources in different disciplines?

What is the difference between "separate" and "connected" ways of knowing? In what specific situations do you use separate and connected thinking?

■ ■ ■ ■ ■ WRITING PROCESSES

By learning and practicing the mental processes on which we focus in Chapters Two and Three, you should be able to base your argumentative positions on a thorough understanding and analysis of the ideas reflected in your sources. But because writing processes—the processes involved in composing and revising multiple drafts of an essay—stimulate reflective thinking, do not be surprised if you refine, modify, or even discover your viewpoint while writing. In an essay entitled "Problem-Solving Strategies and the Writing Process," Linda Flower and John Hayes, who have studied the relationship between thinking and writing, suggest that once you sense the purpose of your essay, you should "turn off the editor and brainstorm," using the first draft to articulate ideas rather than to polish prose (454). According to Flower and Hayes, brainstorming has two rules: "Keep writing and don't try to censor or perfect as you go" (454). In other words, if you have an idea or sentence with which you are not completely satisfied, write it down anyway. Just get your ideas down on paper. In writing the initial draft of an essay, then, you need not concern yourself with paragraphing, smooth transitions, sentence style, or grammatical errors. According to Flower and Hayes, once you have composed a rough draft, you can begin to "test your writing against your own editor" (458), reading the draft as if you were seeing it for the first time. If you read only what you have written, avoiding the temptation to skim over or to fill in unclear passages, you can identify and rework the weak parts of your paper, locating passages that seem confusing, awkward, or incorrect (458). Drafting college papers and revising them call for vastly different types of writing processes.

## Drafting a Paper

When drafting a college paper, you can write down your ideas in the words and sentences that readily come to mind. If you feel pressure to turn out a perfect paper in one pass, you will quickly become frustrated. And according to research on multiple-source writing, when students become frustrated with the initial imperfections of their prose, they can start to rely too heavily on the language of their sources. In an essay entitled "The Composing Process of College Students Writing from Sources," Mary Lynch Kennedy explains that the less fluent writers she studied did not reread their sources or take notes on them before beginning to write essays; rather, these writers referred directly to their sources, drawing heavily from them as they wrote papers (449). On the other hand, the more successful college writers in Kennedy's study worked extensively with their sources before beginning to draft their essays. These more fluent writers first read their sources carefully and took notes, and then they reread the notes before beginning to write. When they began to compose their first drafts, the more successful students set their sources aside and worked almost entirely from notes (448–49).

When you compose a rough draft, you have to integrate information from your sources, but, as we suggest in Chapters Two and Three, you can use a writing log to summarize, synthesize, and analyze the various viewpoints on your topic. In Chapter Four, we explain and illustrate strategies that will help you draft a paper: considering your audience, formulating a thesis statement, integrating information from sources, and organizing a rough draft. Once you have composed a draft, then you can turn to refining your ideas and language.

Revising a Paper

Accomplished writers agree that revision is the most important part of the writing process, but less successful writers spend little or no time revising a paper. Nancy Sommers, a composition expert who has conducted research on how writers revise, suggests that many college students understand revision as a rewording activity, a matter of finding the right diction. In an article entitled "Revision Strategies of Student Writers and Experienced Adult Writers," she quotes writers whom she studied. One first-year student reveals, "I don't use the word rewriting because I only write one draft and the changes that I make are made on top of the draft. The changes that I make are usually just marking out words and putting different ones in" (381). This first-year student and many other college writers tend to approach revision with what Sommers calls a "thesaurus philosophy of writing" (381), crossing out words and replacing them with better ones. On the other hand, experienced writers, according to Sommers, generate more drafts and revise their papers on several levels. Sommers quotes one experienced adult writer who explains, "Rewriting means on one level, finding the argument, and on another level, language changes to make the argument more effective. Most of the time I feel as if I can go on rewriting forever" (384). Focusing first on content and organization, successful writers tend to emphasize sentence-level revisions only after they have discovered the form and argumentative thrust of their essays.

You may already have methods for revising words, but in Chapter Four we explain and illustrate revision techniques for paragraphing; writing introductions, conclusions, and transitions; using active verbs; avoiding nominalization; and using nonsexist language.

**DISCUSSION QUESTIONS**

As you write an academic essay, when do you turn off the editor in your head, and when do you turn it on? Why?

While writing college papers, when do you read your sources, and when do you abandon them? Why?

According to research in composition, how do inexperienced and experienced writers tend to approach revision? How do you revise?

In providing an overview of the thinking and writing processes on which this book focuses, we have tended to separate thinking from writing, reading with empathy from analyzing and evaluating different points of view, and composing the first draft from revising your paper. Let us now acknowledge that this model is misleadingly simple. The writing process does not consist of neat and distinct elements or stages. It is a messy process, one that is idiosyncratic to each individual and to each assignment, and we do not want to lull you into thinking that every writer should always follow the procedures we describe. Nonetheless, recent research, contemporary theory, and our own experiences with teaching college composition have taught us that the strategies we emphasize in this book can help you to master college writing. To illustrate how one student uses these reading and writing strategies during the complex process called *composing*, Chapters Two, Three, and Four include a case study of a student named Jane, who writes a multiple-source paper on the complicated and provocative topic of surrogate motherhood. When you read the next three chapters, following Jane as she reads, thinks, and writes about the divergent points of view on surrogate motherhood, try to determine which of her techniques will help you to improve your own writing process.

## WORKS CITED

Belenky, Mary, Blythe Clinchy, Nancy Goldberger, and Jill Tarule. *Women's Ways of Knowing: Development of Self, Voice, and Mind.* New York: Basic Books, 1986.

Elbow, Peter. *Writing Without Teachers.* London: Oxford UP, 1973.

Flower, Linda, and John Hayes. "Problem-Solving Strategies and the Writing Process." *College English* 39 (1977): 449–61.

Kennedy, Mary Lynch. "The Composing Process of College Students Writing from Sources." *Written Communication* 2 (1985): 434–56.

Sommers, Nancy. "Revision Strategies of Student Writers and Experienced Adult Writers." *College Composition and Communication* 31 (1980): 378–88.

# Chapter Two

# READING WITH

# EMPATHY

*At once it struck me what quality went to form a man of achievement especially in literature and which Shakespeare possessed so enormously. I mean Negative Capability, that is, when man is capable of being in uncertainties, mysteries, doubts, without any irritable reaching after fact and reason.*

*John Keats*

In the nineteenth century, John Keats defined "Negative Capability" in a letter he wrote to his brothers, suggesting that people can understand life only by being open-minded, sympathetic, and receptive to the insights of others. According to Keats, we can resist the urge to reach intellectual closure about abstract and complex issues by temporarily negating our prejudices and preconceptions. Although Keats was arguing that the best poets exercise negative capability, as a student you need to do so also. When you read sources, you must learn how to get inside the heads and hearts of other people in order to understand their ideas fully. However, reading with empathy can be very difficult when people confront ideas and positions about which they already have strong opinions. A pro-choice feminist, for example, would probably find it hard to read empathetically about the ideas of a pro-life candidate for public office, but if the feminist reads with empathy, playing the believing game, he or she will better understand the feelings and arguments that motivate the candidate's opinions. The old adage that you should not judge people until you have walked a mile in their shoes is another way of expressing this idea. Reading with empathy, like walking in another's shoes, should precede judgment.

In this chapter you will learn thinking and writing strategies that will help you to explore and understand other people's viewpoints—that is, to read with empathy. You will learn how to probe your own assumptions and biases about a topic and how to annotate, paraphrase, and summarize sources without distorting them. We explain and illustrate these strategies, as well as those emphasized in Chapters Three and Four, through a case study of one student, Jane, who writes a paper on the intellectually challenging and ethically complex topic of surrogate motherhood. We have chosen to use this case study so that you can see exactly how the thinking and writing strategies in Chapters Two, Three, and Four fit into the entire composing process. Our case study consists of many entries that Jane makes in a writing log as she reads her sources on surrogate motherhood, which we include in Chapter Five. A writing log is simply a journal in which you keep notes about your sources and work through ideas for your paper. For example, after reading and annotating an article, you can paraphrase its main ideas in order to understand the author's argument better. And, as you will see, you can also use a writing log to make connections among several sources. We suggest that you buy a notebook to use as a writing log and that for each of your essays you make entries in it like those that Jane makes in her log.

■ ■ ■ ■ ■  PROBING YOUR OWN ASSUMPTIONS
AND BIASES

In Jane's first entry in her writing log, she acknowledges her preconceptions about surrogate motherhood, probing the assumptions and biases she has about the topic. Although it will sometimes be difficult to externalize preconceptions about a topic, you should try consciously to know how you feel about it before beginning to read any sources. You cannot will your own assumptions and biases out of existence, but if you know what they are and how you developed them, you will be better able to read your sources not with the purpose of criticizing the authors' ideas or of finding evidence to support your own position, but with the purpose of exploring and understanding what the authors really say. You can probe your initial thoughts about a topic by thinking about your current position on it and by reflecting on how you reached that point of view. Begin by asking yourself the following questions:

1. What is my current opinion about the topic?
2. How does this opinion reflect my religious background, political affiliation, or personal experiences?
3. How does my point of view reflect what I have heard my parents or friends say, what I have read, or what I have seen on television?

To answer these questions, write an entry in your writing log that explains what your current perspective is on the topic about which you are writing and how you reached this point of view. In the following passage from Jane's writing log, in which she probes her preliminary thoughts about the topic of surrogate motherhood, notice how she concerns herself not with writing polished prose but with honestly expressing her own ideas.

## CASE STUDY

There are the numerous cases where the surrogate mother decides that she wants to keep the child for her own. This must really hurt the couple who hired her. But it's her child too. In these cases the issues are very complicated. But it's the surrogate mother who really carries the baby, why can't she be allowed to do with it as she pleases? The legality of it. Oh, I don't know. I would have to say that it should be legal. Like I said before, it's a surrogate mother who carries the baby, it's hers to decide what to do with it. No one questions a wife's decision to carry her husband's child, why should they question a woman's decision to carry someone else's, even for money. If both parties are willing, then yes it should be legal. It's no one else's business. The fact that it's even questioned seems ridiculous once I start thinking about it.

My view on surrogate motherhood comes from newspaper and magazine articles and also television. In "Baby M" the judge gave *the child to the infertile couple rather than the surrogate mother, I'm sure this decision influenced my feelings. However, my family has had the largest impact on my views. My mother is a feminist, I'm sure she's had a big influence on how I see this topic.*

Making this preliminary entry in her writing log, Jane realizes that although she has not yet begun to research the topic of surrogate motherhood, she already has some preconceived notions about it. As her log entry indicates, she can understand why an infertile couple would hire a woman to carry and give birth to a child. However, Jane's true sympathy lies with the surrogate mother, whom she believes should be able to birth a child in exchange for money but also to keep the baby if she chooses to do so. Furthermore, Jane realizes that she developed this view in part from following the highly publicized "Baby M" case on television and in newspapers and magazines and in part from adopting some of her mother's feminist values. These acknowledgments can help Jane to recognize her assumptions and biases—to realize that she needs to work at understanding the authors who argue for limiting the rights of surrogate mothers or for banning surrogacy. Once you acknowledge your own opinion about a topic, you too will have a better chance of fully understanding the other viewpoints and arguments you read.

EXERCISE

1. After obtaining a notebook to use as a writing log, write an entry in which you probe your own assumptions and biases about surrogate motherhood (the topic of the readings included in Chapter Five), advertising (the topic of the readings included in Chapter Six), or a topic of your choice, explaining what you think about the topic and how you reached that point of view. Do not worry about writing polished prose. Just try to be honest.

■ ■ ■ ■ ■   ANNOTATING A TEXT

Annotating a text will also help you to understand the divergent perspectives reflected in your sources. *Annotating* means responding to the source by writing in its margins. Although annotations can be either of a connected, believing nature or of a separate, doubting nature, your initial annotations should be empathetic—that is, they should help you to understand a text and not to critique or judge it. The suggestion to annotate sources empathetically might strike you as odd; most academic writing, after all, tends to be rational and argumentative, which seems to suggest that an analytical response is in order. But your first reading should be one in which you do not project anything negative from yourself onto the text, because to evaluate a viewpoint well you must first try to understand it as fully as possible. If you project anything at all in your first reading of an article, make it an attitude of goodwill and sympathy. At least, try to be receptive.

If you ask yourself and try to answer the following two nonevaluative questions when you annotate your sources, you should be able to read more empathetically:

*1. What is the author's position?*

In reading a text that makes an argument, typically begin by asking yourself what position the writer advances. This question might seem so obvious that it hardly needs stating, but to answer it will challenge you if the author gives mixed signals or uses irony. For example, in "Renting Women, Buying Babies and Class Struggles," one of the articles on surrogate motherhood that Jane uses in her paper, Richard Neuhaus writes, "Mary Beth Whitehead is to be discredited and declared an unfit mother because the world of which she is part is unfit for Mr. Stern's baby, or at least not nearly so fit as the world of the Sterns" (18). To read this single sentence, you might think that Neuhaus believes "Baby M" is better off with William and Elizabeth Stern than with Mary Beth Whitehead, but an empathetic reading of this sentence within the context of Neuhaus's whole essay reveals that Neuhaus is speaking ironically—that he in fact sympathizes more with Whitehead.

To identify an author's position as you read and annotate a text empathetically, try underlining the author's thesis and the main ideas in each paragraph that support it. Remember, however, that as in the case of the foregoing sentence from Neuhaus's article, it is sometimes difficult to identify the arguments and supporting points in an essay without first reading it all the way through once. When you read the introductory paragraph of an article for the first time, for example, you might think you recognize the author's thesis and therefore underline a specific sentence. As you read the subsequent paragraphs, however, you might discover that the "thesis" you identified in the introduction is actually an ironic assertion or just a lead-in to get your attention. Therefore, the first time you read an article, try to get a sense of its overall development but do not make annotations. When you read the article a second time, you can identify and select the author's thesis and main points much more easily. Writers often include a thesis statement at the beginning or end of an academic article and express the main point of a paragraph in its first or last sentence, so pay close attention to these parts of a text. In addition to underlining the primary argument of an essay and the main point of each paragraph, jot down next to each paragraph a word or phrase to capture its essence. By underlining an author's thesis statement and main points and briefly expressing them in your own words, you explore the author's argument and begin to understand it.

*2. What are the author's key terms and definitions?*

Many writers advance and support their arguments with key terms. For example, the authors of the articles on surrogate motherhood use terms such as *patriarchy, in vitro fertilization,* and *amniocentesis.* You might need to look up the meaning of some words in a dictionary or to translate a phrase of a foreign language, including a short definition or translation in the margin of your text.

Writers can also use extended definitions that vary from the standard citations in a dictionary. For example, in the essay, "Racism and the White Backlash," Martin Luther King, Jr. defines the concept of *racism* at length to demonstrate why whites, in spite of their good intentions about racial equality and justice, continue to feel ambivalent about the struggle of African-Americans and fail to enforce civil rights laws. As part of his definition, King writes:

> Racism is a philosophy based on a concept for life. It is the arrogant assertion that one race is the center of value and object of devotion, before which other races must kneel in submission. It is the absurd dogma that one race is responsible for all the progress of history and alone can assure the progress of the future. Racism is total estrangement. It separates not only bodies, but minds and spirits. Inevitably it descends to inflicting spiritual or physical homicide on the out-group. (70)

King uses this extended definition of racism to explain that whites use the myth of racial superiority to rationalize the enslavement of African-Americans and that racist attitudes persist because they are so deeply rooted in social attitudes and consciousness. His definition of racism supports and furthers his argument that progress for civil rights has been too slow. When you read extended definitions such as this one, underline them and write the concept they define in the margin.

As you develop and practice the skill of reading and annotating texts empathetically, you might want to experiment with additional kinds of annotations. Some readers, for example, use circles, brackets, or exclamation points to symbolize certain types of responses. For her paper on surrogate motherhood, Jane carefully reads and annotates five sources: four journal articles and a chapter from a book on surrogacy. We include one of these sources, Richard Neuhaus's "Renting Women, Buying Babies and Class Struggles," here with Jane's annotations on it. Read the article, noting where the author places his thesis and how Jane resists the temptation to criticize his ideas even though she probably disagrees with them.

CASE STUDY

■ ■ ■ ■ ■ ■ ■ ■

# RENTING WOMEN, BUYING BABIES AND CLASS STRUGGLES

### Richard John Neuhaus

*1*

*classism*

Quite suddenly, it seems, we have a new form of trade in human beings. It is called surrogate motherhood, and several states have already declared it legitimate by establishing regulations for the trade. Voices have been raised to oppose the baby traders before their business becomes a fait accompli. It may already be too late for that. The *New York Times* has editorially pronounced that regulation is the only way to go since, after all, "the business is probably here to stay." Numerous objections of a moral, legal, and commonsensical nature have been raised to surrogate motherhood. One aspect that has not been sufficiently explored is the way in which the baby trade so rudely rips the veil off class divisions and hostilities in American life.

## Surrogating Today and Yesterday

*2*

*details of "Baby M" case*

*sticking needle into uterus and taking out fluid to check for disease in baby*

The most celebrated, or notorious, case of surrogate motherhood is the one that has swirled around "Baby M" in a New Jersey courtroom. Some of the details are by now well known. Mr. William Stern, a biochemist married to Dr. Elizabeth Stern, a pediatrician who thought pregnancy might be bad for her health, contracted with Mrs. Mary Beth Whitehead to have his baby in return for $10,000 plus an equal amount in expenses. Mrs. Whitehead and her husband Richard, a sanitation worker, agreed. The surrogate contract is not uninteresting, including as it does provisions for amniocentesis and obligatory abortion if Mr. Stern did not like the results of the test. Also, Mrs. Whitehead would not receive the $10,000 but only a small payment for her troubles "in the event the child is miscarried, dies, or is stillborn." The Sterns were taking no chances. But they could not prevent Mary Beth Whitehead from changing her mind. "It's such a miracle to see a child born," she said. "The feeling is overwhelming. All the pain and suffering you've gone through is all gone." Within five minutes she is breastfeeding the baby, the bonding is effected, she runs away to avoid having to turn the baby over to the Sterns, the Sterns hire detectives to snatch the baby, and it all ends up in a court trying to decide who gets to keep the baby.

*3*

*immoral*

The liberal Catholic journal *Commonweal* observes: "Surrogate motherhood is a simple idea. It has become a critical issue today not because of the breakthrough in technology but because of a breakdown in moral understanding— namely, the understanding that human reproduction should be firmly placed in the matrix of personal sexuality, marital love, and family bonds." The point is an important one. Also in religious circles today, there is much prattle about changing moral rules because of technological advances and new discoveries about sexuality. It is highly doubtful that we know anything very significant about sexuality that, say, Saint Augustine did not know. As to surrogate mother-hood, long before the dawn of modern science human males had mastered the technique of impregnating women other than their wives. Genesis 16 tells how Sarah and Abraham chose Hagar to be the surrogate mother of Ishmael. That too turned out badly, although Hagar did get to keep the child. Hagar, of course, was a slave.

*4*    Today it is at least gauche to speak of buying or renting women. The Sterns got over that awkwardness by hiring a Manhattan clinical psychologist who testi-fied, "In both structural and functional terms, Mr. and Mrs. Stern's role as parents to Baby M was achieved by a surrogate uterus and not a surrogate mother." The contract did not call for Mrs. Whitehead to get involved. In fact *she* was supposed to stay out of this deal altogether. Mary Beth's problem, it would seem, is that she was not able to disaggregate herself from her uterus. She did not understand that she could rent out her uterus just as the Manhattan doctor could rent out his certified expertise. The capable lawyers hired by the Sterns had made it all very clear, and for a while she thought she understood, but then somehow the whole thing began to seem surreal. (Not being an educated person, she did not say it seemed surreal. She said it just seemed wrong.)

*[margin note: educated vs. uneducated]*

## Taking Advantage

*5*    True, there are those who argue that there is nothing new in the rich renting the nonrich, whether in whole or in part. A servant or employee, they say, is in effect a rented person. It is hard to argue with people who say such things. More often than not, they are the kind of people who also say that property is theft and tolerance is oppression. One can point out that the employee is free to quit, that a person's work "belongs" to him even if he is paid to do it, that the worker may find fulfillment in the work, and so forth. But such wrongheaded people do have one undeniable point: with respect to the negotiation of worldly affairs, rich people do generally have the advantage of nonrich people. That said, one can only hope it will be acknowledged that there is something singular about the connections between a woman, her sexuality, and her procreative capacity. It is not the kind of acknowledgment people can be argued into, and those to whom it must be explained probably cannot understand. Proabortion proponents of a woman's "reproductive rights" regularly appeal to the uniquely intimate relationship between a woman and her body. Strangely enough, many of them also approve surrogate motherhood as a further step in rationalizing sexual relationships and liberating society from the oppression of traditional mores. The recently discovered constitutional doctrine of "privacy," it would seem, is absolute—unless you have accepted money to have it violated. The inviolably intimate sphere of sexuality is one thing, but a deal is a deal.

*[margin note: child bearing isn't like other activities and services rich pay for]*

*6*    As with abortion, there is another party involved. As is not the case with abortion, everyone here recognizes the other party involved. Baby M, having passed the quality-control tests, is certified as a Class-A member of the species. The question is who owns this valuable product. Presumably ownership is fifty-fifty between Mrs. Whitehead and Mr. Stern. Mr. Stern's case is that Mrs. Whitehead had agreed to sell her share of the baby for $10,000 and then reneged on the deal. A Solomonic decision may be required, except Solomon's proposed solution would likely be found unconstitutional. Mary Beth is perplexed by the ownership conundrum. The following is from a taped telephone conversation admitted in evidence: "WHITEHEAD: I gave her life. I did. I had the right during the whole pregnancy to terminate it, didn't I? STERN: It was your body. WHITEHEAD: That's right. It was my body and now you're telling me that I have no right. STERN: Because you made an agreement . . . you signed an agreement." It is not that nothing is sacred anymore. It is simply that the sacred has been relocated, away from realities such as life and motherhood and placed in a contract signed and sealed by money. Some simplistic types who have not kept up with the demands of cultural change find this repugnant. For example, William Pierce, president of the National Committee for Adoption, flatly says: "If you regulate surrogate motherhood, that is making a public statement that it's all right. We decided a hundred years ago we didn't want people bought and sold in this country."

*$*

*slavery*

*7*

That is not the question, says the judge in the Baby M case. The question, the only question, is what is "in the best interest" of Baby M. In other words, who can offer Baby M the better prospect for the good things in life, the Whiteheads or the Sterns? Here, although the word is never used, the question of class takes center stage in the courtroom drama. The relative stability of American society is due in part to our kindly veiling of class distinctions and hostilities. People making $20,000 and people making $100,000 or more have tacitly agreed to say they are middle class. In fact, some are rich and some are not rich and some are poor. In terms of income, the Sterns are upper-middle or upper class, the Whiteheads are low-low-middle class and have at times been poor. Perhaps more important than the criterion of income, the Sterns and their allies in the New Jersey courtroom represent the new knowledge class. The disputes are over symbolic knowledge; that is to say, over how to establish the "meaning" of ideas such as parenthood, love, stability, life opportunity, and psychological well-being. In the symbolic knowledge showdown, Mary Beth Whitehead is pitifully outgunned. She has never even heard of the transvaluation of values, which is what the Baby M trial is all about.

*judge's decision emphasizes class and education*

## Class Struggle

*8*

It is not simply that the Sterns can hire a battery of lawyers, detectives, psychological experts and social workers, while Mary Beth must get along with a lawyer three years out of school whose main experience has been in liability cases. No, the greater disparity is that the Sterns, their hired experts, the judge, and almost everyone else involved represents the new class arrayed against the world of the Whiteheads who represent the bottom side of the working class. In the class war being waged in the courtroom, the chief weapon of the new class is contempt for the world of their cultural inferiors, a world so blatantly represented by the Whiteheads. Mrs. Whitehead must be criticized for her decision to enter into the agreement in the first place. But that is not a criticism employed in the courtroom to discredit Mrs. Whitehead, for it might reflect unfavorably on the other party to the agreement, even suggesting that perhaps Mr. Stern took advantage.

*class bias*

*9*

Rather, Mary Beth Whitehead is to be discredited and declared an unfit mother because the world of which she is part is unfit for Mr. Stern's baby, or at least not nearly so fit as the world of the Sterns. So extensive evidence is presented that the Whiteheads have had a hard time of it financially, even living in a house trailer for a time. More than that, Mrs. Whitehead received welfare pay-

*class*

ments for a few months and her husband underwent a bout with alcoholism some years ago. The mandatory new class attitude under usual circumstances is that there is absolutely no stigma attached to welfare or alcoholism. But that is under usual circumstances. In the class war being fought in the New Jersey courtroom such things are sure evidence of moral turpitude and the Whiteheads' "unsuitability" as parents for the 50 percent wellborn Baby M. In addition, a team of mental health experts has testified that Mrs. Whitehead shows definite signs of "distress," and one psychiatrist bluntly says she is suffering from "mixed personality disorder."

*class bias*

That presumed illness is defined as "traits from several personality disorders but not all the criteria for any one disorder." It is a kind of catchall category in which, one fears, most human beings might be caught. Yet another psychiatrist in the new class alliance attempts to come up with harder evidence. Dr. Judith Brown Greif said that Mrs. Whitehead "often is unable to separate out her own needs from the needs of the baby." Well, there you have it. Mary Beth, in her pathetic ignorance, probably thought that was a sign of being a good mother. Little does she know about the need-fulfilling autonomy of the psychologically mature.

*10*

In order to get empirical support for their class biases a group of mental health and child development experts visited "for several hours" in the Whitehead and Stern homes to observe firsthand how Baby M "related" to the respective parties. At the Whiteheads, Baby M seemed very happy, but their other two children, ages eleven and twelve, were vying for her attention and Mrs. Whitehead exhibited "an inflated sense of self." This, according to Dr. Marshall Schechter, psychiatrist at the University of Pennsylvania, was revealed in her making "an assumption that because she is the mother that the child, Baby M, belongs to her. This gives no credence to or value to the genetic contribution of the birth father." Things were different at the quiet and spacious Stern home. There were no other children to interrupt and, as Dr. and Mr. Stern sat on the living room floor chatting with their mental health visitors, Baby M gave every sign of relating very well to Mr. Stern. Of Mr. Stern one psychiatrist reported. "He is a thoughtful, sensitive man with a deep sense of responsibility and a respect for privacy." He did not need to add that none of those nice things could be said of Mrs. Whitehead.

*bias of the experts*

*11*

Another expert (the one who contributed the distinction between renting the woman and renting the uterus), unequivocally declared that the Sterns are "far and away more capable of meeting the baby's needs than the Whiteheads." This includes of course his professional evaluation of Dr. Elizabeth, the wife. She is also, the experts told the court, very good at relating. In Dr. Stern's extensive court testimony, according to the *Times,* "she spoke of her delights at home with the baby and her disdain for Mrs. Whitehead." Often, she testified, she takes the baby shopping. "She's the cutest thing around. She's always pulling at the clothes in Bloomingdale's, trying to get them off the rack." At Bloomies, of course. You can bet that Mary Beth Whitehead probably doesn't even know where it is.

*experts: Sterns are better than Whiteheads*

*12*

We Americans have a way of declaring something outrageous, repugnant, odious, and beyond the pale—and then concluding that we should regulate it. Surrogate motherhood should not be regulated, it should be outlawed. Some think the buying and selling of human beings was outlawed with the abolition of slavery, and the renting of women with laws against prostitution. But those big questions are bypassed if one agrees with the court, that the only question is, "What is in the best interest of the child?" Then enters the ugly factor of naked class advantage. If "interest" is defined by material well-being, life opportunities,

*outlaw it!*

*★ Thesis*

professionally certified mental and emotional health, and a "lifestyle" approved by the new knowledge class, then clearly the baby must go to the Sterns. By the criteria by which Mary Beth Whitehead is declared an unsuitable mother, millions of (dare we use the term?) lower-class women are unsuitable mothers. (One waits to see whether the court would take her other two children into custody.) By the criteria by which the Sterns are found to be "far, and away more capable of meeting the baby's needs," people of recognized achievement and approved attitudes have a right to the best babies that money can buy.

*Richard John Neuhaus is director of the Rockford Institute Center on Religion and Society in New York City. A Lutheran clergyman, he was for seventeen years senior pastor of a low-income black and Hispanic parish in Brooklyn, New York. He is editor of* Religion and Society Report *and editor-in-chief of* This World: A Journal of Religion and Public Life. *His books include* The Naked Public Square: Religion and Democracy in America *and* The Catholic Moment: The Paradox of the Church in the Postmodern World.

Annotating Neuhaus's article empathetically, Jane explores and begins to understand a point of view with which she probably feels compelled to argue. Even though Jane sympathizes with surrogate mothers and believes that they should be able to do as they please, she now contemplates the view of an author who also sympathizes with surrogate mothers but, as a result of his sympathy, believes that surrogacy should be outlawed. If she had not read and annotated Neuhaus's essay empathetically, Jane might have tried to find evidence to support her own point of view and might have misinterpreted the author's meaning. Now that she is digesting what Neuhaus has written, she will be better able to analyze his argument, as you will see in Chapter Three.

EXERCISE    1. Empathetically read and annotate one or more sources on surrogate motherhood (Chapter Five), advertising (Chapter Six), or another topic. Try to identify and underline the writer's thesis and main points, jotting down phrases in the margins to capture the essence of each paragraph. Remember to read each article all the way through before rereading and annotating it.

## ■ ■ ■ ■ ■  PARAPHRASING SOURCES

Most textbooks on writing view paraphrasing sources—that is, restating an author's sentences in your own words—as replicating meaning. Paraphrasing, however, is more a record of the reader's understanding of a text than a duplicating of an author's meaning. Through paraphrasing, you can demonstrate that you have done your best to appreciate and understand an author's meaning, but as we saw in the ironic passage from "Renting Women, Buying Babies and Class Struggles" quoted on page 14, meaning is always more than all the words in a sentence and their individual definitions. When empathetic readers paraphrase, they look for meaning not only in what authors explicitly state but also in what they imply, examining phrases and sentences within the context of an entire essay, and recognizing how one idea relates to and plays off of another. Because empathetic readers try to construct rather than to replicate meaning, paraphrasing is more than a mechanical operation. It is an art.

By paraphrasing the thesis statement and main points underlined in your sources, you construct meaning—that is, you grapple with the looseness of understanding that is often a part of reading difficult articles. A standard strategy for paraphrasing an author's sentence is to replace its words with synonyms and to invert the syntax. For example, the original sentence that Jane underlined to capture the essence of the first paragraph in Neuhaus's "Renting Women, Buying Babies and Class Struggles" reads as follows:

> One aspect that has not been sufficiently explored is the way in which the baby trade so rudely rips the veil off class divisions and hostilities in American life.

Replacing some of the original words with synonyms, you may come up with the following:

> A part of surrogate motherhood that has not received enough attention is how this practice exposes classism in American culture.

After substituting some of the original words with synonyms, you may restructure the sentence to create a more fully paraphrased sentence:

> How surrogate motherhood exposes classism in American culture has not received enough attention.

By changing diction and syntax, you can sometimes paraphrase a sentence fairly well. However, in a case such as the ironic sentence from "Renting Women, Buying Babies and Class Struggles," this rewording and restructuring strategy would not work. The best way to paraphrase a sentence you have underlined in a source is to read the sentence out loud, to place the text aside, and then to write a completely original statement that reflects your own understanding of the sentence within the context of the author's entire argument. Following this procedure, Jane paraphrases the sentences she underlined in each paragraph of Neuhaus's essay, using her writing log to restate the article's main ideas in her own words. (The numbers that precede each of the following paraphrases correspond to the numbers she has written at the beginning of each paragraph of the article.)

## CASE STUDY

1. The role of classism in surrogate motherhood has not received enough attention.

2. Thinking pregnancy might threaten his wife's health, William Stern paid Mary Beth Whitehead $10,000 plus medical expenses to be a surrogate mother, but when the child was born, Whitehead decided she had a right to keep it.

3. As the journal _Commonweal_ points out, surrogate motherhood has become an important topic today not because of new technology but because of a deterioration in fundamental assumptions about love, family, and sexuality.

4. The educated psychologists and lawyers hired by the Sterns testified that Whitehead should not have grown close to the baby, but she still believed "Baby M" was hers.

5. In business transactions, the rich have always had more power than the poor but surrogate motherhood is different because it involves reproduction and women's sexuality.

6. Surrogacy turns birth into a financial arrangement like slavery.

7. The "Baby M" case illustrates classism because the judge gave the baby to the

couple with the most education and highest income.

8. The "Baby M" case illustrates classism because the "new class" showed contempt for the working class.

9. According to the educated experts, the Whiteheads are economically and psychologically less stable than the Sterns.

10 & 11. Based upon their class biases, the experts who visited the Stern and Whitehead homes concluded that the Sterns "related" better to the baby.

12. Surrogate motherhood should be illegal because it reflects classism.

By paraphrasing the main idea of each paragraph in "Renting Women, Buying Babies and Class Struggles," Jane confronts the looseness of meaning she encountered while reading the essay, grappling especially to understand the ideas that contradicted her own point of view. Through paraphrasing, Jane empathetically explores Neuhaus's ideas and, as you will see in Chapter Four, she ultimately incorporates some of these sentences, as well as paraphrases of other sources, into her own original essay. In general, Jane benefits from paraphrasing Neuhaus's primary points, but because paraphrasing is so difficult, some of her statements could more closely and more smoothly reflect the author's ideas. If you compare the paraphrases Jane writes to the sentences she underlined while annotating the text, you can see how well she does or does not empathetically construct meaning from Neuhaus's article. How hard do you think Jane works at trying to understand Neuhaus's perspective? Do you think she succeeds in delaying judgment about his point of view? How accurately and fairly do you think her paraphrases represent his ideas? Are some of the paraphrases more empathetic than others? After paraphrasing the main points in Neuhaus's argument, Jane goes through the same process for each of her sources on surrogate motherhood.

EXERCISE    1. Working with a source you have already read and annotated, paraphrase the main idea of each paragraph. To get started, you can reread the sentences you underlined in the essay, but then place the original text aside and try to generate your own sentences that represent the author's ideas.

■ ■ ■ ■ ■    SUMMARIZING SOURCES

In summarizing sources, as in paraphrasing individual sentences, writers strive to represent an author's ideas in their own words, working to understand these ideas and ultimately to integrate them into an original paper. A summary, however, differs from a paraphrase in several significant ways. *First,* a summary is much more thorough: It should include not just one but all the main ideas in the original source. *Second,* because it leaves out any repetition in the source, a summary is usually much shorter than the original text. The length of a particular summary depends in part on the length and style of the original. If the source is very concise—if it presents an abundance of information in only a few pages—then you will find it difficult to abbreviate the article without distorting or misrepresenting some of its meaning. On the other hand, if the source is somewhat wordy—if it repeats ideas or presents similar examples—then you can shorten the article without much distorting its meaning. *Finally,* a summary is coherent. Unlike a list of paraphrases, a summary is a group of connected sentences that reflects the relationships among an author's ideas.

If you have written paraphrases of an article's main points, you can transform these sentences into a summary of the entire source. You may use the following steps to write a thorough, succinct, and coherent summary:

1. To write an introductory sentence, combine your paraphrase of the article's thesis with the author's name and the essay's title.

2. Join to this introductory sentence the other ideas you have paraphrased, consolidating the author's points and sequencing them in your own logical order.

3. Use transitional words, phrases, and sentences to connect the author's ideas.

To understand experts' perspectives better and to prepare summaries for later integrating into her own essay, Jane summarizes each of her sources in her writing log. Here, we have included her summary of "Renting Women, Buying Babies and Class Struggles." In reading Jane's summary of Neuhaus's article, notice how she combines her paraphrase of Neuhaus's thesis—the last sentence in her list of paraphrased ideas—with the name of the article and author, and places the new introductory sentence at the beginning of her summary. By comparing Jane's summary to her list of paraphrased ideas, you can also see how she consolidates all of Neuhaus's most important ideas and arranges them coherently. Finally, try to make a mental note of the transitional words Jane uses to lead you from one idea to another.

## CASE STUDY

In "Renting Women, Buying Babies and Class Struggles," Richard Neuhaus argues that surrogate motherhood should be illegal because it reflects classism. He points out, for example, that classism played an important role in the "Baby M" case. Thinking pregnancy might threaten his wife's health, William Stern, "Baby M"'s father, hired Mary Beth Whitehead to be a surrogate mother for his child in exchange for $10,000 plus medical expenses; but when the child was born, Whitehead decided she had a right to keep it. The "Baby M" case illustrates classism, because the judge gave the baby to the couple who could best provide for it, and the experts' class biases led them to favor the upper-class Sterns over the working-class Whiteheads. Based upon their bias in favor of the couple with the highest education and income, the experts concluded that the Sterns "related" better to the baby, that they were financially and psychologically more stable, and that Mary Beth should not have grown close to the baby. The "new class" showed contempt for and took advantage of the working class. According to Neuhaus, the rich have always had *power over the poor in business transactions, but because surrogate motherhood involves reproduction and women's sexuality, it's different: Surrogacy turns the birth of a child into a financial arrangement like slavery.*

Thorough, concise, and coherent, Jane's paragraph in general summarizes Neuhaus's essay quite well, presenting his main points logically and briefly. Jane uses her paraphrase of Neuhaus's thesis for her paragraph's guiding, or topic, sentence. She also incorporates almost all the other sentences she wrote while paraphrasing, but she leaves out those that correspond to the first and third paragraphs of "Renting Women, Buying Babies and Class Struggles," apparently believing that these sentences relate only indirectly to the article's main topic of classism. It is also interesting that she consolidates the sentences that paraphrase the ideas in paragraphs four, nine, ten, and eleven, probably doing so because each of these sentences explains some conclusion that the experts reached. By grouping all the experts' conclusions into one sentence, Jane avoids the repetition of "educated psychologists and lawyers," "educated experts," and "the experts," phrases used in the paraphrases she wrote earlier. Finally, you should also realize how Jane uses transitional sentences, words, and phrases to connect Neuhaus's ideas about classism in surrogate motherhood. The second sentence, for example, connects the topic sentence about Neuhaus's main argument to his extended example of the "Baby M" case. Although we are not sure why Jane concludes her summary with the sentence comparing surrogate motherhood to slavery, she might have done so to end the paragraph with a punch. As you can see, writing a summary is an active process that requires you to make many decisions. With which of Jane's decisions do you agree or disagree? Why?

EXERCISE    1. Summarize one of the sources with which you have already worked, combining your previously written paraphrases into a thorough, concise, and coherent summary. Remember that you may begin your summary with a sentence that presents the source's title, author, and thesis.

■ ■ ■ ■ ■  WRITING A SUMMARY-
RESPONSE PAPER

Many college teachers, especially in the social sciences and humanities, assign summary-response papers. Put simply, writing a summary-response paper entails carefully summarizing an author's major points and thoughtfully responding to a few of them. The purpose of the assignment is to encourage you not simply to complete assigned readings but to interact with them intelligently. Professors often view this assignment as an exercise that can help you during the reading process rather than as a more substantial paper for a course, and they may even ask you to use a writing log to summarize and respond to articles. Although the summary-response essay does not usually require a fully developed argument or substantial research, the assignment is valuable because it gives you a chance to read a source empathetically, to begin thinking about the ideas in it, and to accommodate these ideas in terms of your own evolving position on a topic. An instructor may ask you to agree or disagree with the author, and if you have probed your assumptions and biases about the topic and have read the article empathetically, some of the author's ideas could influence your perspective and lead you to modify your original position.

Although teachers use and define the summary-response assignment differently, they generally agree that it has a dual purpose—to help you to understand and to think about what you have read. Therefore, try to strike a balance between your summary of and response to the author's ideas. After empathetically reading, annotating, and summarizing your source, consider the following two practical suggestions for writing a summary-response essay that balances your ideas and those of the author:

1. *Compose a statement that combines the author's primary argument and several points that you wish to raise about his or her ideas.*

By writing such a statement, you can start to focus your response, choosing one, two, or perhaps three of the author's points to which you can adequately respond. You can address the main argument in the source or respond to several secondary ideas or examples, perhaps adding your own examples that support or challenge the author's position, asking questions that the author seems to avoid, or drawing connections between the author's ideas and your own experiences. You need not write about every single thought the author raises; rather, pick a few ideas that you find interesting. If you limit your response in this way, you should be able to write an essay that briefly summarizes the source and responds to several of the author's ideas in some detail. Furthermore, if you begin your summary-response paper with this type of statement, it can guide not only your own writing but also your audience's reading.

2. *Organize your paper so that it equally emphasizes summary and response and smoothly blends them.*

One way to structure a summary-response paper is to move from the introductory statement, to the summary, and finally to your response. Although you will eventually discover more natural and complex ways to integrate your ideas with those of the author, you may decide to begin with this organizational model. If you do, try to use a transitional sentence or paragraph between the summary of the article and your response to it so that you lead the reader from the first part of your paper to the second.

In writing a summary-response paper about Neuhaus's article on surrogate motherhood, Jane organizes her essay according to this model. As you read Jane's essay, notice how she begins with a sentence that immediately sets up a balance between her summary of Neuhaus's article and her response to it. Notice, too, how she shifts smoothly from summary to response by using a transitional sentence and beginning a new paragraph. Jane's summary-response essay is especially interesting because it reflects the ways she intellectually accommodates Neuhaus's idea about classism in surrogate motherhood.

## CASE STUDY

In "Renting Women, Buying Babies and Class Struggles," Richard Neuhaus argues that surrogate motherhood should be illegal because it's classist. Although Neuhaus argues forcefully that class bias played a strong role in the "Baby M" case, I wonder if it is as prevalent in other surrogate motherhood cases and if we can somehow eliminate it.

Neuhaus points out that classism played an important role in the "Baby M" case. Thinking pregnancy might threaten his wife's health, William Stern, Baby M's father, hired Mary Beth Whitehead to be a surrogate mother for his child in exchange for $10,000 plus medical expenses; but when the child was born, Whitehead decided she had a right to keep it. The "Baby M" case illustrates classism because a judge decided to give the baby to the couple who could best provide for it, and the experts' class biases led them to favor the upper-class Sterns over the working-class Whiteheads. Based upon their bias in favor of the couple with the most education and highest income, the experts concluded that the Sterns "related" better to the baby, that they were financially and psychologically more stable, and that Mary Beth should not have grown close to the baby. The "new class" showed contempt for and took advantage of the working class. According to Neuhaus, the rich have always had power over the poor in business transactions, but because surrogate motherhood involves reproduction and women's sexuality, it's different:

Surrogacy turns the birth of a child into a financial arrangement like slavery.

   Although class bias may have affected the outcome of the "Baby M" case, Neuhaus mentions only this case. And I have heard of less publicized cases in which classism did not seem to play a role. For instance, I remember reading about a case in which a woman volunteered to be a surrogate for her sister, and the child was genetically related not only to the father but to the mother as well. Everything worked out really well! I don't think class played much of a role in this case, because the two women were from the same family, and besides, no money changed hands. If one woman wants to help out another woman by being a surrogate mother, and class bias is not an issue, I don't see why they shouldn't have the right to do what they want to do. If we could somehow eliminate classism from the practice of surrogate motherhood, then I think it should be legal. If we could make it so that cases like "Baby M" could not happen, but cases like the one with the sisters could, then I would definitely be in favor of surrogate motherhood.


   As you can see, Jane chooses to respond to two related issues in Neuhaus's article: his main argument that surrogacy should be outlawed because of classism and his use of the "Baby M" case as an example. Her short, introductory paragraph, which paraphrases Neuhaus's argument and raises the points she wishes to make about it, focuses the essay on both summarizing and responding. Notice also how the first paragraph sets up the rest of the paper—how it helps the reader to anticipate a movement from summary to response. Jane further blends summary and response with the transitional sentence at the beginning of the third paragraph, "Although class bias may have affected the outcome of the 'Baby M' case, Neuhaus mentions only this case," a sentence that refers retrospectively to the summary section and projects forward to her response.

   In content, Jane's summary-response essay is especially interesting because it reflects a slight modification in her stance toward the topic. Although she does not agree with Neuhaus that surrogacy should be outlawed, Jane acknowledges the potential harm that classism can cause the people who participate in surrogate arrangements. In fact, she now endorses only some cases, those that do not seem to involve classism, and she seems to support legalizing surrogacy on the contingency that class bias could somehow be eliminated. In the log entry in which she probed her assumptions and biases about surrogate motherhood, Jane wrote, "The fact that it's even questioned seems ridiculous," but her summary-response paper reflects a more moderate and complex position, one that accommodates Neuhaus's concern with class bias. As you will see in Chapters Three and Four, although Jane never drastically changes her position, she continues to modify and develop it as she reads additional sources and responds to them.

EXERCISE   1. Write a summary-response paper that uses an article on surrogacy (Chapter Five), advertising (Chapter Six), or a topic of your choice. Try to strike a balance between presenting the author's ideas and responding to them.

## WORKS CITED

King, Martin Luther, Jr. *Where Do We Go from Here: Chaos or Community?* New York: Harper & Row, 1967.

Neuhaus, Richard John. "Renting Women, Buying Babies and Class Struggles." *Society* 25 (1988): 8–10.

# Chapter Three

# ANALYZING DIFFERENT

# POINTS OF VIEW

*The believing game needs to be legitimized if only for the sake of the doubting game.*

*Peter Elbow*

In *Writing Without Teachers*, Peter Elbow suggests that by playing the believing game, students place themselves in a better position to play the doubting game. In other words, if you try to believe points of view that challenge your own opinion, acknowledging the value of these competing views, you can understand them more fully and thus analyze them more effectively. As you analyze different perspectives, you could grow to understand why your opinion is better than others, to modify it slightly, or even to change it radically. In all these cases, you develop an informed argument, one based on an awareness of other people's positions and one worth adding to the many voices that already surround your topic. In this chapter, we focus on several thinking processes involved in analysis, processes that will help you to reach reflective judgments that can be justified persuasively in writing. These processes, some of the most important and complex that you will learn in college, are synthesizing multiple perspectives; evaluating authors' evidence, reasoning, and credentials; and, finally, recognizing the limitations of your own argument.

# ■ ■ ■ ■ ■  SYNTHESIZING MULTIPLE PERSPECTIVES

*Synthesizing* is the process that puts together several parts to create a more complex whole. In college, writing assignments often call for synthesizing multiple perspectives in a coherent essay that focuses on several issues in your topic. By synthesizing sources, you can gain a broader viewpoint that will ultimately help you to reach informed judgments about your topic. To begin this process, you can follow these preliminary steps:

*1. Identify the most important issues.*

Typically, if authors are well informed, they will refer to at least some of the most important issues in a topic. Therefore, one way to identify some of these issues in your particular subject is to watch for those that appear in several sources. If several authors discuss the same issue, you can be confident that it is one of the key questions, ideas, or themes involved with your topic. For example, the authors of articles on mandatory drug testing of professional athletes often refer to the question of whether this practice is constitutional. As you know, the Fourth Amendment protects people from unreasonable searches and seizures, and therefore constitutionality is an important issue in the debate over mandatory drug testing. One issue to which several of the included articles on surrogate motherhood refer is classism. As you will see in Chapter Four, in which we include two drafts and the final version of Jane's essay on surrogacy, she focuses on class bias in her paper. Richard Neuhaus emphasizes classism in his article, and the writers who respond to his piece address this issue as well, making it one of the most important subtopics in the larger topic of surrogate motherhood. When reading sources about other controversial subjects, you will see that it is not unusual for experts to refer directly to each other's ideas about crucial issues.

*2. Clarify authors' views on the important issues.*

To identify what the authors say about the relevant issues in their topics, students sometimes annotate their sources with a felt-tip marker, highlighting passages that refer to the same issue. This is a fairly passive, and therefore easy, way to synthesize multiple perspectives, but such a synthesis is hard to develop into a paper. By highlighting your sources in different colors of ink, maybe you could even identify the authors' views on several issues, but when you began writing your paper and integrating the writers' perspectives into it, you would need to flip through and perhaps reread your sources. To write out in your log what experts believe about the important issues in a topic takes more time at first, but it is usually more beneficial because you have to think about the authors' ideas and perhaps even begin to make connections among them. Furthermore, writing out the authors' viewpoints is ultimately much more efficient because this procedure allows you easily to collect and organize authors' views when you begin drafting an essay. To make a writing log entry on what the authors of your sources think about an issue in your topic, write down a word or phrase in your log that expresses the issue. Then sketch brief explanations of what each author says about it, keeping the multiple perspectives straight in your mind by writing down each source's title and author. For example, if you were writing a paper about the mandatory drug testing of athletes, you could use your writing log to synthesize what the authors of your sources say about the Fourth Amendment, noting each writer's view of the constitutionality of such testing.

*3. Characterize authors' evidence.*

You can also synthesize multiple perspectives by characterizing the evidence authors use to support their arguments. When experts argue from particular instances to general conclusions or from causes to effects, they rely on evidence such as specific examples, empirical observations, statistics, or references to other authorities. For example, Richard Neuhaus refers to a specific example, the "Baby M" case, to support his argument that surrogate motherhood is classist. Scientists, on the other hand, frequently make claims based on empirical evidence they have accumulated in laboratories or through observation. An astronomer, for example, can base a prediction of a lunar or solar eclipse on knowledge of past eclipses and planetary orbits. Sometimes an author uses statistical data to support an argument and makes generalizations based on this type of evidence. A sociologist might predict the approximate number of murders in Detroit for a given year, basing the estimate on the number of murders in past years and on current trends in homicide. Furthermore, writers often refer to other authorities who have special expertise in specific areas. For example, to support his view against regulating surrogate motherhood, Neuhaus quotes William Pierce, president of the National Committee for Adoption, who says, "If you regulate surrogate motherhood, that is making a public statement that it's all right. We decided a hundred years ago we didn't want people bought and sold in this country" (qtd. in Neuhaus 18).

*4. Characterize authors' reasoning.*

In addition to considering their evidence, you can characterize the authors' reasoning. If you are writing about the constitutionality of testing athletes for drugs, for example, you might find that the author of one article supports the practice by arguing that random drug testing is not an unreasonable search because coaches should require an athlete to be medically certified as fit for competition. And to enable coaches to do so, team owners must reserve the right to conduct whatever tests are necessary to protect athletes' health and safety. To complement this type of reasoning, the author might present evidence in the form of specific cases of drug abuse in the National Football League (NFL) or the National Basketball Association (NBA), such as the famous 1974 case involving eight players from the San Diego Chargers. The author of another article, however, might argue that mandatory drug testing is unreasonable because the testing procedures are inaccurate. The author could support such reasoning by referring to informed doctors who have found that urinalysis cannot always distinguish between legal medications and illegal substances—that it cannot, for example, distinguish between some anti-inflammatory drugs and marijuana.

You can use your writing log to synthesize multiple perspectives—to clarify authors' views on an important issue in your topic and to characterize the evidence and reasoning that they use to support these views. Writing a log entry about classism in surrogate motherhood, Jane synthesizes her sources in terms of this important issue in her topic. As you read her entry, notice that she first sketches the authors' positions concerning classism and then briefly tries to describe their evidence and reasoning, keeping the sources straight in her mind by referring to their authors and titles.

## CASE STUDY

Richard Neuhaus, "Renting Women, Buying Babies and Class Struggles."

Neuhaus says class bias in favor of wealthy, educated people and against poor, uneducated people is a big part of surrogate motherhood. He thinks surrogacy should be outlawed because it's so classist. He supports his argument by referring mostly to the "Baby M" case; he seems to reason that if this case is classist, then so is surrogacy in general. He has a lot of biographical information about the Sterns and Whiteheads. Mr. Stern was a biochemist and Mrs. Stern was a pediatrician, but Mr. Whitehead was a garbage man with no money. He also has details about the surrogate contract, quotations from Mary Beth Whitehead, quotations from the psychologists who testified at the "Baby M" trial, and courtroom testimony from the Sterns. In the trial of this case, Judge Sorkow said it boiled down to which party could provide best for the baby, and the Sterns could obviously provide "Baby M" with more than the Whiteheads. The Sterns could also hire the best lawyers, while Mary Beth Whitehead had to use a court-appointed attorney. The Sterns also hired top-notch psychologists to testify for them, and even the judge was from the educated upper-class like the Sterns. Neuhaus also uses quotations from a Catholic journal called <u>Commonweal</u> and the president of the National Committee for Adoption to support his view.

Barbara Heyl, "Commercial Contracts and Human Connectedness"

Heyl agrees with Neuhaus that classism is an important issue in surrogate motherhood cases. She says the legal system favors the upper class over the lower class and people accept the fact that class plays a big part in surrogate motherhood cases. Heyl refers to the adoption system and the juvenile court system, which have been giving children from poor families to parents from rich ones for a long time. She also mentions a public opinion poll of the "Baby 'M'" trial which shows that the public agreed with the judge's decision to give the baby to the Sterns.

Monica Morris, "Reproductive Technology and Restraints"

Morris points out class is not part of all surrogate motherhood court cases. She also argues that we need regulations if we are going to protect innocent, lower-class women from being used by upper-class couples. Morris describes a surrogacy case in Great Britain where the judge also based his decision on which party could provide best for the babies (there were twins). But in the British case, the judge ruled in favor of the surrogate mother because he thought she and the children had already formed a bond and breaking it could be harmful. The British judge did not base his decision on the wealth of the parties. The mother was even unmarried and on social security. Morris also explains laws in Great Britain and Australia that have outlawed commercial surrogacy, which stops rich couples from paying poor women to be surrogate mothers.

Barbara Rothman, "Cheap Labor: Sex, Class, Race — and 'Surrogacy'"

Rothman says surrogacy involves not only class, but also sex and race. Rothman reasons that even rich women can reinforce the patriarchal values in surrogate motherhood. They can pay poor, even Third World, women to carry their eggs and have babies for them. Rich women can own children based on their "seeds" - just like men. Rothman talks about how patriarchal our society is.

Noel Keane and Dennis Breo, "If She's Bright, Beautiful, and Talented and Wants $50,000, Why Not?"

Keane says some of his clients couldn't afford to pay him very much and he didn't want to make his service available to only rich people. Keane refers to biographical details about the people he tried to find surrogate mothers for. He tells us John and Lorelei spent all their savings to give him the $2,000 he charged. John was a driver for the Salvation Army, and Lorelei was a dispatcher for the police. Joseph was a graduate student and a fledgling actor and writer but he was from an upper - class family and obviously had money because he owned a $50,000 stereo. Thomas and Cindy Sue lived in Manhattan and had good jobs in the film industry. They were definitely rich. They even had a place in Paris. Keane says Andy and Nancy were poor, but he doesn't say what their jobs were exactly. Stefan and Nadia had well-paying jobs in the car industry in Detroit, and they were pretty well off. They had two houses, several cars, and a boat.

By synthesizing the authors' views on classism, Jane discovers several new angles on the issue, angles that she will ultimately need to compare and evaluate to reach an informed decision about the topic of surrogate motherhood. In reading this log entry, you might notice that from her new sources Jane learns of laws that regulate surrogacy in other countries and of several additional cases, some of which did not seem to involve class bias. Because these cases and laws address the concerns Jane raised in her summary-response paper, they will play a primary role in her analysis. Why do you think Jane chooses to synthesize authors' perspectives on the particular issue of classism in surrogate motherhood? How accurately does she represent the ideas of Neuhaus, Heyl, Morris, and Keane and Breo? How fairly does she characterize their evidence and reasoning?

EXERCISES

1. After reading two or more sources on surrogate motherhood (Chapter Five), advertising (Chapter Six), or a topic of your choice, identify the issues you think are most important. What are the issues to which several authors refer? If you have already summarized the sources, read the summaries to determine what issues authors raise repeatedly.

2. Try to synthesize several authors' views on one of the issues you identified in the first exercise, writing what the experts say about the issue and how they support their views with evidence and reasoning. Remember to identify the author and title of each source so that you do not confuse one essay with another.

■ ■ ■ ■ ■  WRITING A SYNTHESIS PAPER

College teachers often ask students to write essays that synthesize the multiple perspectives reflected in several sources. Because it draws on more than one source, the synthesis paper is usually longer and more complicated than a summary-response essay. The purpose of writing a synthesis paper is to combine what several authors say into an overview of your topic. But as the writer of this type of paper, you are responsible for fitting the multiple perspectives into a coherent whole—that is, for connecting and comparing many seemingly divergent viewpoints and assembling them into a paper. You play a very active role.

In the previous section of this chapter, you learned how to identify the most important issues in your topic, to clarify authors' views on these issues, and to characterize evidence and reasoning. To write a synthesis paper, follow these same preliminary steps but also make detailed connections and comparisons among viewpoints, evidence, and reasoning. These suggestions should help you get started:

1. *Write a statement that introduces the authors of your sources and the specific ways in which you want to connect and compare their stances.*

You can connect many kinds of material in a synthesis paper. Generally, you will compare authors' attitudes toward what you think are the most interesting and relevant issues in your topic and compare the types of evidence and reasoning you find most significant. More specifically, if writers refer to different facts and examples or interpret the same facts and examples in different ways, you will probably emphasize these differences and similarities. Or, if authors approach issues in your topic from several theoretical or disciplinary perspectives, you might compare these approaches in your paper.

*2. Organize your paper around areas of common ground rather than around authors.*

Beginning college students tend to organize synthesis papers around the authors of their sources, moving from one writer to another as they draft an essay. But this type of structure can hinder you from connecting different writers' perspectives. The best way to organize a synthesis paper is to use common issues, ideas, or evidence that provide a center around which you can compare your sources.

*3. Use transitional words, phrases, and sentences to help the reader understand your connections and comparisons.*

As mentioned, the purpose of a synthesis paper is to make detailed connections and comparisons among the different viewpoints expressed in your sources. When you move from explaining one view to explaining another, or from characterizing one type of evidence to characterizing another, try to use transitional words, phrases, or sentences that describe the relationships among these kinds of material.

As you read Jane's synthesis paper, notice that she begins her essay with a statement that introduces the authors of her sources and the connections she will make among them. Notice, too, that she organizes the synthesis by areas of common ground rather than by author, and that she uses transitions in an attempt to explain her comparisons. Finally, notice that in writing her synthesis paper, Jane works from her previous log entry in which she wrote about the viewpoints on classism in surrogate motherhood.

## CASE STUDY

Richard Neuhaus, Monica Morris, and Noel Keane and Dennis Breo all write about surrogate motherhood. Neuhaus and Morris address the issues of classism and legality, and all the authors refer to different case studies to support their positions.

In "Renting Women, Buying Babies and Class Struggles," Neuhaus says class bias in favor of wealthy, educated people and against poor, uneducated people is a big part of surrogate motherhood. On the other hand, in "Reproductive Technology and Restraints," Monica Morris points out class is not part of all surrogate motherhood arrangements. These writers base their views of class bias in surrogacy on different types of evidence, but they rely heavily on studies of specific surrogate motherhood cases.

In his article, Neuhaus supports his argument by referring mostly to the "Baby M" case. He has a lot of biographical information about the Sterns and Whiteheads. Mr. Stern was a biochemist and Mrs. Stern was a pediatrician, but Mr. Whitehead was a garbage man with no money. He also has details about the surrogate contract, quotations from Mary Beth Whitehead, quotations from the psychologists who testified at the "Baby M" trial, and courtroom testimony from the Sterns. In the trial of this case, Judge Sorkow said it boiled down to which party could provide best for the baby, and the Sterns could obviously provide "Baby M" with more than the Whiteheads could. The Sterns could also hire the best lawyers, while Mary Beth Whitehead had to use a court-appointed attorney. The Sterns also hired top-notch psychologists to testify for them, and even the judge was from the educated, upper class like the Sterns.

In her article, Morris describes a surrogacy case in Great Britain where the judge also based his decision on which party could provide best for the babies (there were twins). But in the British case, the judge ruled in favor of the surrogate mother because he thought she and the children had already formed a bond and breaking it could be harmful. The British judge did not base his decision on the wealth of the parties. The mother was even unmarried and on social security.

Although Keane and Breo, authors of the third source, do not deal directly with the issue of class bias, Keane describes some of the people in the specific cases he was involved with as a lawyer. In "If She's Bright, Beautiful, and Talented and Wants $50,000, Why Not?" he says some of his clients couldn't afford to pay him very much and he didn't want to make his service available to only rich people. Keane refers to biographical details about the people he tried to find surrogate mothers for. He tells us John and Lorelei spent all their savings to give him the $2,000 he charged. John was a driver for the Salvation Army, and Lorelei was a dispatcher for the police. Joseph was a graduate student but he obviously had money because he owned a $50,000 stereo. Thomas and Cindy Sue lived in Manhattan and had good jobs in the film industry. They were definitely rich. They even had a place in Paris. Keane says Andy and Nancy were poor, but he doesn't say what their jobs were exactly. Stefan and Nadia had well-paying jobs in the car industry in Detroit, and they were pretty well off. They had two houses, several cars, and a boat.

Based upon the cases they describe, Neuhaus and Morris reach differing conclusions about the legality of surrogate motherhood. Neuhaus thinks surrogacy should be outlawed because it's so classist. On the other hand, Morris argues that we need regulations if we are going to protect innocent, lower-class women from being used by upper-class couples. Morris also explains laws in Great Britain and Australia that have outlawed commercial surrogacy, which stops rich couples from paying poor women to be surrogate mothers. Great Britain outlaws surrogacy agencies, third-party intervention between couples and surrogates, and advertising for surrogacy. Australia outlaws advertising as well as payments for sperm, eggs, and embryos. In Great Britain, a couple can pay a surrogate for her services, but surrogacy contracts are not legally valid, and in Australia surrogacy contracts are invalid, and it is illegal for a surrogate mother to receive pay for her services.

Neuhaus, Morris, and Keane present specific surrogate motherhood cases as evidence, and on the basis of their case studies, Neuhaus and Morris reach very different types of conclusions about the issues of class and legalization. Neuhaus believes it should be illegal because of classism, and Morris believes it should be regulated to outlaw commercial surrogacy as in Great Britain and Australia.

Jane focuses her synthesis paper on two important issues in surrogate motherhood—classism and legality—and on several authors' use of examples. The first paragraph in her paper introduces these subtopics as well as the specific writers she considers: Richard Neuhaus, Monica Morris, and Noel Keane and Dennis Breo. Notice, however, that she does not organize her paper around these authors' sources but around the subtopics of classism, case-study evidence, and legalization, a strategy that allows her to make connections and comparisons among the writers. In the second paragraph she compares Neuhaus's and Morris's positions on class bias, and in the third, fourth and fifth paragraphs, she connects the kind of evidence that these experts and Keane use to support their opinions. Furthermore, Jane tries to use transitional phrases and sentences to make these comparisons and connections explicit. In her second paragraph, for example, the phrase "on the other hand" expresses the contrast between Neuhaus's and Morris's ideas about classism. And the transitional sentence, "These writers base their views of class bias in surrogacy on different types of evidence, but they rely heavily on studies of specific surrogate motherhood cases," explains how the authors' perspectives on class relate to their use of case studies. What comparisons and connections does Jane make in the rest of her paper, and what transitions does she use to explain them?

EXERCISE    1. Write a synthesis paper in which you make connections among the divergent points of view reflected in the sources on surrogate motherhood (Chapter Five), advertising (Chapter Six), or another topic. Recall that you should try to organize your paper by areas of common ground rather than by authors' sources, comparing experts' perspectives on important issues, uses of evidence, or interpretations of facts and examples.

## ■ ■ ■ ■ ■  EVALUATING MULTIPLE PERSPECTIVES

After making connections and comparisons among your sources, you are ready to start evaluating multiple perspectives. To do so, you can consider how fully the experts support their opinions with evidence and how rationally they explain them with reasoning and logic. Authors can, of course, intentionally try to trick readers, providing deceptive evidence and fallacious logic, but writers more often commit logical errors in their reasoning and use of evidence without knowing it. In either case, you can evaluate authors' evidence and logic to make reflective judgments about their points of view and ultimately to justify your own arguments persuasively in writing.

To start evaluating authors' viewpoints, ask yourself a series of questions that will help you to make judgments about the adequacy of writers' evidence and logic:

*1. Do any authors attack the personal character of another writer?*

If they do, they might be trying to divert your attention from the real issues, or they might simply be exposing their anger, both of which could be signs that their reasoning is problematic. For example, during the half-minute television advertisements that politicians use during a campaign, candidates often attack the character of their opponent, claiming that the person cheated in law school, used family connections to avoid the draft, or smoked marijuana in college. Most of these attacks are irrelevant because they do not relate directly to the important issues at hand, but some attacks seem more appropriate than others. If a political candidate cheated in law school because he or she did not understand legal theory and practice, for example, the candidate might be a poor policymaker. However, even inappropriate attacks on character can sway an unaware public, so always question them.

*2. Do any writers try to appeal to your sense of pity?*

If authors purposely try to arouse your compassion for a person or cause, they can encourage you to accept their positions unreflectively. For example, Richard Neuhaus makes strong appeals to our pity when he characterizes Mary Beth Whitehead as an innocent victim who was taken advantage of by educated lawyers and psychologists. Describing the "Baby M" case, Neuhaus quotes Whitehead as saying, "It's such a miracle to see a child born" and "The feeling is overwhelming" (16). These quotations make us sympathize with Whitehead and view her as a good, caring mother who was labeled "unfit" by cold-hearted psychologists. However, Neuhaus's appeal to pity is not completely inappropriate: The "Baby M" case, as well as the topic of surrogate motherhood in general, involves highly emotional issues, such as the bond between parent and child. How warranted do you think Neuhaus is in arousing our compassion for Whitehead? How could our sympathy for her influence the way we perceive Neuhaus's evidence and reasoning?

*3. Do any authors compare an issue or topic to something else?*

If they do, be especially careful to consider their analogies because analogies are powerful rhetorical devices that can lead you to make unwarranted assumptions. When analogies are appropriate, they compare two things that have several relevant qualities in common. When analogies are inappropriate, they compare two things that have one or more similarities but also very important differences. Inappropriate analogies can lead readers incorrectly to associate one thing's negative qualities with another thing. For example, in "Renting Women, Buying Babies and Class Struggles," the president of the National Committee for Adoption indirectly compares surrogate motherhood to slavery, commenting, "We decided a hundred years ago we didn't want people bought and sold in this country" (qtd. in Neuhaus 18). When analyzing the comparison of surrogacy to slavery, consider carefully the similarities and differences between the two practices. What are some similarities between surrogacy and slavery? What are some important differences? How appropriate do you find this analogy to be?

*4. Do some authors jump to conclusions?*

When comparing experts' viewpoints on an issue, always ask yourself if the evidence is sufficient. In her summary-response paper, Jane, for example, argued that Neuhaus refers only to the "Baby M" case to support his position on classism in surrogate motherhood. After having read Chapter Five's articles on surrogacy or Jane's synthesis of the views on classism, do you think Neuhaus overlooks any other potentially relevant cases? Do you think experts weaken or strengthen their arguments by not referring to examples that challenge their positions?

*5. Do any of the experts use vague language that could lead you to make incorrect assumptions?*

For example, when Barbara Heyl discusses how a child in a surrogate arrangement might experience an identity crisis, she uses language that could mislead an unaware reader. Writing "One nine-year-old adopted child said recently to her adoptive mother, 'People should not be able to give their children away: I don't understand it: it doesn't make sense'" (119), Heyl quotes an actual child. Several sentences later, Heyl asks, "What does the child of a surrogate mother conclude about her? 'She gave me life for $10,000 and relinquished all rights to me so that my father and his wife could raise me?'" (119), using a hypothetical quotation. An alert reader would notice the second quotation's sophistication and question marks, which tell us that Heyl is not suggesting that an actual child spoke these words. But an unaware person, reading the two quotations quickly, could easily assume that the second passage was spoken by a real rather than a hypothetical child.

*6. Do any of the authors assume cause-and-effect relationships without proving them?*

Writers who do not fully explain a cause-and-effect relationship can lead a reader to assume unwittingly that it exists. For example, Neuhaus explains a cause-and-effect relationship well when he argues that the Sterns received custody of "Baby M" because they were from the upper class. Going beyond a mere assertion of this cause-and-effect relationship, he explains that the Sterns' wealth allowed them to hire top-notch lawyers who were better qualified than Mary Beth Whitehead's less experienced, court-appointed attorney; that since the judge and psychologists were from the educated class, they could relate better to the Sterns; and that the judge assumed that the wealthier party could take better care of the child (18–19). Clear in his illustration of this cause-and-effect relationship, Neuhaus carefully explains several connections between the Sterns' upper-class status and the judge's decision.

*7. Do any of the writers give you a choice between only two positions?*

When writers force a reader to choose between two extremes, they could be creating a false dilemma. For example, television news programs and talk shows sometimes take polls, the viewers calling in to the TV stations to answer "yes" or "no" to a sometimes very complex question. Although the sources on surrogate motherhood that we include do not give you a choice between only two positions, what would you think of a writer who asks you to pick between the two alternatives of banning surrogacy completely and allowing it without any restrictions? Are there alternatives to complete banning and complete legalization? Similarly, what do you suppose a teacher would think of a student essay that argues either that surrogate motherhood is completely right or that it is completely wrong?

*8. Do any authors claim more than their evidence can reasonably support?*

For example, television advertisements for health care products often assert, "Doctors recommend that . . ." and "Studies suggest that . . ." without providing any details about their assertions. Most of us quickly recognize that this type of ad does not provide enough evidence to support its claims, but readers might not be as skeptical of scholarly articles. When Heyl writes, "Data indicate that especially during adolescence adopted children show effects of this struggle by having lower indices of self-esteem than children living with their biological parents" (119), some readers might automatically assume that she does in fact have specific data in mind. Indeed, Heyl could know of particular studies, but because she does not summarize and document them, you cannot tell if the evidence supports her claim. (For more information on documenting sources, see Chapter Seven.)

*9. Do any of the authorities use "loaded" terms?*

*Loaded terms* are words that hold almost hidden positive or negative connotations that could mislead an unaware reader. For example, Neuhaus writes that "the Sterns hire detectives to snatch the baby" (16). What connotations does "snatch" have? How could Neuhaus's use of the word mislead an unsophisticated reader to assume that "Baby M" belongs to Mary Beth Whitehead?

*10. Do any writers suggest that if most people agree about something, they must be right?*

When authors make or imply this kind of statement, they commit the *band wagon fallacy:* The fact that many people agree on a point does not mean that it is correct. Sometimes writers refer to opinion polls, but opinion polls, even when researchers do them very carefully, indicate only what people think—not necessarily what is true or best. For example, in "Commercial

Contracts and Human Connectedness," Heyl refers to an opinion poll that indicates the public agreed with Judge Sorkow's decision to award "Baby M" to the Sterns (114). Do you think Heyl uses this poll to suggest only that the public agrees with the judge or to argue that it is not necessarily wrong to pass a child from a poor to a wealthy couple? If writers use an opinion poll to argue that something is right or wrong because the public says so, they commit the *band wagon fallacy*.

By asking yourself these questions about the reasoning and evidence that authors use to support their arguments, you can evaluate multiple perspectives and begin to reach informed judgments about the important issues of your topic.

Furthermore, when you start explaining and justifying your position in writing, you can ask the same questions to evaluate your own logic and evidence: Do I

1. attack another writer's personal character?
2. appeal to the reader's sense of pity?
3. use inappropriate analogies?
4. jump to conclusions?
5. use vague language?
6. assume cause-and-effect relationships?
7. make the reader choose between two extremes?
8. make unwarranted claims?
9. use loaded terms?
10. commit the band wagon fallacy?

If you want readers to take your position seriously, it is important to assess your own evidence and reasoning as well as that of other writers.

## ■ ■ ■ ■ ■  EVALUATING AUTHORS' CREDENTIALS

Although evaluating authors' evidence and logic is the best way to judge multiple points of view, evaluating authors' credentials can also help you to reach a reflective decision about your topic. To consider not only what the authorities say but also who they are and what they have done, think about their educations, careers, and scholarly contributions as well as their evidence and reasoning. At the beginning or end of many articles and books, editors include biographical statements about authors. If your sources include such statements, consult them to see whether writers have the professional credentials to make them credible authorities on the issues in your topic. If your readings do not provide this type of information about authors, ask a librarian to help you find it. However, try not to overemphasize the importance of formal credentials: Some authors might have noncredentialed expertise. For example, a woman who had herself been a surrogate mother would have valuable though nonprofessional expertise about surrogate motherhood.

Imagine again that you are writing about the mandatory drug testing of athletes and that you want to evaluate several authors' views on the constitutionality of such testing. Suppose one writer is associate professor and dean of the College of Physical Education, Recreation, and Health at a large, well-known state university, and that this author has also published a book entitled *How to Live a Healthy Life.* You know that the person has a Ph.D. in physical education and is therefore knowledgeable about health and perhaps about college athletics, but you might question the author's expertise in legal matters related to professional sports, such as applications of the Fourth Amendment to mandatory drug testing of athletes. Similarly, if the author of another one of your sources is a senior editor at *Sports Illustrated*, you know that the writer is well informed about college and professional sports in general, but you have no reason to believe that the person has specialized knowledge in the health or legal issues related to mandatory drug testing. However, assume that the coauthors of your third source are (1) a doctor who specializes in sports medicine and is also the physician for an NBA team and (2) a lawyer who works for the American Civil Liberties Union (ACLU). You can probably assume that the doctor, who earned an M.D., has specialized knowledge and experience in the area of professional athletes' health problems, and you know that the lawyer, who earned a J.D., has experience in constitutional law. Therefore, these authors have special credentials that should make them very reliable sources on the issue of the constitutionality of mandatory drug testing of professional athletes. Although you should never base an evaluation solely on a writer's credentials, considering them can help you to determine the reliability of an expert's point of view.

To consider authors' credentials, Jane studies the biographical statements included in some of her sources and sketches these profiles in her writing log:

## CASE STUDY

Richard Neuhaus
Director of the Rockford Institute Center on
  Religion and Society
Lutheran clergyman
senior pastor of a lower-class, minority
  parish

editor of journals on religion and society
author of several books on religion and
politics

Barbara Heyl

Associate Professor of Sociology at Illinois
State University
Ph.D. in sociology
author of *The Madam as Entrepreneur*
author of several articles on the sociology of
deviance, the sociology of law, and
legislation on handicapped children
recent research on handicapped children and
federal legislation

Monica Morris

Associate Professor of Sociology at California
State University at Los Angeles
Ph.D. in sociology
teacher and researcher in medical sociology,
social interaction, classical and contemporary
theory, and social organization
author of *An Excursion into Creative
Sociology* and *Last-Chance Children:
Growing Up with Older Parents*

Barbara Rothman

Associate Professor of Sociology at Baruch
College and the Graduate Center of the
City University of New York.
Ph.D. in sociology
author of books on obstetrical and
midwifery ideology and on women's

*experiences with new reproductive technology*

*Noel Keane*
*Detroit attorney specializing in surrogate motherhood contracts*
*J. D.*

*Dennis Breo*
*Writer of articles for the <u>Journal of the American Medical Association</u>*

By studying the statements at the conclusion of each of her articles, Jane learns what types of credentials the authors of her sources have. After you have collected information on your authors' advanced degrees, professional experiences, publications, and research, you can begin to evaluate their credentials by asking yourself a series of questions that will help you to determine whether the authors have relevant expertise and special knowledge:

*1. Do any writers hold advanced degrees that suggest relevant areas of expertise?*

Most authors of scholarly articles and books have a Ph.D. in a specific discipline, and if they do, you can assume that they have studied in that field extensively. However, their degrees, and consequently their studies, might not be in the areas about which they write. For example, as an associate professor of sociology at Illinois State University, Barbara Heyl has a Ph.D. in sociology. Her area of study relates well to her argument that surrogacy contracts should reflect the human connectedness that inevitably plays a role in reproduction.

*2. What are the writers' professional experiences?*

You can also gain insights into authors' qualifications by considering where they work and what their responsibilities are. Although professional experiences can give a writer credibility, they can also bias a writer's perspective. For example, as a minister of a low-income parish, does Richard Neuhaus have professional experiences that give him expertise or bias in class-related issues? How could his role of minister influence his view of reproduction and surrogate motherhood? Similarly, as an attorney specializing in surrogate mother contracts, does Noel Keane have professional experience that gives him expertise or bias in the legal dimension of surrogate motherhood? How might his role of lawyer influence his perspective on surrogacy?

*3. In what fields are the authors' publications and research?*

If writers have published articles or books or conducted research in the areas in which they write, they probably have some expertise and specialized knowledge in those areas. For example, Monica Morris has conducted research in medical sociology, social interaction, classical and contemporary theory, and social organization, and she has published in the general field of sociology, as well as in the more specific area of children in nontraditional environments. She has conducted research and published in areas that relate directly to reproductive technology and the effects it can have on the children involved.

After considering experts' evidence, reasoning, and credentials, you should be able to evaluate their viewpoints confidently and fairly, basing your judgments on comparison and analysis rather than on preconceptions. In the following entry in her writing log, Jane evaluates several divergent perspectives on the issue of classism in surrogate motherhood.

## CASE STUDY

Richard Neuhaus presents evidence for classism in surrogate motherhood mostly in the form of facts about the famous "Baby M" case. He shows how the wealthier Sterns used their higher-class status to win the case. Although he proves that class was important in the "Baby M" case, he bases his decision to outlaw surrogacy entirely on this one case. Neuhaus's professional experience as a pastor of a low-income parish has given him insights about how the rich abuse the poor, but he does not seem to have any credentials that would make him an expert in law. Maybe this is why he tries to protect the rights of the poor but doesn't refer to any surrogacy cases that would contradict his argument about classism. I think Neuhaus fails to show the other side of the story. This side is shown by Monica Morris when she talks about a British case that had the opposite result. And even in the United States not all surrogate motherhood cases have classism. Some of the other couples that Noel Keane tried to find surrogates for were not rich. This leads me to the belief that although classism can be found in some surrogacy cases, it is not necessarily part of all of them. Barbara Heyl refers to the adoption system and uses polls to show that people accept the importance of class bias; but just because people accept classism does not mean that it is right. Barbara Rothman uses good reasoning about our patriarchal society to show that surrogacy can limit the rights of women, especially lower-class women of color, but I think that if sound regulations were put into effect, we could limit the ability of rich men and women to take advantage of women of lower classes. Morris mentions some government regulations in England and Australia that control classism in surrogate motherhood. If surrogacy were regulated in the United States to protect women's rights and to stop the importance of wealth seen in some cases, it should be legalized.

According to her log entry, Jane agrees with Richard Neuhaus that classism probably played a significant role in the "Baby M" case, but she also suggests that he inadvertently ignores the cases mentioned by Monica Morris and Noel Keane that did not seem to involve class bias. Attributing

Neuhaus's apparent oversight to his concern for the lower class and to a possible inexperience with legal cases, Jane decides that because he relies so heavily on one case, Neuhaus jumps to the conclusion to outlaw surrogacy. Furthermore, she admits that Barbara Heyl's evidence—the opinion poll about "Baby M" and the references to adoption and the juvenile court system—suggests that many people accept the role that class bias plays in our social and legal systems. Nevertheless, Jane avoids the band wagon fallacy, explaining that she believes classism is unjust despite the fact that many people seem to condone it. She also acknowledges that Barbara Rothman's feminist analysis suggests that the partriarchal structure of American society could affect the rights of working-class women and women of color who want to become surrogate mothers. But her evaluation of the authors' positions leads her to favor regulating surrogate motherhood rather than banning it, because she thinks Morris's information about regulation, if applied in the United States, could allow American women to become surrogates without becoming victims of class bias.

The content of this writing log entry reflects the continuing development of Jane's position toward surrogate motherhood. In her first entry, in which Jane probed her assumptions and biases, she took a dogmatic and absolutist stance in favor of surrogacy. Discussing Neuhaus's concern with racism in her summary-response paper, however, she began to acknowledge the complexity of the topic, to reconceptualize her position, and to take a more tentative stand in support of surrogacy only when class bias does not seem to be an issue. Now, after having read, synthesized, and compared multiple perspectives on the topic, Jane evaluates authors' evidence, reasoning, and credentials to justify her position that surrogacy could indeed be regulated to protect surrogate mothers from class bias. Her present position, although still not completely developed, is informed and reflective. It is interesting that even though Jane keeps modifying her argument, she continues to ground it in the feminist values apparently learned from her mother. Both her original and her most recent stance suggest a strong concern with women's rights.

EXERCISE    1. Evaluate the multiple perspectives reflected in sources on surrogate motherhood (Chapter Five), advertising (Chapter Six), or another topic, asking yourself questions about the authors' evidence, reasoning, and credentials. As you evaluate the writers' views on one or more of the important issues in your topic, try to stake out and justify your own position.

■ ■ ■ ■ ■    RECOGNIZING THE LIMITATIONS
OF YOUR ARGUMENT

If you read your sources empathetically and compare authors' evidence, reasoning, and credentials reflectively, as Jane did, you should feel confident in the judgments you make about your topic. You should be able to argue a position proudly and to justify it persuasively. Nonetheless, Jane's writing log entries reveal not only that you should be confident about your position but also that you should remain somewhat tentative about it. After evaluating the different points of view expressed in your sources, it is time for recognizing the limitations of your argument—that is, for admitting that you might discover ideas or evidence that could change your mind. To write a log entry in which you acknowledge limitations, think about the kinds of events, situations, or facts that could lead you to reevaluate your position on the topic. Jane's log entry looks like this:

## CASE STUDY

> Over the next few years children of surrogate mothers will be old enough to interview. If their parents allow psychologists and sociologists to talk with them, we could get some new information about how children in surrogacy situations grow up and adapt. If the children are unhappy or unhealthy — well, I might have to reconsider my stance in favor of legalizing it. I wouldn't want the children to suffer because of what their parents did.

If you can recognize the limitations of your argument, you will be able to remain open to alternative perspectives as you continue reading about your topic and start drafting and revising a formal argumentative paper. Drafting and revising an argumentative essay will be a learning process in which you further discover, modify, and fine-tune your position. Moreover, by keeping an open mind about your topic, you will be able to produce a final written product that sounds balanced in tone. You do not want your argument to sound weak, but you also do not want it to sound dogmatic. As you try to stake out your position in an argumentative paper, remember that a reflective and persuasive position is always open to discovery and reevaluation.

In Chapter Four, we focus on the writing process in which Jane develops her analysis into a formal, argumentative paper on surrogate motherhood. The chapter includes two rough drafts and the final version of an essay that compares and evaluates several sources.

EXERCISE    1. Try to acknowledge the limitations of your current position on surrogate motherhood (Chapter Five), advertising (Chapter Six), or an alternative topic. What types of evidence, situations, or ideas might you discover that could lead you to reevaluate your argument?

## WORKS CITED

Heyl, Barbara Sherman. "Commercial Contracts and Human Connectedness." *Society* 25 (1988): 11–16.

Keane, Noel P. and Dennis L. Breo. *The Surrogate Mother*. New York: Everest House, 1981.

Morris, Monica. "Reproductive Technology and Restraints." *Society* 25 (1988): 16–21.

Neuhaus, Richard John. "Renting Women, Buying Babies and Class Struggles." *Society* 25 (1988): 8–10.

Rothman, Barbara Katz. "Cheap Labor: Sex, Class, Race—and 'Surrogacy.'" *Society* 25 (1988): 21–23.

# Chapter Four

# DRAFTING AND REVISING

# ARGUMENTATIVE PAPERS

*I think best with a pencil in my hand.*

Anne Morrow Lindbergh

Anne Morrow Lindbergh, author of *Gift from the Sea,* suggests that writing stimulates thinking. When you begin writing an argumentative, multiple-source paper, you will see your topic and your position on it in new ways. For example, in considering the audience for your essay, you will probably work out some of the details and implications of your argument, and you might decide to modify slightly or even drastically change the position you have taken. Therefore, even though you have read your sources empathetically, taken notes on them carefully, and analyzed divergent viewpoints toward your topic, try to remain open to reevaluating your stance as you write. As you will discover while drafting and revising multiple-source essays, the writing process encourages you to keep looking at your argument as you articulate and justify it. A pencil is like a third eye.

In this chapter we refer to the work of our case-study student, Jane, to explain and illustrate strategies associated with drafting and revising college papers. By focusing on the drafting process, we introduce you to strategies such as considering your audience; formulating a thesis statement; integrating information by summarizing, quoting, and paraphrasing; and organizing a rough draft. As we move on to the revising process, you will learn skills for revising on the paragraph level of your essay—skills such as paragraphing, writing introductions, writing conclusions, and using transitions between paragraphs. And as we progress to the sentence and word levels, you will practice strategies such as using active verbs, avoiding nominalization, and using nonsexist language.

# ■ ■ ■ ■ ■ DRAFTING AN ARGUMENTATIVE PAPER

It may at first seem necessary to reread your sources as you begin drafting an argumentative paper; as we briefly explained in Chapter One, however, you should follow your own informed sense of what the important issues are and what you think about them. Rather than rereading your sources during the writing process, try to rely on the notes you have already taken: paraphrases of the main ideas in each paragraph, summaries of entire sources, syntheses of the viewpoints expressed in them, and your analyses of these viewpoints and the evidence and reasoning used to support them. If you have used a writing log to summarize, synthesize, and analyze sources, your notes will be more helpful than the original articles because your notes reflect your own understanding of the authors' most important points. Although you should keep your sources close at hand, try to use them mainly for quoting specific passages.

Furthermore, when you begin drafting, you may feel compelled to focus closely on details such as punctuation and grammar. As we mentioned in Chapter One, however, you should focus first on elements that pertain to the whole essay, not on developing individual paragraphs, crafting eloquent sentences, or choosing the perfect word. If you concentrate on minute details, you are likely to waste time polishing parts of your paper that you will completely delete or totally rewrite later. Instead, set priorities for yourself, moving gradually from the big picture to the more intricate details. Try to think in terms of beginning with the largest unit of text, the entire essay, and then slowly focusing more on smaller units: paragraphs, sentences, and finally words.

## Considering Your Audience

It is complicated to consider the audience for argumentative, multiple-source writing. The first audience to think about is yourself. If you are not interested in your topic, probably nobody else will be curious about it either. And if you are not satisfied with your argument, readers will most likely feel the same way. Therefore, when you make decisions, whether they involve selecting a topic, developing an argumentative stance, or organizing an essay, pay attention to your own reactions and feelings. You can also gain valuable insights from your peers; in fact, many teachers ask students to read and respond to one another's papers.

Although you should always pursue your own interests and consider the advice of your fellow classmates, the most obvious audience for college writing is your teachers. Even if a particular instructor requires class members to comment on rough drafts, the teacher is still the audience for whom you ultimately write. If your classmates respond to your writing, consider their comments carefully. The teacher, however, gives the assignment, has specific requirements and expectations in mind, evaluates your writing, and finally assigns it a grade. You will probably write each of your college papers for a specific instructor, but consider two types of teacher audience: the teacher as evaluator and the teacher as representative of a larger academic group.

To consider the teacher as evaluator—that is, as the person who grades your essays—you need to know the exact requirements of particular assignments and the expectations and pet peeves of individual instructors. For example, some teachers will require you to use a minimum number of sources, and others will not be as specific. Some instructors are relatively unconcerned about grammar and punctuation errors, and others mark every single misplaced comma in a paper. If your teacher provides an oral or written description of a writing assignment, pay close attention to it and ask questions in class about any requirements or expectations that seem unclear. You can also visit your instructors in their offices, asking specific questions about how well your paper responds to an assignment. Most teachers try to be objective about the content of their students' papers, but everybody has biases about certain topics, and college professors are no exception. If your instructor disagrees with your point of view and suggests another one, you do not have to adopt that perspective, but you should acknowledge it in your paper.

Your individual teacher also represents a broader type of audience: an academic community that is highly educated but not necessarily knowledgeable about the details of your particular topic. In considering the audience of teacher as the representative of a larger academic group, you can assume that your reader knows something about your topic in general, but you cannot take it for granted that the teacher has read the sources used in your particular essay. For example, even if you have defined an important term for your writing instructor during a student-teacher conference, you should probably still define that term in your paper, assuming that the larger audience that your teacher represents does not necessarily know what the term means. Furthermore, the larger academic audience is likely to know the conventional rules of argument and to have differing views on your topic, so you will need to avoid logical fallacies of the sort described in Chapter Three and to acknowledge a variety of perspectives. As you can see, college papers present you with an extremely complex problem of audience analysis.

## Formulating a Thesis Statement

The purpose of writing multiple-source, argumentative papers is to analyze several divergent points of view and, in doing so, to stake out and persuasively justify your own position—to add your voice to a conversation taking place among experts. Because your position will probably change as you draft and revise your essay, formulating a thesis statement—that is, a statement of your central argument—is an ongoing process. Nonetheless, if you formulate a thesis early, articulating your position on the topic before starting to write, you will find it easier to make decisions about what to include and exclude in your draft. This is the case because a thesis functions as a guide for the writer as well as the reader. As you write and revise, your central argument will become increasingly clear to you, but try to begin composing by stating the judgment you reached in evaluating experts' viewpoints on your topic. This judgment, or central argument, can serve as a tentative thesis as you write your draft, helping you to focus and to organize your analysis of the various points of view reflected in your sources.

To write an effective thesis, follow these simple suggestions:

*1. State your position clearly.*

Because the purpose of an argumentative paper is to explain and justify what you think about a complex topic, present your opinion clearly to the reader. For example, if you are writing an essay about the controversial topic of animal experimentation, you could use a thesis such as, "Animal experimentation should be legal in medical research but not in research on cosmetics." However, you want to avoid an unclear thesis such as, "Experts have differing opinions about animal experimentation."

*2. State a debatable position.*

An argumentative essay provides an opportunity for you to stake out your own position among other competing perspectives; therefore, generate a thesis that presents a stance that is worth justifying rather than one that people commonly accept as fact. For example, if your teacher asked you to write a paper about capital punishment, you could use a tentative thesis such as, "State legislators should allow capital punishment because it deters crime." Or, you might generate a thesis that states a different point of view: "Because it is discriminatory, state legislators should not allow capital punishment." Both of these stances are debatable. However, you should not begin with a thesis such as, "The question of whether we need capital punishment is a controversial topic in many states." This thesis does not clearly state a position, and it is not debatable.

*3. Limit your position.*

Although you may write about complex topics, try not to argue for positions that are too broad to justify in one paper. Rather, focus your position on important parts of a topic. For example, animal experimentation is a broad, complicated topic, and you could not justify persuasively a thesis that simply took a stand either for or against it. But you could justify a thesis like the first one given on this topic, limiting your position to research on medical treatments and cosmetics. Similarly, capital punishment is a huge topic that has many complicated facets. You could, however, limit your argument, as the first two theses given for this topic do, to the issues of crime deterrence or discriminatory application.

*4. Present your thesis at the beginning of your essay.*

Because your teachers must read many student papers on a regular basis, they appreciate an explicitly stated thesis in the introduction of your paper. If you clearly state your position early in the essay, your reader will know how to interpret the analysis that follows; furthermore, as explained earlier, a thesis located in the introduction can guide your writing and revising process. However, you can also state a thesis at the end of an essay, building climactically to your main point, or you can imply a thesis, never stating it explicitly but allowing your analysis to reflect it. You can experiment with a concluding or implied thesis, but remember that many college teachers view the thesis statement that appears at the beginning of a paper as a convention with an important purpose behind it.

## Integrating Information from Sources

Your thesis will help you to decide what information from sources to include in your essay. As mentioned in Chapter Two, two ways of integrating information from sources are *to summarize* and *to paraphrase*. A third method, which we have not mentioned yet, is *to quote*. All these methods can be appropriate and useful, but they have different purposes.

*1. You can summarize entire sources.*

Imagine, for example, that you are writing a paper on the topic of teenage suicide, arguing first that teenage suicide is indeed a substantial problem and second that parents can take specific steps to help alleviate it. If one of your sources is a recent study that indicates the wide scope of teenage suicides in large cities, you may want to summarize the study, focusing on its methodology and findings, and then to explain why you find it valid. A summary is useful when you want to present an entire source in abbreviated form.

*2. You can paraphrase specific facts and ideas from sources.*

In integrating information, you will probably want to include single ideas or facts more often than you will need to summarize entire sources. If you want to integrate only part of a source, paraphrasing and quoting are better options than summarizing. In general, paraphrasing is more desirable than quoting because when a paper relies heavily on quotations, it has a conglomeration of differing writing styles, and you risk losing your own voice. For example, in writing an argumentative paper about how to prevent teenagers from committing suicide, you would probably consider the various strategies that experts suggest, comparing and analyzing their advice, and ultimately arguing that some strategies are more useful than others. To incorporate preventative strategies, you could paraphrase the original sentences in which they appear.

*3. You can quote short and long passages from sources.*

Although paraphrasing is generally preferable to quoting, sometimes you will need to quote an author. The key is to quote only when you have a very good reason to use a writer's original language. For example, if in writing the essay on teenage suicide, you want to suggest that an author uses loaded terms to manipulate readers, you would need to quote the exact words you think are loaded. If a writer expresses an idea so carefully that in paraphrasing it you risk misrepresenting the author's meaning, you may choose to quote. Or, if in writing about the topic of preventing suicide, you interview a teenager who has attempted suicide and the teen speaks very emotionally about it, you may want to include an exact quotation to capture that emotional intensity. When you have reason to quote a source, you can still maintain the integrity of your own voice and style by quoting words or short phrases and integrating them into your own sentences. Occasionally, however, you will need to quote a long passage from a source. For example, let us assume that in arguing that a certain strategy for discouraging teenagers from committing suicide is unreasonable, you want to show that an author's progression of ideas is illogical. In such a case, you could quote several sentences or a paragraph to present the author's thought sequence before you analyze it.

Whether you summarize, paraphrase, or quote a source, you will almost always need to introduce the passage by identifying its author. When you refer to an author for the first time, include his or her full name but not a title such as "Dr.," "Mr.," or "Mrs." If you want to analyze an author's credentials by emphasizing the person's professional experiences or advanced degrees, you can explain that the writer whom you quote is a doctor, lawyer, or baseball player when you introduce the passage. Subsequent references to the same author should use only the last name. If you follow these simple guidelines, you will refer to the names of men and women in the same manner. In integrating summarized, paraphrased, and quoted information into your paper, you must also cite the source from which it comes. In Chapter Seven, we include details about citing and documenting the sources from which you draw information.

Study the following long quotation, short quotation, and paraphrase. Each is a possible method that you could use to present a passage from Mary Lynch Kennedy's study entitled "The Composing Process of College Students Writing from Sources."

LONG QUOTATION: According to Mary Lynch Kennedy, who researched how different types of writers compose multiple-source papers:

> The more able readers did most of their manipulating of the sources before they set out to compose. They retrieved information, took notes, copied direct quotations, reread their notes, and even revised them at this time. Then, when they composed the essay, they set aside the sources and worked from their notes, rereading them and incorporating them into their piece. They rarely reread the sources, except to retrieve a direct quotation and work it into the essay. (448)

SHORT QUOTATION: According to Mary Lynch Kennedy, who researched how different types of writers compose multiple-source papers, "more able readers" did more "manipulating of the sources" before they began to write a paper, carefully reading and taking notes at this early stage in the writing process. When these students began to draft their essays, they relied on their detailed notes and "rarely" reread their sources except to incorporate a quotation (448).

PARAPHRASE: According to Mary Lynch Kennedy, who researched how different types of writers compose multiple-source papers, the better readers read their sources and took notes on them before they began writing. Once these students started drafting, they relied heavily on their notes, referring to their sources only to find quotations (448).

Each of these methods is technically correct and quite acceptable, but what are the advantages and disadvantages of each? Relying totally on Kennedy's exact words, the long quotation surely reflects her point accurately. However, such a quotation also interrupts your own style, and if you include many long quotations like this one, your voice can become lost. The second example, which integrates quoted phrases and words into your sentences, reflects Kennedy's idea accurately and does not interrupt your own style. The quoted passages could probably be paraphrased without losing Kennedy's meaning, however. The complete paraphrase in the last example also expresses Kennedy's point fairly well, and the paraphrase does not interrupt your style or voice at all. In fact, by paraphrasing the passage, you work at understanding and clarifying the ambiguous terms quoted in the second example.

In reading these three examples, you may have noticed several differences in punctuation. The long quotation is indented 10 spaces from the left-hand margin, and this indentation indicates to the reader that the passage is a direct quotation. The second example uses quotation marks around the words and short phrases that come directly from Kennedy's text, indicating that only these words appear in her article. And in the third example, no quotation marks are used because Kennedy's language is paraphrased. Each of the examples, however, includes in parentheses the number of the page on which Kennedy's idea appears in the original source. Whether you quote several sentences, quote only words and phrases, or completely paraphrase a passage, cite the page from which the author's idea comes. In Chapter Seven, we cover in detail the citation and documentation of sources.

## Organizing a Rough Draft

In organizing a rough draft, as in incorporating information from sources, try to allow your own argument to dictate what you do. If you are writing a paper about surrogate motherhood, arguing, for example, that it is classist but not racist, you could address class in one section and race in another. Remember, however, that each section should not only synthesize what the experts say about an issue but also compare and analyze their viewpoints so as to explain and justify what you think about it. In the section on class, you could paraphrase the views of authorities who find surrogacy to be classist and the views of those who do not, comparing the authors' use of evidence and reasoning to argue for your own perspective. This organizational scheme is often appropriate for argumentative, multiple-source papers because it allows you to synthesize, compare, and evaluate several experts' positions.

In addition to dividing your essay into issues that are important to your argument, consider how these issues relate to each other, sequencing your discussion of them accordingly. For example, if in writing about surrogate motherhood, you want to consider legislation as well as classism and racism, you could first address class and race and then turn to the issue of legislation, arguing that specific laws could or could not solve any potential problems associated with the first two issues. In other words, you could organize your essay around a problem-solution structure. Or, you might find that the focus of your paper suggests another type of organization. For example, if you decide to conduct a detailed analysis of the "Baby M" case, you might want to organize your essay around the stages in the case, beginning with the details of Noel Keane's surrogate mother contract and moving ultimately to Judge Sorkow's decision to award "Baby M" to the Sterns. In writing about any type of process—traveling to Mars, decreasing the number of nuclear weapons, or deciding who receives custody of "Baby M"—you can use a process analysis structure to organize your essay. With this approach, you structure the paper around the succeeding steps in a process, writing the first part on the initial step, the next part on the second step, and so on. Or you could decide to write a paper that focuses almost exclusively on one issue—sexism, for example—arguing perhaps that surrogate motherhood leads to sexism. If this is your decision, you could first explain specific aspects of surrogate motherhood, such as relevant reproductive technology and its legislation, and then argue that their combination can result in certain sexist practices. Whenever you suggest that one thing leads to another—that industrial smoke causes acid rain, that genetic factors contribute to alcoholism, or that poverty leads to crime—you can use a cause-and-effect structure, writing one part of your paper on causes and another section on effects. There are an infinite number of ways to structure an argumentative, multiple-source essay; the key is to let your own argument suggest the organization that is most appropriate.

When drafting her paper on surrogate motherhood, Jane tries to focus on her thesis statement, content, and organization because all these writing elements are essay-level concerns. She does not look up words she cannot spell, try to write a polished introduction, or worry about the unity of her paragraphs. To emphasize these matters would distract her from the paper's argument and overall organization. From reading, thinking, and writing about her topic, Jane knows she wants to focus on the problem of classism and to recommend legislation that addresses this important issue. The following is Jane's first draft.

## CASE STUDY

Thesis statement

I believe surrogate motherhood can be a help for couples who cannot bear children and therefore that it should be legalized. But we do need concrete guidelines if the most important drawback of surrogacy, classism, is to be eliminated.

In "If She's Bright, Beautiful, and Talented and Wants $50,000, Why Not?" Noel Keane, the lawyer who handled the "Baby M" case, and Dennis Breo present five cases involving people who want to have children but for some reason cannot. The first case involves a man named John and a woman named Lorelei. Lorelei could not have children because she had once been a woman in a man's body—what doctors call "semi hermaphroditic." Because

of her problem, she made the decision to have a cross-gender operation that would give her a female sexual organ, but of course
even after the operation she could not have children. John and
Lorelei wanted to have a child, and John wanted one with his
own genes, so surrogacy seemed like the answer. The second case
involved a man named Joseph. He wanted to have a child even
though he wasn't ready for marriage, and he wanted to have a son
with a surrogate because he didn't want to have a sexual relationship with someone he didn't love and want to marry. For their
third case, Keane and Breo give a description of a man named
Thomas and a woman named Cindy Sue. They were both over 40
and had been unable to have a child even though they desperately

SUMMARY    wanted one. Since they weren't getting any younger, they wanted
to have a child by a surrogate mother before it was too late. The
fourth case is about Andy and Nancy. Nancy had two children
from a previous marriage but after that she had a hysterectomy.
The problem was that her second husband, Andy, wanted a child
of his own and Nancy could no longer give birth because of the
operation she had. Last of all, in the fifth case described, there is
Stefan and Nadia from Yugoslavia. They had been trying to have
children for 18 years. But Nadia had blocked Fallopian tubes, and
she had been given a warning that pregnancy would be dangerous
for her. Since Stefan and Nadia were both over 40, they were also
too old to adopt children from an agency, so surrogate motherhood seemed like the last resort for them. All these cases give examples of people who want children but for some reason cannot
have them. According to Keane and Breo, surrogate motherhood
would allow these people to experience the joy of raising a child
that has the genes of at least one parent.

However, surrogacy's propensity for exploitation of people
from lower economic classes is a serious problem. Because of

Paraphrase    this class conflict, Richard Neuhaus, a pastor for a low-income
parish, reaches a decision to outlaw surrogacy altogether (10).
He presents evidence for classism in surrogate motherhood
in the form of facts about the famous "Baby M" case. He uses this

Quotation  evidence to show that surrogate motherhood "rudely rips the veil off class divisions and hostilities in American life" (8). He

Paraphrase  shows how the wealthier Sterns used their higher-class status to win the case (9–10). Although he proves that class was important in the "Baby M" case, he bases his decision entirely on

Analysis  the testimony of this one case, and his analysis is that since the case emphasized class differences, that is what all surrogacy decisions are based on. I think Neuhaus fails to show the other side of the story. This side is shown in "Reproductive Technology and

Paraphrase  Restraints" by Monica Morris, who is a professor of sociology, when she talks about a British case that had the opposite result

SYNTHESIS  (17). Even in the United States not all the surrogate motherhood cases have classism. Some of the people that Keane tried to find surrogates for were not very rich or educated. In "Commercial Contracts and Human Connectedness," Barbara Heyl, another professor of sociology, sees a class bias in surrogacy also, but she

Paraphrase  finds it no different than other aspects of family law, like adoption and juvenile law, and she refers to an opinion poll that indicates most people approved of the judge's decision (11–12). Even though most people show an acceptance of classism in our legal system and surrogate motherhood, I think it is wrong. Classism

Analysis  is not acceptable just because the public thinks it is. However, the British case leads me to the belief that although classism can be found in some surrogacy decisions, it is not necessarily part of all surrogate motherhood cases.

PROBLEM
SOLUTION

I think if sound regulations were put into effect, we could limit the ability of rich men and women to take advantage of women of lower classes. Regulations have become a major issue since the decision came over the "Baby M" case. These new ideas are a reflection on the decision that custody of "Baby M" go to the father because of class reasons. In reference to this though Heyl believes that regulation can help stop this class discrimination,

Quotation  as shown when she says, "We can begin to formulate a creed or policy that could help form public opinion and guide legislature in the near future" (14). This question of regulation is again ad-

Quotation

dressed in the article by Morris for different reasons when she relates her ideas of surrogacy and the future. These ideas are best said when she says, "We could be faced with a Huxleyan society in which making love and making babies are completely separated" (21). It is then through these problems of class and other related issues that could come about with the rise of technology in surrogacy that regulations should be made. These regulations should cover first the rights of the mother, which in my opinion should stress her ability to be able to have contact with her child after it is born. This contact should be the mothers right, she should be able to see her child and hopefully cause a more positive transition for the mother in her giving up her child. This option has

Paraphrase

recently been used in adoptions and so far it has been the trend of the mothers to reduce their visits to the baby after the first year as people start to get back on with their lives (Heyl 15). Another regulation that should be put into effect is that the use of a surrogate mother should be allowed only after all other alternatives have been tried and a doctor has stated that the people who want a baby have failed in all other possible attempts of child bearing. Finally, a regulation needs to be made that outlaws the payment of money to the mother for more than the medical and out-of-work expenses. This last requirement would then be a copy of the Australian law which "prohibits any kind of payment for sperm,

Quotation

eggs, or embryos, other than travel or medical expenses incurred by the donor" (Morris 21). Through the enforcement of the last regulation the appeal to the poor to make money off of surrogacy will not come into effect, therefore stopping some of the class discrimination.

As you probably noticed, Jane does not worry about crafting graceful sentences or choosing perfect words for her first draft. Rather, she concerns herself with the larger issues of formulating a thesis statement, organizing her essay, and integrating information from sources. The first sentence of the short introductory paragraph expresses Jane's argumentative thesis—that surrogate motherhood should be legalized. Furthermore, her introduction also helps the reader to anticipate the major sections of her paper. The first sentence mentions that surrogacy can benefit couples (paragraph two of her draft). The second sentence explains that class bias can nonetheless pose a problem (paragraph three of her draft), and that regulations could address this problem (paragraph four of her draft). The third and fourth paragraphs of Jane's paper work well together because they reflect a problem-solution relationship: She wants to explain what she perceives as a potential problem with surrogacy before suggesting a solution to the problem. Integrating source information into paragraph two, Jane summarizes Noel Keane and Dennis Breo's essay to illustrate that surrogate motherhood can aid couples in a variety of situations. In the rest of her draft, she paraphrases several specific ideas and facts from the articles written by Richard Neuhaus, Monica Morris, and Barbara Heyl, introducing the authors first by their full names and subsequently by their last names only. Quoting the authors as well, Jane integrates some exact words that she chooses not to paraphrase.

You should notice, however, that Jane does not simply integrate information from her sources. In the third paragraph of her draft, she compares and analyzes Neuhaus's and Morris's use of case-study evidence, evaluating their perspectives and justifying her own viewpoint that not all surrogate motherhood cases are classist. And in the fourth paragraph, she synthesizes Heyl's and Morris's ideas about regulating surrogacy to argue for her own view that regulations can solve the potential problem of class bias. Perhaps the most important lesson you can learn from Jane's rough draft is that your thesis determines how to organize a paper and what to include in it. Although she has not yet organized her essay perfectly or developed her argument fully, Jane can continue to work on the structure and content of her paper as she begins to revise it. She is off to a good start.

EXERCISE    1. Using sources on surrogate motherhood (Chapter Five), advertising (Chapter Six), or a topic of your choice, draft an argumentative paper. Remember to formulate a tentative thesis statement that clearly expresses your position on the topic and to let your thesis determine what to incorporate from sources and how to organize it. Do not worry yet about crafting eloquent sentences or choosing perfect words.

■ ■ ■ ■ ■ REVISING AN ARGUMENTATIVE PAPER

In revising an argumentative paper, you begin focusing gradually on small units of text—paragraph, sentence, and word. Concentrating on the paragraph level of an evolving essay, you can revise paragraphs you have already written, write introductory and concluding paragraphs, and add transitions to lead the reader smoothly from one paragraph to another.

## Paragraphing

As you start to emphasize paragraphing, try to keep in mind the following three basic characteristics:

*1. A paragraph should be unified.*

Paragraphs divide an essay into units of text that an audience can easily read and understand. Therefore, each paragraph should be unified around one central idea. To convey each paragraph's central idea to the reader, you can state the topic in the first sentence so that the first sentence of each paragraph indicates to the reader that the essay is shifting from one specific point or issue to another. Although the topic of a paragraph is often stated in the first sentence, another method of revealing a paragraph's point is to state it in the last sentence, to have each sentence build toward a point. A third way to focus a paragraph is to imply its topic without ever explicitly stating it, but this method is less common in college writing.

Read the following disunified paragraph:

> College students need to recognize the importance of disciplined study if they are going to succeed. If they do not study every day, students will not pass their courses or prepare themselves for careers beyond college. Attending parties plays a primary role in the social development of students. When they participate in extracurricular clubs and organizations, students have fun and meet people with whom they share interests. And when they meet people with common interests, students can build enduring friendships. By playing sports, college students learn the value of staying physically fit and of working with a group of people toward a common goal.

This paragraph is not unified because it addresses several different topics: studying, socializing, participating in extracurricular activities, and playing sports. See if you can unify the paragraph by writing a topic sentence that ties all these activities together. Or choose one of the sentences about studies, parties, extracurricular activities, or sports, and use it as a topic sentence in a new, unified paragraph on one activity.

*2. A paragraph should be developed.*

A paragraph is fully developed if it presents evidence such as statistics, examples, references to authority, or facts to support the main point it makes.

Read the following undeveloped paragraph:

> On Saturday mornings each member of my family likes to prepare a different type of breakfast. Although we each like to eat something different and will never agree on what is the best breakfast food, we all enjoy the festive nature of eating together.

This paragraph is not well developed because it does not include examples of the types of breakfast that the writer's family likes to eat. As readers, you cannot picture the scene. Using the first sentence in this paragraph as a topic sentence and the last sentence as a conclusion, try to write several sentences to insert between them. The sentences you write could develop the topic sentence by describing the types of breakfast that members of your family like to make on the weekend. Your sentences should also lead up to the idea in the concluding sentence—that preparing breakfast and eating it together is festive.

*3. A paragraph should be coherent.*

Finally, an easily readable paragraph is coherent—that is, its line of thought is easy to follow. You can organize paragraphs by using the same structures used for organizing entire essays. A paragraph can explain a sequence of steps in a process, illustrate a cause-and-effect relationship, explain a problem and its solution, compare different points of view, or sketch the chronology of an event. Because these are patterns in which people think, readers can readily follow them in your paragraphs.

Slowly read the following paragraph:

> Soon after my father began his new diet, one of his friends stopped by the house with a jar of nuts, a bag of potato chips, and a six-pack of beer. This friend, who was unaware of my Dad's plans to lose weight, opened the snacks and two of the beers. The next morning, my father tore his Weight Watchers' menu calendar off the refrigerator door, tore it up, and threw it in the garbage

can. Darting his eyes around the room, he fell to temptation, and by the time his friend left, the two men had
consumed all the nuts and chips and drunk all the beer.
My father learned that dieting took more willpower
than he was now able to muster.

The last sentence in this paragraph states its topic, and the other sentences describe an event that reflects the idea in the final sentence. But as you probably noticed while reading the paragraph, it is somewhat incoherent. What sentence in the paragraph could you move to make it more coherent? What type of structure does the revised paragraph use?

## Writing Introductions, Conclusions, and Transitions

As you begin writing introductions, conclusions, and transitions, bear in mind that the purpose of an introductory paragraph is to provide pertinent background information, such as definitions of key terms, that will help the audience to understand your argument. For example, if you are writing a paper about surrogate motherhood, you could define the term *surrogate motherhood* carefully at the beginning of your essay so that your readers know exactly what you are writing about. An introductory paragraph usually reveals your thesis statement, or main argument, to the audience as well. Furthermore, in writing argumentative papers about complex topics like surrogate motherhood, you can use an introduction to present differing views on your topic. By writing an introduction that paraphrases several writers' arguments and clarifies your own, you immediately place your position within a context of other voices speaking about your topic. Of course, your introduction should also grab the reader's attention, stimulating the audience to continue reading your essay. Hoping to entice you, for example, we begin each chapter in this textbook with a quotation.

The purpose of a conclusion is to sum up the points you made in trying to explain and justify your argument. But in addition to simply summarizing your own essay, the final section of your paper should draw some type of conclusion, answering the question, "So what?" about your argument. For example, imagine again that you are writing a paper about teenage suicide, a paper in which you argue for specific strategies that parents could use to help alleviate this problem. In your conclusion, you could summarize the strategies that you have argued would be effective, but you could also explore the impact that the strategies would have on the relationship between parent and child. Would they encourage parents and teenagers to communicate better or to respect each other more? Are the strategies based on the assumption that parents should be responsible for their teenage children's emotional stability? If so, are parents of teenagers who have committed suicide then guilty of neglect, or are they even responsible for their child's death? If you are writing an essay about surrogate motherhood, arguing, as Jane does, for regulating it, you could pursue some of the implications of legalized surrogacy. How would it call into question traditional assumptions about marriage and child bearing? How would it affect the future of reproductive technology? What are its implications in terms of human love and sex? A conclusion summarizes your argument and explores its implications. Finally, conclusions should end your paper with a bang, perhaps giving the audience a provocative question, an interesting quotation, or an appropriate analogy to ponder.

In addition to writing introductory and concluding paragraphs and revising all your paragraphs in terms of unity, coherence, and development, pay attention to the relationship of one paragraph to another. Although *you* may know how the point you make in one paragraph relates to the point you make in the next one, you need to explain this relationship clearly to your reader; otherwise, your audience may not follow your sequence of ideas. Study the transitions that Jane writes as she revises her paper on surrogate motherhood. As you read Jane's second draft, notice, too, how she revises paragraphs in an attempt to make them unified, coherent, and developed, and how she frames her essay with an introduction and conclusion.

## CASE STUDY

Definition of terms

Surrogate motherhood allows people who for some reason cannot have their own child in the normal way to have one with the help of another person—a surrogate mother. There are several types of surrogacy. Through in vitro fertilization, human egg and sperm can be combined in a test tube and then transplanted into

INTRODUCTION

a surrogate mother's uterus. It is also possible to freeze embryos created through in vitro fertilization and then to thaw them out later and transplant them into the uterus of a surrogate mother. The most typical kind of surrogacy, however, involves an inser-

Definition of terms

tion of sperm from the father into the surrogate mother with a syringe. This was the type of surrogate motherhood used in the famous "Baby M" case.

Although Noel Keane, the lawyer who arranged the surrogate motherhood situation that led to the creation of "Baby M," and Dennis Breo write about several case studies of people who could benefit from surrogate motherhood, some experts find incredible

Synthesis of
points of view

INTRODUCTION

Thesis statement

problems with surrogacy. Richard Neuhaus, in "Renting Women, Buying Babies, and Class Struggles," sees surrogate motherhood as class conflict, with the courts making a decision that poor parents are unfit to provide for their children (10). In "Commercial Contracts and Human Connectedness," Barbara Heyl says that the problem with surrogacy is that most people do not realize that the bonds between a child, birth mother, and birth father cannot and should not be separated by a legal contract (15). Monica Morris contends, in "Reproductive Technology and Constraints," that although the technology involved in surrogacy is too important to be outlawed, a high degree of regulation is necessary to prevent the commercialization and exploitation of surrogate mothers (19, 22). Finally, Barbara Rothman objects to the practice of surrogacy due to its encouragement of "Western patriarchal capitalism" (23). I believe that surrogate motherhood can be a help for couples who cannot bear children, and I think it should be legalized. But we do need concrete guidelines if the most important drawback of surrogacy, classism, is to be eliminated.

In "If She's Bright, Beautiful, and Talented and Wants $50,000, Why Not?" Keane and Breo present five cases involving people who want to hire a surrogate mother. The first case involves a man named John and a woman named Lorelei. Lorelei could not have children because she had once been a woman in a man's body—what doctors call "semihermaphroditic." Because of her problem, she made the decision to have a cross-gender operation that would give her a female sexual organ, but of course even after the operation she could not have children. John and Lorelei wanted to have a child, and John wanted one with his own genes, so surrogacy seemed like the answer. The second case involved a man named Joseph. He wanted to have a child even though he wasn't ready for marriage, and he wanted to have a son with a surrogate because he didn't want to have a sexual relationship with someone he didn't love and want to marry. For their third case, Keane and Breo give a description of a man named Thomas and a woman named Cindy Sue. They were both over 40 and had been unable to have a child even though they desperately wanted one. Since they weren't getting any younger, they wanted to have a child by a surrogate mother before it was too late. The fourth case is about Andy and Nancy. Nancy had two children from a previous marriage but after that she had a hysterectomy. The problem was that her second husband, Andy, wanted a child of his own and Nancy could no longer give birth because of the operation she had. Last of all, in the fifth case described, there is Stefan and Nadia from Yugoslavia. They had been trying to have children for 18 years. But Nadia had blocked Fallopian tubes, and she had been given a warning that pregnancy would be dangerous for her. Since Stefan and Nadia were both over 40, they were also too old to adopt children from an agency, so surrogate motherhood seemed like the last resort for them. All these cases give examples of people who want children but for some reason cannot have them. According to Keane and Breo, surrogate motherhood would allow people like these to experience the joy of raising a child that has the genes of at least one parent.

Transition

Even though surrogate motherhood seems to offer a promising solution to people who cannot have children through the normal process, surrogacy's propensity for exploitation of people from lower economic classes is a serious problem. Because of this class conflict, Neuhaus, a pastor for a low-income parish, reaches a decision to outlaw surrogacy altogether (10). He presents evidence for classism in surrogate motherhood in the form of facts about the famous "Baby M" case. He uses this evidence to show that surrogate motherhood "rudely rips the veil off class divisions and hostilities in American life" (8). He shows how the wealthier Sterns used their higher-class status to win the case (9-10). Thinking pregnancy might threaten his wife's health, William Stern hired Mary Beth Whitehead to be a surrogate mother for his child in exchange for $10,000 plus medical expenses, but

UNIFIED AND DEVELOPED PARAGRAPH

when the child was born, Whitehead came to the decision that she wanted to keep it. Classism is an issue in the "Baby M" case because the judge decided the baby should go to the home that could best provide for it. At the judge's request, experts visited the homes of the Sterns and the Whiteheads, and their class biases led them to the conclusion that the Sterns' household was better than the Whiteheads'. Because these experts related more to the upper-class, professional Sterns than they did to the working-class Whiteheads, and because the judge believed the baby should be placed in the home that could best provide for it, wealth and education determined who would receive the baby (9-10). Although Neuhaus shows that class was important in the "Baby M" case, he bases his decision entirely on the testimony of this one case, and his analysis is that since the case emphasized class differences, that is what all surrogacy decisions are based on. I think Neuhaus fails to show the other side of the story.

Transition

This side is shown by Morris, who is a professor of sociology, when she talks about a British case that had the opposite result (17). In this case a surrogate mother gave birth to twins and made the decision to keep them. Even though the mother was single, poor, and on welfare, this judge decided that it would be in the best interest of the children if they were given to the mother because she had already developed a psychological bond with them. The judge made a ruling that the bonds already developed between the mother and her children were more important in considering the best interest of the children than any difference in wealth (Morris 17). Even in the United States not all the surrogate motherhood cases have classism. Some of the other couples that Keane tried to find surrogates for were not rich. For example, Andy and Nancy, who wanted desperately to hire a surrogate mother, were poor (180). The British case leads me to the belief that although classism can be found in some surrogacy decisions, it is not necessarily part of all surrogate motherhood cases. Therefore, I do not see why surrogate motherhood should be outlawed because of the problem of classism.

UNIFIED AND DEVELOPED PARAGRAPH

Transition

I think that if sound regulations were put into effect, we could limit the ability of rich men and women to take advantage of women of lower classes. Regulations have become a major issue since the decision came over the "Baby M" case. These new ideas are a reflection on the decision that custody of "Baby M" go to the father because of class reasons. In reference to this though Heyl, another professor of sociology, believes that regulation can help stop this class discrimination, as shown when she says, "We can begin to formulate a creed or policy that could help form public opinion and guide legislature in the near future" (14). This question of regulation is again addressed in the article by Morris for different reasons when she relates her ideas of surrogacy and the future. These ideas are best said when she says, "We could be faced with a Huxleyan society in which making love and making babies are completely separated" (21). It is then through these problems of class and other related issues that could come about with the rise of technology in surrogacy that regulations should be made. These regulations should cover first the rights of the mother, which in my opinion should stress her ability to be able to have contact with her child after it is born. This contact should be the mothers right, she should be able to see her child and hopefully cause a more positive transition for the mother in her giving up her child. This option has recently been used in adoptions and so far it has been the trend of the mothers to reduce their visits to the baby after the first year as people start to get back on with their lives (Heyl 15). Another regulation that should be put into effect is that the use of a surrogate mother should be allowed only after all other alternatives have been tried and a doctor has stated that the people who want a baby have failed in all other possible attempts of child bearing. Finally, a regulation needs to be made that outlaws the payment of money to the mother for more than that of medical and out-of-work expenses. This last requirement would then be a copy of the Australian law which "prohibits any kind of payment for sperm, eggs, or embryos, other than travel or medical expenses incurred by the donor" (Morris 21). Through the enforcement of the last regulation the appeal to the poor to make money off of surrogacy will not come into effect, therefore stopping some of the class discrimination.

Transition     As Neuhaus has persuasively argued, classism was a problem in the "Baby M" case. Referring to a British case, however, Morris provides proof that surrogacy does not have to involve class division. Through the use of regulations, I believe that the

CONCLUSION

major problem of classism that made Neuhaus want surrogacy to be outlawed can be solved. Although the question of class will probably always be a problem in our society, it doesn't have to remain one in the practice of surrogate motherhood. If we regulate surrogate motherhood, we would allow people who cannot have children to have them, and we would also avoid the problem of classism that has been seen in surrogacy. Although the future cannot be foreseen, it is quite possible that new discoveries could be made that will make surrogacy obsolete, but until that time comes some types of regulations are needed on this topic. Man has always tried to use science to harness nature to his advan-

Provocatve question

tage. Why should he not continue to do so with surrogate motherhood?

In reading Jane's revision, you probably noticed that she adds two paragraphs to introduce her topic to the reader. In the first one, Jane defines "surrogate motherhood" because although most people have heard of some surrogacy cases, she knows her audience may not understand the different types of reproductive technology involved. In the second paragraph, Jane explains the major arguments set forth by the authors of her sources and states her thesis, adding her contribution to the ongoing debate about the topic.

Jane also revises the third paragraph of her original draft because it was not well unified or developed. Although the paragraph focused on classism, the first part emphasized classism in the "Baby M" case, the second part addressed the lack of class bias in other cases, and the third part touched on classism in the adoption and juvenile court systems. Since the paragraph shifted emphasis, Jane breaks it into two paragraphs, one focusing on the "Baby M" case, another focusing on cases that do not seem to involve class bias. Notice, too, that she deletes the reference to adoption and juvenile court because it strays slightly from her topic of surrogate motherhood. Adding facts about the surrogacy cases to illustrate her points about them more fully, Jane includes enough evidence to persuade an audience that is unfamiliar with the cases. In revising the section of her paper on classism, Jane develops and unifies her paragraphs.

Furthermore, Jane adds a conclusion that summarizes her analysis, but she also attempts to go beyond a mere summary, asking a provocative question about the role of science in our lives.

Finally, trying to lead the reader from one paragraph to another, Jane writes transitional sentences. Notice, for example, the sentence that leads the reader from the section on class bias to the section on regulation: "I think that if sound regulations were put into effect, we could limit the ability of rich men and women to take advantage of women of lower classes." A major transition, this sentence explains the relationship between classism and regulation, connecting them in terms of problem and solution. Jane also connects the two paragraphs on classism with transitional sentences that explain the relationship between the "Baby M" case and other cases: "I think Neuhaus fails to show the other side of the story. This side is shown by Morris, who is a professor of sociology, when she talks about a British case that had the opposite result." What transitional sentences does Jane use to connect the introduction to the body of her paper, and the body of the essay to its conclusion?

EXERCISE    1. Revise your essay on the paragraph level, stressing the coherence, development, and unity of your introduction, body, and conclusion paragraphs.

After emphasizing the paragraph level, you can begin revising sentences and words. To revise your prose, we suggest you concentrate initially on active and passive voice, nominalization, and sexist language. Passive voice and nominalization can plague the writing style of college students—and teachers. Although passives and nominalizations *sound* sophisticated, they usually make your writing style weaker, less precise, and overly wordy. Masculine gender nouns and pronouns can create imprecise as well as sexist language.

## Using Active Verbs

In trying to impress the teacher with your academic writing, you can fall into the trap of relying too heavily on the passive voice. Passive verbs sound sophisticated, but in most cases an active verb is stronger and more concise than a passive one. Passive constructions include a form of the weak verb "to be" and often a prepositional phrase beginning with "by." In addition to sounding more forceful and less wordy, active verbs are often less ambiguous than passive ones because active constructions always identify the person or thing doing an action. To revise verbs from passive to active voice, read your prose carefully, watching for forms of the verb "to be" followed by verbs in the past tense. Read the following examples and notice why the revisions are stronger, less wordy, and more precise than the original sentences.

PASSIVE: Mary Beth Whitehead was hired to deliver a child.

ACTIVE: William Stern hired Mary Beth Whitehead to deliver a child.

PASSIVE: The surrogacy contract was voided by Judge Sorkow.

ACTIVE: Judge Sorkow voided the surrogacy contract.

It is generally a good idea to revise the passive voice to the active. However, sometimes you can use a passive rather than an active verb, such as when the doer of the action is unimportant or very obvious. For example, in the following case, you could use a passive verb rather than an active one.

PASSIVE: Scott was rushed to the hospital!

ACTIVE: An ambulance rushed Scott to the hospital!

In this sentence, a passive construction works well because who went to the hospital is more important than how he got there and because it is obvious that an ambulance could have taken him.

## Avoiding Nominalization

In trying to make your writing sound sophisticated, you may also rely too heavily on nominalization. Nominalization weakens your prose by placing the action of a sentence in a noun instead of in a verb and by using unnecessary, multisyllabic words. To revise your prose in terms of nominalization, locate the action of a sentence in a verb rather than in a noun. Read the following examples, noting that the revisions use strong verbs to avoid passive voice and nominalization.

NOMINALIZATION AND PASSIVE VOICE: After close analysis of the home lives of the Sterns and the Whiteheads, the psychologists reached the decision that the child should be awarded to the Sterns.

STRONG VERBS: After analyzing the home lives of the Sterns and the Whiteheads, the psychologists decided the judge should award the child to the Sterns.

NOMINALIZATION AND PASSIVE VOICE: After I did an evaluation of the authors' different views, I reached the belief that surrogate motherhood should be outlawed.

STRONG VERBS: After evaluating the authors' different views, I believed the federal government should outlaw surrogate motherhood.

## Using Nonsexist Language

Although authors who write in the English language have for many years used masculine gender nouns such as "man" and pronouns such as "he" to represent both men and women, today many writers try to use nonsexist language. Because sexist language is a political and ideological issue as well as a stylistic one, it may seem inappropriate to include a section on such language in a writing textbook. But using masculine gender words to represent women is imprecise as well as sexist. Masculine pronouns such as "he," "him," and "himself" seem to cause the most problems.

Attempting to solve these problems, conscientious writers have experimented with many creative, although sometimes cumbersome, alternatives. Consider, for example, these proposed alternatives to the masculine pronoun:

> he/she rides
> s/he rides
> her/his bike
> he (or she) rides
> he, or she, rides
> his—or her—bike

The first three alternatives, which use slashes, are awkward because they are distracting to read silently and difficult to pronounce out loud. The last three options, which use parentheses, commas, or dashes, are troublesome because they seem to patronize women. To use nonsexist language well, try to avoid alternatives that employ slashes, dashes, parentheses, or commas.

Some other alternatives to sexist language seem equally problematic. You may have noticed in your own reading that some writers alternate pronouns from paragraph to paragraph, using "he" in one and "she" in the next; this method can confuse readers, making them wonder if the writer is talking about two different individuals. Besides, if you alternate "he" and "she" from paragraph to paragraph as you draft an essay, when you revise your paper and move the paragraphs around, you spend extra time correcting the pronouns each time you reorganize. Other writers use "she" to represent both men and women, reasoning that since people have used "he" for so many years to represent women, the switch is fair. But writers who use "she" exclusively seem just as guilty of using inaccurate and sexist language as those who use only "he."

You can resolve the foregoing problems simply and gracefully by using other options. For example, by using "or," you can add the feminine to the masculine pronoun without relying on dashes, slashes, or parentheses. For example:

> she or he rides
> he or she rides
> her or his bike
> his or hers

When it seems appropriate, you can also use the first person pronoun:

> I ride
> my bike

        mine
        we ride
        our bike
        ours

Or the second person pronoun:

        you ride
        your bike
        yours

One of the best options is to use a plural pronoun:

        they ride
        their bike
        theirs

Sometimes you can even revise sentences to use an article instead of a pronoun, as in:

        a bike
        the bike

Try writing several sentences that use first person, second person, or plural pronouns to avoid sexist and inaccurate language.

Revising her paper on the sentence and word levels, Jane carefully changes passive constructions to active ones, nominalizations to strong verbs, and sexist language to gender-inclusive language. Read her final draft now, and see how she improves her prose.

## CASE STUDY

Title    Surrogate Motherhood: Avoiding Classism through Regulation

Active
voice

Today people who for some reason cannot have a child in the normal way can have one with the help of another person—a surrogate mother. There are several types of surrogacy. Through in vitro fertilization, doctors can combine human egg and sperm in a test tube and then transplant the fertilized egg into a surrogate mother's uterus. It is also possible to freeze embryos created through in vitro fertilization and then to thaw them out later and transplant them into the uterus of a surrogate mother. In the most

Strong verb    typical kind of surrogacy, however, doctors insert sperm from the father into the surrogate mother with a syringe. This was the type of surrogate motherhood used in the famous "Baby M" case.

Although Noel Keane, the lawyer who arranged the surrogate motherhood situation that led to the creation of "Baby M," and Dennis Breo write about several case studies of people who could benefit from surrogate motherhood, other writers find incredible problems with surrogacy. Richard Neuhaus, in "Renting Women, Buying Babies and Class Struggles," sees surrogate motherhood as

Strong verb    class conflict with the courts deciding that poor parents are unfit to provide for their children (10). In "Commercial Contracts and Human Connectedness," Barbara Heyl says that the problem with

Active voice    surrogacy is that most people do not realize a legal contract should not and cannot separate the bonds between a child, birth mother, and birth father (15). Monica Morris contends, in "Reproductive Technology and Constraints," that although legislators should not outlaw the important technology involved in surrogate motherhood,

Strong verbs    they need to regulate the practice strictly so people from the upper class do not commercialize and exploit surrogate mothers (19, 22). Finally, Barbara Rothman objects to the practice of surrogacy because it encourages "Western patriarchal capitalism" (23). I believe that surrogate motherhood can help couples who cannot

Active voice    bear children and therefore that the government should legalize it. However, we need concrete guidelines if we are to eliminate the most important drawback of surrogacy—classism.

In "If She's Bright, Beautiful, and Talented and Wants $50,000, Why Not?" Keane and Breo present five cases involving people who want to hire a surrogate mother. The first case involves a man named John and a woman named Lorelei. Lorelei could not have children because she had once been a woman in a man's body—what doctors call "semihermaphroditic." Because

Strong verb    of her problem, she decided to have a cross-gender operation that would give her a female sexual organ, but of course even after the operation she could not have children. John and Lorelei wanted to have a child, and John wanted one with his own genes, so surrogacy seemed like the answer. The second case involved a man named Joseph. He wanted to have a child even though he wasn't ready for marriage, and he wanted to have a son with a surrogate because he didn't want to have a sexual relationship with someone he didn't love and want to marry. For their *Strong verb* third case, Keane and Breo <u>describe</u> a man named Thomas and a woman named Cindy Sue. They were both over 40 and had been unable to have a child even though they desperately wanted one. Since they weren't getting any younger, they wanted to have a child by a surrogate mother before it was too late. The fourth case is about Andy and Nancy. Nancy had two children from a previous marriage, but after that she had a hysterectomy. The problem was that her second husband, Andy, wanted a child of his own, and Nancy could no longer give birth because of the operation she had had. Last of all, in the fifth case described, there are Stefan and Nadia from Yugoslavia, who had been trying to have children for *Active voice* 18 years. Because Nadia's Fallopian tubes were blocked, <u>doctors</u> *and strong verb* <u>had warned</u> her that pregnancy would be dangerous. Since Stefan and Nadia were both over 40, they were also too old to adopt children from an agency, so surrogate motherhood seemed like *Strong verb* the last resort for them. All these cases <u>exemplify</u> people who want children but for some reason cannot have them. According to Keane and Breo, surrogate motherhood would allow these people to experience the joy of raising a child that has the genes of at least one parent.

*Strong verbs*      Even though surrogate motherhood <u>promises to solve</u> the problems of people who cannot have children through the normal process, surrogacy becomes a serious problem when it <u>exploits</u> people from lower economic classes. Because of this class conflict, Neuhaus, a pastor for a low-income parish, <u>decides</u> to outlaw surrogacy altogether (10). He presents evidence for classism in surrogate motherhood in the form of facts about the famous "Baby M" case. He uses this evidence to show that surrogate motherhood "rudely rips the veil off class divisions and hostilities in American life" (8). He shows how the wealthier Sterns used their higher-class status to win the case (9–10). Thinking pregnancy might threaten his wife's health, William Stern hired Mary Beth Whitehead to be a surrogate mother for his child in exchange

*Passive voice*

*Strong verbs*

for $10,000 plus medical expenses, but when the child was born, Whitehead decided she wanted to keep it. Classism is an issue in the "Baby M" case because the judge decided the baby should go to the home that could best provide for it. At the judge's request, experts visited the homes of the Sterns and the Whiteheads, and their class biases led them to conclude that the Sterns's household was better than the Whiteheads'. Because these experts related more to the upper-class, educated Sterns than they did to

*Active voice*

the working-class Whiteheads, and because the judge believed he should place the baby in the home that could best provide for it, class determined who would receive the baby (9–10). Although Neuhaus shows that class was important in the "Baby M" case, he bases his decision entirely on the testimony of this one case,

*Strong verb*

*Active voice*

assuming that since this case emphasized class differences, all surrogacy decisions are classist. I think Neuhaus fails to show the other side of the story.

*Active voice*

   Morris, a professor of sociology, shows this side when she talks about a British case that had the opposite result (17). In

*Strong verb*

this case a surrogate mother gave birth to twins and then decided to keep them. Even though the mother was single, poor, and on welfare, this judge decided that it would be in the best interest

*Active voice*

*Strong verb*

of the children if he gave them to the birth mother because she had already bonded with them psychologically. The judge ruled that the bonds already developed between the mother and her children were more important in considering the best interest of the children than any difference in wealth (Morris 17). Even in the United States not all the surrogate motherhood cases have classism. Some of the couples that Keane tried to find surrogates for were not rich. For example, Andy and Nancy, who wanted desperately to hire a surrogate mother, were poor (180). The British

*Strong verb*

*Active voice*

case leads me to believe that although some surrogacy decisions illustrate classism, it is not necessarily part of all surrogate motherhood cases. Therefore, the government should not outlaw surrogate motherhood because of the problem of classism.

I think if legislators effectively regulated surrogacy, we could limit the ability of rich men and women to take advantage of women of lower classes. Regulations have become a major issue since Judge Sorkow decided the "Baby M" case. Referring to this, though, Heyl, another professor of sociology, believes that regulation can help stop this class discrimination, as shown when she says, "We can begin to formulate a creed or policy that could help form public opinion and guide legislature in the near future" (14). Morris also addresses this question of regulation but for different reasons when she relates her ideas of surrogacy and the future, writing, "We could be faced with a Huxleyan society in which making love and making babies are completely separated" (21). Because of the problems involved with surrogacy, we should regulate it. These regulations should cover first the rights of the mother, which in my opinion should stress her ability to be able to have contact with her child after it is born. This contact should be the mother's right; she should be able to see her child and then find it easier to part with the baby gradually. Women who wanted to give up their children for adoption have used this option recently, and so far they have tended to reduce their visits to the baby after the first year (Heyl 15). Legislators should also require that people can use surrogate motherhood only after they have tried all other alternatives and a doctor has stated they failed. This regulation would prevent surrogate motherhood from getting out of control. Finally, lawmakers need to stop people from paying the mother more than her medical and out-of-work expenses. This last requirement would copy the Australian law which "prohibits any kind of payment for sperm, eggs, or embryos, other than travel or medical expenses incurred by the donor" (Morris 21). If we can enforce the last regulation, some of the class discrimination will stop because poor people will not have an economic incentive to become surrogate mothers.

As Neuhaus has persuasively argued, classism was a problem in the "Baby M" case. Referring to a British case, however, Morris proves that surrogacy does not have to involve class divi-

*Strong verb and active voice*

*Strong verbs*

*Active voice*

*Passive voice*

*Strong verb*

*Active voice*

*Strong verbs*

Strong verbs

Active voice

sion. I believe the government can <u>regulate</u> surrogate motherhood <u>to solve</u> the major problem of classism that made <u>Neuhaus want to outlaw</u> surrogacy. Although the question of class will probably always be a problem in our society, it doesn't have to remain one in surrogate motherhood. If we regulated surrogacy, we would allow people who cannot have children to have them, and we would also avoid the problem of classism that <u>critics of surrogacy point out</u>. Although <u>we cannot know</u> the future, it is quite possible that

Active voice
and strong verb

<u>new discoveries could soon make</u> surrogacy obsolete, but until that time comes <u>we need to regulate</u> it. People have always tried to

Nonsexist language

use science to harness nature to their advantage. Why should <u>we</u> not continue to do so with surrogate motherhood?

Works Cited

Heyl, Barbara Sherman. "Commercial Contracts and Human
    Connectedness." <u>Society</u> 25 (1988): 11–16.

Keane, Noel P. and Dennis L. Breo. <u>The Surrogate Mother.</u> New
    York: Everest House, 1981.

"Works Cited" page

Morris, Monica. "Reproductive Technology and Restraints." <u>Society</u>
    25 (1988): 16–21.

Neuhaus, Richard John. "Renting Women, Buying Babies and
    Class Struggles." <u>Society</u> 25 (1988) 8–10.

Rothman, Barbara Katz. "Cheap Labor: Sex, Class, Race—and
    'Surrogacy.'" <u>Society</u> 25 (1988): 21–23.

    Completing her final draft, Jane is ready to submit her paper on surrogate motherhood to the teacher. By comparing the passages annotated in Jane's finished essay to the same passages in her earlier draft, you can see the changes she makes in sentence and word levels. You will notice, for example, that in the first paragraph she changes "Through in vitro fertilization, human egg and sperm can be combined in a test tube and then transplanted into a surrogate mother's uterus," to "Through in vitro fertilization, doctors can combine human egg and sperm in a test tube and then transplant the fertilized egg into a surrogate mother's uterus." The first sentence uses a passive verb; the second sentence uses an active one. The revised sentence is stronger and more accurate because it does not include the weak verb "to be" and because it does include the doer of the action. In the same paragraph, Jane also changes "The most typical kind of surrogacy, however, involves an insertion of sperm from the father into the surrogate mother with a syringe," to "In the most typical kind of surrogacy, however, doctors insert sperm from the father into the surrogate mother with a syringe." The first version of this sentence relies on nominalization, but the second version places action in a strong verb rather than in a noun. In the last paragraph of her essay, Jane changes "Man has always tried to use science to harness nature to his advantage. Why should he not continue to do so with surrogate motherhood?" to "People have always tried to use science to harness nature to their advantage. Why should we not continue to do so with surrogate motherhood?" The original sentence uses sexist language, and the revision uses gender-inclusive language. The revised sentence is more accurate because it uses "people" and "we" rather than "man" and "he" to refer to people in general. What other revisions does Jane make? What additional changes do you think she should make?

EXERCISE

1. Revise your essay again, focusing this time on sentences and words. Begin by reading for passive verb constructions, which you can identify by a form of the verb "to be" followed by a verb in the past tense. After changing passive verbs to active ones, revise your paper in terms of nominalization, placing the action of your sentences in strong verbs rather than in nouns. Finally, make sure that your word choices, especially your pronouns, are nonsexist.

You probably noticed that Jane includes a list of "Works Cited" at the end of her finished paper. Include such a list at the end of your multiple-source papers as well. In Chapter Seven, which focuses on researching sources, we explain and illustrate the details of citing and documenting.

## WORKS CITED

Kennedy, Mary Lynch. "The Composing Process of College Students Writing from Sources." *Written Communication* 2 (1985): 434–56.

# Chapter Five

# WRITING ABOUT

# SURROGATE MOTHERHOOD

*Am I describing Paradise or Purgatory, a Golden Age or a Brave New Nightmare?*

*Phyllis Chesler*

The readings in this chapter include four of the works that Jane used as she prepared to write her paper: three of the four articles originally published together in *Society* and a chapter from Noel Keane and Dennis Breo's *The Surrogate Mother.* (The fourth article from *Society* has already appeared in Chapter Two, pages 16 to 20.) In addition to these works, we include the first chapter from Phyllis Chesler's *The Sacred Bond: The Legacy of Baby M,* which provides an excellent introduction to the Baby M case. Chesler also raises some thought-provoking questions that may further stimulate your critical thinking on the topic. And we include "The Terror of Surrogate Motherhood," an essay by Isadore Schmukler and Betsy Aigen, who address the ongoing legal issues confronting state and federal legislators. By reading these additional works, you will have two more perspectives than Jane had when she wrote her paper on surrogate motherhood.

Along with the articles by Barbara Heyl, Monica Morris, and Barbara Rothman, we include the biographical information for each author that originally appeared in *Society.* In Chapter Three, Jane used this information to consider the credentials of the authors of her sources. Heyl, Morris, and Rothman are sociology professors; Neuhaus is a clergyman. In 1990, two years after his article was published in *Society*, Neuhaus changed his religion. He left the Lutheran Church and was ordained a Roman Catholic priest.

Keane, the attorney who helped couples find surrogate mothers in the 1980s, practices law in Michigan. His coauthor, Breo, has written many articles that have appeared in the *Journal of the American Medical Association*. Their book *The Surrogate Mother* describes Keane's efforts in 1979 and 1980 to help desperate infertile couples find surrogate mothers. We include the ninth chapter of the book, "If She's Bright, Beautiful, and Talented and Wants $50,000, Why Not?" The names of people in the book have been changed to protect their privacy.

The authors of our two additional readings, Phyllis Chesler, Isadore Schmukler, and Betsy Aigen, provide you with opposing perspectives on the issue of surrogate motherhood. Chesler has a Ph.D. in psychology. She has written numerous articles and books including *Women and Madness* and *Mothers on Trial: The Battle for Children and Custody*. Throughout her book *The Sacred Bond: The Legacy of Baby M*, Chesler argues against surrogate-parenting agreements because they violate both state and federal laws against indentured servitude—that is, laws stating people cannot be forced to perform against their will, even if they have signed a contract. Chesler also argues that such agreements violate the Thirteenth and Fourteenth Amendments to the Constitution, which prohibit slavery and ensure due process under the law.

Betsy Aigen, Psy.D., and Isadore Schmukler, Ph.D., both work for the Surrogate Mother Program of New York. In their article they argue that viable legislation supporting surrogate mother agreements is possible and desirable. They disagree with the New Jersey Supreme Court decision to outlaw surrogacy contracts and suggest humane standards and guidelines other states could use to legislate surrogacy.

■ ■ ■ ■ ■ ■ ■ ■ ■
# THE CREATION ASSIGNMENT

### Phyllis Chesler

On February 6, 1985, Mary Beth Whitehead, a twenty-eight-year-old housewife and mother of an eleven-year-old boy and a nine-year-old girl, signed a pre-conception or surrogate-parenting contract with lawyer Noel Keane's Infertility Center of New York (ICNY).

The Agreement provided that she (the "Surrogate") would not smoke, drink, or take any drugs during pregnancy; that she would assume any and all medical risks—including death—and that she would submit to amniocentesis and/or abortion upon the demand of thirty-eight-year-old biochemist Bill Stern (the "Natural Father") and his wife, thirty-eight-year-old physician Betsy Stern.

Mary Beth was to receive no compensation if, after trying, she failed to conceive; one thousand dollars if she miscarried or gave birth to a stillborn; and ten thousand dollars if she gave birth to Bill's healthy baby—and legally surrendered custody to him, i.e., if she signed the adoption papers. Noel Keane was to receive seven thousand five hundred dollars for his services. Thus, the Sterns were to pay a minimum of seventeen thousand five hundred dollars, "plus all medical expenses not covered by [Mary Beth's] present health insurance," so that Betsy could legally adopt Bill's genetic child.

On April 26, 1984, ten months before the Sterns selected Mary Beth from a photograph, ICNY's own psychologist, Dr. Joan Einwohner, had written that she was concerned about Mary Beth's "tendency to deny feelings." Dr. Einwohner "thought it would be important to explore with [Mary Beth] in somewhat more depth whether [Mary Beth] will be able to relinquish the child at the end. [Mary Beth's] husband Rick [a Vietnam Veteran and sanitation worker] has had a vasectomy. [Mary Beth] may have more needs to have another child than she is admitting." The Sterns were not informed about Dr. Einwohner's concerns.

Inseminations began the same day in February that the Sterns and the Whiteheads signed the contract. Bill drove Mary Beth in to ICNY from New Jersey. Mary Beth was inseminated. They repeated this procedure nine times until, in July 1985, Mary Beth became pregnant. Betsy decorated the Stern bathroom with pink and blue party streamers. In August, the Sterns bequeathed the bulk of their estate to the six-week-old fetus.

In November 1985, Bill and Betsy wanted Mary Beth to undergo an amniocentesis test. The Sterns did not want a defective child. Mary Beth did not want amniocentesis but felt she had to allow it because of her contractual obligations. In addition, she developed phlebitis and was bedridden for three weeks. Having to take the test made her angry and she refused to disclose the child's sex to the Sterns. Now, Mary Beth also changed her mind about allowing the Sterns to be present at the birth.

On March 27, 1986, accompanied by her husband, Mary Beth gave birth to a daughter—whom she thought looked just like herself. Instantly Mary Beth knew that she'd made a mistake, that she couldn't abandon or sell her own flesh and blood, that she must keep and raise her child. Mary Beth and Richard named the baby Sara Elizabeth Whitehead and, as required by law, filed the birth certificate in their own names. (A husband is automatically the legal father of all his wife's children whether she becomes pregnant by him, by artificial insemination, or by adulterous intercourse.)

According to Mary Beth, she called Noel Keane from the hospital and informed him of her change of heart. He reportedly assured her that "the Sterns might want visitation rights, at the very least." Mary Beth said she would not object to this. She began breast-feeding Baby Sara.

Mary Beth refused to take the ten thousand dollars or to sign the adoption papers. She took Sara home and baptized her in the Catholic Church.

On March 30, Easter Sunday, three days after she delivered, the by-now distraught Sterns pressured Mary Beth into letting them have the baby. After a sleepless and agitated night, Mary Beth implored the Sterns to give her baby back to her. Moved by her suffering they did so. From that day on, Mary Beth refused to part from Sara. On April 12, 1986, after many phone conversations, Mary Beth finally informed the Sterns that she could not surrender Sara to them. The Sterns hired a lawyer, Gary Skoloff, who sought court intervention. On May 5, 1986, when Sara had already been breast-feeding for forty days, Judge Harvey Sorkow issued an ex parte order granting the Sterns sole custody immediately, on the grounds that Mary Beth was allegedly "mentally unstable," i.e., *she couldn't give Sara up!* The Sterns believed that Mary Beth was so "mentally unstable" that she might even exercise her constitutional right to move elsewhere. Sorkow issued his custody order without interviewing Mary Beth and without giving her a chance to hire a lawyer.

On the evening of May 5, the Sterns, accompanied by the police, arrived at the Whitehead home with an order for "Melissa Elizabeth Stern" (the name the Sterns had picked for Bill's genetic child). The Whiteheads showed them the birth certificate, which identified Mary Beth's biological and her husband Rick's legal child as "Sara Elizabeth Whitehead." Then Mary Beth went into the bedroom and passed the baby out the window to Rick. When the police discovered that the baby was gone, they handcuffed Mary Beth and led her into the back seat of the squad car. The police, with no legal basis for arresting her, released her. Within twenty-four hours, Mary Beth and her family fled to Florida and took refuge with her parents, Catherine and Joseph Messer.

Bill knew that Mary Beth was hiding somewhere in Florida. She kept calling him in distress. Judge Sorkow had frozen the Whitehead bank account. Rick and Mary Beth had run out of money; the bank was about to foreclose on the mortgage to their New Jersey home. On July 15, Bill taped the following conversation:

MARY BETH: Bill, you think you got all the cards. You think you could do this to people. You took my house. I mean, we don't even have a car anymore. I can't even afford the car payments. You took everything away from me. Because I couldn't give up my child? Because I couldn't give up my flesh and blood, you have the right to do what you did?

BILL: I didn't freeze your assets. The judge froze your assets. He wants you in court. I want my daughter back.

MARY BETH: And I want her, too, so what do we do, cut her in half?

BILL: No, no, we don't cut her in half.

MARY BETH: You want me, you want me to kill myself and the baby?

BILL: No, that's why I gave her to you in the first place, because I didn't want you to kill yourself.

MARY BETH: I didn't anticipate any of this. You know that. I'm telling you from the bottom of my heart. I never anticipated any of it. Bill, please, stop it. Please do something to stop this.

BILL: What can I do to stop it, Mary Beth?

MARY BETH: Bill, I'll let you see her. You can have her on weekends, Please stop this.

BILL: Oh, God. I can live with you visiting. I can live with that, but I can't live with her having a split identity between us. That'll hurt her.

MARY BETH: What's the difference if I visit or you visit? I've been breast-feeding her for four months. Don't you think she's bonded to me?

BILL: I don't know what she's done, Mary Beth.

MARY BETH: She's bonded to me, Bill. I sleep in the same bed with her. She won't even sleep by herself. What are you going to do when you get this kid that's screaming and carrying on for her mother?

BILL: I'll be her father. I'll be a father to her. I am her father.

MARY BETH: Bill, she knows my smell, she knows who I am. You cannot deny that. Don't I count for anything? Nine months I gave life to this baby. If it wasn't for me, Bill, she wouldn't even be here.

BILL: That's true. She wouldn't be here if it weren't for me either.

MARY BETH: Oh, come on, Bill, it's a little bit different.

BILL: No. I want my daughter back.

MARY BETH: Well, Bill, how about if there's no daughter to get back?

BILL: What do you mean by "no daughter to get back"?

MARY BETH: I took care of myself the whole nine months. I didn't take any drugs. I didn't drink alcohol. I ate good. And that's the only reason that she's healthy, Bill. I gave her life. I did. I had the right during the whole pregnancy to terminate it, didn't I Bill?

BILL: It was your body.

MARY BETH: That's right. It was my body, and now you're telling me that I have no right.

BILL: Because you made an agreement. You signed an agreement.

MARY BETH: Forget it, Bill. I'll tell you right now I'd rather see me and her dead before you get her.

BILL: Don't, Mary Beth, Please don't do—

MARY BETH: I'm going to do it, Bill. You've pushed me to it. I gave her life. I can take her life away. If that's what you want, that's what I'll do.

BILL: No, Mary Beth, no, Mary Beth, wait, wait. Please.

MARY BETH: You've pushed me.

BILL: Please don't—I don't want to see you hurt. I don't want to see my daughter hurt.

MARY BETH: My daughter too. Why don't you quit doing that, Bill, okay? It's our daughter. Why don't you say it, "our daughter"?

BILL: All right, our daughter. Okay, Mary Beth, our daughter.

MARY BETH: That's right. Bill, I can't live like this anymore.

BILL: Please, Mary Beth, please.

MARY BETH: Please forgive me. Tell Betsy to please forgive me. Tell Betsy that I always really cared about you two.

BILL: Where are you Mary Beth? Please, Mary Beth, don't hang up.

MARY BETH: I'm sorry, I'm sorry. Good-bye Bill.

On July 28, 1986, when Mary Beth was hospitalized in Florida with a severe infection, Sara had already been breast-feeding for four months or 123 days. On July 31, while the Sterns waited at the police station, detectives armed with an order for Melissa entered Catherine Messer's home. They allegedly knocked the grandmother down, took Sara from her crib, and pushed away her older sister, Tuesday, who was screaming and hitting an officer on the leg with a hairbrush.

Judge Sorkow did not permit Sara and Mary Beth to see each other for five and a half weeks. Sara was weaned that day by the police, per Judge Sorkow's order. Then, in mid-September, he allowed Sara to see her mother twice a week, for an hour each time. He forbade Sara to breast-feed. The visits took place in a state institution, in a room approximately twelve-by-fourteen feet with an armed guard and a nurse matron in constant attendance. Sara was not permitted to see her half-sister Tuesday, her half-brother Ryan, or her legal father, Rick, except for two hours at Christmas and for three hours on March 29, 1987.

A year after Mary Beth gave birth, ten and one-half months after Sorkow first awarded temporary custody to the Sterns, eight months after his order went into effect, and seven months after a stressful public trial, the judge upheld his own ex parte order of May 5, 1986. On March 31, 1987, Sorkow terminated Mary Beth's parental rights, not because she was in any way unfit but in the "best interests" of the child; he legalized the surrogacy contract; gave permanent custody to the Sterns; and he allowed Betsy Stern to legally adopt Baby M, "Melissa Elizabeth Stern."

Who is a child's true mother? The woman who gives birth to her? Or the woman married to the child's father? The woman who actually takes care of her? Or the woman who can offer her the most money?

Is a child's true mother really her father? Does a child need a biological mother, if her father wants to take exclusive care of her—without involving any women?

Are most biological mothers "unfit" or are they less fit than genetic fathers or adoptive mothers? Should biological motherhood be abolished in the "best interests" of the child? What is a "fit" mother? Who should decide?

Would each child be better off served by a minimum of four "mothers": she who donates the egg, she who incubates the fetus and gives birth, she who legally adopts the newborn, and she who is the child's primary caregiver?

What if compartmentalizing "mother" into specific functions actually enlarges and enhances our experience of both motherhood and childhood? What if such vivisection allows both men and women, the infertile and the fertile, the single and the married, to "mother" children? Would it be civilized—or barbaric—if everyone were to take nurturing and economic responsibility for children, even if they're not bound by blood or suited by temperament to do so?

What would replace the mother-infant bond—the oldest and strongest bond known to a man (and obviously to woman)? Would the absence of this very specific blood bond ultimately weaken and destroy us as a species? Or is the ability to "let go" of this bond precisely what will free us to control our destiny more scientifically?

We must decide: Is a biological mother a human being with a heart, a mind, and an eternal soul—or is she only a surrogate uterus? Is a biological mother the best possible person to mother her baby? If she *is* a fit mother, what entitles a sperm donor or even a legal husband to *sole* custody of her child? Must every woman become a mother? Is every biological mother who is fit to do so obliged to raise her child?

We must decide: Is a father only an income-generating sperm donor? Or is he as "maternal" as any biological mother? If he is, then should biological mothers and genetic fathers "parent," that is, should they both mother and generate income in equal or identical ways? If a custody battle erupts, which "parent" is presumed entitled to custody?

Must every man become a father? Is every genetic father who is fit to do so obliged to raise his child?

Should any blood relative: a grandparent, sibling, aunt, uncle, even a distant cousin, be entitled to sole custody of a child "for its own good," e.g., if they have more money or less troubled relationship with the child (or with the state) than a biological or genetic parent does?

Is a child a "thing" that blood relatives are entitled to fight over? Does a biological mother or genetic father "own" a child? Perhaps all biological families are unfit, i.e., too possessive, too invested in owning each other.

Should we abolish the biological family in the "best interests" of the human race? Should we more readily honor the custodial claims of any adult or group not related to the child by blood, for instance, a foster, adoptive, step- or co-parent? On what grounds should we do this?

Should the male-dominated state replace the father-dominated biological family entirely? Should we have baby-breeding farms and children's houses staffed by trained and paid employees chosen for their "fitness"? Would children be better off if those who took care of them had decent working conditions and had to meet certain standards?

Should parenting become a blue- or a white-collar occupation? If so, should poor or otherwise disadvantaged women be paid to "incubate" babies for higher-income women who are sterile, have chosen careers, or wish to avoid the risks of pregnancy?

Should male-dominated science clean up the imperfect "mess" of human reproduction and traditional family-style child-rearing? Should each child of the future be born at scientifically timed intervals with its sex, personality, skin-and-eye color all carefully preselected?

This scenario has its advantages. For example, if people were *produced* technologically and impersonally instead of *reproduced* biologically and personally, then neither abortion nor involuntary motherhood would have to exist. No human being would have to get pregnant, stay pregnant, or have an abortion.

No one would have to suffer from sterility. How could one? No human being would be personally engaged in biological reproduction; no one gene pool would be used for technological production of the next generation. (Docility might come from one gene pool, the shape of a smile from another, hand size from a third.)

No one would have to marry in order to reproduce. Families as we know them would probably become as extinct as the dinosaur. Racism and sexism could be eliminated. We could all be identical: biologically (male) and racially (white).

Am I describing Paradise or Purgatory, a Golden Age or a Brave New Nightmare? We aren't there yet, but on our way to the future, there are some immediate questions to answer.

If a woman has a legal and moral right to her own body, isn't she free to exercise that right in any way she deems fit? Doesn't she have the legal right to rent her vagina or her uterus, or to sell her one-of-a-kind and irreplaceable heart—or unborn child?

If a woman has the legal right to terminate a pregnancy *because she and no one else has a right to her body,* then at what point does her (pregnant) body cease to be hers alone? When does a sperm donor, an unwed boyfriend, a legal husband or the state, on behalf of the fetus, have the right to prevent a woman from having an abortion on the grounds of their future right to custody? One minute after conception?

Or does a pregnant woman retain the right to her own body until she is five months pregnant? After this, does the sperm donor or legal husband have the right to force her into an amniocentesis test or an abortion?

Does the state have the right to try a woman for murder if her child is born dead—and it is viewed as her fault because she drank alcohol, smoked tobacco, thought "bad thoughts"? Will the state start imprisoning pregnant women for "fetal abuse"? Will the state automatically take custody of these children at birth, wall them up in institutions, sell them to the highest bidder?

The Baby M case raises all these questions—and more. The case is about the reproductive rights of women and men; about biology, human bonding, parental rights and parental obligations; about surrogacy, legal contracts, indentured servitude, and slavery; about mother-blaming among psychiatrists—particularly those involved in custody battles; about the increase in sterility in North America and the consequent increase in custody battles, adoptions, and new reproductive technologies; about the role of the media and legislation in our daily lives—the list is a long one indeed.

The Baby M case is also the story of two women and one man, all united by their passion for the same child. The story has no heroes and no heroines: only monstrously flawed—i.e., ordinary—human beings.

Which makes the issues even more important.

All over the country, people argued and took sides. We tended to "like" and "feel sorry for" Bill and Betsy, and to "hate" Mary Beth. Everyone felt very strongly about who should "get" Baby M—as if we really knew or were entitled to decide; as if this rather public spectacle was, in essence, a family affair. And it was.

We were all "voting" on the future of motherhood and on the future of the human family.

Most of us wanted our future mothers and families to be educated, solidly middle class, and in scientific control of their lives. According to two separate polls, between 74 percent and 92 percent of Americans agreed with the decision to place Baby M with her biochemist father (Bill is employed by the Unigene Corporation) and his pediatrician wife (Betsy's Ph.D. is in human genetics) where, as the child of scientists, she would have the kind of life that would inoculate her against the bad teeth, bad grades, bad health, and bad luck that characterize life among the hard-working, working-class poor.

We were also "voting" on the past collective performance of mothers. We blamed them (not our fathers or presidents or even Our Father Who Art in Heaven) for failing to love us completely enough and for failing to save us from unhappiness. We were Americans. We believed we had a constitutional right to happiness and prosperity.

We were all so angry at mothers (they were the ones, after all, who'd birthed us) that any media "fact" that couldn't be used to condemn Mary Beth didn't register. Other "facts" canceled it out. We heard it—but we promptly forgot it. ("Oh, she refused the ten thousand dollars? But she did sign the contract, didn't she?" "Oh, she really was breast-feeding? But didn't she want to kill the baby?" "Oh, no one ever proved that she was an unfit mother? But the Sterns can offer the child so much more.")

Add to this the "fact" that the media, like everyone else, were also biased in favor of the educated middle class and had more sympathy for the problem of middle-class sterility than for the problem of either working-class *fertility* or sterility.

Sterility has increased—probably due to the combined effects of birth-control technology, delayed childbearing, and an increase in environmental toxicity. Simultaneously, abortion and birth control have led to a "shortage" of adoptable white babies. Many of the journalists, as well as the lawyers, judges, psychiatrists, and social workers involved in the case either themselves were or knew other middle-class people who were sterile, or adoptive parents, or who had experienced great difficulty in trying to adopt a "desirable" baby. The infertile had our "sympathy vote"—at least superficially.

At a deeper level, most people refused to question their own genetic narcissism. For example, no one demanded that *fertile* people adopt a child-in-need before they'd be allowed to reproduce themselves. We were quick to blame the infertile for not wanting to adopt "flawed" children, but we, the fertile, were not about to overturn either adoption procedures or the definition of what constitutes a family.

We (or the entrepreneurs among us) preferred to profit from the suffering of the newly sterile by strip-mining the fertility of the poor, i.e., by industrializing polygamy or surrogacy.

Everyone in America focused on *one* custody battle (Baby M's) as a way of denying (or as the unacknowledged symbol for) the *millions* of custody battles and legal kidnappings that raged all around us. Men (and higher-income couples) were fighting women (and lower-income couples) for custody of the children birthed by unwed or impoverished Third-World mothers—and also by marriage-contract mothers.

The Baby M case is what a custody battle is really like. Marriage constitutes the most common reproductive contract between a woman and a man; a wife may have as much (or as little) right to contested custody of her child as Mary Beth Whitehead—or any other "surrogate uterus" does. Marriage contracts don't exist, but are enforced anyway. Ask any divorced woman about the covenant she so eagerly signed with all of patriarchy, but never read or understood.

According to most Americans, not all contracts are created equal. A football or a movie star's employment contract may be amended or broken, but a woman's contract with a man about his sperm may not be overturned—at least not without threatening our "procreative liberties," the "joys of parenthood," and our "loving homes."[*]

Ultimately, the Baby M case is important for what it teaches us about ourselves.

## Questions for Empathy and Analysis

1.  Chesler gives a list of dates and facts about the Baby M case. Does she organize the list in chronological order? How much time lapses from the date that Mary Beth Whitehead signs the contract with Noel Keane's Infertility Center of New York (ICNY) and the date

---

[*]These phrases are lawyer Gary Skoloff's, from his appeal brief for the Sterns.

that Judge Sorkow terminates Whitehead's parental rights? In a summary of Chesler's list, which dates would you select to convey empathetically Chesler's orientation to the topic? Do Chesler's selection and organization of facts predispose you to feel a certain way toward Mary Beth Whitehead? Do the facts speak for themselves?

2. Around what subjects does Chesler organize her questions and in what order? Do any specific word choices in the questions make you feel a certain way or predispose you toward a certain answer? After reading these questions empathetically, how do you think Chesler would answer her question: "Am I describing Paradise or Purgatory, a Golden Age or a Brave New Nightmare?" (93)

3. Chesler says that polls showed that most people supported the judge's decision to award Baby M to the Sterns. What does she think this indicates about us?

4. Chesler claims that certain "facts" important in the Baby M case did not register on people's minds. Why does she think people ignored certain aspects of the case? Does her presentation of the "facts" encourage you to agree with her claim about the media and their bias toward the middle class? Did the media omit too much? Does Chesler herself omit or slant evidence in an unfair way?

■ ■ ■ ■ ■ ■ ■ ■ ■

# "IF SHE'S BRIGHT, BEAUTIFUL, AND TALENTED AND WANTS $50,000, WHY NOT?"

## Noel P. Keane and Dennis L. Breo

Things opened up in 1980. Suddenly, some of my clients were legally offering $10,000 fees to find surrogate mothers. Introduced into the drama of surrogate parenting were, among others, a transsexual housewife, a single male Hollywood scriptwriter who wanted a son through sperm-splitting and sex-selection techniques, an East Coast "tomboy," a celebrity couple big in films and country music, a Texas midwife with a cause, a California forest ranger, an immigrant couple with everything but a baby, and a physician-supervised clinic specializing in surrogate mothers.

Five of my new cases in 1980 represented the unusual cross-section of people that now are seeking out this new option. Each represented a new challenge for me. There were:

John and Lorelei, a married couple from Connecticut. Lorelei is a transsexual. This couple had to institute a cross-country hunt to Southern California to find a surrogate mother. And Rita, the woman they thought was the answer to their prayers, was to make their lives a nightmare. It was Bill and Bridget and Diane all over again. After John and Lorelei suffered great anguish and expense Rita became pregnant. But, in a dramatic turnaround, she then vowed never to give up the baby. The baby is due in the spring of 1981, and I think that this case will make legal history. Unless Rita changes her mind, a court will be asked to decide whether the baby born to a surrogate mother belongs to the natural mother or to the natural father and his wife.

Joseph, a single man from Hollywood, California, who is both a student and scriptwriter. At the age of thirty, he decided he was ready to start a family, but there was one catch. He was not yet ready to get romantically involved with a woman. He wanted a surrogate mother to give him a child. Beyond that, he wanted a son. To increase the probability of having a son, he wanted to have his sperm split in a laboratory procedure to enhance the male-carrying chromosomes and to have the surrogate mother inseminated with the male-enriched sperm. Since he would not have to adopt (he would already be the father) he is legally able to pay a fee and is prepared to pay what is becoming the standard rate at Dr. Levin's new clinic in Kentucky—$10,000. (Joseph, however, as a single man would not be eligible to find a surrogate mother at Dr. Levin's clinic, which works only with married couples.) Since Joseph's case adds three unorthodox new dimensions—the payment of a fee, the splitting of sperm for sex-selection, and single parenthood—to what is already a controversial subject, I knew there was but one way to argue Joseph's cause: on television. Sure enough, when Joseph spent an hour on "The Phil Donahue Show," the female audience began by wanting to eat him alive. But by the show's end, they had come around to his point of view. A few even volunteered to be the surrogate mother! But Joseph is a fastidious man, and we were to find the search for the surrogate mother to be slow going.

Thomas and Cindy Sue, a film couple from Manhattan. He is a producer of enormously successful TV commercials and industrial films and she is a Southern belle who is well known on the country music scene. They were to spend frustrating months trying to impregnate their surrogate mother, Donna, an East Coast "tomboy" who grew up on a farm and desperately wanted to get pregnant for someone else. The only problem was that she either couldn't get pregnant, or on two occasions when she did, she could not carry a child to term. It was to be a case of extreme determination and extreme frustration.

Andy and Nancy, a laid back couple from the mountains of eastern California. The surrogate mother they found, Jeannette, is unusual for two reasons. She is married and entered into the agreement with her husband's blessing. And she is a midwife who publicly announced her decision in an effort to spread the good news about midwifery. This case represents the ultimate in coincidence. Andy and Nancy called me one afternoon looking for a surrogate mother, and, ironically, Jeannette had contacted me that same morning to volunteer as a surrogate mother. Within days, Jeannette was inseminated by Nancy with Andy's sperm and, it subsequently was confirmed, became pregnant.

Stefan and Nadia, an immigrant couple from Yugoslavia on whom time was running out in their relentless search for a baby. The surrogate mother was their last resort, and they had the money to pay a fee. This was the first couple I sent to

Dr. Levin in Kentucky to be matched with a surrogate mother, who would remain anonymous to the adoptive couple. Their baby, I am happy to say, is also due this spring and you would have to look far and wide to find a happier couple.

These five new cases are a mixed bag of motives and personalities that run the gamut of human experience. The surrogate-mother marketplace is becoming a rather exotic bazaar.

I will describe these cases in detail but they are only the tip of the iceberg. Calls and letters come in daily from people representing every aspect of the human condition. There are a lot of surrogate mothers who—both with and without a fee—want to have these babies. This is not only my experience. But it is also the experience of surrogate mothers in Dr. Levin's clinic.

Each new case represented to me a new legal nuance, a new challenge to be surmounted. But, in addition to the legal intricacies, I have been fascinated by the motives of the people involved, both those who want to have children and those want to carry them. Through the surrogate-mother issue, I have met more interesting people than I have in all my other legal work combined.

When you talk to people about having babies, you are unlocking their strongest feelings. In discussing their hopes, the people in these pages bared their souls so that others like them might have it a little easier.

One factor that should not be overlooked in the surrogate-mother story is the extraordinary effort required on the part of everyone involved, often against enormous odds.

It took surrogate mother Sally a full year of repeated monthly inseminations before she finally became pregnant. And she was prepared to go another year, including visits to a fertility clinic if necessary. She was not paid a penny, other than routine expenses, by adoptive couple Richard and Aralee who had been looking for a way to have a baby for years before even hearing of a surrogate mother. (Their first candidate for surrogate mother, Jill, strung them along before bowing out with an alleged heart murmur.) They persisted with Sally and their hopes—and efforts—never wavered.

I was absolutely delighted when Sally told me she was pregnant. Later, Richard would explain to me how trying their quest had been.

"Sally had free flying privileges and would often fly down to Virginia for the inseminations," he said. "But just as often, Aralee and I or just myself would fly to Detroit. It was becoming very expensive, and we are not wealthy people. Although we both have professional positions, let's face it, the universities do not pay that much. And we both are still paying off heavy educational debts.

"Sally's cycle was so irregular that it was very difficult to calculate her fertile period. We tried temperature charts to pinpoint the precise time of ovulation, but it was all very haphazard. The first two inseminations were witnessed by the Detroit doctor, but that procedure got to be very inconvenient. The most opportune times were often on the weekends, and the doctor would be out of town or off duty. The doctor wasn't doing anything we couldn't do for ourselves, so we just started to do it ourselves. We even went to a fertility clinic in Virginia to get some added advice.

"Sally would perform the inseminations herself. If it were being done in Detroit in a motel, which was another expense, I would discreetly go into the bathroom and fill a syringe and bring it to her and then leave the room. If it were being done in our home in Virginia, I would give the syringe to my wife and she would take it into the other bedroom to Sally.

"Then would begin the long wait. We knew that Sally's period is usually around the first of the month. So we would just sit around and wait for the phone to ring. Every time it rang around the first of the month, we would think, 'Oh, no, that's Sally calling to say she's started her period. We have to do it all over again.' That was the pattern month after month.

"But Aralee and I both believe in extraordinary effort for the things that we want. We are prepared to pour all our energy and money into something worth having. We never gave up, and, fortunately, never did Sally. She did get a little discouraged. At one point, she was feeling guilty, thinking that maybe she wasn't capable of conceiving and that she was wasting our time. She went to a gynecologist, who said there was no apparent problem, but that, perhaps, there was some subtle technique that needed to be worked out. Sally decided that if things didn't hit by the end of 1979, she would go to a fertility clinic in Michigan. I was prepared to go back to the fertility clinic in Virginia to see if there was some extra technique or medication we could try.

"But December was our month. The phone never rang when we feared it might, and we started to cross our fingers. About a week later, Sally called. Our hearts sank. We thought, 'She's calling to say her period was a week late.' But, no, she said, 'Nothing yet, keep your fingers crossed.' She had bought a home pregnancy kit and was going to do the test the following week. It was positive, and her doctor later verified it. Her next call was what we had been waiting to hear for years. 'We've done it! I'm pregnant.' What a Christmas present! Aralee and I have been all smiles ever since.

"And, Noel, you know Sally called us on the night of December 18th. She said she had called your home, too, but your son said you were at an office party. Sally didn't want to bother you, but Aralee and I insisted. We knew you would want to know as soon as possible. After all, you helped make this whole thing possible."

I spent very little time worrying about how Richard and Aralee and Sally would come out. I knew they were right on. My five new cases, however, were not moving so smoothly.

Lorelei sent me a long letter, lovingly handwritten on floral stationery. She said, in effect, that nature had played her a "dirty trick," that for twenty-one years she had the soul of a woman imprisoned in the body of a man, but that the minute she came of age corrective surgery was performed to change her gender. I am neither a physician nor a psychiatrist and was in no position to appraise the validity of her claims. She was recently married and wanted children. With her background, there was but one real option—the surrogate mother. I told her my fee was $2,000—nonrefundable—and that I would require personal interviews with her and her husband, and affidavits from her parents and physicians.

"Do you still want to proceed?" I asked. Lorelei shot back, "You've got it. This is the answer to our prayers."

An appointment was scheduled, but before Lorelei and John came to Detroit, I received a letter from her father. Knowing that Lorelei Michele spent the first twenty-one years of her life as Loren Michael, I was curious as to what her father made of this. His letter was both touching and reassuring.

Hello, Mr. Keane,

My daughter, Lorelei Michele _____, née Loren Michael _____, informs me that you have requested a letter from my wife and me, saying, in effect, that we know all about what she did and is doing, and approve. In view of the fact that Lorelei is twenty-six years old and a married woman, I assume that this is professional courtesy on your part and not a requirement.

Of course, we approve. Surrogate parenthood runs in the family. I am an adopted son, and Lorelei's older brother is also adopted. That is to say, in both cases there were a natural mother and a second-husband father. But I could not have been more loved nor better reared than I was by my Dad, Mom's second husband. And my oldest son is a source of great pride and joy to me. I think my wife and I must have done something right. All our kids still love us. And we them.

What this all boils down to is, again, a philosophical conviction that parental love doesn't happen biologically. It is a creation of minds and hearts interacting over months and years, giving and receiving to and from each other. My parents believed and demonstrated that. My wife and I have always believed it, and I think we have passed it on to our children. If I am right, then it's an accomplishment I take pride in.

Lorelei, therefore, will certainly have no difficulty loving for and rearing "another woman's child," because being the kind of person she is and having the background she has, she will never think of the child as anyone's but hers and John's. The fact that half the chromosomes will be John's is mere icing on the cake.

And speaking for my wife and me, the child will certainly have doting grandparents to visit and get spoiled by.

The letter was signed by both father and mother. I noticed that in Lorelei's formal application to me, she described her father as a decorated fighter pilot during World War II. He was a big Swede, six-foot-three and 245 pounds. Ironic, I thought, that his son should turn out to be a girl.

Whatever remaining doubts I might have had about Lorelei disappeared when I interviewed her and her husband. They are good folks and happily married. Period. However, I had to ask them some tough questions.

John is a dark man and Lorelei is a big blond woman. To the untrained eye, she would certainly "pass" as a normal woman, though a trifle big-boned. Her disposition, however, is decidedly feminine. She speaks quickly and without affectation. Hers is a particularly moving and unusual story.

"I spent the first twenty-one years of my life as a boy," she began. "And I was a very strange-looking boy, OK. In high school, I finally got to the point where I stood there in front of the nurse and said, 'Is this the body of a boy?' And she said, 'Have you seen a doctor?' And I said, 'Well, no, I have never been sick.' She said, 'You have never had a medical examination?' I replied, 'Not since I was six. In my family, you just don't go for medical checkups unless you are sick. A little cold or flu going around, we don't go to the doctor.' My family couldn't afford it. I had never been sick. Well, the nurse wrote a note to my gym teacher excusing me from gym class because it had gotten to the point where I was looking pretty strange, you know. Nothing was developing as it should and some things were developing that shouldn't have been.

"So, when I was twenty, I started preparing for the fact that at twenty-one I would legally be able to do anything to my body that I wanted. I went to a doctor and asked for hormone tests. I told the doctor, 'I think like a woman, walk like a woman, and act like a woman. If there is something wrong with me, I want to know it. I cannot live my life as a man, much less as a boy.' He took hormone tests and, sure enough, I was a semihermaphroditic. Later, the doctors approved me for corrective surgery to cross genders and become a woman. At the time I went in for the surgery, I was performing in a dance company as a female. I was pretty much naked most of the time on stage, skimpy leotards and tights, and I was with all the girls in the dressing room, and no one ever had an idea that it was going to take surgery to make me a real woman. I was the featured dancer in this show—I had been a theatre major in college—and when I went to the hospital for the surgery, the whole dance company would come to my room for rehearsals. They all thought I was there to have fibroid tumors removed.

"What was I like as a boy? Well, I was thoroughly celibate. One of the doctors asked me, 'Have you ever been to bed with a woman?' I replied, 'Are you kidding? I may be a lot of things, but I am not a lesbian!' Physically, I simply did not develop as a man. I sang soprano in the choirs. I was terrific in gymnastics. I was good in swimming. I had Daddy's hands and Daddy's feet. My life going through school was pure hell. You know how cruel kids can be. I always felt like a girl in the boy's locker room. I spent my entire life in fear of being brutalized by the bullies. I would wait in the school library until the bus came and then make a mad dash for the bus. I was terrified. When I was fifteen, I almost had a nervous breakdown. How I got through it, I will never know. But I was in school plays and other dramatic arts. I made a name for myself within the school.

"You know, my father and my two brothers are all big Swedish horses. Very athletic, very macho. My older brother is a doctor now, and he never paid that much attention to me. But I think my younger brother always knew my problem, because I always babied him. After I had the surgery, he told me, 'I've always thought of you as more of a sister than a brother.' That's because I always acted like a mother to him. Our mom worked and when she came home from work, she was exhausted. I was trained as a little girl. I did all the cooking, all the cleaning. My older brother, the doctor today, would have nothing of it and my little brother was too young, so I did all the housework. I bathed the dog. I did everything. I was a housewife from the time I was seven. I fed the baby, and when my younger brother started to toddle, I took him around with me. I taught him the things I learned from church and school. You know how little girls like to play Mama. Well, that's what I did.

"When the doctors told me what my problem was, I wanted the surgery right away. Normally, it is a two-year wait, but for me they waived it to six months, the absolute minimum. I had suffered enough, they told me. While I was waiting, I moved out of state and took a job as a beautician. In my off hours, I sang in a band and danced in a road show. I worked myself to death. I dreamed of making it big in Los Angeles. The surgery took seven-and-a-half hours and was incredibly painful, but I was euphoric. Free at last. When they cut the stitches—they were metal because they had to form the labia from what they had to work with—the nurses were amazed that I didn't scream in pain. But I had already done the real screaming during those first twenty-one years of hell. The doctors said I was a joy to work on because the dancing had put me in good physical condition. I lost twenty pounds in the hospital. Before I had always looked like a tall, thin, hairless, feminine boy. Now, I looked like death on a cheese cracker. I was very skinny—it's only since I became a happy housewife that I've been fat. But anyway, when I left the hospital, I was very, very happy.

"I met my husband while tending bar. I was filling in for a girlfriend. It was a beer-and-wine type place. No problem. John came in with a buddy, and both were pretty looped. He asked me out and I said no. The next night, he came in and asked me out again. I said no. This must have gone on five or six times. Just to get him off my back, I said OK. The rest is history. We hit it off right away.

"He is a good man. Very intelligent. I am absolutely crazy about my husband. He's a terrific person."

I looked across the desk at John, this big, good-looking bull of a man, and started to ask the obvious, when Lorelei anticipated my question.

"Well, after about two months of dating, he finally coaxed me into the sack. After a few weeks of sleeping together, I was staying overnight at his place and going to work from there. He said, 'Are you on the pill, or something?' I said, 'Oh, no.' He asked, 'Well, what if you get pregnant? Will you keep the baby?' He was thinking of us as a married couple. It was obvious he had no idea of my background. I decided I had to tell him before he decided he was in love with me. I didn't want to hurt him. So, one night I made a big dinner, and told him, 'Look, it's time I told you something....'

"Step by step, I started to tell him the whole thing. Halfway through, he cut me off. 'I've heard enough,' he said. 'I need some time to think about it. But let's face it, I've been to bed with you and I don't know the difference. I find it difficult to believe and I don't know why you bothered to tell me, but....' Now, I cut him off. 'Because,' I said, 'there are people in this town who know and I don't want you to learn from them.'

"The next day he called and said, 'It makes no difference to me. I love you [this was the first time he had told me he loved me]. You are a woman to me. You have never been anything different. I don't need to know or hear anything else about it.' "

I looked at John. He simply nodded in agreement. Lorelei added, "That dinner was in May. Two months later, we were married.

"We knew we could never have children, but at first it was no big deal. John said, 'Maybe someday we can adopt.' After a couple years, I started to bug him, 'Are we ready to adopt a baby?' He hedged and then said, 'Well, I would like to have my own child.'

"Now, I really don't know why, but somehow the term 'surrogate mother' had stuck in my mind. But I couldn't remember where. So I called the library. They looked up a back copy of *People* magazine and your name was in it. And here we are."

Knowing what Lorelei had gone through and how sincere she is, I made a snap judgment. I would try to help them, bizarre background or not. Lorelei is as solid a housewife as I have met in a long time. And their marriage seemed secure.

They did not have a lot of money. They had owned a saloon, but the lease ran out. Lorelei was a dispatcher for the police department and John was a driver for the Salvation Army. ("He ran the rag route," Lorelei joked. "You know, driving around and picking up old clothes that people donate. But, don't worry, next month he moves on to bigger things. The appliance route.") Lorelei concluded, "We are not wealthy people, but we can afford the things we really want. And this is what we really want."

Their $2,000 check to me wiped out two years of savings. "It's worth it," Lorelei said. "Worth double that. Now, we have hope."

I shuffled through the papers on my desk and came up with the letter from Rita. She lived in Southern California and had recently written to me volunteering as a surrogate mother. She does not want money, I thought. Carefully, I read her letter.

"I have been wanting to do this for some time," Rita had written in that first letter, "and thought perhaps you could help me as I don't know how to find a couple who are looking for a surrogate mother. Do you know of any couples who are interested? I would appreciate your help very much. Thank you. Very sincerely. Rita _____."

There was a phone number at the bottom of the letter. It was now four P.M. in Detroit, one P.M. on the West Coast. I dialed the number. Rita seemed very cool and very decisive about what she wanted to do. I would later think that she sounded very much like surrogate mother Diane. All good con artists have the ability to fool you. But at the time, I was anxious to help the couple sitting in front of me. Rita said she was twenty-seven, divorced with three children. She said that having children was very easy and very pleasurable for her, and that she wanted to help a couple who could not have this pleasure.

I called in Martha and dictated a letter:

Dear Ms. _____:

To confirm our telephone conversation, you are hereby authorizing me to give your name to a couple who are in need of a surrogate. I would also like to repeat myself in that you will not receive a fee for being a surrogate mother, but that all expenses will be paid by the couple.

Sincerely,
Noel P. Keane.

I handed a copy of Rita's letter to Lorelei and John. The phone number was included. "Think about it for a while," I said. "Then let me know what to do."

They floated out of my office. Martha took a long, hard look at Lorelei, but by now she was not one to judge. "Noel," she said, "all your cases are unusual. Let's hope your luck holds."

In this case, it did not, but we are getting ahead of the story.

Money was not a problem with my next two clients, Joseph, the single student and scriptwriter from Hollywood, and Thomas and Cindy Sue, the celebrity couple from Manhattan. But still, they were to have the same problem as Lorelei and John. Finding the right surrogate mother.

When Joseph called me with his proposal, I knew we would be breaking new ground. On the surface, his request seemed outrageously selfish. All he wanted was to stay single, find a woman who would give him a child, find a sex selection specialist who would split his sperm so there would be maximum potential for that child to be a boy, and, oh yes, the woman had to be superperfect. He was prepared to pay a fee and since he would not have to adopt, I could legally assist him in paying a fee.

By now, I was accustomed to doing fairly in-depth interviewing of all potential adoptive couples. I wanted to assure myself that they were mature enough to take on the responsibilities. Now, the obvious question is: Why didn't we also go into the motives of the potential surrogate mothers? That would have eliminated someone like Diane. Well, as an attorney, I was representing the people who wanted to find a surrogate mother. I would do preliminary screening by phone and questionnaire of the potential surrogate mother, and I would give advice but the buck stopped with the people who wanted a baby. They had to choose their own surrogate mother. For reasons of law and common sense, I did not think I should make the decision for them.

Joseph came to Detroit for a consultation, and I liked him immediately. I knew that critics would say we were playing God, but I believed his reasoning that he was simply trying to find a practical solution to his own situation.

Joseph is slender and attractive. A New York Yankees baseball cap covers the beginnings of his hair transplant. He is an occasional actor who is pursuing a doctorate in political science and writing a screenplay.

He began telling me about himself, "I would like to settle down and have a family. Now, it so happens that I have not fallen in love. I haven't met the right woman, and I don't think I should be restricted by the traditional guidelines set by society. I want a boy because I know the trials and tribulations of growing up as a boy. If it is a girl—wonderful, fantastic. I want to artificially inseminate because I would have a very difficult time doing it otherwise. After all, we are talking about getting into a situation with a woman I do not know."

Why did he want a child, especially a boy?

"I think the psychological vacuum of growing up without my father has a lot to do with my decision. My father was a famous actor and comedian—the 'Charlie Chaplin of Puerto Rico,' they used to call him. He was a beloved figure. His casket was carried through the town square, streets are named after him.

"I never really got to know him. He died when I was six years old, struck down by a brain aneurysm when he was only forty-seven. I only know what other people tell me about him.

"I guess that is the biggest regret of my life, never getting a chance to know my father. But I loved him. He was a theater man, a life of wine, women, and song. The stories they tell about him! He had his tombstone engraved, 'Excuse me for not getting up!' He was somewhat of a rake, and my mother was his third wife. She would get on him about this womanizing, and he once told her, 'Dear, to me you are like a great cathedral. All the other women are but country churches.' I mean you have to like a man like that.

"I want to give my son all the loving I never received from a father."

Was he sure?

"This is a very cold and calculated decision, to have a child. I want to have one now—at thirty—while I'm still young enough to share things. Unfortunately, I'm not ready to settle down with a woman yet and may not be for five or ten years. Why should I wait? This decision is very calculated. But all the calculations and coldness stop when I have my son. I have a lot of love to give and this will be a loved child."

Could he afford a child?

"Money will not be a problem. I am not wealthy, but I am comfortable. Comfortable. I had a very privileged upbringing—European vacations, school in Switzerland and all that. I have invested my money wisely. Everything in my life is being structured to care for a child. I will work and study out of my home. Everything will be built around my son."

Why didn't he find a woman first?

"Maybe I'm selfish right now and simply do not want to share my son with anybody else. I realize it would be easy to put down my motives. To say I'm being narcissistic. But that isn't the way I work. Music, the theatre, and sports are my passions. I have a $50,000 stereo setup, not because it costs that much but because I wanted the best in music. I drive an old car and wear old clothes. The hair transplant is for professional reasons. Why should I look thirty-five when I am thirty? I go all out for things I care for. That's why my stereo system is the best that money can buy. I love to listen to good music. And I get up many mornings at four A.M. to play the piano. What kind of woman is going to want to put up with that?

"I have seen a lot of unhappiness in marriage. I saw that with my parents, brothers, and relatives. When there are children, divorce hurts them. Relationships can be sticky and messy. I'm a neat person. I guess I want to be in control of my situation."

What if something went wrong?

"My mother is very worried for me, that things may not turn out. But I have made up my mind. If the child is born retarded, that is still my child. I accept the risk."

I had no more questions. Joseph, it seemed to me, knew what he wanted to do.

To find a woman for this new twist to the surrogate mother story, we went on "The Phil Donahue Show." It was to prove one of Donahue's highest-rated shows since Debbie, Sue, and George returned with their "gift child," Elizabeth Anne.

We sat there right in front of hundreds of astonished women, Joseph in his Yankee baseball cap, myself in a three-piece suit (Kathy, who was sitting a few feet away, had selected it for me), and Ronald Ericcson, Ph.D., president of Gametrics, Inc., a reproductive biology clinic in Sausalito, Calif., that among other things separates sperm for sex-selection.

The audience quickly went to the attack.

"What makes him think he is going to be a good parent?" one woman asked.

In his inimitable style, Donahue responded, "Why wouldn't he be a good parent?" Added Joseph, "How did you know you were going to be a good parent?"

Another woman listened to Dr. Ericcson's description of sperm-splitting to try to get a boy and envisioned "a 'brave new world' where everybody wants the perfect kid."

Donahue joked, "Hey, if you can get the perfect kid, why not?"

As Dr. Ericcson described the lab techniques to separate and capture the male-carrying Y chromosomes, the audience broke into an uproar. One woman asked Joseph, "What kind of qualities are you looking for in a woman?"

Joseph: "She has to be attractive. She has to be psychologically sound. She has to be...."

Audience uproar.

Another question: "Why don't you just do what comes naturally—get married and have children?"

Audience uproar.

And, "Why artificially inseminate? Why not just pick out a woman and, you know, it would be more fun, wouldn't it?"

Audience uproar.

Buzzing swept up and down the studio crowd and questions swept down to the three of us throughout the full hour of prime TV time.

"Why don't you adopt? There are now single adopting parents." And, "I think you want the love of a child when you should first be looking for the love of a woman." And, "You have to question the emotional stability of a woman who could let herself be used this way." And, "It is adultery for a woman to be artificially inseminated with your sperm."

Patiently, Joseph answered one and all. He had anticipated the questions. After all, we had already discussed most of them in my office. Slowly, he won over the crowd of women.

The clincher came from a caller to the show. It was a man and he said, "This man wants a family based on love. There are plenty of single women who do it—raise children on their own, provide a loving home, care for their kids, take the full responsibility. I can't believe you people are against a man doing it, too."

Audience uproar.

As we drove down Chicago's Kennedy Expressway from Donahue's studio at WGN-TV on the city's northwest side to the Merchandise Mart offices of NBC-TV for a network "Today Show" taping of the same topic, Kathy told me, "Noel, you're finally getting it down. Today, you looked good on camera. And, you sounded halfway good, too."

I had now been on Donahue five times, plus countless other TV appearances, and the thrill had long ago worn off. I now went on shows like Donahue for a simple reason. Other than placing classified ads, the only effective way of finding surrogate mothers was through television and news articles. The true fathers of the surrogate-mother story, perhaps, are the "The Phil Donahue Show" and *People* magazine. Time and again, people have come to me for help with the opening, "I read about you in *People* magazine," or, "I saw you on Donahue." This TV show and this magazine have built their success on knowing what people want to know. And, clearly, the people continue to want to know about surrogate mothers.

We had said that Joseph was prepared to pay $10,000 for a surrogate mother. Now we would have to sit back and wait.

Finding a surrogate mother is one problem. Getting her pregnant, as we were to find with Richard and Aralee and Sally, is another. And, as we were to find with Thomas and Cindy Sue and their surrogate mother, Donna, keeping her pregnant is yet a third. The fourth and biggest problem, of course, is keeping her happily pregnant. But again, we are getting ahead of our stories.

Money was of small matter to Thomas and Cindy Sue, the Manhattan film couple. They had plenty. Once Thomas said jokingly, "Noel, when we find a surrogate mother, why don't we just send her to France. I have a small place in Paris, and she can stay there until she's ready to give birth." I was firm. "No, you people will want to adopt and there's no way you can give a surrogate mother anything of value and then adopt her baby. You can pay expenses, period."

Thomas was forty-two, Cindy Sue forty-one, and their time was running out. They had put their hopes on Donna, the tomboy from the East Coast.

By definition, most surrogate mothers are pretty independent women. But of all the actual and potential surrogate mothers I have met, none are as strong-willed as Donna.

Her father wanted a boy, and he never let her forget it. She grew up on a farm and in a determined effort to win her father's approval learned to out-macho the boys. As I talked to her, she was alternately sunny and sullen, insightful and flip. She had answered an ad I placed in the *Washington Post*.

Why did Donna want to be a surrogate mother?

"I really don't know what is driving me, except there is this woman who cannot have a baby. I can—at least as far as I know. When I was growing up [she is now twenty-one], a friend of my mother's could never have children. I remember how upset she was and during my early teens I used to think, 'If I ever get pregnant, I'll give the baby to her.' Now, I had never heard of 'surrogate mother,' but that's what I wanted to be. When I saw your ad, I thought, 'Fantastic.' I mean this is what I want to do. I believe in it.

"Now, I would never want to get paid. I believe in it too much to take money. And I would never do it for an anonymous couple. I have to know and like the couple for whom I am having a baby."

She had started out trying to be surrogate mother for a Delaware dentist and his wife and became pregnant on the first insemination. But nine weeks later, the child was stillborn. Donna was crushed but she tried twice more for the dentist and his wife. In the meantime, a resourceful reporter who had noticed our ad called to see if there had been any takers. I asked Donna if she wanted to talk with this reporter. She did, and a few days later her story and high school graduation picture were on the front page of the *Washington Post.*

Instant notoriety. The dentist, a private professional, was aghast. He had words with Donna. This was shortly after her traumatic miscarriage, and she wanted support, not criticism. She broke off the arrangement. Months later, she called and said, "Noel, get me another couple. I'm ready to try again." Thomas and Cindy Sue were waiting in the wings. For six consecutive months now, Donna had flown to Manhattan to be artificially inseminated at the Idant sperm bank with the frozen sperm deposited by Thomas. For six consecutive months, nothing happened. She was back in town for another attempt and as we sat in a midtown Manhattan hotel, I wondered how long her resolve would hold. She had been at it for better than a year now. She is an attractive, sexy woman and, in all her time of trying to be a surrogate mother, she had sworn off sex. Or at least sexual intercourse. She was under tremendous pressure from her friends and family to forget this crazy idea.

What did her parents think?

"When my parents first found out, it was a complete disaster. When my mother found out I was pregnant, she thought it was a boyfriend or something like that. When I told them what I was doing, they wanted me out of the house. My father threw me around, beat me up. After the miscarriage, though, they just kind of accepted it. I mean, they wish someone else were doing it, but at least they have quit abusing me. They think surrogate motherhood is a great idea, but not for their daughter. Every time I get my period, my father applauds. He tells me, 'Congratulations!' They keep hoping I'll come to my senses.

"I guess all my problems go back to one thing. I was the firstborn and I was a girl. My father wanted a boy. The birth announcements were made up by a friend of my father's. The front cover had a blue baby outfit, blue rattle, blue hat, blue booties, and it read, 'We knew he was coming.' You open the card and on the inside there are pink booties and things. It reads, 'And here she is.' No doubt about it, he wanted a boy."

Donna is crying, but she continues.

"My father coaches football and track. I guess I made up my mind to be my father's son. I knew he could never tolerate anyone weak. I am a very strong person. I grew up with the boys. I used to go to all the practices with him. I ran on the track team. I lifted weights. There wasn't a guy around I couldn't beat up. I could outlift them, outplay them, outrun them. Almost all my friends were boys.

"But I never really dated or anything like that. My father wouldn't let me. I was dating this guy named Jim for awhile. He was gorgeous, or at least I thought he was. He ran track and he was one of the fastest kids around. Jim's parents were divorced and his father lived in Florida, so my father kind of took him under his wing. He sort of adopted him. But my father restricted me from seeing Jim. It was a way of punishing me. But I was a pretty rebellious girl. I saw Jim anyway. I was going to show my father. We grew up on a farm and it was fantastic. I used to ride horses every day. At one time, I wanted to train show horses. I would get on the tractor and plow the fields. I played football. I would wrestle with the guys. I was one of the gutsiest girls you would ever want to meet. I was going to prove things to my father. But when he wouldn't let me go out with Jim, that really hurt. In fact, it probably hurt me more than anything, other than the miscarriage.

"The miscarriage was absolutely horrible. I am a nurse and I believe in abortion and I see aborted fetuses every day, but this really got to me. I was bleeding and getting ready to go to the hospital. Every time I would urinate, the bleeding would get worse. So I refused to go to the bathroom. Finally, I had to. I figured I better go before I left for the hospital. When I did, that's when I lost the baby. I could feel it wrench within me. I screamed for my mother. When she walked in I was kneeling down at the toilet with the fetus in my hand. It was about ten weeks old and maybe an inch or two long. It was unmistakably human. What happened? I really don't know. I had been running, riding horses, dancing, being active. Maybe it was just God's will. I can't describe the feeling. I was really down. There are two parts to my head. The nurse part said 'It's good that you lost it. It must not have been normal.' But the woman part said, 'Oh, my God, I've lost my baby.' I asked my mother for a plastic container, and I took the fetus with me to the hospital. I was surprised at how powerful my feelings were. I mean, I had been saying to myself all along, 'It's their baby. It's Judy's baby, I'm only carrying it for them.' I was depressed for weeks. That was the beginning of the end for me and the dentist and his wife. I guess I expected them to send me a flower or a card or at least ask, 'Donna, how are you?' But it was like they didn't give a damn. I tried twice again to get pregnant for them, but my heart wasn't in it. After the second time, when the insemination didn't take, I told them, 'I don't want to do this anymore.' We didn't have a contract or anything, just the written agreement you prepared. Well, the dentist got down on his knees and begged. 'I want to have a baby. We want you to have a baby for us. Please. Please. Please.' I cannot stand a weak man. My father's influence, I guess. He was begging. I just walked away.

"Then, through you I met Thomas and Cindy Sue. They care about me, and it shows. I really want to give them a baby."

I asked, "How about the men in your life?"

"I have no use for men. Well, I mean, I do only once in a while. I do not want a full-time relationship with a man. I do not want to get married, until I'm seventy or eighty, anyway. I have plenty of male friends, but I do not need a steady relationship. I have been trying to get pregnant as a surrogate mother for one year now. It would not be fair to get involved with a man. I mean I could not go to bed with him. I am prepared to go another year to have a baby for Thomas and Cindy Sue.

"Do my parents respect me? I don't know. I don't respect them. I hate my father and I hate my mother. My mother is very, very weak—she takes whatever my father dishes out—and my father never shows any affection at all. I cannot stand them.

"But this I know. I want to be a surrogate mother. I am a very strong-willed person, and I always get what I want. Always."

There you have it, a conversation with surrogate mother-hopeful Donna. What would the psychiatrists say? Would they want her as a surrogate mother? Was she a good risk?

I had my doubts if surrogate motherhood were in her best interests. Certainly, with her enormous drive, Donna could have been a success at anything, once she pulled herself together. For now, she seemed determined to have a baby for someone else. I decided, all right, let's try it one more time. But, privately, I was developing serious reservations about her participation.

So unusual are the motivations of these first three cases—Lorelei, the transsexual housewife; Joseph, the single man who wants a surrogate mother, sex-selection, and a son; and Donna, the surrogate mother as crucified avenger—that it almost makes my other cases seem serene by contrast. But three of these—Richard, Aralee, and Sally; Andy, Nancy, and Jeannette, their Texas midwife turned surrogate mother; and the Yugoslavian couple referred to Dr. Levin's Kentucky clinic—also added new dimensions to the story.

The Andy-Nancy-Jeannette linkup is unusual in the legal challenge—Andy and Nancy's California adoption must overcome the Texas legal presumption that Jeannette's husband, Marshall, is the father of the child—and in the missionary zeal with which the surrogate mother approaches her task. Jeannette wants nothing less than the "perfect birth." But I'll let her explain.

"My husband and I have a private joke that we would like to give birth over and over again until we got it right, but what in the world would we do with all the kids. At that time, of course, we had never heard of the 'surrogate mothers,' that there actually were women who gave birth and then gave the babies away. When our son, Christopher, was born, we both felt that several things had gone wrong. I ended up in the hospital, for one thing, and I wanted to give birth at home, attended by a midwife. The baby was separated from us for two to four hours for an observation period, and we do not approve of that. And he was given supplemental vitamin injections, which we didn't think were necessary. So, all in all, we didn't think it had been a 'perfect birth.'

"About two weeks after the birth, I saw you on 'The Phil Donahue Show' and heard about 'surrogate mothers' for the first time. My husband, Marshall, said, 'Well, here it is, the chance to have the perfect birth. Why don't you give him a call?'

"Now, I'm one of the last of the great procrastinators. Two years went by, and then I happened to pick up a copy of *Science Digest.* I had never heard of the magazine before, but it happened to have an article about Noel Keane and the surrogate mothers. The topic had always been in the back of my mind and I mentioned it to Marshall. He said, 'Call him.' Two weeks went by and, still, I did nothing. But Marshall kept reminding me. Finally, I called your office, and your office manager, Martha, told me to write a long letter describing myself and my motivations. I sat down that very afternoon, wrote the letter, and life has never been the same since."

Jeannette's letter ran fourteen handwritten pages and is a model of purposefulness and thoroughness. It covered everything from her family and medical history to her strongly held beliefs on how a surrogate-mother pregnancy and birth should be conducted. Enclosed was a photo of her and her son Christopher. I read the letter one morning, and called Jeannette to get verbal permission to give her name to prospective adoptive couples. Then I went to lunch. The minute I walked back into my office, the phone rang.

It was Andy, calling from California. He and his wife, Nancy, had just seen a rerun of the CBS television documentary, "The Babymakers," which featured a segment about myself and surrogate mothers. Nancy had two teenaged daughters from a first marriage, but a subsequent hysterectomy ruled out children for her and Andy.

At first, this did not bother Andy, but as he got older, he began to want his own child. He was a father to Nancy's two daughters, but he also wanted his own.

I asked, "Have you tried to adopt?"

Andy replied, "Yes, and they told me it would take at least three years just to get on the list. Then, once on the list, there is a probationary period of at least a year. Then, you wait for a baby and you will be lucky if you get one. I'm thirty and my wife is thirty-five. Besides, I have two stepdaughters from my wife's previous marriage. That's sort of like adopting right there. The only reason I haven't adopted them is because their natural father is dead and the children collect Social Security. I have a desire and a need for my own child."

I said, "Well, by coincidence, I just talked this morning to a woman in Texas who thinks she would like to have a baby for another couple. Let me read you her letter."

Andy listened patiently to Jeannette's recitation of why and how she wanted to be a surrogate mother. Then, his voice almost cracked, "I knew that somewhere in the world there had to be a woman who would understand," he said. "I had no idea it might happen so quick."

"Would you like her number?" I asked.

"You bet."

I read off the Texas telephone number. Within a week, Andy's baby would be on the way, carried by surrogate mother Jeannette. Their story is a model, I think, of how the surrogate-mother arrangement can work. Andy and Nancy are poor people, and there is no way they could have paid a fee. But Jeannette would not have heard of a fee. She was doing this for her own intensely personal reasons. All she asked was that the adoptive couple care about children and be able to care for them. Her only financial request is payment for the services of a midwife.

The human story is a warm one. The legal story is complicated, but I think we are on top of it.

But at the end of that call, I simply told Andy, "Let me know what happens."

The story of Stefan and Nadia is one of persistence and eventual success. He is forty-three, she thirty-nine. They came to Detroit from Yugoslavia eleven years ago, and both have good jobs in the auto industry.

He is the oldest of five children, she of eight. They had been trying to have their own children for eighteen years.

As they sat across my desk, Nadia recalled their ordeal.

"We never gave up," she said. "Never. The problem is blocked Fallopian tubes. I have had four major surgeries. One tube was completely removed. But I still had the other. The doctors told me it was very bad, but there was a slight chance I could get pregnant. I went to the fertility clinics and took the medication. Nothing happened. Once I had a tubal pregnancy. This was my last tube. The doctor repaired the tube, and said it was still OK. But I never got pregnant. Twice more, the doctor opened me up to check the tube and see if it were possible for me to have a baby. The second time, he told me, 'I don't want you to try to get pregnant anymore.'

"I quit seeing the doctor for three or four years. I kept hoping a miracle would happen. But nothing did. So, this year, I made an appointment with one of the best fertility experts in the country, [S. J. Behrman, M.D. who testified during the adoption proceedings for Elizabeth Anne and Debbie, Sue, and George]. He put me in the hospital, opened my navel, and checked the tube. 'Give up,' he said, 'The tube is really diseased. And you are too old.' We have been married eighteen years, eighteen years of trying to have children, and he tells us to give up."

Stefan adds, "The doctor took us back to his office and had a long talk with us. He explained we shouldn't try anymore. It was terrible. Nadia was crying. And, I am not ashamed to admit, I cried, too. We sat there and cried like babies."

Nadia: "Before I made the appointment with Dr. Behrman, I had written a letter to England, asking about the 'test-tube' babies. I got a letter back saying they were not accepting any candidates over thirty-six. Then, I wrote to the clinic in Norfolk, Virginia, where they are studying test-tube procedures, and they told me the same thing—'We are not accepting anyone over thirty-three.' I had heard of Dr. Seed and the embryo-transfer procedures in Chicago, so I called him. This seemed the absolute last hope. The answer was the same. The technology is too new and I am too old."

Stefan: "It was like a miracle. We turned on the TV one day, and we saw you talking about surrogate mothers. My wife wrote down the phone number."

Nadia pulls from her purse a tattered, yellowed clipping. It is the 1978 *People* magazine article about my involvement with Debbie, Sue, and George. I am pictured tossing Elizabeth Anne into the air, and, in another photo, out in the front yard with Kathy and my sons hosing down my vintage roadster. Nadia said, "I read about you two years ago, about how that lady had a baby for her friend and how you helped them. I have never left that clipping out of my sight.

"After Dr. Behrman told me there was really nothing left, I gave up. I was very upset. It was like my life was over. All my friends and family tried to comfort me. They felt sorry for me because they knew what I had gone through with the four surgeries. Most women would never have gone through what I did to try to have children. Really, I was desperate to have a child. Even my doctor said, 'I have never seen such courage.' He was amazed that I would go through all the pain.

"And for nothing. There was nothing left. We are too old to adopt. Then, I saw you on TV a few nights ago. I got out the magazine article and read it again. Very carefully. I thought that, 'Well, maybe, here is a new hope.' That is why we are here."

I explained to them the basic procedures, and emphasized there are no guarantees. A surrogate mother, if found, can always change her mind. They were ready to run the risk.

As one consequence of not having children, Stefan and Nadia are fairly well off. They own two homes, several cars, and a large boat. They could afford to pay a surrogate mother. And, by this time, Dr. Levin's Surrogate Parenting Associates, Inc. was ready for business in Kentucky.

"Are you prepared to spend some money to find a mother for your baby?" I asked.

They were.

Quickly, I figured it up. "It will cost you up to $22,000," I said. "That's $10,000 for the surrogate mother, $5,000 for the medical care, $5,000 for the legal fees, including the services of an attorney in Kentucky, and $2,000 in miscellaneous expenses. Plus, you'll have to sell your house and move to Kentucky. If you're going to adopt your baby, you'll have to first become residents of Kentucky."

Stefan said, "What is $22,000? A car costs $15–$16,000 and what have you got? One wrong turn and it's smashed up. It is nothing of real value. This is a human life. We will go anywhere and do anything."

I had some preliminary talks with Dr. Levin and his attorney, Katie Brophy, and knew the general outlines of their program. The physician's intention was to limit surrogate mothers to married women with children, to pay them $10,000 and to keep them anonymous to the adoptive couple. The cost to the adoptive couple, covering air fares to Kentucky, psychiatric evaluations, insurance policies to protect surrogate mother and child, and medical and legal fees, would run between $13,000 and $20,000. And up.

Of course, first he had to find surrogate mothers. How?

I asked Stefan, "If you are prepared to go, we'll start by placing an ad. That's the first step in finding a surrogate mother. Should we do it?"

"Go."

I called Katie Brophy, and, together, we quickly worked out the wording of an ad to be placed in the *Louisville Courier-Journal.*

The search for my second paid surrogate mother was on. The other one, of course, is to find a surrogate mother for Joseph.

The surrogate-mother trail was now at a broad fork in the road.

In one direction, there were the traditional steps I had been following of trying to find a volunteer who would be a surrogate mother for medical expenses and the chance to help somebody else.

In the other, there were the steps opening up in Kentucky—and everywhere if we win our lawsuit—of being able to pay a woman to become a surrogate mother.

We were going to have to blaze both trails, I decided. There is merit in both approaches and different people want different options.

In the coming months, my clients would see me as both sinner and savior. Some of them found success and some found only sawdust. Some of those paying money found happiness and some did not.

The money angle, however, was putting a new perspective—and new publicity—on the issue. In one perhaps prophetic remark, Katie Brophy told a reporter, "Well, if a potential surrogate mother volunteers and she's bright, beautiful, and talented and wants $50,000, why not?"

Well, for one thing, I thought, because the kind of people I got into this to help them can never afford $5,000, let alone $50,000. Others could; however, I was very concerned that this hope of last resort for the barren not be limited to those with the highest barter.

In the meantime, I continued to work with my new clients. Some I helped, some not yet. Let's take the bad news first. As everyone keeps telling me, "Noel, no one ever said it would be easy!"

## Questions for Empathy and Analysis

1. Keane lists the five new cases he had in 1980. Do he and co-author Breo try to make you feel any particular way about the cases through specific word choices and selection of detail? Are you able to read about these cases empathetically? Or do you feel an urge to analyze and judge? If you find yourself judging the cases as soon as you read them, what might your judgments indicate to you about your possible assumptions and biases?

2. Keane says that he has been fascinated by the motives of the people involved. How is this fascination reflected in the portrayal of these five cases? How does Keane judge their motives? Do you agree with his judgments? Why does Keane spend more time judging the motives of the couples rather than those of the surrogate mothers? Do you think potential surrogate mothers should be screened concerning their motives? What motives would you find most acceptable? How do you evaluate Keane's motives?

3. Do you think lawyers or professionals who find surrogate mothers for couples should receive fees of $10,000 or more? Or less? In terms of services rendered, how does their labor compare with that of a surrogate mother? Can you compare them?

4. Do you think that a transsexual or a single man or woman should be permitted to obtain a child through a surrogacy arrangement? Does it seem that Joseph will be a suitable father?

5. Given Donna's reaction to her miscarriage in her first attempt to become a surrogate mother, do you think a psychiatrist would have advised her to try again? Do you think we need legislation to provide screening for surrogate mothers?

■ ■ ■ ■ ■ ■ ■ ■ ■

# COMMERCIAL CONTRACTS AND HUMAN CONNECTEDNESS

## Barbara Sherman Heyl

The contract written by the agency in the Baby M case was designed to cut the connections of the Sterns and the baby to Mary Beth Whitehead after the baby was born. Specifically it states in Provision 1: "Mary Beth Whitehead understands and agrees that in the best interest of the child, she will not form or attempt to form a parent-child relationship with any child or children she may conceive, carry to term and give birth to . . . and shall freely surrender custody to William Stern." The Sterns wanted the baby free and clear from any tie to Mary Beth. The flaw in this plan is that the lives of these biological parents are in fact bound together through the baby, who is alive and well and who will, as she grows up, make her own judgments of all this cutting apart of what is connected. That Judge Sorkow upheld the contract as it was written has signaled an alert to society to consider what factors explain this situation and what the implications are of continuing in this direction.

My discussion probes the role of class factors in the practice of surrogacy and in the debates over social meanings and legal interpretations of surrogacy. Then four issues of the rights and risks of the key parties involved in these arrangements will be explored, ending with a challenge that if surrogate agreements are made, they should integrate and balance these rights and risks, rather than use contracts to deny the connections these biological parents and their families have to each other and to the child they have brought into this world.

Richard John Neuhaus's essay puts front and center the marked class differences between surrogate mothers and families wanting babies. Along with other commentators, Neuhaus finds it unsettling that the court's decision, based on "the best interest of the child," openly reveals a class bias that favors middle-class homes over lower-class homes. This finding should hardly be surprising to observers of family law in action. For example, this bias has run through our juvenile court system since its inception at the turn of the century; it is supported by public opinion (polls indicated general agreement with the judge that the baby would be better off with the Sterns); and it is built into our adoption system in which the class difference between the birth mother and adoptive families is openly utilized by everyone in the system to explain why the baby was given up by the birth mother in the first place. (The birth mother relinquishes her child because the adoptive family can provide it with more life chances, and this explanation is communicated to the child to demonstrate that the birth mother indeed loved her child enough to give it up for a better life.) So the passing of babies from poorer family settings to more financially secure ones, and the court's sanction of this practice, is nothing new.

What may be new about the Baby M case—and the practice of surrogacy contracts in general—is the exercise of class power on the part of the family wanting the baby. It was especially the use of their greater financial resources, superior education, and knowledge of the legal system that empowered the Sterns over Mary Beth Whitehead. In the adoption system an agency (or in private adoptions, an attorney or a doctor) serves as the buffer between the power of the middle- or upper-class couple desperately seeking a white infant and the birth mother. Fifty states have laws prohibiting payment to the mother in adoption cases precisely to help protect a vulnerable, pregnant woman from undue pressure to give up her baby. But, as advocates of surrogacy point out, a surrogacy contract allows for payment to the mother "for her services," and differs from adoption on several grounds, including the fact that the woman agrees before getting pregnant to give up her baby and accept the money and is therefore presumably free of any undue pressure from the financial resources of the couple wanting the baby. Moreover, surrogacy has been legally distinguished from adoption by noting that the person putting up the money is the biological father—so he is not adopting his child (even though his wife will be). As can be seen from this latter point and the claim that the payment is for "services" and not the baby, a battle is being waged over definitions. Neuhaus is absolutely correct in noting that the "disputes are over symbolic knowledge," and in this arena "Mary Beth Whitehead is pitifully outgunned." The symbolic knowledge of the courtroom and of the surrogacy contract belongs to the educated monied classes, and its power is wielded predominantly by male professionals.

It becomes clear after reading the incredible outpouring of editorials, essays, and law review articles on the Baby M case and surrogate mothering that far outside the New Jersey courtroom a battle is being waged as to how surrogacy will be defined and what the rules should be regarding this practice. If surrogacy has been legally distinguished from adoption, then to what is it similar? The National Committee for Adoption has likened surrogacy to baby selling. Is surrogacy, then, closer to prostitution ("contract for services"), to exploitation of women, to commodification of babies and mothers, to trafficking in human beings? Does the contract free the woman to decide what she will do with her body, including her uterus, or does it deprive her of her ultimate freedom to decide about the baby she is nurturing in her body? What do developments in new means of reproduction mean for the definition of parenthood? Alvin Toffler looks at the biological revolution, of which the technology for surrogacy is one small part, and asks the ultimate definitional question in his June 4, 1987, *Christian Science Monitor* essay: "What is human now?" Toffler notes that given the revolutionary developments in genetic engineering, "it is now possible, in principle, to transfer human traits to animals and animal traits to humans." So what will be seen as unequivocally human? He goes even further: "If we can sell parts of our body, why not the entire body—for 21st-century bioslavery?" Who will decide who are the humans and who are the subhumans, who are the masters and who are the slaves? Who will be the human incubators of these biological units, and who will decide on a given day that even these baby-makers are obsolete?

We are now in the middle of the social construction of this biological revolution. We are negotiating the meaning to be given to each of these new developments. With questions as far-reaching as those I have mentioned, it is no wonder that everyone is getting involved: lawyers, journalists, ordinary people writing letters to their newspapers and columns in church newsletters, the Vatican, and even social scientists. Toffler sums it up nicely: "The issues are far too important to be left to the decisions of judges who may base them on obsolete precedent . . . biotechnology businessmen whose commercial instincts may override humane concern . . . specialists who may be too confident of the technologies over which they preside . . . or regulatory bureaucrats. Each may have a role to play, but no one group is wise enough or selfless enough to make decisions of this order." But we must acknowledge that some groups clearly have more power than others to get their definitions translated into public policy, as the sociologists of the labeling and conflict approaches have made clear for some time. Neuhaus is correct that class and class-based language have won some of the early rounds.

When Judge Sorkow decided that the Stern-Whitehead contract was enforceable, that "a deal is, after all, a deal," it signaled a major symbolic shift toward the language of the marketplace and away from the long-held rights of the natural mother in our society—rights protected in family law. Fundamentally, there are four issues raised by this shift, all related to consideration of the rights and risks incurred by the key people involved in these contracts. The first issue is the impact on the traditional rights of birth mothers; the second addresses the psychological impact on the birth mothers of agreeing and being held to these commercial contracts; the third focuses on the children who are the products of these contracts; and the fourth considers the unrealistic expectations of the couple contracting for the baby.

Looking first at the shift away from traditional rights of mothers, the argument appears to be that she has the right to sign away these rights for money. The jury will be out on this issue for a while. Judge Sorkow decided that Mary Beth had signed away her rights, but an indicator of legal opinion running against Judge Sorkow on this point is this: Of ten lawyers asked to write hypothetical decisions on the Baby M case for the February 26, 1987, issue of the *New Jersey Law Journal* (published while Judge Sorkow was deliberating his decision), seven said that the contract should not be enforced so that Mrs. Whitehead would lose her parental rights. Only one author concluded that the contract was enforceable, while two other authors did not articulate a position on the contract. One of these latter authors, Mary Joe Frug, applauds the symbolic shift away from traditional privileges granted to biological mothers. She sees the surrogacy contracts as a way to help "loosen the constraints traditionally associated with biological motherhood. . . . No matter how valuable sex role presumptions occasionally seem, their overall effect on women as well as men is crushingly oppressive." Interestingly, Derek Morgan, in an analysis in the *Journal of Law and Society* of Great Britain's outlawing of commercial surrogacy in the Surrogacy (Arrangements) Act of 1985, sees some evidence that surrogacy is being perceived by men as undermining traditional sex-role expectations. Morgan hypothesizes that the bill received remarkably strong support and was passed "with almost universal blessing" because the predominantly male British Parliament was reacting to the assault that surrogate motherhood represents to traditional notions of women's responsibilities in childbearing and child-rearing. Morgan concludes, however, that commercial surrogacy shifts motherhood into the male-dominated world of the marketplace: "A voice of law which is a predominantly male voice, articulating predominantly male concerns and values will produce a male model of the moral economy of women. Maternity and motherhood will be made and remade male." It may be that surrogacy trades one kind of oppression for another.

By accepting the contract as essentially a business deal, Judge Sorkow precluded adoption law from applicability in this case. Joan Heifetz Hollinger in her opinion in the *New Jersey Law Journal* objected to such abandonment (in surrogacy cases) of rights granted to mothers in other areas of family law.

> Even if the court concludes that Mrs. Whitehead *did* give an informed and voluntary consent [an absolute requirement in waivers of constitutional rights], there remains the amorphous but relevant "unconscionability" doctrine that equitable remedies are not available to enforce contracts that are excessively one-sided, or to enforce particularly harsh terms. A woman's promise before birth, indeed before conception, to relinquish her child at birth is arguably such a term. In more traditional custody or adoption cases, *no state holds a biological mother to a pre-birth contract to surrender her child.* (italics added)

By granting priority to the contract, Judge Sorkow was treading new legal ground, depriving women of some of the power they have needed in child custody fights with men (who typically have greater economic resources for such fights). Indeed, if class operates as Neuhaus and other observers indicate it does in surrogacy cases, then the court's endorsement of the contract cements the deal in favor of the party with the most resources—the couple wanting the baby who can stipulate the conditions under which they will and will not pay the surrogate mother and accept the child. The commercial contract in surrogacy cases turns the old capitalist warning, "let the buyer beware," on its head. It is the seller of her "services" as a surrogate mother who must beware; the middle-class biological father is well protected.

One of the murky issues in all of this is what happens to the women who seek out this risky commercial enterprise. Robert Gould, a psychoanalyst, argues in the *New York Times* that the man's desire to have a child who carries his own genes "cannot justify the pain and scarring that would be inflicted upon the natural mother's other children, the baby itself and the mother, whether she recognized it (as Baby M's mother belatedly did) or not. No mother can voluntarily give away her child, let alone *sell* it, without suffering guilt and loss on a deep psychological level—wounds that may never heal." Gould's language may be excessive, and the reader may wonder about all those birth mothers who put their babies up for adoption over the years. Did they really suffer such pain? Joan Heifetz Hollinger, in the *New Jersey Law Journal,* cites a study of birth mothers who gave up their children for adoption and a study of parents whose children have died and concludes that these studies "suggest a high risk of serious, perhaps permanent harm to women who have become closely attached to their child during pregnancy and after birth." It is true that 95 percent of the mothers in surrogate mother cases gave up their babies without contest, but the lack of legal fights is not a full indicator of their feelings at the time of relinquishment or months later. Elizabeth Kane, one of the best known surrogate mothers, after her appearances on talk shows and interviews in 1980 that showed her to be enthusiastic and untroubled about the surrogacy process at the time, decided only much later that she had been mistaken. In *Commonweal* in January 1987 she stated, "All you're doing is transferring the pain from one woman to another, from a woman who is in pain from her infertility to a woman who has to give up her baby."

One thing the surrogate mothers had probably not expected was the new language being used to describe them, their rights, and their role in the process of creating new life. In her April 4, 1987, *Washington Post* column, Ellen Goodman noted the language used by Judge Sorkow in extolling the advantages of surrogate motherhood for childless couples. He called it "an alternative reproduction vehicle." Goodman responds, "An alternative reproduction vehicle? An ARV? Isn't this what has been so troubling about the whole matter? Those of us less focused on the child or the children hear the mechanistic language and flinch at the idea that there are women—ARVs—who will be recruited professionally to manufacture children." Shari O'Brien, in the winter 1987 issue of the *Utah Law Review,* also identifies the implications of moving motherhood into the market economy:

> Those who argue that the natal mother is adequately reimbursed for serving as a mere "incubator," a sort of ambulatory system of plumbing, ratify a technocratic/capitalistic construct of the world that fosters perceiving the human being as a piece of machinery and the human body as an assemblage of commodifiable parts.

What does being treated like a piece of machinery for producing a salable product do to the self-esteem of these women, to their relationship with their own children—ones they bear and keep and ones they bear and relinquish? Regardless of what interesting explanations come with the commercial surrogacy arrangements, these women live in, and the children grow up in, a culture, yes, even a global setting, that defines motherhood in nonmarket terms. The individual woman's struggle to be comfortable with the payment and the contract's demand to separate cleanly from the baby must necessarily involve psychological effort in the face of global expectations of mother-child connections. (This effort is in addition to managing to bypass the power summarized in the term mother-child *bonding*.) We know from the sociology of deviance that one strategy used by people who regularly violate conventional norms of their society is to isolate themselves from much contact with members of conventional society. The subculture, with its own explanations for the behavior in question and its built-in supportive social network, serves them well. But where are these surrogate mothers to go to avoid the prevalent definitions of motherhood? When the fancy legalese of the contract fades, the notion of being the "natural mother" of the child to whom she contributed half the genetic make-up and whom she carried to full term and delivered will remain.

While we are addressing consequences, we need to consider what the effects may be on the child given away in such a contract. Forming an identity is a crucial and complex process that provides direction in life. We know from the literature on adoptions that even children growing up in loving, nurturing adoptive homes struggle with the questions of their origins and roots—notions that play a crucial role in addressing those existential questions of "Who am I, and what am I doing here?" Data indicate that especially during adolescence adopted children show effects of this struggle by having lower indices of self-esteem than children living with their biological parents. One nine-year-old adopted child said recently to her adoptive mother, "People should not be able to give their children away; I can't understand it; it doesn't make sense." Younger children often wonder if they are not to blame. "Was it me?" Older children begin to consider that their being put up for adoption is reflective more of the behavior of their birth parents. "If it wasn't me, then what does it say about them that they left me behind?" It is a difficult thing not to be able to think well of your birth parents. If this is true about adoption, which has a great deal of public support, surrogacy has the potential of posing greater problems for acceptance of birth parents. What does the child of the surrogate mother conclude about her? "She gave me life for $10,000 and relinquished all rights to me so that my father and his wife could raise me?" And the biological father? "He paid my mother $10,000 to have me on the condition that she would then get out of my life, and the contract he signed protects him from having to pay her or to accept me if I had been handicapped? Who *are* these people, and if I am from them, who am I?"

This latter point indicates that the biological father, whose rights may be well protected by the contract, may be incurring risks involving his relationship with his child and his child's biological mother that he had not considered. His expectations may be unrealistic. It was Katha Pollitt in her May 23, 1987, article in *The Nation* who summed up so well the unprecedented demands that Stern's contract laid out.

> What William Stern wanted, however, was not just a perfect baby; the Sterns did not, in fact, seriously investigate adoption. He wanted a perfect baby with his genes and a medically vetted mother who would get out of his life forever immediately after giving birth. That's a tall order, and one no other class of father—natural, step-, adoptive—even claims to be entitled to. Why should the law bend itself into a pretzel to gratify it?

Stern did succeed in getting the law to approve of his conditions, but surely at a greater cost than he had thought. One part of the contract had not gone according to plan: the mother had refused to disappear quietly. What if the baby had not been born perfect? We could hypothesize the court would also have sanctioned those clauses in the contract that imply that he would not have to assume custody of such a child. Does he live his life knowing that Mary Beth is raising his handicapped child whom he abandoned? So what recommendations can be made at this point, when we can only attempt to assess future costs and do not yet know what the long-term effects will be on parents and children? Despite the call for immediate legislation that appears in editorials and law reviews, some caution is in order. It would only add to the confusion to have fifty different pieces of legislation on surrogacy, with couples crossing state lines to contract the agreement they prefer. In the meantime, we can begin to formulate a creed or policy that could help form public opinion and guide legislatures in the near future.

This generation has more data than any previous generation on a phenomenon we might call the interconnectedness of life. Building recognition of this into our approach to social policies may help us move our thinking about surrogacy away from the market economy that can call for moving separate biological units here and there and toward a morality of responsibility, one that puts respect for human interrelationships at the heart of these agreements. The data on our interconnectedness come to us now from every conceivable level of analysis. What data am I thinking about? First, making a cosmic leap in our frame of reference for a moment, consider that we are connected at the level of the universe. We are all made of the stuff of the stars, as the molecules that make us up as individuals can be traced back to the origins of the universe. On the frontispiece of one of my father's old astronomy books is the following poem attributed to Hagedorn, written long before Carl Sagan was here to promote similar ideas.

> Here is life's secret,
> Keep the upward glance,
> Remember Aries is your relative,
> The moon is your uncle,
> And those twinkling things,
> Your sisters and your cousins and your aunts.

Second, coming down to our planet, it is even easier to acknowledge that we on this globe are interconnected. What happens on one side of the world—be it Chernobyl, a kidnapping in the Middle East, a revolution somewhere, a new scientific discovery, a natural disaster, or an economic or public policy shift—each affects neighboring nations, allies, enemies, and ripples around the globe. Our interconnectedness becomes increasingly salient as the peoples of the globe confront that our planet is threatened with nuclear destruction and widespread pollution.

Third, taking just one of these items, scientific discovery, we are coming to see how what happens in the laboratory, which seems so technical and out of reach, transforms the world in which we live, forcing us to scramble to make sense of the new conditions created—conditions that include fresh new sources of social and political power. The current biological revolution, of which surrogacy is only one small part, provides a fine example of this different kind of interconnectedness—the linking of the work in the laboratory to the policymakers and citizenry trying to assimilate and predict the implications of that work while at the same time being affected by it. Bruno Latour's research reveals that by carefully documenting this interrelationship between laboratory science and the broader social context, the distinction typically followed in the sociology of science between microlevel studies of science and policymaking responses becomes blurred.

Fourth, in our lives we are looking for connections to others. We examine our family connections to find the explanations of our roots, and we look to those near and dear to us to give meaning to the present and future. Saul Bellow's latest novel, *More Die of Heartbreak,* is premised on the idea that we of the modern Western world think we are autonomous, can doggedly pursue whatever we want, and consequently deal in transience rather than in permanent relationships, and are thereby violating some fundamental needs for genuine connectedness over time.

Fifth, at the level of the individual, the interconnectedness of our minds and bodies, our emotional well-being and our physical well-being, is also being increasingly well documented. Holistic medicine, while not yet permeating traditional medicine, is gradually gaining more acceptance as data on diseases previously considered exclusively physiologically-based show influence from the individual's state of mind, including stress. Medical professionals seem more willing to consider the connections of mind and body, and more citizens seem willing to accept greater responsibility for their own state of health.

What does the recognition of the interconnectedness of life mean for surrogate motherhood? First, it should alert us to the risk taken in asking the woman to ignore the connections she will feel to the baby she carries and gives birth to, or as Neuhaus said so well, to "disaggregate herself from her uterus." The separation can be accomplished, although at some cost, but there may be ways to show respect for what the woman is experiencing. For example, the adoption system is moving toward increasing openness in the adoption process, facilitating connections between the birth mother and the adoptive family, depending on the desire of the birth mother regarding such contact and communication. After the allotted period given in adoption proceedings for the birth mother to change her mind, relinquishment occurs. The baby is then permanently in the custody of the adoptive parents, but with the new openness the families may stay in contact, as the birth mother seeks out such contact, which tends to occur especially during the child's first year. In practice, the birth mothers tend to reduce visits to the family as people get on with their lives. But the choice to continue contact and the resulting communication seem to facilitate a more positive transition for parents and child. If surrogacy is allowed, it should minimally leave these protections and innovations from the adoption system. It is not the coldly enforced clarity of a commercial contract signed before pregnancy that is needed. Indeed, such a contract should be declared unenforceable in a court of law. Consumers in New Jersey have forty-eight hours to reconsider a contract they have signed to buy a car. Surely surrogate mothers should have at least that long after the baby is born to reconsider any agreement made and should be able to have contact with the baby after relinquishment.

This brings us to the interconnections of the major participants in the drama. What Stern failed to realized was that he would forever be connected to Mary Beth through Melissa (Baby M). Some of Melissa's individual characteristics will be noticeable gifts from Mary Beth. How will he and his wife respond to Melissa, as she grows up revealing those similarities and traits, when they look down on the mother who passed them directly to her? It is a paradox that these couples, desperately seeking connection to a baby, deny connection to the other biological parent. Perhaps it is because these couples are middle class or above and have lived so much of their lives in private homes or riding in automobiles that separate them from everyone else, that they come to believe they are autonomous. Since it is money that has facilitated the homes, cars, freedom to travel independently, it should not surprise us that they believe they can use that money to get what they want under precisely the controlled conditions they want. The problem is that to get what they want this time involves two other human beings—the mother and the child, with rights and feelings. It is risky for the couple to reach out of their autonomous lives in order to be connected to a child—to extend them further into time, make them a family, and thereby give more meaning and fulfillment to their lives—without also wanting connection to the child's mother, who agreed to carry and bear this dream come true.

Melissa will learn who her mother is. We cannot track our molecules back to the stars in the galaxies, but we can and do follow our connections to our sisters, cousins, and aunts of this world. Melissa will grow up in a society that attaches significance to the concept of natural mother, even if the contract does not. Somehow she will have to sort out the meanings of her origins. The anger and disdain the Sterns have expressed for Melissa's mother could come back to haunt them. This should be a warning to all those couples considering using someone else's egg, sperm, or uterus. If we are going to do this, we need to choose people we respect and like enough to be connected to through time, to include them in our lives and our children's lives. The cold, legal contract cannot buy us the connection we seek. Only warmth and respect and caring can. Surely, Unamuno's beautiful words should speak to us here: "No, not more light, but more warmth. Men die of cold, not of darkness. It is the frost that kills and not the night." If we are not ready to respect the interconnectedness of life at this point, then we had better outlaw surrogacy until we are.

## *SUGGESTED READINGS*

Finkelstein, Joanne, and Clough, Patricia. "Foetal Politics and the Birth of an Industry." *Women's Studies International Forum* 6 (1983).

Hollinger, Joan Heifetz. "Informed Consent Needed for Specific Performance." *New Jersey Law Journal* 119 (February 26, 1987).

Morgan, Derek. "Making Motherhood Male: Surrogacy and the Moral Economy of Women." *Journal of Law and Society* 12 (Summer 1985).

O'Brien, Shari. "The Itinerant Embryo and the Neo-Nativity Scene: Bifurcating Biological Maternity." *Utah Law Review* (Winter 1987).

Pollitt, Katha. "The Strange Case of Baby M." *The Nation* (May 23, 1987).

Tofler, Alvin. "What Is Human Now?" *Christian Science Monitor* (June 4, 1987).

*Barbara Sherman Heyl is associate professor of sociology at Illinois State University. She is author of* The Madam as Entrepreneur *and has published articles in the fields of the sociology of deviance and the sociology of law. Her recent research and publications have been on the legal impact of federal legislation in the education of handicapped children.*

## Questions for Empathy and Analysis

1. Why does Heyl think that the contract between the Sterns and Mary Beth Whitehead was flawed? Empathetically paraphrase the first two paragraphs of Heyl's article. What expectations does she establish in her introduction?

2. Heyl says that class bias in our court system and adoption is not new. What is new as far as Heyl is concerned?

3. In paragraph four Heyl speaks of the battle being waged over definitions. How does Heyl's use of the word *definition* relate to her use of the phrase *symbolic knowledge*? How does her use of the word *definition* relate to her use of the phrase *social construction*? Can you think of an instance when your definition of something conflicted

with someone else's? How did you decide whose definition was better? What is the relationship between language and social reality? Can language create a reality or only describe the reality that is there?

4. What does Heyl mean when she says that Judge Sorkow's decision "signaled a major symbolic shift toward the language of the marketplace and away from the long-held rights of the natural mother in our society"? Do you agree with her that the "language of the marketplace" is male-dominated? Can you think of any specific examples?

5. How does Heyl's example of the expression "alternative reproduction vehicle" serve to advance her arguments about language? How does society typically define a mother? How would you define her?

6. Heyl argues that there is an interconnectedness to life and cites many examples. Which examples do you think are most effective in advancing her overall argument? Do you think that couples seeking surrogates are likely to want to include the surrogate mother in their future plans? If they are, how might this be legislated? Should specific custody arrangements be worked out when the contract is signed?

■ ■ ■ ■ ■ ■ ■ ■ ■

# REPRODUCTIVE TECHNOLOGY AND RESTRAINTS

## Monica B. Morris

We are on the edge of a biotechnical revolution as profound in its implications as was the Industrial Revolution—and we are as unprepared for this one as we were for that. To believe we can outlaw surrogate parenting is to believe with the Luddites that the Industrial Revolution could be stopped by wrecking the machinery that made it possible.

Many thinkers, including Richard John Neuhaus, are adamant that surrogate motherhood should be outlawed. The reasons they give are many and, for the most part, sensible and humane. For Neuhaus, the main objection to surrogate motherhood is that it is a form of trade in which those with money exploit poor, or poorer, women and that, in the United States, in deciding matters like the Baby M case, money speaks louder than morality, ethics, or compassion.

As we spill gallons of ink on paper in discussion of social class and exploitation in the Baby M case, technological advances continue and the topic widens and deepens to include a dozen more issues, so that the "problem" becomes not one but many, so densely interwoven that solutions become ever more elusive. The speed of new discoveries and of refinements to existing technology becomes apparent when the kind of arrangement between Mary Beth Whitehead and the Sterns is referred to in a recent edition of the television program, "Nova," as "traditional surrogacy." This "traditional" surrogacy has been going on for over a decade.

## Reproductive Technology Yesterday and Today

Artificial insemination by a donor has been used for several decades, some say centuries: in vitro fertilization, in which an embryo is created by combining the parents' egg and spermatozoon outside the mother's body and then transplanting it in her uterus to complete its gestation, was first successful in 1978 in England. Since then, thousands of healthy babies worldwide have resulted from this technique. Technology developed in Australia and now used in several other countries makes it possible to freeze embryos produced in vitro and later to thaw and transplant them into their biological mother's uterus or into the uterus of a surrogate mother who is not biologically related to the child she will carry. In 1987, in England, a Mrs. Mary Wright gave birth to "twins" eighteen months apart. The babies were conceived in a petri dish at the same time some years before and transplanted in her uterus at different times, simulating a "normal" interval between the babies.

Possible now, too, and practiced, is the donation of eggs from one woman to another who, although infertile or whose own eggs carry some genetic flaw, can sustain a pregnancy. The eggs are fertilized by artificial insemination before being removed and transplanted, or they can be fertilized in vitro and then transferred.

These biotechnical achievements are miraculous, offering hope to couples who long to have children but who, until now, have not been successful. Estimates of infertility vary between one in seven and one in five couples, and one must feel compassion for those who want children and cannot have them. Those so placed talk of their suffering, their pain, their "obsession," with having a baby. Women give up jobs, careers, to devote all their time to fertility treatments. There has even been a play on the subject. David Rudkin's bitter *Ashes,* that depicts one infertile couple's obsessive and, ultimately, fruitless efforts to procreate.

Human-made miracles appear to offend some who believe that only God can work miracles. Yet, since its beginning, technology has attempted to conquer nature and make it work for us rather than against us. Scientific discoveries, from the time of Copernicus on, have been strongly resisted as against the will of God or as sacrilegious. According to the scriptures, women are to bring forth offspring in "sorrow"; science has eased our sorrow, and it has reduced the dangers that came "naturally" before we understood enough to wash our hands before plunging them into the bodies of women delivering babies.

Science, as has been repeatedly, and often passionately, argued, cannot determine morality. Given the large numbers of couples in despair over their infertility, the deep pool of poor women who might be recruited as surrogate mothers or as egg donors, and the skill of entrepreneurs in generating "needs" as yet unrealized, the potential for misuse of the reproductive technology, and for the abuse and exploitation of all parties, is vast. It raises disturbing questions about how we are to manage our technological marvels. How can we assure they are used for good? What, indeed, is "good," and for whom is it good?

## Best Interests of the Child

The United States is not the only country grappling with these problems. A widely reported surrogacy case was ruled upon in Great Britain at about the same time as the Baby M case was going through the New Jersey Courts. On March 12, 1987, a surrogate mother was granted custody of six-month-old twins, a boy and a girl, conceived by artificial insemination. Like Mary Beth Whitehead, after the birth the surrogate refused to hand the babies over to the father and his wife. The judge, Sir John Arnold, said he had heard nothing that "might be taken to outweigh the advantages to these children of preserving the link to the mother to whom they are bonded and who has exercised a satisfactory degree of maternal care." Sir John saw nothing shameful in the arrangements between the parties but that "ultimately, the welfare of the children is the first and paramount consideration which the court must, by statute, take into account and that is what I do." Unlike Judge Sorkow, in deciding the best interest of the child, Sir John did not weigh the wealth of the father as important. The birth mother was unmarried and on social security; one reason she offered herself as a surrogate mother was to raise money to bring up her seven-year-old son. At last report, the mother was seeking child support for the twins from their father who, under present legislation may have to pay maintenance costs until the twins are sixteen years old, even though he has no parental rights. Appeals by the father may set precedents in this hitherto uncharted area.

Although both Judge Arnold and Judge Sorkow stated their concerns with the children in these custody cases and what would be best for them, each ruled differently. For Judge Arnold, the best interest of a child lies in preserving the link to its mother. For Judge Sorkow, the close bonding of Mary Beth Whitehead to her child was dismissed as irrelevant. Under the terms of the contract, she should not have allowed herself to become emotionally involved. Yet, in discussing custody of children in adoption cases, when birth mothers change their minds and want to keep their babies, adoption and child-development experts, as well as judges, have seen some risk of long-term emotional disturbance to a child who is taken from the care of one woman and given into the care of another at between six months and two-and-a-half years of age. The adult most suited to making a child feel wanted is the one with whom the child has already had, and continues to have, an affectionate bond. This would seem to apply to Baby M, whose mother nursed her from birth and who was with her for most of the first several months of her life.

Given the Baby M case and, perhaps, similar cases to follow, how can we determine the best interest of the child? In the United States, will the Ph.D. always win out over the high-school dropout? One problem is that we do not yet have children of these arrangements who are old enough to be studied. The best we can do is consider "scholarly" opinions as well as extrapolate from what we know about children who have grown up in other unusual or nontraditional circumstances; these might include adopted children, children of gay parents, and children born to mothers, including unmarried mothers, who chose artificial insemination by a donor.

Looking again at Great Britain, the British Medical Association (BMA) has flipped, then flopped, then flipped again on surrogate motherhood, most recently considering the practice not in the best interests of the children. In February, 1984, the association recommended that doctors not become involved in any "rent-a-womb" surrogacy scheme, whether the surrogate is paid or not and regardless of whether the baby was conceived by artificial insemination or in vitro and is genetically the couple's child. It seemed not to object to the use of in vitro fertilization to allow another woman to donate an egg for a couple with an infertile wife.

In December, 1985, the British Medical Association voted to support surrogate motherhood under "careful controls," but the May 7, 1987, report by the association's Board of Science and Education states that the baby born to a surrogate mother is "doomed to second best from the start by being deliberately deprived of one of its natural parents," and that the practice should not be supported. The report concluded that the interests of such children cannot be guaranteed and their welfare is more important than the wishes of infertile couples. This may not be the last word on surrogacy from the BMA, and its vacillation is not surprising given how little is known about surrogacy's effects on its products.

Information is sparse, too, on children resulting from artificial insemination by a donor. Researchers have found it difficult to follow the progress of such children largely because the legal parents have resisted study. As with traditional adoption, secrecy has generally been the rule. Some children of these arrangements, discovering their unorthodox origins—and estimates indicate about half of such children are later told or find out—have been vocal in expressing their anger. One, Suzanne Rubin, has been particularly visible on television talk shows and in magazine articles. She, like others in her situation, is dismayed at the lack of information available to her about her father's genetic background. She expresses horror that men like her father are able to sell their sperm without any responsibility for the lives they will help create. Discovering their origins in adolescence or in adulthood has the effect of destroying all their past lives as unreal, as fictional. These days, single women choosing artificial insemination by a donor are more likely to speak out about their decision and, presumably, will tell their offspring as much as they know about the donor. Openness is now thought to be desirable in attuning the children to their condition and in helping them accept it with minimum trauma.

Adoption agencies, too, have been recommending more openness between birth mothers and adopting couples than once was the rule. Agency research indicates that many adopted children have suffered substantial emotional anguish at their inability to trace their biological mothers, an anguish that has discolored their lives. One of my students, J, a married man with several children of his own, told me of his desperation to find his "real" mother and father, despite the great love and appreciation he felt for his adoptive parents. Records had been sealed, but after years of effort and with much ingenuity and some guile, J did trace his mother, long-married and with other children, to a city on the other side of the country. His father, also married and with grown children, was also tracked down.

The father, angry at first, refused to see J. Successful in business and fearful of schemes that might deprive his legitimate children of their inheritance, he resisted. J, risking arrest, pushed his way into his father's office and confronted him. In time, J's wife and children were accepted by the families of both his biological parents. "I can't tell you what it meant," he said, "to look into my mother's face and see my little daughter's face there! And to find all those brothers and sisters I never knew I had!" Biological ties can be important, it seems, and while William Stern's "compelling need" appears to have been in continuing his family "blood line," neither the feelings of Mary Beth Whitehead's older children at losing their sister, nor the existence of Baby M's older siblings and the meaning of their loss to her life have been considered of significance in the Baby M case. Baby M also has a "blood line," independent of her father's.

Research on the well-being of children of gay parents is also scarce; such children seem to cope well with their unconventional family life. They appear to understand and accept homosexuality and are able to discuss it calmly with their parents and with interviewers. Some are reluctant to let schoolmates other than close friends know their situation, their experience informing them that this will lead to ridicule or ostracism.

My own explorations into what it feels like to be the child of older parents, prompted by the current trend toward deferred parenting, also indicates the difficulties children face when they are different in any way from most of their peers. Having one's parents mistaken for one's grandparents, or realizing that Dad is not able to play catch with the lads like the other guys' dads may not seem terrible hardships, but to the children involved they can cause embarrassment and sadness. The fear of losing parents while one is still a child is real. The now-adult subjects offered suggestions about how today's older parents might ease the problems for their children. These included being open with children about such worrying matters as the possibility of early responsibility for ailing, elderly parents, and about the likelihood of being left without parents, especially without fathers, sooner than most of their peers. The need for openness is emphasized in all kinds of nontraditional or less-than-usual family patterns. Children of older parents also emphasized their need for their parents' time. Those whose parents had been generous in discussion and in time and attention were far less likely to be troubled in any way by their parents' ages than those whose parents were less open and less available. That older parents are more likely to be financially comfortable than younger ones was noted by several subjects as an advantage, but one that is outweighed by many other factors.

The requirement for subjects in my research was that their mothers were at least thirty-six-years-old when the subjects were born; the fathers' ages ranged from thirty-five to over fifty. Although little has been said on the matter, it cannot be overlooked that the Sterns are older parents, each forty or forty-one when Baby M was born, making her an ideal candidate for my research later on—were she not weighted down with a passel of problems unrelated to her parents' age.

Parents' age is seen as important in, for instance, the choice of adoptive parents for infants. Adoption counselors in three different agencies have told me, unofficially—officially they do not discriminate on the basis of age—that, given a choice of adoptive parents for an infant, they would probably not give the child to a couple aged forty or over. One reason among several is that while the couple might be energetic in their forties, by the time the baby was a teenager, they would be in their mid-fifties or older and perhaps less able to cope with stresses and strains of adolescence than would younger parents.

## Reproductive Technology Today and Tomorrow

In the matter of Baby M, all the participants have been hurt, and they may never be entirely free of pain. We cannot assess how Baby M's life will be colored or, rather, discolored by her origins and by the publicity arising from the case for her custody. In light of the repugnance generated by talk of rented wombs and the commercialization of birth, of baby-selling, of children as commodities to be contracted for, and the outrage felt by many that an infant can be wrested from its birth mother against her will because of a bill of sale, it is not unreasonable for Neuhaus and others to call for an end to surrogate mothering. But, even were it possible to stop surrogacy completely, it would be a mistake. It is possible and, given the doubts about the future well-being of the offspring, of vital importance that it be very tightly controlled and used only in special circumstances which should be clearly specified.

Why should we not outlaw surrogacy? The technology involved is a vital step toward solving other problems. Surrogate mothering, artificial insemination by a donor, in vitro fertilization, embryo suctioning and transplanting, embryo freezing, have been developed by researchers as part of the quest not only to help infertile couples but also to diminish life-long suffering of children with serious genetic conditions. For some time, we have been able to perform certain surgical procedures on fetuses in utero; now, an embryo suctioned after a few days of gestation can be examined for genetic flaws before replanting in its mother's uterus. These techniques, while still experimental, may become routine. Instead of waiting until the second trimester of pregnancy for amniocentesis, a pregnant woman may know within days of conception if the embryo will develop normally. The choice to abort is rarely easy; it is particularly difficult at sixteen or eighteen weeks of gestation.

Some of the most recently reported advances in reproductive technology are in ways to battle male infertility—believed to be the cause of 40 percent of all fertility problems. Microfertilization, or microinjection, or zone drilling, involve direct injection of sperm into egg (in vitro) so that men with low sperm counts will be able to father their own children. In effect, it gives nature a boost. For some such men, the only solution to childlessness has been for their wives to be artificially inseminated by a donor. So, in time, and with more research, some of the presently used techniques may be replaced by those that raise fewer ethical and moral questions.

Why must we regulate surrogacy and other procedures? Regulation is needed, not only to control exploitation of poor women but also to avoid the widespread misuse of these technologies. Neuhaus is right to deplore using one class of women for the benefit of those of another social class. This exploitation will know no bounds if allowed free rein. The ability to transplant a couple's own embryo into the uterus of a third party means that the third party need not be of the same race or ethnicity as the embryo. A black woman could bear a white child who has no genetic relationship to its "incubator." Gena Corea, author of *The Mother Machine,* raises the possibility that women in the Third World could be induced to provide baby-bearing services for far less money than American women, making the procedure attractive to couples who could not otherwise afford it. Rather than expressing horror at this idea, the studio audience of the Donahue show on which Corea appeared on August 7, 1987, as well as the rest of the panel, dismissed her as radical and shrill. Women in the audience, and those who called in, were attracted to the idea of surrogate mothering. One caller wanted to know how she could become a surrogate. A member of the audience suggested that a computerized list of would-be surrogates be made nationally available for couples to choose from. Another regarded surrogacy as "a wonderful option" for people who marry late and want children. This latter statement drew hearty applause from an audience that could gain little understanding of the implications of what they applauded from the superficial handling of the topic on a television talk show. These kinds of entertainments stir up enthusiasm and create markets. Manufacturers have not been slow to turn to workers in the Third World to keep labor costs down; entrepreneurs in the baby business will seize the same opportunities if they are cost-effective—and if they are allowed to do so.

## Lack of Regulation

Unlike those of several other countries, the United States government has been slow to fund—and hence to regulate—research in reproductive technologies. It has been slow, too, to regulate the "private" areas of family and procreation, leaving both research and surrogacy wide open for commercial exploitation. Without regulations, lawyers and businessmen have been able to raise capital—even to sell public stock—to operate sperm banks, reproduction and fertility clinics, surrogacy agencies, and to promote the idea of "franchises" that will use patented techniques. This means that royalties would be paid to the patent holders every time a particular tool—a specialized catheter, for instance—were used. A company spokesman for Fertility and Genetic Research, Incorporated, in a sales pitch to stockbrokers, spoke of plans to tap the affluent market for egg donation. Market researchers, hired to survey the availability of women willing to serve as regular donors for $250 a procedure, discovered that "Donor women exist in cost-effective abundance." Another entrepreneur, lawyer Noel P. Keane, whose infertility center made the match between Mary Beth Whitehead and the Sterns, has a thriving business finding surrogates. His fee is about $10,000 for each match; this is apart from the fee paid to the surrogate and the cost of prenatal care and delivery, all of which is paid by the negotiating couple. It is reported that Keane is now expanding his services to include a pool of egg donors as well as surrogate mothers. The donors are available, as is a ready market of affluent couples willing to do almost anything to have children. Why not put the two together and make everybody, especially the money men, happy? It is the American way.

Indeed, Americans have not shown any great dismay or disgust with the profiting from these arrangements. Seventy-five percent of those polled by the Roper organization felt Judge Sorkow's ruling to give Baby M to the Sterns was right. "After all," people responded. "A contract is a contract." Business, in fact, is business. Only 20 percent of the personal sympathy of those polled lay with Mary Beth Whitehead. The contract for a woman to bear a child to give to another couple was viewed as no different from any other exchange of services for money.

A small part of this reasoning may be due to some, not all, feminists' insistence that women are to be treated under the law exactly as men are treated, that women should have control over their own bodies, including the right to use them to make money, and that to suggest that women's biological makeup might affect their emotions is to be sexist and paternalistic. Since the Baby M case, feminist thinking has converged and several prominent feminists, including Gloria Steinem, Betty Friedan, Phyllis Chesler, and Marilyn French, have joined with other groups to file an amicus curiae brief arguing that the commercialization of surrogate parenthood violates the Constitution and the dignity of women.

In making this distinction between surrogacy and commercial surrogacy, the feminists are following the guidelines of already established regulations in some other countries. As one example, under the Surrogacy Arrangements Act of 1985, Great Britain outlaws surrogacy agencies. It outlaws third-party intervention of any kind between a couple and the woman who is to bear a baby for them. Advertising for surrogacy arrangements is a criminal offense by the publisher or the distributor. Commercial surrogacy, then, is against the law, and although it is legal for a woman to be paid for bearing a child for someone else, contracts between the parties are not legally enforceable.

It is fascinating to watch how those profiting from surrogacy have attempted to subvert, or find loopholes, in the British law. The London *Sunday Times* reports that British women are being sought by one Washington-based agency to travel to the United States to serve as surrogate mothers for British couples, also being recruited, who are prepared to pay as much as £20,000 (approximately $32,000) for a child, thus removing the entire transaction from the United Kingdom. It may well be, as Patrick Steptoe, the pioneer in in vitro fertilization, has said, that we need international, rather than local, legislation.

### Regulating Reproductive Technology

Guidelines on regulating surrogate mothering and all the other techniques are urgently needed. The lag between our technology and our social policy grows wider by the moment. At the very least, prospective parents should meet the criteria for eligibility to adopt a child under the current laws. Couples should not be able to arrange for a child, as they might arrange for an entertainment center or a BMW, simply because they want one and can afford it. Certainly, the doctrine of informed consent should prevail. That is, all parties should recognize and accept the risks and benefits involved and enter voluntarily, free of any kind of coercion. The psychological as well as the physical risks of childbearing must be understood by all and it should also be acknowledged that the emotional involvement in carrying a fetus to term and delivering it is of a different order from that involved in milking sperm into a jar. Informed consent is no simple matter; people do not always know in advance of an event how they will feel about it when it occurs.

We do not have to start with a blank sheet. We can look to countries more advanced than ours for guidelines to legislation. Britain, as already mentioned, has outlawed commercial surrogacy; the Australian state of Victoria, in The Infertility (Medical Procedures) Act of 1984 has also set firm limits, both on who is eligible for the procedures and on just how far the scientists may go. Control is firmly in government hands. Among other criteria, patients must have been under treatment for infertility for at least twelve months to assure they are seeking a "last resort" and that there is no other possibility of a pregnancy, or that the woman seeking treatment could pass on a hereditary disorder. The law prohibits any kind of payment for sperm, eggs, or embryos, other than travel or medical expenses incurred by the donor. It sets strict rules on the use by scientists of embryos in experiments, and makes it an offense, punishable by up to two years in prison, to give or receive payment for acting as a surrogate mother. Like the British law, it forbids advertising for surrogates or for offering to act as one and it declares void all contracts between the parties.

Even more unclear than the long-term effects on all the parties to surrogate parenting are the implications of technology that could make surrogacy obsolete. According to Surgeon General C. Everett Koop, it is not inconceivable that total extrauterine life will be possible within the next ten years; the gap between in vitro fertilization and the maintenance of premature babies will narrow. This possibility, too, must be addressed publicly—and soon—or we could be faced with a Huxleyan society in which making love and making babies are completely separated, "childbearing" is a loathsome obscenity, and "father" is a dirty word.

The Luddites' fear of the machine was well founded. Industrialization eventually raised the standard of living for millions, providing them with shoes and dishes and clothing and other goods of a quality once reserved for the rich; but at the beginning the factory system and the shift from rural to urban areas brought untold misery. Men, women, and children were hideously exploited, separated from their roots, forced to work long hours for little pay in filthy, back-breaking, and dangerous conditions. In many parts of the world, where they remain unregulated, working conditions and pay are still appalling. Regulation of surrogacy does not necessarily "make a public statement that it is all right." Good laws and regulations protect those who are least able to protect themselves or who are unaware of the implications of their actions. They also serve to protect a society from its own folly.

*SUGGESTED READINGS*

Andrews, Lori B. "Yours, Mine and Theirs." *Psychology Today* (December 1984).
Goldstein, Joseph, Freud, Anna and Solnit, Albert J. *Beyond the Best Interests of the Child.* Glencoe, N.Y.: The Free Press, 1973.
Groth, Mardel et al. "An Agency Moves Toward Open Adoption of Infants." *Child Welfare* (May/June 1987).
Guest, Ted. "Finally a Ruling—'M' is for Melissa." *U.S. News and World Report* (April 13, 1987).
Singer, Peter. "Making Laws on Making Babies." *Hasting Center Report* (August 1985).

*Monica B. Morris is associate professor of sociology at California State University, Los Angeles. Her teaching and research interests include medical sociology, social interaction, classical and contemporary theory, and social organization. She is author of* An Excursion into Creative Sociology *and from Columbia University Press* Last-Chance Children: Growing Up with Older Parents.

## Questions for Empathy and Analysis

1. Empathetically summarize Morris's section on "Reproductive Technology Yesterday and Today." What is the author's orientation to

her topic? Do you expect she will argue that surrogate motherhood is good or that it is bad? Why does she think surrogate motherhood should be regulated?

2. In considering the best interests of the child in surrogate motherhood cases, Morris compares the offspring of surrogates first to children resulting from artificial insemination, second to adopted children, third to children of gay parents, and finally to children of older parents. In terms of her organization of ideas, how does she weigh the effects on a child born and raised in unusual circumstances? What does she suggest is in the best interests of a child? Do you agree or disagree with her comparisons?

3. Morris argues that we should not outlaw surrogacy because it is a "vital step toward solving other problems." Do you think that it would be impossible to develop techniques of embryo suctioning and transplanting, embryo freezing, or microfertilization if surrogate motherhood were outlawed? How interdependent are these reproductive technologies?

4. In what ways is surrogate motherhood analogous to the Industrial Revolution? How does Morris's analogy support her argument? Are there any ways in which the analogy could work against her?

■ ■ ■ ■ ■ ■ ■ ■ ■
# CHEAP LABOR: SEX, CLASS, RACE—AND "SURROGACY"

## Barbara Katz Rothman

"Surrogacy" is an issue that cannot be reduced to a question of class. Although neither, as Richard John Neuhaus persuasively argues, can we leave out questions of class. Sex, class and race—this issue has them all: it is truly an issue on which to hone our analytic capabilities.

The concept of surrogacy is deeply rooted in essential patriarchal concepts and ideology governing reproduction. In the old days of patriarchy, the days before things got complicated and subtle, men owned women and owned all of the fruits of their labor, most especially their children. To have children a man had to have a wife or otherwise own and control a woman. This is the context in which Abraham used Hagar. A "surrogate" is a substitute. We can speak of Hagar as a "surrogate," but not as a surrogate mother for Ishmael. She was unquestionably the mother of that child. Sarah was not Ishmael's adoptive, foster, or any other kind of mother. She was Abraham's wife, and Hagar was the mother of the child. The point was, so what? It hardly mattered who was the mother: the real question was who was the father. Abraham needed a child, a son really, and he needed a woman as a route to a son. When Sarah did not work out, he substituted Hagar.

3    Back in those days, children were believed to grow of men's "seed." We are still left with remnants of that thinking in our language. We tell children that "Daddy plants a seed in Mommy." We say that Mrs. John Smith bears John Smith, Jr., and women themselves speak of having a man's baby.

4    Modern reproductive technology has been forced to go beyond the sperm as the seed. Modern science has had to confront the egg as seed. On one level, that is the end of the patriarchal assumption: modern medical thinking cannot possibly hold onto old notions of women as nurturers of men's seeds. A doctor who has spent time "harvesting" eggs from women's bodies for in vitro fertilization cannot deny the significance of women's seed. But that does not mean the end of the cult of the seed—the belief that seeds, genes, are everything, all that matters in the making of a baby.

5    The old cult of the seed had a clear place for women: as nurturers of men's seeds, as containers, the soil in which seeds grow. When forced to acknowledge that women's genetic contribution is equal to men's genetic contribution, there were two choices available to support patriarchy: to continue to denigrate the significance of everything about women, which would mean losing the cult of the seed and denying the significance of genetic ties; or to extend to women some of the privileges of patriarchy. That is, the choice can be to recognize women's paternity rights in their children. Women too can be seen to own their children, just like men, based not on their unique nurturance, the long months of pregnancy, the intimate connections with the baby as it grows and moves inside her body, passes through her genitals, and sucks her breasts. No, women can be said to own their babies, have "rights" to them, just like men do—based on their seed.

6    Neuhaus buys right into that. Recognizing that the baby has become a commodity, he questions who owns this valuable product and answers "Presumably ownership is fifty-fifty between Mrs. Whitehead and Mr. Stern." Presuming exactly what? That babies are half egg, half sperm, and might as well have grown in the backyard.

7    Mary Beth Whitehead (Mrs? Why does Neuhaus keep reminding us that she is *Mrs.* Whitehead?) herself buys into much of the culture of patriarchy, not really challenging dominant ideology. For one thing, while the "experts" may claim that she denied the significance of the "genetic contribution of the birth father" (whatever is a birth father?), it was the Whitehead family that was asking for joint custody, and the Sterns who wanted "all or nothing." But her acceptance of patriarchal thinking, like Neuhaus's, is more insidious than that. Neuhaus quotes her as saying "It's such a miracle to see a child born." She did not just "see" that baby born: she birthed it. The emphasis on "seeing" babies born came out of middle-class humanizing modifications of obstetrical practices. Women wanted to be socially acknowledged during births. Doctors agreed; women could watch the births in mirrors, along with their husbands.

8    The alienation of women from their bodies, the ability of a woman to "disaggregate herself from her uterus" is not unique to surrogacy. It is what modern obstetrics asks of all women, as they are to watch their fetuses on sonograms, "identifying" with the baby on the television screen; to watch their births in a distant

mirror, the baby emerging through a pile of laundry "draped" there to keep the dirty woman away from the sterile baby; and to speak of holding their babies for the "first time" when they hold them in their arms.

9    Neuhaus talks of "bonding" being "effected." Whitehead talked about bonding too. I guess we are all talking about it these days; but we are talking about it as if the baby arrives from Mars and then "bonds" to someone and someone "bonds" to it. We talk of the moment of birth, when one becomes two—a separation so profound it can only be done in blood and in pain—as a moment of "bonding," of "attachment." Reality is turned on its head: the cord is cut, severed, and we talk of bonding. That is an outsider's view, a man's eye view of birth: the baby "arrives," "enters" the world. The woman feels the baby leave.

10    It is in this crazy world, in which men's experience defines women's reality, that "surrogacy" is at all understandable. Babies are sperm grown up: Noel Keane, who wrote the Stern-Whitehead contract, speaks of the "surrogate" as giving the baby "back" to the father. The homunculus theory never really left us. Men need somewhere to plant this precious sperm, these seedling babies. If one patch of soil is barren, they can hire themselves another.

11    What of the first wives, the Sarahs of these stories? Unlike the original Sarah, the Elizabeth Sterns are expected to be social mothers to these children. Never mind all those pictures of Mr. Stern carrying the baby into the court house: it was Elizabeth who took her off to Bloomies in her stroller. How secure are these women in their social motherhood? What if Mr. Stern had turned to his wife when the judge was ready for Elizabeth to adopt the baby and said, "Never mind. I want a divorce." If she were no longer Mrs. Stern, what would be her claim to Baby Stern? Are not all of these social mothers of children born out of "surrogacy" contracts just one divorce away from childlessness?

12    Those are the issues of patriarchy that Neuhaus omits; but it is indeed more complicated than just this. The technology of the Stern-Whitehead case was the simple "turkey baster" technology of artificial insemination, in use with humans for over a hundred years. The newer technology allows eggs to be transferred from one woman to another woman. Like artificial insemination, it can be used to allow social parenthood to begin with a pregnancy: one uses another person's genetic material to become a parent starting with pregnancy—one's own pregnancy in the case of egg donations, one's wife's pregnancy in the case of artificial insemination. The woman pregnant with another woman's egg donation is the birth mother, although not the genetic mother, of the baby she bears. In the case of artificial insemination, the man who is physically, socially, and emotionally present for the pregnancy and birth (in the case in question that would be Richard Whitehead) is the social or, I would think, birth father, but not genetic father of the baby.

13    The technology of egg donation or embryo transfer, like the technology of artificial insemination, can be used in this newer "surrogacy" model, to hire a pregnancy, rent a womb. In this instance, some of the privileges of patriarchy are extended to upper-class women: rich women too can hire women to grow their seed for them. Women with money and power can exercise their rights of "paternity," declaring ownership of a baby grown of their seed in another woman's body, in a "rented uterus."

14    Here is where we go beyond sex and class and have to deal with issues of race as well: such a "rented uterus" need not be of the same race as the fetus

*[handwritten margin note: racism]*

she bears. And so we have the specter of women of color—the same women who push white babies in their strollers, white elderly in their wheelchairs—growing white people's babies for them, for a fee. Picture what the Baby M case would have looked like had Mary Beth Whitehead been a black woman. The end could not have been much worse, but I bet we would have gotten there faster.

*[handwritten margin note: * Thesis — men are dominant, women submissive (unimportant in births?)]*

(15) Race, class and sex—these are not three separate systems. They are deeply entwined, in their functioning and in their ideology. Our American focus on genetics, on seeds, is equally there in our attitudes toward race and sex, in our patriarchal ideology that genetics are our essence, nurturance merely the "dirt," or "soil," things grow in. In that sense, surrogacy is not a new idea: it is the reductio ad absurdum of Western patriarchal capitalism.

*[handwritten note: → reduced to absortion?]*

*Barbara Katz Rothman is associate professor of sociology at Baruch College and the Graduate Center of the City University of New York. Her publications include an analysis of obstetrical and midwifery ideology,* In Labor: Women and Power in the Birthplace, *published in paperback as* Giving Birth; *and a book on women's experiences with new reproductive technology:* The Tentative Pregnancy: Prenatal Diagnosis and the Future of Motherhood.

## Questions for Empathy and Analysis

1. What does Rothman mean by "patriarchy" and the "cult of the seed"? What is the tone of her essay in the beginning paragraphs? Empathetically paraphrase the fourth and fifth paragraphs. How does paraphrasing help you to understand the tone of her essay?

2. Rothman claims that Mary Beth Whitehead accepted patriarchal thinking without questioning it. How does Whitehead do this, according to Rothman? How did the experts accept patriarchal thinking, too? Would you agree with experts that William Stern is the "birth father"? How does Rothman define a "birth father" later in her essay? Do you find her method of returning to this point persuasive?

3. What, for Rothman, is the difference between a man's eye view of birth and a woman's eye view of birth?

4. Rothman raises the question of the rights of social mothers and genetic mothers. What rights do foster parents, adoptive parents, or stepparents have in relation to the children they nurture? What rights do you think they ought to have?

5. Rothman briefly touches on the issue of race at the end of her essay. She claims that if Whitehead had been a black woman "the end could not have been much worse, but I bet we would have gotten there faster." How do you interpret this statement?

■ ■ ■ ■ ■ ■ ■ ■

# THE TERROR OF SURROGATE MOTHERHOOD
## Fantasies, Realities, and Viable Legislation

### Isadore Schmukler and Betsy P. Aigen

Why does surrogate motherhood create so much antagonism and anger? Why should there be such outrage against women who are willing to help an infertile couple create a family of their own, especially if these women enjoy childbearing, already have children of their own, and can significantly increase their self-esteem in the process? And what is so evil about paying someone for this?

It is becoming increasingly clear that surrogate motherhood arouses panic and fear because it is seen as challenging cherished cultural values, such as the sanctity of motherhood and the family, and is being forbidden on that basis. We feel that this is an effort to legislate morality, equivalent to past efforts against drinking or abortion, most likely promoting similar results. Certain conservative and religious groups are attempting again to define for all of us what we should believe as right and wrong, what we can and cannot do. The legislature should question whether they have the right to eliminate people's freedom because others have a different idea about what is moral or correct.

In addition, the couples, the surrogates, and the intermediary agencies are accused of many evils, such as exploitation, ruthlessness, and encouraging mothers to desert their children. This is most often done in complete ignorance of the actual motives and feelings of the participants. Ignorance allows glib labels such as "reproductive prostitution" and "baby-selling" to be hurled at the surrogacy process with impunity. It is quite amazing to us when, for example, we hear charges that the surrogate is exploited, that those making these charges never provide evidence by asking the surrogates. Of course not! The surrogates would tell them that they are *not* being exploited. Who wants to hear *that*? All the critics seem to *know* that surrogacy exploits women. They know it *a priori,* without the chore of having to find out. If surrogate motherhood has the *potential* for exploitation, that's good enough for them.

Let's take a closer look at the corruption of morals that surrogacy is accused of. Protection of these morals has been labeled "public policy," and the recent New Jersey Supreme Court decision regarding the Baby M case outlines two basic aspects of such policy: (a) "that children be brought up by their natural parents, the surrogacy contract guaranteeing the separation of the child from its natural mother," and (b) "that adoption not be influenced by the payment of money, the surrogacy contract being based on such payment" (New Jersey Supreme Court, 1987, p. 2). Surrogate motherhood is seen by the court as violating each of these two aspects of public policy.

These policies appear to us primarily as cultural values that have been accorded legal status. It is our position that these values are a product of pervasive irrational fears. Experiences such as surrogacy, which are seen as undermining these values, are forbidden. Critical examination of such values is becoming increasingly important because the legitimacy of surrogacy is being determined by them. Additionally, they fuel very moralistic, self-righteous positions because they represent cherished cultural ideals whose correctness is seen as self-evident.

## Abandonment Fears

> The surrogacy contract guarantees permanent separation of the child from one of its natural parents. Our policy, however, has long been that to the extent possible, children should remain with and be brought up by both of their natural parents. That was the first stated purpose of the previous adoption act.... "It is necessary and desirable (a) to protect the child from unnecessary separation from his natural parents." (New Jersey Supreme Court, 1987; p. 42)

Harold Cassidy, Mary Beth Whitehead's lawyer, has said:

> The single most important issue that ought to emerge from the Baby M case is the need for society to preserve and protect the ties between mothers and children.... Society must not sanction a public policy that would encourage mothers to "abandon" their children. (*New Jersey Record,* 1988, p. 14)

It becomes clear that surrogacy is seen as encouraging the evil of maternal abandonment. Surrogacy is portrayed as a form of stealing children, of forcing ordinary mothers to hand over their beloved children to "baby snatchers." Even in the absence of the payment of a fee to the surrogate, there is a clear moralistic underpinning to the arguments against surrogacy, which is rarely stated overtly: That choosing to have a baby for someone else is reprehensible because it represents a rejection of the infant by its biological mother. Society sees the cherished ideal of mother love and the mother-infant bond being threatened, and surrogacy is the corrupting agent.

Well, isn't all that true? By viewing the surrogate as just another woman carrying a child that she wants to get rid of by giving it to a couple for adoption, the courts and the press have perpetrated and perpetuated such an image.

Situations like surrogacy inevitably stimulate deep anxiety and discomfort on a massive level because they evoke one of our primal fears as human beings: Being rejected and thrown away by our mothers. We identify with the infant and perceive him as being orphaned by his mother, whom we see as "using" him. This is the way surrogate mothers have most often been portrayed both in the press and by critics. This unconscious fantasy of rejection is fueled by the negative feelings we all have about our mothers and by fears of not having been totally "wanted."

It is, of course, true that, biologically, the surrogate is the "real" mother. But this ignores the circumstances and motivation for her pregnancy, as if these were irrelevant details. However, these are precisely the central points about being a surrogate mother. The court and others fervently deny the possibility of a woman's wanting to bear a child for someone else, a child that she therefore does not consider primarily as "hers." If a woman sees herself as a stand-in or double for another woman for whom she is bearing the child, and feels from the beginning of conception that this child belongs to the other woman and her husband, the biological father, rather than to herself, what type of abandonment is this? It is because the woman has chosen to biologically substitute for an infertile woman less fortunate than herself that she defines the experience for herself as an act of "giving" rather than "giving away" and rejecting a child.

This is the real emotional state and attitude of the surrogate, and it has been totally denied by and distorted by the New Jersey Supreme Court. For instance, "She [the child] is the offspring of someone who gave birth to her only to obtain money" (New Jersey Supreme Court, 1987, p. 51). "It [surrogacy] takes the child from the mother regardless of her wishes and her maternal fitness, and it does all of this, it accomplishes all of its goals, through the use of money" (p. 53). How does surrogate motherhood take a child from the mother "regardless of her wishes or maternal fitness"? The court is on a one-way track: It keeps trying to see the surrogate mother as wanting this child for herself. What does the surrogate mother's "maternal fitness" have to do with anything? It can have relevance only in a process that is seen as forcibly separating a child from its mother against her wishes. The court cannot absorb or deal with a situation where this is not the case, and it keeps addressing and judging the entire surrogate experience as if it were.

In a similar way, the surrender of parental rights, from the *surrogate's* experience, merely makes legal what has been her primary belief from the beginning: that the child is for the couple, not for herself. Unfortunately, because of the emotional power of the "bad mother" fantasy that surrogacy evokes, critics do not wish to know the *reality* of how surrogates themselves feel. Under the guise of protecting surrogates' rights, such critics really wish to proclaim the obligations of biological motherhood, regardless of what women actually want to do or how they feel. They refuse, for example, to allow a surrogate mother to surrender her parental rights, claiming that they are fundamental legal rights that cannot be relinquished by contract. This is tantamount to changing a right to be a mother into an obligation to be one. It is as if these people were saying, "The law says you have to be a good mother and raise this baby, and the baby is yours, whether you think so or not." Critics use the idea of a right as a method of coercing the surrogate mother to fulfill what they think is her obligation to her child. This makes a travesty of the concept of rights; it curtails freedom of choice instead of expanding it.

It is one thing to have a public policy that protects the rights of biological parents to raise children whom they are attached to and want, or that defends the child from "unnecessary separation from his natural parents." But to use such a policy to forbid experiences to which it was never meant to apply is a travesty. The court is implying that the biological mother is morally obligated to raise the child, purely by virtue of the biological relationship, and that experiences like surrogacy are inherently wrong, exactly because they create situations in which this biological mother doesn't want to raise this baby. Well, why is *that*? *Is* it better for a woman not to help others to have a baby, just to avoid such a situation? Is *that* what is meant by the public policy of the adoption law that the court refers to? Or is it the private view of the judges or others that is being held up as "public policy," as common law and value? Is this the widely held value that the court says it is? Where are the polls or referendums to show it?

## Fears of Being Used as an Object

The second major aspect of public policy that the courts feel is violated by surrogacy is "that adoption not be influenced by the payment of money." Because of the need to deny the crucial differences between the surrogate pregnancy and the typical unwanted pregnancy, in which a woman wants to surrender her child, the courts have pushed surrogacy into adoption law, which forbids payment to the mother. The original intent of this law was to prevent poor women from being pressured to give up their babies, making their decision "involuntary."

It is clear, however, that the introduction of money into such situations involves other values.

> There are, in a civilized society, some things that money cannot buy . . . .
> The long term effects of surrogacy contracts are not known, but feared—
> the impact on the child who learns her life was bought, that she is the off-
> spring of someone who gave birth to her only to obtain money; the impact
> on the natural mother as the full weight of her isolation is felt along with
> the full reality of the sale of her body and child. (New Jersey Supreme
> Court, 1987, pp. 50-51)

The real evil of money emerges: Its power to corrupt and seduce human beings to treat each other as commodities, as objects to be bought and sold, coldly and without feeling; a mother sells herself and her baby as objects.

The examples the New Jersey Supreme Court lists as "things that money cannot buy" in a "civilized society" are the following:

> Employers can no longer buy labor at the lowest price they can bargain
> for, even though that labor is "voluntary" . . . or buy women's labor for less
> money than paid to men for the same job. . . . or purchase agreement of
> children to perform oppressive labor . . . or purchase the agreement of
> workers to subject themselves to unhealthful working conditions. . . . There
> are, in short, values that society deems more important than granting to
> wealth whatever it can buy; be it labor, love, or life. Whether this principle
> recommends prohibition of surrogacy, which presumably sometimes re-
> sults in great satisfaction to all parties, is not for us to say. (New Jersey
> Supreme Court, 1987, p. 51)

Thus, although the court admits that "the great satisfaction to all of the parties"—which has actually occurred in almost all surrogate outcomes—would put surrogacy in a different category, it goes on to ignore this consideration and suggests that surrogacy is another example of human oppression and exploitation. It seems to us that the mind of the court is menaced by any thought of buying human services. This is quite understandable in that the court, like all of us, lives in a "civilized society" where money buys "human labor" and an endless variety of human services every day.

Money allows human beings to indulge their impulses to be served or serviced by others, without any sympathy or feeling for those being "used." Actually, one need only review the examples offered by the court of what "money cannot buy" to realize that all of these abuses were perpetuated for centuries against victims such as workers, children, and women. One need only think of the long use of slavery to understand the powerful wish to use others, and it is no wonder that there are laws against "baby-selling." These abuses are all fueled by human impulses, impulses that are common and only recently banned by the introduction of "civilized laws." It is our understanding that the introduction of money in surrogacy provokes repressed guilt over wishes to use others as objects. As Freud said, the repressed impulse always pushes for return, and society as hypervigilant against any situation that gives even the appearance of exploitation or devaluation.

Because surrogacy has the *potential* for abuse, the court assumes that such abuses are constantly occurring in practice. "The negative consequences of baby-selling are potentially present in the surrogacy context, especially the potential for placing and adopting a child without regard to the interest of the child or the natural mother" (New Jersey Supreme Court, 1987, p. 27). The comparison is to babies being sold into slavery, to be exploited: "In surrogacy, the highest bidders will presumably become the adoptive parents regardless of suitability, so long as payment of money is permitted" (New Jersey Supreme Court, 1987, p. 48). The implication of a slave auction, complete with "bidders," is clear. The actual reality of helping very adequate couples to have children is completely lost sight of.

The court wishes to exorcise what it considers to be "bad" motives. "Nowhere does this Court find any legal prohibition against surrogacy when the surrogate mother volunteers, without any payment, to act as a surrogate and is given the right to change her mind and to assert her parental rights" (New Jersey Supreme Court, 1987, p. 94). This seems to mean that surrogacy is okay if one's motives are "pure," untainted by financial gain, and shows the crucial role that moralistic judgments of character have played in the court's decision. If money is eliminated, the surrogate no longer is mercenary or heartless, the couple is no longer exploitative, the infant is no longer an object or a commodity being either sold to or stolen by the couple. The evil is exorcised, and the results are now benign.

Once surrogacy is judged to be in the category of evil human impulses and activities, stereotyped images of the motives and characters of the participants are made.

> The child . . . is the offspring of someone who gave birth to her only to obtain money; the impact on the natural mother as the full weight of her isolation is felt along with the full reality of the sale of her body and child; the impact on the natural father and adoptive mother, once they realize the consequences of their conduct. (New Jersey Supreme Court, 1987, p. 51)

Thus, all parties are seen as morally corrupt, sinners who should be hanging their heads in shame. In this type of primitive caricature, the characterizations are black and white, in this case all "bad"; there is no allowance for complexity, for other "good" motives being attributed to anyone involved. Roles are attributed to the participants that do great violence to the facts. The court cannot see that surrogates most often are not poor, are not "forced" into anything, are not deprived or degraded, and that, on the contrary, they feel enhanced and emotionally gratified. The couples are not unfit, "unsuitable," corrupt, or exploitative. The surrogates do not want to keep these children, not because they are heartless deserters but because they consider these children to belong to others.

## The Psychology of Feminist Criticism of Surrogate Motherhood

Some feminists attack surrogacy as degrading and dehumanizing in reducing women to being "biological objects" and "breeders." They claim that surrogacy exploits women by seducing them with money to engage in "a form of prostitution."

The terms used to describe the role of the surrogate mother are identical with those used originally to attack the subjugation of women by men. Feminists react to surrogacy as a male conspiracy to "use" women. The fee paid to the surrogate mother, who offers her biological identity as a childbearer, has somehow been confused with a man's payment to a woman for the sexual use of her body. These feminists react to surrogate arrangements as if the husband in the infertile couple is "cheating" on his wife and paying for the reproductive "favors" of another woman.

To cast surrogate motherhood in sexual terms is a gross distortion of reality. It neglects the infertile wife's vital and often dominant role in choosing surrogacy as a solution to her own infertility, as well as the advantages she feels in being able to "have" her husband's child through a surrogate. On the other side, the surrogate is often more identified with the plight of the woman than the man, and sees herself as wanting to be a surrogate primarily for the wife of the couple.

Surrogacy provides a role for women that causes discomfort among people who have difficulty accepting women's biological identity. Feminists have a long history of ambivalence toward women's being defined as childbearers, and they have an equally long history of rebellion against such a definition of themselves. It has been difficult for many women to perceive being a "breeder" in a positive way, and the term itself betrays contempt and devaluation of the childbearing role.

It is threatening for women to proclaim that childbearing—the use of their biology and physiology—is a source of such great personal value that they fulfill themselves. The issue of personal fulfillment is never addressed by feminist critics; its omission reduces surrogates to reproductive objects. The actual lived experience of the surrogate mothers is never referred to.

Many feminists, although espousing the principle of women's rights to control their bodies and to "reproductive freedom," wish to deny such rights to women in specific instances, when they do not like the choices other women are making. In other words, women should be able to have abortions, under the principle of freedom of choice and control of their own bodies, but should not bear a child for someone else.

At a moral level, it is amazing to us to see feminists fervently proclaim a woman's right to abort and thus destroy a potential life, yet deny a woman the right to create a life that wouldn't otherwise exist, and a life that is desperately wanted by another woman. It is unclear why women helping other women is exploitative, or why women who love being pregnant and pride themselves on their capacity to give birth are not acceptable. Many feminists seem to have "bought into" traditional cultural definitions and ideas about motherhood in an unquestioning way. It is certainly no accident that on the issue of surrogacy, feminists are in bed with churchmen, two groups that have rarely desired each other in the past.

## Legislating Surrogacy—What Works and What Doesn't

Surrogate parenting has been practiced in the United States for over 37 years.[1] Twelve years ago the first surrogate contract was arranged. *The New York Times* (1987) estimated 2000 births. The American Organization of Surrogate Parenting Practitioners is able to document approximately 1000 births. It is difficult to establish a specific number for two reasons: New babies are born each month, and many arrangements are done privately, not through agencies, and are not recorded as surrogate births. Of all the births that have taken place, only six birth mothers have not relinquished the babies.[2] The Baby M trial gave surrogacy national attention, albeit in an extremely negative perspective.

Without knowledge, understanding, or facts about the process, many states have rushed into legislation with a knee-jerk reaction to the Baby M trial. Bills originating in Florida, Indiana, Kentucky, Louisiana, Michigan, and Nebraska have tried to discourage surrogacy by declaring contracts invalid or banning fee payment. Michigan's legislation is currently being challenged, while Arkansas and Nevada have passed pro-surrogacy legislation.

In the states that have attempted to end surrogacy, the surrogate agencies report that the practice is still flourishing, but without legislation to protect it. In the next few years, other states will be dealing with forming legislation. We would like to critique the negative legislation in a constructive manner while making specific suggestions for regulation of surrogacy.

There are strong, paid professional antisurrogacy lobbies—i.e., the National Coalition Against Surrogacy, the National Committee for Adoption, in addition to the Catholic Church—that are attempting, entirely on the basis of prejudice and ignorance of surrogacy, to influence legislators to draft bills. The pro-surrogacy point of view is infrequently heard, while the antisurrogacy position is sensationalized and is favored by the press in its so-called objective reporting. Moreover, both couples and surrogate birth mothers understandably prefer anonymity and seldom speak out.

Two examples of bills that have been influenced by this lobby that have currently been introduced are California's Assembly Bill 3200, and New York's bill introduced into the Assembly and the Senate as A.10851-A and S.9134, respectively. I am vehemently opposed to any bill that (1) makes contracts void and unenforceable, (2) prohibits payment to surrogates, (3) bans agencies from being involved with surrogacy, and (4) makes surrogacy a criminal offense with criminal penalties (fine and/or jail) for those involved. This type of bill, in reality, attempts to end surrogate parenting as an option for childless couples who wish to build

[1] Vicky and Eric Solo, born in Chicago, February 1954 and February 1958, by the same surrogate.
[2] Survey compiled by American Organization of Surrogate Parenting Practitioners, Indianapolis, Indiana.

their families. It would be poor public policy to allow private surrogacy without the benefit of an experienced agency's being responsible for prescreening, couple/surrogate matching, counseling, and guidance, and without contracts to protect all parties involved. It would be poor public policy not to allow any compensation to the surrogate beyond the most basic pregnancy expenses. This would most certainly reduce the quality of the interested and available women and would leave all parties unprotected.

Surrogate parenting is not a new way to build families. In many cultures and at other times in our history, surrogacy has been seen as a positive solution to a societal problem. Several children now in their 30s, such as Eric and Vicky Solo (see footnote 1), have come forward to say how grateful and proud they are of their parents' courage, a courage that gave them existence and life that they would not otherwise have had.

Antisurrogacy legislation assumes that surrogate mothers, infertile couples, and all the children involved will be emotionally damaged by such arrangements to build families. There is absolutely no research to show that this is the case. On the contrary, published accounts show that in over 99% of the surrogate births that have occurred, all of the participants were satisfied with the results. Contrary to distorted and biased opinion, less than 1% of all surrogates to date have regretted their decision (see footnote 2). Furthermore, the authors of this type of bill have clearly not studied, or chosen to recognize, any of the current studies examining motivations of surrogate mothers, which have found surrogates to be capable, informed, stable, and competent women who are able to make conscientious and careful decisions regarding surrogate parenting. Nor have they bothered to read any of the six postpartum studies available. Surrogates overwhelmingly report emotional satisfaction and self-growth owing to their participation (Einwohner, in progress; Forst, 1988; Hanafin & Reading, 1989; Hardwick, 1989; Schwartz, 1989; Ulrich-Resnick, 1989).

These results are different in many respects from those gathered about the traditional adoption population, to which people have liked to *force* a comparison.[3] Assumptions about, and laws pertaining to, surrogate parenting cannot be drawn from analogies to adoption, which is in reality very different from surrogacy.

Several provisions of this type of bill create potentially disastrous consequences for future participants:

1. All those considering participating in a surrogate mother pregnancy are prohibited from availing themselves of knowledgeable professionals, such as mental health experts or surrogate agencies. Peer group support provided by the agency is extremely important for both couple and surrogate. In addition, the psychological counseling and guidance of a program can help participants solve their problems in a dignified and humanitarian manner.

2. Surrogacy is seen as *legal,* but professionals helping those parties to perform this "legal" act are seen as felons and liable to criminal penalties (i.e., fine and/or jail terms).

---

[3]Andrews, Lori B., Esq., Balboni, Michael, Esq., and Podell, Richard J., Esq.; Testimony before Assembly Standing Committee on Judiciary Assembly and Task Force on Women's Issues; December 6, 1988.

3. All surrogate contracts are void and unenforceable. Couples are allowed to engage in surrogacy but *only by themselves,* without any support or aid. Each arrangement would have to be worked out in isolation, as if it were the first. All the hard-won experience of 2000 preceding births would be unavailable to them. Inevitably, mistakes that could have been avoided will be made, frequently with damaging results. Allowing a woman to become a surrogate mother only so long as she does not enter into any type of agreement as to the responsibilities of the parents or the future of the child is clearly an act of political irresponsibility and neglect. It seems malevolent in its intent and would certainly be malevolent in its consequences.

4. Prohibiting payment to the surrogate will lead to the most feared outcome regarding surrogacy. Fewer women will volunteer, and these will not necessarily be the best qualified; yet they will be chosen, without the appropriate medical and psychological safeguards, because couples with no choice will feel even more desperate than they already do. Wealthier couples who can afford going out of state will be favored, and surrogacy will ironically become an arrangement for the rich. *The worst result will be in the coercion and pressure by childless couples on their friends and family members to "volunteer" to be a surrogate for them.* This will inevitably lead to disastrous outcomes, including custody battles, broken families, and emotional trauma for all parties. Such outcomes have been avoided until now because of fee payment, and because of the overseeing of most arrangements by responsible agencies and experienced professionals.

5. The result of all this is to leave all participants in surrogate arrangements in an extremely vulnerable position. Surrogate parenting is a complicated emotional, legal, interpersonal agreement that needs experienced professional supervision and support to prevent the occurrence of potential problems. Psychological screening of surrogates and couples, counseling on typical emotional reactions that can arise for the couple and the surrogate, and matching of specific couples with specific surrogates for the best "fit" all provide safeguards against poor outcomes. Outlawing such safeguards by making felons of the professionals who provide them cannot possibly improve the situation for individuals engaging in surrogacy.

6. Legislation that does not distinguish between surrogacy using a surrogate's egg and *in vitro* fertilization using the infertile couple's embryo is primitive. The denial of such differences points to the philistine level of understanding behind bills of this kind.

7. At a legal level, this type of bill unnecessarily interferes with the right to procreate, which encompasses the right to conceive, bear, and rear children, and the right to contract. The bill further violates the right of couples and surrogates to be aided by professionals. If tested, such a bill would be found unconstitutional.[4]

For all of these reasons, individuals should consider the reality of surrogacy in light of the existing facts, and not be swayed by hysterical and confounded fears and prejudices. This type of bill would eliminate an important option now

[4]*Family Law Quarterly,* Surrogate Parenthood and Adoption Statutes: Can a Square Peg Fit into a Round Hole? (Chicago, Illinois: Volume XXII, Number 2, Summer 1988), p. 199.

available to infertile couples. Instead of limiting or eliminating surrogacy, it will merely drive the entire practice underground. Infertile couples will still reach out to surrogacy, but in secret, and without professional help or accountability. A bill that neglects regulation and hides from its responsibilities will certainly result in future tragedies.

What we need is bold, thoughtful, creative legislation that will provide standards and guidelines pertaining to the rights of voluntary surrogates, infertile couples, and the babies born by these arrangements.

After two years of work, the American Bar Association Family Law Section has written a Model Surrogacy Act, including specific recommendations for the regulation of surrogacy.[5] The American Organization of Surrogate Parenting Practitioners is also working to set standards for professional surrogate services, including screening, counseling, and legal protection for both couples and surrogates. The group unanimously agreed to support the American Bar Association's Family Law Section Model Surrogacy Act. We have proposed several standards to the organization that are already included in the surrogate mother program that we run, and a number of which are included in the American Bar Association Act. For example:

1. The birth mother does not sign away her parental rights before the delivery.

2. The birth mother has the opportunity to change her mind after the birth of the child. This would put the onus on the surrogate mother agencies to do more extensive screening. It would also serve the best interest of the child, who would be settled in a permanent home and not be "treated like a Ping-Pong ball," in the very rare instances of dispute.

3. The birth mother's bodily integrity must be respected, and she must have control of all medical decisions, such as a choice of doctor, hospital, medication, and method of birthing, and, specifically, that no contract can dictate whether she should abort or not.

4. The surrogate should be paid for her services a fee to be calculated by the month. Therefore, if she has a miscarriage in her fourth month or her seventh month, she is paid until that time. If she delivers a deformed child or if the baby is delivered stillborn, she should be paid the full $10,000 because she went through the full nine months of pregnancy. This dispels the "baby-selling" argument; there may be no baby.

5. A surrogate must be represented by her own independent attorney.[6]

In contrast to the image of surrogate agencies carelessly accepting surrogates without regard for their welfare, it takes three to six months to be accepted into our program. We accept only one-third of the women who apply, and only after they pass three rigorous screening interviews. They are provided with read-

[5] *Family Law Quarterly,* Draft of American Bar Association Model Surrogacy Act (Chicago, Illinois: Volume XXII, Number 2, Summer 1988), p. 123.

[6] Provisions included in the Surrogate Parenting Agreement of the Surrogate Mother Program of New York, 1989.

ing material for and against surrogacy, and they have the option of speaking with other surrogates. We also meet with their husbands and families. The surrogates receive psychological counseling throughout the pregnancy, and they may continue counseling for up to a year after birth, not only for themselves but for their families, if necessary.

Fears of exploitation are often voiced by opponents of surrogacy when they link it with adoption. There are incomparable differences in profiles and life circumstances between a woman caught in a crisis situation with an unwanted pregnancy, who feels forced to give up her baby for adoption, and a surrogate who enters into a cooperative birthing arrangement voluntarily. The surrogate has legal, psychological, and medical counseling, and deliberates an average of two years before entering the agreement.

Women placing their children for adoption frequently (1) are in their teens, (2) have not had any other children, (3) are not married, (4) do not have a supportive home environment, and (5) are in poor financial circumstances and cannot support the child. In contrast, surrogate mothers (1) are older, with an average age of 26 to 27 years, (2) have birthed before and have children of their own, (3) are married or have a supportive home, (4) have an average income of $25,000, and(5) have a stable home environment (Aigen & Schmukler, 1987).

It is ironic, if not actually bizarre, that some people can favor a woman's having the right to abort and kill a potential life yet oppose that same woman's having the right to choose to create a life that would not otherwise exist, and one that is so desperately wanted by another woman. Women are doing this to allow other women to become mothers.

Surrogacy's worst opponents can point to only a handful of failures. Out of over 1000 documented births over the past 12 years in the United States, only six women have not relinquished the babies, and only about 12 others have had regrets. This is a 99% success rate.[7] Contrary to popular opinion, birth mothers generally report profound gratification, a feeling of heroism, and a long-standing sense of achievement. To date there have been six postpartum studies of surrogate mothers. All of them have found these women to have been emotionally gratified and without regrets. Every woman who has birthed in our program has asked to birth a second time.

Notions of family and motherhood are changing. Surrogacy is needed, and it works. People will continue to seek out this last chance to build a family, and surrogate parenting should not be forced underground. Much unnecessary misery will be created by short-sighted, narrow-minded legislation. It is possible to deal responsibly with the medical, moral, emotional, and legal issues so that the rights of all parties are protected. There is no inherent conflict between the participants. Typically, the surrogate experience is joyful and gratifying for everyone involved.

## Authors' Notes

The following are recommendations for anyone, and particularly legislators, interested in an objective investigation of surrogacy. The purpose is to gain a

[7]Survey compiled by American Organization of Surrogate Parenting Practitioners, Indianapolis, Indiana, Spring 1988.

diversified perspective of the issues before forming an opinion or presenting a bill for legislation.

1. A body of scientific data now exists of studies with surrogate birth mothers. This includes motivational, socioeconomic, and six follow-up studies of women after they have birthed. This objective material is vital for anyone interested in a true investigation of the issue. (See References and Additional Reading.)

2. Legislators should speak directly with at least a dozen surrogates as well as with couples that have gone through the process. Surrogates can be contacted through their two national organizations: Surrogates by Choice, located in Dearborn, Michigan, and the National Association of Surrogate Mothers, in Los Angeles, California.

3. The American Organization of Surrogate Parenting Practitioners in Indianapolis, Indiana, should be contacted, and three or four member agencies should be interviewed. This will offer a full and different perspective of the realities and complexities involved in these arrangements. In this regard, the 50-page Surrogate Parenting Contract of the Surrogate Mother program of New York can clarify how many sensitive issues can be adjudicated in a humanitarian way.

4. *The Family Law Quarterly,* Volume XXII, Number 2, Summer 1988, should be read in its entirety (see footnotes 4 and 5). It is completely devoted to legal issues involving surrogacy and includes a draft of the American Bar Associations' Model Surrogacy Act as drafted and approved by the Family Law section. In addition, Lori B. Andrews, project director of medical law at the American Bar Foundation, has been studying and writing extensively on surrogacy. She is a highly respected legal expert in the field, and no consideration of surrogacy would be complete without including her work. She testified at four of the five hearings of the New York State Assembly and Senate (see also Andrews, 1981, 1984, 1987, 1989).[8]

5. New York State Senator John R. Dunne, chairman of the Judiciary Committee, and Senator Mary Goodhue, chairman of the Child Care Committee, have spent over a year investigating surrogacy. They held three public hearings that included testimony from national experts with diverse opinions. They compiled a brief titled "Surrogate Parenting in New York: A Proposal for Legislative Reform" and outlined a bill, S.1429. While we do not agree completely with the bill, it is a notable effort at dealing with the complex issues of regulating surrogacy. Because

---

[8]Public Hearing of Assembly Standing Committee on Judiciary and Assembly Task Force on Women's Issues (New York: December 6, 1988); New York State Joint Public Hearing of New York State Assembly and New York State Judiciary Committee. Hearing on surrogate parenthood and new reproductive technologies (New York: October 16, 1986); New York State Senate Child Care Committee. Public hearing on surrogate parenting (White Plains, New York: April 10, 1988); New York State Senate Child Care Committee. Public hearing on surrogate parenting (Albany: May 7, 1988); New York State Senate Judiciary Committee, Senator John R. Dunne, Chairman. Surrogate parenting in New York: A proposal for legislative reform (Albany: January 1987).

of its national scope, it can be used by any state as a model for drafting surrogacy legislation.

6. The complete testimony of the five legislative hearings listed in footnote 8 can be obtained by contacting the respective legislative offices. While New York and California hearings are cited, the witnesses included experts from across the country.[9] A wealth of information, for and against surrogacy, is included in this testimony.

7. The Congress of the United States Office of Technological Assessment published a report on infertility in May 1988 (U.S. Congress, 1988). While the section on surrogacy was already out of date with respect to agencies and number of births when printed, the report contains a great deal of information. Additionally, a survey of the surrogate mother agencies was conducted by Amy Zuckerman-Overvold and is published in her book, *Surrogate Parenting* (1987).

## The Future

Surrogate motherhood, since its inception, has had the legitimate goal of allowing new families to be created. The primary reaction, however, has been terror, as if the process were a deliberate effort to undermine society's most cherished ideals, to encourage mothers to abandon their children, to steal children from their mothers and sell them into slavery. The culture has felt assaulted and has reacted in a typically paranoid way, attributing to the participants malevolent motives that correspond to these perceived "evil" goals. Thus, the couples are seen as mercenary, the intermediaries as ruthless "baby brokers," and the surrogates as both deluded and heartless.

We have tried to show that frightening human impulses and painful early experiences are "stirred up" by the idea of surrogate arrangements, to the point where these impulses and experiences are "seen" in surrogacy, rather than the more benevolent reality. As legislatures begin to grapple with the legitimacy of surrogacy, it is crucial that they do not mistake their fantasies for reality, or biased subjective views for the facts. Is this a case of selling babies as commodities or slaves, or does it have more to do with enabling couples to become families by enabling parenthood? Is this a case of an underprivileged, deprived woman being paid for using her procreative capacity, a capacity she values and gains great satisfaction in using, particularly to allow others to enjoy what she has enjoyed: Children?

Regulation of potential abuses is a legitimate concern that should be addressed. But the possibility of *potential* abuses, of *potential* difficulties that may arise, should not lead to the mistaken belief that abuses are inevitable or in any way typical. Surrogate motherhood is based not on a conflict of interest but on mutuality of interests among the participants. Out of over 900 surrogate births (750 registered; 150 to 200 estimated additionally, undocumented; see Overvold, 1987), only seven have encountered difficulties, a very small fraction. Is it possible that this is because surrogacy has been a "successful" experience for almost all who have participated?

[9]California Assembly Judiciary Committee. Public hearing on surrogacy (Sacramento: April 8, 1988).

*REFERENCES*

Aigen, B. P., & Schmukler, I. (1987). Motivations of surrogate mothers: Parenthood and self-actualization. Unpublished.

Andrews, L. B. (1981). Removing the stigma of surrogate motherhood. *Family Advocate, 4,* 20.

Andrews, L. B. (1984). *New conceptions.* New York: St. Martin's Press.

Andrews, L. B. (1987). The aftermath of Baby M: Proposed state laws on surrogate motherhood. *Hastings Center Report, October/November.*

Andrews, L. (1989). *Between strangers.* New York: Harper & Row.

Einwohner, J. L. (n.d.). Additional study in progress, unpublished.

*Family Law Quarterly* (Summer 1988). Volume XXII, Number 2.

Forst, K. (1988). *Grief experiences: Social support networks of surrogate mothers.* Masters dissertation, Colorado State University.

Hanafin, H., & Reading, A. (1989). *Assessing the anxiety level and attitudes towards pregnancy in surrogates.* Los Angeles: Cedars-Sinai, Department of Psychological Studies.

Hardwick, S. (1989). Doctoral dissertation in process. Hofstra University.

*New Jersey Record.* (1988). Surrogate motherhood. January 14, p. 14.

New Jersey Supreme Court. (1987, September term). In the case of Baby M.

*The New York Times.* (1987). Surrogacy.

Overvold, A. Z. (1987). *Surrogate parenting.* New York: Pharos.

Schwartz, S. (1989). *Study on infertile women choosing adoption vs. surrogacy.* Doctoral dissertation, Cambridge School.

Ulrich-Resnick, R. (1989). *Surrogate mothers: Relationship between early attachment and the relinquishment of a child.* Doctoral dissertation, Fielding Institute.

U.S. Congress, Office of the Technology Assessment (1988, May). *Infertility: Medical and social choices* (OTA-BA-358). Washington, DC: U.S. Government Printing Office.

*SUGGESTED READINGS*

Aigen, B. P. (1986). In the matter of Baby M. (Amicus curiae brief on behalf of Dr. Betsy P. Aigen, Psy.D., submitted by Annette Tobia, Esq.). Trenton, NJ: Supreme Court of New Jersey, Docket No. 27,050, Civil Action.

Aigen, B. P. (1988-1989). All benefit from cooperative birthing arrangements (Decree). New York: American Adoption Congress, Volume 7, Number 1.

American Bar Association (1989). National Conference of Commissioners on Uniform State Laws, Docket 113B.

American Organization of Surrogate Parenting Practitioners, Indianapolis, IN.

Dunne, J. R., and Goodhue, M. (1988). *Surrogate parenting in New York: A proposal for legislative reform* (S.1429)

Einwohner, J. L. (1987, August).*Psychological characteristics of surrogate mothers.* Paper presented at the annual convention of the American Psychological Association, New York.

Franks, D. D. (1981).*Psychiatric evaluation of women in a surrogate mother program* (Vol. 138, pp. 1378–1379). New York: Academic Press.

Hanafin, H. (1984). *Surrogate mother: Exploratory study.* Doctoral dissertation, California School of Professional Psychology, Los Angeles.

Hanafin, H. L. (1984, August). Paper presented at a meeting of the American Psychological Association.

Hollos, M. (1987, August 31). Paper presented at the annual meeting of the Association.

Parker, P. J. (1987). Motivation of surrogate mothers: Initial findings. *American Journal of Psychology 140,* 117–118.

Parker, P. J. (n.d.) Additional study, unpublished.

Taub, N. & Cohen, S. (1989). *Reproductive laws for the 1990s.* Clifton, NJ: Humana Press.

## Questions for Empathy and Analysis

1. Schmukler and Aigen begin with a series of questions. What specific word choices help them to establish their position, and what do you expect will follow?

2. Schmukler and Aigen contrast the New Jersey Supreme Court's view of surrogacy contracts with the view of surrogate mothers. Empathetically summarize the surrogate mother's view as the authors describe it. Do you think most surrogate mothers share this view?

3. Schmukler and Aigen refer to surrogate mothers as "surrogates" or "the surrogate" throughout their article. How does this word choice support their position?

4. In the section of the article dedicated to discussing the payment of money, the authors argue that "society is hypervigilant against any situation that gives even the appearance of exploitation or devaluation." Why do they choose the word "hypervigilant"? Do you agree with this statement?

5. Empathetically summarize Schmukler and Aigen's account of the feminist criticism of surrogate motherhood. In what ways are feminists hypocritical?

6. Schmukler and Aigen emphasize how surrogacy entails women helping women. Do you think surrogacy might enable us to achieve a more balanced or matriarchal society?

7. The authors claim that not to allow any compensation would reduce the quality of the interested women. What does this suggest about the motives of surrogate mothers?

8. Who pays for the service of the psychologists and mental health experts of the surrogate agencies? If these professionals are paid by the couples looking for surrogates, do you think such professionals have a conflict of interests?

9. Do you agree with the argument that outlawing surrogacy will not stop it but will only force it underground? Who is most likely to be left unprotected by secret, illegal surrogacy arrangements?

10. What is your reaction to the Model Surrogacy Act? Why should a surrogate be represented by her own attorney?

11. Schmukler and Aigen claim that the reality of the majority of surrogate motherhood cases is a positive, benevolent outcome. What evidence do they use to support this claim? How reliable is their source of information?

## Questions for Comparison and Synthesis

1. (*Chesler–Keane*) While describing his many cases, Keane urges that the "extraordinary effort required on the part of everyone in-

volved" not be overlooked. Do you think surrogate mothers should be paid for their time and effort involved in attempting to conceive even if they are not successful? Chesler notes that Mary Beth Whitehead would not have received any fee if she had not conceived. Do you think that surrogate mothers who want to donate themselves, free of charge, should be permitted to do so? Should legislation regulate payment for services rendered? Should surrogate mothers receive minimum wage for each hour they spend in producing the baby? What would Keane answer in response to these questions? What would Chesler? How do they compare?

2. *(Heyl–Neuhaus)* When Heyl says in her fourth paragraph that "the symbolic knowledge of the courtroom and of the surrogacy contract belongs to the educated monied class," what do you think she means by "symbolic knowledge"? Heyl refers to Neuhaus's use of "symbolic knowledge." Find Neuhaus's reference and read it to determine Heyl's meaning. In light of your understanding, what do you think Heyl means by "the social construction of the biological revolution"?

3. *(Heyl–Chesler)* Both Heyl and Chesler ask many questions about the definition of parenthood and of motherhood in particular. In what ways do their questions about defining motherhood overlap?

4. *(Heyl–Keane)* Heyl considers the future effects on the child. In the cases Keane describes, to what extent do the couples and surrogate mothers consider such effects? What do they assume about their relationship to the child?

5. *(Morris–Chesler)* What does Morris mean by "commercial surrogacy"? How does she define it? Morris claims that feminists, including Phyllis Chesler, make a distinction between surrogacy and commercial surrogacy. What is this distinction? Is surrogacy unconstitutional because money is exchanged or because a woman cannot sign a contract that deprives her of her rights as a citizen, that is, her right to due process under the law (a right Whitehead was denied when her baby Sara was taken away by law officials) and her right not to be a servant or a slave against her will? Do feminists think that surrogacy is right if the woman chooses to become a surrogate mother without pay?

6. *(Morris–Neuhaus)* Do you think Morris's comparison of Neuhaus to the Luddites is well founded? Do you think Morris's Industrial Revolution analogy works well?

7. *(Rothman–Neuhaus)* In paragraph six of her essay, Rothman criticizes Neuhaus's view that a mother and a father have equal rights to their child on the basis of the idea that since each parent contributed fifty percent of the genetic material, each has fifty percent ownership of the child. What does she find so troubling about a

concept that endorses equality? What alternative view does she endorse instead?

8. *(Rothman–Morris)* Morris emphasizes that surrogacy is a new technology, an irreversible revolution. In sharp contrast, Rothman emphasizes that surrogacy is as old as biblical times when Abraham used Hagar as a surrogate for Sarah. How do the emphases of the authors help to support their arguments? How "old" or "new" do you think the issue of surrogate motherhood is?

9. *(Rothman–Morris)* Morris claims in her section "Lack of Regulation" that some feminists support surrogate motherhood because "women should have control over their own bodies, including the right to use them to make money, and that to suggest that women's biological makeup might affect their emotions is to be sexist and paternalistic." But other feminists, she says, oppose it because it is commercialized. Where would you place Rothman, a feminist, in Morris's description? How do you imagine Rothman would respond to this description?

10. *(Schmukler and Aigen–Neuhaus–Rothman)* Schmukler and Aigen give a number of reasons why critics condemn surrogate motherhood. Since you have read Neuhaus and Rothman, both of whom condemn the practice, would you say that Schmukler and Aigen include them among these critics? If so, do they accurately describe these authors' positions?

11. *(Schmukler and Aigen–Morris)* Compare Schmukler and Aigen's argument about maternal abandonment to Morris's discussion about the best interests of the child.

12. *(Schmukler and Aigen–Rothman)* Schmukler and Aigen argue that critics want to obligate a surrogate mother to raise the child she bears. If surrogate mothers were so obligated, would they still be surrogate mothers? What does it mean to have a "right to be a mother"? How do you think Rothman would respond to this idea?

13. *(Schmukler and Aigen–Rothman)* Schmukler and Aigen argue that surrogate motherhood is women helping women. But Rothman argues that the infertile wife is just a divorce away from childlessness. How vital and dominant a role do you think wives such as Betsy Stern can actually play? How may their rights be best served?

14. *(Schmukler and Aigen–Neuhaus–Chesler–Rothman)* Schmukler and Aigen claim that "on the issue of surrogacy, feminists are in bed with churchmen." Compare Neuhaus to Chesler and Rothman. In what ways do the feminists and this churchman agree? In what ways do they differ?

# Chapter Six

# WRITING ABOUT

# ADVERTISING

*Advertising does not of course exist in isolation from the rest of society; it mirrors in some way the "reality" that surrounds it.*

*Sut Jhally*

The readings in this chapter are on the topic of advertising, a subject that touches us all, interests many, and reflects different points of view. The readings we have selected represent to some extent the range of information you might find if you were to research this topic on your own. Once you have gathered your materials, your challenge is to discern the ways in which the readings relate and speak to one another. You can evolve new and original ideas by paying close attention to the points of intersection among the articles, essays, and books on a given topic. When you explore the overlapping ideas that suggest areas of commonality and importance, you are on the path that leads to fresh insights and discoveries.

As you read these articles and excerpts on advertising, keep your writing log close at hand. You may begin by jotting down your own assumptions and ideas on advertising. As you read, use the methods of believing, annotating, paraphrasing, summarizing, and analyzing that we described in Chapters Two and Three. We have selected these readings because they simulate the diversity of approaches you would encounter if you were in the library doing research on this topic. You will discover that each reading comes from its own unique context and that the authors have very different backgrounds and credentials. As an empathetic reader of these texts, suspend judgment and try not to let your own ideas about advertising interfere with your understanding. As an active reader, make connections among the readings that lead you to new insights. We have grouped the readings to aid the process of making connections, and our questions at the end of each reading encourage empathetic reading and active thinking.

In America today we cannot escape from advertising. Our newspapers and magazines, television and radio programs are filled with ads; our streets and highways are lined with billboards. Given the ubiquity of advertisements, we ask: What purpose do they serve? Obviously, ads promote goods and services, but do they do more than this? The essays included in this chapter all address the question of the broader social role of advertising. The points of view represented here encompass the economic, political, historical, linguistic, psychological, sociological, and anthropological ramifications of advertising. The points of view are divergent, but frequently they overlap in significant ways. Taken together, they help us to see that the images of advertising surround us like a room filled with mirrors. We are invited to separate the reflection from the reality, the dream from the nightmare.

# ■ ■ ■ ■ ■ ■ ■ ■ ■
# ADVERTISING:
## The Magic System

### Raymond Williams

The British literary critic, Raymond Williams (1921–1988), wrote many articles and books on literature and drama, and on theories of culture and cultural production. An expert in Marxist theory, Williams explored the elaboration of "cultural materialism" in contemporary societies. In "Advertising: The Magic System," first published in 1960 in *New Left Review,* Williams argues that advertising is an integral part of capitalist society: The one could not exist without the other. The magic system of capitalism and advertising creates an "ideal of consumption" that obscures real human needs and satisfactions, especially those that are social, such as health care and education. The magical illusion of humans as individual "consumers" of goods obscures and subjugates the reality of humans as social "users" of goods. Williams's criticism of advertising strikes at capitalism as being an irresponsible economic system.

## History

It is customary to begin even the shortest account of the history of advertising by recalling the three thousand year old papyrus from Thebes, offering a reward for a runaway slave, and to go on to such recollections as the crier in the streets of Athens, the paintings of gladiators, with sentences urging attendance at their combats, in ruined Pompeii, and the flybills on the pillars of the Forum in Rome. This pleasant little ritual can be quickly performed, and as quickly forgotten: it is, of course, altogether too modest. If by advertising we mean what was meant by Shakespeare and the translators of the Authorized Version—the processes of taking or giving notice of something—it is as old as human society, and some pleasant recollections from the Stone Age could be quite easily devised.

The real business of the historian of advertising is more difficult: to trace the development from processes of specific attention and information to an institutionalized system of commercial information and persuasion; to relate this to changes in society and in the economy; and to trace changes in method in the context of changing organizations and intentions.

The spreading of information, by the crier or by handwritten and printed broadsheets, is known from all periods of English society. The first signs of anything more organized come in the seventeenth century, with the development of newsbooks, mercuries and newspapers. Already certain places, such as St. Paul's in London, were recognized as centres for the posting of specific bills, and the extension of such posting to the new printed publications was a natural development. The material of such advertisements ranged from offers and wants in personal service, notices of the publication of books, and details of runaway servants, apprentices, horses and dogs, to announcements of new commodities available at particular shops, enthusiastic announcements of remedies and specifics, and notices of the public showing of monsters, prodigies and freaks. While the majority were the simple, basically factual and specific notice we now call 'classified', there were also direct recommendations, as here, from 1658:

> That Excellent, and by all Physicians, approved China drink, called by the Chineans Tcha, by other nations *Tay* alias *Tee*, is sold at the Sultaness Head Cophee-House in Sweeting's Rents, by the Royal Exchange, London.

Mention of the physicians begins that process of extension from the conventional recommendations of books as 'excellent' or 'admirable' and the conventional adjectives which soon become part of the noun, in a given context (as in my native village, every dance is a Grand Dance). The most extravagant early extensions were in the field of medicines, and it was noted in 1652, of the writers of copy in news-books:

> There is never a mountebank who, either by professing of chymistry or any other art drains money from the people of the nation but these arch-cheats have a share in the booty—because the fellow cannot lye sufficiently himself he gets one of these to do't for him.

Looking up, in the 1950s, from the British Dental Association's complaints of mis-leading television advertising of toothpastes, we can recognize the advertisement, in 1660, of a 'most Excellent and Approved DENTIFRICE', which not only makes the teeth 'white as ivory', but

> being constantly used, the Parties using it are never troubled with the Tooth-ache. It fastens the Teeth, sweetens the Breath, and preserves the Gums and Mouth from Cankers and Imposthumes.

Moreover

> the right are onely to be had at Thomas Rookes, Stationer, at the Holy Lamb at the east end of St Paul's Church, near the School, in sealed pa-pers at 12d the paper.

In the year of the Plague, London was full of

> SOVEREIGN Cordials against the Corruption of the Air.

These did not exactly succeed, but a long and profitable trade, and certain means of promoting it, were now firmly established.

With the major growth of newspapers, from the 1690s, the volume of adver-tisements notably increased. The great majority of them were still of the specific 'classified' kind, and were grouped in regular sections of the paper or maga-zine. Ordinary household goods were rarely advertised; people knew where to get these. But, apart from the wants and the runaways, new things, from the latest book or play to the new kinds of luxury or 'cosmatick' made their way through these columns. By and large, it was still only in the pseudo-medical and toilet advertise-ments that persuasion methods were evident. The announcements were conven-tionally printed, and there was hardly any illustration. Devices of emphasis—the hand, the asterisk, the NB—can be found, and sailing announcements had small woodcuts of a ship, runaway notices similar cuts of a man looking back over his shoulder. But, in the early eighteenth century, these conventional figures became too numerous, and most newspapers banned them. The manufacturer of a 'Spring Truss' who illustrated his device, had few early imitators.

A more general tendency was noted by Johnson in 1758:

> Advertisements are now so numerous that they are very negligently perused, and it is therefore become necessary to gain attention by mag-nificence of promises and by eloquence sometimes sublime and some-times pathetick. Promise, large promise, is the soul of an advertisement. I remember a washball that had a quality truly wonderful—it gave *an exquisite edge to the razor*! The trade of advertising is now so near to perfection that it is not easy to propose any improvement.

This is one of the earliest of 'gone about as far as they can go' conclusions on advertisers, but Johnson, after all, was sane. Within the situation he knew, of newspapers directed to a small public largely centred on the coffee-houses, the natural range was from private notices (of service wanted and offered, of things lost, found, offered and needed) through shopkeepers' information (of actual goods in their establishments) to puffs for occasional and marginal products. In this last kind, and within the techniques open to them, the puffmen had indeed used, intensively, all the traditional forms of persuasion, and of cheating and lying. The mountebank and the huckster had got into print, and, while the majority of advertisements remained straightforward, the influence of this particular group was on its way to giving 'advertising' a more specialized meaning.

## Development

There is no doubt that the Industrial Revolution, and the associated revolution in communications, fundamentally changed the nature of advertising. But the change was not simple, and must be understood in specific relation to particular developments. It is not true, for example, that with the coming of factory production large-scale advertising became economically necessary. By the 1850s, a century after Johnson's comment, and with Britain already an industrial nation, the advertising pages of the newspapers, whether *The Times* or the *News of the World*, were still basically similar to those in eighteenth-century journals, except that there were more of them, that they were more closely printed, and that there were certain exclusions (lists of whores, for example, were no longer advertised in the *Morning Post*).

The general increase was mainly due to the general growth in trade, but was aided by the reduction and then abolition of a long-standing Advertisement Tax. First imposed in 1712, at one shilling an announcement, this had been a means, with the Stamp Duty, of hampering the growth of newspapers, which successive Governments had good reason to fear. By the time of the worst repression, after the Napoleonic Wars, Stamp Duty was at 4d a sheet, and Advertisement Tax at 3s 6d. In 1833, Stamp Duty was reduced to 1d, and Advertisement Tax to 1s 6d. A comparison of figures for 1830 and 1838 shows the effect of this reduction: the number of advertisements in papers on the British mainland in the former year was 877,972; by the later date it stood at 1,491,991. Then in 1853 the Advertisement Tax was abolished, and in 1855 the Stamp Duty. The rise in the circulation of newspapers, and in the number of advertisements, was then rapid.

Yet still in the 1850s advertising was mainly of a classified kind, in specified parts of the publication. It was still widely felt, in many kinds of trade, that (as a local newspaper summarized the argument in 1859)

it is not *respectable*. Advertising is resorted to for the purposes of introducing inferior articles into the market.

Rejecting this argument, the newspaper (*The Eastbourne Gazette and Fashionable Intelligencer*) continued:

Competition is the soul of business, and what fairer or more legitimate means of competition can be adopted than the availing oneself of a channel to recommend goods to public notice which is open to all?

Advertising is an open, fair, legitimate and respectable means of competition; bearing upon its face the impress of free-trade, and of as much advantage to the consumer as the producer.

The interesting thing is not so much the nature of this argument, but that, in 1859,
it still had to be put in quite this way. Of course the article concluded by drawing
attention to the paper's own advertising rates, but even then, to get the feel of the
whole situation, we have to look at the actual advertisements flanking the article.
Not only are they all from local tradesmen, but their tone is still eighteenth-century,
as for example:

To all who pay cash and can appreciate
GOOD AND FINE TEAS
CHARLES LEA

Begs most respectfully to solicit a trial of his present stock which has
been selected with the greatest care, and paid for before being cleared
from the Bonded warehouses in London . . .

In all papers, this was still the usual tone, but, as in the eighteenth century, one class of product attracted different methods. Probably the first nationally advertised product was Warren's Shoe Blacking, closely followed by
Rowland's Macassar Oil (which produced the counter-offensive of the antimacas-
sar), Spencer's Chinese Liquid Hair Dye, and Morison's Universal Pill. In this
familiar field, as in the eighteenth century, the new advertising was effectively
shaped, while for selling cheap books the practice of including puffs in announcements was widely extended. Warren's Shoe Blacking had a drawing of a cat
spitting at its own reflection, and hack verses were widely used:

The goose that on our Ock's green shore
Thrives to the size of Albatross
Is twice the goose it was before
When washed with Neighbour Goodman's sauce.

Commercial purple was another writing style, especially for pills:

The spring and fall of the leaf has been always remarked as the periods
when disease, if it be lurking in the system, is sure to show itself. (Parr's
Life Pills, 1843).

The manner runs back to that of the eighteenth-century hucksters and
mountebanks, but what is new is its scale. The crowned heads of Europe were being signed up for testimonials (the Tsar of all the Russias took and recommended
Revalenta Arabica, while the Balm of Syriacum, a 'sovereign remedy for both
bodily and mental decay', was advertised as used in Queen Victoria's household).
Holloway, of course a 'Professor', spent £5,000 a year, in the 1840s, spreading
his Universal Ointment, and in 1855 exceeded £30,000.
    Moreover, with the newspaper public still limited, the puffmen were going
on the streets. Fly-posting, on every available space, was now a large and orga-

nized trade, though made hazardous by rival gangs (paste for your own, black-ing for the others). It was necessary in 1837 to pass a London act prohibiting posting without the owner's consent (it proved extremely difficult to enforce). In 1862 came the United Kingdom Billposters Association, with an organized sys-tem of special hoardings, which had become steadily more necessary as the flood of paste swelled. Handbills ('throwaways') were distributed in the streets of Victorian London with extraordinary intensity of coverage; in some areas a walk down one street would collect as many as two hundred different leaflets. Adver-tising vans and vehicles of all sorts, such as the seven-foot lath-and-plaster Hat in the Strand, on which Carlyle commented, crowded the streets until 1853, when they were forbidden. Hundreds of casual labourers were sent out with placards and sandwich boards, and again in 1853 had to be officially removed from pave-ment to gutter. Thus the streets of Victorian London bore increasingly upon their face 'the impress of free trade' yet still, with such methods largely reserved to the sellers of pills, adornments and sensational literature, the basic relation be-tween advertising and production had only partly changed. Carlyle said of the hatter, whose 'whole industry is turned to *persuade* us that he has made' better hats, that 'the quack has become God'. But as yet, on the whole, it was only the quack.

The period between the 1850s and the end of the century saw a further expansion in advertising, but still mainly along the lines already established. After the 1855 abolition of Stamp Duty, the circulation of newspapers rapidly increased, and many new ones were successfully founded. But the attitude of the Press to advertising, throughout the second half of the century, remained cautious. In particular, editors were extremely resistant to any break-up in the column layout of their pages, and hence to any increase in size of display type. Advertisers tried in many ways to get round this, but with little success.

As for products mainly advertised, the way was still led by the makers of pills, soaps and similar articles. Beecham's and Pears are important by reason of their introduction of the catch-phrase on a really large scale: 'Worth a Guinea a Box' and 'Good morning! Have you used Pears Soap?' passed into everyday language. Behind this familiar vanguard came two heavily advertised classes: the patent food, which belongs technically to this period, and which by the end of the century had made Bovril, Hovis, Nestlé, Cadbury, Fry and Kellogg into 'household names'; and new inventions of a more serious kind, such as the sewing-machine, the camera, the bicycle and the typewriter. If we add the new department-stores, towards the end of the century, we have the effective range of general advertising in the period, and need only note that in method the patent foods followed the patent medicines, while the new appliances varied between genuine information and the now familiar technique of slogan and association.

The pressure on newspapers to adapt to techniques drawn from the poster began to be successful from the 1880s. The change came first in the illustrated magazines, with a crop of purity nudes and similar figures; the Borax nude, for example, dispelling Disease and Decay; girls delighted by cigarettes or soap or shampoos. The poster industry, with its organized hoardings, was able from 1867 to use large lithographs, and Pears introduced the 'Bubbles' poster in 1887. A mail-order catalogue used the first colour advertisement, of a rug. Slowly, a famil-iar world was forming, and in the first years of the new century came the coloured electric sign. The newspapers, with Northcliffe's *Daily Mail* in the lead, dropped their columns rule, and allowed large type and illustrations. It was noted in 1897 that '*The Times* itself' was permitting 'advertisements in type which three years ago would have been considered fit only for the street hoardings', while the front page of the *Daily Mail* already held rows of drawings of rather bashful women in combinations. Courtesy, Service and Integrity, as part of the same process, acquired the dignity of large-type abstractions. The draper, the grocer and their suppliers had followed the quack.

To many people, yet again, it seemed that the advertisers had 'gone about as far as they can go'. For many people, also, it was much too far. A society for Checking the Abuses of Public Advertising (SCAPA) had been formed in 1898, and of course had been described by the United Bill Posters Association as 'super-sensitive faddists'. SCAPA had local successes, in removing or checking some outdoor signs, and the 1890s saw other legislation: prohibiting uniform for sandwich-men (casual labourers, dressed as the Royal Marine Light Infantry or some other regiment, had been advertising soaps and pills); regulating skyline and balloon advertisements; restricting flashing electric signs, which had been blamed for street accidents. It is a familiar situation, this running fight between traditional standards (whether the familiar layout of newspapers or respect for building and landscape) and the vigorous inventiveness of advertisers (whether turning hoardings into the 'art-galleries of the people', or putting an eight-ton patent food sign halfway up the cliffs of Dover). Indeed ordinary public argument about advertising has stuck at this point, first clarified in the 1890s with 'taste' and 'the needs of commerce' as adversaries. In fact, however, even as this battle was raging, the whole situation was being transformed, by deep changes in the economy.

## Transformation

The strange fact is, looking back, that the great bulk of products of the early stages of the factory system had been sold without extensive advertising, which has grown up mainly in relation to fringe products and novelties. Such advertising as there was, of basic articles, was mainly by shopkeepers, drawing attention to the quality and competitive pricing of the goods they stocked. In this comparatively simple phase of competition, large-scale advertising and the brand-naming of goods were necessary only at the margin, or in genuinely new things. The real signs of change began to appear in the 1880s and 1890s, though they can only be correctly interpreted when seen in the light of the fully developed 'new' advertising of the period between the wars.

The formation of modern advertising has to be traced, essentially, to certain characteristics of the new 'monopoly' (corporate) capitalism, first clearly evident in this same period of the end and turn of the nineteenth century. The Great Depression, which in general dominated the period from 1875 to the middle 1890s (though broken by occasional recoveries and local strengths), marked the turning point between two modes of industrial organization and two basically different approaches to distribution. After the Depression, and its big falls in prices, there was a more general and growing fear of productive capacity, a marked tendency to reorganize industrial ownership into larger units and combines, and a growing desire, by different methods, to organize and where possible control the market. Among the means of achieving the latter purposes, advertising on a new scale, and applied to an increasing range of products, took an important place.

Modern advertising, that is to say, belongs to the system of market-control which, at its full development, includes the growth of tariffs and privileged areas, cartel-quotas, trade campaigns, price-fixing by manufacturers, and that form of economic imperialism which assured certain markets overseas by political control of their territories. There was a concerted expansion of export advertising, and at home the biggest advertising campaign yet seen accompanied the merger of several tobacco firms into the Imperial Tobacco Company, to resist American competition. In 1901, a 'fabulous sum' was offered for the entire eight pages of *The Star*, by a British tobacco advertiser, and when this was refused four pages were taken, a 'world's record', to print 'the most costly, colossal and convincing advertisement ever used in an evening newspaper the wide world o'er'. Since the American firms retaliated, with larger advertisements of their own, the campaign was both heavy and prolonged. This can be taken as the first major example of a new advertising situation.

That this period of fundamental change in the economy is the key to the emergence of full-scale modern advertising is shown also by radical changes within the organization of advertising itself. From the eighteenth century, certain shops had been recognized as collecting agencies for advertisements, on behalf of newspapers. In the nineteenth century, this system (which still holds today for some classified advertisements) was extended to the buying of space by individual agents, who then sold it to advertisers. With the growth in the volume of advertising, this kind of space-selling, and then a more developed system of space-brokerage, led to a growth of importance in the agencies, which still, however, were virtually agents of the Press, or at most intermediaries. Gradually, and with increasing emphasis from the 1880s, the agencies began to change their functions, offering advice and service to manufacturers, though still having space to sell for the newspapers. By the turn of the century, the modern system had emerged: newspapers had their own advertising managers, who advanced quite rapidly in status from junior employees to important executives, while the agencies stopped selling space, and went over to serving and advising manufacturers, and booking space after a campaign had been agreed. In 1900 the Advertisers Protection Society, later the Incorporated Society of British Advertisers, was formed: partly to defend advertising against such attacks as those of SCAPA, partly to bring pressure on newspapers to publish their sales figures, so that campaigns might be properly planned. Northcliffe, after initial hesitations about advertising (he had wanted to run *Answers* without it), came to realize its possibilities as a new basis for financing newspapers. He published his sales figures, challenged his rivals to do the same, and in effect created the modern structure of the Press as an industry, in close relation to the new advertising. In 1917 the Association of British Advertising Agents was founded, and in 1931, with the founding of the Audit Bureau of Circulations, publishing audited net sales, the basic structure was complete.

It is in this same period that we hear first, with any emphasis, of advertising as a profession, a public service, and a necessary part of the economy. A further aspect of the reorganization was a more conscious and more serious attention to the 'psychology of advertising'. As it neared the centre of the economy, it began staking its claims to be not only a profession, but an art and a science.

The half-century between 1880 and 1930, then, saw the full development of an organized system of commercial information and persuasion, as part of the modern distributive system in conditions of large-scale capitalism. Although extended to new kinds of product, advertising drew, in its methods, on its own history and experience. There is an obvious continuity between the methods used to sell pills and washballs in the eighteenth century ('promise, large promise, a quality truly wonderful') and the methods used in the twentieth century to sell anything from a drink to a political party. In this sense, it is true to say that all commerce has followed the quack. But if we look at advertising before, say, 1914, its comparative crudeness is immediately evident. The 'most costly, colossal and convincing advertisement' of 1901 shows two badly-drawn men in tails, clinking port-glasses between announcements that the cigarettes are five a penny, and the slogan ('The Englishman's Toast—Don't be gulled by Yankee bluff, support John Bull with every puff') is in minute type by comparison with 'Most Costly' and 'Advertisement'. Play on fear of illness was of course normal, as it had been throughout quack advertising, and there were simple promises of attractiveness and reputation if particular products were used. But true 'psychological' advertising is very little in evidence before the First War, and where it is its techniques, both in appeal and in draughtsmanship and layout, are crude. Appropriately enough, perhaps, it was in the war itself, when now not a market but a nation had to be controlled and organized, yet in democratic conditions and without some of the older compulsions, that new kinds of persuasion were developed and applied. Where the badly-drawn men with their port and gaspers belong to an old world, such a poster as 'Daddy, what did you do in the Great War' belongs to the new. The drawing is careful and detailed: the curtains, the armchair, the grim numb face of the father, the little girl on his knee pointing to her open picture-book, the boy at his feet intent on his toy-soldiers. Alongside the traditional appeals to patriotism lay this kind of entry into basic personal relationships and anxieties. Another poster managed to suggest that a man who would let down his country would also let down his sweetheart or his wife.

The pressures, of course, were immense: the needs of the war, the needs of the economic system. We shall not understand advertising if we keep the argument at the level of appeals to taste and decency, which advertisers should respect. The need to control nominally free men, like the need to control nominally free customers, lay very deep in the new kind of society. Kitchener, demanding an Army, was as startled by the new methods as many a traditional manufacturer by the whole idea of advertising, which he associated with dubious products. In both cases, the needs of the system dictated the methods, and traditional standards and reticences were steadily abandoned when ruin seemed the only alternative.

Slowly, after the war, advertising turned from the simple proclamation and reiteration, with simple associations, of the earlier respectable trade, and prepared to develop, for all kinds of product, the old methods of the quack and the new methods of psychological warfare. The turn was not even yet complete, but the tendencies, from the twenties, were evident. Another method of organizing the market, through consumer credit, had to be popularized, and in the process changed from the 'never-never', which was not at all respectable, to the primly respectable 'hire-purchase' and the positively respectable 'consumer credit'. By

1933, a husband had lost his wife because he had failed to take this 'easy way' of providing a home for her. Meanwhile Body Odour, Iron Starvation, Night Starvation, Listlessness and similar disabilities menaced not only personal health, but jobs, marriages and social success.

These developments, of course, produced a renewed wave of criticism of advertising, and, in particular, ridicule of its confident absurdities. In part this was met by a now standard formula: 'one still hears criticism of advertising, but it is not realized how much has been done, within the profession, to improve it' (for example, a code of ethics, in 1924, pledging the industry, *inter alia* 'to tell the advertising story simply and without exaggeration and to avoid even a tendency to mislead'. If advertisers write such pledges, who then writes the advertisements?). The 'super-sensitive faddists' were rediscovered, and the 'enemies of free enterprise'. Proposals by Huxley, Russell, Leavis, Thompson and others, that children should be trained to study advertisements critically, were described, in a book called *The Ethics of Advertising*, as amounting to 'cynical manipulation of the infant mind'.

But the most significant reply to the mood of critical scepticism was in the advertisements themselves: the development of a knowing, sophisticated, humorous advertising, which acknowledged the scepticism and made claims either casual and offhand or so ludicrously exaggerated as to include the critical response (for example, the Guinness advertisements, written by Dorothy Sayers, later a critic of advertising). Thus it became possible to 'know all the arguments' against advertising, and yet accept or write pieces of charming or amusing copy.

One sustained special attack, on an obviously vulnerable point, was in the field of patent medicines. A vast amount of misleading and dangerous advertising of this kind had been repeatedly exposed, and eventually, by Acts of 1939 and 1941, and by a Code of Standards in 1950, the advertisement of cures for certain specified diseases, and a range of misleading devices, was banned. This was a considerable step forward, in a limited field, and the Advertising Association was among its sponsors. If we remember the history of advertising, and how the sellers of ordinary products learned from the quack methods that are still used in less obviously dangerous fields, the change is significant. It is like nothing so much as the newly-crowned Henry the Fifth dismissing Falstaff with contempt. Advertising had come to power, at the centre of the economy, and it had to get rid of the disreputable friends of its youth: it now both wanted and needed to be respectable.

## Advertising in Power

Of the coming to power there was now no question. Estimates of expenditure in the inter-war years vary considerably, but the lowest figure, for direct advertising in a single year, is £85,000,000 and the highest £200,000,000. Newspapers derived half their income from advertising, and almost every industry and service, outside the old professions, advertised extensively. With this kind of weight behind it, advertising was and knew itself to be a solid sector of the establishment.

Some figures from 1935 are interesting, showing advertising expenditure as a proportion of sales:

| | |
|---|---|
| Proprietary medicines | 29.4% |
| Toilet goods | 21.3% |
| Soaps, polishes, etc. | 14.1% |
| Tobacco | 9.3% |
| Petrol and oil | 8.2% |
| Cereals, jams, biscuits | 5.9% |
| Sweets | 3.2% |
| Beer | 1.8% |
| Boots and shoes | 1.0% |
| Flour | 0.5% |

The industry's connections with its origins are evident: the three leading categories are those which pioneered advertising of the modern kind. But more significant, perhaps, is that such ordinary things as boots, shoes and flour should be in the table at all. This, indeed, is the new economy, deriving not so much from the factory system and the growth of communications, as from an advanced system of capitalist production, distribution and market control.

Alongside the development of new kinds of appeal came new media. Apart from such frills as sky-writing, there was commercial radio, not yet established in Britain (though the pressure was there) but begun elsewhere in the 1920s and beamed to Britain from the 1930s. Commercial television, in the 1950s, got through fairly easily. Among new methods, in this growth, are the product jingle, begun in commercial radio and now reaching classic status, and the open alliance between advertisers and apparently independent journalists and broadcasters. To build a reputation as an honest reporter, and then use it either openly to recommend a product or to write or speak about it alongside an advertisement for it, as in the evening-paper 'special supplements', became commonplace. And what was wrong? After all, the crowned heads of Europe, and many of our own Ladies, had been selling pills and soaps for years. The extension to political advertising, either direct or by pressure-groups, also belongs, in its extensive phase, to this period of establishment; in the 1950s it has been running at a very high rate indeed.

The only check, in fact, to this rapidly expanding industry was during the last war, though this was only partial and temporary, and the years since the war, and especially the 1950s, have brought a further spectacular extension. It is ironic to look back at a book published in wartime, by one of the best writers on advertising, Denys Thompson, and read this:

> A second reason for these extensive extracts is that advertising as we know it may be dispensed with, after the war. We are getting on very well with a greatly diminished volume of commercial advertising in wartime, and it is difficult to envisage a return to the 1919–1939 conditions in which publicity proliferated.

Mr Thompson, like Dr Johnson two centuries earlier, is a sane man, but it is never safe to conclude that puffing has reached its maximum distension. The history, rightly read, points to a further major growth, and to more new methods. The highly organized field of market study, motivation research, and retained sociologists and psychologists, is extremely formidable, and no doubt has many surprises in store for us. Talent of quite new kinds is hired with increasing ease. And there is one significant development which must be noted in conclusion: the extension of organized publicity.

*'Public Relations'*

Advertising was developed to sell goods, in a particular kind of economy. Publicity has been developed to sell persons, in a particular kind of culture. The methods are often basically similar: the arranged incident, the 'mention', the advice on branding, packaging and a good 'selling line'. I remember being told by a man I knew at university (he had previously explained how useful, to his profession as an advertiser, had been his training in the practical criticism of advertisements) that advertisements you booked and paid for were really old stuff; the real thing was what got through as ordinary news. This seems to happen now with goods: 'product centenaries', for example. But with persons it is even more extensive. It began in entertainment, particularly with film actors, and it is still in this field that it does most of its work. It is very difficult to pin down, because the borderline between the item or photograph picked up in the ordinary course of journalism and broadcasting, and the similar item or photograph that has been arranged and paid for, either directly or through special hospitality by a publicity agent, is obviously difficult to draw. Enough stories get through, and are even boasted about, to indicate that the paid practice is extensive, though payment, except to the agent, is usually in hospitality (if that word can be used) or in kind. Certainly, readers of newspapers should be aware that the 'personality' items presented as ordinary news stories or gossip, will often have been paid for, in one way or another, in a system that makes straightforward advertising, by comparison, look respectable. Nor is this confined to what is called 'show business;' it has certainly entered literature, and it has probably entered politics.

The extension is natural, in a society where selling, by any effective means, has become a primary ethic. The spectacular growth of advertising, and then its extension to apparently independent reporting, has behind it not a mere pressure-group, as in the days of the quacks, but the whole impetus of a society. It can then be agreed that we have come a long way from the papyrus of the runaway slave and the shouts of the towncrier: that what we have to look at is an organized and extending system, at the centre of our national life.

## The System

In the last hundred years, then, advertising has developed from the simple announcements of shopkeepers and the persuasive arts of a few marginal dealers into a major part of capitalist business organization. This is important enough, but the place of advertising in society goes far beyond this commercial context. It is increasingly the source of finance for a whole range of general communication, to the extent that in 1960 our majority television service and almost all our newspapers and periodicals could not exist without it. Further, in the last forty years and now at an increasing rate, it has passed the frontier of the selling of goods and services and has become involved with the teaching of social and personal values; it is also rapidly entering the world of politics. Advertising is also, in a sense, the official art of modern capitalist society: it is what 'we' put up in 'our' streets and use to fill up half of 'our' newspapers and magazines: and it commands the services of perhaps the largest organized body of writers and artists, with their attendant managers and advisers, in the whole society. Since this is the actual social status of advertising, we shall only understand it with any adequacy if we can develop a kind of total analysis in which the economic, social and cultural facts are visibly related. We may then also find, taking advertising as a major form of modern social communication, that we can understand our society itself in new ways.

It is often said that our society is too materialist, and that advertising reflects this. We are in the phase of a relatively rapid distribution of what are called 'consumer goods', and advertising, with its emphasis on 'bringing the good things of life', is taken as central for this reason. But it seems to me that in this respect our society is quite evidently not materialist enough, and that this, paradoxically, is the result of a failure in social meanings, values and ideals.

It is impossible to look at modern advertising without realising that the material object being sold is never enough: this indeed is the crucial cultural quality of its modern forms. If we were sensibly materialist, in that part of our living in which we use things, we should find most advertising to be of an insane irrelevance. Beer would be enough for us, without the additional promise that in drinking it we show ourselves to be manly, young in heart, or neighbourly. A washing-machine would be a useful machine to wash clothes, rather than an indication that we are forward-looking or an object of envy to our neighbours. But if these associations sell beer and washing-machines, as some of the evidence suggests, it is clear that we have a cultural pattern in which the objects are not enough but must be validated, if only in fantasy, by association with social and personal meanings which in a different cultural pattern might be more directly available. The short description of the pattern we have is *magic:* a highly organized and professional system of magical inducements and satisfactions, functionally very similar to magical systems in simpler societies, but rather strangely coexistent with a highly developed scientific technology.

This contradiction is of the greatest importance in any analysis of modern capitalist society. The coming of large-scale industrial production necessarily raised critical problems of social organization, which in many fields we are still only struggling to solve. In the production of goods for personal use, the critical problem posed by the factory of advanced machines was that of the organization of the market. The modern factory requires not only smooth and steady distributive channels (without which it would suffocate under its own product) but also definite indications of demand without which the expensive processes of capitalization and equipment would be too great a risk. The historical choice posed by the development of industrial production is between different forms of organization and planning in the society to which it is central. In our own century, the choice has been and remains between some form of socialism and a new form of capitalism. In Britain, since the 1890s and with rapidly continuing emphasis, we have had the new capitalism, based on a series of devices for organizing and ensuring the market. Modern advertising, taking on its distinctive features in just this economic phase, is one of the most important of these devices, and it is perfectly true to say that modern capitalism could not function without it.

Yet the essence of capitalism is that the basic means of production are not socially but privately owned, and that decisions about production are therefore in the hands of a group occupying a minority position in the society and in no direct way responsible to it. Obviously, since the capitalist wishes to be successful, he is influenced in his decisions about production by what other members of the society need. But he is influenced also by considerations of industrial convenience and likely profit, and his decisions tend to be a balance of these varying factors. The challenge of socialism, still very powerful elsewhere but in Britain deeply confused by political immaturities and errors, is essentially that decisions about production should be in the hands of the society as a whole, in the sense that control of the means of production is made part of the general system of decision which the society as a whole creates. The conflict between capitalism and socialism is now commonly seen in terms of a competition in productive efficiency, and we need not doubt that much of our future history, on a world scale, will be determined by the results of this competition. Yet the conflict is really much deeper than this, and is also a conflict between different approaches to and forms of socialism. The fundamental choice that emerges, in the problems set to us by modern industrial production, is between man as consumer and man as user. The system of organized magic which is modern advertising is primarily important as a functional obscuring of this choice.

### 'Consumers'

The popularity of 'consumer', as a way of describing the ordinary member of modern capitalist society in a main part of his economic capacity, is very significant. The description is spreading very rapidly, and is now habitually used by people to whom it ought, logically, to be repugnant. It is not only that, at a simple level, 'consumption' is a very strange description of our ordinary use of goods and services. This metaphor drawn from the stomach or the furnace is only partially relevant even to our use of things. Yet we say 'consumer' rather than 'user', because in the form of society we now have, and in the forms of thinking which it almost imperceptibly fosters, it is as consumers that the majority of people are seen. We are the market, which the system of industrial production has organized. We are the channels along which the product flows and disappears. In every aspect of social communication, and in every version of what we are as a community, the pressure of a system of industrial production is towards these impersonal forms.

Yet it is by no means necessary that these versions should prevail, just because we use advanced productive techniques. It is simply that once these have entered a society, new questions of structure and purpose in social organization are inevitably posed. One set of answers is the development of genuine democracy, in which the human needs of all the people in the society are taken as the central purpose of all social activity, so that politics is not a system of government but of self-government, and the systems of production and communication are rooted in the satisfaction of human needs and the development of human capacities. Another set of answers, of which we have had more experience, retains, often in very subtle forms, a more limited social purpose. In the first phase, loyal subjects, as they were previously seen, became the labour market of industrial 'hands'. Later, as the 'hands' reject this version of themselves, and claim a higher human status, the emphasis is changed. Any real concession of higher status would mean the end of class-society and the coming of socialist democracy. But intermediate concessions are possible, including material concessions. The 'subjects' become the 'electorate', and 'the mob' becomes 'public opinion'.

Decision is still a function of the minority, but a new system of decision, in which the majority can be organized to this end, has to be devised. The majority are seen as 'the masses', whose opinion, *as masses* but not as real individuals or groups, is a factor in the business of governing. In practical terms, this version can succeed for a long time, but it then becomes increasingly difficult to state the nature of the society, since there is a real gap between profession and fact. Moreover, as the governing minority changes in character, and increasingly rests for real power on a modern economic system, older social purposes become vestigial, and whether expressed or implied, the maintenance of the economic system becomes the main factual purpose of all social activity. Politics and culture become deeply affected by this dominant pattern, and ways of thinking derived from the economic market—political parties considering how to sell themselves to the electorate, to create a favourable brand image; education being primarily organized in terms of a graded supply of labour; culture being organized and even evaluated in terms of commercial profit—become increasingly evident.

Still, however, the purposes of the society have to be declared in terms that will command the effort of a majority of its people. It is here that the idea of the 'consumer' has proved so useful. Since consumption is within its limits a satisfactory activity, it can be plausibly offered as a commanding social purpose. At the same time, its ambiguity is such that it ratifies the subjection of society to the operations of the existing economic system. An irresponsible economic system can supply the 'consumption' market, whereas it could only meet the criterion of human use by becoming genuinely responsible: that is to say, shaped in its use of human labour and resources by general social decisions. The consumer asks for an adequate supply of personal 'consumer goods' at a tolerable price: over the last ten years, this has been the primary aim of British government. But users ask for more than this, necessarily. They ask for the satisfaction of human needs which consumption, as such, can never really supply. Since many of these needs are social—roads, hospitals, schools, quiet—they are not only not covered by the consumer ideal: they are even denied by it, because consumption tends always to materialize as an individual activity. And to satisfy this range of needs would involve questioning the autonomy of the economic system, in its actual setting of priorities. This is where the consumption ideal is not only misleading, as a form of defence of the system, but ultimately destructive to the broad general purposes of the society.

Advertising, in its modern forms, then operates to preserve the consumption ideal from the criticism inexorably made of it by experience. If the consumption of individual goods leaves that whole area of human need unsatisfied, the attempt is made, by magic, to associate this consumption with human desires to which it has no real reference. You do not only buy an object: You buy social respect, discrimination, health, beauty, success, power to control your environment. The magic obscures the real sources of general satisfaction because their discovery would involve radical change in the whole common way of life.

Of course, when a magical pattern has become established in a society, it is capable of some real if limited success. Many people will indeed look twice at you, upgrade you, upmarket you, respond to your displayed signals, if you have made the right purchases within a system of meanings to which you are all trained. Thus the fantasy seems to be validated, at a personal level, but only at the cost of preserving the general unreality which it obscures: the real failures of the society which however are not easily traced to this pattern.

It must not be assumed that magicians—in this case, advertising agents—disbelieve their own magic. They may have a limited professional cynicism about it, from knowing how some of the tricks are done. But fundamentally they are involved, with the rest of the society, in the confusion to which the magical gestures are a response. Magic is always an unsuccessful attempt to provide meanings and values, but it is often very difficult to distinguish magic from genuine knowledge and from art. The belief that high consumption is a high standard of living is a general belief of the society. The conversion of numerous objects into sources of sexual or pre-sexual satisfaction is evidently not only a process in the minds of advertisers, but also a deep and general confusion in which much energy is locked.

At one level, the advertisers are people using certain skills and knowledge, created by real art and science, against the public for commercial advantage. This hostile stance is rarely confessed in general propaganda for advertising, where the normal emphasis is the blind consumption ethic ('Advertising brings you the good things of life'), but it is common in advertisers' propaganda to their clients. 'Hunt with the mind of the hunter', one recent announcement begins, and another, under the heading 'Getting any honey from the hive industry?', is rich in the language of attack:

> One of the most important weapons used in successful marketing is advertising.

> Commando Sales Limited, steeped to the nerve ends in the skills of unarmed combat, are ready to move into battle on any sales front at the crack of an accepted estimate. These are the front line troops to call in when your own sales force is hopelessly outnumbered by the forces of sales resistance . . . .

This is the structure of feeling in which 'impact' has become the normal description of the effect of successful communication, and 'impact' like 'consumer' is now habitually used by people to whom it ought to be repugnant. What sort of person really wants to 'make an impact' or create a 'smash hit', and what state is a society in when this can be its normal cultural language?

It is indeed monstrous that human advances in psychology, sociology and communication should be used or thought of as powerful techniques *against* people, just as it is rotten to try to reduce the faculty of human choice to 'sales resistance'. In these respects, the claim of advertising to be a service is not particularly plausible. But equally, much of this talk of weapons and impact is the jejune bravado of deeply confused men. It is in the end the language of frustration rather than of power. Most advertising is not the cool creation of skilled professionals, but the confused creation of bad thinkers and artists. If we look at the petrol with the huge clenched fist, the cigarette against loneliness in the deserted street, the puppet facing death with a life-insurance policy (the modern protection, unlike the magical symbols painstakingly listed from earlier societies), or the man in the cradle which is an aeroplane, we are looking at attempts to express and resolve real human tensions which may be crude but which also involve deep feelings of a personal and social kind.

The structural similarity between much advertising and much modern art is not simply copying by the advertisers. It is the result of comparable responses to the contemporary human condition, and the only distinction that matters is between the clarification achieved by some art and the displacement normal in bad art and most advertising. The skilled magicians, the masters of the masses, must be seen as ultimately involved in the general weakness which they not only exploit but are exploited by. If the meanings and values generally operative in the society give no answers to, no means of negotiating, problems of death, loneliness, frustration, the need for identity and respect, then the magical system must come, mixing its charms and expedients with reality in easily available forms, and binding the weakness to the condition which has created it. Advertising is then no longer merely a way of selling goods, it is a true part of the culture of a confused society.

## Questions for Empathy and Analysis

1. Williams's use of some English words may seem foreign to you because he is British. What words do you find that are used in unfamiliar ways? How do you deduce from the context of the sentence the meaning of some of these words?

2. How do you determine, when reading the first few paragraphs of the essay, its thesis and what the essay is going to be about? How does the essay fulfill the expectations it sets up in terms of its overall structure?

3. In terms of history, what for Williams is the major change that occurred in advertising practice in Great Britain at the time of the Great Depression (1875 to the middle 1890s)?

4. What does Williams mean by "puffery"? Why is it "never safe to conclude that puffing has reached its maximum distension"? Do you agree with Williams? Do you think that advertisers will continue to develop more deceptive methods?

5. On page 166, Williams claims that advertising is criticized for creating a society that is too materialistic, but he counters that our society is, paradoxically, not materialistic enough. What do you think he means by this? In what way could you say that our U.S. society fails to bring to us the "good things of life"?

6. What does advertising sell, and for Williams, why is it magic?

7. Do you think too many decisions that determine how our U.S. society functions are left up to capitalists? To what extent does our society as a whole decide on how goods are produced and dis-

tributed? Think of specific examples and illustrations to support your claims.

8. What is Williams's definition of a *consumer*? Why does he think we ought to find the term repugnant?

9. Would you agree with Williams that the social purpose of addressing human needs has been obscured by the purpose of maintaining capitalism as an end in itself? Do you think the "consumption ideal" has been destructive of American values and social objectives?

10. Williams says that the notion that high consumption reflects a high standard of living is a general belief of a capitalist society. How could one have a high standard of living without high consumption?

11. To what extent do you feel that advertising is a beneficial service to you? To what extent do you feel assaulted by advertising?

12. Williams claims that advertisers must bind "the weakness to the condition that created it." How does advertising create weakness? Paraphrase the final paragraph to interpret and clarify your understanding of what Williams means by "weakness."

■ ■ ■ ■ ■ ■ ■ ■ ■

# THE EMERGENCE OF NEW CONSUMER PATTERNS:
## A Case Study of the Cigarette

### Michael Schudson

In his book, *Advertising, The Uneasy Persuasion: Its Dubious Impact on American Society* (1984), Michael Schudson, a professor who has taught courses on the subject of advertising at the University of Chicago and the University of California, San Diego, defends advertising against many of the criticisms leveled against it. Schudson disagrees with the argument that advertising created a "consumer society" and led people to buy products that they did not really need. He believes that the influence of advertising is far less insidious than many think it is. Consumers are skeptical and often inattentive to the commercials around them. Moreover, they are motivated to buy things for many more compelling reasons than because they saw or read an ad.

Schudson sees advertising as related to, but finally distinct from, consumer society. In the following excerpt from the sixth chapter of his book, "The Emergence of New Consumer Patterns:

A Case Study of the Cigarette," he argues that women began smoking in large numbers in the 1920s not because they were manipulated by ads but because they found cigarettes an inexpensive and convenient way to demonstrate their independence. According to Schudson, advertisers respond to cultural change but rarely create it.

The United States became the first consumer society beginning in the late nineteenth century with the growth of the department store and the rise of national advertising.

And the United States became the first consumer society in the 1920s with the development of installment buying, the mass marketing of the automobile, and the creation of common national tastes through the movies and radio.

And the United States became the first consumer society in the 1950s with the rapid rise in real family income, the suburbanization of the population and the establishment of new social norms of home ownership and two-car ownership, and the emergence of television as a powerful new advertising medium.

And—the United States never was the first consumer society because England became a consumer society in the eighteenth century. Most of the major industries of early industrialization were consumer goods industries and a wave of "fashion" spread from the aristocracy to the middle class in everything from clothing to crockery to books and clocks.

Not all of these positions can be right, though good arguments can be made for any of them. Carving a conceptual category—"consumer society"—out of the flux of history is to some degree an arbitrary task. There has not been an overnight revolution in the habits or views of Americans (or the British, for that matter) regarding material goods. For instance, a traditional Christian belief in the virtue of thrift still influences American thought and feeling, even though some observers see its death presaged in the expansion of consumer credit in the 1920s, others see it as having been killed by the "me" generation of the 1970s, and others observe that it has been under heavy fire since the 1700s when traditional views of "luxury" were overturned in economic thought. There is no single point in history before which we were all nature's children, after which we became the sons and daughters of commerce.

I will not go any further in attempting to date the birth of an American consumer culture. Instead, I want to say something about the character of that culture and the nature of modern consumption, visible by the 1920s if not earlier. I want to explore what I shall call the democratization of goods and the emergence of "convenience" as a desirable product characteristic. Convenience is a desired attribute of goods primarily in socially democratic and relatively affluent societies. I will develop this point through a case study of the growing popularity of the cigarette in the 1920s and, in doing so, will make a second point: that major consumer changes are rarely wrought by advertising. Advertising followed rather than led the spread of cigarette usage and it was the convenience and democracy of the cigarette, coupled with specific, new opportunities for its use, that brought the cigarette into American life.

## The Democratization of Goods

Everywhere in the 1920s, it seems, there was discussion of the "fast pace" of modern life, a quickened heartbeat to the whole social order. Historian James Truslow Adams, among others, wrote of the quickening "tempo":

> Whether any more "events" are happening in the universe now than in earlier times would lead us into unfathomable bogs of metaphysics, but for our purpose it is enough to grant that more events are happening to each man of which he is conscious. In other words, a resident of New York today is getting more sensations and of a more varied sort than the Neanderthal or early man of several hundreds of thousands of years ago. Owing to this number and variety of sensations and his constantly shifting environment, modern man is also called upon to make a far greater number of adjustments to the universe than was his remote relative in the caves and forests of Germany or Java. It is the number of these sensations and adjustments in a given time that makes the tempo of life. As the number and variety of sensations increase, the time which we have for reacting to and digesting them becomes less, as it does also for adjusting ourselves to our environment when that alters at an advancing rate. The rhythm of our life becomes quicker, the wave lengths, to borrow a physical concept, of that kind of force which is our mental life grows shorter.

By the 1920s, lives could be led not only in different ways, depending on class and ethnicity and region, but at different *paces*. There was a new sense of the scarcity of time, accelerated by the increasingly large array of choices available to people. There was more choice, or the sense of more choice, in part because the newspapers, movies, and radio brought to people a strong sense of other social worlds, other possibilities. The advances in mass production methods made goods and luxuries unheard of a generation before potentially available to large numbers of people. In the supermarket there were more product categories, and within these more brands to choose from. Brands proliferated. One study of small-town Midwestern consumers found 101 different brands among 210 purchased pianos and equally impressive numbers of brands of cars, radios, phonographs, and washing machines.

At the same time, there was a democratization of goods. As Daniel Boorstin has observed, products that once held some kind of uniqueness by being available only at certain times of the year or only in certain parts of the country were increasingly available year-round and throughout the country, thanks to canning, refrigerated railroad cars, and other technological and social developments. Not only the means of production but the modes of consumption became "continuous process." Extending Boorstin's observation, products are democratized in three other ways.

First, they become more standard as they come to be produced for a mass audience. They are easier to handle, easier to "do it yourself" without great skill on the part of the user; both a mediocre cook and a great cook make equally good cakes from a cake mix. Both an adept smoker and a novice smoker can get about the same satisfaction from a cigarette, but this is much less so with a pipe or cigar. Both a French chef and an ordinary citizen can order an acceptable meal at McDonald's without a faux pas, but this is not true at Maxim's. Standard products and standard situations for shopping make it easier for the unskilled consumer to avoid embarrassment and to become equal to the adept consumer.

Second, products become not only more standard but milder and easier to use. They become convenient. I will try to suggest in this chapter that convenience is a democratic quality. Convenience is an attribute that has as much to do with the social uses and social meaning of a product as with its engineering. The more convenient a good, the more it is equally available for the use of men and women, adults and children, the hardy and the dainty, the veteran and the novice.

Third, there is democratization when goods are consumed in increasingly public ways. This happened in many respects in the 1920s as the *Middletown* study suggests. Lunch became a meal consumed away from home, in the presence of nonfamily members. For the middle class, the spare time of adolescents increasingly became time away from home, in cars and at the movies. A decline in the dependence on the domestic servants was coupled with increasing reliance on a national market for consumer goods for washing, cooking, and cleaning chores. There was a growth in business luncheons, club memberships, and other voluntary associations for both men and women, providing more extrafamilial public occasions. Media—notably the women's magazines—quickly became consumption tutors, taking over for mother and grandmother—and for good reason. Mother and grandmother could adequately advise so long as the young person's sphere of movement did not extend far beyond the family circle. With changes in employment, mobility (brought on the by the automobile), and exposure to a wider world by way of movies and other mass media, mother and grandmother were no longer quite so relevant. Public, rather than private, standards of consumption became more salient. People increasingly saw their own consumption pattern in comparison to a wide group of other people. And one could see not only people of "one's own sort" but could peek at the consumption pattern of very different people. The social order, as the Lynds put it, began to shift from a set of plateaus to a single slope and so there was both a democratization of vision and, as I have already suggested, a democratization of envy.

Another change underlines all of these. Products become more democratic when people become more equal. Manufacturers can try to expand the market for a product whose use has traditionally been limited to one sex, class, race, region, or age group when the relevant social distinction changes its character or loses its force. In the 1920s, this happened as women gained ground toward social and civic equality. Their movement into new social roles made them more than ordinarily susceptible to the siren call of the marketers. Women were newly *public* people and needed, more than before, social currencies acceptable in the public world defined by men. The cigarette was one such social coin and a particularly convenient one: cheap, visible, an identifying mark, both easily flaunted and easily hidden, a topic of talk, a token of comradeship and, to boot, a comfort in anxious moments.

The spread of cigarette smoking, particularly among women, was one of the most visible signs of change in consumption practices in the 1920s, and one that has been cited frequently as evidence of the new powers of advertising and marketing. Between 1918 and 1940, American consumption grew from 1.70 to 5.16 pounds of cigarette tobacco per adult. During the same period, advertising budgets of the tobacco companies bulged, movies pictured elegant men and women smoking, and public relations stunts promoted cigarettes.

Some contemporary observers concluded that advertising *caused* the increase in cigarette smoking among women. For instance, in 1930, Clarence True Wilson, board secretary of the Methodist Episcopal Church, declared: "If the advertising directed to women ceased, it is probable that within five years the smoking woman would be the rare exception." Scholars in recent years have accepted a similar view. Erik Barnouw, for instance, holds that advertising was responsible for bringing women into the cigarette market.

This conclusion is difficult to sustain for a number of reasons, the most obvious of which is that tens of thousands of women began smoking cigarettes in the 1920s *before* a single advertisement was directed toward them. It is more accurate to observe that cigarette smoking among women led tobacco companies to advertise toward the female market than to suggest that advertising created the market in the first place. The mass media played a role in spreading the cigarette habit among women, but it was primarily the information conveyed in news stories, not the persuasion attempted in advertisements, that helped in the first instance to legitimate smoking among women in the 1920s.

The power of the mass media in influencing taste and consumption patterns must be seen in context. If advertising and news helped legitimate smoking among women, what began the social trend in the first place? To answer that, I will consider the sociology of consumption more broadly, examining the variety of factors that underlie changes in consumption patterns.

But the question of women smoking cigarettes is only half of the puzzle of tobacco consumption in the 1920s. There is a second key issue. If it was a cultural revolution for women, who had never smoked at all in large numbers, to turn to cigarettes, it was also a revolution for men, who had smoked cigars and pipes, to turn to the "feminine" cigarette. At the beginning of the twentieth century cigarettes were banned in the U.S. Navy at the same time that the cigar was widely accepted. The cigarette was regarded as "a debasement of manhood." The *New York Times* in 1925 made note of the growth of smoking among women but felt that the importance of this trend "has been greatly overestimated.... The women smokers probably do not account for more than a billion of the 72,000,000,000 cigarettes we use up." Industry sources estimated that women smoked as much as 12 or 14 per cent of all cigarettes by 1930, an important quantity but still a small proportion of the total.

Men were switching to cigarettes at a rapid rate. Cigarette tobacco outsold pipe tobacco for the first time in 1919; it passed cigars in 1921 and it outsold chewing tobacco for the first time in 1922. A measure of the relative importance of cigarette smoking for men and women comes from "The Fortune Survey" in 1935. The survey separated men from women and people over forty from those under forty and reported what percentage of each group smoked cigarettes:

|          | Men  | Women |
|----------|------|-------|
| Under 40 | 65.5 | 26.2  |
| Over 40  | 39.7 | 9.3   |

Clearly, many more men than women smoked cigarettes, and younger people were more likely than older people to have adopted the cigarette habit.

While cigarette consumption grew enormously during the years between the wars, total tobacco consumption remained stable. In 1918 the total tobacco consumption (cigarettes, cigars, pipe tobacco, chewing tobacco, and snuff) was exactly the same as it would be twenty-two years later in 1940—9.12 pounds per adult. The rise of cigarette smoking was accompanied by the *fall* in other tobacco uses. Not only did women begin to smoke, but men changed their smoking preference in droves. What accounts for the movement of men to cigarettes? This is the second puzzle.

## The Public Legitimation of Cigarettes for Women

For all practical purposes, the story of cigarettes begins in 1881, when James Bonsack patented a cigarette-making machine that manufactured up to forty times what the best skilled workers could produce by hand. Within a decade, the cost of producing a cigarette was reduced to one-sixth of what it had been. When James Buchanan Duke turned exclusively to machine production in 1885, he quickly saturated the American market. Production was no longer a problem; the only task was to sell.

Cigarette smoking grew steadily from 1880 on. By 1890, the use of cigarette tobacco ran even with that of snuff. This state continued into the 1890s, but cigarette use declined in the period 1900-1905 and only equaled snuff again in 1911. It did not reach the level of consumption of any other tobacco form until the early 1920s, when it passed pipe tobacco, cigars, and chewing tobacco. By 1935 cigarettes represented more than half of all tobacco consumption.

The cigarette is distinguished from other tobaccos by its mildness. After the 1870s, cigarette tobacco was flue- rather than fire-cured. The barns where tobacco is dried and cured are heated with flues running through them rather than with open wood or charcoal fires, making the tobacco milder. It produces a slightly acid rather than alkaline smoke. In alkaline form, nicotine can be absorbed through the linings of the mouth and nose without inhaling, as with chewing tobacco, pipe tobacco, and snuff. All of these forms permit a gradual intake of nicotine without inhaling. Flue-cured tobacco, in contrast, must be inhaled if nicotine is to be absorbed because only in the lungs will the acid smoke be converted to alkaline. The result is a smoke not only mild but more addictive than other tobaccos.

Cigarette tobacco after World War I became milder than that which was available before the war. Just before the war, blended tobaccos had come into use, replacing some of the stronger Turkish tobaccos. When the war interrupted trade and cheaper Turkish brands lost out completely, the newer, mild cigarettes came to dominate the market. After the war, import and revenue duties were high, Turkish tobacco production declined sharply, and American cigarette production grew quickly, from 30 billion cigarettes in 1917 to 60 billion in 1923.

This change to a milder cigarette, it is reasonable to assume, reduced the cost of "trial" of new smokers; that is, because the cigarette was milder, the discomfort for trying it was reduced and the chances of being initially disgusted by it and not taking up the habit as a result, minimized.

If the war helped provide a more palatable cigarette, it also provided many young men and women with their first smoking experience. The tobacco industry was fond of quoting General "Black Jack" Pershing: "You ask me what we need to win this war. I answer tobacco as much as bullets." Boxcars from the tobacco states moved toward the seaports with signs painted on their sides, "Roll Your Own Into Berlin," "The Makings for U.S., the Leavings for the Kaiser," "America's Best for America's Bravest," and "When Our Boys Light Up the Huns Will Light Out." Following the lead of the French and the British, American military leadership recommended that soldiers receive tobacco rations in addition to food and drink rations. When the War Department approved this suggestion, "a wave of joy swept through the American army," according to the *New York Times.* Rations were issued at .4 ounces of tobacco per day with one hundred cigarette papers for every four ounces, or, alternatively, four ready-made cigarettes per day, or .4 ounces of chewing tobacco per day. Not only military authorities but volunteer groups supplied soldiers with tobacco. The Y.M.C.A. and the Red Cross lifted their opposition to smoking during the war and sent cigarettes to the soldiers overseas.

No promotional scheme could have matched a war for spreading the cigarette habit, connecting it emotionally with relief and comradeship in the most trying of circumstances, associating a feminized product with the ultimately masculine endeavor. Its use in wartime was favored over other tobacco because of its convenience: One did not have to carry along a pipe nor did it take the time and attention of a cigar. It could be picked up and put down or stubbed out quickly. (The war stimulated other conveniences, too. For instance, the Gillette Company sold the War Department 3.5 million razors and 32 million blades and this strongly encouraged the relatively new habit of self-shaving.)

Women as well as men took up the smoking habit during the war:

> Women war-workers took up the habit abroad, and women at home in their men's jobs and new-found independence did likewise. Within the next three or four years cigarette smoking became the universal fashion, at least in cities, and children born since the war take smoking mothers for granted.

This contemporary observation is clearly an exaggeration, but there is no reason to doubt that some women who had never smoked learned that the physical threshold to smoking was lowered by the mild tobacco and that the social threshold was lowered when laboring in a war industry.

While observers of the social scene in the 1920s most often pointed to the war or to the changing status of women as reasons for the growth of cigarette smoking, tobacco manufacturers themselves explained the trend by citing the large-scale manufacture of mild, blended tobacco. In fact, all of these elements played a part; it would be hard to know which one contributed most decisively.

While the cigarette was mild, resistance to it was not, especially with regard to women smokers. Throughout the 1920s, controversy over women smoking was a salient news item. This was notably so in reports on smoking in colleges and on public transportation.

Take the case of women's colleges, which the *New York Times* covered closely. The *Times* reported as early as 1921 that the University of Chicago banned smoking among women students. By 1925 such stories were front page news. Women who were allowed to smoke at home felt their liberties were infringed upon at school. The Vassar College students' council, in response to agitations over a rule prohibiting smoking, polled students on whether they smoked away from school, whether their parents approved of their smoking, and what school regulations for smoking should be adopted. A week later the results were in and the *Times* provided front-page coverage: 433 Vassar girls liked cigarettes; 524 did not smoke; about 400 sets of parents disapproved of their daughters' smoking; 302 approved according to the daughters; 278 students voted to continue the smoking prohibition; 539 favored more lenient rules. A month later the students nonetheless banned smoking on the grounds that "smoking is not yet established as a social convention acceptable to all groups throughout the country."

The *Times* in 1925 also reported on smoking at Radcliffe and at Smith. It was front page news that M.I.T. permitted women to smoke at dances, while Goucher College prohibited students from smoking both on campus and in public places in Baltimore. A study at Bryn Mawr showed that less than half of Bryn Mawr women smoked, but the Self-Government Association petitioned the college president to set aside a smoking room in each dormitory. President Marion Edwards Park consented, saying that a change in attitude toward smoking by women had come about and that it was natural for this change to be reflected among college students. She repealed the 1897 ban on smoking. The *Times* editorially endorsed the Bryn Mawr decision, though in condescending tones, hoping that by allowing cigarettes in certain places, "what once was a feat of defiance becomes rather a bore . . . . "

These accounts reinforce the conclusion of historian Paula Fass that "smoking was perhaps the one most potent symbol of young woman's testing of the elbow room provided by her new sense of freedom and equality." Fass shows that, while the *Times* may have approved the Bryn Mawr decision, many other opinion leaders were shocked. The president of Kansas State Teachers College said that "nothing has occurred in higher education that has so shocked our sense of social decency as the action at Bryn Mawr," and many other college presidents and deans agreed. But however shocked the authorities were, the Bryn Mawr decision was a recognition of the social fact that by 1925 large numbers of college women smoked cigarettes. One-third of the women at Ohio State said that they smoked at least occasionally; a student leader at Rhode Island State in 1924 claimed that "practically all the girls smoke." The student newspaper at the University of Illinois covered the smoking issue often in 1924 and made it clear that enlightened student opinion felt it perfectly acceptable for women to smoke.

By the end of the twenties, there was still opposition to women smoking on campus. At their 1929 conventions, sororities Pi Beta Phi and Alpha Gamma Delta voted to ban smoking in chapter houses. But more and more, colleges were coming to accept smoking among women students. Goucher, which just a few years before had banned smoking, reversed itself in 1929. Acting President Hans Froelicher said, "This practice has become so general that public opinion in the student body demanded the change in the rule to bring it within the law, for fear that disregard for this law would breed disrespect for all laws enacted under the student government."

The campus was not the only locus of social conflict and comment over women smoking. A second center of conflict was public transport. News coverage in the *New York Times* dates to 1921 when a news item noted that the Canadian Pacific Railroad had installed smoking compartments for women in its cars. A reporter in 1923 took a seat in a smoker between New York and Philadelphia and noted that many of the forty men, but none of the ten women in the car were smoking. An hour out of the station one woman lit up. "There was a general straightening of backs and turning of heads. The fat man opposite the woman dropped his paper and frankly stared." The reporter concluded that it was still socially unacceptable for women to smoke in public: "It is being done, because railroads are opening their smoking cars to women, but it is not being done comfortably." Pullman Company bulletins in 1923 were announcing that if women's smoking could not be curbed, women's smoking compartments would have to be installed. In 1925 the Chicago, Milwaukee, and St. Paul Railroad added a women's smoker to its Chicago-Seattle run. The Detroit streetcar system ruled that women could smoke on the streetcars, a development the *New York Times* bemoaned in an editorial. Women were allowed in the smoking room of the White Star Liner *Homeric*, despite men's complaints dating back several years that women occupied seats in the smoking rooms. The Erie Railroad decided to allow smoking in the dining car because women requested it.

Part of the reason for agitation by women for smoking inside is that smoking outside was still unacceptable. It was a shock for the people of Dayton, Tennessee, to see women smoking openly in the street as visitors streamed in for the Scopes "monkey" trial in 1925. As late as 1937 a market research firm found that 95 percent of male smokers smoked in the street but only 28 percent of them believed it right for women to do likewise. That women smoking outside was an issue is suggested by this 1928 report:

> A few years ago an enterprising taxi driver did a thriving business in the Wall Street district during the noon hour by driving around women who wanted to smoke a cigarette or two before returning to their offices. None of the women rode any considerable distance. But the taxi driver had a continued run of passengers.
>
> The taxi was about the only place these women could smoke with any sense of freedom. In the restaurants they would have felt conspicuous. In the offices it was quite out of the question. An unwritten law said that women must not smoke in the business houses. Today there is hardly any place except the street where a woman cannot smoke with equanimity.

Women were conspicuous as smokers because people were not used to seeing women smoke. But they were conspicuous also because, wary of smoking outdoors where they feared disapproval, they smoked inside in places where men had never smoked—railroad diners, retail stores, and art galleries. Frances Perkins took out after women smokers in an essay in the *New Republic,* "Can

They Smoke Like Gentlemen?" She noted that President Nielson of Smith College had announced that smoking would be restricted to two fireproof rooms after several dormitory fires were caused by cigarettes. He said, "The trouble is, my dear young ladies, you do not smoke like gentlemen." Perkins wholeheartedly agreed, complaining of women who smoke in restaurants all through their dinners and in railway dining cars; men, she observed, always politely retire to the smoking car. In years of gallery going, she added, she had never seen a man smoke at an art exhibition. "It remained for a couple of plain middle-aged women to mess up the floor and haze up the air, successfully obscuring the exquisite colors of Georgia O'Keeffe at a recent showing." Her main concern was that women smoked in retail stores, including the major department stores. In men's clothing shops, hardware stores, or florist shops, she wrote, there was, by custom, no smoking. But in stores frequented by women, the prevalence of smoking was a serious fire hazard.

The colleges' establishment of smoking rooms in dormitories and creation of liberal smoking regulations and the streetcars', railroads', and shipping lines' provisions for women smokers helped legitimate the cigarette for women. Further, these changes were covered prominently in the press and this surely gave support to the spread of the cigarette for women. In times past, smoking has been associated only with scandalous women but now one could read in the newspaper that prominent, young, wealthy women smoked. In 1925 an inspection report on the New York Women's Workhouse in New York showed that smoking was very common among the inmates, but it refused to recommend that smoking be prohibited on the grounds that "if a recent canvass of Vassar College showed nearly 50 percent of the girls to the manor born smoking, this is not surprising in a women's workhouse." It is possible, of course, that New York is a special case or that the *New York Times* is an unrepresentative source, although the data from the Midwest colleges lend support. The South and West to this day differ from the East and Midwest in patterns of tobacco use. Still, I think this evidence is a good basis for the presumption that women in large numbers were smoking cigarettes by the mid-1920s.

## Cigarette Advertising and the Meaning of Smoking to Women

Meanwhile, cigarette manufacturers were cautious in appealing directly to women. Curtis Wessel, editor of the *United States Tobacco Journal,* wrote in 1924 that "all responsible tobacco opinion" found the habit of women smoking so "novel" that "it would not be in good taste for tobacco men as parties in interest to stir a particle toward or against a condition with whose beginnings they had nothing to do and whose end, if any, no one can foresee."

When advertisers did begin to address women directly, they did so cautiously. The first notable cigarette ad directed toward women was a Chesterfield ad in 1926 showing a romantic couple at night, the man smoking, the woman sitting next to him, with the caption, "Blow Some My Way." Most ads for cigarettes, even ads with an audience of women in mind, showed only men smoking. The *New Yorker* in 1926 printed a full page ad for Miltiades Egyptian cigarettes that featured a drawing captioned, "After Theatre," with a man and a woman in evening dress. The man is smoking and says to the woman, "Somehow or other Shakespeare's heroines seem more feminine in modern garb and smoking cigarettes...." He advises her to exercise care in choosing a cigarette—but she, as usual, is not shown smoking. A Camel cigarette ad in *Time* in 1926 shows two men lighting up, two women looking on. An ad in *Time* for Fatima Turkish Cigarettes claims, "It's What the Younger Crowd Thinks About It!" and shows a man and a woman waterskiing, but only the man smoking. A Camel cigarette ad in *The Outlook* in 1927 shows two men and a woman at a nightclub, both men smoking and the woman not smoking.

In 1928 and 1929, R.J. Reynolds ran a series of back cover full-color ads in *Time* for Camel cigarettes. Some of these continued to show men smoking, women looking on. But some made it clear that women smoke Camels too, although the ads do not always go so far as to show women smoking. In one ad, "Don't Be Selfish," an elegantly dressed man offers a cigarette to his fashionable woman companion. In another, a woman is shown in a classy shop, buying a box of Camels which the clerk is carefully wrapping. The caption says, "Camels, of course. The more you demand of a cigarette, the quicker you come to Camels." Another ad, "Well Bred," dares to show two women smoking at the track. The copy compares horses and women in its praise of "breeding" and "a capacity for selection."

I examined the *New York Times,* the *San Diego Union,* and *Time* magazine and found no ads picturing women smoking or obviously appealing to women as smokers before the late 1920s. (I examined four weeks of each year for *Time* from 1923 through 1935 and two weeks for each newspaper for the years 1918, 1921, 1924, 1927, 1930, and 1933.) In the late twenties, appeals to women appear and in a few years become very direct. American Tobacco's campaign for Lucky Strike was the most notable, emphasizing in testimonial ads featuring women that Luckies were not harsh to the throat. One ad in the *New York Times* in 1927 showed opera star Ernestine Schumann-Heink recommending Lucky Strike as soothing to the throat; another pictured actress Florence Reed also recommending the cigarette that offered "no throat irritation." Beginning in 1928, American Tobacco advertised Lucky Strike as a good alternative to eating candy. Their famous slogan, aimed at the female consumer, was "Reach for a Lucky instead of a sweet." Chocolate manufacturers feared that women were doing exactly what the tobacco makers urged and the complaints of confectioners made news.

The confectioners were not alone in opposing cigarettes. There was a strong anti-cigarette movement that enrolled Henry Ford and several notable academics and public health leaders, among others. It was especially influential among women's groups. The national Women's Christian Temperance Union (W.C.T.U.) was active in opposing the use of cigarettes among women and children. Their 1921 annual report noted that Iowa's anti-cigarette law had been weakened, North Dakota's had been strengthened, Oregon had instituted a law against smoking where foods are exposed for sale, and Minnesota was working on a similar law. The Union's Anti-Narcotics Department resolved to campaign for strict enforcement of laws forbidding the sale of tobacco to minors, to increase its efforts against misleading advertising, and to attack the increasing habit of smoking among women.

By 1927, the Anti-Narcotics Department reported that chapters had sponsored 6,699 anti-smoking programs that year, nineteen state poster contests, and the distribution of 580,223 pages of anti-smoking literature. In essay contests, over 27,000 anti-smoking essays had been submitted. In Portland, Oregon, the W.C.T.U. successfully protested the decision of the leading department store to show a female mannequin in the window holding a cigarette. The women convinced the store to have the mannequin hold a rose. In campaigns, the nature of which the reports of the W.C.T.U. does not specify, members crushed 219,560 cigarette stubs and 39,713 cigar stubs. The Mt. Vernon, New York, chapter urged that women's smoking be confined to private places. Despite W.C.T.U. agitation, the Atlantic City School Board refused to bar women who smoke from teaching in the public schools. The W.C.T.U. helped lobby for laws prohibiting smoking in places where food was displayed for sale, and by 1927 twenty-one states had such laws. But some legislation was going the other way. In 1927 Kansas legalized cigarette sales, repealing a twenty-year-old statute, though retaining a prohibition on all cigarette advertising and cigarette sales to minors.

When cigarette advertising to women became more prominent, there was a backlash—just as the tobacco companies had feared. Bills to restrict cigarette advertising were introduced in the legislatures in states including Illinois, Michigan, and Idaho. Efforts sprang up around the country to protest an American Tobacco billboard that featured a "girl of tender years actually smoking cigarettes." The National Education Association passed a resolution at its annual meeting in 1930 condemning "the fraudulent advertising of certain manufacturers in their efforts to foster cigarette-smoking." It urged schools to select for school libraries periodicals that did not carry tobacco advertising. Both the Cleveland Boy Scouts Council and the Sioux Falls, South Dakota, City Commission objected to billboards that pictured women smoking. Protest reached the floor of the U.S. Senate in 1929 when Senator Smoot rose to say: "Not since the days when public opinion rose in its might and smote the dangerous drug traffic, not since the days when the vendor of harmful nostrums was swept from our streets, has this country witnessed such an orgy of buncombe, quackery and downright falsehood and fraud as now marks the current campaign promoted by certain cigarette manufacturers to create a vast woman and child market for the use of their product." Advertising, it appears, precipitated criticism of tobacco companies and, at least for a time, intensified public opposition to women smoking.

Why did women take to cigarettes in the 1920s? I have approached the question indirectly. I have not presented the extensive literature on why people take up smoking, what kind of satisfaction they get from it, why they tend to begin as teenagers, and so on. Those questions examine the psychology of the individual smoker and ask why someone would deviate from a healthful norm to take up smoking. My interest, in contrast, is to understand how the norm itself changed, how smoking became socially acceptable.

What did smoking mean for women? In Sinclair Lewis's *Babbitt,* published in 1922, there are several mentions of women smoking, and this in the decidedly uncosmopolitan town of Zenith, Ohio. George Babbitt's teenage son Ted, fighting with his girl friend Veronica, exclaims: "It's disgusting of you to smoke cigarettes..." Babbitt's wife does not touch tobacco, but Babbitt himself has an affair with Tanis Judique, who, to his surprise, is a smoker:

> "Do give me a cigarette. Would you think poor Tanis was dreadfully naughty if she smoked?"

"Lord, no, I like it!"

He had often and weightily pondered flappers smoking in Zenith restaurants, but he knew only one woman who smoked—Mrs. Sam Doppelbrau, his flighty neighbor. He ceremoniously lighted Tanis' cigarette, looked for a place to deposit the burnt match, and dropped it into his pocket.

"I'm sure you want a cigar, you poor man!" she crooned.

"Do you mind one?"

"Oh, no. I love the smell of a good cigar; so nice and—so nice and like a man."

For men, cigarettes meant refinement—a feminine sensibility. Had there been a Marlboro man in 1922, he would have smoked a cigar. For women, on the other hand, cigarettes suggested some naughtiness, some sexual openness, an allegiance to and association with younger, stylish women. Of course, it depended where one was coming from. For Shirley Polykoff's mother, a Ukrainian immigrant, smoking meant American-ness. She wanted to become American as quickly and fully as possible and so "she was one of the first ladies in her tenement to smoke a cigarette." In a 1922 piece of magazine fiction, "Women Cigarette Fiends," Mr. and Mrs. John Smith, affluent Middle Westerners, visit their daughter at a fashionable finishing school in New York. Mrs. Smith, active in the Anti-Tobacco League, refuses to eat in the hotel dining rooms where women smoked openly. To her horror, she learns that her daughter has become expert in smoking and that there are even smoking rooms set aside for the girls at the school. Again, the cigarette is connected to the young, the cosmopolitan, and the naughty.

Smoking a cigarette was a social symbol of considerable power in the 1920s. Women used cigarettes to mark themselves as separate from the past, different from past women. In all human societies, there are markings that distinguish people in their social identity—men are different from women, children from adolescents, adolescents from adults. These are physical differences, of course, but they are also social stations, always reinforced and restated culturally by clothing or other body markings and differentiated, socially mandated forms of behavior. In modern societies, people mark themselves not only in social space but in social time. Through goods, they indicate their relationship to one another and also accent their relationship to the spirit of the times. They display their modernity or their resistance to modernity. They mark their allegiance to groups that embrace social change or to groups that hold to tradition. In the 1920s, cigarettes came to be a personal and social marker for "the new woman," a sign of divorce from the past and inclusion in the group of the new, young, and liberated.

This was the cultural theme that public relations agent Edward Bernays tried to capitalize on when, in 1929, working for American Tobacco's Lucky Strike brand, he organized a contingent of women in New York's Easter Parade. Each woman smoked a Lucky and the cigarettes were touted as "torches of liberty." Bernays takes credit for having significantly promoted smoking among women by this feat, but his self-congratulatory claim cannot be taken at face value. As we have seen, women by 1929 were smoking in public (though not in the street) in large numbers and advertisers were appealing openly to the female market. If Bernays was not especially perceptive in seeing that cigarettes represented independence to women, he was nonetheless commercially correct to pick up on the theme.

Symbols may not only confirm members of an emergent social group in a new identity but, at the same time, may be likened to a prism in concentrating light on a subject, generating heat and even fire. The cigarette was such a symbol in the 1920s, a focus of anxiety and antagonism toward the "new woman" and the changing sex roles she embodied. Cigarette advertising provided a way to legitimate and naturalize women's smoking. It was a weapon in the fight among tobacco companies for market share, of course, but it was, like most advertising, conservative, venturing to challenge established ways in the population only when evidence of new market patterns was in plain view. Despite the importance of the commercial interests involved in spreading the use of cigarettes among women, the change that occurred was a cultural one. It was made possible by changes in the cigarette product itself, by World War I's transformation of social habits, and by a new class of women who sponsored the cigarette in its political and social battles. In the 1920s, a cigarette in the hands of a woman meant a change in the language of social interaction. Such changes may be vigorously contested. They were at that time, just as they have been more recently when "Ms" and "he or she" entered the spoken language and came to be used, at least in some circles, naturally. That advertising has played a role since the late 1920s in promoting smoking among women should not blind us to the fact that this change in consumption patterns, like many others, has roots deep in cultural change and political conflict that advertising often responds to but rarely creates.

## Questions for Empathy and Analysis

1. For Schudson, a consumer culture is marked by a "democratization of goods" and the emergence of "convenience" as desirable. What does Schudson mean by the "democratization of goods"? How does the cigarette fit into the categories he describes?

2. What are the causes that Schudson lists for the increase in cigarette smoking among women? How persuasive do you find these causes to be? Do you think that Schudson undermines his case at all when he claims that tobacco manufacturers say that the increase was caused by the manufacture of mild, blended tobacco? Why or why not?

3. What evidence does Schudson use to support his claim that advertising was not responsible for the increase in cigarette consumption among women? Do you think that Schudson has chosen a representative sample of newspapers and magazines?

4. Schudson explains the considerable opposition that arose in response to the increasing habit of smoking among women and to advertisements that promoted it. For what reasons did many people oppose it? In what ways does emphasizing this opposition further his position that advertising did not cause women to smoke? In what ways does it undercut it?

5. What was the symbolic value of smoking, according to Schudson? Do you think the analogy Schudson makes in his final paragraph when he compares the symbolism of smoking to linguistic changes such as using "Ms." or "he or she" is effective?

6. Do you think that a change in cultural values and sexual politics is the most significant cause for the increase in smoking? How would you weigh the cause of cultural change against the other causes Schudson lists? Can you think of any causes that Schudson omits? In terms of cause-and-effect analysis, do you think that the cause of cultural and political change is both sufficient *and* necessary? That is, would this cause have been sufficient to create the change? Given the other factors involved in the change, would you say that this cause was a necessary one? Could the change have occurred without this particular cause?

■ ■ ■ ■ ■ ■ ■ ■ ■
# WHY BIG TOBACCO WOOS MINORITIES

## Shaun Assael

Although we tend to think of consumer goods as beneficial to society, we know that some goods, such as alcohol and tobacco, are hazardous. In the past few years, the advertising of products that pose clear health or safety risks has met with increased consumer resistance and, in some instances, governmental regulation. Once the link between cigarette smoking and lung cancer and heart disease was clearly demonstrated, cigarette advertisements were banned from television and radio, and many smokers succeeded in giving up the habit. As Shaun Assael reports in this article from *Adweek Marketing News* (January 29, 1990), a beleaguered tobacco industry is devising even more ingenious advertising strategies to maintain the demand for its products. A look at the industry's methods reveals that some advertising influences political realms as well as social areas.

If the product were different, or even the timing, it might merely have come off as a botched job. The costly embarrassment of aborting a product test would only have served to reinforce an old tenet—never, ever discuss a test.

But R.J. Reynolds Tobacco Co. not only announced Uptown cigarettes, it divulged its strategy with unprecedented candor. The new cigarette was developed, packaged and marketed specifically for blacks. What followed was a surprisingly swift and powerful backlash that forced the company to eat its words and cancel its plans. And instead of just blowing millions of dollars, RJR blew the lid off an industry dilemma that has been building for years.

Tobacco companies have to target minorities because whites have been kicking the habit at a much faster pace. But the Uptown defeat raises the question of whether cigarettes will become unmarketable. Has public opposition and activism gained so much momentum that tobacco companies can't ever target demographic groups again? Of more immediate concern to tobacco marketers is whether this latest triumph for anti-smoking activists will pave the way for further ad bans and restrictions.

One by one, the doors are closing. Cigarette companies have long faced limitations in the messages they sent to consumers and in the media they used to reach them. Now a specific brand has been forced out of a specific market. For RJR, Uptown is the second failed attempt at niche marketing in less than a year. Last March the company pulled its smokeless Premier cigarette—a $300-million pitch to the environmentally conscious that failed because smokers couldn't inhale it.

With Uptown, however, RJR sparked a cigarette revolt like none before. For the first time, widespread protest tore into a single consumer brand. The company got it from all sides—community groups, medical associations, minority groups and even the Secretary of the Department of Health and Human Services, Dr. Louis Sullivan. And for the first time, a cigarette company bowed in a very public way.

Uptown isn't the first cigarette directly or even indirectly to target minorities. Name brands like Virginia Slims, More, Rio, Dorado, Salem and Newport are heavily marketed in the inner city. Most are supported by advertising as well as billboards and promotions.

Last year saw a rash of new generic and sub-generic cigarettes, including American brands' Montclair, Liggett Group's Pyramid and Philip Morris' Bristol. Two weeks ago Lorillard Inc. introduced a price-value brand called Heritage. The makers of these cigarettes have never said they were targeting minorities. But their critics have.

"These new very low-priced cigarettes are an effort by the tobacco industry to bring in or keep in the market blacks, Hispanics and children—particularly black and Hispanic children because they are the most price-sensitive," says Matthew Myers, staff director of the Coalition on Smoking or Health.

The price-value category accounted for 15% of the total cigarette market last year, compared with 11% in 1988 and just 3% in 1983. Unlike Uptown, however, the introduction of generics and sub-generics did not prompt a major public backlash. They didn't move a Cabinet member to denounce their marketing and morality. These brands are still on the market or in test. Despite their pervasiveness in minority communities, they have escaped the national attention and criticism that came crashing down on Uptown. But their prevalence has not gone entirely unnoticed.

Long before Uptown, health advocates and anti-smoking activists railed against cigarette marketing in the inner city. Just weeks before RJR made its announcement, Dr. Harold Freeman strode past the entrance of Harlem Hospital in New York City, where he is director of surgery. Above him the motto "Quality health care for all" stretched across a blue awning. At a bus stop not a half-dozen feet away, an ad beckoned transit riders to try Virginia Slims.

"It's terrible," says Freeman, former president of the American Cancer Society. "I looked at it in disgust for a full three minutes and asked myself, 'How can this be?' "

Of the cancer patients at Harlem Hospital, 22% suffer from lung cancer, 10% from esophageal cancer and 6% have head and neck cancer. All are smoking-related diseases.

According to Simmons Market Research Bureau, nearly 44% of black adults smoke, contrasted with 37% of the white population. Data compiled by The National Center for Health Statistics suggests that the higher percentage of minority smokers has a direct impact on smoking-related diseases. While the statistics are clouded by poverty, malnutrition and generally poor healthcare, the incidence of smoking-related disease is much higher for minorities. Black men contract heart disease 20% more often than white men, while black women are afflicted 50% more often than white women. Black women contract lung cancer 58% more frequently than white women.

Figures for Hispanics are even more dramatic. In New Mexico, deaths from lung cancer tripled for Hispanic males between 1958 and 1982, according to the *American Journal of Public Health*. The rate for white males doubled in the same time period. Similar results were found in both Colorado and Denver. These studies by the Center for Science in the Public Interest (CSPI) concluded that the worst is yet to come, since the incubation period for lung cancer is 20 years.

For tobacco companies, it has ceased being an issue of market share. They need new smokers. Government data suggests the most likely recruits will be Hispanics and black women—groups that have not kept pace with the national move toward quitting.

The campaign to maintain and even increase the base of minority smokers goes well beyond billboards. Event marketing abounds, such as the sponsorship by Philip Morris' Marlboro of Mexican rodeos in California. Tobacco companies also donate to such groups as the National Black Caucus and the National Association of Hispanic Journalists.

Tobacco companies have been lavishing money on black arts and political groups since the 1950s. But as their overall market shrinks, they have turned up the heat under the Hispanic market. California's *Hispanic Business* magazine reports that Philip Morris was the second largest advertiser in Hispanic media for fiscal year 1989, spending $8.6 million. In 1988 PM topped the list. Last year the National Association of Hispanic Publications named Philip Morris the company of the year.

The tobacco industry has become sophisticated at cloaking its patronage. Anti-smoking activists say it is increasingly difficult to know what tobacco interests are behind these days.

Consider the case of Emilio Carrillo, a faculty member at Harvard Medical School and the director of a smoking-prevention group for Puerto Rican teens. In the summer of 1988 Carrillo decided that the annual Puerto Rican Festival in Boston would provide a captive audience for his non-smoking literature. He called up one of the festival organizers and asked for booth space. He was turned down.

Carrillo was stunned by the reason. As he recalls it, the festival organizer said, "We're getting sponsored by this tobacco company for $30,000, and this may be a problem." The company was Philip Morris.

After Carrillo began calling Mayor Raymond Flynn's office and writing to community groups, the festival organizer came back to him with two options—put up the $30,000 himself or shut up. Carrillo kept up the pressure, and eventually got a final offer from the organizer.

"He said that because of the mess we made they'd lost their sponsor, and we were barred," Carrillo says. "I felt anger and frustration because, in a sense, we won, but we didn't win."

In addition to event marketing, tobacco companies are visible in their overtures to minority political and social organizations. And despite the high cancer rates among their constituents, these organizations have few qualms about accepting tobacco money. In fiscal 1989, for example, the United Negro College Fund picked up $286,500 from RJR Nabisco, $200,500 from Philip Morris and $65,000 from an employee donation program at Brown & Williamson. UNCF board member Hugh Cullman is a retired vice chairman of Philip Morris. Other major contributions include:

- $4.4 million to the National Urban League from cigarette concerns for each of the past three years;
- $60,000 a year to the National Black Caucus of State Legislators (which represents about 400 black state lawmakers) from Philip Morris, RJR and the Tobacco Institute, an industry lobbying arm with a budget of more than $25 million;
- $50,000 to the Congressional Hispanic Caucus for an internship program in public policy from tobacco companies in 1989.

"The industry has bought the silence and complacency of the black community," says Dr. Alan Blum, director of Doctors Ought To Care, an anti-smoking project in Houston.

"Has anyone ever called Lincoln Center and asked why they haven't turned tobacco money down?" retorts Donald Hense, vice president of development at the National Urban League. "There's $4 billion dollars out there in cigarette money, and you come asking me about a piddley $400,000?"

Harriet Schimmel, a spokeswoman for the National Urban League, rejoins in a voice made weary by answering the same question too many times. "We don't advocate anything but putting kids in school," she says.

But non-minority groups that accept funding from tobacco companies usually are not saddled with the charge that they are selling out their constituents.

Ironically, when state legislatures began imposing restrictions on smoking in offices and other public areas, minority groups protested. Such laws, the groups said, would most adversely affect workers who did not have private offices. And more often than not, that meant minorities. Anti-smoking laws, therefore, were discriminatory.

Tobacco companies, in turn, also play up issues of discrimination and civil liberties when it comes to minorities. RJR blasted critics of Uptown with charges that they had eroded free enterprise. It also suggested that anti-smoking "zealots" were limiting the choices for blacks and implying that minorities couldn't make choices for themselves. Philip Morris, in its much-maligned sponsorship of the Bill of Rights Bicentennial last fall, seems to speak to minorities with an equally libertarian message.

Across the country, the inflated images of cigarettes reign over inner cities. The Coalition on Scenic Beauty in Washington, D.C. reports that four of the five biggest billboard advertisers in the country are tobacco companies. They are, in order, RJR, Philip Morris, Batus Industries and American Brands.

The Coalition estimates that 30% of all billboards feature cigarettes. And the research shows that most of them are in minority-filled ghettos. In 1988 Washington, D.C. junior high school students discovered that the city's Wards 7 and 8—where 95% of the black population lives—had more than half of all cigarette ads in Washington. The predominantly white Ward 3, meanwhile, had the fewest.

In a 1989 survey, the Detroit Planning Commission found that cigarettes and alcohol accounted for about 55% of billboards "in lower-income Detroit." In suburban districts, the figure was about 38%.

"We're outraged about tobacco," says Alberta Tinsley Williams, a commissioner in Wayne County, Mich. "There's a disparate amount of advertising of it in poor communities....They're everywhere, right inside the stores, exposed to children. It's constant reinforcement of their messages."

In Detroit, as in many urban areas, consumers can buy cigarettes individually. They usually sell for a dime apiece at the local "party stores" that sell cigarettes, beer and sometimes crack.

And the level of penetration into minority communities goes even deeper. Dr. Freeman of Harlem Hospital recalls that in 1988, a black vice president at Philip Morris arranged for the company to sponsor a retirement party at the Waldorf-Astoria Hotel in New York for a Harlem businessman. "Philip Morris cigarettes were on all the tables," Freeman says.

Tobacco companies have also made inroads into college campuses, where black fraternities and sororities are eager to have their parties sponsored. A guide to black organizations produced by Philip Morris lists hundreds of fraternities and sororities. The company also produces a similar guide for Hispanics.

Larger-scale promotions include the Kool Jazz Festival, the Kool Achievement Awards for inner-city leaders and the Marlboro Soccer Cup. The *Ebony* Fashion Fair was sponsored by More until recently, when public pressure forced the magazine to drop the cigarette.

The burgeoning Hispanic market has led the tobacco industry in a new direction. According to *Marketing Disease to Hispanics*, published by the Center for Science in the Public Interest in Washington, D.C., Liggett & Myers was especially innovative in the 1988 launch of Dorado. Liggett hired a marketing consultant in New Mexico who helped arrange promotions at state fairs, at a hot-air balloon festival and at the annual Santa Fe Fiesta.

The CSPI also reports that Philip Morris spent $350,000 on a traveling art tour called "The Latin American Spirit: Arts and Artists in the United States, 1920–1970."

Despite the long-standing prevalence of cigarette marketing in urban areas, the Uptown incident seems to have galvanized minority groups and other activists into action. RJR's reaction suggests that the most effective anti-cigarette strategy is to target a specific brand. And now Dr. Sullivan of Health and Human Services is hinting that he will lead the anti-smoking movement.

At Harlem Hospital, Dr. Freeman is still fighting on a grass-roots level. He decided that the Virginia Slims ad must come down. He sent letters to Mayor David Dinkins and New York City's health commissioner, David Axelrod, as well as to State Senator David Patterson. Freeman is investigating legal action against the cigarette company, its ad agency or even the city's transit authority. Until then, the ad remains a sore spot. "We're treating some of the sickest people in the city, because they smoked," says Freeman. "Then this thing appears, right at our door. I believe legally the community should have some control."

## Questions for Empathy and Analysis

1. Why do you think minorities have been slower to give up smoking than whites?

2. What does the brand name Uptown connote? Why do you think R. J. Reynolds felt this would be an effective brand name? What connotations do brand names like Virginia Slims, More, Rio, Dorado, Salem, Newport, Montclair, Pyramid, Bristol, and Heritage have, especially for their targeted markets?

3. Advertisers are sometimes defended because they are so responsive to consumer needs. This responsiveness seems to indicate that they may respond to markets more than create them. Do you think that R. J. Reynolds is justified in responding to these consumer needs? How do you feel about their efforts to sell low-cost cigarettes to black and Hispanic teenagers?

4. The patronage of tobacco companies of minority political groups and cultural events raises a number of ethical issues. Do you think that advertisers should be permitted to support these groups and events? Many television programs on the Public Broadcasting System's stations are supported by corporations; do you think this is acceptable? Are some kinds of support more acceptable than others? If so, should governmental restrictions be imposed?

5. Assael writes that the failure of Uptown and RJR's reaction suggest that "the most effective anti-cigarette strategy is to target a specific brand." Do you agree with this idea? If so, how could consumer activists proceed?

■ ■ ■ ■ ■ ■ ■ ■ ■
# MORALS AND ETHICS
# IN ADVERTISING

## John Crichton

John Henderson Crichton (1919-1977), a former president of the American Association of Advertising Agencies, defends advertising against its most common criticisms. He also attempts to dispel some of the myths about advertising. The world of advertising, for

Crichton, is orderly, businesslike, accurate, and openly persuasive. Its role is economic, and it functions within a circumscribed and regulated subsidiary realm.

The problems of ethics and morality in advertising are partially those of any form of communications, and some are unique to advertising.

## Advertising Restrictions

For example, advertising usually works in confined units of space and time. A poster relies on illustration and a minimum of words; the 30-second television commercial will probably have no more than 65 words of copy or dialogue; even the newspaper or magazine page is compressed and pruned to keep the written copy as terse and relevant as possible. In classified advertising, the language may be reduced to short-hand, or agreed-upon symbols, like "wbf" for *wood-burning fireplace*. So advertising tends to be brief, and perhaps alone of communications media is intended for the casual glance, the preoccupied ear, and the inattentive mind.

Further, advertising—with the exception of outdoor advertising and direct mail—usually occupies a subsidiary position to the news and entertainment and information of the medium which carries it. Its position adjacent to, or following, editorial matter presumes that the reader, viewer or listener will transfer some part of his attention to the advertising. Advertising *competes* with the editorial material which surrounds it for the attention of the audience.

It is clear that some advertising is as useful to people served by the medium as the bulk of its editorial material; on the other hand, by circumstance much advertising has to be *injected* into the reading or viewing or listening pattern of the audience. It is either an added benefit, or a burden, depending on one's viewpoint. As an example of the difference, it is an ominous development if a newspaper starts to lose department store advertising, which is an important part of its circulation allure. On the other hand, research suggests that the interruptive quality of television commercials is a major factor in the irritation some viewers report about television advertising.

Again, advertising as communication is preliminary to another transaction, or communication translation. Most advertising—mail order, or direct response advertising, is a notable exception—is premised on a subsequent visit to a supermarket, drug store, hardware store, book store, or gasoline station. As communication, then, it attracts interest and asks for action, but in most cases that action will be beyond the scope of the advertising.

Automobile manufacturers expect the advertising to build traffic in the showrooms, where the automobiles themselves, the sales literature, and the dealer's salesmen will be the convincing factors which lead to the sale. Grocery manufacturers expect that the coupons in their advertisements will be redeemed at the food store. Department stores sometimes offer mail and telephone service on items featured in advertising, while listing which of their branch stores have the items being advertised.

Finally, advertising alone among communication media has both statutory and self-regulatory mechanisms aimed at preserving its truthfulness. Some classifications of advertising are specifically required by law to state various pieces of language relevant to the real estate or financial community. The advertising of some products—cigarettes, for example—is circumscribed by law or self-reg-ulation. Cigarettes were removed by law from broadcast advertising; they carry warn-ing notices in advertising (Warning: "The Surgeon General Has Determined . . .") and tar and nicotine percentages in advertisements. Liquor advertising, by volun-tary agreement, does not appear in broadcast media, and it is customary to clear advertising campaigns with a branch of the Treasury Department. State laws as well deal with liquor advertising, a reflection of the legislation which accompa-nied the repeal of the Eighteenth Amendment. Automobiles are required to use Environmental Protection Agency figures for gasoline consumption in advertising.

Most broadcast advertising is screened by individual networks, which re-quire substantiation for individual advertisement claims. The National Association of Broadcasters' Code Authority inspects and clears all advertising for toys, pre-miums, and feminine hygiene products.

All national advertising may be challenged on a truth and accuracy basis through the National Advertising Review Board, an industry apparatus set up by advertising associations to handle complaints about specific advertisements or campaigns.

The federal government is represented by the Federal Trade Commission, which since 1914 has had a mandate to encourage competition by preventing unfair trade practices, of which deceptive advertising is held to be one. Since 1938, it has had specific powers over deceptive, misleading, and unfair advertising. Other government departments and bureaus have powers over specific segments of advertising (e.g., the Civil Aeronautics Board over airline advertising; the Food and Drug Administration over prescription drug advertising; the Department of Housing and Urban Development over some kinds of real estate construction and development).

The point is that advertising as communication operates in a much more circumscribed sense than most of the rest of communications. The circumscription comes in space and time, in its relationship to accompanying editorial or program material, in its prefatory role to a final selling transaction, and in an array of private and governmental bodies which exercise some control over its content and techniques. . . .

Advertising is essentially an economic process. It is not primarily a political or social process, although it has been used for both political and social ends. It is essentially an instrument for sellers trying to reach buyers. . . .

## Myths about Advertising

Advertising often symbolizes the impersonality of modern selling. It is re-ceived in an atmosphere of curiosity and skepticism. In recent years various oc-cult powers have been imputed to advertising. These are deeply held concerns about "subliminal" advertising, or "motivational research." The first suggests that advertising can be successful by operating beneath the ordinary level of com-prehension; the second suggests that systematic exploration of the psyche can produce advertising which successfully manipulates people because it is directed toward their most susceptible areas of mind and personality.

Alas for the fable! The human mind is remarkable, and eye and memory can be trained to receive and retain and identify messages or objects flicked on for a split second. The aircraft identification techniques of World War II are a good example. There is no recorded research which testifies in any respect to the successful use of subliminal advertising in selling. It remains in fact one of those hideous nonsense notions which haunt our fear-filled society.

The motivation research story is more complex. Research will reveal that products, services, and institutions have a personality. Their users and non-users have opinions about the products, sometimes from experience, sometimes from conversations with other users (particularly family and friends); there are publications specializing in analysis of products and their performance, like *Consumer Reports*; some magazines and newspapers have analytical columns which test and review new products.

In short, experience with and opinions about products may be formed from many influences other than advertising.

It is, however, a marketing axiom that people buy satisfactions, not products. As Professor Levitt of the Harvard Business School has said, people don't buy quarter-inch drills, they buy quarter-inch holes. By extension, they don't buy soap, they buy cleanliness; they buy not clothing, but appearance. It is both efficient and ethical to study the public's perception of a product, and to try to alter or reinforce it, and it may frequently lead to product reformulation or improvement in order to effect the desired change in attitude, buying, and satisfaction leading to repurchase.

## Three Problem Areas

There remain three areas which are usually items of vehement discussion with regard to advertising, and its morals and ethics.

The first is *advocacy*. Advertising always advocates. It pleads its case in the strongest and most persuasive terms. It is neither objective nor neutral. It makes its case, as dramatically as possible, with the benefit of words, pictures, and music. It asks for attention, absorption, conviction, and action.

This disturbs critics, who feel that advertising ought to be objective, informative, and dispassionate. They wish advertising not to be persuasive, but informative. Their model for advertising is the specification sheet, and they have to some degree confused *advertising*, which must interest large numbers of people, with *labeling*, which is for the instruction of the individual purchaser, and performs a much different function.

If morals and ethics stem from public attitudes, it may be interesting that the public both perceives and appreciates the advocacy of advertising. It understands clearly that "they are trying to sell me something," and their attitude is appropriately intent and skeptical. Typically they are well-informed about the product and its competitors. It is a useful attitude in a democracy.

Research tells us that the public is both interested in and derisive about advertising. It is interested in the products which are being sold. It finds elements of the selling process entertaining. The public is, however, quickly bored and inattentive when the products or the way they are sold are unattractive to them.

The second problem area is *accuracy*, used here instead of "truth" because its elements are somewhat easier to define. Most advertising people believe advertising should be accurate; that is, they believe the product should not be sold as something it is not, nor should promises be made for its performance which it cannot fulfill.

In general, advertising's accuracy is good. The dress one sees advertised in the newspaper is available in the sizes and colors listed, and at the price advertised. The headache remedy will alleviate headache pain. It could hardly have been on the market for five decades if it did not. The orange juice looks and tastes like fresh orange juice. The instant coffee cannot be distinguished in blindfold tests from ground coffee which has been percolated. The anti-perspirant reduces perspiration.

Beyond accuracy, the question is often one of perception. It is true that the dress in the advertisement is available in the sizes, colors and price advertised—but will the dress make the purchaser look like the slim young woman in the ad? Answer, only if the purchaser looks like her already. There is no magic in advertising, and no magic in most products. The satisfaction with that dress cannot be literal, and most research suggests that in the public mind no such literal translation exists. It is not expected that the purchase of the dress will make the purchaser look like the person in the ad.

And while frozen orange juice may look and taste like fresh orange juice, it will not have the pulpy texture of freshly squeezed juice, and therefore to many people will never be its equivalent. Therefore the purchaser must decide whether the texture means enough to him to squeeze the oranges. But the accuracy is not the question, it is the extended perception of what the words mean, so that accuracy becomes equivalency.

The third area is *acquisitiveness*. It is felt by many critics that advertising is a symbol of the preoccupation of our society with material things, and that preoccupation preempts the most important spiritual values. It is felt by critics that the steady drum-fire of advertising and advertising claims, the constant parade of products and services, serve to bewitch and beguile the viewer and reader, who gradually is corrupted into being either a hedonist or a consumptionist.

Of this criticism, two things should be said. The first is that the more material a society has, the greater its support for matters and institutions of the mind and spirit. It is the affluent societies of history to which one must look for the art, architecture, music, universities, hospitals, and cathedrals.

The second is that man is acquisitive. Plato again, as the Athenian speaks: "Why, Clinias my friend, 'tis but a small section of mankind, a few of exceptional natural parts disciplined by consummate training, who have the resolution to prove true to moderation when they find themselves in the full current of demands and desires; there are not many of us who remain sober when they have the opportunity to grow wealthy, or prefer measure to abundance. The great multitude of men are of a clean contrary temper: what they desire they desire out of all measure; when they have the option of making a reasonable profit, they prefer to make an exorbitant one...."

It is difficult to imagine that without advertising one would have an elevated society, one in which acquisitiveness had gradually disappeared. What one knows about such diverse tribes as the Cheyennes and the Kwakiutl of the Northwest is that both took individual wealth seriously, whether in stolen horses or gifts to be given ostentatiously in a Potlatch. Acquisitiveness is innate, as Plato suggested; what advertising does is to channel it.

Daniel Bell, in "The Cultural Contradictions of Capitalism," argues that advertising is a sociological innovation, pervasive, the mark of material goods, the exemplar of new styles of life, the herald of new values. It emphasizes glamour, and appearance. While Bell concedes that a society in the process of quick change requires a mediating influence, and that advertising performs that role, he also sees that "selling became the most striking activity of contemporary America. Against frugality, selling emphasized prodigality; against asceticism, the lavish display." It is his judgment that "the seduction of the consumer had become total," and he believes that with the abandonment of Puritanism and the Protestant Ethic, capitalism has no moral or transcendental ethic, and he points to the conflict between the workaday habits which require hard work, career orientation, and delayed gratification, and the private life in which (in products and in advertisements) the corporation promotes pleasure, instant joy, relaxing, and letting go. "Straight by day," and a "swinger by night," in Bell's capsule summary.

But Bell also sees "in Aristotle's terms, *wants* replace *needs*—and wants, by their nature, are unlimited and insatiable."

Probably no more haunting problem exists for society than motivating people. The system of motivation and rewards within a society is critical to the kind of society it will ultimately be, and to the welfare and happiness of the people in it. The drive for material goods which characterizes most Western societies may be less admirable than a different kind of reward and motivation set of goals. The fact is that the system works, and that it does both motivate and reward people. If it appears to critics that the motivations are inferior, and that the rewards are vulgar, it must be remembered that at least the people have their own choice of what those rewards will be, and observation tells us that they spend their money quite differently. It is essentially a democratic system, and the freedom of individual choice makes it valuable to the people who do the choosing. One man's color television set is another man's hi-fidelity system; one man's summer cottage is another man's boat; and one man's succession of glittering automobiles is another man's expensive education of his children. In each case, the choice of the distribution of rewards is individual.

## Three Important Reservations

Morals and ethics in advertising have engaged the interest of working advertising people as long as there has been an advertising business in this country. Much of the discussion has pivoted around three ideas:

1. While most advertising is accurate because the advertisers, the advertising agencies, and the media insist that it be so, there is a fourth compelling force. Almost all products depend upon repeat purchases for success. It is the experience of the consumer—his or her ultimate satisfaction with the product in relation to its promises in advertising, its packaging, its price, etc.—which is crucial. A satisfied consumer has future value, a dissatisfied consumer has none.

2. There are some problems associated with particular kinds of products and purchasers. There are people who feel strongly that advertising directed to children takes advantage of a child's trusting nature, and his inability to distinguish advertising from entertainment, and his undiscriminating wish for products simply because they are attractively presented to him. Further, the fact that the child is induced by advertising to bedevil parents to buy him or her products is annoying to parents. There are two solutions: one is to ban advertising to children, presumably

still realizing that products will continue to be sold to children, that children will want these products, and that they will continue to cajole their parents for them. The second is to take the view that the child is socialized in the process—that learning about what to buy, learning to evaluate claims, learning to make discriminating decisions, is an important part of growing up, particularly in a free society which offers so many choices, political and social. The second choice seems more sensible.

3. Advertising is a means of influencing the media of communication; it distorts or subverts the publications and broadcast media which carry it. Experience suggests that this is an overblown issue. There have been publications which have forsworn advertising, in the belief that it would make possible a kind of journalism impossible so long as the "interests of the advertisers" had to be taken into account. None of the publications survived; the truth was that their editorial content was not sufficiently different from those which carried advertising to assure their success. There clearly is a problem with the demand of media for large audiences, because large audiences are able to command larger advertising support. But quality and responsiveness of the audience is also important. It is worth remembering that the *New York Times* survived in New York when it was the fourth largest in circulation in a seven-newspaper city.

## Summary

Advertising has particular problems of ethics and morality among communications media because it is essentially a method of selling. It has the ethical obligation to be accurate, and it has the unusual circumstance of extensive voluntary and statutory restrictions, some arranged to protect competitors from unfair practice, others to be sure consumers are fairly treated.

Advertising is a weapon of competition, and it suffers from some of the defects of competition. The late General Sarnoff once said that competition brings out the best in products and the worst in men, and advertising's constant competitive effort is often wearing to people who wish for a quieter world.

Nevertheless, that competition is, in some respects, a public safeguard. The need for repeat purchases requires that advertising present the product so that the purchaser finds the product's performance satisfactory. The pressure of different products and services pushes and pulls the public mind in different ways: fly and get there quickly, take the bus and save money; spend your money and go to the Caribbean, buy a savings certificate and earn 8 3/4%; try the newest coffee, switch to tea. What the consumer has is the misery of choice.

## Questions for Empathy and Analysis

1. Crichton argues that advertising occupies a distinct realm, one that is subsidiary to the news and other media that surround it. It competes for attention with the other media and functions in a much more circumscribed world than do the other media. Do you agree with his position? Do you think that most Americans would agree with this definition?

2. Crichton says that people buy satisfactions; for example, they don't buy soap, they buy cleanliness. What does this suggest about the

needs of people? Think of examples that suggest other kinds of needs that people have.

3. Do you agree with Crichton that advertising is accurate? Do you think the editors of *Consumer Reports* would also agree with Crichton's claim? Read several issues of *Consumer Reports* and find examples either of accuracy in advertising or of misleading advertising. On balance, would you say that accurate advertising is more prevalent than misleading advertising?

4. Crichton claims that the more materialistic a culture is, the more spiritual it is also. The affluent societies are those that have the most museums, churches, and cultural institutions. How do you define "affluence"? What examples of other societies, both in history and today, can you think of that either support or negate his claim?

5. Crichton concedes that there are problems with advertising directed to children, but he argues that learning how to discriminate among products is an important thing for children to learn. Watch a Saturday morning cartoon show or two, and analyze the kinds of advertising directed toward children. In light of your findings, would you say that it is enough for children to learn that the buyer should beware? Or should there be more restrictions placed on advertising to protect children while they are in the process of learning?

■ ■ ■ ■ ■ ■ ■ ■ ■
# SEX, LIES & ADVERTISING

## Gloria Steinem

In 1972, encouraged by the success of the women's movement, Gloria Steinem helped to found *Ms.* magazine and gave it direction as one of its editors. The magazine heralded a change in women's roles and provided vision for feminist activism. For 17 years, *Ms.* struggled to secure advertising and to change the stereotypical attitudes of advertisers toward women. During the 1980s, financial pressures made *Ms.* more vulnerable to the demands of advertisers, many of whom insisted that the content of the magazine reflect a more traditional attitude toward women. When *Ms.* made compromises, however, it lost many of its readers. In November 1989, *Ms.* was sold to Dale Lang, owner of *Working Mother* and *Working Woman,* and publication stopped with the November issue. Readers expressed such a sense of loss that Lang was impressed, and Steinem felt encouraged to suggest an experiment: a *Ms.* that would be editorially free, reader-supported, and with no advertising. Lang agreed and readers enthusiastically responded, including many who had canceled subscriptions. This article, which appeared in the premier issue of the new *Ms.* (July/August 1990), gives an account of the history of *Ms.* and its advertisers. Steinem is a consulting editor of *Ms.* Her most recent book, *Revolution from Within: A Book of Self-Esteem,* was published in 1991.

About three years ago, as *glasnost* was beginning and *Ms.* seemed to be ending, I was invited to a press lunch for a Soviet official. He entertained us with anecdotes about new problems of democracy in his country. Local Communist leaders were being criticized in their media for the first time, he explained, and they were angry.

"So I'll have to ask my American friends," he finished pointedly, "how more *subtly* to control the press." In the silence that followed, I said, "Advertising."

The reporters laughed, but later, one of them took me aside: How *dare* I suggest that freedom of the press was limited? How dare I imply that his newsweekly could be influenced by ads?

I explained that I was thinking of advertising's media-wide influence on most of what we read. Even newsmagazines use "soft" cover stories to sell ads, confuse readers with "advertorials," and occasionally self-censor on subjects known to be a problem with big advertisers.

But, I also explained, I was thinking especially of women's magazines. There, it isn't just a little content that's devoted to attracting ads, it's almost all of it. That's why advertisers—not readers—have always been the problem for *Ms.* As the only women's magazine that didn't supply what the ad world euphemistically describes as "supportive editorial atmosphere" or "complementary copy" (for instance, articles that praise food/fashion/beauty subjects to "support" and "complement" food/fashion/beauty ads), *Ms.* could never attract enough advertising to break even.

"Oh, *women's* magazines," the journalist said with contempt. "Everybody knows they're catalogs—but who cares? They have nothing to do with journalism."

I can't tell you how many times I've had this argument in 25 years of working for many kinds of publications. Except as moneymaking machines—"cash cows" as they are so elegantly called in the trade—women's magazines are rarely taken seriously. Though changes being made by women have been called more far-reaching than the industrial revolution—and though many editors try hard to reflect some of them in the few pages left to them after all the ad-related subjects have been covered—the magazines serving the female half of this country are still far below the journalistic and ethical standards of news and general interest publications. Most depressing of all, this doesn't even rate an exposé.

If *Time* and *Newsweek* had to lavish praise on cars in general and credit General Motors in particular to get GM ads, there would be a scandal—maybe a criminal investigation. When women's magazines from *Seventeen* to *Lear's* praise beauty products in general and credit Revlon in particular to get ads, it's just business as usual.

## I.

When *Ms.* began, we didn't consider *not* taking ads. The most important reason was keeping the price of a feminist magazine low enough for most women to afford. But the second and almost equal reason was providing a forum where women and advertisers could talk to each other and improve advertising itself. After all, it was (and still is) as potent a source of information in this country as news or TV and movie dramas.

We decided to proceed in two stages. First, we would convince makers of "people products" used by both men and women but advertised mostly to men—cars, credit cards, insurance, sound equipment, financial services, and the like—that their ads should be placed in a women's magazine. Since they were accustomed to the division between editorial and advertising in news and general interest magazines, this would allow our editorial content to be free and diverse. Second, we would add the best ads for whatever traditional "women's products" (clothes, shampoo, fragrance, food, and so on) that surveys showed *Ms.* readers used. But we would ask them to come in *without* the usual quid pro quo of "complementary copy."

We knew the second step might be harder. Food advertisers have always demanded that women's magazines publish recipes and articles on entertaining (preferably ones that name their products) in return for their ads; clothing advertisers expect to be surrounded by fashion spreads (especially ones that credit their designers); and shampoo, fragrance, and beauty products in general usually insist on positive editorial coverage of beauty subjects, plus photo credits besides. That's why women's magazines look the way they do. But if we could break this link between ads and editorial content, then we wanted good ads for "women's products," too.

By playing their part in this unprecedented mix of *all* the things our readers need and use, advertisers also would be rewarded: ads for products like cars and mutual funds would find a new growth market; the best ads for women's products would no longer be lost in oceans of ads for the same category; and both would have access to a laboratory of smart and caring readers whose response would help create effective ads for other media as well.

I thought then that our main problem would be the imagery in ads themselves. Carmakers were still draping blondes in evening gowns over the hoods like ornaments. Authority figures were almost always male, even in ads for products that only women used. Sadistic, he-man campaigns even won industry praise. (For instance, *Advertising Age* had hailed the infamous Silva Thin cigarette theme, "How to Get a Woman's Attention: Ignore Her," as "brilliant.") Even in medical journals, tranquilizer ads showed depressed housewives standing beside piles of dirty dishes and promised to get them back to work.

Obviously, *Ms.* would have to avoid such ads and seek out the best ones—but this didn't seem impossible. *The New Yorker* had been selecting ads for aesthetic reasons for years, a practice that only seemed to make advertisers more eager to be in its pages. *Ebony* and *Essence* were asking for ads with positive black images, and though their struggle was hard, they weren't being called unreasonable.

Clearly, what *Ms.* needed was a very special publisher and ad sales staff. I could think of only one woman with experience on the business side of magazines—Patricia Carbine, who recently had become a vice president of *McCall's* as well as its editor in chief—and the reason I knew her name was a good omen. She had been managing editor at *Look* (really *the* editor, but its owner refused to put a female name at the top of his masthead) when I was writing a column there. After I did an early interview with Cesar Chavez, then just emerging as a leader of migrant labor, and the publisher turned it down because he was worried about ads from Sunkist, Pat was the one who intervened. As I learned later, she had told the publisher she would resign if the interview wasn't published. Mainly because *Look* couldn't afford to lose Pat, it *was* published (and the ads from Sunkist never arrived).

Though I barely knew this woman, she had done two things I always remembered: put her job on the line in a way that editors often talk about but rarely do, and been so loyal to her colleagues that she never told me or anyone outside *Look* that she had done so.

Fortunately, Pat did agree to leave *McCall's* and take a huge cut in salary to become publisher of *Ms.* She became responsible for training and inspiring generations of young women who joined the *Ms.* ad sales force, many of whom went on to become "firsts" at the top of publishing. When *Ms.* first started, however, there were so few women with experience selling space that Pat and I made the rounds of ad agencies ourselves. Later, the fact that *Ms.* was asking companies to do business in a different way meant our saleswomen had to make many times the usual number of calls—first to convince agencies and then client companies besides—and to present endless amounts of research. I was often asked to do a final ad presentation, or see some higher decision-maker, or speak to women employees so executives could see the interest of women they worked with. That's why I spent more time persuading advertisers than editing or writing for *Ms.* and why I ended up with an unsentimental education in the seamy underside of publishing that few writers see (and even fewer magazines can publish).

Let me take you with us through some experiences, just as they happened:

■ Cheered on by early support from Volkswagen and one or two other car companies, we scrape together time and money to put on a major reception in Detroit. We know U.S. carmakers firmly believe that women choose the upholstery, not the car, but we are armed with statistics and reader mail to prove the contrary: A car is an important purchase for women, one that symbolizes mobility and freedom.

But almost nobody comes. We are left with many pounds of shrimp on the table, and quite a lot of egg on our face. We blame ourselves for not guessing that there would be a baseball pennant play-off on the same day, but executives go out of their way to explain they wouldn't have come anyway. Thus begins ten years of knocking on hostile doors, presenting endless documentation, and hiring a full-time saleswoman in Detroit; all necessary before *Ms.* gets any real results.

This long saga has a semihappy ending: foreign and, later, domestic carmakers eventually provided *Ms.* with enough advertising to make cars one of our top sources of ad revenue. Slowly, Detroit began to take the women's market seriously enough to put car ads in other women's magazines, too, thus freeing a few pages from the hothouse of fashion-beauty-food ads.

But long after figures showed a third, even a half, of many car models being bought by women, U.S. makers continued to be uncomfortable addressing women. Unlike foreign carmakers, Detroit never quite learned the secret of creating intelligent ads that exclude no one, and then placing them in women's magazines to overcome past exclusion. (*Ms.* readers were so grateful for a routine Honda ad featuring rack and pinion steering, for instance, that they sent fan mail.) Even now, Detroit continues to ask, "Should we make special ads for women?" Perhaps that's why some foreign cars still have a disproportionate share of the U.S. women's market.

■ In the *Ms.* Gazette, we do a brief report on a congressional hearing into chemicals used in hair dyes that are absorbed through the skin and may be carcinogenic. Newspapers report this too, but Clairol, a Bristol-Myers subsidiary that makes dozens of products—a few of which have just begun to advertise in *Ms.*—is outraged. Not at newspapers or newsmagazines, just at us. It's bad enough that *Ms.* is the only women's magazine refusing to provide the usual "complementary" articles and beauty photos, but to criticize one of their categories—*that* is going too far.

We offer to publish a letter from Clairol telling its side of the story. In an excess of solicitousness, we even put this letter in the Gazette, not in Letters to the Editors where it belongs. Nonetheless—and in spite of surveys that show *Ms.* readers are active women who use more of almost everything Clairol makes than do the readers of any other women's magazine—*Ms.* gets almost none of these ads for the rest of its natural life.

Meanwhile, Clairol changes its hair coloring formula, apparently in response to the hearings we reported.

■ Our saleswomen set out early to attract ads for consumer electronics: sound equipment, calculators, computers, VCRs, and the like. We know that our readers are determined to be included in the technological revolution. We know from reader surveys that *Ms.* readers are buying this stuff in numbers as high as those of magazines like *Playboy*; or "men 18 to 34," the prime targets of the consumer electronics industry. Moreover, unlike traditional women's products that our readers buy but don't need to read articles about, these are subjects they want covered in our pages. There actually *is* a supportive editorial atmosphere.

"But women don't understand technology," say executives at the end of ad presentations. "Maybe not," we respond, "but neither do men—and we all buy it."

"If women *do* buy it," say the decision-makers, "they're asking their husbands and boyfriends what to buy first." We produce letters from *Ms.* readers saying how turned off they are when salesmen say things like "Let me know when your husband can come in."

After several years of this, we get a few ads for compact sound systems. Some of them come from JVC, whose vice president, Harry Elias, is trying to convince his Japanese bosses that there is something called a women's market. At his invitation, I find myself speaking at huge trade shows in Chicago and

Las Vegas, trying to persuade JVC dealers that showrooms don't have to be locker rooms where women are made to feel unwelcome. But as it turns out, the shows themselves are part of the problem. In Las Vegas, the only women around the technology displays are seminude models serving champagne. In Chicago, the big attraction is Marilyn Chambers, who followed Linda Lovelace of *Deep Throat* fame as Chuck Traynor's captive and/or employee. VCRs are being demonstrated with her porn videos.

In the end, we get ads for a car stereo now and then, but no VCRs; some IBM personal computers, but no Apple or Japanese ones. We notice that office magazines like *Working Woman* and *Savvy* don't benefit as much as they should from office equipment ads either. In the electronics world, women and technology seem mutually exclusive. It remains a decade behind even Detroit.

■ Because we get letters from little girls who love toy trains, and who ask our help in changing ads and box-top photos that feature little boys only, we try to get toy-train ads from Lionel. It turns out that Lionel executives *have* been concerned about little girls. They made a pink train, and were surprised when it didn't sell.

Lionel bows to consumer pressure with a photograph of a boy *and* a girl—but only on some of their boxes. They fear that, if trains are associated with girls, they will be devalued in the minds of boys. Needless to say, *Ms.* gets no train ads, and little girls remain a mostly unexplored market. By 1986, Lionel is put up for sale.

But for different reasons, we haven't had much luck with other kinds of toys either. In spite of many articles on child-rearing; an annual listing of nonsexist, multi-racial toys by Letty Cottin Pogrebin; Stories for Free Children, a regular feature also edited by Letty; and other prizewinning features for or about children, we get virtually no toy ads. Generations of *Ms.* saleswomen explain to toy manufacturers that a larger proportion of *Ms.* readers have preschool children than do the readers of other women's magazines, but this industry can't believe feminists have or care about children.

■ When *Ms.* begins, the staff decides not to accept ads for feminine hygiene sprays or cigarettes: they are damaging and carry no appropriate health warnings. Though we don't think we should tell our readers what to do, we do think we should provide facts so they can decide for themselves. Since the antismoking lobby has been pressing for health warnings on cigarette ads, we decide to take them only as they comply.

Philip Morris is among the first to do so. One of its brands, Virginia Slims, is also sponsoring women's tennis and the first national polls of women's opinions. On the other hand, the Virginia Slims theme, "You've come a long way, baby," has more than a "baby" problem. It makes smoking a symbol of progress for women.

We explain to Philip Morris that this slogan won't do well in our pages, but they are convinced its success with some women means it will work with *all* women. Finally, we agree to publish an ad for a Virginia Slims calendar as a test. The letters from readers are critical—and smart. For instance: Would you show a black man picking cotton, the same man in a Cardin suit, and symbolize the antislavery and civil rights movements by smoking? Of course not. But instead of honoring the test results, the Philip Morris people seem angry to be proven wrong. They take away ads for *all* their many brands.

This costs *Ms.* about $250,000 the first year. After five years, we can no longer keep track. Occasionally, a new set of executives listens to *Ms.* saleswomen, but because we won't take Virginia Slims, not one Philip Morris product returns to our pages for the next 16 years.

Gradually, we also realize our naiveté in thinking we *could* decide against taking cigarette ads. They became a disproportionate support of magazines the moment they were banned on television, and few magazines could compete and survive without them; certainly not *Ms.*, which lacks so many other categories. By the time statistics in the 1980s showed that women's rate of lung cancer was approaching men's, the necessity of taking cigarette ads has become a kind of prison.

■ General Mills, Pillsbury, Carnation, Del Monte, Dole, Kraft, Stouffer, Hormel, Nabisco: you name the food giant, we try it. But no matter how desirable the *Ms.* readership, our lack of recipes is lethal.

We explain to them that placing food ads *only* next to recipes associates food with work. For many women, it is a negative that works *against* the ads. Why not place food ads in diverse media without recipes (thus reaching more men, who are now a third of the shoppers in supermarkets anyway), and leave the recipes to specialty magazines like *Gourmet* (a third of whose readers are also men)?

These arguments elicit interest, but except for an occasional ad for a convenience food, instant coffee, diet drinks, yogurt, or such extras as avocados and almonds, this mainstay of the publishing industry stays closed to us. Period.

■ Traditionally, wines and liquors didn't advertise to women: men were thought to make the brand decisions, even if women did the buying. But after endless presentations, we begin to make a dent in this category. Thanks to the unconventional Michel Roux of Carillon Importers (distributors of Grand Marnier, Absolut Vodka, and others), who assumes that food and drink have no gender, some ads are leaving their men's club.

Beermakers are still selling masculinity. It takes *Ms.* fully eight years to get its first beer ad (Michelob). In general, however, liquor ads are less stereotyped in their imagery—and far less controlling of the editorial content around them—than are women's products. But given the underrepresentation of other categories, these very facts tend to create a disproportionate number of alcohol ads in the pages of *Ms.* This in turn dismays readers worried about women and alcoholism.

■ We hear in 1980 that women in the Soviet Union have been producing feminist *samizdat* (underground, self-published books) and circulating them throughout the country. As punishment, four of the leaders have been exiled. Though we are operating on our usual shoestring, we solicit individual contributions to send Robin Morgan to interview these women in Vienna.

The result is an exclusive cover story that includes the first news of a populist peace movement against the Afghanistan occupation, a prediction of *glasnost* to come, and a grass-roots, intimate view of Soviet women's lives. From the popular press to women's studies courses, the response is great. The story wins a Front Page award.

Nonetheless, this journalistic coup undoes years of efforts to get an ad schedule from Revlon. Why? Because the Soviet women on our cover *are not wearing makeup.*

■ Four years of research and presentations go into convincing airlines that women now make travel choices and business trips. United, the first airline to advertise in *Ms.*, is so impressed with the response from our readers that one of its executives appears in a film for our ad presentations. As usual, good ads get great results.

But we have problems unrelated to such results. For instance: Because American Airlines flight attendants include among their labor demands the stipulation that they could choose to have their last names preceded by "*Ms.*" on their name tags—in a long-delayed revolt against the standard, "I am your pilot, Captain Rothgart, and this is your flight attendant, Cindy Sue"—American officials seem to hold the magazine responsible. We get no ads.

There is still a different problem at Eastern. A vice president cancels subscriptions for thousands of copies on Eastern flights. Why? Because he is offended by ads for lesbian poetry journals in the *Ms.* Classified. A "family airline," as he explains to me coldly on the phone, has to "draw the line somewhere."

It's obvious that *Ms.* can't exclude lesbians and serve women. We've been trying to make that point ever since our first issue included an article by and about lesbians, and both Suzanne Levine, our managing editor, and I were lectured by such heavy hitters as Ed Kosner, then editor of *Newsweek* (and now of *New York Magazine*), who insisted that *Ms.* should "position" itself *against* lesbians. But our advertisers have paid to reach a guaranteed number of readers, and soliciting new subscriptions to compensate for Eastern would cost $150,000, plus rebating money in the meantime.

Like almost everything ad-related, this presents an elaborate organizing problem. After days of searching for sympathetic members of the Eastern board, Frank Thomas, president of the Ford Foundation, kindly offers to call Roswell Gilpatrick, a director of Eastern. I talk with Mr. Gilpatrick, who calls Frank Borman, then the president of Eastern. Frank Borman calls me to say that his airline is not in the business of censoring magazines: *Ms.* will be returned to Eastern flights.

■ Women's access to insurance and credit is vital, but with the exception of Equitable and a few other ad pioneers, such financial services address men. For almost a decade after the Equal Credit Opportunity Act passes in 1974, we try to convince American Express that women are a growth market—but nothing works.

Finally, a former professor of Russian named Jerry Welsh becomes head of marketing. He assumes that women should be cardholders, and persuades his colleagues to feature women in a campaign. Thanks to this 1980s series, the growth rate for female cardholders surpasses that for men.

For this article, I asked Jerry Welsh if he would explain why American Express waited so long. "Sure," he said, "they were afraid of having a 'pink' card."

■ Women of color read *Ms.* in disproportionate numbers. This is a source of pride to *Ms.* staffers, who are also more racially representative than the editors of other women's magazines. But this reality is obscured by ads filled with enough white women to make a reader snowblind.

Pat Carbine remembers mostly "astonishment" when she requested African American, Hispanic, Asian, and other diverse images. Marcia Ann Gillespie, a *Ms.* editor who was previously the editor in chief of *Essence*, witnesses ad bias a second time: having tried for *Essence* to get white advertisers to use black images (Revlon did so eventually, but L'Oréal, Lauder, Chanel, and other companies never did), she sees similar problems getting integrated ads for an integrated magazine. Indeed, the ad world often creates black and Hispanic ads only for black and Hispanic media. In an exact parallel of the fear that marketing a product to women will endanger its appeal to men, the response is usually, "But your [white] readers won't identify."

In fact, those we were able to get—for instance, a Max Factor ad made for *Essence* that Linda Wachner gives us after she becomes president—are praised by white readers, too. But there are pathetically few such images.

■ By the end of 1986, production and mailing costs have risen astronomically, ad income is flat, and competition for ads is stiffer than ever. The 60/40 preponderance of edit over ads that we promised to readers becomes 50/50; children's stories, most poetry, and some fiction are casualties of less space; in order to get variety into limited pages, the length (and sometimes the depth) of articles suffers; and, though we do refuse most of the ads that would look like a parody in our pages, we get so worn down that some slip through.... Still, readers perform miracles. Though we haven't been able to afford a subscription mailing in two years, they maintain our guaranteed circulation of 450,000.

Nonetheless, media reports on *Ms.* often insist that our unprofitability must be due to reader disinterest. The myth that advertisers simply follow readers is very strong. Not one reporter notes that other comparable magazines our size (say, *Vanity Fair* or *The Atlantic*) have been losing more money in one year than *Ms.* has lost in 16 years. No matter how much never-to-be-recovered cash is poured into starting a magazine or keeping one going, appearances seem to be all that matter. (Which is why we haven't been able to explain our fragile state in public. Nothing causes ad-flight like the smell of nonsuccess.)

My healthy response is anger. My not-so-healthy response is constant worry. Also an obsession with finding one more rescue. There is hardly a night when I don't wake up with sweaty palms and pounding heart, scared that we won't be able to pay the printer or the post office; scared most of all that closing our doors will hurt the women's movement.

Out of chutzpah and desperation, I arrange a lunch with Leonard Lauder, president of Estée Lauder. With the exception of Clinique (the brainchild of Carol Phillips), none of Lauder's hundreds of products has been advertised in *Ms.* A year's schedule of ads for just three or four of them could save us. Indeed, as the scion of a family-owned company whose ad practices are followed by the beauty industry, he is one of the few men who could liberate many pages in all women's magazines just by changing his mind about "complementary copy."

Over a lunch that costs more than we can pay for some articles, I explain the need for his leadership. I also lay out the record of *Ms.:* more literary and journalistic prizes won, more new issues introduced into the mainstream, new writers discovered, and impact on society than any other magazine; more articles that became books, stories that became movies, ideas that became television series, and newly advertised products that became profitable; and, most important for him, a place for his ads to reach women who aren't reachable through any other women's magazine. Indeed, if there is one constant characteristic of the ever-changing *Ms.* readership, it is their impact as leaders. Whether it's waiting until later to have first babies, or pioneering PABA as sun protection in cosmetics, *whatever* they are doing today, a third to a half of American women will be doing three to five years from now. It's never failed.

But, he says, *Ms.* readers are not *our* women. They're not interested in things like fragrance and blush-on. If they were, *Ms.* would write articles about them.

On the contrary, I explain, surveys show they are more likely to buy such things than the readers of, say, *Cosmopolitan* or *Vogue*. They're good customers because they're out in the world enough to need several sets of everything: home, work, purse, travel, gym, and so on. They just don't need to read articles about these things. Would he ask a men's magazine to publish monthly columns on how to shave before he advertised Aramis products (his line for men)?

He concedes that beauty features are often concocted more for advertisers than readers. But *Ms.* isn't appropriate for his ads anyway, he explains. Why? Because Estée Lauder is selling "a kept-woman mentality."

I can't quite believe this. Sixty percent of the users of his products are salaried, and generally resemble *Ms.* readers. Besides, his company has the appeal of having been started by a creative and hardworking woman, his mother, Estée Lauder.

That doesn't matter, he says. He knows his customers, and they would *like* to be kept women. That's why he will never advertise in *Ms.*

In November 1987, by vote of the Ms. Foundation for Education and Communication (*Ms.*'s owner and publisher, the media subsidiary of the Ms. Foundation for Women), *Ms.* was sold to a company whose officers, Australian feminists Sandra Yates and Anne Summers, raised the investment money in their country that *Ms.* couldn't find in its own. They also started *Sassy* for teenage women.

In their two-year tenure, circulation was raised to 550,000 by investment in circulation mailings, and, to the dismay of some readers, editorial features on clothes and new products made a more traditional bid for ads. Nonetheless, ad pages fell below previous levels. In addition, *Sassy*, whose fresh voice and sexual frankness were an unprecedented success with young readers, was targeted by two mothers from Indiana who began, as one of them put it, "calling every Christian organization I could think of." In response to this controversy, several crucial advertisers pulled out.

Such links between ads and editorial content was a problem in Australia, too, but to a lesser degree. "Our readers pay two times more for their magazines," Anne explained, "so advertisers have less power to threaten a magazines' viability."

"I was shocked," said Sandra Yates with characteristic directness. "In Australia, we think you have freedom of the press—but you don't."

Since Anne and Sandra had not met their budget's projections for ad revenue, their investors forced a sale. In October 1989, *Ms.* and *Sassy* were bought by Dale Lang, owner of *Working Mother*, *Working Woman*, and one of the few independent publishing companies left among the conglomerates. In response to a request from the original *Ms.* staff—as well as to reader letters urging that *Ms.* continue, plus his own belief that *Ms.* would benefit his other magazines by blazing a trail—he agreed to try the ad-free, reader-supported *Ms.* you hold now and to give us complete editorial control.

## II.

Do you think, as I once did, that advertisers make decisions based on solid research? Well, think again. "Broadly speaking," says Joseph Smith of Oxtoby-Smith, Inc., a consumer research firm, "there is no persuasive evidence that the editorial context of an ad matters."

Advertisers who demand such "complementary copy," even in the absence of respectable studies, clearly are operating under a double standard. The same food companies place ads in *People* with no recipes. Cosmetics companies support *The New Yorker* with no regular beauty columns. So where does this habit of controlling the content of women's magazines come from?

Tradition. Ever since *Ladies Magazine* debuted in Boston in 1828, editorial copy directed to women has been informed by something other than its readers' wishes. There were no ads then, but in an age when married women were legal minors with no right to their own money, there was another revenue source to be kept in mind: husbands. "Husbands may rest assured," wrote editor Sarah Josepha Hale, "that nothing found in these pages shall cause her [his wife] to be less assiduous in preparing for his reception or encourage her to 'usurp station' or encroach upon prerogatives of men."

Hale went on to become the editor of *Godey's Lady's Book*, a magazine featuring "fashion plates": engravings of dresses for readers to take to their seamstresses or copy themselves. Hale added "how to" articles, which set the tone for women's service magazines for years to come: how to write politely, avoid sunburn, and—in no fewer than 1,200 words—how to maintain a goose quill pen. She advocated education for women but avoided controversy. Just as most women's magazines now avoid politics, poll their readers on issues like abortion but rarely take a stand, and praise socially approved lifestyles, Hale saw to it that *Godey's* avoided the hot topics of its day: slavery, abolition, and women's suffrage.

What definitively turned women's magazines into catalogs, however, were two events: Ellen Butterick's invention of the clothing pattern in 1863 and the mass manufacture of patent medicines containing everything from colored water to cocaine. For the first time, readers could purchase what magazines encouraged them to want. As such magazines became more profitable, they also began to attract men as editors. (Most women's magazines continued to have men as top editors until the feminist 1970s.) Edward Bok, who became editor of *The Ladies' Home Journal* in 1889, discovered the power of advertisers when he rejected ads for patent medicines and found that other advertisers canceled in retribution. In the early twentieth century, *Good Housekeeping* started its Institute to "test and approve" products. Its Seal of Approval became the grandfather of current "value added" programs that offer advertisers such bonuses as product sampling and department store promotions.

By the time suffragists finally won the vote in 1920, women's magazines had become too entrenched as catalogs to help women learn how to use it. The main function was to create a desire for products, teach how to use products, and make products a crucial part of gaining social approval, pleasing a husband, and performing as a homemaker. Some unrelated articles and short stories were included to persuade women to pay for these catalogs. But articles were neither consumerist nor rebellious. Even fiction was usually subject to formula: If a woman had any sexual life outside marriage, she was supposed to come to a bad end.

In 1965, Helen Gurley Brown began to change part of that formula by bringing "the sexual revolution" to women's magazines—but in an ad-oriented way. Attracting multiple men required even more consumerism, as the Cosmo Girl made clear, than finding one husband.

In response to the workplace revolution of the 1970s, traditional women's magazines—that is, "trade books" for women working at home—were joined by *Savvy*, *Working Woman*, and other trade books for women working in offices. But by keeping the fashion/beauty/entertaining articles necessary to get traditional ads and then adding career articles besides, they inadvertently produced the antifeminist stereotype of Super Woman. The male-imitative, dress-for-success woman carrying a briefcase became the media image of a woman worker, even though a blue-collar woman's salary was often higher than her glorified secretarial sister's, and though women at a real briefcase level are statistically rare. Needless to say, these dress-for-success women were also thin, white, and beautiful.

In recent years, advertisers' control over the editorial content of women's magazines has become so institutionalized that it is written into "insertion orders" or dictated to ad salespeople as official policy. The following are recent typical orders to women's magazines:

■ Dow's Cleaning Products stipulates that ads for its Vivid and Spray 'n Wash products should be adjacent to "children or fashion editorial"; ads for Bathroom Cleaner should be next to "home furnishing/family" features; and so on for other brands. "If a magazine fails for 1/2 the brands or more," the Dow order warns, "it will be omitted from further consideration."

■ Bristol-Myers, the parent of Clairol, Windex, Drano, Bufferin, and much more, stipulates that ads be placed next to "a full page of compatible editorial."

■ S.C. Johnson & Son, makers of Johnson Wax, lawn and laundry products, insect sprays, hair sprays, and so on, orders that its ads *"should not be opposite extremely controversial features or material antithetical to the nature/copy of the advertised product."* (Italics theirs.)

■ Maidenform, manufacturer of bras and other apparel, leaves a blank for the particular product and states: "The creative concept of the _____ campaign, and the very nature of the product itself appeal to the positive emotions of the reader/consumer. Therefore, it is imperative that all editorial adjacencies reflect that same positive tone. The editorial must not be negative in content or lend itself contrary to the _____ product imagery/message (e.g., *editorial relating to illness, disillusionment, large size fashion, etc.*)." (Italics mine.)

■ The De Beers diamond company, a big seller of engagement rings, prohibits magazines from placing its ads with "adjacencies to hard news or anti/love-romance themed editorial."

■ Procter & Gamble, one of this country's most powerful and diversified advertisers, stands out in the memory of Anne Summers and Sandra Yates (no mean feat in this context): Its products were not to be placed in *any* issue that included *any* material on gun control, abortion, the occult, cults, or the disparagement of religion. Caution was also demanded in any issue covering sex or drugs, even for educational purposes.

Those are the most obvious chains around women's magazines. There are also rules so clear they needn't be written down: for instance, an overall "look" compatible with beauty and fashion ads. Even "real" nonmodel women photographed for a women's magazine are usually made up, dressed in credited clothes, and retouched out of all reality. When editors do include articles on less-than-cheerful subjects (for instance, domestic violence), they tend to keep them short and unillustrated. The point is to be "upbeat." Just as women in the street are asked, "Why don't you smile, honey?" women's magazines acquire an institutional smile.

Within the text itself, praise for advertisers' products has become so ritualized that fields like "beauty writing" have been invented. One of its frequent practitioners explained seriously that "It's a difficult art. How many new adjectives can you find? How much greater can you make a lipstick sound? The FDA restricts what companies can say on labels, but we create illusion. And ad agencies are on the phone all the time pushing you to get their product in. A lot of them keep the business based on how many editorial clippings they produce every month. The worst are products," like Lauder's as the writer confirmed, "with their own name involved. It's all ego."

Often, editorial becomes one giant ad. Last November, for instance, *Lear's* featured an elegant woman executive on the cover. On the contents page, we learned she was wearing Guerlain makeup and Samsara, a new fragrance by Guerlain. Inside were full-page ads for Samsara and Guerlain antiwrinkle cream. In the cover profile, we learned that this executive was responsible for launching Samsara and is Guerlain's director of public relations. When the *Columbia Journalism Review* did one of the few articles to include women's magazines in coverage of the influence of ads, editor Frances Lear was quoted as defending her magazine because "this kind of thing is done all the time."

Often, advertisers also plunge odd-shaped ads into the text, no matter what the cost to the readers. At *Woman's Day*, a magazine originally founded by a supermarket chain, editor in chief Ellen Levine said, "The day the copy had to rag around a chicken leg was not a happy one."

Advertisers are also adamant about where in a magazine their ads appear. When Revlon was not placed as the first beauty ad in one Hearst magazine, for instance, Revlon pulled its ads from *all* Hearst magazines. Ruth Whitney, editor in chief of *Glamour*, attributes some of these demands to "ad agencies wanting to prove to a client that they've squeezed the last drop of blood out of a magazine." She also is, she says, "sick and tired of hearing that women's magazines are controlled by cigarette ads." Relatively speaking, she's right. To be as censoring as are many advertisers for women's products, tobacco companies would have to demand articles in praise of smoking and expect glamorous photos of beautiful women smoking their brands.

I don't mean to imply that the editors I quote here share my objections to ads: Most assume that women's magazines have to be the way they are. But it's also true that only former editors can be completely honest. "Most of the pressure came in the form of direct product mentions," explains Sey Chassler, who was editor in chief of *Redbook* from the sixties to the eighties. "We got threats from the big guys, the Revlons, blackmail threats. They wouldn't run ads unless we credited them.

"But it's not fair to single out the beauty advertisers because these pressures came from everybody. Advertisers want to know two things: What are you going to charge me? What *else* are you going to do for me? It's a holdup. For instance, management felt that fiction took up too much space. They couldn't put any advertising in that. For the last ten years, the number of fiction entries into the National Magazine Awards has declined.

"And pressures are getting worse. More magazines are more bottom-line oriented because they have been taken over by companies with no interest in publishing.

"I also think advertisers do this to women's magazines especially," he concluded, "because of the general disrespect they have for women."

Even media experts who don't give a damn about women's magazines are alarmed by the spread of this ad-edit linkage. In a climate *The Wall Street Journal* describes as an unacknowledged Depression for media, women's products are increasingly able to take their low standards wherever they go. For instance: newsweeklies publish uncritical stories on fashion and fitness. *The New York Times Magazine* recently ran an article on "firming creams," complete with mentions of advertisers. *Vanity Fair* published a profile of one major advertiser, Ralph Lauren, illustrated by the same photographer who does his ads, and turned the lifestyle of another, Calvin Klein, into a cover story. Even the outrageous *Spy* has toned down since it began to go after fashion ads.

And just to make us really worry, films and books, the last media that go directly to the public without having to attract ads first, are in danger, too. Producers are beginning to depend on payments for displaying products in movies, and books are now being commissioned by companies like Federal Express.

But the truth is that women's products—like women's magazines—have never been the subjects of much serious reporting anyway. News and general interest publications, including the "style" or "living" sections of newspapers, write about food and clothing as cooking and fashion, and almost never evaluate such products by brand name. Though chemical additives, pesticides, and animal fats are major health risks in the United States, and clothes, shoddy or not, absorb more consumer dollars than cars, this lack of information is serious. So is ignoring the contents of beauty products that are absorbed into our bodies through our skins, and that have profit margins so big they would make a loan shark blush.

## III.

What could women's magazines be like if they were as free as books? as realistic as newspapers? as creative as films? as diverse as women's lives? We don't know.

But we'll only find out if we take women's magazines seriously. If readers were to act in a concerted way to change traditional practices of *all* women's magazines and the marketing of *all* women's products, we could do it. After all, they are operating on our consumer dollars; money that we now control. You and I could:

- write to editors and publishers (with copies to advertisers) that we're willing to pay *more* for magazines with editorial independence, but will *not* continue to pay for those that are just editorial extensions of ads;

- write to advertisers (with copies to editors and publishers) that we want fiction, political reporting, consumer reporting—whatever is, or is not, supported by their ads;

- put as much energy into breaking advertising's control over content as into changing the images in ads, or protesting ads for harmful products like cigarettes;

- support only those women's magazines and products that take *us* seriously as readers and consumers.

Those of us in the magazine world can also use the carrot-and-stick technique. For instance: pointing out that, if magazines were a regulated medium like television, the demands of advertisers would be against FCC rules. Payola and extortion could be punished. As it is, there are probably illegalities. A magazine's postal rates are determined by the ratio of ad to edit pages, and the former costs more than the latter. So much for the stick.

The carrot means appealing to enlightened self-interest. For instance: there are many studies showing that the greatest factor in determining an ad's effectiveness is the credibility of its surroundings. The "higher the rating of editorial believability," concluded a 1987 survey by the *Journal of Advertising Research*, "the higher the rating of the advertising." Thus, an impenetrable wall between edit and ads would also be in the best interest of advertisers.

Unfortunately, few agencies or clients hear such arguments. Editors often maintain the false purity of refusing to talk to them at all. Instead, they see ad salespeople who know little about editorial, are trained in business as usual, and are usually paid by commission. Editors might also band together to take on controversy. That happened once when all the major women's magazines did articles in the same month on the Equal Rights Amendment. It could happen again.

It's almost three years away from life between the grindstones of advertising pressures and readers' needs. I'm just beginning to realize how edges got smoothed down—in spite of all our resistance.

I remember feeling put upon when I changed "Porsche" to "car" in a piece about Nazi imagery in German pornography by Andrea Dworkin—feeling sure Andrea would understand that Volkswagon, the distributor of Porsche and one of our few supportive advertisers, asked only to be far away from Nazi subjects. It's taken me all this time to realize that Andrea was the one with a right to feel put upon.

Even as I write this, I get a call from a writer for *Elle*, who is doing a whole article on where women part their hair. Why, she wants to know, do I part mine in the middle?

It's all so familiar. A writer trying to make something of a nothing assignment; an editor laboring to think of new ways to attract ads; readers assuming that other women must want this ridiculous stuff; more women suffering for lack of information, insight, creativity, and laughter that could be on these same pages.

I ask you: Can't we do better than this?

## Questions for Empathy and Analysis

1. How does beginning with an anecdote about Soviet journalism help Steinem to establish the tone and thesis of her essay?

2. When the journalist says that women's magazines are catalogs, what do you think he means? Where in Steinem's essay does she explain the historical events that turned women's magazines into catalogs?

3. What does Steinem mean when she says on page 198 that her article "doesn't even rate as an exposé"?

4. Steinem discusses her early goal of making *Ms.* a forum for improving advertising. Did you feel on your first reading of this essay that her goal and expectations were reasonable? How does her chronological ordering of events lend force to her overall argument?

5. To what extent do you feel you are in Steinem's shoes as she takes you through these experiences? How do you imagine that her presentation advocating the advertising of sound systems was received at the JVC trade show, given the context in which it was presented? How do you think she may have felt? In light of your imaginings, do you think her account of this incident is stated objectively, understated, or overstated?

6. Why do you think the advertisers were so resistant to change? Do you agree with Steinem that their resistance probably cost sales to some of them, such as the auto dealers or the toy train manufacturers?

7. Why does Steinem think that magazines like *Working Woman* that are geared toward women working in offices are antifeminist? How does the institution of advertising imprison publishers? How does Steinem extend her analogy of advertising to imprisonment?

■ ■ ■ ■ ■ ■ ■ ■ ■ ■

# ROCK VIDEO, MTV AND THE "COMMERCIALISATION" OF CULTURE

## Sut Jhally

Sut Jhally has written extensively on advertising in *Social Communication in Advertising* (1986) and in *The Codes of Advertising* (1987), from which the following is excerpted. For Jhally, modern advertising has emerged as a discourse about objects and through objects. Jhally believes that advertising is one of our most influential institutions of socialization, structuring in profound ways mass media content, gender identity, the needs of family members and their relation to one another, political strategy, public policy issues, and cultural institutions such as sports and popular music. Jhally relates the social role of advertising to the economics of capitalism and the symbolic dimensions of culture and human needs. In an advanced stage of capitalism, the economic and the symbolic are "symbiotically intertwined" through advertising. One compelling illustration of such an intertwining is found in the rock video.

The most important development in the realm of popular culture in the 1980s has undoubtedly been the emergence of the phenomenon termed 'rock video' or 'videomusic'. Rock videos are song-length clips of video that use a track from a musical album as soundtrack. Their prime function is to act as a commercial for the album, to help boost the sales of records. The most direct indication of their status is the fact that the money for the production of videos comes from the advertising budget of record companies. Indeed, the rock video has taken over in large part from the heavy costs incurred by record companies of financing a tour by a new band in conjunction with the release of an album. Like commercials in general, there are huge sums expended on these videos. It is not unusual today for videos of the more popular bands to cost a quarter of a million dollars and more. Indeed Michael Jackson's 'Thriller' video (directed by film director John Landis) cost over one million dollars to produce. The video, then, is primarily a *marketing* tool used in the sale of record albums. John Kalodner of Geffen Records says: 'Rock video is not the art form. Rock video markets the art form.' Similarly Simon Fields, the head of a major video production company notes: 'We have to remember that we are making a sales tool. These are little commercials. It is our job to make an artist look good.'

There are two principal places where these promotional pieces are seen: on broadcast television where the networks have their own video shows (such as 'Friday Night Videos'), and, more importantly, on cable television. For the latter, one cable network, Music Television (MTV) has dramatically changed the nature of the popular music industry in the United States. Formed in 1981, MTV is run much like a radio station. In its early years MTV got videos free from the record companies who hoped that exposure would increase record sales. Recently, however, MTV has started to negotiate with the major record labels for exclusive rights to the videos of some bands, for which it pays a considerable fee. Its revenue is derived from charging cable operators a fee for each subscriber to the service and, of course, by selling advertising time to the manufacturers of non-musical commodities. Although MTV lost money for the first few years of its existence, by 1984 it was being seen in 2,900 cable markets and had 24.2 million subscribers. For the first nine months of 1984 it had profits of $7.3 million on revenues of $46.9 million. Beyond its profitability, however, the importance of MTV for the analysis of popular culture rests in the unique position it holds now in the marketing of popular music. In a very short time MTV has become the vital factor in the marketing of rock groups.

The emergence of MTV is not a fluke of the marketplace—indeed, MTV was the most researched station ever to be formed. The basic premise of its foundation was that an important segment of the market, music enthusiasts aged between 14 and 34, were proving very difficult for advertisers to reach. As Ron Katz, director of media concepts for the J. Walter Thompson advertising agency noted: 'You can't put commercials on the records they buy, and they don't watch much regular TV' (USA Today, 27 December 1984). MTV's goal would be to capture this elusive market for advertisers. To this end there was wide and extensive research conducted at all levels of the market. Six hundred 14- to 34-year-olds were interviewed to establish if there would be interest in a channel that showed nothing but rock video. An astonishing 85 percent responded positively. Research was also conducted on which artists should be shown and on the lifestyles and attitudes of the potential MTV audience so that the choice of settings, clothes and veejay personalities could reflect this. On the business side, surveys of advertising agencies were conducted to see if they wanted to reach this audience and record companies were contacted to establish if they would supply MTV with videos. MTV's selling point to the record companies was simple—they were offering them free publicity for their commodities. As Bob Pittman, chief operating officer of MTV remarks: 'If you look at our advertising rate card, we're giving them a million dollars worth of exposure for a hit song.' Indeed it was very easy to show record companies how MTV increased record sales. Six weeks after MTV started, sales of certain artists who were being strongly featured started to rise in places that had MTV available on cable. Steven Levy (1983, p. 35) writes:

> Like any good television commercial, the videos had their effect—MTV viewers went out and bought the records. You could almost make a tactical map of the country, darken the MTV areas and see the sales of certain records increasing in those areas.

The bands to benefit most from this new exposure were new English bands that were not getting airplay on the radio and who had sophisticated videos already available. (The rock video field was more developed in England than in the USA in the early 1980s.) Groups such as Duran Duran owe their enormous success to MTV. For instance, their album *Rio* was noted to be selling extremely well in Dallas, but it was selling well in only half of the record stores, not all of them uniformly. The areas where it was selling well coincided remarkably with areas of the city that were wired for cable and MTV. That MTV is now a vital factor in the success of an album was reinforced by an A.C. Nielsen poll that showed that MTV viewers averaged 9 album purchases a year and that 63 percent of these viewers said that MTV influenced their purchasing decisions. A hit video now is an indispensable part of the process of producing a hit record. The music is no longer enough. Record albums owe their success or their failure to the production (or non-production) of the commercial video.

This, however, has deep implications for the type of music that people will be exposed to in this new media environment for, like any advertising-based service, MTV's programming will have to 'reflect' the desires of its demographic target audience. In this particular case, the targeted audience is largely *white suburban teenagers*. As Steven Levy (1983, p. 35) writes, MTV's purpose is

> not to provide the best, most challenging music possible, but to ensnare the passions of Americans who fit certain demographic or, as Pittman puts it, 'psychographic' requirements—young people who have the money and the inclination to buy things like records, candy bars, videogames, beer and pimple cream.

Early in its history MTV was involved in a heated controversy over the failure to play the music of *black* bands and artists. The basic decisions were not based on musical considerations but on a fear of 'alienating the white kids in the suburbs, who according to research, didn't like black people or their music' (Levy 1983, p. 36). The huge success of Michael Jackson with both black and white audiences has temporarily alleviated this problematic area for MTV, although even now the best and most challenging black music is not featured. Just as in network television, it is the demographics (and psychographics) that determine the 'programme' content. Black audiences (who tend to be largely poor with little money to spend on the kind of things that MTV advertisers want to sell) in this case are simply undesirable, as is their music.

On MTV the 'blurring' of the content between programmes and advertising is complete on both the objective and subjective levels. On the *objective* level we can see that, viewed from an economic perspective, on MTV everything is a commercial. Videos are promotional pieces for record albums while the commercials that appear between these are promotions for other commodities. Further indication that the videos are nothing more than advertisements is provided by the fact that when a particular video does not make it on to MTV's playlist, the record company can pay MTV to play it just like any other commercial. Thus at one level MTV is based upon the extraction of *absolute* surplus-value in that the entire twenty-four hours of the viewing day is commercial time. However, because MTV also sells the time of a particular segment of the audience (and not a heterogeneous mass) it [is] also based upon the extraction of *relative* surplus-value.

This 'blurring' is also clearly observable at the *subjective* level. In the actual viewing of the messages transmitted by MTV it is sometimes impossible to distinguish between programming and non-programming, between video and advertisements. Style, pacing, visual techniques, fantasies and desires are all interchangeable in the MTV messages. Lionel Ritchie switches from a Pepsi rock video to one of his own that mimics the style of the commercial (or is it vice versa?). Similarly directors of commercials (such as Bob Giraldi and George Lois) become directors of videos, fusing the two together with their distinctive styles. Videos (like commercials and unlike other programmes) employ such things as storyboards to sketch the action prior to shooting. While on network television it is relatively easy to distinguish between programme and advertisement, narrowcasting such as MTV dramatically intensifies the 'blurring'. Indeed, advertisers are trying to place commodities *in* rock videos. Brian Harrod, Vice President of McCann Erickson in Toronto says: 'The rock video thing is very exciting. We start to advertise subtly (like public TV now). It is a tough audience to get hold of. They don't read too much, it's part of the TV generation. We've got to get ourselves into the rock video or we won't have a way to talk to them.'

> MTV's most stunning achievement has been in domesticating the relatively media-primitive field of rock and in coaxing it into the ultracommercial video arena, where products lose identity as anything but products, where it is impossible to distinguish between entertainment and sales pitch.
>
> MTV is perfect for a generation never weaned from television, because its videos contain few lines between fantasy and reality. Sexual fantasies blend with a toothless gossip about a rock community that does not exist, having dissipated maybe a decade ago. It doesn't matter. There are no dissenting opinions or alternative views telecast on MTV. Profit-making television creates an unreal environment to get the people into what is called a 'consumer mode': MTV as its executives boast is pure environment. It is a way of thought, a way of life. It is the ultimate junk-culture triumph. It is a sophisticated attempt to touch the post-Woodstock population's lurking G spot, which is unattainable to those advertisers sponsoring *Wc Got it Made*. . . . After watching hours and days of MTV, it's tough to avoid the conclusion that rock and roll has been replaced by commercials (Levy 1983, p. 33).

Given this search for environment and the stress of demographics and psychographics, it should not be surprising that more and more advertisers are starting to produce commercials specifically for MTV.

There are four important effects that emerge from MTV's valorisation of audience time. First, signing and touring. The effect of the central place that rock videos now hold in the marketing of artists goes beyond whether a particular record will be successful. It also extends to who record companies will sign to contracts in the first place. Companies check out the 'video potential' of artists before committing to contracts, and artists, too, recognising the importance of video, ask for commitments about video promotion. In such a situation record companies are more likely to finance a group if they have the potential for successful exposure on MTV. Cindy Lauper was signed to CBS partly because of her video performance. Increasingly, new bands are going to have to come up with not only a demonstration record or tape but a demonstration video. As Keith Richards of the Rolling Stones says: 'If new bands have to worry about the cost of making a record and also about making a video, how is that going to weigh out?' In addition, concert promoters negotiate with bands on the basis of their MTV performance.

Second, composition. Given the central importance of video in the contemporary music scene, it should not be too surprising to hear that many writers of popular music are beginning to write with the video specifically in mind. In 1983 Rickie Lee Jones reported that she was writing the songs and the video simultaneously while Olivia Newton-John actually hired a video writer to develop a script that songwriters would later fill in with music. Billy Joel says: 'I've written songs sometimes just thinking about a visual.' Former Doobie Brother's member Patrick Simmons, when asked if he will write specifically with video in mind, replied: 'Definitely, I think that's just the natural progression for music to take at this time. It's really exciting. I want my MTV.' The point here is that the commercial for the music is actually affecting the music itself. As David Marshall (1984) notes:

> With the move into the realm of the dominant visual image for success, the artist effectively abdicates much of his control of his message.... If that abdication is true, then the introduction of video can be seen as the loss of *potential* free expression and opposition in favour of corporate commodification.

Third, consumption. Similarly, the way audiences consume the cultural products of the popular music industry is affected by the video technology of its marketing. For instance, we have a different experience of a song when we have only listened to it. We can give a personal interpretation to the song, link it up to particular times in our lives, specific places, ideas and moods. The conceptual circle of consumption is in some way left *open*. Listening to a song after we have viewed the visual images completely changes the nature of our consumption. The visual interpretation of the song tends to fix the *meaning* that it comes to have for the audience. 'MTV is a context that seems to abolish context, removing the freedom of the record listener to edit his or her experience, or the radio listener to imagine the music as playing some indirect part of his life' (Gehr 1983). Steven Levy (1983) writes: 'In the pre-MTV world we used to construct our own fantasies to music, provide our own images rich in personal meaning. Now mass images are provided for us.' David Byrne of the group Talking Heads, one of the few musicians who directs his own videos, says of this link between visuals and music: 'I tend to like to have relatively few visual links to the lyrics of the song. I feel that you pigeon-hole the song that way, that you detract from the lyrics by interpreting them.' Most bands, however, have not been this thoughtful about the style and contents of their videos. Largely they have abdicated responsibility for this to video specialists. This may be the reason why, in many videos, the visuals seem not to be connected with the subject of the song. It is almost as if video directors are choosing images that are powerful for the audience but are divorced from the musical content. This should not be too surprising given that video directors know that they are not involved in making art, but in marketing the art form.

> The primary criterion for choosing these images is not artistic validity or even what the songwriter had in mind, but what might sell the song. MTV and the advertisers who fund the service hope that the effect of these rock images will be to put us into the mood to buy anything that comes to our attention, from chewing gum to MTV satin jackets, yours for only a modest $49.95. MTV has turned rock & roll songs into advertising jingles (Levy 1983, p. 78).

Working within the conventions of the advertising industry, video writers, producers and directors have access to a limited pool of images that are known to work in the selling of commodities. 'It sometimes appears on MTV that each group is handed a menu of images and is then told to pick five to be used in their video. The list includes beautiful Caucasian women, cats, high-heeled shoes, hotel rooms, fog, leather, snow, detectives, and beautiful Oriental women—the comic-book fantasies of adolescent males and James Bond fans' (Gehr 1983, p. 40).

Fourth, videos and the consumer ethic. Although videos are primarily commercials for records, they are located within a curious context in the structure of narrowcasting for they are at the same time, of course, the programme material of MTV. Their function at one level is to reorganise the watching population along demographic and psychographic dimensions so that audience time can be sold to advertisers, and at another level it is to provide a suitable environment for the commercials of those advertisers. In this way MTV videos are the same as network programmes—they should reflect the ethics of consumption. Thus not any video by a popular rock band will make it onto MTV—Duran Duran, The Rolling Stones, and The Cars have all had their videos refused on the grounds of 'indecency'. Arlene Zeichner (1983, p. 39) writes:

> The sex on MTV probably never will get really hot: Pittman runs a tightly censored ship. According to rock critic John Pareles, Pittman rejected The Tubes 'White Punks on Dope' because it pictured scantily-clad women and a pro-drug message.... The fevered spirit of teen rebellion against family, school, and state, which energised rock music from Buddy Holly to The Clash, is sorely lacking at MTV.

MTV sells advertisers not only audiences but pure environment, a form that is 'nonlinear, using mood and emotion to create an atmosphere' (Pittman, cited in Levy 1983). In its early history, MTV frightened off some mainstream advertisers because of its programming environment, but since then the advertising industry has learnt that, with compatible commercials, MTV offers a unique consumption environment. As it attracts more mainstream advertisers MTV videos will become

| ADVERTISERS FOR | VIDEOS FOR | SIGNING AND TOURS |
|---|---|---|
| CANDY, BEER, ETC. $\longrightarrow$ | MTV $\longrightarrow$ | COMPOSITION |
| RECORD companies | | CONSUMPTION OF MUSIC |
| | | SELLING AUDIENCE TIME |

even more middle-of-the-road while selling the illusion of 'sex and drugs and rock & roll' to the huge consumer teenage suburban market.

MTV stands at the centre of modern popular culture. Its use-value in the realm of meaning is immensely important. Yet what drives it is the valorisation of audience time. While the audience derives meaning from rock video (use-value), the context within which this takes place is dominated and structured by the system of exchange-value within which rock video is located.

Further, the influence of MTV is not limited to the messages emanating from its own channel. MTV Networks in 1984 launched another video service called VH–1 which would be targeted at an older audience (aged 25–54). The videos here featured older artists and musical styles (country, soft rock, ballads) not available on MTV. MTV has even made itself felt on network television with shows such as 'Miami Vice' where content is totally abandoned in the search for style and young affluent audiences. It may in fact be the only show on television where certain colours (red and brown) are not allowed to be shown. As Michael Mann of NBC notes of the show, 'the secret of its success? No earthtones. We want to feel electric.' Similarly, many motion pictures (for example, *Flashdance*) today are little more that glorified rock videos. MTV has tapped the heart of teenage America with a message format that is pure commercial and is derived from the accumulation dynamic of advanced capitalism. Not content to languish on the sidelines any more, the 1980s has seen the ultimate triumph of the 'commercialisation' of culture.

*SUGGESTED READINGS*

1. Steven Levy, "Ad-Nauseum: How MTV Sells Out Rock & Roll," *Rolling Stone*, Dec. 8, 1983.
2. David Marshall, "Videomusic and Interface: The Conforming Nature of Technological Innovation and Cultural Expression," unpublished paper, Simon Fraser University, 1984.
3. R. Gehr, "The MTV Aesthetic," *Film Comment*, vol. 19, no. 4, 1983.
4. A. Zeichner, "Rock 'n' Video," *Film Comment*, vol. 19, no. 4, 1983.

## Questions for Empathy and Analysis

1. Jhally argues that rock videos are really commercials for record albums. Do you agree with him? Do you think most viewers are aware of this or experience the rock video as a commercial? If rock videos are not perceived by some as being commercials, do you think this makes them more or less susceptible to influence by advertisers?

2. Jhally states that initially MTV excluded black bands because market research indicated that their presence might alienate white suburban teenagers. While this was true in the mid-1980s, in the 1990s blacks have a prominent place on MTV with programming dedicated specifically to rap music and with black artists featured regularly each day. What do you think has accounted for this change?

3. Do you think that television programmers are discriminatory in determining programs by market analysis? Should they be permitted

to let market forces alone govern the creation and airing of programs? How responsible should television be in assuming leadership that would work for positive social changes?

4. To what extent do you think that commercial sponsorship of television programming determines what gets aired? Can you think of any programs that corporations have refused to sponsor? To what extent do advertisers determine the content of the programs?

5. Jhally says that advertisers now want to get commodities into the rock videos. This technique is also being used in films, where a product is held by an actor or actress as if it were just a normal part of the represented environment. Do you think this kind of advertising is harmful? Is it ethical?

6. Jhally shows how the medium of MTV has caused new artists to be signed on to record contracts only if they will look good on video. Many artists now write songs for the medium. To what extent do you think these practices limit artistic and cultural freedom? In what ways could you argue that these are positive developments?

7. Jhally says that watching a video tends to fix the images in our mind, so that if we listen to the music, we see those images rather than imagining our own. Do you feel that your own freedom in listening to a rock song is restricted once you have seen the video?

8. Jhally says that what drives MTV is "the valorisation of audience time" (216). To *valorize* means to enhance the price, value, or status of something by organized action. What does Jhally mean, more specifically, by his use of this word?

9. Jhally says that MTV is pure commercial and is derived from the "accumulation dynamic of advanced capitalism" (219). What do you think he means by this phrase?

■ ■ ■ ■ ■ ■ ■ ■ ■
## AD-MEDIA SFPs

### Wilson Bryan Key

No author in American society today is more outspoken than Wilson Bryan Key about the manipulative techniques of advertising that are made possible by technology. Key has written four books on the ways advertisers use subliminal messages to manipulate the public in ways its members are usually not aware of, *Subliminal Seduction* (1973), *Media Sexploitation* (1977), *The Clam-Plate Orgy and Other Subliminal Techniques for Manipulating Your Behavior* (1981), and most recently, *The Age of Manipulation* (1989). According to Key, the subliminal techniques that advertisers use are numerous, ranging from the optical illusions created by figure-ground reversals, to the weaving of words such as *SEX* into paper stock, to tachistoscopic displays in which words and pictures can be flashed at 1/3000 of a second in a film or video tape, to special uses of background sound or low-volume sound, to double entendres in language. Against this high-tech arsenal of advertising, Key argues that the best defense is awareness, but our culture tends to train us in the opposite direction, to visual illiteracy and ignorance of the way language works.

In the excerpt from *The Age of Manipulation* that follows, Key argues that advertisers manipulate the psychological phenomenon of the self-fulfilling prophecy. Self-fulfilling prophecies are predictions or assumptions that seem to cause an event to occur. Such predictions or assumptions thus confirm their own accuracy. A woman dreams of a car accident, and the next week she is in one. A student assumes that a classmate will behave in a friendly way, and the student's predisposition to encounter friendliness actually induces a friendly response in the classmate. The classic example is Oedipus, who, in the Greek tragedy by Sophocles, discovers that, against all his efforts to avoid the prophecy that he will murder his father and sleep with his mother, he has unknowingly committed the acts he most feared.

In advertising, self-fulfilling prophecies work by promising to fulfill the positive expectations of an individual while actually playing on the individual's deepest fears. The Catch-22 of such advertising is that use of the product will actually help bring on what is most feared; hence, the ad works as a self-fulfilling prophecy. Ads that use SFPs, Key's abbreviation for self-fulfilling prophecies, are most frequently those for tobacco and alcohol, products known to be harmful.

As manufacturer of cultural value systems, commercial mass media set up the society for a nightmare of unfulfilled and unfulfillable expectations, tragic self-fulfilling propehcies, and a myriad of self-sealing premises. Constant pandering through sensory manipulation devalues, dehumanizes, and mechanistically sexualizes everything that is sold or purchased. The self-fulfilling prophecies of the ad media, however, are the opposite of what they appear. The reverse, or negative, side of the expectation is fulfilled. Ads say little about products or brands. The pitch is based upon flattering, patronizing, idealized descriptions of consumers and what the product has done for them. Consumers are endlessly stereotyped as happy, fulfilled, successful, sexually desirable and available, independent, young, knowledgeable, and emotionally secure—a message of flattery. "Mirror, mirror on the wall, who is the fairest of them all?"

"Narcissus Narcosis" was Marshall McLuhan's description of the media-induced stupor where audiences sit mindlessly before the tube, projecting themselves into the video mirror. Narcissus was the Greek god who fell in love with his reflection in a pool of water. He was eventually destroyed by the wise, noble, kind, good, honest, and beautiful creature who smiled lovingly at him from the reflection. He never discovered he had fallen in love with himself.

The self-flattering platitudes of ad media are constant anesthesia against the intrusion of reality into daily life. The implied cause-and-effect reward for purchases is the healthy, handsome, good life with inexhaustible sexual opportunity and abundant sources of sensual gratification reflected by the highly paid, successful, idealized models—the most beautiful of people. Unfortunately for hapless consumers, these rewards are either nonexistent or unobtainable. Real life, as well as anyone can perceive it, is never this simple or consistent. The large-bosomed model cannot be sexually enjoyed or obtained along with the shoe polish she is employed to advertise. If consumers were really capable of thinking for themselves, as they believe they do, they would avoid any product hyped with large mammary glands as a lie. The only sensual indulgence available through an ad illustration would be a masturbatory fantasy.

Joyous, friendly, social acceptance as a strong, independent man or woman does not magically occur via the purchase of a light beer. Just the opposite is closer to reality. Most beer drinkers, especially those in bars, are lonely, isolated, dependent, insecure individuals. Ad models are paid to seem as though a drink or cigarette enhances their consummate social popularity. These fantasies are usually the opposite of the consumer's reality. That is the reason they work. Ads promise that if you buy the product, it will make up for your deficiencies. Uncertain individuals who fall into the ad trap are often conformists who constantly seek the fantasized adulation and approval conformity supposedly brings. The next time an opportunity arises, watch someone reveal their social apprehensions and dependence with a cigarette as a social prop. During the addiction-withdrawal period, anti-smoking clinics utilize videotapes of patients smoking as reinforcement. Smokers find these tapes emotionally very disturbing. Once the smoker perceives what other people have perceived—the ill-at-ease, dependent, nervous, infantile sucking behaviors involved in smoking—kicking the habit becomes easier.

Stereotypical role models from ads, motion pictures, TV, or rock music—perhaps desirable images on the surface—disintegrate into a nightmare of unfulfillable human expectations on close examination. The media image is a lie, but if not examined too carefully it promises eroticized fantasies vastly more enchanting and narcotizing than anything available in reality.

Consumers eventually discover the fantasies were merely hype, but blame themselves for their deficiencies. The good life never materializes, even after endless product purchases and loyalties. The unfulfilled promise must then be internalized. Consumers slowly acquire the self-perception of losers. Hopelessly entrapped in purchasing behavior syndromes, the well-trained consumer will buy something when depressed, disappointed, frustrated, angry, rejected, lonely, and bored, having been exhaustively trained to deal with problems of emotional adjustment through purchasing. But the expectations the ad promotes are never fulfilled. At best, relief is short-term. Effect becomes indistinguishable from cause—the snake again bites its tail. The well-integrated consumer perceives a world where everyone is getting it all—everyone, that is, except the loyal, generous, trusting, obedient consumer who has metamorphosed into a buying machine. Another product and brand is tried, another lover chosen, another social group discovered, a new hairstyle tried, another job found, another residence purchased, another fantasy pursued, and another, and another, and another, and another. . . . Reality perceptions fade and superimpose upon one another further and further into the fantasies of media.

False expectations ensure ultimate disappointment and failure—the diametric opposite of what the ad media presents. To the advertiser, fulfilled consumers are undesirable. Satisfied consumers might withdraw, disengage from the system, stop buying.

## The Twentieth-Century Sisyphus

The consumer slowly evolves into a modern Sisyphus, trained to push the heavy boulder of hope for an identity, for purpose, acceptance, happiness, and fulfillment, to the summit of a steep hill. The boulder then rolls, once more, to the bottom. The consumer pushes it again to the top—again, again, and again until the end. The motto of a consumer society reads, "I consume, therefore I exist!" The expectations promoted by the ad media, which lead to the self-fulfilling prophecies, emphasize the short-comings, deficiencies, and weaknesses individuals perceive in themselves. Negative self-esteem is constantly reinforced. The consumer evolves from loser into superloser.

Drug and alcohol addiction have their roots in ads. For nearly a century, the U.S. population was ad-educated to seek chemical solutions to problems of emotional adjustment. Booze, tobacco, pills, dope—all serve the same objective. There is no reason, the ads teach, to experience the slightest discomfort, depression, or pain. Be happy, well-adjusted, ever optimistic, tranquil, self-assured, socially accepted, and loved—on top of the world. If you cannot get there through alcohol, try tobacco, or pick up analgesics, antidepressants, tranquilizers, or happy pills of several dozen varieties. There is a drink or pill for every minor or major symptom. Once integrated, you do not need the symptom, only an *expectation* of the symptom. Ads introduced, rationalized, validated, legitimated, and authorized chemical-drug consumption at staggering levels. It is a very profitable business, except for users—many of whom end up as addicts.

Every political administration over the past century has, at least in words, taken a strong position against illegal drug usage. It is comparable to being against sin, child molestation, and welfare cheats. Legal drugs, that profitable business, are ignored. Distinction between *legal* and *illegal* is another of the perceptual fictions, but a real vote getter. At unconscious perceptual levels, where ads have their most powerful impact, consumers are propagandized to favor the good life you get from drug-chemical products. *Perceived product benefits*, not legal distinctions, motivate and enrapture consumers. While manufacturers and politicians play games with legalisms, ads milk consumers to accept and integrate drug-chemical consumption into U.S. culture.

As the consumption of *legal* drugs—alcohol, tobacco, and pharmaceutical products—proliferated over the past half century, so did the *illegal* drugs—marijuana, heroin, LSD, and more recently cocaine and crack. Illegal drug consumption in the U.S. is now estimated to be a $220 million daily business by the

National Institutes of Health. It is curious no one in public life has noted the parallel increase in consumption of both legal and illegal drugs. Judicial distinctions have nothing to do with psychological distinctions. The death wish is regularly manipulated at the subliminal level by alcohol, tobacco, and pharmaceutical ads. The mere designation *illegal* provides powerful consumption appeal for many individuals. Illegal consumption is romantically perceived as an act of liberation from imposed restrictions, a defiance of authority. During 1986, there were an estimated 4 million cocaine addicts, with 5,000 new users added daily to the population.

The Chivas Regal "What's News?" ad appeared for over five years in numerous magazines—*Time, U.S. News & World Report, Newsweek, Business Week,* et cetera—at an estimated cost of $4 to $5 million for space. With its copy, "Can you think of anything that gives you a better return on your investment?" the ad objective is to establish Chivas Regal as a complement to business, a large portion of which is supposedly conducted over Scotch. The return on your investment of time, effort, and entertainment will be improved with Chivas Regal twelve-year-old Scotch whiskey. The implied prophecy is success, money, power—approved objectives of business. Who could argue against the logic, truth, and good sense of such an ad, even though placed in a periodical context of frivolous appeals to sensuality, indulgence, and superficial distractions? Chivas drinkers are leaders who appreciate the best. Drinking Scotch smooths the climb to the top, helps ensure success. The prophecy appears clear, at least at one level of perception.

The *Wall Street Journal*, with its daily front-page feature, "What's News?" is an icon of business. The Chivas bottle beside it is open, the contents less than full. Presumably the Scotch on the rocks has just been poured. Curiously, the painted replica of the *Journal*, not the real thing, has been indistinctly lettered, as if out of focus. Except for the words *Business and Finance* and *World*, the lettering is obscured . . . .

The word *sluts* can be perceived in the third line of the headline in the left column. Part of a paragraph in the left-column story is distinct and readable, part undecipherable. One word in the text stands out, *banning*. These appear, at first, isolated and irrelevant words, but they have been carefully crafted into the newspaper replica. The words would never be perceived by a reader consciously. Unconsciously, however, even the smallest, most inconspicuous detail could be very important.

Painted obscurely into the ice cubes and glass are various skulls. One is in the center left of the glass, anamorphically distorted. Another skull appears upside down under the liquid surface just left of center. Skulls and other dead imagery are common in alcohol ads. They appeal to the death wish.

Just to the right of the anamorphic skull appears a standing, robed figure, wearing a peaked cap. Few people wear peaked caps—Catholic bishops, cardinals, and the Pope. Kneeling before him appears a woman. Her face is surrounded by long hair, her shoulders are bare, her gown having slipped off her shoulders. The waist of her gown appears above her billowing skirt. The woman's right arm extends downward from her exposed shoulder, her forearm extends upward. She appears to be holding something with her right hand pointed at her open mouth.

Fellatio with the Pope in an ice cube: a bizarre subliminal strategy to manipulate consumers into the purchase of Chivas Regal Scotch. Most readers will find the embedded obscenity unsettling, at the very least. Considering the kind of world that has been constructed in the name of unrestrained enterprise, with every neighborhood boasting its so-called "adult bookstore," fellatio in an ice cube may have become a normal expectation.

One additional surprise appears in the Scotch on the rocks. Just to the right of the two figures appears a familiar version of Christ, patiently observing the action in the adjacent ice cube.

Though quite small in proportion to the bottle and glass, inconspicuously located, these images will be perceived instantaneously at the unconscious level by anyone who even glances at the ad. At no point in the perceptual process would meaning and significance emerge in conscious awareness. The obscene and taboo representations have a powerful and enduring unconscious effect on those who perceive the ad for even an instant. This ad would have its most powerful motivating effect upon individuals who have strong inhibitions about sex coupled with conservative religious convictions. The two perspectives often go together.

The real name of the game, of course, is sensual indulgence, the reward for success both in business and quality Scotch. The Scotch provides a transport to the "banned" "sluts" mentioned in the *Wall Street Journal*. The taboo world of sex, death, the Christ figure, the skulls, and self-destruction is an end to the hypocrisy and conflicting value systems of modern life. If the businessman happens to be going that way, as many appear to be, Chivas Regal—as the ad suggests—is the way to go. Chivas delivers!

At one level, the conventional road to success—work, preoccupation with Wall Street, business, and finance. On another level, self-destructive, guilt-ridden indulgence that invariably defeats success or achievement. Anyone in business, government, finance, or the professions today who is perceived a drinker turns on warning lights in the heads of peers and superiors. Contrary to ad misrepresentations, the alcohol drinker is publicly perceived as a pathetic loser, not as a great guy.

Simplistic, verbalized notions of cause and effect, if strongly believed, lead humans toward self-fulfilling prophecies. The SFP, once established, takes on a life of its own, creates its own reality, which would not have developed without the initial cause-and-effect assumptions. SFP expectations often bring about what was most feared and anticipated. Mathematician Nigel Howard offered a counterstrategy to SFPs: "If persons become aware of a theory concerning their behavior, they are no longer bound by the theory. They are free to disobey. The best theory is powerless in the face of antitheory."

## Questions for Empathy and Analysis

1. Key claims that ads convey little information about products but instead reflect to consumers ideal images of how they would like to see themselves. To what extent do you think this is an accurate account of the advertisements you have seen or read recently?

2. Behind the stereotypes, says Key, is a host of nightmares. Look at advertisements for alcohol and tobacco and consider what nightmares are implied as a negative fulfillment of what the ads promise.

3. Key develops his argument through use of an analogy. Ads work as a narcotic *because* they cannot fulfill the promised satisfactions. But the response to this lack of fulfillment is to buy more in a spiral of hope and expectation. How effective an analogy do you think this is?

4. Would you agree with Key that one of the major causes of alcoholism and drug dependence in this country is advertising? What other factors could be said to cause alcoholism? For Key, the rise in alcoholism is parallel to the increased use of illegal drugs such as cocaine and heroin. Key believes that advertising has led to increased use of both legal and illegal drugs by exploiting individuals and making them believe that buying is the solution to their problems. Do you agree with Key? Could you argue that the fact there is no advertising for illegal drugs shows that drug and alcohol dependency does not depend on advertising?

5. Do you believe Key's description and analysis of the Chivas Regal ad? Why or why not? Do you think that advertisers use these techniques? If so, how prevalent do you think they are?

6. Although the public knows that advertisers of liquor, beer, and cigarettes lie, do you think people are aware of the use of techniques such as those Key sees in the Chivas Regal ad? Would lack of awareness make them more susceptible? Is the skepticism consumers already have sufficient to protect them from being manipulated?

7. Analyze the two Dewar's advertisements for scotch whiskey (pages 227 and 228), which are directed to a male audience, and the advertisement for Grand Marnier Liqueur (page 229) directed to a female audience for the self-fulfilling prophecies contained in them. Read the printed profiles of the "lounge lizard" and of Paul Binder the ringmaster. On the basis of these profiles, what kind of men do you think drink Dewar's? What special features of each photograph do you note? What feeling is created by the smoke in front of the lounge lizard's face? What might be the significance of the small bottle in the middle of the ashtray? What is the effect of the light on the venetian blinds? What feeling does Paul Binder encircled by fire create or suggest? What message do you think is conveyed by these ads but not explicitly suggested? Study the Grand Marnier Liqueur ad. What is happening in this ad? What kind of love is suggested, and how might it be grand? How might this ad work as a self-fulfilling prophecy?

# DEWAR'S PROFILE:

**LOUNGE LIZARD**

PROFESSION: Spirits Columnist, New York Daily News.

HOBBY: Leading the fight against drinks with silly names. "Bars were invented as places where man could go to drink, not to be theme parks."

LATEST ACCOMPLISHMENT: Six hours of sleep.

WHY I DO WHAT I DO: "Because so far nobody's told me I can't."

QUOTE: "It only costs a few dollars more to fly first class."

LAST BOOK READ: *Oh, What a Paradise it Seems*, by John Cheever.

PROFILE: Primordial, nocturnal and unpretentious. Comfortable with any crowd, though values his anonymity. "I guess it could be said I'm a reptile to all men."

HIS SCOTCH: Dewar's "White Label". "How?...in a glass."

227

# DEWAR'S PROFILE:

**PAUL BINDER**

HOME: Rhinebeck, NY

AGE: 46.

PROFESSION: Ringmaster, artistic director, founder, The Big Apple Circus.

HOBBY: "I always want to play golf, but I'm never in one place long enough to join one of those clubs."

LAST BOOK READ: *The Tin Drum*, Günter Grass.

LATEST ACCOMPLISHMENT: "The Circus. Last night's performance, and tomorrow's. So maybe it should say ongoing accomplishment."

WHY I DO WHAT I DO: "Everyone jumps through hoops for a living; I've just found some that are more fun."

QUOTE: "The circus is magic, and one of the few things the world can use more of is magic."

PROFILE: Extroverted, creative and highly organized. With 102 people and 43 vehicles to look after, he has to be.

HIS SCOTCH: Dewar's® "White Label," with soda. "When the tent is dark and the roar of the greasepaint is just a memory, it's time for my Scotch to take center stage."

Love
is
Grand.

229

■ ■ ■ ■ ■ ■ ■ ■

# FETISHISM: DISTORTED COMMUNICATION IN THE WORLD OF GOODS

### William Leiss, Stephen Kline, and Sut Jhally

Leiss, Kline, and Jhally see in advertising for national consumer products one of the great vehicles of social communication. In this excerpt from *Social Communication in Advertising*, they argue that in modern society people speak to each other through things as much as they speak through language. In speaking to each other through things, they in some sense continue the ancient practice of *fetishism*, a practice whereby African tribes used objects to bring about a change in the behavior or condition of individuals. Although the social communication of advertising is continuous in this way with older practices, modern practices reveal significant differences as well, particularly in the distorted and indirect ways that our contemporary "fetishes" communicate. Such distortions, however, do not suggest to the authors that advertising is inherently deceptive. Although the authors portray advertising as a positive form of communication in this selection, one of them, Sut Jhally, has changed his position and writes more negatively about advertising in his book *The Codes of Advertising* (1987). An excerpt from his book appears on pages 213 to 219.

The objects we acquire, display, or simply admire are a powerful medium for the circulation of messages about ourselves to others, and for learning the forms of expression for social interactions (the status symbols, clothing styles, and so forth) that appear to be sanctioned at any one time. This ensemble can be said to represent, in Marshall Sahlin's words, "man speaking to man through the medium of things." Presumably, most of us, most of the time, strive to convey our intentions and perceptions truthfully; but evasions, outright lies, and honest mistakes are not unknown. More important, the subjective bias with which we all operate inevitably colors our reading of events. So we must ask: Is the discourse through and about things spoken with forked tongues?

In considering this question we will continue to look chiefly at the place of objects in social interactions, and pay little attention to the role they might play in the psychological development of individuals. (For an excellent discussion of this point, see Part I of *The Meaning of Things* by Csikszentmihalyi and Rochberg-Halton [1981].) There are stages in childhood where a fixation on particular objects seems to be both a necessary and normal process that, so far as we know, occurs universally. However, in some cases an abnormal fixation on objects can occur in which, for example, a male cannot perform sexually under normal conditions, and seeks to use what psychoanalytic theory terms a "fetish object" such as a woman's shoe as a catalyst to reaching orgasm.

The notion of fetish, as we shall see, is helpful for investigating to what extent the discourse through and about objects contains elements of distortion and misrepresentation. The Portuguese coined the terms "fetish" and "fetishism" as a result of the European encounter with African societies beginning in the fifteenth century. They were describing the widespread practice they observed of addressing or employing material objects in order to effect a change in the condition or behavior of another. Traditional ceremonies involving fetishes persist to the present. Of special interest are practices that blend old fetishisms with other elements in response to pressures exerted by twentieth century market forces operating on a global scale. The anthropologist Michael Taussig tells of Bolivian tin miners who have called upon a mixture of folklore and Christian doctrine to construct a representation of what has happened to traditional ways of life, particularly in the domain of producing goods. The tin miners' mythic structure explains that the people have been seduced away from their traditional agricultural pursuits by the promise of great wealth in the mines. But the mine owner is actually the devil who has deluded the workers. To protect themselves from the dangers of the mines, the miners adapted peasant sacrifice rituals to their new situation, seeking to propitiate the devil-owner with gifts and ceremonies, chewing coca together and offering it to the icon that represents the devil-owner.

> *His body is sculptured from mineral. The hands, face, and legs are made from clay. Often, bright pieces of metal or light bulbs from the miners' helmets form his eyes. The teeth may be of glass or crystal sharpened like nails, and the mouth gapes, awaiting offerings of coca and cigarettes. The hands stretch out for liquor. In the Siglo XX mine the icon has an enormous erect penis. The spirit can also appear as an apparition: a blond, bearded, red-faced* gringo *wearing a cowboy hat, resembling the technicians and administrators. . . . He can also take the form of a succubus, offering riches in exchange for one's soul or life. (Taussig 1980, 143)*

Thus materials from older fetishistic practices were adapted and transformed to provide a workable representation of what the introduction of wage labor meant for the relationship between humans and the material world. The personification (the devil) of the agent behind these changes is anchored in the concept of "seduction" when, lured by material wealth, people accept the rules of the game in a market economy founded on working for wages and producing tin for world markets.

What prompts cultures to create such representations is the need to supply a coherent account (however implausible it may appear to outside observers) of changes that have a major impact on established ways. Social relations oriented around long-standing modes of production and exchange—subsistence agriculture, extended family or kinship groups, barter—began to dissolve as private capitalists and market economics took control. But what is *visible and tangible* about these changes? It is not capital investment decisions, international stock exchange fluctuations, or profit targets set by multinational corporations for their operations in foreign countries. It is loss of access to land, cash wages determined and paid by strangers, radically different types and conditions of work, and the breakdown of kinship groups. For the indigenous peoples of Bolivia just as for the peoples of Europe a century earlier, structures of life and experience familiar to countless generations suddenly disintegrated before their very eyes. It is hardly surprising that they should suspect the devil of having a hand in it.

For the objects of the material world and the activities needed to sustain life no longer make sense by the accepted standards of judgment. The establishment of a market economy unravels and discards not only specific things, habitual routines, and norms but also the integument holding them together, the sense of a collective identity and fate. At first no new means for binding together the experience of the material world is proferred. It appears only as an "immense and astonishing collection of goods."

That phrase is from the opening sentence of Karl Marx's *Capital*. In reading the many tomes on political economy published in his day, Marx noticed something peculiar about how social commentators described the emerging market society and its advantages. They seemed to regard the domain of material production, when governed exclusively by the rules of "free markets," as something beyond human control, obeying only its own inherent principles, almost as if the economy possessed a "life of its own...."

Marx saw in this philosophy an analogy between the propensities of religion and the new way of thinking about a market economy that had been developing since the eighteenth century. In religious thought "the products of the human brain appear as autonomous figures endowed with a life of their own, which enter into relations both with each other and with the human race. . . . [So] it is in the world of commodities or goods with the products of men's hands. I call this the fetishism which attaches itself to the products of labor as soon as they are produced as commodities, and is therefore inseparable from the production of commodities" (Marx [1867] 1976, 165).

This is a remarkable statement, especially considering when it was penned; except for some perceptive comments on related topics made around the turn of the twentieth century by Thorstein Veblen and Georg Simmel, two of the founders of modern sociology, about a hundred years passed before this theme was seriously taken up again. What connects Marx's notion with our earlier discussion of fetishism is that he too encountered the idea by reading a book (in his case, one published in the eighteenth century) about European voyages to then unfamiliar places. He detected a similarity between the fetishistic practices in African societies, where certain material objects were regarded as embodying forces that could affect human behavior, and the way the political economists of his own day described the operations of a market economy as an independent force in society, steered by its own mechanisms (the so-called "laws of supply and demand") that compelled all sensible men and women to act in accordance with its dictates. Those who protested against poverty or degraded working conditions were told that there was a "natural" level for wages, determined by the marketplace itself, and that neither labor unions nor legislation could interfere with its mysterious ways. Any notion of tampering with the wild, roller-coaster ride of the business cycle in the nineteenth century was resisted just as strenuously.

Marx argued that this conception of the economy and its "laws" was regressive, because it left most people at the mercy of unmastered forces. But his argument also contains a particular point of special relevance for this chapter, namely that *the misrepresentation about production and consumption in a market economy is embodied in material objects themselves.* And should such a fundamental misrepresentation be found to exist, it necessarily would call into question the power of goods to serve as meaningful communicators of personal intentions, motives, and objectives.

To live according to the principles of a market economy is to be immersed in buying and selling transactions every day, where everything one has (especially one's mental skills and physical energies) and everything one wants or needs has a price. In other words as a market-industrial economy expands, more and more elements of both the natural environment and human qualities are drawn into the orbit of exchanged things, into the realm of commodities. Everything has some use to someone (or so it is hoped), and likewise everything has a price at which it can be acquired.

When elements of nature and humanity are ever-increasingly absorbed into the market's orbit, becoming exchanged things, they begin to appear to us as objects, or at least as *objectified forms*. Fewer and fewer aspects of our environment and ourselves remain "outside" the domain of buying and selling. By and large in earlier times individuals were expected to adjust their behavior to role requirements, and in the early phases of our modern economy occupational structures dictated the behavioral standards to which people were expected to conform. More recently, however, we are commonly told to "market" ourselves, to regard our qualifications and experiences as components that we can "repackage" in various ways to suit the demands of changing employment patterns.

The process of converting more and more elements of natural environments and human qualities into objectified forms, into commodities, constitutes the very essence of an expanding market-industrial economy. This busy enterprise has yielded abundant fruit, which is why the social wealth produced by it appears, in Marx's words, as an "immense and astonishing collection of goods." This is what strikes us immediately, overwhelmingly, as we look about us and consider just how much *more* there is now than at any other time. So strong is this impression that it is easy not to notice that what is missing, what does not appear immediately to us, what remains hidden beneath the surface in the vast world of goods, is any adequate representation of the *social* character of production and consumption activity.

With the progressive specialization of labor most of us work at a narrow range of tasks, and in industrialized nations today the majority of the labor force has no direct involvement in the production of any material objects, although upon reflection we know that we work in an integrated production system and that what we do is connected somehow with the overall economic result. For the most part we encounter objects as users and consumers; since in these settings we usually have specific aims in mind (the accomplishment of certain tasks or the gratification of particular wants), the social processes through which these objects came to be produced as appropriate for consumption remain in the background.

In our political rhetoric we worry a good deal about the condition of our economy as a whole, but this is a rather abstract and "distant" concern. The point is that we tend to allow the economy itself, as the sphere in which the world of goods is produced and consumed, to represent what binds us together as a society. Goods themselves do provide some of the major lines of communication for our system of social relations. But the lines are buried, so that we sometimes run the risk of focusing too much interest on the surface attractions of things and too little on their more important communicative functions: "If things attract our attention excessively, there is not enough psychic energy left to cultivate the interaction with the rest of the world" (Csikszentmihalyi and Rochberg-Halton 1981, 53).

This point may be clearer if we recall the "double symbolic process." On one side businesses incorporate their understanding of consumer preferences (and how they might be changed) into the physical and symbolic characteristics of the product, though the design and marketing strategies are not necessarily visible or obvious to consumers, nor are they meant to be. Meanwhile consumers construct their own self-images and preference patterns out of an enormous array of symbolic associations and behavioral codes that manufacturers are not always able to anticipate or decode. Thus what we get is not the whole story.

Marx did not see the consumer society emerge, but he did spot the first forms of this peculiar feature in a market economy, remarking that the objectified forms for what is produced and consumed there have an "enigmatic" or "mysterious" character: although marketed goods have a richly textured social composition, involving co-ordinated production, distribution, and consumption on a global scale, their social character is not immediately apparent. Thus commodities are "sensuous things which are at the same time supra-sensible or social," a combination of features that we can see, touch, and smell, on the one hand, and of the complex but hidden social relations orchestrated by the market economy on the other hand.

Commodities are, therefore, a unity of what is revealed and what is concealed in the processes of production and consumption. Goods reveal or "show" to our senses their capacities to be satisfiers or stimulators of particular wants and communicators of behavioral codes. At the same time they draw a veil across their own origins: products appear and disappear before consumers' eyes as if by spontaneous generation, and it is an astute shopper indeed who has much idea about what most things are composed of and what kinds of people made them.

Marx called the fetishism of commodities a disguise whereby the appearance of things in the marketplace masks the story of who fashioned them, and under what conditions. Is it important for us to hear this story? Are we, in being deprived of it, experiencing a systematic distortion of communication within the world of goods itself?

The story matters not because we would necessarily act differently once we heard it, but because it draws attention to some otherwise unnoticed aspects of a market economy, including the role of advertising in it. Although goods serve as communicators of social meanings, they do not do so in straightforward or unambiguous ways. Goods are communicators in a market-industrial society, just as they have always been in human cultures; but precisely what they communicate—and, equally as noteworthy, fail to communicate—is something that can be determined only by close analysis.

Commodities tell us a great deal about themselves, at least insofar as their surface features are concerned, especially in advertisements. But, unlike goods in earlier societies, they do not bear the signatures of their makers whose motives we might assess because we know who they are, nor do they tell us how we should behave with them as they do in societies with closed spheres of exchange.... Among the Siane people in New Guinea "no commodity can be used in an ambiguous situation" (Salisbury 1962, 103). In contrast, a market economy revels in ambiguities that flow from the double symbolic process, and under their sway the discourse through and about objects must be, in some important measure, systematically distorted—a passage through a carnival hall of mirrors.

The distortion arises primarily on account of what is omitted at the surface level of representations about needs and commodities. Neither the conditions of production, nor the manufacturer's marketing strategies, nor the subtle ploys of the ad agency's "creative" department is meant to attract our attention as the object presents itself to us. On the other hand, although most people seem willing at least on occasion to indulge their fantasies in stores, market researchers can find no simple correlations between personality traits and ordered arrays of consumer preferences. Like producers, consumers too draw a veil across the sources of their enterprise.

A market society is a masked ball. Here we bring our needs to dance with their satisfiers (goods) in close embrace to the melodies of an unseen orchestra. The costumes serve products well, for they hide the fact that so many of them are just ordinary chemical compounds tarted up in fancy packages; our disguises are equally advantageous, shielding from others' gaze our many disappointments—as consumers—in our partners' performances.

There are distorted patterns of communication imprinted on the collection of goods circulating in a market-industrial society because some important aspects of producing and consuming activities generally remain out of view. The discourse through and about objects is carried on from behind elaborate masks; advertisers and marketers fashion huge numbers of masks, and in selecting some, consumers allow themselves to be persuaded that they can serve their needs. At social events conversations are customarily limited to polite remarks about superficial matters, and discourse in the marketplace generally confines itself to the surface qualities of objects and of our possible reasons for being interested in them.

In fashioning masks for goods marketers and advertisers use all the available media of communication to move back and forth across the interface between the production and consumption spheres, restlessly creating and refurbishing zones of encounter between needs and products. . . . Advertising mirrors the identifying sign of the consumer society—the unending play with new possibilities for satisfaction. This sign is reflected concretely in the general characteristics of goods themselves—changing qualities, styles, materials, and modes of appeal. As represented in advertisements, goods are active, potent ingredients in social interactions; they are bearers of powers that can affect us and assist us in affecting others. In advertising we encounter a lush and entertaining realm of fetishes.

Certainly our fetishes do not serve us in the same way as those used in primitive societies serve them. Another important point is that in modern society goods themselves are not fetishes, except in unusual or abnormal circumstances. Rather, through marketing and advertising goods are fitted with masks that "show" the possible relations between things on the one hand and human wants and emotions on the other. These masks are our fetishes. They make things come alive, make them able to act—almost literally—as participants in social interactions. They encipher goods in codes that we can read and act upon.

This perspective enables us to understand two interrelated features of the consumer society, the ambiguous sense of satisfaction experienced by individuals and the role that marketing and advertising plays in its formation.

Distorted communication is a structural component of the world of goods itself. In a market-industrial society the domain of communication is indeed systematically misleading because it makes so few direct references to many essential aspects of our producing and consuming activities. Any direct connection between goods and the enduring sources of contentment in life is concealed: The happiness surveys report that people regard earlier generations (which had a noticeably lower material standard of living) as being more contented than they are today but also that most would not wish to live as people did in those times.

Certainly advertising seeks to link goods with images of happiness and content by designing masks for things which display such linkages. Sometimes the designs are actually false or misleading, but this is not one of their inherent features: Legislation and industry guidelines (at least in western societies) have tended to reduce considerably the extent of overtly untruthful or deceptive practices. While the masks are meant to influence consumer behavior, it is certain that they do not and cannot control it. Thus we do not contend that modern society's realm of fetishes is generally harmful or manipulative in general. The vital issues about advertising today are specific ones, such as the wisdom of promoting alcohol and tobacco products, stereotyping, and directing messages at children.

### REFERENCES

Csikszentmihalyi, M., and E. Rochberg-Halton. 1981. *The Meaning of Things*. Cambridge: Cambridge University Press.
Marx, Karl. (1867) 1976. *Capital*. Harmondsworth, Middlesex: Penguin.
Salisbury, Richard. 1962. *From Stone to Steel*. London: Cambridge University Press.
Taussig, M. 1980. *The Devil and Commodity Fetishism in South America*. Chapel Hill: University of North Carolina Press.

## Questions for Empathy and Analysis

1. How was the mine owner "fetishized" by the Bolivian tin miners? Why did they feel the need to create this fetish? How did the fetish function as a symbol?

2. Why might the "immense and astonishing collection of goods" have been disturbing to people in an early capitalist society? Do you think advertising played a role in helping to make coherent sense of the proliferation of goods? Does the appearance of goods seem to you to be governed by mysterious forces beyond your control?

3. Do you think capitalism operates by laws of supply and demand and its own independent mechanism? If so, do you think that its operation is inherently just, or dangerous?

4. What do you think the authors mean when they say that "the misrepresentation about production and consumption in a market economy is embodied in material objects themselves"? How would you relate this statement to their claim that the world of goods lacks "any adequate representation of the social character of production and consumption activity" (233)?

5. The authors quote and explain Karl Marx's idea that in religious thought "products of the human brain appear as autonomous figures endowed with a life of their own" (232). What did Marx, an atheist, mean by this? How do the authors relate it to their own theory about advertising?

6. What is meant by the "double symbolic process"?

7. In what ways are goods as communicators of meaning ambiguous? What do they show? What do they hide? In what ways do consumers show and hide? Do you think the analogy to the masked ball is an effective analogy for the double symbolic process?

8. If advertising fits goods with masks that "show" the possible relations between things and human needs, would you describe advertising as being informative or persuasive?

9. Do you think it is possible for a means of communication, such as advertising, to distort and misrepresent and still be a valuable and positive social force? How?

■ ■ ■ ■ ■ ■ ■ ■ ■

# ADVERTISING: STRONG FORCE OR WEAK FORCE?
## Two Views an Ocean Apart

### John P. Jones

In this article from the June 1990 issue of the *International Journal of Advertising*, John P. Jones, a professor at Syracuse University in New York, addresses the needs of graduates from advertising programs of U.S. universities. Jones argues that tomorrow's advertisers will need to approach their profession in a much more efficient and scientifically rigorous way if they are to survive and enhance their career development. Advertisers need to be able to measure the effects of their advertising much more precisely and to cut down on waste. In arguing for a change in university education, Jones details two opposing theories concerning advertising's effectiveness: what he terms the *Strong Theory* and the *Weak Theory*. As someone who has worked in the advertising business, Jones provides a useful frame of reference for analyzing the points of view of others who write about advertising.

*This article reviews the conventional view of advertising—the* **Strong Theory**—*which is all but universally believed in the United States and which*

*sees advertising as a dynamic force operating as an engine for brand inno-
vation and other types of change in the market-place. In contrast, there is the
theory developed over the years with increasing persuasiveness by Andrew
Ehrenberg of the London Business School, that sees advertising as a weak
force, one that cannot act as a prime mover in the capitalist system, but which
is used defensively by most advertisers as a means of protecting the status
quo. This essay argues that a good deal of mischief has been caused by an
uncritical belief that the* **Strong Theory** *operates in all circumstances. As a result, advertising has been associated too much with over-promise and under-
delivery. The article's focus is then directed to education for advertising as it is
carried out in American universities. It is argued that much of the research carried out in these universities is not concerned in any rigorous fashion with the
measurement of advertising's effects. Partly because of this, universities have
adhered unquestioningly to the* **Strong Theory,** *and the exclusive teaching of
this theory has led to grave deficiencies in the education of graduates from advertising programmes.*

Advertising and controversy seem to be inseparable. But there is one aspect of advertising at least about which there is very little dispute: the fact that it
accounts for very large quantities of money each year. In 1989, a sum of more
than $70 billion was spent in the United States on advertising in the main media
alone (newspapers, magazines, television, radio and billboards). This is equivalent to 1.5 per cent of the gross national product. If such an amount of money were
to be deployed in different circumstances—under an alternative type of economic
organization—it would be large enough to make a significant difference to investment levels in activities with a high social priority, such as health care or military
hardware. To this $70 billion should be added equivalent or greater investments
(albeit more difficult to estimate) devoted to what in the jargon of the business is
called 'below-the-line' activity: direct mail, and retail promotions of different types
(temporary price reductions, coupons, sweepstakes, gifts, premiums), together
with all the advertising used to support and reinforce these activities.

What return does society receive for this money and for all the noise it
generates, noise whose ubiquity acts as a constant reminder of advertising's very
considerable use of resources?

Advertising makes two contributions to society. First, it influences the individual manufacturer's sales to some degree. Sales have a multiplier effect in that
they generate incomes and total demand in the economy; and insofar as advertising does influence sales, it affects, to at least a moderate extent, the overall
level of economic activity. It has this 'macro' influence on the economy as a result
of the sum of individual 'micro' effects—those stemming from the productivity and
growth of individual firms. At the same time, advertising lubricates the competitive
system by telling consumers about the differences between competing brands.
(It should be understood that such differences are real, and that they are both
functional and non-functional.) Indeed, it would be difficult to visualize the operation of competitive capitalism without advertising. Many people including myself
believe that this type of economic organization has many advantages despite
its imperfections; and to the extent that capitalism yields a net gain in the economic and social equation (measured by the sum of its advantages over the sum
of its disadvantages), advertising is entitled to a small share of the credit. This is in

spite of the likelihood that much advertising is used defensively; it is part of the system, and not a completely unimportant part of it.

The second point about advertising is that it contributes a substantial subsidy to the media, a subsidy that is overwhelmingly, although not completely, benevolent in its social effects. The ability of the media to 'inform, educate and entertain' (to quote Reith's famous words which were used as guiding precepts at the BBC) becomes possible in the United States because of advertising dollars. However, how well the media actually succeed in carrying out these admirable tasks is a different question altogether, although the media's effectiveness is limited more by their own inefficiencies and weaknesses than by advertisers' willingness to invest the money. Advertisers do this of course to boost their own sales, but their expenditure has the side benefit of financing the media, thereby making a transfer payment to all members of society as users of television, radio, newspapers and magazines.

These two points have a general application and taken together they represent a substantial justification for at least some advertising—perhaps a moderate level of it. They cannot however be taken to extremes to justify advertising in all its aspects, and in particular to justify completely the enormous sums of money spent on it every year. Indeed, most people, including the majority of knowledgeable practitioners, acknowledge a vast degree of waste in the advertising process. The well-known aphorism attributed variously to Lord Leverhulme and John Wanamaker (Ogilvy, 1984) that 'half the money I spend on advertising is wasted, and the trouble is I don't know which half' represents, in my experience, a gross overestimate of the amount of advertising that has a discernible effect on sales. But even if this celebrated estimate that half of all advertising expenditure is wasted is anywhere near the truth, we are facing an annual wastage valued at approximately $35 billion!

It would start a lively and provocative academic debate to argue the economic advantages of cutting out advertising altogether and making advertisers send the subsidy direct to the media. (Think of the saving in salaries and in the energy of talented people, not to speak of cutting out all the irritating television advertisements we have to sit through, and eliminating the ulcers which grow so richly on Madison Avenue.) I have however resisted the temptation to take this extreme position, even for the sake of argument. But I fully intend to address the waste that we all associate with advertising, and I shall do this with the object of examining specifically the contribution that universities might make to scaling down this waste to more manageable proportions. But it is worth stating now that universities will only be able to make such a contribution if and when they move nearer to the leading edge of knowledge than they are at present. This is an important matter to which we shall return.

### 'The Power of Advertising' (Advertising Age title, 1988)

Our knowledge of advertising, in particular our knowledge of how it actually works, is extremely imperfect. Many aspects of it have been studied for a long time, but with results that are far from conclusive. One sensible inference that has been drawn from all this investigation is that certain types of advertising almost certainly work in one way, and other types in another. The case-by-case inductive approach that has been used to a limited degree is probably the way in which our corpus of reliable knowledge will be significantly augmented in the future. But the trouble is that to date we have made very little real progress along the path to enlightenment. Many people have made efforts to discover a general theory. However, the fact that none of those hypothesized have been proved to be correct suggests that the effects of advertising may eventually be demonstrated by a multiplicity of specific theories, each relating to small numbers of circumstances, rather than by any single unified theory. Recent empirical work supports this view, although it admits to important interconnections and similarities between the way advertising works in disparate cases.

An assumption underlying the majority of studies of advertising's effectiveness is that advertising *is* effective, and that we only need to develop more sophisticated measurement tools and we shall then be able to quantify the payoff. In particular, we shall do better if and when we separate more efficiently than we can at present advertising's effects from those of all the other stimuli that influence sales of a brand. Strangely enough, nobody is much interested in the circumstances in which advertising has *no* effect, although reliable knowledge of these circumstances would be very interesting to manufacturers; for if manufacturers managed to eliminate ineffective advertising, the money saved would increase profit, in some circumstances to a dramatic degree.

An instinctive (and in most cases unsubstantiated) belief in the power of advertising is a truism of the advertising business, and is an article of faith devoutly accepted by observers of all persuasions, whether defenders or opponents of the art. It permeates the trade press and also the professional schools in universities where advertising is taught. Study the following randomly selected quotations:

> Turn off the advertising spigot and see what happens to sales, production, jobs, to the all-important marketing strategy that was carefully pieced together (Danzig, 1988).

> Advertising—the use of paid media by a seller to communicate persuasive information about its products, services or organization—is a potent promotional tool (Kotler, 1984).

> The marketing process depends upon advertising and promotion for its dynamic energy (Winters and Milton, 1982).

> Radio and more especially television have . . . become the prime instruments for the management of consumer demand (Galbraith, 1978).

> (I)t is tempting to put one's faith in education, and to hope that as fresh generations grow up to be more discriminating and critically-minded in their reading, viewing and spending, the mass-persuaders will be compelled to raise their sights and to reduce their reliance upon cheap emotional manipulation (Whitehead, 1975).

> (T)he customer will be influenced by advertisement, which plays upon his mind with studied skill, and makes him prefer the goods of one producer to those of another because they are brought to his notice in a more pleasing or more forceful manner (Robinson, 1950).

Readers will have no difficulty in inferring that the first three of the above quotations were written by protagonists of advertising, and the last three by antagonists. But note the similarity in each author's belief in advertising's potency as a persuasive force. This arresting notion was first raised by Professor Andrew Ehrenberg, whose name will recur in this article. The quotations are typical of how advertising is viewed by large numbers of observers who are interested enough in the business (quite often at an emotional level) to publish their words of praise or condemnation.

Readers may also guess (although they may not be closely familiar with the work of these authors) that they are all well-known commentators on advertising, or on economic matters in which advertising plays a role. However, the authors are all either academics or journalists, and not advertising practitioners (past or present). None of them in fact has ever had to earn a living practising the business. If they had, it would have added a measure of credibility to their words, since the authors would then have been in a position to evaluate at first hand just how powerful a force advertising actually is.

Although practitioners know an insufficient amount about how advertising operates, they are, not surprisingly, more knowledgeable than lay people. In particular, they are constantly reminded that it operates in sometimes unexpected and subtle ways. Practitioners also have the great advantage over members of the general public, even intelligent and educated ones, in that their minds are less confused by the myths that advertising has always generated. The most delightful of these is surely the concept of 'subliminal' effects. These were originally the main feature of a British newspaper hoax, subsequently popularized by a journalistic book on advertising (Packard, 1979) and finally taken up—devastatingly seriously—by the American academic establishment.

## Two Theories

For obvious reasons, we can use the phrase *The Strong Theory* to describe advertising as it has been illustrated by the six quotations in the last section. The implications of this theory can be summarized along the following lines:

- Advertising increases people's knowledge and changes people's attitudes; as a result of these changes, it is capable of persuading people who had not previously bought a brand to buy it, at first once and then repeatedly.

- Advertising is a prime mover in the capitalist system and acts as a driving force for the engine of demand.

- Advertising is capable of increasing sales not only of brands but also of complete product categories (e.g., cigarettes); growth in markets is assumed to be common.

- Advertising is often able to manipulate the consumer by the use of psychological techniques that destroy the consumer's defences; in some cases these techniques are not even perceptible to the conscious mind.

- If the advertiser is to be successful, his strategic posture must generally be attacking and aggressive—he should 'sell hard' and increase advertising pressure with the expectation that sales and profits will rise as a direct consequence; as a rule repetition pays.

■ In general, consumers are apathetic and rather stupid, in line with the old adage that no one ever lost money by underestimating public taste.

It is not too extreme an extrapolation of these points to conclude that advertising deserves (depending on one's point of view) the most exalted praise for its contribution to the benefits of the capitalist system, or the most trenchant condemnation for its contribution to its evils. According to the Strong Theory, advertising plays a centrally important part in the economic system of a country like the United States.

As I have pointed out, the Strong Theory is the theory of advertising that receives the widest support, although I believe it is accepted more by default than by active endorsement. Observers of advertising, strangely enough, do not dwell on how advertising works (which is why we have learned so little that is reliable). When they do so, they are generally inclined to accept advertising as a powerful force because they have never contemplated any alternative.

There *is* however another theory which has been articulated in Europe, and which has been developed with increasing confidence and persuasiveness over the course of the last three decades. I shall call this *The Weak Theory*. It is associated virtually exclusively with the name of Andrew Ehrenberg, who holds a Research Chair at the London Business School. He is a mathematician and statistician with a formidable battery of business experience. The theory is strongly rooted in empiricism. The words Awareness-Trial-Reinforcement (A-T-R) are used to describe it. According to the Weak Theory, advertising has the following characteristics:

■ It is capable of increasing people's knowledge and stimulating trial of a brand. But consumers are not very interested in viewing/hearing/reading advertisements, most people who do so being users of the brand advertised (a phenomenon associated with selective perception). These advertising watchers already know the characteristics of the advertised brand; because of this, advertising's role in communicating information is of limited importance.

■ Advertising is not strong enough to convert people; or to persuade people whose beliefs are different from what is claimed in the advertising. Advertising is generally *not* capable of overcoming resistant attitudes. The difficulty that advertising faces is twofold. First, an advertising argument is extremely constricted (to 30 seconds—60 words—in the case of most television commercials). Second, and even more important, people very easily switch off their mental engagement (through the operation again of selective perception). Without enticing the audience, advertising cannot communicate. Without an interested audience, the advertiser will indeed find it difficult to lure and seduce, let alone browbeat.

■ Most consumer goods markets in developed countries have stopped growing except for the market increase associated with population growth; a brand can therefore only increase at other brands' expense, and manufacturers are naturally aware of this.

■ As a result, most advertising is employed defensively. This means that it is not used actively to increase sales by bringing new users to the brand advertised. It is more commonly used to retain existing users; and any advertised brand which has a significantly above-average market share benefits from an above-average frequency with which buyers buy it—something that can be stimulated by advertising. Existing users are already fairly well-disposed towards a brand (because they buy it), and advertising merely reinforces this preference. The high cost of advertising is paid reluctantly, but paid nevertheless through fear of the consequences if the advertiser were to stop or seriously reduce it. Most advertising is addressed to existing users of a brand, not least because these people are more likely to pay attention to the advertising for it. Achieving continuous business from existing users is a lucrative marketing strategy for many brands, particularly large ones, which have an extensive user base. Advertising is a driving force for continuity rather than change.

■ Advertising which attempts to operate in an opposite direction to existing psychological and behavioural tendencies is in effect attempting to fight human nature. Such advertising will not be effective, and a devastating waste of resources will result.

■ We should not forget that members of the public commonly claim to be uninfluenced by advertising. Why should we assume that they are always telling lies? Most practitioners and ex-practitioners, including myself, are only too conscious of the difficulty of persuading the public to do anything at all.

■ As stated, advertising can on occasion make people aware of a new brand or a restaging of an existing brand, and it can stimulate trial. Nevertheless, people tend to learn about new brands more from promotions (particularly sampling) and from word-of-mouth than from brand advertising (King, 1980).

■ In general, consumers are apathetic and rather intelligent.

Some readers of this article may consider the whole question of whether advertising works according to the Strong or the Weak Theory to be essentially an unimportant matter, comparable with the debates of the disputatious medieval schoolmen about how many angels can stand on the head of a pin. To most of the general public, advertising is an activity of trivial importance. They are only too conscious of the waste that is inseparable from it, and may believe instinctively that it is not worth the effort to do anything about this.

However, as a student of advertising and a former practitioner, I cannot in any way share this view. This article opened with an illustration of the massive quantity of resources devoted to advertising. The size of the investment requires that, if advertising is to be carried out at all, it should be planned and executed with the highest skills we can bring to bear, and with the most economical use of resources. It is only by doing this that the endemic waste in the system can be brought down to less unacceptable levels; and knowledge of how advertising works is a *fundamental first step* to more efficient planning of specific campaigns. What is difficult to comprehend is how a business that has been practised increasingly widely and in a supposedly increasingly sophisticated fashion for more than a century, has taken such a time to realize basic truths.

The purpose of this article is not to attempt to prove the general validity of either the Strong or the Weak Theory, although I shall shortly give a personal view. Its purpose is to consider the role of the university in advertising research and advertising education in relation to the waste engendered by the system. But before we can discuss this aspect, there are a few additional points about the Strong and Weak Theories that must be disposed of first. Let us start with some facts.

We know a number of things at a detailed level about the degree to which people respond behaviourally to advertising; and other things can be strongly inferred. However, what we know is neither comprehensive enough nor sufficiently sharply and specifically directed, to prove decisively that either the Strong or the Weak Theory is definitive. Nevertheless, a number of pieces of robust evidence can be brought to bear, and here are a few of the more important ones:

1. The vast majority of new brands fail. There is some controversy about the actual figure (depending as it does on the criterion for success or failure), but it has been estimated to be as high as 95 per cent (Jones, 1986, pp. 64–6). In many of the failures, advertising has been directly responsible; and in all other cases, advertising has not proved itself a strong enough force to compensate for other weaknesses in the marketing 'mix'.

2. There is evidence from a large sample of cases that in about 70 per cent of them, any sales effect (however small) generated by advertising is the direct and exclusive result of the amount of money that is spent. There is a good statistical regression linking variations in advertising pressure and sales, irrespective of campaign changes (Jones, 1986, pp. 88–90). The creative content (i.e., persuasive power) of the advertisements themselves does not therefore appear to exercise any influence. Furthermore, there is much experimental evidence from tests of unusually elevated advertising pressure that such increases have a disappointing effect on sales and are rarely profitable (i.e., the sales increases are very small and generate far less profit than is needed to fund the increased advertising).

3. In the market for repeat purchase packaged goods (the product category which accounts for the largest single share of total advertising dollars), consumers' purchases show an astonishing degree of regularity and predictability. In the majority of cases, each consumer during the course of a year buys a group of competing brands (known technically as the consumer's repertoire). The proportions of total purchases represented by the different brands within the repertoire show little variation over time, and new brands join the repertoire only in the most exceptional circumstances. Most significantly, it appears that the consumer's habits are a more important determinant of brand purchasing than either advertising or promotions. This has been Professor Ehrenberg's main field of study. The operational implications of his work have been discussed in my own published writing (Jones, 1986, Chapter 5). As already mentioned, the majority of individual markets for consumer goods in developed countries do not increase in size by more than one or two per cent in any year (a situation known technically as stationary conditions). This means that all marketing activity in such categories is entirely concerned with manipulating brands' market shares. Advertising is generally unable to increase the size of any market (nor does a reduction in total advertising cause a decline in the size of any market).

4. If advertising worked generally according to the Strong Theory, advertising investments would almost certainly increase continuously over time. In fact, when measured in real terms, the opposite is the case (*Advertising Age*, 17 October 1988; Jones, 1986, Chapter 11).

Where does all this wide-ranging but rather fragmentary evidence take us? I have an opinion, and although it is based on prolonged study of much empirical material, readers of this paragraph and the four succeeding ones should bear in mind that they are reading a personal view. I believe that the Strong Theory probably works in a small minority of circumstances (in certain defined product fields and with advertising employing certain specific media). However, the Weak Theory has a far wider application. It operates virtually universally in fields in which advertising investments are considerable in absolute terms—where consumer purchasing is high and where advertising is an important component of the marketing 'mix.'

But it is going too far to suggest that even in these fields the Weak Theory operates in quite the extreme way described by Ehrenberg; it is too much to claim that advertising is *never* a prime mover, *never* a dynamic force. My particular field of study is the empirical evaluation of specific cases in which advertising might be shown to have a measurable marginal effect in the market-place. Such examples are to be found in what are sometimes very important product categories, and markets like these can often be shown to contain minor dynamic elements within the overall pattern of stationary conditions (Jones, 1989). In these, advertising occasionally goes beyond the reinforcement role, and even beyond the awareness and trial roles propounded by Ehrenberg. It can exploit sales growth in a more positive way; indeed, such growth can provide advertising with a real opportunity to yield a dividend.

In these narrowly defined circumstances, advertising often has a pronounced effect, which can be accurately tracked and its results evaluated, sometimes even by a relatively precise estimate of the marginal increment of profit generated. But the circumstances in which such demonstrable results are apparent are exceptional, despite the fact that they are intensely interesting to advertising practitioners. It would be fair to say that these exceptions—important though they may be—serve generally to prove the rule, which is that in the majority of cases, advertising can be more persuasively explained by the Weak Theory than by the Strong one. Ehrenberg is generally more often right than wrong.

Where advertising can be shown to have an effect, I know large numbers of cases that demonstrate that advertising can pay for itself by achieving a behavioural response from only a tiny proportion—perhaps one per cent or less—of the audience to which it is addressed. But such a response can only be achieved by some sort of intellectual or emotional engagement; advertising must be seen and must evoke initially some psychological response. In general, strongly persuasive advertising (often called 'hard selling') cannot achieve this. Advertising normally acts as a simple and low-key reminder stimulus to purchase, so that when the consumer is next shopping for a brand in the category (ideally in the supermarket the next day), he or she will pick up the brand advertised, and not one of the two or three other brands he or she commonly uses. In most product fields, choosing one brand rather than another is not a weighty decision (it is known technically as a 'low involvement' process). Rational consideration of the pros and cons rarely takes place.

There is also evidence, certainly in the case of existing brands and established advertising campaigns, that such advertising is capable of working on a 'single exposure' basis, and fresh advertising exposures have little perceptible cumulative effect on the psyche of the consumer. The long-term effect of advertising is generally the result of repeat purchasing through habit, once an advertised brand joins a consumer's repertoire. (Repeated 'hard selling' is not only distasteful; it is unnecessary). And although advertising can on occasion communicate in subtle ways, by emphasizing certain emotional stimuli rather than others—matters which are usually carefully researched—it does not employ the black arts (e.g., 'subliminal seduction').

## 'How Ridiculously Little We Really Know Despite the Bravado of Lecture and Textbook' (Lilienthal, 1950)

It is obvious from the issues that have been discussed in this article that although we know a few things about how advertising works, we have vastly more to learn. However, it is a sad fact that American universities—the organizations that in all other fields of learning are among the leading torch-bearers in the pursuit of knowledge—are not especially interested in contributing to this particular debate. There seem to be three reasons for this.

The first reason is by far the most important. Rather surprisingly, the Weak Theory has not penetrated. It originated in Europe; and although it is believed or at least half-believed by some of the more important advertisers and advertising agencies in the United States, the theory is *terra incognita* in at least 95 per cent of business and communications schools. It is not easy to comprehend why this should be so, but I have no doubt at all that it is true, and it symbolizes in a rather dramatic fashion the position of business and communications educators in relation to the advertising profession. In all substantial respects, the profession leads and the universities follow. Most people in advertising education will find nothing uncomfortable or surprising about this. But they should consider the position of their colleagues in the natural sciences, in particular medicine. The notion that in its contributions to increasing our knowledge the work carried out in the research laboratory and the teaching hospital is less important than that done in general practice, is frankly bizarre. And yet it is accepted as the norm in advertising.

We should also remember that Ehrenberg's seminal work was carried out in an academic environment. Admittedly his work has been sponsored (both financially and through the supply of empirical data) by more than forty American and British companies, including Procter and Gamble, Colgate Palmolive, General Foods, General Mills and M. & M. Mars. But his work of analysis, synthesis and model-building was and is carried out in a place far detached physically and psychologically from the pressures of the business world. His work does however rely completely on huge data inputs from this world.

The second reason why interested parties have not pursued the Weak Theory is that some people who are aware of the theory reject it on non-rational grounds. This is true in my personal observation of people in some advertising companies and agencies, and profesional organizations—men and women whose resistance is due to their emotional commitment to the advertising enterprise. Advertising represents the mainspring of their lives and professional endeavours, and these people reject without serious examination any notion that devalues or undercuts it. I suspect that some university professors also share this view.

The third point is a very practical matter. Those universities where advertising is studied are not fully geared (technically at least) to handle the type of research needed to advance our knowledge. The advertising faculties in communications schools have developed instructional skills, but for the most part they have never practised in the professional world except perhaps as juniors or interns. As a result, they are not as conscious as are practitioners of the most salient issues that call for investigation. Not surprisingly, academics are unused to handling the data bearing on these issues (even if they manage to obtain access to it). Their own research activities range over many topics that interest them, and these are often related to advertising's social effects (although this again involves begging a question—they assume that advertising *does* have social effects.) Their inquiries are however not usually germane to improving the efficiency of professional practice. Their published work is startlingly devoid of data on the *sales* effects of advertising (American Academy of Advertising, 1988).

I believe emphatically—on the basis of the academic research I read every day from business and communications schools in all parts of the United States— that the interests of academic researchers are in fields far removed from those covered in the research that is carried out routinely by major advertisers and agencies, little of which is published. However, these latter investigations have led to the progress (small though it is) that we have made towards an understanding of advertising.

There is no point in lamenting this situation; proselytizing and crusading would be a frustrating and almost certainly fruitless endeavour. The advice I give myself is to pursue my own research which (as readers will have no difficulty in guessing) is devoted to analysing hard data from real advertisers, with the aim of exploring the Strong and Weak Theories on a case-by-case basis, and operating inductively to tease out general patterns. I shall have more to say about research, and I intend to revert to it after giving some attention to a different but closely related topic.

There is in fact a very substantive matter that leads directly out of the dispute about the relative validity of the Strong and Weak Theories—something with an immediate bearing on what goes on in universities in general and in communications schools in particular (as the places where the majority of advertising instruction is concentrated). This concerns how the controversy affects our *educational* endeavours. Are there significant differences between what we will be teaching our students according to whether our doctrine is embedded in either the Strong or the Weak Theory? I believe that there are very significant differences indeed.

Since (as explained) the Strong Theory receives by far the wider endorsement in universities, I shall first hypothesize the sorts of beliefs that graduates who have been imbued with the Strong Theory will take into the real world as part of their intellectual baggage.

Such graduates will believe instinctively in the great power of advertising. They are likely to be imaginative and have some talent; they will also be energetic and aggressive. They will be proponents of 'strong selling' as a means of switching consumers from brand to brand, and—very important—they will push the general policy of increasing advertising investments. If they manage to stay in the business, and if their professional status improves in it, their recommendations to their clients will gain progressively in weight and authority. Most of the advertising industry is not efficient at, nor very interested in, evaluating the effectiveness of campaigns in a scientific and rigorous fashion. As a result, optimism and enthusiasm may be accepted uncritically for extended periods, and the consequences of wasteful over-expenditure may take years to come home to roost.

However, in the inflationary conditions of the 1970s and with the heated competitive climate and profit pressures of the 1980s, the folly of over-promise and the gross waste to which it contributes have almost invariably become evident sooner or later. This has always seemed to me the best explanation for two unpleasant phenomena of the advertising business.

The first is the lack of stability in the relationships between clients and their advertising agencies. It is difficult to make accurate estimates of the average number of years advertisers work with their agencies, and the figures are to some extent biased by the deliberate policies of a small number of important but exceptional advertisers to build relationships which last for decades. Outside these cases, observation of the business discloses plentiful evidence of extreme volatility; there is little doubt that the average length of a manufacturer's relationship with his advertising agency is far shorter than his relationships with his other professional advisers, such as his accountants and his lawyers (Mitchell, 1988). For the agency, lost business is followed almost immediately by lost jobs.

This second phenomenon—reduced employment levels in the industry—is of considerable personal significance to the individual (and in consequence to the university that educates him or her).

There have been two other important influences on this reduction in numbers and the consequent threat to employment prospects for new graduates. The first is a lack of growth in advertising when measured in real terms (a point already mentioned). This has been caused mainly by manufacturers reducing their advertising in the main media to enable them to increase their expenditure on promotions, something that has meant in effect relatively less advertising and relatively more price-cutting. The second influence has been amalgamations between major agencies during the present decade, an important manifestation of the business's response to overall lack of growth, excessive competition and pressure on profits.

As a result of these forces in the market, the advertising business is characterized—to a far greater degree than any other business with which I am personally familiar—by abruptly and sometimes tragically terminated careers. I shall avoid dwelling on the scores, perhaps hundreds, of specific cases that I have encountered. It is enough to say that it could cause deep disquiet in all universities where advertising is taught, to contemplate the extraordinary numbers of graduates (sometimes the most promising ones) who find themselves stranded 'on the beach' in their thirties and forties, often with only the smallest prospects of re-entering the profession.

How would the situation be different if we made an effort to teach our students (at the very least) that the Weak Theory exists, and may apply to some—perhaps the majority—of the brands on which they will be working during their professional careers? I can only hypothesize the likely long-term effect of this change in our teaching emphasis, but I have not the smallest doubt that graduates would approach their professional endeavours with a far greater realism, sense of caution, and willingness to experiment.

We should begin by emphasizing to our students that advertising is a tough and competitive business to break into and in which to maintain a career with any upward progression. Although advertising is unquestionably exciting, interesting, and well-paid, it is a calling that makes high demands on brains, imagination and resilience. The first thing we should always do with our students is to test the strength of their motivation as well as their understanding of the realities of the business.

Students who comprehend the Weak Theory will also have a different and greater technical understanding of the business than have those people who understand the Strong Theory alone. Specifically they will be sceptical of the value of 'hard-sell' advertising. They will be open-minded about the possibility of increasing their clients' profits by *reducing* advertising investments. (The resultant effect on sales can be evaluated with reasonable accuracy by market-place experimentation.) They will learn to operate advertising—and also encourage their clients to operate advertising—with economy of force. They will use advertising as a rapier and not as a bludgeon. They will learn by experience and base recommendations on cool evaluation and an increasing knowledge rather than on an unremitting bullishness.

The business will almost certainly operate at a lower and less heated level than at present, with less advertising overall. The force of competition will continue strongly but will be based more on objectively verifiable performance than at present, and the probable result will be less neurosis among both clients and agencies. It is inevitable that waste will be reduced as a general result of these changes, and there will be less 'career fallout' among advertising practitioners. These changes will certainly result in significant social benefits.

One factor that is working in favour of practitioners who apply finesse and caution to their clients' advertising is the rapid decline of the agency commission system. When this system was universal, advertising agencies could only increase their incomes by persuading their clients to push up their advertising budgets. This system is giving way to greatly more sensible procedures in which agencies earn fees based on time spent on operating their clients' advertising (Weilbacher, 1983).

The methods of working described in the last three paragraphs represent major changes, and for universities to play a part we must of course tackle the problem of educating the educators before we educate the students. This brings us back to the all-encompassing role of the university, in particular in the quest for knowledge.

To my mind, it would be grossly inadequate for the university simply to learn about the Weak Theory (or any other theory) and then to teach it. The university cannot in good conscience earn its keep unless it participates in the frustration and excitement of the exploration and the discovery. It is only by doing this that the university will say anything new, and provide insights that the practitioner will be interested in sharing. I cannot see how the university can, without deep inner dissatisfaction, accept its present subordination to the practitioner, who is so clearly the person at the leading edge of knowledge. If inhabitants of the communications schools, because of weaknesses in their enterprise and skills, have to continue to accept the technical leadership of the practitioner, there is the inevitable prospect that their status will continue to sink. This will have an obvious bearing on the respect accorded to the educational programmes offered by advertising departments and in the quality of the students whom these will attract. The American advertising business in any event recruits as extensively graduates in the liberal arts as people with a more vocational education.

Unlike most schools of medicine and architecture, engineering and advanced technology, the advertising departments of university communications schools are in a position of some vulnerability, and there they will remain until at least some practitioners are persuaded to beat a path to the doors of some universities to learn something new about the 'state of the art'. The traffic is progressing too much in the opposite direction at the present time.

*REFERENCES*

*Advertising Age* (1988) Special issue title, 9 November.
*Advertising Age* (1988) Anon. (editorial) The ad 'crash' of '85, 17 October.
Danzig, F. (ed.) (1988) Advertising and progress. *Advertising Age* special issue, 9 November.
American Academy of Advertising (1988) Proceedings of the Conference.
Galbraith, J. K. (1978) *The New Industrial State*, Second Edition, p. 213. Harmondsworth, Middlesex: Penguin Books.
Jones, J. P. (1986) *What's in a Name? Advertising and the Concept of Brands*. Lexington, MA: Lexington Books.
Jones, J. P. (1989) *Does It Pay to Advertise? Cases Illustrating Successful Brand Advertising*. Lexington, MA: Lexington Books.
King, S. (1980) *Advertising as a Barrier to Market Entry*, p. 15. London: Advertising Association.
Kotler, P. (1984) *Marketing Management, Analysis, Planning and Control*, Fifth Edition, p. 658. Englewood Cliffs, NJ: Prentice-Hall.
Lilienthal, J. I. Jr. (1950) Liberal education and medicine. *Freedom and the University*, p. 89. Ithaca, NY: Cornell University Press.
Mitchell, P. (1988) Account Switching. *Journal of Advertising Research*, June/July, p. 38.
Ogilvy, D. (1984) *Confessions of an Advertising Man*, p. 59. New York: Atheneum.
Packard, V. (1979) *The Hidden Persuaders*, pp. 41–42. Harmondsworth, Middlesex: Penguin.
Robinson, J. (1950) *The Economics of Imperfect Competition*, p. 90. London: Macmillan.
Weilbacher, W. M. (1983) *Current Advertiser Practices in Compensating Their Advertising Agencies*. New York: Association of National Advertisers.
Whitehead, F. (1975) 'Advertising'. In Michael Barnes (ed.) *The Three Faces of Advertising*, p. 54. London: Advertising Association.
Winters, A. A. & Milton, S. F. (1982) *The Creative Connection*, p. 4. New York: Fairchild Publications.

## Questions for Empathy and Analysis

1. According to Jones, how is advertising a part of the system of capitalism, and how does it benefit capitalism? In his first paragraph, Jones entertains the idea that a redeployment of the billions of dollars spent on advertising to other areas of social priority, such as health care, might give us a better return on the money invested in advertising. Strategically, how does the opening paragraph work in terms of the way Jones sets up his argument?

2. If it is true, as Jones speculates, that more than half of the money spent on advertising is wasted, do you think it would make sense for advertisers to subsidize the media directly, without going to the expense of making commercials for programming? How ironic do you think Jones is when he makes this suggestion?

3. Examine your own point of view and biases about advertising. To what extent have you assumed that advertising is effective? Have you felt that this effectiveness accounted for the prevalence of advertising in the media?

4. Summarize the *Weak Theory* of advertising as Jones explains it. On the basis of your knowledge of advertising, do you think that most advertising is used defensively? Does it seem that advertisers are more concerned with keeping existing users than with attracting new ones?

5. How persuasive do you find Jones to be when he argues that practitioners of advertising are less confused about the strength and power of advertising than journalists or academics?

6. When, for Jones, is advertising most effective? Why does he believe that "hard selling" is not an effective marketing technique?

7. Why does Jones think that the *Weak Theory* has not been given much credence at universities? What are the research interests of academics in advertising? What are the consequences of academics' interests for graduates?

8. After reading Jones's article, would you advise a friend to pursue a career in advertising? Would you be more or less likely yourself to pursue such a career?

## Questions for Comparison and Synthesis

1. *(Williams–Key)* Williams claimed in 1960 that the highly organized field of market study and motivation research would have many surprises in terms of developing methods to deceive us. What developments have taken place since 1960 that seem to confirm Williams's fears? How does Key support Williams's claim? Given the technological advancements of the past 20 years, what new technological methods might be used to trick or persuade consumers?

2. *(Williams–Jhally–Steinem)* Williams claims that the borderline between advertising and ordinary news is increasingly difficult to determine. Do you think that newspaper articles, news photos, and television newscasts are objective? What determines what counts as news? Who pays for the news? Compare Williams's claim about the lack of distinction to Jhally's claims about the "blurring" effect of MTV. Compare Williams's claim about the lack of distinction to Steinem's claims about women's magazines. Watch MTV,

examine a women's magazine, and try to determine if the programs and the articles are related to the advertising placed near them. What does the relationship between programs and features suggest to you about men and women as "consumers" and about capitalism as a system of censorship and control?

3. *(Williams–Assael)* In his discussion of public relations, Williams claims that patronage is a natural extension of advertising in a society where selling has become a primary ethic. Do you think that the to- bacco companies' patronage of minority political groups and cultural events supports Williams's position that advertising is an organized system integral to our social and economic system?

4. *(Williams–Schudson)* Williams sees a consumer society and its adver- tising as interdependent, but Schudson believes that, although they are interrelated, one can separate them to analyze people's motiva- tions to buy. Do you think that human need led to the production of mild cigarettes, or did the production of mild cigarettes lead manufac- turers to create a demand for them? Could women have found other convenient and democratic means to symbolize their newfound inde- pendence? How do you think Williams would argue against Schud- son? How would Schudson argue against Williams?

5. *(Schudson–Assael)* Although some people considered cigarette smok- ing to be a health hazard even as early as the 1920s, there was little substantial evidence to document the ill effects. Nevertheless, Schud- son describes a backlash against smoking by women and says that "bills to restrict cigarette advertising were introduced in the legisla- tures in states including Illinois, Michigan, and Idaho. Efforts sprang up around the country to protest an American Tobacco billboard that featured a 'girl of tender years actually smoking cigarettes.'" In what way is this backlash similar to the backlash against Uptown described in Assael's article? How is it different?

6. *(Schudson–Assael)* How do you think Schudson would explain the role of advertising in promoting cigarettes today? Would the same argument about democratization of goods apply, or have consumer attitudes and beliefs about the symbolic value of cigarettes changed? What do you see as being the most important similarities and differ- ences?

7. *(Schudson–Assael)* Women in the 1920s began smoking in part to symbolize their freedom and independence and their equality with men. Even today, smoking remains an issue that concerns free- dom and equality. What issues of civil liberties and discrimina- tion are mentioned in Assael's article? To what extent do you think this is similar to what was happening in the 1920s? How is it different?

8. *(Schudson–Crichton)* In what ways does Crichton's position support Schudson's?

9. *(Schudson–Steinem)* Do you think Steinem would agree or disagree with Schudson's argument that advertising has a relatively small influence on the consumer behavior of women? In Steinem's view, do advertisers promote social change?

10. *(Crichton–Williams)* Crichton says that "advertising is essentially an economic process. It is not primarily a political or social process, although it has been used for both political and social ends" (192). Contrast Crichton's position with that of Raymond Williams. What are the most important lines of disagreement between them?

11. *(Crichton–Williams)* Crichton says that the more affluent a society, the more it supports institutions of the mind and spirit. How do you think Raymond Williams would respond to this statement in light of his distinction between "consumers" and "users" of goods? How does American society compare with others in terms of institutions of health care, education, welfare, and culture? Which institutions seem most progressive in relation to those of other societies? Which seem most backward? Could the economic or social role of advertising have had any impact, positive or negative, on the progress or lack of progress of any of these institutions?

12. *(Crichton–Williams)* Crichton emphasizes the freedom of choice that the public has with regard to advertising. Evaluate his argument against Raymond Williams's claim that "decision is still a function of the minority, but a new system of decision, in which the majority can be organized to this end, has to be devised" (168).

13. *(Crichton–Williams)* Crichton says that advertising is a weapon of competition but that it functions also as a safeguard. Analyze Crichton's comment about competition in relation to Raymond Williams's criticism of advertising's hostile stance toward consumers and the aggressive warlike language of "make an impact" and "smash hit." Do you think that competition can lead advertisers to be aggressive against and protective of consumers at the same time?

14. *(Jhally–Williams)* Raymond Williams provides a historical account of the development of advertising in Great Britain. If the history of advertising in the United States paralleled that of Great Britain in terms of a transformation away from isolated, local, and short informational bits of advertising to a more global, systemic mode of advertising, then is the rock video a logical extension of this change?

15. *(Jhally–Williams)* Williams writes that advertising is "the official art of modern capitalist society" and that we can understand our society if we take "advertising as a major form of social communication" (165–166). If the rock video is a form of art, what does its commercialization tell us about our society? Watch three or four rock videos on MTV, and analyze them in terms of their messages. In these videos, does the imagery support or work against the content of the songs? What social values and ideals are suggested by the content and imagery of each video? Do these values support a capitalist economy or work against it in any way?

16. *(Jhally–Schudson)* How much power do you think the rock video has to persuade viewers to buy rock albums? In terms of the rock video, would you agree with Schudson's argument that advertising usually follows cultural change rather than leading it? Did advertising follow the consumption of rock music rather than cause it? Is MTV a response to consumer needs more than it is an effort to determine those needs?

17. *(Leiss, Kline, and Jhally–Key)* Leiss, Kline, and Jhally argue that the masks of advertising hide only social processes and not deception: "While the masks are meant to influence consumer behavior, it is certain that they do not and cannot control it" (236). What reasons do the authors give for their belief? How would Wilson Bryan Key respond to this claim and the reasons supporting it? Which position seems to make more sense to you? Why?

18. *(Leiss, Kline, and Jhally–Steinem)* Leiss, Kline, and Jhally argue that the world of goods is structured by distorted communication. Steinem supports their argument when she quotes Joseph Smith of Oxtoby-Smith Inc.,who claims that "broadly speaking, there is no persuasive evidence that the editorial context of an ad matters" (207). In what other ways does Steinem's article support the arguments of Leiss, Kline, and Jhally?

19. *(Steinem–Jones)* How do you think Steinem would respond to Jones's claim that the ability of the media to educate and inform "becomes possible in the United States because of advertising dollars" (239). Would she agree with Jones that the subsidy to the media is benevolent in its social effects?

20. *(Jones–Key–Leiss, Kline, and Jhally)* How persuasive do you find Jones to be when he argues that practitioners of advertising are less confused about the strength and power of advertising than are journalists or academics? What do you think his attitude would be toward Key's arguments concerning subliminal seduction? What do you think his attitude would be toward Leiss, Kline, and Jhally's arguments, especially in light of his comment that academics are not interested in the issues that call for investigation?

Jones claims that the academics' "own research activities range over many topics that interest them, and these are often related to advertising's social effects (although this again involves begging a question—they assume that advertising *does* have social effects)" (247). Whose authority on these matters would you rely on more: the practitioners' or the academics'? Who do you think is likely to be more objective?

21. (*Jones–Steinem*) In what ways does Steinem's article support the *Weak Theory* of advertising? According to Jones, how does advertising work as a "driving force for continuity rather than change" in terms of women's roles (243)?

22. (*Jones–all other Chapter Six authors*) Which of the authors you have read in this chapter implicitly support the *Strong Theory* of advertising as Jones describes it? Which of the authors implicitly support the *Weak Theory*?

# Chapter Seven

# RESEARCHING THE

# ARGUMENTATIVE PAPER

*All language is "new" and "used" at once.*

*David Bleich*

In this quotation from *The Double Perspective* (120), David Bleich, an English professor, invites us to consider language in two ways simultaneously. Once you begin researching and writing multiple-source papers, you will have a better feel for how language is both "new" and "used" at once. When you wrote papers in high school using sources such as magazines, newspapers, and books, you probably reported what you had discovered by summarizing, paraphrasing, and quoting the ideas of others. Your efforts were more of a reuse of language than an original and "new" formulation of it. At the college level, you continue to refine those skills that enable you to summarize, paraphrase, and quote effectively. But you also develop skills of finding sources and of analyzing and synthesizing arguments. All of these skills combined enable you to contribute your own "new" thoughts on a topic. The key to writing a successful college paper is to demonstrate that you have gathered sources with strong arguments reflecting multiple points of view and have, after reading and thinking about the arguments, formed your own perspective.

Some college students feel paralyzed when they first confront the multiple opinions of experts and professionals. Faced with scholarly ideas and the polished prose of practiced writers, you may feel that the best you can do is to string citations together, borrowing a line from this source and a paragraph from that. This chapter focuses on skills that will enable you to control the research process rather than having it control you—skills such as using research to brainstorm; finding a topic; searching for argumentative works in indexes, card catalogs, and sources outside the library; avoiding plagiarism; and documenting sources.

When you research a paper, you become involved in a sustained process of gathering, selecting, and responding to information and ideas. Generally, you evolve a topic of interest or question for inquiry from course materials and then seek additional sources on the topic. But you may soon discover how difficult finding sources can be. The college library can seem an obstacle course of electronic data bases, indexes, references, and filing systems that hold the lock and key to dusty tomes in labyrinthine corridors. And even direct interviews or empirical observation seem hard when you consider the hassles of setting up appointments or establishing controls and sampling procedures. Given such obstacles, you may flounder in the preliminary stages of your project and write papers without the benefit of the best sources or sufficient data. But if you spend time learning how the library is organized and learning procedures for gathering data, you will improve the quality of your research. We aim to inform you about what the library has to offer as well as to explain the active critical thinking that goes on while you conduct a library search. Once you are aware of strategies for selecting sources, library research need not be a nightmare; research can open exploration, discovery, and even adventure.

## ■ ■ ■ ■ ■ USING RESEARCH TO BRAINSTORM

Just as the experienced writer uses the process of writing as a tool for discovering and developing ideas, so too does the experienced researcher use the process of gathering information as a tool for learning and brainstorming on ideas for a topic. The first stage of the writing process is known as the *invention stage*; research is a vital component of that stage. In choosing a topic to research, begin with some initial interests and questions to give the research direction. Early in your research, you can define possible topics rather broadly. Your research will provide you with additional information and insights to help you narrow a topic to a more suitable size for the assignment. Once you have discovered information on the topic, you may decide to shift the emphasis of the initial questions or to change to another topic altogether.

Your research will be more focused and fruitful if you begin by asking yourself a series of questions on the research topic. The place where you begin your research in the library, whether it is the reference room, the indexes, the online catalog, or the periodicals, depends in part on the type of information you are seeking. Start by asking yourself about the kind of information you need (e.g., facts, opinion, analysis) and about the subject(s) or subject disciplines that are relevant to your topic. Will you need historical information or the most current information?

You can determine the kind of information you need by doing some preliminary research in the reference section of your library. Encyclopedias can familiarize you with the terminology, trends, concepts, and facts of a topic. Encyclopedia entries also often contain bibliographies that can lead you to useful sources of information. Encyclopedias are most useful when they are consulted as an initial step in a more lengthy research process to gain an overview on a topic. For example, if you were writing a paper on the Persian Gulf War in Iraq and Kuwait, you may consult the *Encyclopedia Americana* to get a sense of the history, culture, peoples, natural resources, and economy of these two countries, along with some initial references to general books published on them.

You are probably already familiar with general encyclopedias such as the *World Book Encyclopedia*, the *New Encyclopaedia Brittanica*, and *Collier's*. Although these encyclopedias may be good places to begin, their entries tend to be too brief to serve the purposes of college research. But there are numerous specialized encyclopedias that concentrate on specific subject areas that can help you to gain background information as well as references to other sources. Among these specialized encyclopedias are those for such disciplines as philosophy, psychology, and the social sciences. Once you identify the discipline(s) relevant to your topic, it will be useful for you to consult these encyclopedias. For example, if you are interested in pursuing the topic of aboriginal music in Australia, the *New Grove Dictionary of Music and Musicians* would be the best place for you to begin. Notice that the term *dictionary* is often used synonymously with *encyclopedia* because both tend to be arranged alphabetically.

There are also specialized encyclopedias on different cultural groups, ethnic groups, and other groups of people. Two examples are the *Dictionary of Black Culture* and *Women's Studies*. Some encyclopedias, such as the *Quotable Woman*, *Rock Record*, and *Homosexuality: A Research Guide*, are highly specialized. The librarian at your reference desk can provide a list of the encyclopedias your library holds and advise you which ones are likely to be most useful.

EXERCISE

1. In a group of three or four students, generate approximately six to eight general subjects of interest to the group. After class hours, go as a group to the reference section of your campus library and find dictionaries and encyclopedias that seem to be promising sources of information. As a group, generate a list of the best reference works for each subject. Appoint a recorder for the group who will explain briefly in writing why you found each work helpful.

# ■ ■ ■ ■ ■   NARROWING A TOPIC FOR THE ARGUMENTATIVE PAPER

Having brainstormed on a broad topic of interest, you now need to evolve some **inquiry questions** that are open to differences of opinion and that lead to a range of possible answers. If a question that you evolve on your topic leads to obvious or indisputable answers, then you probably should abandon it. For example, a student named Greg was interested in the topic of steroids, and his question for inquiry was, "Are steroids harmful?" He discovered with some preliminary research an overwhelming body of data showing that steroids can cause acne, impotence, and a number of other health problems. If Greg had narrowed his topic further and written a paper using this question, he would have written a report about the harm steroids can cause instead of an argumentative paper. Although some questions can lead to dead ends, others can lead to argumentative inquiry. Greg recast his question into, "What policies should sports programs implement in order to monitor possible steroid use by athletes?" This question led him to speculate on possible differences of opinion and directed his research into sports administration, taking him away from research into medical findings on the effects of steroid use. Greg was still able to use his preliminary research, however, because while pursuing this research he had discovered that medical tests for steroid use would fail if those tested had refrained from using steroids a day or two before the test was given. His medical data could support a position in favor of mandatory unannounced testing. Sometimes even false leads can yield valuable, useful information.

Although the ideas you already have on your topic may give you some clues to what may be most worthwhile or controversial, learning a few invention strategies can help you to think systematically about potential ways of formulating a research question and of exploring and developing your paper. Writers develop arguments through reason and evidence, and they employ methods that are best suited to their topics. Knowing these methods can help you to brainstorm systematically and strategically.

Particular types of inquiry questions can help you direct your research and focus your topic. These questions emphasize defining a topic, comparing it to something else, and analyzing cause-and-effect. The questions are: (1) "What is X?" (2) "What is X like or not like?" and (3) "What are the causes of X?" or "What does X cause?"

1. The **definition question,** or "What is X?" invites you to think about the meaning of terms. As an invention strategy, the definition question looks beyond an obvious clarification of terms. The definition question helps you to focus on those words and meanings that are open to dispute and that must be stipulated in a given way in order to develop your argument. People do not argue about dictionary definitions, but they do argue about the more

general significance of human relationships, especially when such significance has a bearing on the outcome of their arguments.

For example, the topic of surrogate motherhood can be explored productively using the definition questions, "What is a surrogate mother?" or "What is a mother?" The answer to either question is open to dispute. Can a mother be called a "surrogate" if she is in fact the genetic mother of a child? The answer to this question had definite legal as well as psychological implications for Mary Beth Whitehead. Phyllis Chesler, in *The Sacred Bond*, asks a series of definition questions that model an effective use of this invention strategy:

> Who is a child's true mother? The woman who gives birth to her? Or the woman married to the child's father? The woman who actually takes care of her? Or the woman who can offer her the most money?
>
> Is a child's true mother really her father? Does a child need a biological mother, if her father wants to take exclusive care of her—without involving any women?
>
> Are most biological mothers "unfit" or are they less fit than genetic fathers or adoptive mothers? Should biological motherhood be abolished in the "best interests" of the child? What is a "fit" mother? Who should decide? (92)

Chesler's answers to these questions are vital to the development of her argument against surrogate motherhood. And the way that she asks the questions implies that she has already answered them in a certain way, for the framing of the questions is slanted to reinforce her viewpoint. In her finished piece of writing, she organizes the questions as a rhetorical and persuasive strategy, but at some point in her initial research, she probably asked herself these definition questions in a more open-ended and exploratory way. Chesler provides a good illustration of the way that invention strategies may themselves be later translated into rhetorical, persuasive strategies in developing an argument while writing a paper.

Definition questions about surrogate motherhood are good examples of questions which cannot be answered by using a dictionary. The criteria for defining a "mother" or "surrogacy" are not absolute and are open to debate. The authors who write on this issue and focus on the meaning of surrogacy must establish the criteria they find to be most relevant, and these criteria will be useful in furthering the positions they take. Phyllis Chesler defines a mother in biological terms and emphasizes the sacred bond that is created through the act of giving birth and nursing a child. Her definition furthers her position that surrogacy should be outlawed, because she believes we should not rationalize away something so essential to our humanity.

Against Chesler's definition, authors Isadore Schmukler and Betsy P. Aigen in "The Terror of Surrogate Motherhood" define surrogacy as the triumph of reason and humanity over the limitations of biology:

> If a woman sees herself as a stand-in or double for another woman for whom she is bearing the child, and feels from the beginning of conception that this child belongs to the other woman and her husband, the biological father, rather than to herself, what type of abandonment is this? It is because the woman has chosen to biologically substitute for an infertile woman less fortunate than herself that she defines the experience for herself as an act of "giving" rather than "giving away" and rejecting a child. (138)

By arguing that surrogacy is an act of self-definition for the surrogate mother, Schmukler and Aigen can themselves define *surrogacy* as an act of liberation rather than an act of oppression. If you choose to write on surrogate motherhood, you may also want to consider these issues of definition.

Some topics lend themselves to questions of definition more so than others. When you choose a topic that interests you, determine whether definition questions are pertinent for the purpose of exploring your topic. Sometimes, even if they are pertinent and help you to explore your topic, you may finally decide that you want to develop your paper using other kinds of argumentative strategies.

Asking questions of definition as an invention strategy helps an author to establish useful criteria for the meaning that is in dispute. These criteria are usually not "necessary" criteria. It may be necessary for animals to have hair and nourish their young with milk to be defined as mammals, but this is not an issue for argumentation. Arguments tend to focus on criteria that are stipulated as being "sufficient" to define a thing or concept. For example, you could argue that for a woman to be defined as a *mother*, it is sufficient for her to raise and love a child. Someone else might argue that for a woman to be defined as a *mother*, it is sufficient for her to give birth to a child. You will achieve clarity in your exploration of a topic if you try to separate the criteria that seem relevant and analyze them as independent variables.

2. **The comparison question**, or "What is X like or not like?" invites you to think about analogies. In an analogy, two or more X's—where each X may be something as complicated as an event or as simple as an object— are shown to be alike in several ways. From this similarity it is inferred that they are alike in other ways as well. For example, in his article "Death and Justice: How Capital Punishment Affirms Life," which appeared in *The New Republic*, Ed Koch, the former mayor of New York City, draws an analogy between executing a convicted criminal and finding a cure for cancer:

Admittedly, capital punishment is not a pleasant topic. However, one does not have to like the death penalty in order to support it any more than one must like radical surgery, radiation, or chemotherapy in order to find necessary these attempts at curing cancer. Ultimately we may learn how to cure cancer with a simple pill. Unfortunately, that day has not yet arrived. Today we are faced with the choice of letting the cancer spread or trying to cure it with the methods available, methods that one day will almost certainly be considered barbaric. But to give up and do nothing would be far more barbaric and would certainly delay the discovery of an eventual cure. The analogy between cancer and murder is imperfect, because murder is not the "disease" we are trying to cure. The disease is injustice. (13)

Arguments based on analogies are never watertight because there are usually differences as well as similarities between the two things being compared. Still, if there are enough similarities in the comparison, analogies can be very persuasive, even though the reader needs to make an inductive leap from one point to another. Also, analogies can help a reader to see from a fresh perspective. Koch's argument from analogy helps the reader to consider the truth of the paradox that putting murderers to death affirms life. And, to keep the analogy from leaking, he skillfully anticipates an objection the reader may have. But to finally be persuaded, the reader must accept not only that cancer is like the injustice of murder but also that capital punishment is related to the injustice of murder in the same way that chemotherapy is related to cancer—that is, that capital punishment can function as *the* cure for murder.

By asking comparison questions about your own topic, you can invent new arguments. For example, if you are writing on the topic of surrogate motherhood, ask: What is surrogate motherhood like? Or, what issues concerning surrogate motherhood are like other issues that women face in similar situations? Although your answers to these questions may not finally take you in the direction for argumentation that you think is best, at least they allow you to explore a fuller range of possible arguments. The resemblance question on the issue of surrogate motherhood is one that seemed promising to Phyllis Chesler. In *The Sacred Bond*, Chesler pursues the analogy between a surrogate mother who gives up her child and a mother who gives up her child for adoption. She provides evidence for the long-term pain that women suffer when they give up a child for adoption. She argues, by analogy, that the surrogate mother, even if she feels positive about giving up the baby, will probably suffer the same agony. For Chesler, brainstorming on the resemblance question gave her strong arguments for her position against surrogate motherhood.

3. **The cause-and-effect questions** "What are the causes of X?" or "What does X cause?" are also powerful for inventing ideas on a

topic. These questions can lead you to arguments that show relationships between cause and effect. Such arguments are chronological in emphasis, for they show how past or current events are related to present or future events. They try to demonstrate that a particular cause has led or will lead to a particular effect or that a particular effect has happened because of a particular cause.

Some topics lend themselves well to cause-and-effect analysis. For example, the question of whether to legalize drugs in the United States has to be answered with demonstrations of relationships between cause and effect. If you have chosen this topic, you can brainstorm productively by exploring as many cause-and-effect relationships as you can think of. For example: Has the fact that drugs are illegal led to more crime and drug abuse, or less? Would making drugs legal lead to an increase of crime and drug abuse? When brainstorming on these questions, you need to decide which questions seem to be the most promising. After brainstorming, you may decide that your best approach will be to argue from past causes to present effects—for example, that making drugs illegal has led to a significant increase in organized crime and that crime is the issue to be addressed. Or you may decide to argue from present causes to future effects—for example, that the current illegality of drugs may have contributed to crime but that it has contained drug abuse. You may project that legalizing drugs would increase drug abuse and addiction enormously, and for this reason, you would adopt the position that drugs should not be legalized.

Asking questions about cause and effect can help you to open up a topic in ways you had not considered previously. Whether you decide to argue from present effects to past causes or from present causes to future effects will depend on the strength of the evidence you find. Although some causes lead necessarily to certain effects (e.g., placing wood in a fire will cause it to burn), such necessary relationships are rarely found in argumentative writing. If they were, you probably would not have anything to argue about! Instead, cause-and-effect relationships usually hinge on partial causes, or on more than one cause leading to an effect, or on a cause leading to more than one effect.

To illustrate this complexity, consider again the question of whether drugs should be legalized in the United States. Does the illegality of drugs have a cause-and-effect relationship on actual drug use? Do people use drugs because drugs are forbidden? Perhaps some people want to try things they are prohibited from doing. In analyzing this cause-and-effect relationship, ask if desiring the forbidden is in itself enough to guarantee drug abuse. Are there other reasons people may use drugs? Considering other possible causes may make it clearer that, although desiring the forbidden may be cause enough, there are probably other causes for drug use as well, such as emotional distress, poverty, and illness. And even though there may be evidence supporting a link between this cause and its effect, there is no necessary connection between them. People may desire the forbidden, but they will not necessarily incur the risk of criminal charges in order to act on their desires. Although the limitations of this cause-and-effect link become evident from such considerations, you do not have to rule out using it altogether. The evidence you provide in support of the argument can make it seem more plausible and probable to your reader. Although the argument has limitations, it may be effective if you support it with evidence and combine it with other arguments in support of the position.

EXERCISES

1. Read over the following inquiry questions on contemporary American issues:
   a. Should the sale of handguns be prohibited?
   b. Should the sale of drugs such as cocaine or heroin be legalized?
   c. Should the sale of pornographic materials that use children be banned?
   d. How should genetic engineering be regulated?
   e. Should English be the national U.S. language?
   f. What are the limits of free speech?
   g. Is legislation for "comparable worth" a workable means of achieving equal pay?
   h. Should it be legal for homosexuals to marry?

   On which of these issues would you want to ask questions of definition? Of resemblance or comparison? Of cause and effect? Discuss these issues and then write two questions of definition, comparison, or cause and effect for each topic—whichever kind you think is best suited for the topic. In a small group of three to five students, pool all the questions for each topic. As a group, make a list of the questions you think would be most useful to help a writer develop arguments about the topic.

2. Evolve three inquiry questions on topics that interest you. In a small group of three to five classmates, share your inquiry questions and together analyze (a) whether they are open to differences of opinion and belief and (b) whether they lead to different possible answers needing support of evidence and reason. Each member of the group should then rank all the inquiry questions according to their potential for developing arguments.

3. Choose an inquiry question that you are interested in answering. In a small group, share your inquiry questions with the other members. Then, as a group, brainstorm collectively and write questions of definition, comparison, and/or cause and effect for each inquiry question. As a group, determine which kinds of invention strategies and questions would work best for each inquiry question.

# ■ ■ ■ ■ ■ SEARCHING FOR ARGUMENTATIVE WORKS IN INDEXES

Once you have chosen the one or two inquiry questions that seem most promising or interesting to you, you are ready to begin searching for argumentative works in indexes at the library. Although encyclopedias and general reference works can provide background information that will help you determine your inquiry questions, these sources are not as likely to help you search for arguments related to your topic. To find arguments, you need to search indexes that can help you find magazine and journal articles, newspaper articles, and books.

Strategically, you can begin your search by looking at indexes of periodicals (i.e., indexes of magazines and journals that are published periodically) rather than at the on-line catalog for books, since the argumentation in book-length studies is often more complicated, lengthy, and sustained than that in magazine articles and scholarly journals. If you gather books in these initial stages, you may feel overwhelmed and spend too much time reading them and sifting out relevant ideas. However, collections of articles in book form can be useful. Looking for collections in books may be a logical step after searching indexes of articles.

Many students begin, as they did in high school, by looking at the *Readers' Guide to Periodical Literature*. Although indexes for magazines and popular journals may also be a good place to begin at the college level, you will probably overlook the important reliable sources in more scholarly periodicals if you end your research with these indexes. Make a point, then, of checking at least two or three indexes other than the *Readers' Guide*. Browse through the index section of your library. Libraries' indexes are grouped by subject areas, such as history, education, and general indexes. Once you have familiarized yourself with the indexes in your library, you will have a better sense of what your options are. If you still are unable to find a more specialized index for your topic, do not hesitate to ask the reference librarian for help. For any given research topic, you will probably find both basic and specialized index tools that will be useful. To give you a sense of what kinds of general indexes your library is likely to have, we include the following annotated list:

## Indexes to Periodicals and Newspapers

### GENERAL

*Readers' Guide to Periodical Literature*. Available in most libraries on computer terminals, the *Readers' Guide* indexes popular magazines such as *Time* and *Sports Illustrated* and covers all fields.

*Magazine Index*. Indexing more than twice as many popular "newsstand" periodicals as does the *Readers' Guide*—more than 400—its comprehensiveness makes it a useful reference. If the *Magazine Index* is not available in your library on a computer database, it is probably available on microfilm.

*Academic Index.* This index complements the *Magazine Index*, both of which are published by the Information Access Company. The *Academic Index* expands the coverage found in the *Magazine Index* by providing references in art, anthropology, economics, education, ethnic studies, government, history, literature, political science, science, psychology, religion, sociology, and leisure. Its coverage represents the most commonly held periodical titles in over 120 university and college libraries.

*NewsBank.* *NewsBank* accesses articles from newspapers in over 450 U.S. cities. It also provides full-text articles selected from the newspapers on the basis of their research value. These full-text articles are printed on microfiche each month. A printed index to the microfiche is published monthly.

*National Newspaper Index.* This resource covers the *Christian Science Monitor*, the *Los Angeles Times*, the *New York Times*, the *Wall Street Journal*, and the *Washington Post*.

## EDUCATION

*Current Index to Journals in Education.* Begun in 1969, it covers approximately 760 major education and education-related journals. It is part of the ERIC family of reference publications sponsored by the Educational Resources Information Center.

*Education Index.* If you need to take a historical approach to your subject, you will find this index useful because it dates back to 1929. The *Education Index* includes such subject areas as administration, pre-school through adult education, teacher education, counseling services, computers in education, health and physical education, library and information science, multicultural and ethnic education, special education, and rehabilitation.

*ERIC: Educational Resources Information Center.* The National Institute of Education of the U.S. Department of Education has been compiling this index since 1964. The ERIC database can at first seem complicated to use, but it is worth learning the procedure. To use ERIC, you begin with the *ERIC Thesaurus* of descriptors, which provides subject headings and cross-references. These subject headings help you to use the *RIE: Resources in Education* index, which provides both titles and abstracts for articles. By reading the abstracts for the titles that seem promising, you can save time because the abstracts summarize articles. After deciding which articles you want, you can go to the journals or to the microfiche to read the complete articles.

## HUMANITIES

*Humanities Index.* Covering approximately 350 English-language periodicals in the fields of archaeology, area studies, classical studies, folklore, history, journalism, language and literature, political criticism, performing arts, philosophy, and theology, it indexes interviews, reviews, and bibliographies as well as articles.

*MLA International Bibliography.* This index falls within the broader field of the humanities and focuses more specifically on critical articles on literary works in the modern languages.

*Historical Abstracts.* It contains abstracts to scholarly articles on world history, excluding American history, from more than 2,100 journals published in over 80 countries.

*America: History and Life.* Abstracting and indexing scholarly articles on American and Canadian history, area studies, and current affairs literature, it covers history related to interdisciplinary studies and topics in the social sciences.

## LAW

*Legal Resources Index.* Compiled by the American Association of Law Libraries, this index covers nearly 800 legal periodicals.

*Monthly Catalog of the United States Government Publications.* Dating back to 1895, it includes references to congressional debates and hearings, decisions by the Supreme Court and other federal courts, and documents issued by executive departments and the office of the president.

## SOCIAL SCIENCES

*Social Sciences Citation Index.* This tool indexes scholarly English-language periodicals in the fields of anthropology, area studies, community health and medical care, consumer affairs, human ecology, economics, environmental studies, geography, gerontology, international relations, law and criminology, minority studies, nursing, pharmacology, police science and corrections, policy sciences, political science, psychiatry, psychology, public administration, social work and public welfare, sociology, and urban studies.

*Sociofile.* It contains abstracts to articles in over 1,500 journals in sociology.

*Public Affairs Information Service Bulletin.* This index covers the areas of public policy and political and international affairs more fully than the *Social Sciences Index.*

*PsycINFO.* This database, the most comprehensive index for psychology, is published by Psychological Abstracts Information Services. To use the database you must begin with its special thesaurus of descriptors to find subject headings that will work for retrieval of abstracts.

## HEALTH SCIENCES

*Index Medicus.* The most comprehensive index for the health sciences, it covers articles in approximately 3,000 journals.

SCIENCES

*General Science Index.* Although you cannot search it by author, only by subject, the *General Science Index* covers periodicals in the fields of astronomy, atmospheric sciences, biological sciences, botany, chemistry, earth sciences, environment and conservation, food and nutrition, genetics, mathematics, medicine and health, microbiology, oceanography, physics, physiology, psychology, and zoology.

*Applied Science and Technology Index.* Although you can search it only by subject, the *Applied Science and Technology Index* covers the fields of aeronautics, chemistry, computer technology, construction industry, electricity, energy research, engineering, environmental sciences, fire prevention, food industry, geology, industrial and mechanical arts, machinery, mathematics, metallurgy, oceanography, petroleum and gas, physics, plastics, telecommunications, textile industry and fabrics, and transportation.

## Additional Indexes

BUSINESS

*Business Periodicals Index*

BIOGRAPHY

*Biography and Genealogy Master Index*

HUMANITIES

*Art Index*
*Index to Art Periodicals*
*Film Literature Index*
*International Guide to Classical Studies*
*International Bibliography of Historical Sciences*
*Music Article Index*
*Popular Music Periodical Index*
*Index to Religious Periodical Literature*
*Philosopher's Index*
*Index to Black Periodicals*

LAW

*Index to Legal Periodicals*

SOCIAL SCIENCES

*Anthropological Index*
*Population Index*

*International Bibliography of Economics*
*International Bibliography of Political Science*
*Environment Index*
*Sociological Abstracts*
*International Bibliography of Sociology*
*Women's Studies Abstracts*
*Alternative Press Index*

SCIENCES

*Biological and Agricultural Index*
*Biological Abstracts*
*BioResearch Index*
*Chemical Abstracts*
*Computer and Control Abstracts*
*Bibliography and Index of Geology*
*Physics Abstracts*

## Computer Databases

Computers are powerful tools for researchers, enabling them to find more sources in far less time than formerly. You can find more sources than you would doing a manual search because computer databases can rapidly cross-reference you to related subject headings. In this way you can find related works under headings you might not even have considered. Some databases are able to search by keyword, so that you can locate a word appearing in a title or bibliographic entry. This capability enables you to locate possibly relevant sources even when you do not have the exact citations or know the subject headings. Computer searches are also more efficient than manual searches in a number of ways. Instead of checking each annual volume of an index for all the relevant citations over the course of a few years, you now may find all of those in the past five to ten years just by touching a few keys. Most computers are connected to printers, and you can quickly print out the citations you want. The time you spend learning the search functions of a given database will richly reward you by providing efficient and effective access to the sources you need.

The *Readers' Guide to Periodical Literature* is now available in many libraries either through a database called *InfoTrac General Periodicals Index* or the *Wilson Database*. These databases may be available either online, with computer terminals linked by telephone lines to the service, or on disk. Your library will have a number of databases that you can use free of charge; it is worth checking to see which ones are available.

Your library may subscribe to the *Dialog Information Retrieval Service*, the most powerful online service of them all. Through the Dialog Service you can access more than 380 databases, including databases that contain the complete text of books, journals, and newspapers. In addition to full-text sources such as the *King James Bible, Motortrend, Who's Who in America*, and *AP (Associated Press) News*, you can access directories such as *Books in Print, Peterson's College Database*, and *Ulrich's International Periodicals Directory*. And there are scores and scores of bibliographic databases, including indexes such as *Chemical Abstracts, Child Abuse and Neglect, Dissertation Abstracts Online, Medline*, and *Nursing and Allied Health*. You may have to pay a fee to use the Dialog Service, but the time you save will reward your investment.

If you discover that the source you are looking for is not available in your library, you may be able to find it in another library in your region by searching in a computer database called the Online Computer Library Center (OCLC). Nearly 4,000 libraries participate in this shared-cataloging network, making it easy to see which of them owns a source. (Records in the OCLC can be searched by author or title only.) Once you discover who holds a source, you may be able to have it sent to your library through an interlibrary loan.

Although each database has its own particular capabilities and key functions, which are usually explained by a tutorial program built into the index, some general features tend to be common to all computer databases, including the computerized version of your library's card catalog. In a database, items of information are stored according to fields. A database that indexes articles and books contains the fields of subject, author, title, and keyword. You can search within a field, a very simple procedure if you are looking for a single subject, author, or title. You can also search within a field by combining items. For example, you can link two subject headings in the subject field. You can also search by combining fields. When you want to link items within a field or to link two fields, you must use logical and positional operators.

The logical (or Boolean) operators AND, OR, and NOT make computer searches more precise by searching for overlapping categories, inclusive categories, or exclusive categories. When searching within a field, you can link two items with AND, and the computer will retrieve only those citations referenced by both terms. The operator OR is useful when you want to expand a search, since it retrieves records that contain any of the terms separated by OR in the search statement. The operator NOT helps to exclude information.

The positional operators SAME, WITH, and ADJ help to make a search statement even more specific by linking terms that are often found in close proximity to each other. The operator SAME searches for terms $X$ and $Y$ in the same field. This operator is especially useful when you are searching by keyword through titles, abstracts, or subject headings. The operator WITH specifies that terms $X$ and $Y$ must be found in the same sentence or subject heading. The operator ADJ searches for terms $X$ and $Y$ when they are adjacent to each other. Logical and positional operators are useful when you search within a field, and you can also use them to gather records from more than one field at a time.

Libraries of the future will certainly contain many full-text databases. One can imagine a library in the not too distant future that has no books at all! Although some people may find this to be a sad thought, full-text databases may finally be the key to preserving our libraries' holdings. Each year, millions of books on acid paper disintegrate because of oxidation, and many are lost forever, just as absolutely as the books of the Alexandrian library were lost to us when the Roman Emperor Aurelian razed it early in his reign, around 270 A.D.

■ ■ ■ ■ ■   SEARCHING YOUR LIBRARY'S CATALOG

After you have checked indexes to magazines, popular and scholarly journals, and newspapers, and have pursued whatever leads they offer, you will be in a much better position to search the card catalog or its electronic version in your library. Reading articles may help you to define and clarify your topic further. As you read, jot down keywords that can lead you to related subject headings relevant to your topic.

### The *Library of Congress Subject Headings*

Before you begin a search of works catalogued in your library, look in the three-volume *Library of Congress Subject Headings* (LCSH), located near the card catalog. Computer catalogs for libraries use the LCSH in their subject fields. If you type in a subject and it is not there, you can check the LCSH to find subjects that will work. The three LCSH volumes contain the standardized headings that librarians have evolved to catalog the holdings of libraries in the United States. These volumes are particularly useful in determining the exact spelling and word choice for subjects in which you are interested. Your knowledge of Library of Congress subject headings is crucial for your search in the card catalog or online catalog. It is also helpful when you are using basic indexes to journals because many, though not all, of these indexes use the Library of Congress subject headings for their vocabulary control. You can probably save time if you begin your search by looking in the LCSH.

Imagine, for example, that you are researching the topic of marijuana and its legalization. If you type in "marijuana" as a subject on the online catalog of your library's holdings, you will be disappointed because the LCSH spells this "marihuana." But if you first look up "marijuana" in the LCSH, you will find the direction "USE marihuana."

The LCSH can also help you to narrow your choice of search terms for your subject so that you find the most relevant information efficiently.

For example, a student, Joshua, is interested in writing a research paper on the topic of prejudice and the ways that people are stereotyped and labeled. He has decided to focus on the negative prejudicial names that people call one another, names like "nigger," "wop," "chick," "kike," and "spick." But when he types in the search term "name" as a subject on the online catalog, he finds to his dismay that there are more than 900 items in the subject guide under this subject heading, and, as he begins to scan through the guide display, he sees that most of the subheadings deal with names of nationalities, such as "African," "Ainu," "Anglo-Saxon," "Celtiberian," and "Circassian." Because his computer screen will list only 18 of these subheadings at once, it would take him a long time to scan through to see if there are any subheadings related to his topic. A quick check of the LCSH yields useful information to help him narrow his subject heading. There Joshua finds the subject "Names" (see Figure 7.1). As he scans through all the related subject subheadings, he finds "RT Epithets," which indicates to him that he could look up the related term "epithets" in the LCSH. To find out what "epithet" means, he looks up the word in the dictionary and finds that one sense of the word means an abusive word or phrase. He concludes that "epithets" may lead him to items dealing with pejorative, prejudiced names. He also finds "Ethnic Names" in the LCSH and learns he could use the term "Names, Ethnological."

## Subject, Author, and Title

With the information gleaned from the LCSH, Joshua can now go back to the online catalog and type in subjects or identify numbered lines on the guide display of subject headings that provide more promising leads to the information he seeks. If, for example, Joshua types in the subject "epithets," he will find the following work among the sources listed on his screen: Allen I.L., *The Language of Ethnic Conflict*. When Joshua commands the computer to give him more information on this work, a bibliographic record display appears (Figure 7.2). If Joshua looks in the card catalog for the subject card "Epithet," he will find the Allen work listed there also. Both the computer bibliographic record display and the subject card include at the bottom the related subject headings under which this work is categorized. The title page of the book also includes this information. (Sometimes, the card or the display indicates that a book contains a bibliography. A book's bibliography may provide additional sources of information by listing relevant authors and titles of works, so it is helpful to notice.)

Before you begin your own search for subjects on the computer, consult whatever information your library has available on procedures for searching online. These procedures vary from library to library.

In addition to searching the catalog by subject, you can search by author and by title. If you use a computerized version of the card catalog, you should again familiarize yourself with the library's information on

**Names** *(May Subd Geog)*
   UF   Nomenclature
          Proper names
          Terminology
   BT   Language and languages—Etymology
   RT   Epithets
   SA   *subdivisions* Name *or* Names *under subjects, e.g.*
          America—Name; Catholic Church—Name; United
          States—History—Civil War, 1861–1865—Name;
          Jews—Name; Sects—Names; Stars—
          Names
   NT   Boat names
          Business names
          Code names
          House names
          Love names
          Names, Geographical
          Names, Personal
          Onomastics
          Ship names
          Terms and phrases
   — Etymology
          USE   Onomastics
   **— Pronunciation**
   **— Transliteration**
**Names, African**
   UF   African languages—Names
          African names
   BT   African languages—Etymology—Names
**Names, Ainu**
   UF   Ainu language—Names
          Ainu names
   BT   Ainu language—Etymology—Names
**Names, Amharic**
   UF   Amharic language—Names
          Amharic names
Names, Anglo-Saxon
   USE   Names, English (Old)
**Names, Arabic**
   UF   Arabic language—Names
          Arabic names
**Names, Bete** *(May Subd Geog)*
   UF   Bete language—Names
          Bete names
**Names, Celtiberian**
   UF   Celtiberian names
**Names, Chinese** *(May Subd Geog)*
   UF   Chinese language—Names
          Chinese names
Names, Christian
   USE   Names, Personal
**Names, Circassian** *(May Subd Geog)*
   UF   Circassian languages—Names
          Circassian names
   BT   Circassian languages—Etymology—Names
Names, Code
   USE   Code names
**Names, Cornish** *(May Subd Geog)*
   UF   Cornish language—Names
          Cornish names
Names, Corporate (Cataloging)
   USE   Corporate headings (Cataloging)

**Names, Dagari** *(May Subd Geog)*
   [DT510.42 (Ghana)]
   UF   Dagari language—Names
          Dagari names
          Names, Dagari (African people)
Names, Dagari (African people)
   USE   Names, Dagari
**Names, Dutch** *(May Subd Geog)*
   UF   Dutch language—Names
          Dutch names
   BT   Dutch language—Etymology—Names
**Names, English**
   UF   English language—Names
          English names
   NT   English language—Etymology—Names
**Names, English (Old)**
   UF   Anglo-Saxon names
          English language—Old English, ca.
             450–1100—Names
          English names, Old
          Names, Anglo-Saxon
          Names, Old English
          Old English names
Names, Ethnic
   USE   Names, Ethnological
**Names, Ethnological** *(May Subd Geog)*
   UF   Ethnic group names
          Ethnological names
          Ethnology—Names
          Names, Ethnic
          Names of peoples
          Tribal names
   BT   Onomastics
Names, Family
   USE   Names, Personal
Names, Fictitious
   USE   Anonyms and pseudonyms
**Names, French**
**Names, Geographical** *(May Subd Geog)*
   [G104-G108]
   UF   Geographical names
          Names, Geographical—Dictionaries
          Place-names
   BT   Names
          Onomastics
   RT   Geography—Terminology
          Toponymy
   SA   *subdivision* Name *under names of*
          *countries, cities, etc.*
   NT   Andover (Name)
          Elgin (Name)
          Europa (Name)
          Field names
          Hamilton (Name)
          Hanover (Name)
          Hydronymy
          Street names
          Tatsuta (Name)
   — Cataloging
          USE   Names, Geographical (Cataloging)
   — Dictionaries
          USE   Names, Geographical

**FIGURE 7-1** Library of Congress Subject Headings

```
Search Request:  S=EPITHET
BOOK - Record 14 of 19 Entries Found              Long View
--------------------- + Screen 1 of 2 ------------------
Author:       Allen, Irving L., 1931-

Title:        The language of ethnic conflict : social
              organization and lexical culture / Irving
              Lewis Allen.

Published:    New York : Columbia University Press, 1983.
Description:  162 p. ; 23 cm.

SUBJECT HEADINGS (Library of Congress: use s=):
              English Language--Etymology--Slang.
              Epithets
              English language--Etymology
              English language--United States--Social aspects
              Nicknames--United States.
              United States--Ethnic relations

Notes:        Includes index.
              Bibliography: p. [143]-155.

ISBN.         0231055560
              0231055579 (pbk.)
--------------------- + Screen 2 of 2 ------------------
      LOCATION:         CALL NUMBER:        STATUS:
1.  GRADUATE LIBRARY    PE2846. A441 1983   Overdue
2.  UNDERGRADUATE       PE2846. A441 1983   Not checked out
```

**Figure 7.2** Bibliographic Record Display

procedures. If you use a card catalog, notice that some libraries separate their card catalogs so that the author cards are in separate drawers from the subject and title cards. If they are not separate but are all together in the same drawers, you can distinguish them by looking at the first line. Subject cards begin with headings in capital letters. Author cards begin with a name, followed by the title. (Authors are not always individuals. An author can also be an institution or an organization.) Title cards begin with the title, followed by the author and then the title again. This information is particularly helpful when the work is biographical.

When searching your library's catalog, be aware that your library probably contains materials other than books and printed sources. Although the word *library* comes from the Latin *liber*, meaning book, libraries also contain films, microfilms, videotapes, records, compact disks, and slides. These materials are often catalogued according to the same general principles as books, but they may be held in separate collections. If these materials are of possible relevance to your research, ask a librarian how to find them.

## Call Numbers

You probably were introduced to the *Dewey Decimal System* and the *Library of Congress System* before coming to college, but familiarizing yourself with the branches of knowledge represented by the call numbers will aid you in determining which books are likely to be most useful for your research. Both systems are designed to keep books together by subject, but the older system of the two is the Dewey Decimal System. When Melvil Dewey introduced this system in 1876, he advanced the classification of books substantially.

### THE DEWEY DECIMAL SYSTEM OF CLASSIFICATION

The Dewey system divides all knowledge into 10 large categories using numbers from 000 to 999:

| | |
|---|---|
| 000–999 | general works (encyclopedias, periodicals) |
| 100–199 | philosophy, psychology |
| 200–299 | religion |
| 300–399 | social sciences |
| 400–499 | language |
| 500–599 | science |
| 600–699 | technology |
| 700–799 | fine arts |
| 800–899 | literature |
| 900–999 | history, geography, biography |

Most libraries are now replacing the Dewey Decimal System with the even more flexible and expandable Library of Congress System, which allows for more specific categories of subjects by combining letters and numbers. Given the exponential expansion of knowledge in the twentieth century, an expansion that has challenged libraries throughout the United States, the Library of Congress System has become the mainstay of classification for college libraries in this country. But it is still helpful to know the Dewey Decimal System because in some libraries books that were originally classified under this system are still shelved according to its call numbers. You may have to go to two different places in your library to find books grouped together on a specific subject. One bonus of those libraries that have switched classification sytems without entirely replacing the Dewey Decimal System is that the most current books, those published in the past 10 to 15 years, are grouped together under the Library of Congress call numbers. This can enable some students to find up-to-date sources just by pursuing call numbers for their area of interest in the Library of Congress stacks. Serendipitous research discoveries are frequently made by browsing through the stacks, although obviously this is not by itself a fail-safe or reliable method of research.

### THE LIBRARY OF CONGRESS SYSTEM OF CLASSIFICATION

| | |
|---|---|
| A | general works (encyclopedias, periodicals) |
| B | philosophy, psychology, religion |
| C | history—auxiliary sciences |
| D | history and topography (excluding America) |
| E–F | history, America |
| G | geography, anthropology, sports |
| H | social sciences |
| J | political science |
| K | law |
| L | education |
| M | music |
| N | fine arts |
| P | language and literature |
| Q | science |
| R | medicine |
| S | agriculture |
| T | technology |
| U | military science |
| V | naval science |
| Z | bibliography, library science |

The system is expanded by dividing these large general classes into more specialized ones indicated by a second letter. For example, the letter P for language and literature is further subdivided using P–PA for linguistics and Classical languages and literatures, PB–PH for modern European languages, and so on. The science letter Q is further subdivided using QA for mathematics, QB for astronomy, QC for physics, and so on. Each of these subdivisions is further subdivided by adding numbers and letters so that within the broader category of mathematics, those subjects related to algebra and arithmetic will be grouped together.

EXERCISES    1. In a group of eight students, choose one topic or inquiry question to pursue in the library. Choose (a) two members of the group to pursue research in encyclopedias and reference works, (b) two to research indexes to periodicals and scholarly journals, (c) two to search newspapers and also films, videocassettes, and other nonprint sources, and (d) two to search the online catalog of books and the OCLC catalog. After working in the library, pool your resources. Each two who worked on the same category of research should compare their findings. Then the entire group should discuss its process of research, focusing on difficulties encountered and sources found. Which sources proved most useful? What does this indicate to you about a general research strategy that an individual working alone on this topic might undertake?

2. In a group of eight students, continue the work you began in Exercise 1. Choose two sources from each of the categories you researched: (a) encyclopedias and reference materials, (b) periodicals and scholarly journals, (c) newspapers and nonprint sources, and (d) books and the OCLC catalog. Locate the sources and bring them (or copies of them) in for the group as a whole to see. Evaluate your sources according to the guidelines detailed in Chapter Three. Who are the authors of these sources, and what are their credentials? Who are the publishers, and what kind of reputation does each of them have? What about the quality of evidence and ideas in each source? Is the information presented in each source up to date? Are the arguments developed through sound reasoning? Is the evidence supporting the reasoning well researched and documented? Is the evidence balanced or biased? As a group, rank the sources in terms of their overall reliability.

3. Choose an inquiry question. Form a group and divide into two subgroups. Have one subgroup conduct a manual search of the *Readers' Guide to Periodical Literature* (or some other designated index such as the *Monthly Catalog of the United States Government Publications*). Have the other subgroup do a computer search of *InfoTrac* or the *Wilson Database* (the *GPO Monthly Catalog* is the database that corresponds to the *Monthly Catalog*). Some possibilities for corresponding print indexes to computer databases include:

| Print Indexes | Data base Indexes |
|---|---|
| America: History and Life | America: History and Life |
| American Banker | American Banker Full Text |
| American Men and Women of Science | American Men and Women of Science |
| Arts & Humanities Citation Index | Arts & Humanities Search |
| Dissertation Abstracts | Dissertation Abstracts Online |
| Index of Economic Articles | Economic Literature Index |
| National Organizations of the U.S. | Encyclopedia of Associations |

| | |
|---|---|
| Resources in Education | ERIC |
| Current Index to Journals in Education | ERIC |
| Everyman's Encyclopedia | Everyman's Encyclopedia |
| Facts on File | Facts on File World News Digest |
| Index Medicus | Medline |
| MLA Bibliography | MLA Bibliography |
| Philosopher's Index | Philosopher's Index |
| Psychological Abstracts | PsycINFO |
| Oxford Dictionary of Quotations | Quotations Database |
| Index to Religious Periodical Literature | Religion Index |
| Social Science Citation Index | Social Scisearch |

## ■ ■ ■ ■ ■  SEARCHING OUTSIDE THE LIBRARY

In addition to library research, you may want to do some primary research by gathering your own information and by making some firsthand observations. Among those researchers who rely heavily on primary research methods are social scientists, journalists, counselors, and biographers. Social scientists in particular have evolved many systematic methods for the scientific observation of individuals and society, including methods for doing field research, studying causality, measuring events and behavior, and sampling. The most common method for gathering information is through interviews of individuals, and since this method requires less advanced training, we discuss some techniques you may use to conduct interviews.

An interview is a process of planned, purposeful questioning. An interviewer's objective is principally to gather and receive information from a respondent, although occasionally an interview is designed to facilitate an exchange of information. An interview can range from being nondirective and unstructured, more of a free-flowing conversation, to being highly structured so that all questions are carefully planned in advance and always read in the same order.

### The Empathetic Interview

In the empathetic interview, the interviewer sets out with only a general goal in mind, leaving the individual interviewed to determine the direction and course of the conversation. The interviewer tries to create a warm climate that will allow the respondent to express ideas and information without fear of being judged or evaluated. Methods of empathetic reading that we stressed in Chapter Two also work well in this kind of interview. In listening to the respondent, the interviewer tries to record and understand what is said. Carl Rogers, the clinical psychologist, used this method of interviewing to understand his patients. His general goal was to provide a safe setting where the patients in telling their life stories would set the tone and determine the content of the interview. The interviewer's skill comes out through the warmth and acceptance that enable the individual interviewed to respond openly without fear of disapproval.

The empathetic interview is particularly well suited for gaining autobiographical information. Respondents can feel safe to share their life stories without fear that interviewers will rush to interpret and objectify the information they share. You may incorporate information that you gather from interviews into your paper on the condition that respondents have granted their permission. Because interviews often focus on the emotional or even moral aspects of life events, they can help you generate and develop ideas for a paper and can provide illustrations and personal testimonies that support your points.

By conducting an empathetic interview, you discover how others see and interpret life events. While you are asking questions, you should be as unobtrusive as possible. For example, if you ask an undergraduate what she enjoys most about living in the dorm, she may answer "my roommate." At this point, you would not want to prompt her with a question such as, "Are you and your roommate close friends?" This might direct the student to think along lines she had not thought of and would substitute your categories for hers. Instead, you should follow up by asking an open-ended question such as, "What do you enjoy about your roommate?" The student is then free to give information that allows her own perspective to emerge. Perhaps she may say something like "My roommate comes from a very different background than I do. She's from inner-city Detroit and has had to work much harder than I have to go to college. She's a work-study student, too, and so must be very organized to get all her work done. I've always had trouble being organized, and she's been a good influence on me. I like her upbeat approach to life."

Other follow-up questions can ask the respondents to expand or clarify a statement or to explain changes in their perspectives or attitudes. Such questions can help you to show interest, establish trust, and move toward a fuller understanding of the individuals' lives as they have experienced them.

To conduct an empathetic interview, you can follow these steps:

*1. Set up a time and place to interview the appropriate people.*

For example, a student named Vanessa wants to write about the effects of unemployment on workers who have been laid off their assembly line jobs at a General Motors plant. She calls two unemployed workers who are acquaintances of her uncle to interview them about the layoff, arranging to meet the workers at a restaurant in their town.

### 2. Decide whether to tape the interview.

Vanessa realizes that the demands of active listening may make it difficult to take many notes during the interview. She considers the option of taping the interview but decides against it, fearing that the workers would be more hesitant to disclose how they feel about their situation. Instead she plans to record the interview in writing as fully as she can shortly after it ends.

### 3. Write a brief explanation of your objectives.

Because Vanessa is particularly interested in how the workers have supported themselves after the layoff, she decides to focus on financial matters and on career changes they may have made. She considers how she will present her objectives in a way that promotes trust and a willingness to participate, and she considers what can be talked about in the amount of time agreed upon for the interview.

### 4. Draw up several initial questions.

Vanessa draws up three or four general questions that will help to trigger discussion as well as directly serve her objectives. She decides she will ask, "Has General Motors been helpful to you in any way since the layoff?" "How long do your unemployment benefits run?" and "Has General Motors been willing to provide any education or training that might help you readjust to your new situation?" Vanessa considers the sequencing and pacing of her questions. She decides that the question "How long do your unemployment benefits run?" should come later in the interview, since it may create anxiety in the workers.

### 5. Consider possible follow-up questions.

Vanessa imagines her role as an empathetic listener and the questions that would help those interviewed to describe and to reflect upon their experience. She decides to ask: "What career alternatives have you considered?" "Who do you perceive as being most supportive of you at this time?" "In what ways are they supportive?" and "How do you feel about their support?"

### 6. Think about how you will end the interview.

Vanessa decides she will give a clue that she is approaching the end of the interview by stating, "I have two more questions." She decides she will offer to give the workers a copy of her paper when she thanks them for cooperating.

If, like Vanessa, you decide to follow this procedure for empathetic interviewing, you may want to practice by role-playing with one of your peers in or outside the classroom. In normal conversation, we tend to ask directive questions, because our interests determine what we want to hear about. The empathetic interviewer, however, must try to let the respondent determine the flow of the conversation, to refrain from making judgments, and to listen actively.

■ ■ ■ ■ ■  KEEPING TRACK OF YOUR RESEARCH

As you conduct your research you need to keep track of the sources you find, the promising ideas or arguments you encounter as you skim and read sources, and the ideas sparked in your own mind that have potential as arguments. Although there is no set method of achieving this goal, we recommend that you keep a writing log and follow the steps that Jane took in Chapters Two and Three. In your writing log, probe your own biases and assumptions on a topic; paraphrase, summarize, and respond to the authors' ideas; compare, synthesize, and evaluate their ideas; and develop your own perspective.

In the earliest stages of research, when you are gathering the materials that you will reflect upon in your writing log, you can save time by following these three tips:

1. Use computer terminals that have a printer when you use a database. Make notes in the margins of the printout about which sources proved most promising. You can also paste individual citations from the printout on note cards.

2. Photocopy articles or sections of books and annotate the photocopy. Make sure to write the full citation for the journal or book at the top of the first page of the photocopy.

3. For books that you check out of the library, use Post-Its (notepaper with adhesive backing that does not stick permanently) to mark pages with ideas or quotations that you may want to think about. Write subject headings or the beginning and ending words of the quotation on the Post-It.

These simple procedures allow you to work efficiently without damaging library property.

Shortcuts you should never use are to write in a library book or periodical and to rip pages out of a book. Unfortunately, defaced library materials indicate that researchers use these shortcuts far too frequently. Such acts permanently mar the library's holdings, making research more difficult not just for the next person but for researchers in years to come. Library policy prohibits defacing library materials, and penalties are exacted against those caught doing so.

■ ■ ■ ■ ■   AVOIDING PLAGIARISM

In writing papers from sources, you need to be very careful about avoiding plagiarism. When exploring and evaluating authors' divergent points of view, you will probably find positions you already held or with which you agree. How, then, do you distinguish shared ideas from those you gained from reading? Occasionally, students are so fearful about plagiarizing that they document almost every sentence in a paper, even those ideas that belong to the realm of common knowledge. If you go to this extreme, however, you undervalue your own insights and contributions. But how do you distinguish between legitimately incorporating others' ideas and illegitimately plagiarizing them? In general, you can follow these four guidelines:

*1. You need not document ideas that are common knowledge.*

For example, important historical dates and facts, such as the date of John F. Kennedy's assassination or the year of the Norman conquest are common knowledge. Well-known concepts and theories, such as the Oedipus complex, the domino theory, and existential angst, also fall into this category. Well-known arguments on current issues also count as common knowledge; for example, most of us know the popular arguments supporting and opposing abortion, the death penalty, and gun control. In fact, in Chapter Two, we asked you to probe your own biases and assumptions because, although the knowledge you bring to your reading and writing can be an asset, it can also interfere with your ability to analyze and evaluate authors' arguments.

*2. You must document quoted, summarized, and paraphrased passages from sources.*

Plagiarism is using someone else's words or ideas without acknowledging or documenting them. Incorporating an author's exact words without using quotation marks and a citation is one clear-cut case of plagiarism. Summarizing or paraphrasing an author's ideas without attributing them to the writer by name or without documenting them also constitutes plagiarism. To help you better understand what constitutes plagiarism, read the following two excerpts from the readings on advertising in Chapter Six.

The first excerpt is from Michael Schudson, "The Emergence of New Consumer Patterns: A Case Study of the Cigarette," page 175:

The spread of cigarette smoking, particularly among women, was one of the most visible signs of change in the consumption practices in the 1920s, and one that has been cited frequently as evidence of the new powers of advertising and marketing. Between 1918 and 1940, American consumption grew from 1.70 to 5.16 pounds of cigarette tobacco per adult. During the same period, advertising budgets of the tobacco companies bulged, movies pictured elegant men and women smoking, and public relations stunts promoted cigarettes.

Some contemporary observers concluded that advertising *caused* the increase in cigarette smoking among women. For instance, in 1930, Clarence True Wilson, board secretary of the Methodist Episcopal Church, declared: "If the advertising directed to women ceased, it is probable that within five years the smoking woman would be the rare exception." Scholars in recent years have accepted a similar view. Erik Barnouw, for instance, holds that advertising was responsible for bringing women into the cigarette market.

This conclusion is difficult to sustain for a number of reasons, the most obvious of which is that tens of thousands of women began smoking cigarettes in the 1920s *before* a single advertisement was directed at them. It is more accurate to observe that cigarette smoking among women led tobacco companies to advertise toward the female market than to suggest that advertising created the market in the first place. The mass media played a role in spreading the cigarette habit among women, but it was primarily the information conveyed in news stories, not the persuasion attempted in advertisements, that helped in the first instance to legitimate smoking among women in the 1920s.

This second excerpt is from Shaun Assael, "Why Big Tobacco Woos Minorities," page 187:

For tobacco companies, it has ceased being an issue of market share. They need new smokers. Government data suggests that the most likely recruits will be Hispanics and black women—groups that have not kept pace with the national move toward quitting.

The campaign to maintain and even increase the base of minority smokers goes well beyond billboards. Event marketing abounds, such as the sponsorship by Philip Morris' Marlboro of Mexican rodeos in California. Tobacco companies also donate to such groups as the National Black Caucus and the National Association of Hispanic Journalists.

Tobacco companies have been lavishing money on black arts and political groups since the 1950s. But as their overall market shrinks, they have turned up the heat under the Hispanic market. California's *Hispanic Business* magazine reports that Philip Morris was the second largest advertiser in Hispanic media for fiscal year 1989, spending $8.6 million. In 1988 PM topped the list. Last year the National Association of Hispanic Publications named Philip Morris the company of the year.

The tobacco industry has become more sophisticated at its patronage. Anti-smoking activists say it is increasingly difficult to know what tobacco interests are behind these days.

Now, imagine that a student incorporated information from these excerpts in the following fashion:

Advertising is the most significant cause of smoking among women and minorities. The advertising budgets of tobacco companies have bulged, and these companies will stop at nothing to ensure that people keep smoking. The campaign to sustain and augment the base of minority smokers goes well beyond billboards. Event marketing is plentiful. In California, Philip Morris' Marlboro has sponsored Mexican rodeos.

Without advertising, women and minorities could kick the habit. For instance, Clarence True Wilson, board secretary of the Methodist Episcopal Church, declared, "If the advertising directed to women ceased, it is probable that within five years the smoking woman would be a rare exception" (Schudson 175).

Notice how the student paraphrases Shaun Assael and then uses Michael Schudson's quotation of Clarence True Wilson to support Assael's point. A reader could wonder how the student knows about Mexican rodeos in California. By not documenting the paraphrased material, the student plagiarizes. Furthermore, the closing quotation could lead a reader to assume that the student did the research on Clarence True Wilson. Typically, you should not use material quoted in a source but rather refer to the original article. When only an indirect source is available, then you can write "qtd. in," short for "quoted in," before the source you cite in your parenthetical reference.

3. *Be careful to distinguish quotations from paraphrase or summary by using quotation marks.*

When you are writing in your log, make sure you do not inadvertently copy word for word when paraphrasing or summarizing a source. As we described in Chapter Two, a paraphrase and a summary should be in your own words. If you are not careful, when you reread your log and draft your paper, you could mistakenly assume that the author's words are your own.

Imagine that a student, working with the above excerpts, makes such a mistake:

> Did advertising cause women to take up the habit of smoking in the 1920s? Although many would like to blame the tobacco industry for bringing women into the cigarette market by advertising, this conclusion is difficult to sustain for a number of reasons, the most obvious of which is that tens of thousands of women began smoking cigarettes in the 1920s before a single advertisement was directed toward them (Schudson 175). Still, given the current efforts of tobacco companies to lure minorities into the habit—the campaign to maintain and even increase the base of minority smokers goes well beyond billboards to event marketing and patronage (Assael 187)—one might readily assume that the tobacco industry was just as wily and crafty then as they are now.

In this sample, notice how the student does cite the author and would probably document the complete reference on the "Works Cited" page. But this is still plagiarizing because the lack of quotation marks leads the reader to assume that the writer is using his or her own words rather than the actual words of the author.

4. *Look for evidence of synthesizing, analyzing, and evaluating the ideas of others.*

To what extent do you go beyond quotation, paraphrase, and summary and develop your own ideas on a topic? Even though you may agree with the arguments of others and want to incorporate them into your paper, overall your own prose style and argumentative position should shape an essay. A student who is careful about documentation and who understands how to highlight an analysis of the material may approach the above excerpts in this way:

> Can advertising cause people to take up the habit of smoking? Michael Schudson is one analyst of advertising who believes its role is limited. In "The Emergence of New Consumer Patterns: A Case Study of the Cigarette," he argues that women in the 1920s began smoking because they wanted to symbolize their

new found independence. Many women, he claims, began smoking in the 1920s before the advent of cigarette advertising directed specifically at them (Schudson 175). Still, I can't help wondering if advertising wasn't more of a contributing cause than Schudson thinks it was. If women wanted to be more like men, perhaps they were influenced by cigarette ads directed at men. And advertisers may have had some cagey ways of speaking to women through the men's ads. After all, look at the wily ways today's tobacco advertisers have of getting minorities to take up smoking. Not only do they bombard them with billboard ads in the inner cities but they also secretly fund minority arts and political events. As Shaun Assael remarks in his article, "Why Big Tobacco Woos Minorities," "The tobacco industry has become sophisticated at cloaking its patronage. Anti-smoking activists say it is increasingly difficult to know what tobacco interests are behind these days" (187). I think advertisers were probably devising ingenious ways to get women to start smoking as early as the turn of the century, and I have studied cigarette ads in some popular magazines from 1910 to 1915 to analyze them for possible double messages.

This student has taken charge, analyzing the sources to advance an argument. Furthermore, the parenthetical citations and quotation marks acknowledge authors' ideas and words clearly and correctly. The student's writing is credible and convincing.

EXERCISE

1. In a peer-editing group, go over the draft of each member's research paper. Pay close attention to the way each author has quoted, paraphrased, and summarized. What does the author seem to do especially well? What could the author do to improve the methods of synthesizing and interweaving sources into the paper? Discuss each author's draft with the aim of helping him or her to improve.

■ ■ ■ ■ ■   DOCUMENTING YOUR SOURCES

Whether you quote, paraphrase, or summarize your sources, you need to document them. The best method is to use parenthetical references in the text, followed by a list at the end of the paper of the works you actually use. Parenthetical citations work better than footnotes or endnotes because they are less distracting. Footnotes or endnotes, for example, can indicate a citation, but they can also indicate that there is further explanation or amplification of the text. Because footnotes or endnotes function in both of these ways, a reader will usually look at such notes; if the information is only a citation, however, a glance down to the bottom of the page or the end of the paper needlessly interrupts the flow of reading. Your reader's way is smoothed, then, if you give brief citations in the text, and use footnotes or endnotes only when you do want to further explain or amplify a portion of your text. Your reader can easily refer to the list of sources, alphabetically arranged at the end of the paper, to get the full citation.

Although there are a number of formats you can use to document sources, in this textbook we cover only two of them—the Modern Language Association (MLA) documentation style and the American Psychological Association (APA) documentation style. Use the MLA style when writing a paper for an English composition or literature course. It also applies to other disciplines in the humanities such as art history, linguistics, philosophy, and religious studies, but in writing for other courses always check with your instructor concerning the style to use. The APA style is most frequently used in the social sciences, such as psychology and economics. It emphasizes publication date because the time an idea or discovery emerged is important to an understanding of scientific development and progress.

## The Modern Language Association Style for Parenthetical References

Since 1984, the MLA has preferred the use of parenthetical references to endnotes or footnotes for works published in the humanities. The parenthetical reference should be placed in the paper where it is needed, and should contain enough information so a reader can locate the full citation without difficulty in the alphabetical list of works cited. Usually, this means giving only the authors' last names and the page numbers within parentheses. The parenthetical information is treated as a part of the sentence and should go within the period if it falls at the end of the sentence. For example:

Euphemisms such as little girl's room may seem funny, but according to one linguist they are really "outward and visible signs of our inward anxieties, conflicts, fears" (Rawson 314).

If you include the name of the author in the sentence, you can omit it from within the parentheses:

Euphemisms such as little girl's room may seem funny, but according to Rawson they are really "outward and visible signs of our inward anxieties, conflicts, fears" (314).

When a quotation runs more than four typewritten lines, indent 10 spaces, double-space, and treat as a block quotation. Set it off from your text by adding a colon to the preceding sentence and beginning a new line. No quotation marks are used in block quotations, and since block quotations usually are longer than one sentence, the parenthetical information goes outside of the period of the last sentence quoted. For example:

Euphemisms may seem funny and trivial, but according to one linguist:

> Euphemisms are society's basic lingua non franca. As such, they are outward and visible signs of our inward anxieties, conflicts, fears, and shames. They are like radioactive isotopes. By tracing them, it is possible to see what has been (and is) going on in our language, our minds, and our culture. (Rawson 314)

The MLA parenthetical format is simple and logical, but sources are often complicated because there is more than one author of a work, more than one volume of a work, more than one work written by an author, and any other number of possible complications. Complications frequently encountered by students when they begin to interweave sources into their papers are discussed below.

### A source quoted in another

To cite a source quoted in another source, use the abbreviation for "quoted in." For example: (John W. Dean III qtd. in Rawson 317). In this example, the abbreviation helps the reader to understand that the quotation from Dean appears in a source written by Rawson. If you lift a quotation appearing in one source and do not cite both sources, you can confuse your readers. They might, for instance, think that you have read the quoted source. If you can find and read the source that is quoted in another, you should do so, citing directly from it. Your understanding of the source an author has quoted may be different from that author's understanding once you view it in a fuller context.

### A source with more than one author

The names of multiple authors should appear as they do in the list of works cited, which is also the way they appear on the title page of their work. If the title page does not list the names alphabetically, then you should follow whatever order is used there. The works are indexed and cataloged in the library following the order on the title page, so by following this order, you can help your reader find your source. For example: (Lakoff and Johnson 35–36).

### *Two authors with the same last name*

When you have two different sources by authors with the same last name, distinguish them by including their first names. For example: (Michael Johnson 44) (Barbara Johnson 102)

### *A source with no author*

Use the title in abbreviated form. Begin with the word by which it is alphabetized in the list of works cited.

### *Multiple sources by the same author*

Abbreviate the titles. When citing articles from newspapers, magazines, or scholarly journals, make sure you abbreviate the title and not the name of the periodical. For example, in working with two articles by Annie Dillard on jokes, "The Leg in the Christmas Stocking: What We Learned from Jokes" (*The New York Times Book Review*, Dec. 7, 1986) and "Mother Told Jokes" (*Reader's Digest*, Oct. 1987, 122–125), you should *not* abbreviate *The New York Times Book Review* or *Reader's Digest*. Instead abbreviate the titles: (Dillard, "The Leg") and (Dillard, "Mother" 123).

### *Sources with editors or translators*

In general, it is best to cite the author who appears in an edition, anthology, or translation and not the editor, compiler, or translator. For example, if one of your college readers has a collection of articles on the topic of capital punishment and you quote from David Bruck's "Decisions of Death," then in parentheses give the name of the author of the article or excerpt and the page number (Bruck 95). Your full bibliographic citation will alert your reader to the editor and edition:

Bruck, David.  "Decisions of Death."  <u>The Informed Argument</u>.
    Ed. Robert K. Miller.  2nd ed.  Harcourt Brace Jovanovich,
    1986.  90-101.

If you quote from the editor's preface or introduction, however, you would cite the editor: (Miller 5). Again, the full bibliographic citation would indicate to the reader the editor as "author." For example:

Miller, Robert K., ed.  "An Introduction to Argument."  <u>The Informed</u>
    <u>Argument</u>.  2nd ed.  Harcourt Brace Jovanovich, 1986.

*Multivolume works*

If you cite from a book with more than one volume and you actually use more than one of these volumes in your paper, you must distinguish them in your parenthetical note, for example: (Husserl 1:163) and (Husserl 2:199) to cite:

Husserl, Edmund.   Logical Investigations.   Trans. J. N. Findlay.
　　2 vols.   London: Routledge & Kegan Paul, 1970.

*Sources without pages*

For works without pages, such as television programs, videocassettes, films, and recordings, cite the title of the work only. For example: (*Triumph of the Will*). In your bibliography, you would give the full citation:

Triumph of the Will.   Videocassette.   Dir. Leni Reifenstahl.   Indi-
　　anapolis: Video Classics, Inc., 1984.

Occasionally, in the instance of recordings, you may want to emphasize the artist, in which case you may cite the name only, or the name and an abbreviated title as in (Rose, *Liszt* 4) for:

Rose, Jerome.   Liszt Piano Music.   4 Vols.   New York.   Vox, 1974.

　　Use your judgment and remember that the important thing is to help your reader to find your full citation on the list of works cited. In the case of speeches, interviews, or articles reproduced on microfiche, give the name of the speaker, the person interviewed, or the author of the article only.

## MLA Style for the "Works Cited" Page

　　The "Works Cited" page appears at the end of the paper and includes only those works you actually cite. This list is most appropriate for the five- to twenty-page papers students write at the undergraduate level. If, however, you are asked to include relevant works that you consulted while researching that you do not actually cite, you will need to list the "Works Consulted." The format given here for "Works Cited" can also be used for "Works Consulted."

## Sources in Periodicals

　　What follows are sample citations for articles and other materials found in periodicals. List your citations in alphabetical order according to authors' last names. Start the first line of each entry flush with the left margin, and indent subsequent lines five spaces from the left margin. We include those forms you are most likely to have questions about. If you encounter a special case that we have not covered, check your library or local book store for the *MLA Handbook for Writers of Research Papers*, 3rd edition.

An entry in the list of works cited has three main divisions, each followed by a period and two spaces. These divisions are: the author(s), the title, and the publication data.

The format for articles is:

Name of Author. "Title of Article." *Name of Periodical* volume number (date): page numbers.

**Name of author,** in inverse order. When there is more than one author, list only the first name in inverse order and give authors in the order as given in the publication. Follow the name(s) with a period.

**Title of article,** in quotation marks. Place the period at the end of the title within quotation marks. Use normal title capitalization (even if it appears in small caps in the periodical) and separate a title from a subtitle with a colon.

**Name of periodical,** underlined and given in full without abbreviation.

**Volume number,** without intervening punctuation in Arabic figures. If each issue of the periodical is paginated separately, give both the volume number and the issue number (e.g., 13.2, for volume 13, issue 2), but if the volumes are paginated consecutively, you need only the volume number. If there is no volume number but only issue numbers, give the issue number.

**Date.** For scholarly journals place the date within parentheses. For magazines and newspapers that are issued weekly, bimonthly, or monthly, you do not need the volume number, only the date. Give the full date (e.g., *Newsweek* 28 May 1991) and omit parentheses. Follow the date with a colon and page numbers.

**Page numbers,** of the entire article. Sometimes a magazine has an article that begins at the front and is continued at the back. In this case, inclusive page numbers are misleading, so give the first page number only and follow it by a plus (+) sign, leaving no intervening space before the plus sign (e.g., 6+). Page numbers in newspapers often include the section letter (e.g., section B). Give page numbers as they appear in the newspaper (e.g., 4C). End with a period.

As you compile your list, remember that the objective is to help your readers not only witness your research but pursue it if they should so desire. Make your citations complete enough to enable a reader to find your sources in the library without difficulty. Strive for consistency and clarity, but if you have a question or doubt, err on the side of inclusiveness. Be scrupulous, then, in recording details about volume numbers, issue numbers, dates, and page numbers when you conduct your research.

## Some Typical Entries

*Scholarly journals*

Baron, Dennis E.   "The Epicene Pronoun: The Word that Failed."
   American Speech 56.2 (1981): 83-97.

Bem, Sandra L., and Daryl J. Bem.   "Does Sex-biased Job Advertising 'Aid and Abet' Sex Discrimination?"   Journal of Applied
   Social Psychology 3 (1973): 6-18.

Scott, Patricia Bell.   "The English Language and Black Woman-
   hood: A Low Blow at Self-Esteem."   The Journal of Afro-American
   Issues 2 (1974): 218-225.

*Magazine and newspaper articles*

Kunen, James S.   "Childless Couples Seeking Surrogate Mothers
   Call Michigan Lawyer Noel Keane—He Delivers."   People Weekly
   30 Mar. 1987: 93+.

Gladwell, Malcom and Rochelle Sharpe.   "Baby M Winner: Meet
   the Surrogacy Entrepreneur."   The New Republic 16 Feb.
   1987: 15-18.

Milne, David.   "Surrogate Contracts Ruled to Be Unenforceable."
   American Medical News 12 Feb. 1988: 11.

*An editorial*

Wall, James M.   "The Battle Over Baby M.   " Editorial.   The Christian
   Century 4 Feb. 1987: 99.

*Letter to the editor*

Flitterman-King, Sharon.   Letter.   Ms. Apr. 1988.

*Anonymous article*

"Legal in New Jersey: Surrogate Motherhood."   The Economist 4
   Apr. 1987: 2.

*Anonymous editorial*

"There Ought to Be a Law."   Editorial.   Commonweal 26 Feb 1988:
   100-101.

*Review*

Dunham, Janice.   Rev. of <u>Surrogate Motherhood: The Ethics of</u>
<u>Using Human Beings</u> by Thomas A. Shannon.   <u>Library</u>
<u>Journal</u> 114 (Feb. 1, 1989): 77.

Note: If the review has a title, include it in quotation marks with a period right after the reviewer's name.

*A personal interview*

Johnson, Barbara.   Personal Interview.   22 Feb. 1991.

## Sources in Books

The format for books is:

Name of Author. *Title of Book*. Series, volume number, or number of volumes (if applicable). Edition (if not the first). City of publication: Name of Publisher, year of publication. Page numbers.

Page numbers are included only if you are citing part of a book, such as an essay in a collection or a short story.

**Name of author** in inverse order. If there is more than one author, list the first author's name in inverse order and the other names in the normal order, and follow the same sequence as given on the title page. Give the names in full as they appear on the title page. If you have more than one listing for an author, type three hyphens and a period in place of the author's name after the first listing. An editor as "author" can also be placed at the beginning of the citation, but remember to include ed. after the name (e.g., Smith, Marvin, ed.) If an editor or translator is named in addition to an author, type Ed. or Trans. after the title followed by the person's name in normal order. Follow the name(s) with a period.

**Title of book**, underlined. Use a colon to separate a title from a subtitle. Use normal capitalization for titles, even if the title page has unusual typographical characteristics. End with a period and two spaces. If you are using an edition other than the first, identify it by 2nd ed., 3rd ed., or by year, 1990 ed. If it is a multivolume work, include total number of volumes (e.g., 5 vols.). Your parenthetical reference has already identified the specific volume you used.

**City of publication**. If more than one city is specified on the title page, use the first one. If the city is not well known, include the postal service abbreviation for the state. If the city is outside the United States, include an abbreviation for the country (e.g., Lancaster, Eng.). Follow the city with a colon and the name of the publisher.

**Name of Publisher**. Strive for brevity. Eliminate "Inc.", "Ltd.", and "Company." Abbreviate University Press to UP. Follow the name of the publisher with a comma.

**Year of publication**. Use the original year of publication, even if the work has been reprinted. If the work is in a new revised edition, however, identify the edition in your entry by number (e.g., 2nd ed.), right after the title and include the name of the editor. Use the year of the revised edition instead of the original publication date after the publisher's name. Follow the year with a period.

**Page numbers of the entire selection**. Use page numbers only if you have cited an essay or an entitled excerpt that is part of a larger collection or anthology. Your parenthetical notes have already identified the specific pages of reference so you do not need them here. End with a period.

### Some Typical Entries

*One author*

Farb, Peter. Word Play. New York: Alfred A. Knopf, 1974.

*Single author with more than one listing*

Mandelstam, Nadezhda. Hope Abandoned. Trans. Max Hayward. London: Collins and Harvill, 1974.

- - -. Hope Against Hope. Trans. Max Hayward. London: Collins and Harvill, 1971.

*Two or more authors*

Schilling, Warner, Paul Y. Hammond, and Glenn H. Snyder. Strategy, Politics, and Defense Budgets. New York: Columbia UP, 1962.

*Collection or anthology with editor(s)*

Knepler, Henry and Myrna Knepler, eds. Crossing Cultures: Readings for Composition. 3rd ed. New York: Macmillan, 1991.

*Essay in a collection*

Angelou, Maya. "Graduation." Crossing Cultures: Readings for Composition. Eds. Henry Knepler and Myrna Knepler. 3rd ed. New York: Macmillan, 1991. 3-14.

*Book with translator*

Derrida, Jacques. Dissemination. Trans. Barbara Johnson. Chicago: U of Chicago P, 1981.

*More than one volume*

Husserl, Edmund.  Logical Investigations.  2 vols.  Trans. J. N.
    Findlay.  London: Routledge & Kegan Paul, 1971.

Note: If you use only one volume, list as follows:

Husserl, Edmund.  Logical Investigations.  Vol. 1.  Trans. J. N.
    Findlay.  London: Routledge & Kegan Paul, 1971.

Note: If an author or editor titles each volume of a multi-volume set differently, list the volumes you use singly as follows:

Copleston, Frederick.  Modern Philosophy: Descartes to Leibniz.
    Vol. 4 of A History of Philosophy.  Garden City NY: Image
    Books, 1963.

*Book with new editions*

Spurgin, Sally De Witt.  The Power to Persuade.  2nd ed.  Engle-
    wood Cliffs NJ: Prentice Hall, 1989.

*Government documents*

U.S. Congress.  Senate.  Committee on Foreign Relations.  Causes,
    Origins, and Lessons of the Vietnam War: Hearings.  92nd
    Cong., 2nd sess., 1972.

U.S. National Military Establishment.  Annual Report of the Sec-
    retary of the Army: 1948.  Washington: GPO, 1949.

## The American Psychological Association Style for Parenthetical References

The APA style for parenthetical references includes the date of publication. As in the MLA format, you give page numbers for direct quotations.
The APA style differs from the MLA style in that you do not need page numbers to accompany paraphrases and summaries. Parenthetical references in
the APA style correspond to a "References" list at the end, which is similar
to the MLA's "Works Cited" list.

As in the MLA style, parenthetical information is treated as a part of
the sentence and so should go within the period if it falls at the end of the
sentence. The APA style differs from that of the MLA in terms of punctuation within parentheses. The APA style (1) uses commas to separate name
from date, (2) uses p. and pp. to indicate page and pages, and (3) uses an
ampersand (&) instead of *and* when more than one author appears in a note.
Because APA parenthetical references include publication date, your text
will be more readable if you include the authors' names in the text. For
example:

Mantsios (1988) argues that many myths govern our concepts about class in America; the most prevalent myth is that "we are, essentially, a middle-class nation" (p. 58).

When a work has more than one author, mention them all the first time you cite a source.

Belenkey, Clinchy, Goldberger, and Tarule (1986) describe the learning experiences women have had at universities in the United States.

If you name the authors in parentheses, do not forget to use the ampersand for "and."

A team of researchers has studied the learning experiences of women at universities in the United States (Belenkey, Clinchy, Goldberger, & Tarule, 1986).

When there are more than two authors, you need to identify them all only once. In subsequent citations, use the first author's name followed by "et al."

Belenkey et al. also showed how women students often expressed a belief that they had latent knowledge (p. 217).

If two authors have the same last name, use initials to distinguish them. If the author of a work is not given, use the complete title when you refer to it in your text, or use the first two or three words when you refer to it in your parenthetical notation.

## APA Style for the "References" Page

In APA style, title your list of cited works as "References." List your citations in alphabetical order according to authors' last names (or first words of title, excluding *A*, *An*, *The*). Begin each entry flush with the left margin, and indent subsequent lines three spaces. For the sake of brevity, we include those forms you are most likely to have questions about.

Articles, Books, and Other Materials

The format for articles is:

Name of Author. (Date). Title of article. *Name of Periodical* , *volume number,* page numbers.

The format for books is:

Name of Author. (Date). *Title of book.* City of publication: Publisher.

**Name of author**, in inverse order. When there is more than one author, invert *all* authors' names. Use initials instead of first names, and use commas to separate authors' surnames and initials. Use an ampersand (&) instead of "and" when there are two or more authors. Do not use "et al." Include all authors' names. Follow the name(s) with a period. (If an author's initial ends the name(s), do not add an extra period.) If a book is an edited book, place the name(s) of the editor in the author position and include the abbreviation "Ed." or "Eds."

**The date.** Place the date in parentheses and follow with a period.

**Title.** Capitalize only the first word of the title and subtitle, and all proper nouns and adjectives. Separate a title and subtitle with a colon. End the title with a period. For articles: Do not underline. For books: Underline, and include additional information about edition or volume number in parentheses before the period.

**Publication information for articles.** Include the *Name of the periodical* underlined and given in full. Capitalize the first, last, and all major words in the title and subtitle. End the name of the periodical with a comma. The *Volume number* follows and, for periodicals, is also underlined. If you include the issue number, do not underline it, but place it in parentheses. Follow volume and issue numbers with a comma. *Page numbers.* With the APA style, you do not always use the abbreviation "p." for page or "pp." for pages, so listing works requires some care in this regard. The rule is to use the abbreviation "p." or "pp." before page numbers of newspaper and magazine articles but not to use the abbreviation "p." or "pp." before page numbers of scholarly journals. Include the page numbers of the entire article.

**Publication information for books.** Give the city and include the U.S. Postal Service abbreviation for the state (or abbreviate the name of the country) if the city is not well known or has the same name as another city. Follow the city with a colon. Give the name of the publisher, omitting Co. and Inc. and end with a period.

## Some Typical Entries

*Scholarly journal article*

Ibrahim, H., and Morrison, N.  (1976).  Self-actualization and
self-concept among athletes.  The Research Quarterly,
47(1), 68-79.

*Magazine and newspaper articles*

Klerman, G. L.  (1979, April).  The age of melancholy?  Psychology
Today, 12(11), pp. 36-38, 42, 88.

Coleman, D.  (1991, July 16).  New ways to battle bias: Fight
acts, not feelings.  New York Times, pp. B4, B9.

*Anonymous article*

Legal in New Jersey: Surrogate motherhood.  (1987, April 4).
The Economist, p. 2.

*Article in an anthology*

Kaplan, H. S.  Androgyny as a model of metal health for women:
From theory to therapy.  (1976).  In A. G. Kaplan and J. P.
Bean (Eds.), Beyond sex-role stereotypes: Readings toward
a psychology of androgyny (pp. 353-362).  Boston: Little
Brown.

*Multiple works by an author published
the same year*

Horner, M. S.  (1970a).  Femininity and successful achievement:
A basic inconsistency.  In J. M. Bardwick, E. Douvan, M. S.
Horner and D. Gutman, Feminine personality and conflict
(pp. 45-74).  Belmont, CA.: Brooks/Cole.

Horner, M. S.  (1970b).  The motive to avoid success and changing aspirations of college women.  In Women on campus: 1970
a symposium (pp. 12-23).  Ann Arbor, MI.: Center for the
Continuing Education of Women.

*Book by single author*

King, M. L., Jr.  (1968).  The trumpet of conscience.  New York:
Harper & Row.

*Two or more books and articles by the same
author*

Mead, M.  (1935).  <u>Sex and temperament in three primitive
societies.</u>  New York: Dell.

Mead, M.  (1949).  <u>Male and female.</u>  New York: Dell.

Mead, M.  (1974).  On Freud's view of female psychology.  In J.
Strouse (Ed.), <u>Women and analysis: Dialogues on psycho-
analytic views of femininity</u> (pp. 95-106).  New York:
Grossman.

List works in chronological order by date if there are two or more articles
by the same author.

*Book, corporate author, author as publisher*

American Medical Association. (1977). <u>Judicial Council opinions and reports: Including the principles of medical ethics
and rules of the judicial council.</u>  Chicago: Author.

*Edited book, second edition*

Barnet, S. & Bedau, H. (Eds.). (1990).  <u>Current issues and enduring questions: Methods and modes of argument</u> (2nd
ed.).  New York: St. Martin's.

*Article or chapter in an edited
and translated book, volume in a multivolume
work*

Freud, S.  (1959).  Female sexuality.  In J. Strachey (Ed.), J.
Riviere (Trans.), <u>Collected papers of Sigmund Freud</u> (Vol.
5, pp. 252-272).  New York: Basic Books.  (Original work
published in 1931).

Note:When you have two dates, your in-text citation would look like:
(Freud, 1931, 1959).

*Article or chapter in an edited book, reprinted
from another source*

Koch, E. I.  (1990).  Death and justice: How capital punishment
affirms life.  In Barnet, S. & Bedau, H. (Eds.).  <u>Current
issues and enduring questions: Methods and modes of</u>

argument. (2nd ed.).   New York: St. Martin's.   (Reprinted
from The New Republic, 1984, July 30).

*Interview, review, film, videotape, recording*

State the kind of medium in brackets after the title but before the
period. For example:

Buckley, B. (Director).   (1983).   Never turn back: The life of
Fanny Lou Hamer [16mm film].   New York: Rediscovery
Production Inc.

Hoffman, R.   (1990, Dec. 30).   Everybody's mother's ghost [Re-
view of Family by J. California Cooper].   The New York
Times Book Review, p. 12.

## Suggestions for Using Parenthetical References

Students can err either by using too many parenthetical references or
by using too few. If you have many, ask yourself: (1) Do I rely too heavily
on my sources without giving myself enough of an opportunity to develop
my own ideas on the topic? Sometimes numerous references are appropriate, especially if you are developing a complicated argument using evidence
from a number of sources. But too many references can also be a crutch,
indicating that you are piecing ideas together rather than synthesizing
them and developing your own perspective. You should also ask yourself:
(2) Are some of these references needlessly repetitive? Can I eliminate or
condense them in any way? If you refer to the same source several times in
the same paragraph, you can use just one parenthetical reference at the end
of the paragraph, giving a range of page numbers rather than listing each
page number specifically; for example—(Johnson 44–48). Or you can double the notes within parentheses; for example—(Johnson 44–48; Maxwell
264). Sometimes you can eliminate the parenthetical reference altogether if
it refers to general knowledge or well-known information.

Too few references may indicate other problems. Ask yourself:
(1) Have I sufficiently researched the topic? and (2) Do I acknowledge
sources when I paraphrase and summarize as well as when I quote? Failure to acknowledge paraphrased and summarized sources can result in
plagiarism.

## Footnotes and Endnotes to Explain or Inform

Occasionally, you may want to do more than cite or refer to a source
in your paper. You may want to add a footnote or endnote to offer an explanation, to write in greater detail about an idea, or to provide some relevant
piece of information. In both MLA and APA styles, you may use content

notes that offer comment or explanation the text cannot accommodate. You are encouraged, however, to avoid using these notes. In MLA style you may also use bibliographic notes that offer information or evaluation of sources. To provide either of these two kinds of notes, place a superscript Arabic numeral in your text which matches the numeral of a footnote or endnote. Whenever possible, place the superscript numeral at the end of a sentence or, at least, at the end of a clause. Some sample content and bibliographic notes follow:

*Content Notes*

[1] We have little knowledge about the intimate lives of lower-class women during this period. Few of them could write and their letters were rarely preserved.

[5] Hoosier is a common name for residents of the state of Indiana.

*Bibliographic Notes*

[2] For reference to Egypt as "the land of Ham," see Psalm 105, verses 23 and 27, which describe the Israelites' slavery in Egypt.

[1] For more on the psychological considerations of competition, see Alfie Kohn, No Content: The Case Against Competition (Boston: Houghton Mifflin, 1986) 96-131.

When using bibliographic notes in MLA style, the form of the citation is slightly different from the form on the "Works Cited" page. This form has a period only at the end of the reference, as in the above example citing Alfie Kohn's book.

## Suggestions for Compiling Your List

Compile your "Works Cited" or "Reference" list while you work on your paper. The work involved is painstaking and it is best not to leave it for those last moments when you are rushing to type your paper. Record all the information needed on index cards while you write your paper, or keep an independent file on your computer for your list, updating it as you go along. Keep an index card with the basic format written out for articles and books, or include the basic format in your computer file where you can easily erase it when you have finished. There are programs available for some computers, such as Zenith and MacIntosh, that will format this information for you according to MLA or APA style once you have entered it into the program's file.

**EXERCISE**

1. In the process of conducting your research, begin to compile your list of references or works cited. Photocopy your list for the members of the

group. As a group, discuss the range and quality of research that appears to be represented by the list. Are the works listed up to date, reflecting current scholarship? Are any of the authors well-known? Does the list inspire confidence? After answering these questions, edit the list so that it conforms to MLA or APA documentation style.

## WORKS CITED

Allen, Irving Lewis. *The Language of Ethnic Conflict: Social Organization and Lexical Culture.* New York: Columbia UP, 1983.

Assael, Shaun. "Why Big Tobacco Woos Minorities." *Adweek's Marketing Week* 29 Jan. 1990: 20–30.

Bleich, David. *The Double Perspective: Language, Literacy and Social Relations.* New York: Oxford UP, 1988.

Chesler, Phyllis. *The Sacred Bond: The Legacy of Baby M.* New York: Times Books, 1988.

Koch, Edward I. "Death and Justice: How Capital Punishment Affirms Life." *The New Republic* 15 Apr. 1985: 12–14.

Schmukler, Isadore, and Betsy P. Aigen. "The Terror of Surrogate Motherhood: Fantasies, Realities, and Viable Legislation." *Gender in Transition: A New Frontier.* Ed. Joan Offerman-Zuckerberg. New York: Plenum, 1989. 235–48.

Schudson, Michael. *Advertising, the Uneasy Persuasion: Its Dubious Impact on American Society.* New York: Basic, 1984.

## SELECTED WORKS CONSULTED

Achtert, Walter S., and Joseph Gibaldi. *The MLA Style Manual.* New York: MLA, 1985.

Adams, Gerald R., and Jay D. Schvaneveldt. *Understanding Research Methods.* White Plains, NY: Longman, 1985.

American Psychological Association. *Publication Manual of the American Psychological Association.* 3rd ed. Washington: APA, 1983.

Dillard, John M., and Robert R. Reilley, *Systematic Interviewing: Communication Skills for Professional Effectiveness.* Columbus, OH: Merrill, 1988.

Gibaldi, Joseph, and Walter S. Achtert. *MLA Handbook for Writers of Research Papers.* 3rd ed. New York: MLA, 1988.

Mann, Thomas. *A Guide to Library Research Methods.* New York: Oxford UP, 1986.

McCracken, Grant. *The Long Interview: Sage University Paper Series on Qualitative Research Methods.* Vol. 13. Newbury Park, CA: Sage, 1986.

# Chapter Eight

# READING FOR

# FURTHER ANALYSIS

T his chapter consists of fourteen additional readings: seven on waste management and seven on sports culture. These selections reflect diverse points of view on interesting topics in science and sociology, providing you with further opportunities to synthesize, analyze, and evaluate multiple sources. The essays on waste management discuss the challenges of our solid waste crisis and explore a variety of solutions including landfills, incinerators, recycling programs, composting sites, and waste reduction. The essays on sports culture examine ways that sports have changed in relation to spectators' needs and players' evolving athletic abilities. We invite you to read, think, and write about these pertinent topics—to propose a solution to the solid waste crisis and to form a theory about the social role of sports.

# ■ ■ ■ ■ ■  WRITING ABOUT WASTE MANAGEMENT

*People want a quick and easy path to reduce waste, but there is no quick fix.*

—*Ellen Harrison*

In 1988 the sight of a garbage barge searching for a port along the East Coast forced most Americans to acknowledge the seriousness of the solid waste crisis. But as Ellen Harrison, associate director of the Cornell Waste Management Institute, suggests, many people do not understand how difficult it will be to find an adequate solution, one that is environmentally safe and economically feasible. The authors of the following sources propose a variety of solutions, and we invite you to analyze their proposals and to reach your own judgment about waste management.

In the first selection, "The State of Garbage in America," Jim Glenn and David Riggle overview the crisis, explaining exactly what percentage of solid waste finds its way to landfills, incinerators, recycling programs, and composting sites. As writers for *BioCycle*, Glenn and Riggle highlight the trend toward starting recycling programs and closing landfills. In "Trends in Landfill Planning and Design," however, Larry Schaper, a professional engineer, argues that landfills are a logical part of waste management; according to Schaper, Environmental Protection Agency (EPA) regulations have led engineers to design environmentally sound landfill liners and caps, leachate treatment systems, and gas collection devices. Furthermore, in "Air Pollution Control and Waste Management," Mario Gialanella and Louis Luedtke, executives in sales and marketing of gas removal systems, assert that as landfills reach capacity, well-designed and efficiently operated incinerators become an increasingly important option. Gialanella and Luedtke suggest that incinerators using recent advances in emissions control technology not only meet but exceed EPA guidelines for clean air. But in "The Dioxin Deception," published by *Greenpeace Magazine*, Joe Thornton and John Hanrahan claim the EPA bases its pollution regulations on political and economic considerations rather than on scientific research. According to Thornton and Hanrahan, the EPA refuses to acknowledge the health hazard of dioxin, a chemical formed and released through incineration, because doing so would open the federal government to lawsuits and undercut its advocacy of garbage incinerators.

The next two selections on waste management present case studies of New York City and Seattle. Nancy Shute, author of "The Mound Builder," explains that New York produces 20,000 tons of solid waste every day, over

80 percent of which is buried at Fresh Kills, a landfill on Staten Island that rapidly grows closer to capacity and regularly violates a number of EPA regulations. According to Shute, city officials plan to recycle 25 percent of New York's garbage by 1995 and to build five large waste-to-energy incinerators, but heated debate has delayed construction of the incinerators. Moreover, she adds that even if all five incinerators were built, they would accommodate only 12,000 tons of garbage a day, and even if the city could incinerate 40 percent and recycle 40 percent of its waste, the remaining 20 percent would eventually fill Fresh Kills. Should New York design new landfills and modern incinerators based on recent technological advances, or is recycling the best approach to waste management?

In "Better Homes and Garbage," Jerome Richard writes that when Seattle's two landfills began to near capacity and to discharge methane gas, city officials considered incineration but decided on a comprehensive recycling system. He describes the facilities of two companies that process recyclables in Seattle, where residents recycled 16 percent of their waste in 1989 and hope to recycle or compost 60 percent by 1998. Although Richard praises Seattle's successful program, he also anticipates financial shortcomings: the supply of recycled materials may soon overwhelm demand, making the system economically unfeasible, and the pilot project for recycling plastic bottles cost Seattle $6,000 a year more than it cost to dispose of them in a landfill. Should Seattle develop sophisticated landfills or incinerators to offset the financial burden of recycling, or do environmental concerns outweigh economic ones?

Finally, in the last reading on waste management, "What Has Happened to Waste Reduction?" Anne Magnuson insists that even though recycling is important, a cheaper solution is to generate less waste in the first place. She suggests that by using cloth towels instead of paper ones, photocopying on both sides of paper, removing names from junkmail lists, and reusing items such as drinking cups, air filters, clothing, bags, boxes, and cars, people could not only reduce waste but save money.

Waste reduction strategies, high-tech landfills and incinerators, and comprehensive recycling programs all need to be evaluated carefully if America is to solve its waste management crisis.

■ ■ ■ ■ ■ ■ ■ ■ ■

# THE STATE OF GARBAGE IN AMERICA

## Jim Glenn and David Riggle

We all begin to wonder when it will all stop—or at least slow down. When will the increase in recycling programs slow to a trickle? How long can yard waste composting sustain a 40 to 50 percent growth rate? No one really knows, but certainly 1990 was another good year, actually, another excellent year in the push to change wastes into resources.

Curbside recycling programs in place increased by almost 80 percent in 1990. That climb followed more than a 40 percent jump in 1989. In total, since our 1988 survey, the number of programs has gone from just over 1,000 to more than 2,700. Even more rapid growth has occurred in the development of materials recovery facilities (MRFs). Over the past year, the number of MRFs has more than doubled to 92. The 1988 survey identified 16. Yard waste composting facilities also are exhibiting sustained growth. In 1990, more than 1,400 yard waste facilities were operating. That is an increase of more than 40 percent over 1989 and about 120 percent more than 1988.

It's fortunate that this growth is occurring because the number of landfills continues to shrink, dropping below 6,400 by the end of 1990. This equals out to a loss of about 1,000 operating landfills, or a total approximate loss of 1,500 since the end of 1988.

Despite the encouraging news, the picture is not all rosy. Last year, the glutted paper market cast a pale [sic] over recycling. This year, it is the general state of the economy and its affect [sic] on state and local budgets. While conducting this survey, there were frequent mentions of state budget deficits in the billions of dollars. Dealing with red ink of this magnitude has led to cuts in state solid waste staff and financial and technical assistance to local governments.

This first part of *BioCycle's* third annual survey, "The State of Garbage in America," examines how much waste is going into U.S. landfills and incinerators, and highlights the growth of programs and facilities used to recycle and compost a portion of that material. All the data are for programs in operation by the end of 1990. . . .

As with last year's survey, the vast majority of information was provided by the agency principally responsible for solid waste management in each state. That information in some cases was augmented with data from other sources.

## How Big Is the Pile?

According to the survey, the amount of solid waste produced and/or disposed of in municipal facilities was approximately 293,000,000 tons in 1990. This figure is significantly more than the U.S. Environmental Protection Agency's estimate for municipal waste generation which is just under 180,000,000 tons for the year 1988.

Probably the most substantial difference between the two figures is that often, some of the waste that goes into municipal facilities is not defined as municipal waste by EPA. This includes such materials as nonhazardous industrial waste, construction and demolition waste, and sewage sludge. While some states establish estimates of the amount of waste generated (most times using the EPA figures), a majority use "disposed of" figures, i.e. what is actually being placed in municipal processing and disposal facilities.

Despite the fact that the amount of waste generated and/or disposed jumped more than 23,000,000 tons when compared to 1989, the percentage of the total solid waste reported going to the landfill declined from just under 84 percent to 77 percent.

Where did it go? It appears that incineration and recycling are picking up the slack. The amount of waste incinerated increased from approximately 8.5 to

**TABLE 1.** Waste Generation/Disposal and Methods of Disposal (by State)

| State | MSW (tons/year) | Recycled (%) | Incinerated (%) | Landfilled (%) |
|---|---|---|---|---|
| AL[d] | 4,400,000 | 5 | 2 | 93 |
| AK[b] | 511,000 | 6 | 9 | 85 |
| AZ | 3,100,000 | 5 | 0 | 95 |
| AR[b] | 2,000,000 | 5 | 3 | 92 |
| CA[f] | 50,000,000 | 11 | 2 | 87 |
| CO[d] | 2,000,000 | 20 | 0 | 80 |
| CT | 2,900,000 | Unk | 59 | 41 |
| DE[c] | 875,000 | 20 | 43 | 37 |
| DC | 755,000 | 8 | 29 | 63 |
| FL | 18,300,000 | 15 | 21 | 64 |
| GA | 4,400,000 | 5–10 | 5 | 85–90 |
| HI[f] | 1,200,000 | 4 | 13 | 83 |
| ID[f] | 850,000 | 3 | 2 | 95 |
| IL[f] | 13,100,000 | 6 | 2 | 92 |
| IN | 5,500,000 | 5 | 20 | 75 |
| IA[d] | 2,300,000 | 7–10 | 2 | 88–91 |
| KS[a] | 1,600,000 | 5 | 0 | 95 |
| KY[d] | 4,600,000 | 3–10 | 3 | 87–94 |
| LA[f] | 3,500,000 | 3 | 0 | 97 |
| ME | 922,000 | 16 | 45 | 38 |
| MD[f] | 7,200,000 | 10 | 17 | 73 |
| MA[e] | 10,000,000 | 16 | 47 | 37 |
| MI | 11,700,000 | Unk | 4 | 96 |
| MN[a] | 4,200,000 | 22 | 25 | 53 |
| MS[f] | 1,800,000 | Unk | 4 | 96 |
| MO[b] | 6,000,000 | <10 | 0 | 90 |
| MT[e] | 600,000 | 6 | 4 | 90 |
| NB | 1,100,000 | 10–12 | 0 | 88–90 |
| NV | 1,000,000 | 5 | 0 | 95 |
| NH[d] | 1,000,000 | 8 | 24 | 68 |
| NJ[b] | 14,000,000 | 39 | 9 | 52 |
| NM | 1,200,000 | 1 | 0 | 99 |
| NY[f] | 22,000,000 | 15 | 15 | 70 |
| NC[d] | 6,000,000 | 5 | 1 | 94 |
| ND | 450,000 | 3–4 | 0 | 96–97 |
| OH[a] | 14,000,000 | 9 | 10 | 81 |
| OK | 3,600,000 | 2 | 13 | 85 |
| OR[d] | 2,200,000 | 20–25 | 10 | 65–70 |
| PA | 9,200,000 | 4–5 | 6–7 | 88–90 |
| RI[d] | 1,000,000 | 18 | 0 | 82 |
| SC[e] | 2,500,000 | 8 | 6 | 86 |
| SD | 500,000 | 1 | 0 | 99 |
| TN[d] | 5,400,000 | Unk | 6 | 94 |
| TX | 18,000,000 | 8 | 1 | 91 |
| UT | 1,100,000 | 10 | 12 | 78 |
| VT | 350,000 | 15–18 | 15 | 67–70 |
| VA[a] | 9,000,000 | 10 | 10 | 80 |

**TABLE 1.** *(continued)*

| State | MSW (tons/year) | Recycled (%) | Incinerated (%) | Landfilled (%) |
|-------|-----------------|--------------|-----------------|----------------|
| WA | 5,600,000 | 28 | 8 | 64 |
| WV | 1,700,000 | 5–10 | 0 | 90–95 |
| WI[a] | 7,000,000 | Unk | 4 | 96 |
| WY[b] | 300,000 | 3 | 0 | 97 |

| **Total** | **293,613,000** | | | |

a—includes some industrial waste
b—includes demolition waste
c—includes some sewage sludge and industrial waste
d—includes some demolition and industrial waste
e—includes some sewage sludge and demolition waste
f—includes some demolition waste, some industrial waste and sewage sludge

11.5 percent. Likewise, the percentage of waste recycled climbed from just under eight to 11.5 percent. Composted municipal solid waste (not including yard waste) remained at a fraction of a percent.

Fourteen states (plus Washington, D.C.) landfill 75 percent or less of their waste—two more than last year. Four of those—Connecticut, Delaware, Maine and Massachusetts—have reduced their dependence on landfills to under 50 percent, joining D.C. and Minnesota which incinerate 25 percent or more of their waste.

As would be suggested by the increased recycling nationwide, a number of states have reported an increase in their individual rates. Last year, only Washington and Oregon had rates of 20 percent or above. This year, Colorado, Delaware, Minnesota and New Jersey have reached that level as well. Another 11 states have rates between 10 and 20 percent.

These or any stated recycling rates should be taken with a grain of salt. Often, rates are simply a "guesstimate" based on a person's experience in the field. Even if the rate were based on actual amounts, the question becomes amounts of what? For instance, last year New Jersey estimated it had an 18 percent recycling rate, excluding leaf composting. This year, the state claims a 39 percent rate. Was there that dramatic an increase in recycling? No. Officials simply included materials that had never been included in the calculation previously. So when comparing states' recycling rates, make sure it's a fair comparison.

## Landfill Numbers Down, Cost Up Slightly

The number of municipal waste landfills in this country continues to decline at a steady rate. By the end of 1990, there were approximately 6,326 operating landfills, a net loss of more than 1,000 from last year's total of 7,379. The 1990 figure represents a 20 percent drop from 1988 when there were nearly 8,000 operating landfills.

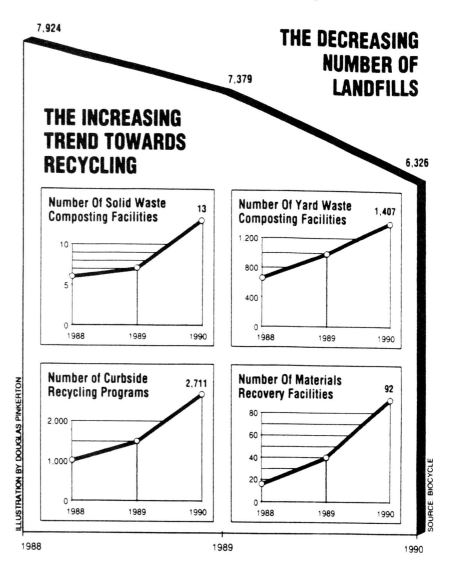

The decrease in landfills is not spread equally among the regions of the country. In the Northeast, states are continuing to lose sites, but at a slower pace than in the past. Last year, Pennsylvania led the decline in the region with a loss of 24 landfills.

The West experienced the sharpest decline. Over the past two years, California has culled almost half of its landfills from the rolls, although it still has 330 remaining. Montana and Nevada lost 50 each.

As we all know, large numbers of landfills don't necessarily translate into adequate disposal capacity which, of course, is what is truly important. Of the

**TABLE 2.** Disposable Capacity, Number of Facilities and Tipping Fees (by State)

| State | Landfills | | | Incinerators | | |
| | Number | Cost/Ton $ | Remaining Capacity (years) | Number | Cost/Ton $ | Daily Capacity (tons/day) |
|---|---|---|---|---|---|---|
| Alabama | 107 | 5.25 | <4 | 1 | 20 | 225 |
| Alaska | 740 | up to 120 | 20 | 3 | up to 120 | 100 |
| Arizona | 92 | up to 22 | n/a | 0 | – | – |
| Arkansas | 73 | 15–20 | 7 | 2 | n/a | n/a |
| California | 330 | 10–28 | n/a | 3 | 21–29 | 2500 |
| Colorado | 140 | up to 22 | 20 | 0 | – | – |
| Connecticut | 60 | 60–100 | n/a | 6 | 60–85 | 4700 |
| Delaware | 3 | 35–45 | 20+ | 1 | 35–45 | 600 |
| Dist of Columbia | 1 | 42 | 4 | 1 | 42 | 600 |
| Florida | 170 | 5–60 | <5 | 13 | 40–60 | 13,000 |
| Georgia | 180 | 10–27 | 3–4 | 1 | n/a | 500 |
| Hawaii | 17 | 17–54 | 5 | 1 | 54 | 2000 |
| Idaho | 85 | up to 10 | 10 | 1 | n/a | 50 |
| Illinois | 117 | 12–38 | 8 | 1 | n/a | 1200 |
| Indiana | 83 | 12 | 7 | 1 | 18 | 3000 |
| Iowa | 82 | up to 30 | 10 | 1 | 37 | 125 |
| Kansas | 130 | 4–14 | 15–20 | 0 | – | – |
| Kentucky | 75 | 10–28 | 3 | 1 | n/a | 400 |
| Louisiana | 32 | 15–30 | 10+ | 0 | – | – |
| Maine | 185 | 40–75 | n/a | 5 | 40–60 | 1400 |
| Maryland | 42 | up to 85 | 7 | 4 | 40–60 | 5000 |
| Massachusetts | 150 | 45–65 | 3–5 | 9 | 45–65 | 8600 |
| Michigan | 71 | n/a | n/a | 3 | n/a | 1250 |
| Minnesota | 51 | 35 | 5–10 | 12 | 54 | 4500 |
| Mississippi | 85 | 16–25 | <4 | 1 | 20 | 200 |
| Missouri | 84 | 13 | 9 | 0 | – | – |
| Montana | 90 | 5–15 | n/a | 1 | n/a | 60 |

39 states estimating the amount of landfill capacity remaining, 12 have five or less years of disposal capacity and another 11 have between five and 10 years. Disposal capacity in 17 states was estimated to be in excess of 10 years, with nine of those having 20 or more years of capacity.

Although most people would identify the Northeast as the region with the worst disposal problems, it appears from the survey that in fact the South is in the worst shape. Of the 10 southern states that estimate disposal capacity, only Arkansas and South Carolina had 10 years or more. The other eight average less than five years. Perhaps in the Northeast, after years of planning and program development, the "crisis" is starting to stabilize.

The Western states appear to be in the best shape of all the regions in terms of capacity. In fact, most state officials in the West say they don't have a disposal problem at all. Most have in excess of 10 years of capacity. The only states that don't are Hawaii, with five years, and New Mexico, with somewhere between two and five years of capacity.

**TABLE 2.** *(continued)*

| State | Landfills | | | Incinerators | | |
|---|---|---|---|---|---|---|
| | Number | Cost/Ton $ | Remaining Capacity (years) | Number | Cost/Ton $ | Daily Capacity (tons/day) |
| Nebraska | 40 | 4–13 | 8–10 | 0 | – | – |
| Nevada | 100 | up to 10 | 20 | 0 | – | – |
| New Hampshire | 51 | 18–60 | n/a | 16 | 37–60 | 900 |
| New Jersey | 31 | 50–150 | n/a | 4 | n/a | 3315 |
| New Mexico | 130 | n/a | 2–5 | 0 | – | – |
| New York | 233 | n/a | 9 | 15 | 0–85 | 12,750 |
| North Carolina | 125 | 10–25 | n/a | 2 | 45–50 | 250 |
| North Dakota | 47 | 15 | 20+ | 0 | – | – |
| Ohio | 88 | 20+ | 8–10 | 7 | 20+ | 3750 |
| Oklahoma | 147 | 8–15 | 15 | 3 | 0–45 | 1250 |
| Oregon | 94 | 26–50 | 20+ | 2 | n/a | 650 |
| Pennsylvania | 48 | n/a | 5+ | 3 | n/a | 1550 |
| Rhode Island | 1 | 13–59 | 4 | 0 | – | – |
| South Carolina | 76 | 5–10 | 10 | 2 | 40 | 700 |
| South Dakota | 36 | 3–4 | 10–15 | 0 | – | – |
| Tennessee | 96 | up to 26 | n/a | 3 | n/a | 1150 |
| Texas | 934 | 12 | 15 | 9 | n/a | 200 |
| Utah | 50 | up to 22 | 20 | 1 | 35 | 350 |
| Vermont | 60 | 20–67 | 3 | 0 | – | – |
| Virginia | 291 | 20 | n/a | 9 | 35 | 5000 |
| Washington | 49 | 35 | 40+ | 6 | 60–65 | 1200 |
| West Virginia | 44 | 15–30 | 5 | 0 | – | – |
| Wisconsin | 180 | n/a | n/a | 10 | n/a | 1000 |
| Wyoming | 100 | up to 10 | 20+ | 0 | – | – |
| **Total** | **6,326** | **164** | | **81,775** | | |

n/a—Figure not available

The South may be inheriting the title of "Disposal Crisis King" from the Northeast. But it is still far costlier to dump garbage in the Northeast than anywhere else in the country. In general, although there have been some moderate increases in tipping fees, the rise has been small.

## Incinerators

In the past year, the number of operating incinerators increased by only 10, from 154 to 164. The increase was half of what it was the previous year. While the rise in the number of plants was small, those 10 facilities added more than 13,000 tons per day of capacity, almost a 19 percent increase. By the end of 1990, there was just under 82,000 tons per day of incinerator capacity in the country.

Like last year, Florida and New York head the list in the amount of incinerator capacity available with 13,000 and 12,750 tons/day respectively. Florida's total increased approximately 3,800 over the last year and New York's went up by about 2,900. Three other states—Maryland, Massachusetts and Virginia—

have at least 5,000 tons of daily capacity and 15 others have 1,000 tons or more.

## Curbside Recycling

Given the year curbside recycling had in 1989, with over a 45 percent increase in the number of operating pilot and full-scale programs, it wasn't reasonable to expect that 1990 would be better. Well, in the immortal words of Gomer Pyle, "Surprise! Surprise!" The number of programs increased at a 79 percent clip.

According to reports from the states, by the end of 1990, there were at least 2,711 municipalities with curbside service. Almost 1,200 programs were added to the list in 1990. (The actual figure is undoubtedly higher, but Wisconsin could not provide any estimate of the number of operational curbside programs.)

Eight states now have more than 100 municipalities with curbside programs. This year, Florida (150+), Illinois (175) and New York (162), joined New Jersey (492), Pennsylvania (412), Minnesota (381), California (254) and Oregon (108), the five states on the 100-plus list last year.

Of those eight, New Jersey, Pennsylvania, Minnesota and Oregon all are at least fairly well along in the process of implementing state legislation that requires their municipalities to provide recycling services. The other three states have passed some form of similar legislation, although the deadline for implementation has not been reached.

By the end of 1990, only Alaska and Delaware did not have at least one curbside recycling program. Hawaii, Montana, Nevada, New Mexico, North Dakota, South Dakota, Utah and West Virginia all added one or more programs during the year.

Over the past year, five states added over 100 programs. Minnesota topped that list by adding 196, Pennsylvania jumped 167, California increased 151 and Illinois added 110. Florida added at least 100 programs. And although the gross numbers aren't as impressive, other states have had substantial increases in the number of programs. For instance, Indiana identified three programs in 1989. There are 28 this year. Iowa now has 17, up from two in 1989. West Virginia went from zero to 14 during the course of the year. Georgia began 1990 with six programs and now has 20.

Based on information from the 28 states that were able to provide it, more than 37,000,000 people nationwide are served by curbside recycling programs. Nine states have programs that service at least 1,000,000 people:

New Jersey—7,000,000
California—6,475,000
Pennsylvania—5,500,000
Florida—5,000,000
Illinois—2,200,000
Minnesota—2,200,000
Oregon—2,000,000
Virginia—1,200,000
Ohio—1,000,000

**TABLE 3.** Curbside Recycling Programs (by State)

| State | Number | Population Served | Mandatory | Voluntary |
|-------|--------|-------------------|-----------|-----------|
| Alabama | 6 | n/a | 0 | 6 |
| Alaska | 0 | – | – | – |
| Arizona | 6 | 50,000 | 0 | 6 |
| Arkansas | 3 | 100,000 | 1 | 2 |
| California | 254 | 6,475,000 | 24 | 230 |
| Colorado | 7 | 285,000 | 0 | 7 |
| Connecticut | 80 | n/a | 80 | 0 |
| Delaware | 0 | – | – | – |
| Dist of Columbia | 1 | 630,000 | 1 | 0 |
| Florida | 150+ | 5,000,000 | n/a | n/a |
| Georgia | 20 | n/a | | 18 |
| Hawaii | 2 | 25,000 | 0 | 2 |
| Idaho | 1 | 100,000 | 0 | 1 |
| Illinois | 175 | 2,200,000 | 0 | 175 |
| Indiana | 28 | 125,000 | 2 | 26 |
| Iowa | 17 | n/a | 11 | 16 |
| Kansas | 5 | n/a | 0 | 5 |
| Kentucky | 10 | n/a | 0 | 10 |
| Louisiana | 10 | 500,000 | 10 | 10 |
| Maine | 7 | 70,000 | 1 | 6 |
| Maryland | 37 | n/a | 1 | 36 |
| Massachusetts | 23 | 890,000 | 18 | 5 |
| Michigan | 40 | n/a | 7 | 33 |
| Minnesota | 381 | 2,200,000 | 44 | 337 |
| Mississippi | 12 | n/a | 0 | 12 |
| Missouri | 16 | n/a | 2 | 14 |
| Montana | 4 | 3,000 | 0 | 4 |
| Nebraska | 1 | 300 | 0 | 1 |
| Nevada | 1 | 8,500 | 0 | 1 |
| New Hampshire | 18 | n/a | 0 | 18 |
| New Jersey | 492 | 7,000,000+ | 492 | 0 |
| New Mexico | 2 | 20,000 | 0 | 2 |
| New York | 162 | n/a | 76 | 86 |
| North Carolina | 25 | n/a | 0 | 25 |
| North Dakota | 2 | 7,500 | 0 | 2 |
| Ohio | 56 | 1,000,000 | 3 | 53 |
| Oklahoma | 8 | n/a | 0 | 8 |
| Oregon | 108 | 2,000,000 | 0 | 108 |
| Pennsylvania | 412 | 5,500,000 | 274 | 138 |
| Rhode Island | 23 | 640,000 | 22 | 1 |
| South Carolina | 4 | 75,000 | 0 | 4 |
| South Dakota | 1 | n/a | 0 | 1 |
| Tennessee | 8 | n/a | 0 | 8 |
| Texas | 10 | n/a | 0 | 10 |
| Utah | 1 | n/a | 0 | 1 |
| Vermont | 8 | 10,000 | 0 | 8 |
| Virginia | 25 | 1,200,000 | 3 | 22 |
| Washington | 34 | n/a | 0 | 33 |

**TABLE 3.** (*continued*)

| State | Number | Population Served | Mandatory | Voluntary |
|---|---|---|---|---|
| West Virginia | 14 | 50,000 | 0 | 14 |
| Wisconsin | n/a | – | – | – |
| Wyoming | 1 | n/a | 0 | 1 |
| **Total** | **2711** | **37,054,300** | **1052** | **1507** |

n/a—Figure not available

Of the curbside programs identified this year, only 44 collect a single material. The majority—99 percent—are multi-material programs, up from 96 percent in 1989.

Over the past several years, there has been a significant increase in mandatory curbside programs in the U.S. By the end of 1989, there were 592 mandatory programs. One year later, there were at least 1,054, a 78 percent increase. Voluntary programs are growing at an even greater rate. This year 1,507 were identified, as compared to 541 last year—an increase of 179 percent in one year. Mandatory programs were in the majority (52 percent) in 1989, but by the end of 1990, almost 59 percent of all programs were voluntary.

The Northeast has the largest concentration of mandatory programs. All of New Jersey's 492 programs are mandatory. Pennsylvania has 274. Connecticut, New York, Rhode Island and Massachusetts have 80, 76, 22 and 18 respectively. Outside of the Northeast, only California (24) and Minnesota (44) have mandatory programs.

### Materials Recovery Facilities

Tied closely to the increase in curbside recycling programs is the development of materials recovery facilities (MRFs). (For this discussion MRF is a facility that sorts materials from commingled recyclables collected principally from the home.) Just two years ago, MRFs were largely an East Coast phenomenon. Not any more. Today there are 92 MRFs operating in 24 states, from Maine to California, from Florida to Washington. Last year's survey identified only 40 operating facilities. The year before that only 16 existed.

While the seed has spread, clearly the Northeast has the mother lode. New Jersey, New York and Pennsylvania account for 36 of the total number of facilities. Each has 12 in operation presently. There are 50 MRFs located north of the Mason-Dixon line and east of Ohio.

At least for the short term, it appears that MRFs will continue to be built at roughly the same pace as last year. Currently, 17 facilities are under construction and another 20 are in procurement. At least 49 other MRFs are being considered.

### Mixed Waste Processing

When municipalities and private firms began to struggle with the lack of disposal capacity and state requirements to reduce what is headed for landfills and incinerators, the first push was to develop source separation programs. Certainly, given the number of curbside programs, a lot of people have moved in that direction. Of late, however, the thought of sorting recyclables from mixed waste, although not a new idea, has been getting increased attention. While the mere mention of such a notion rankles recycling purists, facilities attempting such activity have begun to spring up in locations throughout the U.S. If they can perform at acceptable levels, chances are they will be here to stay.

In doing the survey last year, there were enough mentions of mixed waste processing that we queried states this year on their operations. Surprisingly, there was a lot more activity than expected. Twenty operating mixed waste processors (MWP) were identified. Another four MWPs were under construction and one was in construction. At least 14 more are in the planning stages.

## Municipal Solid Waste Composting

In 1989, there were only seven operating mixed municipal solid waste facilities operating in this country. By the end of 1990, that figure had increased to 13. While on the whole it's onward and upward with MSW composting, one facility (Skamania County, Washington) closed its doors last year. Additionally, in early 1991, the Agripost project in Dade County, Florida—the largest composting facility in the country to date—was, at least temporarily, closed down.

Currently, Minnesota is the hotbed of composting activity in the country, with five operational facilities and another three under construction. No other state has more than a single operating facility.

At the end of 1990, there were 10 facilities under construction. In addition to the three mentioned in Minnesota, both Florida and Iowa have two projects under construction. Missouri, Oregon and Texas have one each. Portland, Oregon's project, which will be the largest composting facility in the country, at 800 tpd, is scheduled to come on line early in 1991.

The growth in MSW composting should continue for some time. Beyond the 10 facilities under construction, another 10 are in some phase of procurement. And an almost unbelievable 72 projects are under consideration. States having the most interest in composting include Florida, Massachusetts, Maryland, Minnesota, New Hampshire, New York and Washington.

## Yard Waste Composting

Spurred on largely by state bans on disposal, yard waste composting continues to escalate at roughly the same rate as curbside recycling programs. This year's total of 1,407 facilities is up 43 percent from 1989's figure of 986, and more than 116 percent over the number found in 1988. One or more facilities can be found in 44 states. Only Alaska, Arizona, Nevada, New Mexico, Texas, Wyoming and Washington, D.C. indicated in the survey that yard waste was not being composted in their respective states.

Seven states have 100 or more yard waste composting facilities (Illinois—106; Massachusetts—160; Michigan—150; Minnesota—212; New Jersey—243; New York—170; and Pennsylvania—102). In 1989, only Massachusetts, Michigan, Minnesota and New Jersey topped the 100 level.

Over the past year, Illinois has experienced the greatest growth in the numbers of projects. At the end of 1989, there were only 20 yard waste composting

**TABLE 4.** Yard Waste Composting Programs (by State)

| State | All YW | Leaves Only | Total # | State | All YW | Leaves Only | Total # |
|---|---|---|---|---|---|---|---|
| AL | 1 | 2 | 3 | MT | 0 | 4 | 4 |
| AK | 0 | 0 | 0 | NB | n/a | n/a | 10–15 |
| AZ | 0 | 0 | 0 | NV | – | – | 0 |
| AR | – | – | n/a | NH | 0 | 37 | 37 |
| CA | 20 | 1 | 21 | NJ | 40 | 203 | 243 |
| CO | – | – | n/a | NM | – | – | 0 |
| CT | 0 | 44 | 44 | NY | n/a | n/a | 170 |
| DE | 2 | 0 | 2 | NC | – | – | n/a |
| DC | – | – | 0 | ND | 5 | 0 | 5 |
| FL | 15 | 0 | 15 | OH | n/a | n/a | 10+ |
| GA | 0 | 1 | 1 | OK | 3 | 0 | 3 |
| HI | 1 | 0 | 1 | OR | 7 | 0 | 7 |
| ID | 4 | 0 | 4 | PA | 0 | 102 | 102 |
| IL | 106 | 0 | 106 | RI | 1 | 7 | 8 |
| IN | 6 | 0 | 6 | SC | 1 | 0 | 1 |
| IA | n/a | n/a | 8 | SD | 1 | 2 | 3 |
| KS | n/a | n/a | 5–10 | TN | n/a | n/a | 6 |
| KY | 2 | 1 | 3 | TX | – | – | 0 |
| LA | 2 | 0 | 2 | UT | n/a | n/a | 1 |
| ME | n/a | n/a | 3 | VT | n/a | n/a | 10 |
| MD | 8 | 2 | 10 | VA | 1 | 1 | 2 |
| MA | 50 | 110 | 160 | WA | 6 | 0 | 6 |
| MI | n/a | n/a | 150 | WV | 1 | 0 | 1 |
| MN | n/a | n/a | 212 | WI | – | – | n/a |
| MS | 7 | 0 | 7 | WY | – | – | 0 |
| MO | n/a | n/a | 15 | | | | |
| **Total** | | | | | **294** | **517** | **1407** |

n/a—Figure not available

facilities in the state. By the end of 1990, the figure had grown to 106. The principal reason for this growth was clearly the disposal ban that became effective in July 1990. Other states with dramatic growth include New York, up from 65; Minnesota, which rose from 130; Massachusetts, which added 45; and Pennsylvania, which grew by 39 programs over the last year.

Traditionally, yard waste composting has been limited primarily to leaves. Although no good data exist for prior years, we guesstimate that more than 95 percent of all projects dealt exclusively with leaves. By the end of 1990, a minimum of 294 facilities composted grass (at least) along with leaves. That's about 20 percent of the total.

Direct land application of yard waste is increasing as well. Although there are no firm numbers, the survey found a substantial volume of grass and leaves being handled in this fashion in Illinois, Minnesota, New Jersey and Wisconsin. Additionally, state officials in Iowa and Pennsylvania believe that land application will play a significant part in dealing with yard waste in their respective states.

# ■ ■ ■ ■ ■ ■ ■ ■ ■
# TRENDS IN LANDFILL PLANNING
# AND DESIGN

## Larry Schaper, P.E.
Partner,
Black & Veatch,
Kansas City, Missouri

Professionals responsible for solid waste management have made great strides in landfill planning and design during the last quarter century. As recently as the 1960s, burning dumps were common. Some solid waste from our nation's capital was being burned at Kenilworth Dump, a few miles from the White House. In the early 1970s, the EPA waged a massive campaign to close open dumps.

As the nation progressed from dumps to landfills, landfill design became more complicated. Engineers began incorporating liners and leachate collection systems into the landfill. Because of the leachate's powerful polluting potential, leachate treatment facilities became more common. The transition from open burning dumps to sanitary landfills changed air quality concerns from smoke and particulates to methane, and more recently, to volatile organic compounds.

Landfill planning and design has evolved into a rather complex technology. The trend toward more sophisticated design will continue as long as landfills are an integral part of solid waste management. Although a sanitary landfill is the last choice in the hierarchy of solid waste management alternatives, it remains an essential part of the total waste management program. In this review of waste management, current landfill issues and the direction of landfill planning and design in the 1990s are discussed with seven important facets of landfill development.

## Siting

Siting has always been one of the most difficult aspects of sanitary landfill planning and design. Unfortunately there are no indications this will change in the future. Successful landfill siting approaches include public involvement, improved selection procedures, and in some cases, special compensation for the residents or government entity where the site is to be located.

Just two decades ago, an EPA regional administrator took the position that landfills could be located almost anywhere and any site deficiencies could be addressed through site design. Current EPA thinking regarding landfill siting is provided in the proposed Subtitle D regulations, which constrain landfill development near airports or in flood plains, wetlands, certain fault areas, seismic impact zones, and unstable areas. There is also major concern about siting landfills in areas near important groundwater aquifers. The threat of potential multi-million dollar expenditures for groundwater cleanup has convinced landfill operators that sites should be located as far as practical from major aquifers.

Landfill siting studies should reflect the degree of public acceptance, environmental impact, and cost. It is best to assign dollar values to criteria whenever possible, with point ratings for other items. Weighing the relative importance of point and economic ratings requires judgement and experience. This rating system assumes that none of the potential sites are in areas prohibited by applicable regulations.

Landfill siting considerations would include:

- SOCIAL POLITICAL CRITERIA

    Adjacent land use
    Haul route suitability
    Conformance with planning documents
    Offsite visibility
    Zoning

- PHYSICAL CRITERIA

    Impact on wetlands
    Cover material availability
    Acreage available
    Flood zone impact
    Proximity to water supply

- ECONOMIC CRITERIA

    Land cost
    Site development cost
    Haul cost

The social and physical criteria would be assigned point values. The economic criteria would be developed as actual cost values in dollars. As siting becomes more difficult and expensive, few companies or agencies have the necessary resources and fortitude to do the entire project. Thus there is a trend toward fewer and larger landfills to serve metropolitan areas. Extra costs may be incurred for host compensation. Especially when landfills are located in remote areas, there is merit in the landfill operator/owner compensating the city or county. A few dollars per ton of waste received can produce millions of dollars per year that can be used for schools, libraries, and other public amenities. The extra funds can soften the psychological impact for being the "dumping ground" for a metropolitan area.

## Liners and Caps

In the early 1970s, the EPA funded innovative projects that demonstrated new and improved technology. One such project was a sanitary landfill located in a densely populated, low-income neighborhood in Kansas City, Kansas. The landfill design included a clay liner, leachate collection, and a methane collection system. Project success was symbolized by a plaque presented to the Mid-America Regional Council, which coordinated and managed the project. The plaque was presented by the Kansas City, Kansas Chapter of the National Association for the Advancement of Colored People in appreciation for the work on the demonstration sanitary landfill project. The NAACP represented many of the people living near the site.

In the two ensuing decades, many technological developments have occurred in liner and cap design and this trend will undoubtedly continue. Using geosynthetics in landfill construction introduced many new words and techniques to the field. Geomembranes, geotextiles, geogrids, geonets, and geocomposites are examples finding their way into landfill design.[1] Using these products has changed design procedures and greatly increased the need for quality control during installation.

Geosynthetics use is still relatively new, and improved products and design techniques will undoubtedly continue to be introduced. The EPA has sponsored extensive research to aid the development of liner technology. The proceedings from technical programs at major solid waste organizations' technical conferences provide excellent technology transfer materials. One example is the proceedings from the recent Landfill Technology Conference sponsored by National Solid Waste Management Association.[2]

The availability of new products offers many options to landfill designers. In addition, old products packaged in new ways have new value in landfill design. For example, bentonite has been used as a pond liner for decades. It can now be purchased from several sources as a geocomposite, offering several potential advantages over conventional bentonite liners.

The exact nature of future landfill liners and caps will be closely tied to the requirements and constraints of applicable regulations. As concern for groundwater protection grows and the liability for groundwater cleanup increases, there is a strong driving force to improve landfill liner and cap technology.

## Leachate Treatment

Just as some good medicines have side effects, so do some good regulations. A side effect of regulations requiring liners and leachate collection systems is the resulting need for leachate treatment. Leachate treatment facilities have a significant initial cost and a continuing operation and maintenance cost.

In general, the simplest leachate management approach is to discharge the leachate to a sanitary sewer for treatment at an existing wastewater plant. However, in many cases, pretreatment standards force treating the leachate prior to sanitary sewer discharge. In other cases, sewer fees for organic waste loading are higher than the cost of constructing and operating a pretreatment plant. Thus, building a treatment facility must be factored into the overall project cost.

The pretreatment method is dictated by the constituents to be removed and by economics. Both aerobic and anaerobic treatment processes are used to reduce the quantity of leachate organics. Chemical treatment or membrane technology are sometimes needed to reduce metal levels.

Recirculating leachate in the landfill substantially affects leachate treatment needs. The debate over the desirability of recirculation has continued for years. Editor/consultant Abraham Michaels recently presented the pros and cons of the issue in *The Solid Waste Forum*.[3] If leachate is recirculated, biological treatment of the leachate occurs within the landfill, and leachate leaving the site therefore requires less treatment. Those opposed to the practice generally feel that to minimize leachate potential is to make every effort to keep liquid out of the landfill. The EPA has restricted introduction of liquids into landfills in the proposed Subtitle D regulations, but has exempted leachate recirculation if the landfill has a composite liner, leachate collection, and certain other design features.

Leachate treatment will become a more common part of the overall landfill operation. A treatment plant adds a substantial cost to solid waste disposal, but is an essential element of an environmentally sound landfill facility.

### Methane Gas

Methane gas collection systems are installed to prevent gas concentrations from exceeding dangerous limits in on-site structures or at the property line. In many landfills, energy is recovered from the collected gas. In 1988, the EPA reported that gas is collected and used as recovered energy at approximately 100 landfills.[4] Recovery is frequently feasible at very large and deep landfills. With the current trend toward larger regional landfills, it follows that methane gas collection and energy recovery will also become increasingly common.

Another factor that may hasten the trend toward methane collection and disposal facilities are global warming concerns. Methane can contribute significantly to global warming. Hunter F. Taylor, a recognized authority on resource recovery, reported that a molecule of methane is about 25 times more effective at trapping heat than a molecule of carbon dioxide.[5] If methane gas is collected and burned, it is largely converted to carbon dioxide.

### Volatile Organic Compounds

Historical concern with landfill gas was usually limited to the safety hazards associated with methane. Landfill gas typically consists of about 50 percent methane, 50 percent carbon dioxide, and traces of volatile organic compounds. In recent years, concern about volatile organic compounds has increased. California focused attention on this issue by passing legislation requiring evaluating the gas emissions from landfills; specific concerns center on the toxic and/or carcinogenic nature of compounds such as benzene, toluene, and trichloroethylene. Depending on how they leave a landfill, these gases pose a potential threat to either the air or groundwater. Because most current data is from old landfills, it is difficult to tell how much of the gases are from industrial wastes that are no longer placed in municipal landfills. The EPA states, in the preamble to the proposed Subtitle D regulations, its intent to regulate air emissions under the clean air act or in other regulations.

Future landfill design will place greater emphasis on collecting and managing the generated gases. This will result in better control of potentially explosive gas (methane), odor, and volatile organic carbon gases. If energy prices increase significantly faster than inflation, there will be increased use of landfill gas as a fuel to generate electricity.

### CADD

Computer-aided design and drafting is an integral part of contemporary design capabilities. Its use in landfill design is a trend that will continue. Design firms using CADD are driven by the need to be cost competitive. The computer provides the opportunity to improve efficiency as well as reduce design errors.

An inherent advantage in computer use is the ability to economically investigate different alternatives. There are many ways to design a given site. Using the computer allows evaluating multiple options and selecting the best choice.

Computers in landfill design are becoming universal as improved software becomes available. Some of the current software was developed for other applications and is not ideally suited to landfill design. Nevertheless, computers have become an important part of current design practice, and increased future use will yield higher quality and more efficient landfill designs.

## Regulations

The solid waste industry faces an ever-increasing volume of regulations that control disposal practices. The federal government issues proposed regulations, which—even before becoming final—influence state regulations. If and when the federal regulations are promulgated in final form, the states then have a certain time frame to draft their own regulations.

Further complicating the matter are the plethora of other laws and regulations that may be applicable to the landfill design. Other regulations that are—or may become—applicable pertain to volatile organic compound emissions, NPDES permits for liquid discharges, and wetlands encroachment. As our understanding of the environment becomes more sophisticated, the regulations needed to protect it become more numerous and complicated. There is no end in sight to the trend toward more comprehensive regulations.

The rapid progress in landfill planning and design over the last few decades will continue into the 21st century. Despite the great emphasis on reducing the nation's dependence on landfills, the need is not likely to be eliminated. As the industry gains more control over the types of materials going into municipal landfills and landfill designs become more reliable, the public may become more accepting of landfills as a logical part of the solid waste management system. The rapid pace of advancements in sanitary landfill design will challenge design engineers to stay abreast of new developments. Because the need for landfills will not expire, it is essential to develop and use environmentally sound design, construction, and operation techniques.

*REFERENCES*

1. G. N. Richardson, and R. M. Koerner, "Geosynthetic Design Guidance for Hazardous Waste Landfill Cells and Surface Impoundments." EPA/600/S2-87/097, February 1988.
2. National Solid Waste Management Association, Landfill Technologies–Back to the Basics, WasteTech 90 Technical Proceedings. October 23-24, 1990.
3. Abraham Michaels, "The Solid Waste Forum." Public Works, December 1990.
4. U.S. Environmental Protection Agency, Solid Waste Disposal Facility Criteria; Proposed Rule. *Federal Register,* page 33338, August 30, 1990.
5. Hunter F. Taylor, "Municipal Waste-to-Energy Facilities Reduce Greenhouse Gas Emissions." Presented at Institute of Gas Technology Fourth Annual National Symposium on Municipal Solid Waste Disposal and Energy Production, January 1990.

■ ■ ■ ■ ■ ■ ■ ■

# AIR POLLUTION CONTROL AND WASTE MANAGEMENT

Mario Gialanella
and Louis Luedtke

Few environmental concerns have been better publicized recently than air pollution control. Acid rain, ozone depletion and global warming have become front-page news, and the Clean Air Act has received more publicity than most other environmental legislation.

Environmental issues, however, do not appear in a vacuum. Just as the concern over air quality is growing, attention has focused on the solid waste crisis. The image of 1988's wayward garbage barge cruising the Eastern Seaboard in search of a welcoming port brought the problem into focus for millions of Americans. Meanwhile, solid waste professionals struggle with shrinking landfill capacity, growing waste generation and complex environmental protection regulations.

The interest in waste reduction by means of recycling intersects with energy production. The Persian Gulf crisis highlights the nation's dependence on fossil fuels extracted or refined in foreign nations. With some experts insisting that solid waste can provide up to 5 percent of America's total energy requirements annually, the growing waste stream may represent one of the most cost-efficient fuels for producing energy.

This central point—the disposal of solid waste and the generation of energy through the burning of solid waste—is where air pollution control should be addressed. The incineration of solid waste can produce pollutants. If inadequately controlled, these pollutants can pass into the atmosphere, where they pose health and environmental dangers. The operative phrase is "if inadequately controlled"— a phrase that applies equally to the pollutants contained in solid waste disposed of in landfills.

Public opposition to incinerators has been well documented during the '80s. In too many cases, that opposition was justified, based on dismal experiences with incinerators that were inefficiently operated or poorly designed. Unfortunately, much of the opposition was not aimed at individual incinerators, but at incineration as a method, resulting in the overlooking of advances in emissions control technology.

These advances have produced control technologies capable of removing more than 99 percent of specific emissions. The control technologies, many of them applied during the '80s in Europe and the Far East, where emissions control standards were more stringent than those in the United States, now are proven technologies capable of meeting or exceeding requirements of the Clean Air Act.

Increasingly, the public is accepting that there is no single cure-all for the solid waste disposal problem. Waste reduction, recycling, landfilling and incineration serve roles in a comprehensive program to address solid waste management. Each option has its own advantages and disadvantages.

Landfilling no longer is considered to be environmentally benign, because of the potential for groundwater and soil contamination. Equally important, existing landfills are nearing capacity and the prospect of siting new ones in increasingly crowded counties generates strong public opposition regularly.

Recycling has become the most popular alternative to waste disposal. Curbside pickups or neighborhood drop-off bins are appearing in communities throughout the nation. Recycling generally is viewed as a means of reworking a specific product—paper is reprocessed into paper, and plastics are reprocessed into plastics. Little attention is paid to the possibility of "recycling" products into energy or to determining the highest use of a particular product.

Newspapers, for example are recycled, with newsprint extracted and the paper reprocessed into relatively poor quality paper. If the concept of recycling were expanded just slightly, the high thermal value of newspapers might dictate that waste newspaper be used as a fuel source for generating electricity, rather than for reprocessing paper.

Materials recovery is incorporated in many incinerators, as a means of reducing emissions by modifying the waste stream itself. Yard clippings routinely are removed from the waste stream and composted, thereby limiting the production of nitrogen oxides. Batteries often are taken from the waste stream as a means of minimizing mercury emissions. Metal products often are removed to control heavy metal emissions.

Although many materials can be removed from the waste stream, others preclude pre-combustion handling. Potentially pathogenic waste from hospitals, laboratories or biotechnology operations usually is handled at specialized disposal facilities, but the accidental inclusion of such wastes in municipal operations poses the danger of disease transmission. Even when pre-combustion efforts are undertaken, they do not eliminate all targeted emissions. In tests at a Detroit incinerator, the recycling of household batteries reduced mercury emissions by only 50 percent—considerably less than anticipated.

In any discussion about what—or if—to incinerate, the critical consideration remains the ability of an emissions control system to remove potentially harmful pollutants from the flue gas after the waste has been incinerated. The success of an air pollution control system is determined by the quality of the air at the stack, not in the combustion chamber or at the outlet of the post-combustion emissions control equipment.

By its nature, municipal solid waste is complex and variable, producing a range of potentially harmful pollutants, including acid gases, heavy metals and toxic organics. The nation's first federal emissions control regulations were inaugurated in 1971 by the U.S. Environmental Protection Agency through new source performance standards which applied to all incinerators burning more than 50 tpd. These regulations established a maximum emission level only for particulates.

In December 1989, EPA proposed regulations for municipal waste combustors that included performance standards under Section III(b) of the Clean Air Act for new, modified or reconstructed facilities. EPA also proposed new emission guidelines and compliance schedules for states to use in developing control requirements for existing municipal waste incinerators under Section III(d).

These regulations, as well as existing local, regional and statewide legislation to control emissions from municipal incinerators, address three main types of pollutants: those products resulting from incomplete combustion (PICs), including trace organics; particulate matter; and trace metals and acid gases. Some of these pollutants such as dioxins and heavy metals are known to be toxic, while others such as the acid gases are specifically identified as damaging to the environment.

PICs include carbon monoxide and chlorinated aromatic hydrocarbons such as dioxins and furans. About 10 percent of the dioxins and furans, which can be gases or attached to particulates, are suspected toxic compounds. Polynuclear aromatic hydrocarbons and polychlorinated biphenyls (PCBs) are other PICs.

These compounds are generated during the combustion process, and can be controlled to some extent through plant design and operation. Combustion efficiency and an adequate air supply can minimize the production of these pollutants. Post-combustion particulate control equipment is able to remove the particulates on which dioxins and furans have adhered, but the additional 70–80 percent of dioxins and furans in the gaseous phase must be addressed through separate emissions control technologies.

Particulates and heavy metals represent unburned waste, including inorganic materials, and organometallic compounds. Particulates resulting from incomplete combustion are carried in the flue gas, as are inorganic oxides and metal salts that form from high-temperature oxidation.

Inorganic material that will not burn becomes bottom ash, while heavy metals may adhere to the flyash or become part of the bottom ash. Lead and mercury are two of the heavy metals and are regulated under EPA's prevention of significant deterioration regulations. These trace metals may solidify on the flyash or may evaporate at high temperatures.

Other heavy metals include arsenic, cadmium, chromium, copper, manganese, nickel and zinc. Although these and other heavy metals are not regulated, growing public concern is likely to prompt stricter controls.

Acid gases are the most publicized emissions and are formed when constituents in the flue gas combine with water or water vapor. The acid gases include nitrogen oxides, sulfur dioxide, sulfur trioxide, hydrogen chloride and hydrogen fluoride.

Because pollutants form at different points in the incineration process and from different causes, a number of technologies have been developed to address the control of individual types of pollutants. The three categories of technologies are pre-combustion, in-situ and post-combustion.

Pre-combustion, or material recovery, refers to the modification of fuel prior to combustion and can include recycling or chemical modification of the waste stream. In-situ combustion controls refer to the modification or control of the combustion process to limit the generation of pollutants formed in incineration. In-situ methods rely on plant design and operation and are used to control PICs and nitrogen oxides through temperature control, oxygen levels and mixing of combustion gases with fuel.

The accurate control of these factors will achieve near-complete burnout, thereby minimizing PICs. Control of nitrogen oxides is achieved by combining high-nitrogen fuels prior to combustion and controlling the amount and distribution of excess combustion air and temperature.

Post-combustion systems are used to control particulates and gases. Although some of these technologies may be familiar because of their long histories in emissions control, traditional particulate-control workhorses like electrostatic precipitators and baghouses have undergone considerable upgradings recently. Newer technologies, such as the array of scrubbing systems now available, were unknown a decade ago and have become important acid gas control technologies.

Particulates were the first pollutants to be addressed by regulation or science. As early as the first decade of this century, the electrostatic precipitator was developed to capture the particulates that, until then, had billowed in dark streams from smokestacks.

Legislation in 1971 regulated the larger particulates. Since then, scientific research has established the public health danger associated with fine particulates, which are inhaled easily and become lodged in the lungs, contributing to lung disease. Of equal concern is the control of constituents that adhere to particulates. At high temperatures, heavy metals can volatize into gas, later solidifying on particulates as the gas cools.

Two major types of particulate collection systems are used by municipal incinerators—electrostatic precipitators (ESPs) and baghouses.

ESPs were developed early in the history of air pollution control and have continued to serve as the workhorse of the field. They use electricity to ionize gas molecules as the flue gas flows through a large box with rows of electrically grounded plates. The charged ions collide with the flyash particles that are suspended in the gas. The charged particles are drawn to the plates, where they collect in a layer. The particles are then released periodically into an ash hopper.

A number of enhancements and upgrades have been incorporated in the new generation of ESPs. As late as the '60s the internal components of ESPs were vulnerable to corrosion and to what amounted to short-circuits, which resulted in frequent system failures and the corresponding escape of excessive particulate emissions.

Today's ESPs rely on rigid electrodes rather than wires, and have improved dependability and availability. Gas conditioning is another area of enhancement, involving the injection of chemical compounds that reduce the resistivity of the flyash, thereby allowing increased particulate collection.

Similarly, modifications to traditional power supplies allow the adjustment of voltage which is applied to the gas, producing significant energy savings. Some commercial tests of intermittent energization, which allow the base voltage to be turned off during cycles of full-wave or half-wave voltage applications to the discharge voltage, have shown reductions of as much as 50 percent of power consumption. Other enhancements have included wide-plate spacing, which reduces capital costs by reducing the number of plates needed, and the incorporation of micro-processor technology, which provides an added level of control to ESP operation.

Although baghouse popularity grew slowly in the United States, it now represents the fastest-growing of today's basic air pollution control technologies among American industry. Like ESPs, baghouses provide a means of particulate collection, but they also are capable of removing fine particulates and, in some cases, small amounts of heavy metals, dioxins and acid gases.

Flue gas is forced through specially designed fabric filters on which the particles collect. The particle layer forms a "cake" that acts as an additional layer through which air is forced. This cake is not just a side-effect; it actually serves as the primary filtering medium, and the control of its composition and thickness is of critical importance to baghouse efficiency.

Three main types of fabric filters are available, distinguished mainly by their cleaning mechanism: reserve-air, shake/deflate and pulse-jet. All three types have been improved in recent years, partly due to the selection of fabrics for the filters. Fabrics and fabric coatings are sensitive to flue-gas characteristics and the resulting ash; as such, the selection of the appropriate fabric for any individual application determines whether the baghouse will operate efficiently or not.

As the particulate collection mechanism, ESPs and baghouses control particulates and varying degrees of heavy metals. Because they are unable to control acid gases, however, they usually are accompanied by specific technologies that address acid gases.

The emphasis on acid gas control has fueled the development and refinement of a number of technologies, with the most accepted being the scrubbing systems. When used with an efficient particulate collection system, some scrubbing systems have documented removal rates for specific acid gases in the range of 95–99 percent.

The Jackson, Mich., incinerator documents removal rates of 95–97 percent for sulfur dioxide and 98–99 percent for hydrogen chloride through a semi-dry absorption system and baghouse for particulate control. In addition to controlling the acid gases, absorbers are used to control those heavy metals, dioxins and furans that have vaporized and are a part of the flue gas stream.

Of the heavy metals, mercury has been difficult to control because of its volatility. In a number of cases, emissions control devices that have achieved remarkable removal efficiencies for other heavy metals, for particulates and for dioxins have failed to control mercury adequately.

Recently, however, a hospital waste incinerator in Skovd, Sweden, documented mercury removal rates of 97–99 percent, despite the high mercury content of hospital waste. The incinerator uses a system incorporating the injection of a carbonaceous compound for mercury control in addition to the alkaline compound normally used for acid gas control.

Although there are three major types of absorption systems—wet, semi-dry and dry—wet absorption systems are used almost exclusively in industrial applications, where they sometimes provide the dual function of controlling acid gases and producing a gypsum from the system's waste. Because they depend on the injection of a liquid slurry to absorb or scrub the pollutants from the gas stream, they produce wet waste which must be treated prior to disposal.

Semi-dry, or spray-dryer, systems use an alkaline or caustic slurry that is atomized into fine droplets in a spray-dryer and then injected into the flue gas. The droplets mix with hot incoming flue gas, allowing the reagent in the slurry to react with the acid gases while the water evaporates. The dried material then drops to the bottom of the spray-dryer or passes through the dryer to the dust collector, where more acid is removed from the gases. Semi-dry systems have demonstrated removal rates of more than 90 percent for acid gases, up to 99 percent for heavy metals and more than 95 percent for dioxins. The semi-dry systems have been designated as "best available technology" for municipal incinerators.

Dry absorption systems, including dry sorbent injection, initially were applied to industrial and utility operations, but recently have been applied to municipal incinerators. These systems center on the injection of a dry alkali reagent, which reacts with chemicals in the flue gas to absorb the pollutants from the air stream.

Semi-dry absorption systems sometimes are called "dry-scrubbing" systems because the water in the slurry evaporates completely, leaving dry reagent and particulates. Dry sorbent injection, which most frequently uses limestone as reagent, recently was included as a "best available technology" for municipal incinerators.

Solid waste management decisions are complex, bound by technology, economics and public opinion. A single management method is not likely to achieve the desired goals of environmental protection, public acceptance and fiscal responsibility.

Incineration offers an important option that extends beyond mere waste disposal. By utilizing a renewable resource—garbage—in place of nonrenewable fossil incineration provides a means of generating energy while conserving natural resources. A number of states, seeking to stimulate the development of such facilities as part of their intersecting goals of waste management and energy conservation, are enacting legislation geared specifically to providing rate incentives or removing prohibitive surety bond requirements for waste-to-energy plants owned and operated by municipalities.

The field of solid waste management has undergone critical changes in the past 20 years. As air pollution control systems prove their ability to safeguard the environment and public health, the perspective toward waste is likely to undergo similar changes, with waste disposal providing a simultaneous opportunity to generate energy.

*Mario Gialanella is director of sales and marketing, acid gas removal systems, and Louis Luedtke is vice president of sales and marketing for Research-Cottrell Air Pollution Control Division, Branchburg, N.J.*

■ ■ ■ ■ ■ ■ ■ ■ ■
# THE DIOXIN DECEPTION

## Joe Thornton
### Additional Reporting by John Hanrahan

In the 1960s, when scientists discovered that the pesticide DDT was causing reproductive problems among birds and fish, and that the same chemical was building up in the environment and the tissues of U.S. citizens, the government banned it.

In the mid-1970s, scientists found cancer-causing PCBs, chemicals used in electrical transformers, accumulating in the tissues of marine mammals, birds, fish and humans. Although Monsanto, the only U.S. producer of the chemicals, released studies saying PCBs were harmless, Congress banned them.

In the 1980s, scientists discovered the same, and worse, about a class of chemicals called dioxins. But the Environmental Protection Agency (EPA) has allowed dioxin pollution to continue while cooperating with the industries most responsible for it, in an attempt to roll back regulations and reduce public fears.

Why the break from tradition? Dioxin (shorthand for a group of 75 chemicals, but most commonly used to refer to the most toxic form, also known as 2,3,7,8-tetrachlorodibenzo-p-dioxin, or TCDD) is no less dangerous than PCBs or DDT; on the contrary, dioxin is more toxic, longer-lived and even more likely to accumulate in living organisms. But dioxin has many powerful friends. While only a handful of industries were dependent on PCBs and DDT, dioxin is the unintended by-product of dozens of chlorine-based industrial chemicals and processes, including pulp and paper bleaching, garbage and hazardous waste incineration, the manufacture of many pesticides and industrial chemicals, and certain types of wood preserving, oil refining and metal smelting.

An industrial coalition, with U.S. chemical and paper manufacturers in the lead and EPA and lesser industries in tow, has conducted a decade-long campaign to "detoxify" dioxin's image in the public eye. And it is succeeding. "We're failing to deal with dioxin not because of any lack of information about its dangers to human health, but because of political and economic considerations," says Dr. Samuel Epstein, professor of Occupational and Environmental Health at the University of Illinois.

Dioxin has been building up in the environment since the rapid growth of the chlorinated chemicals industry after World War II. But controversy over the contamination didn't erupt until 1979, when EPA suspended use of the dioxin-contaminated herbicide 2,4,5-T on forests, rights-of-way and pastures. The sudden decision was prompted by an EPA study correlating spraying patterns of the herbicide with human miscarriages in western Oregon. Despite a flurry of protests from the chemical industry, EPA then began the long process of canceling 2,4,5-T's registration permanently, arguing that no safe level of exposure to dioxin could be demonstrated and that a ban on the herbicide was necessary to protect the public.

At that point, the agency was on firm scientific ground. Tests on laboratory animals showed dioxin to be among the most poisonous substances known to science. Doses as low as one one-trillionth of an animal's body weight have correlated with cancer, birth defects and reproductive problems. At higher but still tiny doses, it has produced those same effects, plus developmental and nervous and immune system abnormalities, and damage to the kidneys, liver and skin. A 1985 EPA document regards TCDD as "the most potent carcinogen ever tested in laboratory animals."

Even worse, dioxin not only causes cancer itself, but also promotes cancers started by other carcinogens. Since TCDD always occurs in combination with other pollutants, the implications of this "cancer enhancement" are sobering. "Thirty years ago," Dr. Epstein says, "one in four Americans was getting cancer and one in five was dying from it. Today, one in three Americans gets cancer, and one in four dies from it. I have no doubt dioxin must be given some credit for this."

While EPA's pesticide regulators moved to ban 2,4,5-T, other EPA officials realized that a "no safe level of dioxin" policy would have broad implications. For instance, EPA was advocating incinerators for garbage and toxic waste, despite evidence that dioxins were formed and released in the burning process. An EPA memo described the quandary: "What should EPA do—regulate [dioxin] using the Clean Air Act—which could result in closing all resource recovery [garbage incineration] facilities?" Other federal agencies were threatened as well: Waiting in the wings were perhaps billions of dollars in claims from Vietnam veterans exposed during the war to dioxin (as 2,4,5-T) in the defoliant Agent Orange.

While EPA tore itself in two, Dow and Monsanto, the nation's major 2,4,5-T manufacturers, began a scientific and political battle to salvage their herbicide and soothe the public's fear of dioxin. At the same time, the federal government began a research program into Agent Orange's effects on veterans.

In 1980, Monsanto released the first of three studies of workers exposed to dioxin at its 2,4,5-T factory in West Virginia. It concluded that the workers suffered no dioxin-related effects except for chloracne, a painful skin disease. Along with studies conducted by Dow, the German chemical company BASF and the government's Agent Orange project, the Monsanto research laid the foundation for claims that humans were somehow immune to the extraordinary toxicity dioxin had shown in animal tests.

This position was reported approvingly in the media throughout the 1980s, and it soon became accepted wisdom. The Monsanto studies were influential in EPA's dioxin policy, and they played key roles in legal decisions denying compensation to American and Australian Vietnam veterans.

In 1990, information surfaced showing that the Monsanto, BASF and Agent Orange studies were manipulated and scientifically invalid. In each case, the data or methods of the studies appeared to have been massaged to obscure dioxin's effects on exposed workers and veterans. Dr. Cate Jenkins, a chemist in EPA's Regulatory Development Branch, calls Monsanto's research "fraudulent" and refers to "flawed data and the knowing, inappropriate use of such data" in the studies. EPA is now conducting a criminal investigation of Monsanto's conduct, but the policies based on these studies remain. Despite ongoing revelations of this kind, EPA continues to rely on information prepared by industry. "Industry studies are always suspect," says Epstein. "The people who profit should not do the testing."

And, in August 1990, the House Government Operations Committee charged that the Agent Orange study, conducted between 1982 and 1987 by the government-run Centers for Disease Control (CDC), amounted to a "cover-up." According to the report, the CDC study embodied "flawed science" and "political manipulation" by the Reagan White House, which "controlled and obstructed" the study to ensure that Agent Orange was not linked to the veterans' health problems. Representative Ted Weiss (D-NY), who chaired the subcommittee investigation, termed the CDC study "a sham."

Throughout the 1980s, while industry maintained that dioxin was safe for humans, some EPA officials lent a hand by suppressing information to the contrary. In late 1980, the Canadian government began to urge the U.S. to investigate the source of high TCDD levels found in the Great Lakes, and the U.S. and Canada agreed to conduct a joint investigation. Internally, EPA scientists had already predicted increased cancer rates as high as 1 per 100 among people who ate just one meal of Great Lakes fish per week contaminated with dioxin at levels of 10 parts per trillion. Such an estimate, however, would require that the U.S. Food and Drug Administration (FDA) declare a quarantine on Great Lakes fish. EPA kept these figures quiet and successfully pushed FDA to recommend only that people limit their consumption to two meals per month of fish contaminated at a 25–50 parts per trillion "level of concern."

But EPA's Region 5 office, which serves the Great Lakes states, took a harder line. In the spring of 1981, EPA Region 5 prepared a draft report rejecting FDA's "level of concern" and concluding that dioxin in the Great Lakes constituted a grave cancer threat to persons eating fish from the lakes. The report named Dow, manufacturer of 2,4,5-T, as the primary dioxin source and recommended that consumption of fish caught in the region of Dow's Michigan plant "be prohibited."

When EPA released the report, all the damaging information had been deleted. A 1983 congressional investigation found that EPA officials John Hernandez and John Todhunter had forced Region 5 to delete all references to Dow as well as any discussion of health risks posed by eating Great Lakes fish. Also deleted were all mentions of other studies pointing to dioxin's toxicity, including miscarriages in Oregon and the effects of Agent Orange exposure. Both Hernandez and Todhunter resigned in the wake of the scandal.

In addition, documents leaked to the press in 1983 showed that EPA officials had concealed evidence conclusively linking dioxin to the miscarriages in Oregon and had forbidden its scientists to discuss the project with the public or the media. Within two months after the suppressed link came to light, EPA began an internal investigation, Dow "voluntarily" withdrew its opposition to the ban on 2,4,5-T and EPA quietly canceled the herbicide's registration without having to ratify a "no safe level" position.

While industry pushed its position that dioxin was safe for humans, EPA regulators had to take another tack to avoid action because the agency's own science made clear that *any* dioxin exposure was a threat. The new strategy was based on elaborate studies called risk assessments, which attempted to measure the number of cancers in humans caused by dioxin. With these, EPA could make the political judgment that the threat posed by low-level dioxin exposure, while undeniable, was "acceptable." (For a comprehensive look at the politics of risk assessment, see "At Our Peril: The False Promise of Risk Assessment," *Greenpeace,* March/April 1991.)

EPA Chief William Ruckelshaus put the issue in stark terms in a 1983 speech to the National Academy of Sciences, while the 2,4,5-T controversy still raged. "The administrator of EPA," Ruckelshaus insisted, "should not be forced to represent that a margin of safety exists for a specific substance at a specific level of exposure where none can be scientifically established." Instead, he urged the use of risk assessment to calm public "hysteria" and "resolve the dissonance between science and the creation of public policy."

For EPA, this meant fine-tuning the science to harmonize with its political agenda. From this point on, according to Paul Merrell and Carol Van Strum, who have written exhaustive analyses of EPA's dioxin policy for Greenpeace, "Government scientists were expected to tailor their risk assessments to support already-made management decisions on dioxin."

One of the agency's first risk-based dioxin decisions involved the government-financed cleanup of Times Beach, Missouri. Emergency action was clearly necessary, but a no-safe-level position would have set a dangerous precedent. EPA thus declared a one-part-per-billion "level of concern"—requiring cleanup and evacuation at Times Beach but setting the stage for ignoring future sites contaminated below this level.

In an internal briefing document, EPA officials admitted that the level was "based on cost and need for immediate action, not total health protection." But, the document said, this position "allows immediate action for agency, and good press. Buys time: allows time for reassessment of agency risk analysis methods and policies. . . . Allows preparation of public for possible change in policy. Intermediate cost option. . . . Easily implemented, sampling is relatively inexpensive and easy."

Meanwhile, EPA was developing its official cancer potency estimate for dioxin under a court order forcing the agency to issue water quality regulations for dozens of chemicals, including dioxin. The estimate, finished in 1984, used standard methods to extrapolate from tests conducted by Dow on laboratory rats the cancer threat to humans posed by any exposure to dioxin. Once again, the tests showed that dioxin was the most potent synthetic carcinogen ever tested.

But EPA policymakers turned the study on its head, using it to set levels of dioxin exposure they considered "acceptable." Throughout the rest of the 1980s, then, EPA regulators could tell concerned communities that dioxin discharges from an incinerator or chemical factory were "acceptable" on a scientific basis. This risk-based policy also suited the affected industries, who could point to EPA regulations that reflected this new standard of "safety."

Just after EPA policymakers had finished their risk assessment policy, however, new information emerged that sparked the call for emergency action once again. Scientists around the world were finding that dioxin contamination was not limited to those who worked in chemical factories or were sprayed with 2,4,5-T; on the contrary, dioxin was literally everywhere in the environment in alarming quantities.

The findings undermined EPA's "acceptable risk" position. Dioxin exposures were not only universal but they were already greater than EPA's "acceptable" amounts. The entire food supply—especially animal products—now contains so much dioxin that the average American is ingesting from 150 to 500 times EPA's "acceptable" dose on a daily basis. A single meal of Great Lakes fish can contain the "acceptable" dioxin dose for an entire year.

These results are no surprise to anyone familiar with dioxin's behavior in the environment. The chemical is extraordinarily long-lived, resisting natural breakdown processes for many years, even decades. And dioxin's tendency to collect in fatty tissues means that it is found in frightening concentrations in species near the top of the food chain. As a result, fish, birds of prey, marine mammals and people act as living reservoirs for dioxin at levels thousands of times higher than those found in the environment.

Since nursing babies occupy a place even higher on the food chain than adults, they receive the greatest dioxin doses of all. Surveys of mothers' milk in industrialized countries, including the U.S., have found dioxins in alarming quantities. EPA's latest estimate is that breast-fed infants are subject to dioxin doses about 11,000 times greater than the "acceptable" amount daily.

This information put EPA in an impossible position. Suddenly, the agency's level of "acceptable risk" was exceeded by levels of dioxin found in the general public. In response, EPA moved quickly to revise its risk assessment to declare these new, higher doses "acceptable." By July 1986, EPA administrative staff convened a panel to assemble evidence justifying a downgraded estimate.

The pulp and paper industry, whose use of chlorine was just being revealed as a major dioxin source, joined the chemical companies in pressuring the agency. According to paper industry documents leaked to Greenpeace in 1987, the industry mounted a campaign to "forestall major regulatory and public relations difficulties" by pressuring EPA to keep alarming information from the public and to relax the present risk estimate. The briefings said the industry's "short-term objectives" were the following: "Get EPA to 'rethink' dioxin risk assessment. . . . Get EPA to issue statement 'no harm to environment or public health.' "

EPA complied, agreeing to highly unorthodox arrangements with the American Paper Institute to limit access to information on the industry's contribution to dioxin pollution. At the same time, the agency's risk panel had developed a risk proposal that said dioxin's cancer potency was only one-sixteenth what the agency had thought in 1985. The panel was surprisingly frank about the dubious basis of the proposal, noting that "there is considerable uncertainty and controversy about the mechanism by which 2,3,7,8-TCDD causes cancer," and admitting there was "no definitive scientific basis" on which to choose one risk estimate over another. Nevertheless, EPA said its downgraded estimate was "rational, prudent science policy."

The reassessment drew immediate fire. "I believe that the new draft report on dioxin health risk fails to meet the rudimentary requirements of scientific discourse," Dr. Barry Commoner, of the Center for the Biology of Natural Systems at Queens College, told an EPA audience in 1988. "Politics should not hide behind the skirt of bad science." EPA's Science Advisory Board, too, rejected the new risk assessment, finding "no scientific basis for such a change." The proposal was canceled—for the time being, at least.

While EPA and the industry assured the public that dioxin was not a cancer danger, new information emerged that suggested just the opposite. For instance, a 1989 study of a dioxin-exposed community near a chemical factory in Italy found increased rates of brain cancer, leukemia and other cancers. A 1990 study of Swedish pesticide applicators conclusively linked dioxin to high rates of specific, rare cancers. The same year, a panel of eight independent scientists, including Dr. Epstein and Dr. Commoner, surveyed all the information to date and found links between dioxin-contaminated Agent Orange and 10 different kinds of cancer, neurological effects, reproductive problems, immunological abnormalities and liver damage.

The final nail in the coffin for industry's argument came in January 1991, when the National Institute for Occupational Safety and Health (NIOSH) published the results of a 10-year study of thousands of dioxin-exposed workers in the

United States, including the same group studied by Monsanto. This, the most comprehensive epidemiological study of dioxin ever conducted, found conclusive links between dioxin exposure and elevated cancer rates.

With a final gasp, industry tried to dismiss the study. "This is very reassuring," said George Carlo, an epidemiologist who heads a consulting firm that has been retained by the Chlorine Institute. Because the link between cancer and dioxin was clearest at high exposure levels, Carlo asserted that lower levels were safe.

But that conclusion was clearly indefensible. "It doesn't say there is no risk," Marilyn Fingerhut, the study's chief author, says flatly. The study will cause "some weakening of the position of those who believe low levels of [dioxin] exposure are entirely safe for humans," epidemiologist John Bailer wrote in an editorial in the *New England Journal of Medicine.*

Now, according to a flood of new dioxin studies, cancer may prove to be only one of our worries. Because dioxin imitates naturally occurring sex and growth hormones, it can promote the growth of cancers in fledgling stages throughout the body, according to a 1988 EPA document. Even worse, dioxin-altered hormone levels can disrupt the development of the immune system and interfere with fetal development according to Ellen Silbergeld, a University of Maryland toxicologist who is a staff scientist with the Environmental Defense Fund. A damaged immune system can make people vulnerable to a variety of diseases, none of which can be traced to dioxin exposure exclusively.

Above all, hormonal disruption impairs reproduction. Dioxin's effects on sex hormones can inhibit sperm formation, suppress ovulation and decrease libido, Silbergeld says. Michael Fry, a biologist at the University of California, told the *New York Times* in May 1990 that male birds exposed to dioxin-like compounds failed to exhibit normal courtship behavior, developed malformed testes and even began to grow ovaries. "Essentially they were chemically castrated," he said. Vietnamese villages sprayed with Agent Orange are showing high rates of infertility and birth defects years later, and Monsanto workers have reported impotence and decreased libido.

Some of the most sobering of recent research involves dioxin's effects on the development of children. Observation of rhesus monkeys exposed to dioxin prenatally and through mother's milk showed that the infant monkeys were unusually dependent upon their mothers and that the mothers, in turn, treated them as if they were ill or injured. Years later, the dioxin-exposed young had behavioral and mental difficulties. Their performance in memory and other mental tasks was poor, and they seemed unusually apathetic about learning. In peer groups, the dioxin-exposed young were unusually aggressive, initiating violent behavior more often than unexposed monkeys.

"It took us centuries to recognize that lead was impairing our children's mental development," says Pat Costner, Greenpeace's research director. "There's no excuse for sitting back while the same—or worse—happens with dioxin."

Yet EPA's effort to detoxify dioxin persists. In a 1990 internal memo, EPA official Donald Barnes—one of the earliest advocates of slashing the risk assessment by a factor of 16—wrote that if the agency could find a way to adopt the level proposed in 1988, EPA could make a "risk management decision" to allow risks of one in 100,000 instead of one in a million. "EPA's number," Barnes wrote, referring to the "acceptable" dose that would result, would then be "comparable with the 'background' dietary intake level." In other words, levels of dioxin already present in the environment would abruptly, and conveniently, be labeled "safe."

The day NIOSH's 1991 study linking cancer to dioxin exposure among chemical workers was released, an EPA memo leaked to Greenpeace expressed the agency's plan to use the study to reduce the risk assessment. Though NIOSH's research involved no measurement of dioxin doses in any of the workers examined—and, according to the memo, EPA had not yet received the study's data from the author—the agency's intent was clear: "EPA will attempt a new quantitative risk assessment if the data allow (which is likely)."

Also in 1991, a dioxin conference hosted by the prestigious Banbury Center exploded in controversy when the Chlorine Institute declared, in a press packet put out with the help of a public relations firm, that a "consensus" had been reached on a new downgraded estimate of dioxin's danger. Independent scientists who attended the conference bristle at the assertion. "It was not a consensus conference," says Jan Witkowski, Banbury's director. Silbergeld, who gave the meeting's central address on dioxin and risk assessment, says she is "astounded" that anyone is suggesting there was agreement to reduce the cancer potency estimate. "I did not expect to be manipulated by industry or government spokespeople," Silbergeld told *Science* magazine in February.

But EPA apparently is already pushing the fake consensus. Linda Birnbaum, an official in EPA's Health Effects Research Laboratory, is telling the agency that "back of the envelope calculations led to agreement" at the conference that EPA's dioxin risk assessment could be weakened by a factor of as much as 500.

While it prepares to alter its risk assessment, EPA is allowing states to weaken their own dioxin positions. Regulators in seven states have already changed standards to allow greater dioxin levels. The Environmental Defense Fund is now suing EPA for its failure to implement the Clean Water Act.

Some 17,000 studies exist on dioxin's health effects. The controversy over the best way to measure the toxicity will continue. But alternatives are available now for industrial processes that produce dioxin. Paper manufacturers can substitute oxygen-based processes and other methods to eliminate the use of chlorine. Recycling and other waste-reduction strategies can eliminate any need for incinerators, and chlorinated pesticides, plastics, and industrial chemicals can be replaced with safer materials and processes.

Protecting the environment from dioxin means eliminating chlorine from a whole range of industries, and the transition will require major investments from industry and ambitious action from government. For the makers of chlorine and chlorinated chemicals, it means making different products. These are serious changes that will not come easily or, judging from the various industries' questionable efforts, voluntarily. But focusing on lengthy disputes over science and risk assessment has diverted time and money from action and jeopardized public health.

Since PCBs and DDT were banned, their levels in the environment have steadily dropped. There is more than enough information now to justify emergency action to ban dioxin sources, if only the government had the political will to do so. "EPA has been asleep at the wheel on dioxin for far too long," Greenpeace's Costner says. "It's time for the country to wake it up."

■ ■ ■ ■ ■ ■ ■ ■ ■

# THE MOUND BUILDER

## Nancy Shute

Glen Nison, a mild-mannered former New York City park ranger, may well be the city's best hope for unloading 20,000 tons of trash. For the past year, Nison has been prowling the mean streets of the Lower East Side and East Village, dodging crack dealers and winos on his way to tape up fliers and sweet-talk building superintendents. Building by building, block by block, he is preaching a word that even a year ago would have prompted many New Yorkers to let loose a Bronx cheer: recycling.

Nison, until his promotion this spring to supervisor, was one of New York's twenty-five community coordinators, the city's front line in its new mandatory recycling program. In the line of duty, he has addressed church groups and PTA meetings, handed out balloons and blue "I'm a waste watcher, I recycle" buttons at street fairs, and contacted superintendents in every building with more than nine apartments. "Some of them complain, because it's something to complain about," Nison said. "Most people are in favor of it."

The thirty-six year-old Brooklyn native counters those complaints about the inconvenience of sorting trash and storing recyclables until the weekly curbside collection day with two classic New York comebacks: "When the landfill closes, your taxes are going to go up," and "If I can recycle in a small studio apartment, I don't want to hear about it."

"I've had a pretty good time except sometimes when the weather is bad," Nison said. "In New York it's hard to get anything done, but it's working." It is indeed. Although the nation's largest mandatory recycling program began only last year and is still being phased in, New Yorkers are proving themselves more willing to recycle than officials expected. In April, the Department of Sanitation exceeded the legally mandated take of 700 tons of recyclables a day, although it failed to meet its internal goal of 895 tons. Instead, it collected 827 tons of paper, glass, bulk items like refrigerators, and dirt recycled from empty lots. The residential curbside collection of paper, glass, and metal exceeded even the internal goals, with 327 tons collected daily. Apartment buildings did not quite come through with the goods: the city hoped for seventy-nine tons a day from multi-unit dwellings, yet collected only sixty-one.

That did not surprise Ivan Braun, deputy director of the recycling program. Aside from a delay in getting recycling containers to the buildings, Braun attributed the shortfall to the knotty logistics of large building collections, including communicating to residents, coaxing supers to handle recyclables separately, and identifying miscreants. "Seattle has a great recycling program, but they cut off every building with more than six units. We don't have the luxury of doing that. We have pioneered large-apartment home recycling."

So far the yuppie haven of the Upper West Side and the blue-collar Staten Island are posting the best compliance, with about 30 percent of households recycling; not surprisingly, numbers are lower in Harlem and other low-income neighborhoods. A recent late-night tour of West Ninety-Third Street revealed neatly tied bundles of newspapers and corrugated cardboard in front of building after building, awaiting the morning pickup. Amazing, but true.

New York City has gotten religion on recycling for a reason: It is fast running out of places to put its garbage. This is no small matter. New York City, which so loves being biggest and best, is in the unenviable position of being the nation's leader in garbage production—20,000 tons a day, or five pounds for each resident, a number, for reasons that elude the city's trash mavens, that is almost twice that of other U.S. cities. The 20,000 tons is disposed of in time-honored tradition. The bulk of it, more than 80 percent, is carted to the city's Fresh Kills landfill on Staten Island and buried. Most of the rest is burned in small private incinerators, with a fraction—5 percent—recycled, mostly as bottles and can returns through the state's bottle deposit law.

Yet the city is under pressure from the state to close Fresh Kills, and a long-debated plan to build five large waste-to-energy incinerators remains mired in political and environmental controversy. Faced with this unpleasant reality, in 1989 the city passed its first comprehensive recycling law. Compared with other cities such as Seattle [see "Better Homes and Garbage," page 340] and Minneapolis, its goals are modest—25 percent recycling within five years, including composting of leaves and yard waste and recovery of household batteries and tires.

By contrast, New York state's 1987 solid waste management plan aims to reduce the trash stream by 50 percent in ten years. And since 40 percent of all of New York state's trash is generated by New York City, the burden of meeting the state's goal falls heavily on the city.

"The city backed into this crisis because it's running out of landfill space," said Eric Goldstein, director of NRDC's urban environment program and author, with Mark Izeman, of *The New York Environment Book* (Island Press). "Government is crisis oriented. It avoids difficult problems until it has to deal with them. But we're getting to that point now."

If Glen Nison is the future of city sanitation, Fresh Kills is its past. The world's largest landfill rises from the flats of Staten Island like a misdirected Pocono or Catskill, a 3,000-acre grassy lump visible from the West Shore Expressway, from the Staten Island Mall, from the backyards of hundreds of the boxy duplexes that dot this defiantly suburban borough of 40,000 people.

Six days a week, twenty-four hours a day, city barges bring 17,000 tons of trash from nine marine transfer stations in the other boroughs to Fresh Kills, where it is unloaded by large clamshell cranes and trucked to the "bank," the open slope where the garbage is dumped, crushed by compacting tractors and sealed with fill dirt. Despite the milling machines and thousands of sea gulls that wheel in to feed with each new truckload, the scene is remarkably orderly; occasional whiffs of a faint garbage-pail scent and methane and stray plastic bags that blow into wire litter fences are the messiest byproducts of the business at hand.

"Our operation is like a military operation," said Vinnie Ambrosino, a landfill foreman, Staten Island native and twenty-year veteran of the Department of Sanitation. "These guys take a lot of pride in the way they work." To Ambrosino and his colleagues, Fresh Kills is a work of art: they strive to create a level platform to quickly cover the bank, using the highest quality cover dirt. To a casual visitor standing on the edge of the bank, with 150 feet of garbage underfoot and trucks roaring up yards away, Fresh Kills is awe inspiring, a vast monument to the fecundity of consumer culture. Upon completion, this latter-day pyramid of Giza will reach 505 feet, the highest point of land on the Eastern seaboard between Boston and Washington, D.C.

The all-too-visible presence of the Fresh Kills landfill has long been a sore point among Staten Islanders, who cite the smells, dirt, and noise as yet another slight inflicted by the larger and richer boroughs. "We want the damned thing closed down," said Frank Brady, chairman of the Staten Island Chamber of Commerce. "I don't think it will be, because they don't have any alternatives. It's a complete lack of planning. Nobody wanted to touch it. They [the politicians] are all just avoiding it. It's not going to go away."

Ironically, Fresh Kills once seemed the answer to the city's prayers. New York City has often been an innovator in urban solid waste technology, and was the first to build a "sanitary landfill" to replace the malodorous, vermin-plagued open pits prevalent until the 1930s. Prior to that, the city had made other notable experiments in garbage disposal: from 1886 to 1918, New York separated household trash into ash, food waste, and rubbish. The ash was sold for fill; the rubbish was sorted to salvage paper and metal; and the food waste was steamed and separated into grease, which was skimmed off, barreled, and sold to European soap manufacturers, and solids, which were shipped to the South for use as cotton fertilizer. A wartime labor shortage and financial problems led the city to abandon recycling in favor of ocean dumping; it stayed with that easy solution until 1984, when a Supreme Court ruling barred ocean dumping of trash.

Yet the city also has historically depended on incineration and landfilling. It built the nation's first waste-to-energy incinerator in 1905; the electricity generated was used to light the Williamsburg Bridge. By 1934, the city had twenty-two incinerators (despite neighborhood opposition) and eighty-nine operating landfills; the landfills were increasingly relied upon after the ocean dumping ban. In the 1950s, the city turned back to incinerators. Then in the late 1960s, with the advent of air pollution controls, it returned to landfilling. But with space shrinking and the realization that raw garbage creates massive water pollution when dumped into wetlands, landfills were slowly phased out, too. Today, all but two, Fresh Kills and tiny Edgemere in Queens, have gone underground, and now underlie Flushing Meadow Park, Rikers Island, parts of LaGuardia and Kennedy airports, and less notable sites. No new landfill has opened in New York in the past two decades. The city now has, for all purposes, one, Fresh Kills, and it is both salvation and nemesis.

After decades of use, Fresh Kills has become an environmental disaster, consistently in violation of dozens of federal landfill regulations. The site leaches 2 million gallons a day of toxic effluent into the ground water and the Arthur Kill, in violation of federal and state landfill laws; trash often blows from the landfill and the transport barges into the water and onto the New Jersey shore; there is no system for monitoring the gas generated by the landfill, and odors are a problem, particularly in the summer.

The state has increasingly pressured the city about Fresh Kills, and obtained court orders for tighter environmental controls in 1980 and 1985. Yet the state feels the city has yet to do right by Fresh Kills. In November 1989, one day after David Dinkins was elected mayor, state Commissioner of Environmental Conservation Thomas C. Jorling filed a civil complaint against the city over Fresh Kills's environmental violations, seeking $76 million in fines and threatening to close the dump by July 1991.

Then-Mayor Edward Koch lashed out at Jorling, calling him "insane," a "fanatic," and a "hanging judge." Koch's sanitation commissioner Brendan Sexton was less inflammatory, and said the city was willing to spend millions to make Fresh Kills "a damn good landfill." He speculated that the state's move was designed to "put the new mayor in a box." Jorling, for his part, said, "The message I'm trying to communicate is that they have an obligation to manage solid waste."

Since last November, New York City and New York state have retreated to their corners, awaiting the next round of regulatory chicken. Underlying the parrying is a larger question: when will Fresh Kills be filled, and finally force the city's hand? Sexton, a peppery forty-four year-old Staten Islander, laughed when asked when the landfill will be closed. "I think I will cease operations before Fresh Kills does."

By the mid-1970s, it became clear to city officials that landfill space was becoming scarce and that out-of-state landfilling options would be prohibitively expensive. Once again, New York turned to incineration, joining hundreds of other cities across the nation in a rush to build technologically advanced waste-to-energy plants as the ultimate solution. In 1979, the Brooklyn Navy yard was picked as the site for the first of five to eight 3,000 ton-per-day incinerators. Yet after eleven years of administrative hearings and appeals and lengthy negotiations with the state, communities, and environmental groups, the city has yet to build one incinerator.

Last November, one week after New York state cited the city for failure to clean up Fresh Kills, DEC Commissioner Jorling ruled that the city could go ahead with the Brooklyn Navy Yard incinerator if it came up with an acceptable ash disposal site, either in a new clay-lined dump at Fresh Kills or through a five-year contract with a contractor outside the city.

Proponents of the incinerator claimed victory, noting that Jorling had overcome arguments about the health risks of incineration. Yet opponents claimed victory, too, noting that the city's chances of building a landfill that would be acceptable to the state, or finding a willing contractor, are slim. Incinerator ash residue runs up to 30 percent of the volume of original trash and can contain significant amounts of toxic heavy metals and dioxins, enough that it could be classified as hazardous waste, and fall under state and federal statutes for controlling hazardous waste disposal. Earlier city plans to landfill ash on Staten Island or export it to Bucks County, Pennsylvania, were quickly scuttled by environmentalist and community opposition.

The inertia gripping the city's incinerator program is compounded by mixed signals from Mayor Dinkins, who during last year's mayoral campaign proposed a three-year moratorium on incinerator construction until recycling got on its feet. Although the city's capital budget includes almost $800 million for the construction of incinerators, Dinkins's office has been notably silent on the subject. The situation has been further muddied by Dinkins's delay in appointing a sanitation commissioner. Former Metropolitan Transit Authority general counsel and secretary Steve Polan was not sworn into the job until May, six months after the election, and has made no public statements on incineration.

Yet another quandary underlies the incinerator controversy. Even if all five incinerators are up and running at full tilt, they could only burn 12,000 tons of garbage a day, less than half the amount the city now creates.

Thus New York City enters the 1990s only marginally farther ahead in dealing with waste disposal than it was ten years ago, and in the most concrete way—the measuring stick on the garbage mountain at Fresh Kills—farther into the hole. There are no incinerators, no ash disposal site, no solution to pollution from Fresh Kills—and 20,000 tons a day in trash to contend with, an amount that is climbing year after year. What is more, there is no sign that any politician is about to give garbage higher priority than any of the city's other headaches: schools, the homeless, health care, housing, drugs, crime.

Local environmentalists believe that the answer to the city's woes lies in a far more aggressive recycling effort, but worry that the municipality is regarding its 25 percent goal as a ceiling, rather than a floor. The state, with its own 50 percent goal for municipalities, agrees, "We think [25 percent] is a good start," said R.W. Groneman, a spokesman for the state DEC. "We think it is swell they went that far. We want them to go farther."

Yet the efforts of Glen Nison and his little cadre of community coordinators have won praise across the board. "Even the most cynical people in the Department of Sanitation admit that [recycling] works," said NRDC's Goldstein. "There's a real latent potential, where even three years ago people would have said you were nuts."

Nobody is quite sure how far New York City can go with recycling, however. Researchers at the Center for Biology of Natural Systems at Queens College, directed by environmental scientist Barry Commoner, claim that New Yorkers could recycle 73 percent of their household trash, including food waste, which would be composted by the city as in olden days. By landfilling the remaining 27 percent, CBNS estimates that the city could save $20 per ton of disposal cost, paying $167 per ton as opposed to the $195 per ton for the city's target of 25 percent recycling, 51 percent incineration, 14 percent incinerator ash disposal, and 10 percent landfilling. But cities in Europe and Japan have not been able to raise recycling rates above 51 percent, despite considerable experience.

New York's fledgling program faces significant obstacles: no markets for the recovered materials, and no program for the huge amount of commercial trash that is now trucked to cheaper out-of-state landfills. The city plans to double the recycling program budget every year for the next several years, from $43 million in fiscal 1990 to a proposed $73 million for 1991 despite its budget woes, and is currently studying markets and an intensive recycling pilot project demanded by environmentalists. It is also, for the first time, looking at its trash to figure out exactly what the city is throwing away. "The two biggest obstacles are markets and processing," said the Sanitation Department's Stabile. "The same as in any other city, just on a larger scale. I am confident that we are going to make it happen, but it is a challenge."

Like many other East Coast cities, New York has been forced to pay private haulers to take away the paper it collects, to the tune of $15 to $30 per ton. (The city currently charges private haulers at Fresh Kills $100 a ton.) The recycling program's Ivan Braun sees no change in that until paper companies retool plants to use more recycled stock, a response that will take years. "There's going to be a lot of hand-wringing and gnashing of teeth in the next few years while supply and demand chase each other around," Braun said of the newsprint market. "We're going to force that material into the market. The invisible hand out there is going to have to adjust to that." Markets for recyclable glass and metals have proven to be far more elastic.

Shapiro, Goldstein, and other environmentalists remain skeptical. "The only thing the city can tout is recycling," said Goldstein, who is launching a "waste-watchers" program to independently monitor the New York's recycling. "They're boxed in. They must demonstrate now that recycling is more than golden words."

Former Commissioner Sexton dismisses doubts about the city's dedication, noting that even in its infancy stage, New York's is the largest household recycling program in the country. "We're proving people wrong," he said. "Recycling in New York is difficult. Apartment houses recycling is in fact just as difficult as people told us it would be. We're still learning. And we're failing sometimes to do it right.... If we're not the leader now, it's only a question of time until people wake up to how committed we are."

Still, Sexton projects a more grittily pragmatic resolution of New York's garbage crisis. "I think recycling will be a way of life. I believe we'll be incinerating—less than we'll be recycling—but we'll be incinerating a substantial portion of the trash. If we incinerate 40 percent of the trash in New York and recycle 40 percent, leaving only 20 percent, that's still, in this town, 5,000 or 6,000 tons a day. We would still be running one of the biggest landfills in the world."

*Nancy Shute is a free-lance environmental reporter in Washington, D.C.*

■ ■ ■ ■ ■ ■ ■ ■ ■

## BETTER HOMES AND GARBAGE

### Jerome Richard

Seattle's citizens have historically been civic-minded, and for more than a decade, have recycled their household wastes. Until recently, these efforts were entirely voluntary, and were conducted by charities (usually in the form of paper drives) and by small scale entrepreneurs who set up recycling bins in supermarket parking lots. Others went door to door collecting newspaper and aluminum. And at its transfer stations, the city provided drop-off recycling boxes. Through these scattered efforts, Seattle recycled as much as 25 percent of its waste.

But in 1986, when the city's two, nearly full landfills began leaking methane gas off-site, and became Superfund candidates, it was clear that much more needed to be done. The city's short-range solution was to contract with King County to use its landfill, even though this meant a leap in costs from $11 a ton to $31.50 a ton. The merits of incineration were also weighed, but the city eventually decided that recycling was the fastest, cleanest, and safest alternative. Last September, Lorie Parker, recycling program manager for Seattle's Solid Waste Utility, boasted before the Seventh National Recycling Congress that, "no other city in the nation or the world has come close to doing the kind of recycling that we are envisioning." The vision has become reality. Today, Seattle is the recycling capital of the nation, in terms of both per capita and the total tonnage; San Jose is second. By 1998, the city hopes to recycle or compost 60 percent of its waste.

At the inception of the program, Seattle targeted all single through four-unit residences, covering about 75 percent of its residents. After seeking competitive bids, the city awarded contracts through 1992 to two recyclers who proposed different methods.

Recycle America, a subsidiary of Waste Management, Inc., landed the northern half of the city, with about 65,000 eligible households. Residents who signed up for the service received three stacking containers: one for glass, aluminum and tin; one for mixed scrap paper (including junk mail and magazines); and one for newspaper. The brightly colored bins, about the size of milk crates, are picked up weekly. Cardboard cartons can be set out alongside the bins to hold overflow.

The southern half of the city, with about 82,000 eligible households, went to Recycle Seattle, a new subsidiary of Rabanco, a locally owned waste collector. Rabanco provided 60- or 90-gallon wheeled, plastic carts into which residents toss all their recyclables for monthly pick-up.

The official recycling program got off to a bumpy start. In mid-December of 1987, the city sent out sign-up cards, and although the response was good, many of the cards were thought to have been thrown out with the seasonal junk mail. So, in February, a second mailing went out. Those who signed up in December were not sure whether they should sign up again, and confused residents flooded the Solid Waste Utility with calls—over 10,000 in one month. Then, Recycle Seattle had computer trouble, and reportedly lost thousands of sign-ups. When all the paper work was finally settled, Seattle America's processing facility was not ready, and its employees spent the first two months of operation sorting trash in a parking lot.

The city predicted that 40 percent of the residents in the north end and 30 percent of those in the south would sign up. The north end had a greater history of private recycling, more homeowners, and a more highly educated population. (The University of Washington is in the north end.) The south end is home to more ethnic groups—people who are harder to reach, requiring multi-lingual notices— and a greater proportion of renters, who would not feel the bite of higher garbage rates directly.

Officials are delighted to tell you they underestimated the willingness of Seattle citizens to participate in the recycling effort. In the north end, 89.8 percent of eligible households have signed up, and in the south, the sign-up rate is currently 67.3 percent. Parker attributes the goal-breaking sign-up rate to a good job of promotion and to the fact that expectations were based on programs in other cities. In retrospect, the city and the recyclers now agree that if *everyone* had been given a container, whether they signed up or not, the participation rate could be even higher.

Although the program is voluntary, there is a certain amount of financial coercion: those who do not recycle pay higher garbage rates, while the pick up of recyclables is free. Households that separate and cut their wastes from two cans to one save nine dollars a month, at current rates. The loud colors of Recycle America's containers (yellow, lime green, and grass green) make it clear to all who is recycling and who is not, creating a kind of community pressure to participate.

The two contractors' processing facilities are based on slightly different principles, both reportedly satisfactory. Recycle America's facility, relying on source-separated material, is a fairly low-tech operation. At a moving belt, workers sort the glass by color, and a magnet separates "tin" cans from aluminum. Mixed scrap paper, which makes up 20 to 30 percent of the household waste stream, is the most problematic element in the waste stream. The paper is heavy, difficult to handle, and the market for it is poor. San Jose does not bother collecting it, while Seattle does to keep it out of the landfill.

At Recycle Seattle, recyclables arrive unsorted. The mixed wastes are conveyed through a screen, which removes most of the cans and bottles. Farther along the conveyor belt, a blower does a pretty good job of separating mixed scrap paper from the heavier cardboard and newspaper, and at the end of the line, a magnet separates the steel from the aluminum. Between the two mechanical separators, workers sort glass by color and pick out the cans and bottles that escaped the screen.

Recycle Seattle and Recycle America processed 40,732 tons of materials in 1989, or 16 percent of the total amount of residential waste generated. This cost the city $2,980,820 or about $51.50 a ton in payment to the contractors in 1989—more than the immediate cost of landfilling, but larger collections and/or higher prices for recycled goods should make recycling cheaper than landfilling within five years. City tonnage at the landfill was down about 22 percent or 58,600 tons through December, 1989.

Success is something of a mixed blessing. The most immediate threat to the recycling program is that the supply of recycled material may so overwhelm demand that prices become uneconomical. Last year, the price for recycled newsprint dropped from about $60 to $20 per ton. The price has crept back up to $30 per ton, as newspapers up their purchases of recycled newsprint. The solution, says Don Kneass, regional recycling manager for Recycle America, is to develop more markets for recycled products. To this end, the city's Solid Waste Utility has joined the Chamber of Commerce and the King County Commission on Marketing Recyclables in a non-profit recycling venture, with the goal of increasing the markets for recycled materials.

Next on Seattle's recyclables list: yard waste and plastics. As of last year, residents can no longer mix yard wastes with their garbage. They are encouraged to compost or pay extra to have it hauled away for eventual city composting. During 1989, the city collected 31,657 tons of yard waste—12.5 percent of the total residential waste stream.

A pilot project set up to collect mixed plastics at several sites around the city proved that mixed resins are very difficult to reprocess. The city tried shipping the plastics to Thailand, but this proved too expensive. A revised program limits collection to plastic liquor and pop bottles, which are made of polyethylene teraphthalate (PET). Even so, Seattle must pay the recycling companies what it would cost to deposit the bottles in a landfill—plus a $6,000 a year subsidy. A negotiating impasse was broken when a local plastic bottle manufacturer guaranteed the recyclers $320 a ton for the material.

Seattle's recycling success story is rooted in part, in good fortune. Local steel and glass companies provide markets for those materials, and its port is convenient for shipping paper and plastics to the Far East. The city is in an environmentally conscious region with government officials who are enthusiastic about recycling and citizens eager to cooperate in the effort.

"Recycling is still in its infancy," Don Kneass reminds visitors touring the Recycle America plant. Yet Seattle's program has become something of a model for other cities. Officials from municipalities as small as Carlsbad, California and as large as Milwaukee, Wisconsin and Vancouver, British Columbia have visited Seattle to study its recycling methods. As Lorie Parker told that National Recycling Congress: "Keep your eyes on Seattle. We're going to show you how to do it right!"

*Jerome Richard is a free-lance writer based in Seattle.*

■ ■ ■ ■ ■ ■ ■ ■ ■

# WHAT HAS HAPPENED TO WASTE REDUCTION?

## Anne Magnuson

Recycling is the rage today, but whatever happened to waste reduction? U.S. Environmental Protection Agency guidelines are aiming for 25-percent recycling and waste reduction by 1992.

"It is a slippery concept," says Carl Woestendiek, waste reduction planner in Seattle. "It's really a conservation program involving shopping practices and reuse strategies."

Waste reduction, also known as source reduction, is an activity that prevents waste by reusing materials, lengthening a product's life, or precycling (changing buyer or consumer habits). For local governments, this means financial incentives or bans, reduction efforts in municipal offices and workplaces, and aggressive public education. Many locations such as Seattle employ a broader definition which includes municipal or backyard composting and redesigning products to lessen toxicity.

Analysts say the best way to complete this task is to "divide and conquer" all the little details which make up a successful program. Ellen Harrison, associate director of the Cornell Waste Management Institute, says each community's solid-waste plan should include a variety of trash-prevention schemes.

"People want a quick and easy path to reduce waste, but there is no quick fix," she says.

Perhaps the most effective, single method is for communities to reduce the sheer volume of waste by charging residents a flat fee for every trash bag. For example, recycling is voluntary in Woodstock, Ill. A 32-gallon bag for the remaining refuse costs $1.83 at curbside with a weight limit of 50 pounds per bag. David Danielson, assistant city manager, says an independent study tallied source reduction at 38 percent.

In some towns, this personal monetary incentive to reduce trash works best if a mandatory recycling law also is in place. Charging for bags did not lessen the volume of trash noticeably in Ilion, N.Y., until the village mandated the recycling of glass, newsprint and corrugated cardboard. Then the volume of waste fell by one-third, says Debra Greig of the Ilion department of public works.

The price for 30-gallon bags in Ilion is $2 and 20-gallon bags cost $1.75. The Ilion police department issues warnings followed by $250 fines if residents refuse to use the village bags. "Most people have been very cooperative," says Greig. "There have been only 10 violations in three years."

A box of 20 32-gallon bags costs $15.50 in Duluth, Ga. Carlisle, Pa.'s, 18,300 residents pay $2.10 per 30-gallon bags. The variable bag rate became mandatory last July, and the mandatory recycling law took effect in September. Carlisle supplies everyone with containers to collect glass, cans, plastics, news-papers and corrugated cardboard.

Allen Loomis, Carlisle's borough manager, says that quantifying volume reduction is difficult because the community went from numerous haulers to one hauler when it initiated mandatory recycling. The hauling contractor estimates the waste stream has been reduced from 100 tons per week to 70 tons per week. "Pricing the bags helps, but the mandatory recycling law was the motivator," Loomis says.

Beyond charging a fee per bag, municipalities labor toward other waste-reduction practices which take more time and effort. For most communities, re-duction starts in municipal offices and private business establishments. Consultant Pam Winthrop Lauer of Apple Valley, Minn., says her favorite way of encouraging waste reduction is to start a program first in government offices and garages. Then the municipality asks business and industry to join the program while advertising the values of reduction and reuse to the community.

"You go through the steps in your own courthouse and then you go one step further, to help others in the community do the same," she says. "Keep the message in peoples' sights constantly, or else it will be forgotten."

Minnesota reduction guidelines, which Lauer helped formulate, suggest a multitude of reuse strategies for business and municipal offices, many of which save money. In addition, the Minnesota Office of Waste Management's reduction checklist recommends offering incentives to employees for thinking of new ideas to reduce waste.

In Itasca County, Minn., the county courthouse and 16 road and bridge department garages reduced the amount of trash generated last year by about 10 percent. With a landfill tipping fee of $55/ton, the county saved $4,780 in purchasing costs and $104 in disposal costs by weight.

To achieve this reduction success, Itasca County zeroed in on a number of particular savings. It cleaned and reused the 60 stainless-steel air filters in the furnaces and air-filtration systems in the 16 garages and courthouse, and replaced disposable drinking cups with reusable ones.

Junk mail was reduced by employees sending pre-printed postcards to the generators asking to be removed from mailing lists. Mailing 1,000 postcards rep-resenting 20 people costs $173. In the Itasca County zoning office and human resources office, the junk mail dropped from eight pounds per week in February 1990 to 1.5 pounds per week in May.

The county also photocopied on both sides of the paper and bound scratch pads from papers already used on one side. Finally, using cloth roll towels instead of paper towels in the courthouse restrooms avoided 30.24 cubic yards at the landfill for a savings of $971.

A team spirit approach in Itasca County helped maintain motivation for the source-reduction project, says Lauer. Employees shared the workload and Lauer points out that the facility's workers knew best what prevention methods would be most appropriate. The project's facilitator at the Office of Waste Management had never heard of washable, reusable air filters.

Quantifying savings and source reduction is difficult for in-house projects, but it is even more so for communities at large. To estimate the amount of waste reduced, Itasca County compared procurement and disposal weights and volumes. These figures are more precise than measurements of source reduction for entire communities which must estimate the difference in volume of trash discarded by residents, government and commerce. Small communities can judge at drop-off centers or ask haulers whether the amount of trash has lessened.

Seattle traces waste reduction results with an annual 400-household survey initiated last April. "It is not hard numbers but a way for us to track trends in source reduction," says Woestendiek. Although the main purpose of the survey is to compare citizen participation in source reduction yearly, Seattle promotes reduction and education at the same time.

More than 50 percent of the 400 people surveyed already reduce their trash to some degree, according to a report by Karen Brattesani of Research Innovations, Seattle. They reuse bags, buy goods with recyclable packaging, reuse boxes and packaging materials, and repair small appliances at home. One in four Seattle residents compost yard or food waste in their backyards because of the successful composting program the city launched in 1985.

But only 23 percent of those surveyed could define or give an example of waste reduction. In fact, 56 percent identified recycling as a form of waste reduction. The most popular methods for reduction were buying long-lasting goods, repairing rather than replacing small appliances, and buying products with recyclable packaging. The activities least acceptable were renting tools or appliances, reusing bags for produce or bulk goods, buying used clothing, and buying used appliances or furniture.

To further inspire the public, Seattle issues pamphlets such as "Precycling," which gives tips on buying in bulk, avoiding disposable products, and shopping for durability. Other educational pamphlets encourage "Cutting Down on Garbage," give "Other Ideas for Reducing Garbage," describe "Recycling Household Items," and list "Diapering Choices."

Seattle's King County Nurses Association compares methods of treating diapers in its pamphlet. "Diapering Baby: What's the Bottom Line?" Home laundry or employing a diaper service is less expensive than buying disposable diapers which make up 2 percent of the waste stream. The association distributes its fact sheet to young mothers and pediatricians. Also, 60 of the 64 hospitals in the Seattle region now use cloth rather than disposables on maternity and pediatric wards.

Composting has become another popular method that cities and counties are using to reduce the amount of landfilled waste. Brenda Platt of the Institute for Local Self-Reliance in Washington, D.C., recommends local governments distribute backyard composters in the community since yard waste is 15 to 35 percent of the residential waste stream. Platt, director of materials recovery, says training sessions to use the composter are vital to the program's success. West Linn, Ore., has distributed individual composters and holds a symposium, "How to Compost at Home," four times a year.

Some prevention programs, such as the war on packaging, are perhaps best handled by large municipalities or states. According to industry sources, packaging costs for manufacturers climbed from $32 billion in 1980 to $60 billion in 1987. Packaging (one-third of the waste stream) can be reduced by statewide taxing or granting tax credits to manufacturers that cut back on boxes and plastic bubbles.

Denise Lord, director of planning for the Maine Waste Management Agency, says the result of the new law is that more beverages now are available in glass, metal and plastic. Yet some companies have switched to odd plastic resins which are more difficult to recycle, she says.

Portland, Ore., limits polystyrene food containers used by restaurants or other food vendors. For example, prepared foods such as deli sandwiches and take-out salads no longer can be wrapped in polystyrene according to a Portland ordinance which took effect in January 1990. Compliance at the 2,200 restaurants and grocery stores is more than 99 percent, says Catherine Fitch, policy analyst for the city's bureau of environmental services. Some of the restaurants have turned to permanent ware which is the preferred option, she says. Others use plastic and paper products which still go to the landfill.

Fitch says 100,000 tons of plastic including 9,000 tons of polystyrene are landfilled in Portland yearly. "It is difficult to assess how much waste reduction we have achieved by the new law, but we are studying it," she says.

Berkeley, Calif., has enacted a similar law banning polystyrene clam shells, cups, etc., for prepared take-out foods. The ordinance, which also took effect January 1990, is enforced through routine inspections by the environmental health department. Offenders are fined $500. "We have very high compliance," says Arba Goode, assistant manager analyst for Berkeley's recycling division.

Another form of waste reduction which is difficult to achieve locally is preventing toxins from entering the waste stream. The Coalition of Northeastern Governors has a source reduction council working on an array of issues including recent legislation to ban lead, cadmium, mercury and hexavalent chromium in packaging. Lead is found in the solder of cans, tin and wine and liquor bottle caps, and cadmium and chromium in ink pigments on labels or other parts of a wrapper or box. A package, according to the law, includes the label, binding, shipping pallet and secondary or tertiary boxes.

Chip Foley, project director for the council, reports that last spring the new law passed in eight states—Connecticut, New York, Maine, New Hampshire, Rhode Island, Vermont, Wisconsin and Iowa.

The council also has formed a toxics committee to develop a protocol for identifying other toxins in packaging. "There are years of data for lead, cadmium, chromium and mercury," says Foley, "but when you deal with these other things— benzene, arsenic, chlorine, hundreds of things—we don't have the data."

So the committee will form a chart or grid to check off negative and positive attributes for humans, animals and plant life and to address how the chemicals affect landfills and incinerators.

Federally, the government has not enacted legislation to foster source reduction. EPA regards itself as an "information exchange," says Paul Kaldjian, source reduction coordinator in EPA's Office of Solid Waste. EPA offers a 44-page booklet, "The Environmental Consumer's Handbook," which summarizes waste reduction and offers a bibliography of EPA sources.

Kaldjian suggests local officials also subscribe to "Reusable News," a quarterly newsletter put out by EPA's Office of Solid Waste's municipal and industrial solid waste division.

In addition, EPA helps finance packaging and product life assessment (PLAs) studies. Kaldjian says these life-cycle analyses will determine the environmental impacts of different products or packages not only during disposal but also during the manufacture and use phases. This would include risk calculations for natural resources and energy, emissions during manufacture and disposal characteristics.

"The issue of PLAs is a long way from being resolved," says Susan Mooney of Chicago's EPA office. "Environmental impact assessment is a big, black box, and we don't know what's in it and we don't know its borders. The hope is PLAs would provide a systematic way to compare or look at a product or material."

Mooney says grocery shoppers now notice paper and plastic bags, consider where they come from and their biodegradability. Life-cycle analyses for these bags will calculate the whole gamut of environmental effects. "In the end we'll have all the information laid out," she says.

A long time may be needed before these assessments are of practical, everyday use to the public and localities. But the advantage of PLAs from a waste-reduction point of view is to improve labeling programs. This would encourage consumer "smart-shopping."

There are numerous proposed laws regarding waste reduction before state legislatures across the nation which would affect local waste-prevention programs. For example, the waste reduction and packaging law ("the wrap act") to be proposed in New York, would require all packaging to be 50-percent recycled and have a statewide recyclability rate of 60 percent.

An exception would be if the package could be refilled a minimum of five times. The sale in disposable wraps of food to be eaten on the premises would be prohibited, says the bill's author, Judith Enck of the New York Public Interest Research Group. There would be a charge of five cents for each paper or plastic bag used in retail transactions.

With legislation in the wings, localities and residents still want a quick and easy path toward waste prevention. But American cities and counties should resist passing the waste-reduction buck back to the state and federal level, Harrison says. She adds that a tendency exists for local governments to wait for higher action and for the federal government to pass it down.

"In the end, consumers have to do this thing," she says. "In fact, educating the public may be the most important aspect of a waste-reduction program."

*Anne Magnuson is a correspondent for* American City & County *based in Clifton Park, N.Y.*

# ■ ■ ■ ■ ■ WRITING ABOUT SPORTS CULTURE

*So why worry about what the future may bring, particularly since it already seems to be here?*

*Ron Fimrite*

We have selected readings on sports that are certain to stimulate your thinking about the role of sports in your life, in American culture, and in an increasingly technological world. How have sports changed in relation to players' evolving athletic capabilities and to spectators' needs? And what do these changes suggest about what sports in America will be like in the twenty-first century?

In his essay "Football Red and Baseball Green," Murray Ross suggests that spectators seem to prefer more and more the fast-paced, mechanized sport of football to the more leisurely, rural sport of baseball. Ross, an authority in drama who directs the theatre program at the University of Colorado, appreciates the mythic and romantic elements of sports. He believes American spectators are drawn to both of these sports, but he argues that football helps to save us, with heroic exploits, from the chaos we experience in our daily lives. British author Mary Evans, a lecturer in sociology at the University of Kent at Canterbury, agrees with Ross in her essay "Patriarchy at Play" that football reflects American cultures and values, but finds the reflection unflattering.

Americans' changing tastes in sports may also help to explain why basketball is evolving into a fast-paced, slam-dunking sport. Phil Taylor, in his 1991 article from *Sports Illustrated*, "Bashball!" explores these changes and hopes for a future in which the game will still be recognizable in its purer style. Taylor's discussion of changes in basketball provides a context for the two additional readings on basketball: Jeff Greenfield's "The Black and White Truth About Basketball" and Charles Pierce's "The Brother from Another Planet." Both of these essays appeared originally in the men's magazine *Esquire*, Greenfield's in 1975 and Pierce's in 1992. (Greenfield's essay appears here in its updated 1984 version.) Both essays address the issue of "black" and "white" styles of basketball: Greenfield argues that "white" ball is methodical, "black" ball is expressive; Pierce, through his analysis of Boston Celtics player Larry Bird, suggests that "black" and "white" distinctions may blind us to our best possibilities.

The final two essays on sports, Linda Levy's "A Study of Sports Crowd Behavior: The Case of the Great Pumpkin Incident" and Ron Fimrite's "What If They Held a Sporting Event and Nobody Came?" explore the relation of the spectators to sports spectacle. Levy, a professor of sociology at Rutgers University, applies four theories of collective behavior in her analysis of an incident she observed while attending a professional football game. Levy adds another perspective to Ross's and Evans's on what attracts Americans to football games and why spectators behave as they do. Fimrite, in an article that appeared in *Sports Illustrated* in July of 1991, worries less about crowd behavior and conformity among spectators than he does about the trend toward isolation in the viewing of sports. His essay provokes his readers to reflect on whether televised sports will damage social and family relations. Should we as Americans encourage the changes that are taking place in sports and sports-viewing, or should we resist them, holding back the future, as Fimrite would have us do?

■ ■ ■ ■ ■ ■ ■ ■ ■

# FOOTBALL RED AND BASEBALL GREEN

## Murray Ross

Every Superbowl played in the 1980s rates among the top television draws of the decade—pro football's championship game is right up there on the charts with blockbusters like *Star Wars, Batman,* and the *Rockys.* This revelation is one way of indicating just how popular spectator sports are in this country. Americans, or American men anyway, seem to care about the games they watch as much as the Elizabethans cared about their plays, and I suspect for some of the same reasons. There is, in sport, some of the rudimentary drama found in popular theater: familiar plots, type characters, heroic and comic action spiced with new and unpredictable variations. And common to watching both activities is the sense of participation in a shared tradition and in shared fantasies. If sport exploits these fantasies without significantly transcending them, it seems no less satisfying for all that.

It is my guess that sport spectating involves something more than the vicarious pleasures of identifying with athletic prowess. I suspect that each sport contains a fundamental myth which it elaborates for its fans, and that our pleasure in watching such games derives in part from belonging briefly to the mythical world which the game and its players bring to life. I am especially interested in baseball and football because they are so popular and so uniquely *American;* they began here and unlike basketball they have not been widely exported. Thus whatever can be said, mythically, about these games would seem to apply to our culture.

Baseball's myth may be the easier to identify since we have a greater historical perspective on the game. It was an instant success during the Industrialization, and most probably it was a reaction to the squalor, the faster pace, and the dreariness of the new conditions. Baseball was old-fashioned right from the start;

it seems conceived in nostalgia, in the resuscitation of the Jeffersonian dream. It established an artificial rural environment, one removed from the toil of an urban life, which spectators could be admitted to and temporarily breathe in. Baseball is a *pastoral* sport, and I think the game can be best understood as this kind of art. For baseball does what all good pastoral does—it creates an atmosphere in which everything exists in harmony.

Consider, for instance, the spatial organization of the game. A kind of controlled openness is created by having everything fan out from home plate, and the crowd sees the game through an arranged perspective that is rarely violated. Visually this means that the game is always seen as a constant, rather calm whole, and that the players and the playing field are viewed in relationship to each other. Each player has a certain position, a special area to tend, and the game often seems to be as much a dialogue between the fielders and the field as it is a contest between the players themselves: Will that ball get through the hole? Can that outfielder run under that fly? As a moral genre, pastoral asserts the virtue of communion with nature. As a competitive game, baseball asserts that the team which best relates to the playing field (by hitting the ball in the right places) will win.

Having established its landscape, pastoral art operates to eliminate any reference to that bigger, more disturbing, more real world it has left behind. All games are to some extent insulated from the outside by having their own rules, but baseball has a circular structure as well which furthers its comfortable feeling of self-sufficiency. By this I mean that every motion of extension is also one of return—a ball hit outside is a *home* run, a full circle. Home—familiar, peaceful, secure—it is the beginning and the end. You must go out but you must come back; only the completed movement is registered.

Time is a serious threat to any form of pastoral. The genre poses a timeless world of perpetual spring, and it does its best to silence the ticking of clocks which remind us that in time the green world fades into winter. One's sense of time is directly related to what happens in it, and baseball is so structured as to stretch out and ritualize whatever action it contains. Dramatic moments are few, and they are almost always isolated by the routine texture of normal play. It is certainly a game of climax and drama, but it is perhaps more a game of repeated and predictable action: the foul balls, the walks, the pitcher fussing around on the mound, the lazy fly ball to center field. This is, I think, as it should be, for baseball exists as an alternative to a world of too much action, struggle, and change. It is a merciful release from a more grinding and insistent tempo, and its time, as William Carlos Williams suggests, makes a virtue out of idleness simply by providing it:

> The crowd at the ball game
> is moved uniformly
> by a spirit of uselessness
> Which delights them. . . .

Within this expanded and idle time the baseball fan is at liberty to become a ceremonial participant and a lover of style. Because the action is normalized, how something is done becomes as important as the action itself. Thus baseball's most delicate and detailed aspects are often, to the spectator, the most interesting.

The pitcher's windup, the anticipatory crouch of the infielders, the quick waggle of the bat as it poises for the pitch—these subtle miniature movements are as meaningful as the home runs and the strikeouts. It somehow matters in baseball that all the tiny rituals are observed: The shortstop must kick the dirt and the umpire must brush the plate with his pocket broom. In a sense baseball is largely a continuous series of small gestures, and I think it characteristic that the game's most treasured moment came when Babe Ruth pointed to where he subsequently hit a home run.

Baseball is a game where the little things mean a lot, and this, together with its clean serenity, its open space, and its ritualized action is enough to place it in a world of yesterday. Baseball evokes for us a past which may never have been ours, but which we believe was, and certainly that is enough. In the Second World War, supposedly, we fought for "Baseball, Mom, and Apple Pie," and considering what baseball means, that phrase is a good one. We fought then for the right to believe in a green world of tranquility and uninterrupted contentment, where the little things would count. But now the possibilities of such a world are more remote, and it seems that while the entertainment of such a dream has an enduring appeal, it is no longer sufficient for our fantasies. I think this may be why baseball is no longer our preeminent national pastime, and why its myth is being replaced by another more appropriate to the new realities (and fantasies) of our time.

Football, especially professional football, is the embodiment of a newer myth, one which in many respects is opposed to baseball's. The fundamental difference is that football is not a pastoral game; it is a heroic one. Football wants to convert men into gods; it suggests that magnificence and glory are as desirable as happiness. Football is designed, therefore, to impress its audience rather differently than baseball.

As a pastoral game, baseball attempts to close the gap between the players and the crowd. It creates the illusion, for instance, that with a lot of hard work, a little luck, and possibly some extra talent, the average spectator might well be playing, not watching. For most of us can do a few of the things the ball players do: catch a pop-up, field a ground ball, and maybe get a hit once in a while. As a heroic game, football is not concerned with a shared community of new equals. It seeks almost the opposite relationship between its spectators and players, one which stresses the distance between them. We are not allowed to identify directly with the likes of Jim Brown, the legendary running back for the Cleveland Browns, any more than we are with Zeus, because to do so would undercut his stature as something more than human. Pittsburgh's Mean Joe Green, in a classic commercial from the seventies, walks off the battlefield like Achilles, clouded by combat. A little boy offers him a Coke, reluctantly accepted but enthusiastically drunk, and Green tosses the boy his jersey afterwards—the token of a generous god. Football encourages us to see its players much as the little boy sees Mean Joe: We look up to them with something approaching awe. For most of us could not begin to imagine ourselves playing their game without risking imminent humiliation. The players are all much bigger and much faster and much stronger than we are, and even as fans we have trouble enough just figuring out what's going on. In baseball what happens is what meets the eye, but in football each play means eleven men acting against eleven other men: It's too much for a single set of eyes to follow. We now are provided with several television commentators to explain the action to us, with the help of the ubiquitous slow-motion instant replay. Even the coaches need their spotters in the stands and their long postgame film analyses to arrive at something like full comprehension of the game they direct and manage.

If football is distanced from its fans by its intricacy and its "superhuman" play, it nonetheless remains an intense spectacle. Baseball, as I have implied, dissolves time and urgency in a green expanse, thereby creating a luxurious and peaceful sense of leisure. As is appropriate to a heroic enterprise, football reverses this procedure and converts space into time. The game is ideally played in an oval stadium, not in a "park," and the difference is the elimination of perspective. This makes football a perfect television game, because even at first hand it offers a flat, perpetually moving foreground (wherever the ball is). The eye in baseball viewing opens up; in football it zeroes in. There is no democratic vista in football, and spectators are not asked to relax, but to concentrate. You are encouraged to watch the drama, not a medley of ubiquitous gestures, and you are constantly reminded that this event is taking place in time. The third element in baseball is the field; in football this element is the clock. Traditionally heroes do reckon with time, and football players are no exceptions. Time in football is wound up inexorably until it reaches the breaking point in the last minutes of a close game. More often than not it is the clock which emerges as the real enemy, and it is the sense of time running out that regularly produces a pitch of tension uncommon in baseball.

A further reason for football's intensity is that the game is played like a war. The idea is to win by going through, around, or over the opposing team and the battle lines, quite literally, are drawn on every play. Violence is somewhere at the heart of the game, and the combat quality is reflected in football's army language ("blitz," "trap," "zone," "bomb," "trenches," etc.). Coaches often sound like generals when they discuss their strategy. Woody Hayes, the former coach of Ohio State, explained his quarterback option play as if it had been conceived in the Pentagon: "You know," he said, "the most effective kind of warfare is siege. You have to attack on broad fronts. And that's all the option is—attacking on a broad front. You know General Sherman ran an option through the South."

Football like war is an arena for action, and like war football leaves little room for personal style. It seems to be a game which projects "character" more than personality, and for the most part football heroes, publicly, are a rather similar lot. They tend to become personifications rather than individuals, and, with certain exceptions, they are easily read emblematically as embodiments of heroic qualities such as "strength," "confidence," "grace," etc.—clichés really, but forceful enough when represented by the play of a Lawrence Taylor, a Joe Montana, or a Jim Rice. Perhaps this simplification of personality results in part from the heroes' total identification with their mission, to the extent that they become more characterized by what they do than by what they intrinsically "are." At any rate football does not make as many allowances for the idiosyncrasies that baseball actually seems to encourage, and as a result there have been few football players as uniquely crazy or human as, say, Casey Stengel or Dizzy Dean.

A further reason for the underdeveloped qualities of football personalities, and one which gets us to the heart of the game's modernity, is that football is very much a game of modern technology. Football's action is largely interaction, and the game's complexity requires that its players mold themselves into a perfectly coordinated unit. The smoothness and precision of play execution are insatiable preoccupations, and most coaches believe that the team which makes the fewest mistakes will be the team that wins. Individual identity thus comes to be associated with the team or unit that one plays for to a much greater extent than in baseball. Darryl Strawberry is mostly Darryl Strawberry, but Dan Hampton is mostly a Chicago Bear. The latter metaphor is a precise one, since football heroes stand out not only because of purely individual acts, but also because they epitomize the action and style of the groups they are connected to. Ideally a football team should be what Camelot was supposed to have been, a group of men who function as equal parts of a larger whole, dependent on each other for total meaning.

The humanized machine as hero is something very new in sport, for in baseball anything approaching a machine has always been suspect. The famous Yankee teams of the fifties were almost flawlessly perfect, yet they never were especially popular. Their admirers took pains to romanticize their precision into something more natural than plain mechanics—Joe DiMaggio, for instance, became the "Yankee Clipper." Even so, most people seemed to want the Brooklyn Dodgers (the "bums") to thrash them in the World Series. One of the most memorable triumphs in recent decades—the victory of the Amazin' Mets in 1969—was memorable precisely because it was the triumph of a random collection of inspired rejects over the superbly skilled, fully integrated, and almost homogenized Baltimore Orioles. In baseball, machinery seems tantamount to villainy, whereas in football this smooth perfection is part of the unexpected integration a championship team must attain.

It is not surprising, really, that we should have a game which asserts the heroic function of a mechanized group, since we have become a country where collective identity is a reality. Yet football's collective pattern is only one aspect of the way in which it seems to echo our contemporary environment. The game, like our society, can be thought of as a cluster of people living under great tension in a state of perpetual flux. The potential for sudden disaster or triumph is as great in football as it is in our own age, and although there is something ludicrous in equating interceptions with assassinations and long passes with moonshots, there is also something valid and appealing in the analogies. It seems to me that football does successfully reflect those salient and common conditions which affect us all, and it does so with the end of making us feel better about them and our lot. For one thing, it makes us feel that something can be released and connected in all this chaos; out of the accumulated pile of bodies something can emerge—a runner breaks into the clear or a pass finds its way to a receiver. To the spectator, plays such as these are human and dazzling. They suggest to the audience what it has hoped for (and been told) all along, that technology is still a tool and not a master. Fans get living proof of this every time a long pass is completed; they appreciate that it is the result of careful planning, perfect integration, and an effective "pattern," but they see too that it is human and that what counts as well is man, his desire, his natural skill, and his "grace under pressure." Football metaphysically yokes heroic action and technology by violence to suggest that they are mutually supportive. It's a doubtful proposition, but given how we live, it has its attractions.

Football, like the space program, is a game in the grand manner. Homer would have chronicled it; Beowulf would have played fullback. Baseball's roots are at least as deep; it's a variation of the Satyr play, it's a feast of fools. But today their mythic resonance has been eroded by commercial success. Like so much else in America, their character has been modified by money.

More and more, both baseball and football are being played indoors on rugs in multipurpose spaces. It doesn't make good business sense to play outside where it might rain and snow and do terrible things; it isn't really prudent to play on a natural field that can be destroyed in a single afternoon; and why build a whole stadium or park that's good for only one game? The fans in these stadiums are constantly diverted by huge whiz-bang scoreboards that dominate and describe the action, while the fans at home are constantly being reminded by at least three lively sportscasters of the other games, the other sports, and the other shows that are coming up later on the same stations. Both pro football and pro baseball now play vastly extended seasons, so that the World Series now takes place on chilly October nights and football is well under way before the summer ends. From my point of view all this is regrettable, because these changes tend to remove the game from their intangible but palpable mythic contexts. No longer clearly set in nature, no longer given the chance to breathe and steep in their own special atmospheres, both baseball and football risk becoming demythologized. As fans we seem to participate a little less in mythic ritual these days, while being subjected even more to the statistics, the hype, and the salary disputes that proceed from a jazzed-up, inflated, yet somehow flattened sporting world—a world that looks too much like the one we live in all the time.

Still, there is much to be thankful for, and every season seems to bring its own contribution to mythic lore. Some people will think this nonsense, and I must admit there are good reasons for finding both games simply varieties of decadence.

In its preoccupation with mechanization, and in its open display of violence, football is the more obvious target for social moralists, but I wonder if this is finally more "corrupt" than the seductive picture of sanctuary and tranquility that baseball has so artfully drawn for us. Almost all sport is vulnerable to such criticism because it is not strictly ethical in intent, and for this reason there will always be room for puritans like the Elizabethan John Stubbes who howled at the "wanton fruits which these cursed pastimes bring forth." As a long-time dedicated fan of almost anything athletic, I confess myself out of sympathy with most of this; which is to say, I guess, that I am vulnerable to those fantasies which these games support, and that I find happiness in the company of people who feel as I do.

A final note. It is interesting that the heroic and pastoral conventions which underlie our most popular sports are almost classically opposed. The contrasts are familiar: city versus country, aspirations versus contentment, activity versus peace, and so on. Judging from the rise of professional football, we seem to be slowly relinquishing that unfettered rural vision of ourselves that baseball so beautifully mirrors, and we have come to cast ourselves in a genre more reflective of a nation confronted by constant and unavoidable challenges. Right now, like the Elizabethans, we seem to share both heroic and pastoral yearnings, and we reach out to both. Perhaps these divided needs account in part for the enormous attention we as a nation now give to spectator sports. For sport provides one place where we can have our football and our baseball too.

■ ■ ■ ■ ■ ■ ■ ■ ■

# PATRIARCHY AT PLAY

## Mary Evans

The great event of the winter term at Harvard is the Harvard and Yale football game. It is the time when the American elite return to the ivy-clad towers along the Charles river and re-live their youth. For hours before the game, a stream of expensive foreign cars pour into Cambridge, and the parking lots are soon filled with well-dressed people cooking elegant meals on portable microwave ovens and high-powered gas stoves. At a discreet distance sit the ambulances, ready to rush anyone who falls victim to the desire for the hamburgers of their college days to intensive care at Massachusetts General.

What they come to watch is a football game, but what they take part in is a magnificent visual metaphor for American society. The lumbering absurdity of industrial capitalism's most wealthy state, the irrelevance of technology to many human needs, and the absolute dominance of the values of aggression and male physical strength, are all portrayed in a game of incomprehensible grown-up tag. As a demonstration in the way in which each society creates its own culturally specific games (or ways of playing them), and how those games say something about that society, then watching Harvard play Yale says a good deal about the United States.

First and foremost, it suggests that many Americans are having a wonderful time within a fundamentally ridiculous social system. The game itself is a constant succession of little skirmishes: short flurries of feverish, vicious activity as the players try and cross the marked lines with the ball. Within these skirmishes the players, and the spectators, all seem to enjoy themselves immensely, and it is disconcerting to the first-time spectator when everyone leaps to their feet and cheers because someone carrying a ball slipped over.

In the United States, the superlative has become a daily possibility, and applause for every action is an intrinsic part of this culture. Every paperback is the world's number one bestseller, every act of professional competence a major achievement, and every stranger a new, dear friend. These football players do not have to get through the game against a background of apathetic indifference. If they do well, or fairly well, or just what they are told, they are applauded.

Since there is so much applause and apparent friendliness around, it seems almost churlish in America not to do what everyone else does or fall around in raptures at every consumer novelty. Even the everyday language suggests a high degree of constant pleasure. People are always *pleased to have met you* after five seconds' acquaintance. The manners of the service sector are full of tiring exhortations to *have a nice day*, a nice night, nice time, nice meal or even just a nice one.

It is, however, a tribute to the human body—and a reason for genuine applause—that some of these players can move about the pitch at all. Last year's Harvard captain was a slight lad from California who weighed in at 240lb and was six feet five inches tall. And they didn't make him captain just for growing: there were others on both sides who are at least as large.

Padded up in the helmets and body protectors that are part of the uniform, they have little human shape. Only their ankles, and the fact that they still walk around on two legs, suggest that they belong to a familiar species. Like the American soldiers in Vietnam, whose equipment was often unsuitable for fast movement, so these football players seem to be dressed in a way designed to minimise speed.

Yet what these players demonstrate is not only how much the human body can be distorted, but also how much of anything Americans think is necessary to achieve their ends. Anyone in the Politburo, seeing this game, should abandon immediately all hope of nuclear or military comparability with the United States. This country has 79 men on each side of a football team. The metaphorical mathematics become truly appalling. If it takes 79 men to carry a ball 20 yards down a football pitch, what do they think they need to annihilate Russia?

Not, of course, that the Americans would necessarily win through sheer over-production. So highly specialised are many people in this society—and these football teams—that, confronted with issues and situations for which they have not been trained, they simply collapse. Who else except a man used to playing many parts could offer this country appropriate leadership?

But, paradoxically, while they seem to need so many of each other (and so much of those others), Americans also apparently need to protect themselves against each other, and the rigours of existence, to a very high degree. Just like real-life Americans, these football players have done everything they can to keep life at bay. They want to play hard, but they are not prepared, like us resigned Europeans, to envisage knocks and bumps. We have to remember that this is a country which has never known, on its own soil, the realities of 20th century war, and in which the promise of thin thighs in 30 days kept a book at the top of the bestseller list for nine months.

All this self-protection takes place in a country where real men, so the saying goes, do not eat quiche. What they will do is dress up like Martians to play football, and lie on their stomachs in the mud to confound the opposing team. When a sex will go that far to win, it is not surprising that American feminists can be driven to despair by the sheer power of the patriarchy with which they are confronted. The power and form of relationships between men and women is amply demonstrated by people at the match.

The women very occasionally watch the game. More often, they are busily arranging sociability with other wives, and keeping going the social ties that knit any society together. Younger, nubile women are bouncing around as cheer leaders: demanding not that the men cheer them, but that they cheer other men. Come on, they say, we are the pretty girls that your sons will marry, show your enthusiasm for this continuity.

And being part of this continuity is clearly no bad thing. This is not any old football crowd. The clothes are expensive, the rugs and cushions are from Saint Laurent, and the refreshments are bourbon and delicatessen sandwiches. Being the wife of one of these men carries obvious rewards, even if it does involve freezing football games, and the encouragement of bizarre games on the pitch and in the boardroom. The harsh realities of the femininisation of poverty have not gone unremarked by the highbrow American media. These women must know that if they leave the world of men, where the old and young men have all (or most) of the money, then what is outside are earnings that are half those of men, and a world quite unlike the gregarious and very prosperous warmth of the stadium.

And those inside the stadium have a manner which is seductively open and friendly. They are pleased that many have come along to join in the fun. Unlike a gathering of the British elite, this crowd—which probably represents a large part of the corporate power of the United States—is not exclusive in its manner. The spectators cheerfully move up to make room for a couple of shabby latecomers and pass them a programme. They wipe mustard off their minks with good humour, and do not bray at each other in the donkey-rally tones of their British equivalents. If you want to come to the match, then you're one of us.

Welcome, huddled masses: the game is absurd, but we will do everything that we can to preserve it.

*Mary Evans is Lecturer in Sociology, University of Kent at Canterbury.*

■ ■ ■ ■ ■ ■ ■ ■ ■

# BASHBALL!
## The College Game Is Now One of Strength and Power

### Phil Taylor

*Basketball was meant to be a game of finesse and beauty and maneuverability. In its purest form, the game has a flow to it, an elegance.*

—*Former UCLA Coach John Wooden*

*You want to know the theory people play with today? Coaches tell their kids, "All five of you guys go ahead and foul at once, because they can only call one of 'em."*

—*Virginia Commonwealth Coach Sonny Smith*

Someone dug an old game film out of the Providence College archives last season, and coach Rick Barnes, who happened to walk by while it was playing, saw the ancient images flickering on the screen. The footage was from 1973, when the Friars were playing Maryland in the East regional final of the NCAA tournament.

Barnes stopped for a brief glance, but something made him stay. It wasn't so much that the film was filled with future NBA players—Ernie DiGregorio, Marvin Barnes and Kevin Stacom for Providence; Tom McMillen, Len Elmore and John Lucas for Maryland—it was the style of play, the movement and spacing of the players. The arms and legs under the basket weren't nearly as intertwined as those Barnes is used to seeing in today's game. Cutters slid through the lane without looking as if they were running a gantlet, without having to dodge knees, elbows and forearms placed in their paths. The players were gliding through a smoother, freer game.

"It was much more of a pure game," Barnes says. "There wasn't as much body on body, like you see today. There was very little contact, and what there was, was called by the refs. From a technical point of view, it was great to watch. Sometimes you don't realize just how much the game has changed until you look back and see what it was."

College basketball has evolved over the last few years from controlled traffic to bumper cars. Strength and power are in; finesse is out. For all the recent trumpeting about New Age, run-and-gun, transition basketball, there's far more physical contact than there was 20, even 10 years ago, when the game was truly a noncontact sport. Granted, what Lew Alcindor, Bill Walton and other great centers of the past practiced in the paint wasn't exactly ballet, but it's obvious that if they were playing today, they would be performing in a far more permissive—read: brutal—atmosphere.

Bulk has become as important as height for anyone who hopes to score most of his points from near the basket, which is why athletes who might have been linebackers and defensive ends in another era are now power forwards and centers. Oklahoma State's Byron Houston (6' 7", 235 pounds), Southern Mississippi's Clarence Weatherspoon (6' 7", 240), Murray State's Popeye Jones (6' 8", 260) and Wake Forest's Rodney Rogers (6' 7", 235) are fine low-post players whose strength makes them especially well suited to today's game. Teams aren't looking for the next Ralph Sampson; they're looking for the next Larry Johnson.

Partly this is the natural evolution of the game, as inevitable as the growth of a child. Today's players are too big and too fast to be constrained by the old standards of acceptable contact. "Everybody's taking his players and putting 10, 15 pounds of muscle on them with weights and nutrition," says Louisville coach Denny Crum. "Suddenly, you have a bunch of agile 225-pounders jockeying for position, and refs are not going to be able to call the game the same way they once did."

Nearly everyone agrees that these bigger, faster athletes are leaning into, banging and pushing one another more than ever before, yet the number of personal fouls called in college basketball has remained relatively constant for the past two decades. According to the NCAA, in 1970 Division I teams combined for an average of 38.6 fouls per game. By 1990, the average had increased by only one foul, to 39.6.

Fortunately, there are no indications that increased contact has led to more fighting, and it would be hard to argue that today's more physical style has turned off the fans. Attendance figures (which reached a record 34 million in 1990–91) and TV coverage (more games are televised than ever) indicate that the popularity of college basketball is at an alltime high. But the emphasis on strength is threatening the flow and beauty of the game, the aesthetic appeal that Wooden talked about. "It's like a rugby scrum out there," says Xavier coach Pete Gillen.

Houston coach Pat Foster calls the '90–91 season "the most physical year ever." LSU center Shaquille O'Neal nearly jumped to the NBA on the assumption that if he was going to get beaten up regularly by opposing teams, he might as well get paid for it. Oklahoma coach Billy Tubbs describes the game's current style as "push and shove, block and tackle." After a typically rough Missouri–Oklahoma State game last season, Tiger coach Norm Stewart said, "Byron Houston had four takedowns and two reversals. Don't those count for two points each?"

Nowhere is this mutual pounding more evident than in the low post. A typical encounter took place last season between 6' 9", 225-pound Anthony Avent of Seton Hall and 6' 7", 240-pound Marvin Saddler of Providence. Avent set up on offense with his back to the basket, staying so low that he was almost sitting on the court. He leaned back into Saddler with such force that he would have gone skidding out-of-bounds had Saddler taken a step back. Not that Saddler had any intention of doing so. Instead, he tried to move around Avent to guard him from in front, which was hard to do because Avent's right arm was hooked around Saddler's hip in an effort to pin him back. At the same time, Saddler was digging his left knee into Avent's backside and inching him forward the way you might push a box that was too heavy to lift.

Referee Tim Higgins took a few steps back and forth along the baseline, occasionally craning his neck to get a better view of the action between the two men, like a boxing ref observing fighters in a clinch. Eventually Providence regained possession of the ball, and Avent and Saddler nearly fell to the floor trying to untangle themselves.

No foul was called, and by the current standards, probably none should have been. No advantage was gained by either player. The mugging was mutual. Play on.

There was a time when the play of Eastern teams and Big Ten schools was considered rougher than that of the rest of the country, but regional differences have now all but disappeared. In a California-Arizona game last season, Cal center Brian Hendrick and Arizona center Sean Rooks had several interesting skirmishes. At one point Hendrick came down the floor and tried to post up just outside the lane, but Rooks beat him to the spot, and the two bumped shoulders. They stood there for several seconds, pushing against each other like two men trying to move blocking dummies—and all the while they were oblivious to the action going on around them.

When New Mexico played Brigham Young last season, Lobos senior center Luc Longley and BYU freshman center Shawn Bradley locked horns for the first time. Longley proved more skilled in physical battle, and at one point he sent Bradley crashing to the floor as they fought for position. "He gave me a piece of advice later on," Bradley says. "He said to get used to it, because that's how the game is played."

But why? John Guthrie, the Southeastern Conference supervisor of officials, lays part of the blame on his own profession. "There aren't a whole lot of officials who officiate post play on a consistent basis real well," he says. "It's undoubtedly the most difficult area to officiate right now, tougher than the charge or goaltending."

For several seasons, the NCAA has tried to address the problem. The most recent attempt came during the off-season, when Division I officials attending the NCAA's six regional clinics were told about so-called absolutes—fouls that, according to veteran Big Eight and Big Ten referee Jim Bain, "officials are now directed to call every time. Offensive post people backing into a defender—it's a foul. The defender putting a knee in the back or a forearm in the rear—it's a foul, it's absolute. The NCAA recognizes the need to get the post cleaned up."

Many coaches are skeptical. "Every year at the committee meetings and rules seminars the NCAA says this is the year they're going to clean up the post, and every year it seems like it gets more physical," says Southern Mississippi's M. K. Turk.

Then again, most coaches believe officials are to blame for just about everything but the federal budget deficit. "There wasn't as much pushing and shoving 20 years ago, because you called the foul. It's as simple as that," says North Carolina coach Dean Smith. "I think we've got to get back to that."

"In the post, the referees allow the defensive man to use his hip to push the offensive man out of position," says Dayton coach Jim O'Brien. "That's the NBA's defensive philosophy. There's constant contact, and they don't call it. Every team does it, including us, because you can get away with it."

But coaches have to accept some of the responsibility for the slam-dancing atmosphere under the basket. While officials are calling the game loosely, coaches are pushing their players to take full advantage of the freedom.

"It's pretty hard on the refs when we're teaching what we're teaching," says UNLV coach Jerry Tarkanian. "On offense, we teach our guys how to pin their men, that is, pin them without getting caught fouling. If you know what you're doing, you can do a lot in there that won't get called. If our guys are pinning properly, for instance, it's as easy for the ref to call the foul on the defensive man as on the offensive man. I'm not sure there's a whole lot more the officials can do."

Ironically, the emphasis on strength at the expense of skill exists because the average player's skill has improved so dramatically. "Players have gotten so good that if they get the ball in the low post it's an automatic bucket or a foul, so you better do all you can to push them out of there or keep the ball from getting in," says Stanford coach Mike Montgomery.

A basic tenet of Providence's defensive philosophy, according to Barnes, is that "strength negates talent. If you get a great athlete against you who can really run, really jump . . . well, he's not going to run quite as fast or jump quite as high if he's got a body on him all the time."

So what will it take to swing the pendulum in the other direction? First, either all college players' television sets will have to be taken away or the NBA will have to begin all its TV games with a warning: Kids, don't try this yourselves. The pro game, with its no-holds-barred style of play, has influenced the way college players approach the game.

"Guys in college today grew up watching Moses Malone put his rear end into people and back them practically from the foul line to the baseline," says former Iowa State center Victor Alexander, now a rookie with the Golden State Warriors. "Karl Malone, Charles Barkley, Patrick Ewing, all the great inside players use their strength. It's a game of muscle in the NBA, so when you're in college, you figure, if it's good enough for the pros, it's good enough for me."

Several remedies have been suggested, including widening the lane, which would force offensive players to post up farther from the basket and make it less important for defenders to push them out. But not everyone is convinced that such a move would have much effect.

"Widening the lane won't help at all if referees don't start to call the three-second violation and stop people from camping in there," says TCU coach Moe Iba. "The reason it's so physical now is that centers are being taught not only to post up on the low block, but to back into the paint and to catch the ball within two feet of the goal. If you have somebody really working on them while they're doing that, they have to stay in there longer than three seconds, but it's hardly ever called. I have told our players we're going to start playing in the lane until somebody calls it, because everybody does it."

Then there's the three-point line, which was instituted four years ago, in part to relieve the congestion under the basket. It has worked to some extent, stretching defenses and keeping teams from packing everyone into the middle, but the *mano a mano* mayhem still goes on.

"The three-point line has made people defend the perimeter more aggressively," says Barnes. "What that means is that the low-post defender has to push his man out even farther if he wants to get help."

Widening the lane and enforcing the three-second rule would help college basketball regain a purer style of play. But changing the officiating, particularly around the basket, would be the most important step. Players and coaches adjust their styles nightly to fit the circumstances, and there's no reason why they couldn't rebalance the scales that weigh skill and strength. The game will never again be played quite like it was in Wooden's day, and perhaps it shouldn't be. Perhaps the guiding principle should be to make sure that 20 years from now, it will be a game the old coach would still recognize.

■ ■ ■ ■ ■ ■ ■ ■ ■

# THE BLACK AND WHITE TRUTH ABOUT BASKETBALL

## Jeff Greenfield

The dominance of black athletes over professional basketball is beyond dispute. Two thirds of the players are black, and the number would be greater were it not for the continuing practice of picking white bench warmers for the sake of balance. The Most Valuable Player award of the National Basketball Association has gone to blacks for twenty-three of the last twenty-five years. The NBA was the first pro sports league of any stature to hire a black coach (Bill Russell of the Celtics) and the first black general manager (Wayne Embry of the Bucks). What discrimination remains—lack of opportunity for lucrative benefits such as speaking engagements and product endorsements—has more to do with society than with basketball.

This dominance reflects a natural inheritance; basketball is a pastime of the urban poor. The current generation of black athletes are heirs to a tradition half a century old: In a neighborhood without the money for bats, gloves, hockey sticks, tennis rackets, or shoulder pads, basketball is accessible. "Once it was the game of the Irish and Italian Catholics in Rockaway and the Jews on Fordham Road in the Bronx," writes David Wolf in his brilliant book, *Foul!* "It was recreation, status, and a way out." But now the ethnic names are changed; instead of Red Holzmans, Red Auerbachs, and McGuire brothers, there are Julius Ervings and Darryl Dawkinses and Kareem Abdul-Jabbars. And professional basketball is a sport with a national television contract and million-dollar salaries.

But the mark on basketball of today's players can be measured by more than money or visibility. It is a question of style. For there is a clear difference between "black" and "white" styles of play that is as clear as the difference between 155th Street at Eighth Avenue and Crystal City, Missouri. Most simply (remembering we are talking about culture, not chromosomes), "black" basketball is the use of superb athletic skill to adapt to the limits of space imposed by the game. "White" ball is the pulverization of that space by sheer intensity.

It takes a conscious effort to realize how constricted the space is on a basketball court. Place a regulation court (ninety-four by fifty feet) on a football field, and it will reach from the back of the end zone to the twenty-one-yard line; its width will cover less than a third of the field. On a baseball diamond, a basketball court will reach from home plate to just beyond first base. Compared to its principal indoor rival, ice hockey, basketball covers about one-fourth the playing area. And during the normal flow of the game, most of the action takes place on about the third of the court nearest the basket. It is in this dollhouse space that ten men, each of them half a foot taller than the average man, come together to battle each other.

There is, thus, no room; basketball is a struggle for the edge: the half step with which to cut around the defender for a lay-up, the half second of freedom with which to release a jump shot, the instant a head turns allowing a pass to a teammate breaking for the basket. It is an arena for the subtlest of skills: the head fake, the shoulder fake, the shift of body weight to the right and the sudden cut to the left. Deception is crucial to success; and to young men who have learned early and painfully that life is a battle for survival, basketball is one of the few games in which the weapon of deception is a legitimate rule and not the source of trouble.

If there is, then, the need to compete in a crowd, to battle for the edge, then the surest strategy is to develop the *unexpected*; to develop a shot that is simply and fundamentally different from the usual methods of putting the ball in the basket. Drive to the hoop, but go under it and come up the other side; hold the ball at waist level and shoot from there instead of bringing the ball up to eye level; leap into the air and fall away from the basket instead of toward it. All these tactics take maximum advantage of the crowding on a court; they also stamp uniqueness on young men who may feel it nowhere else.

"For many young men in the slums," David Wolf writes, "the school yard is the only place they can feel true pride in what they do, where they can move free of inhibitions and where they can, by being spectacular, rise for the moment against the drabness and anonymity of their lives. Thus, when a player develops extraordinary 'school yard' moves and shots . . . [they] become his measure as a man."

So the moves that begin as tactics for scoring soon become calling cards. You don't just lay the ball in for an uncontested basket; you take the ball in both hands, leap as high as you can, and slam the ball through the hoop. When you jump in the air, fake a shot, bring the ball back to your body, and throw up a shot, all without coming back down, you have proven your worth in uncontestable fashion.

This liquid grace is an integral part of "black" ball, almost exclusively the province of the playground player. Some white stars like Bob Cousy, Billy Cunningham, Doug Collins, and Paul Westphal had it: the body control, the moves to the basket, the free-ranging mobility. They also had the surface ease that is integral to the "black" style; an incorporation of the ethic of mean streets—to "make it" is not just to have wealth, but to have it without strain. Whatever the muscles and organs are doing, the face of the "black" star almost never shows it. George Gervin of the San Antonio Spurs can drive to the basket with two men on him, pull up, turn around, and hit a basket without the least flicker of emotion. The Knicks' former great Walt Frazier, flamboyant in dress, cars, and companions, displayed nothing but a quickly raised fist after scoring a particularly important basket. (Interestingly, the black coaches in the NBA exhibit far less emotion on the bench than their white counterparts; Al Attles and K. C. Jones are statuelike compared with Jack Ramsey or Dick Motta or Kevin Loughery.)

If there is a single trait that characterizes "black" ball it is leaping agility. Bob Cousy, ex-Celtic great and former pro coach, says that "when coaches get together, one is sure to say, 'I've got the one black kid in the country who can't jump.' When coaches see a white boy who can jump or who moves with extraordinary quickness, they say, 'He should have been born black, he's that good.' "

Don Nelson, former Celtic and coach of the Milwaukee Bucks, recalls that in 1970, Dave Cowens, then a relatively unknown Florida State graduate, prepared for his rookie season by playing in the Rucker League, an outdoor Harlem competition that pits pros against playground stars and college kids. So ferocious was Cowens' leaping power, Nelson says, that "when the summer was over, everyone wanted to know who the white son of a bitch was who could jump so high." That's another way to overcome a crowd around the basket—just go over it.

Speed, mobility, quickness, acceleration, "the moves"—all of these are catch-phrases that surround the "black" playground style of play. So does the most racially tinged of attributes, "rhythm." Yet rhythm is what the black stars themselves talk about; feeling the flow of the game, finding the tempo of the dribble, the step, the shot. It is an instinctive quality, one that has led to difficulty between systematic coaches and free-form players. "Cats from the street have their own rhythm when they play," said college dropout Bill Spivey, onetime New York highschool star. "It's not a matter of somebody setting you up and you shooting. You *feel* the shot. When a coach holds you back, you lose the feel and it isn't fun anymore."

Connie Hawkins, the legendary Brooklyn playground star, said of Laker coach Bill Sharman's methodical style of teaching, "He's systematic to the point where it begins to be a little too much. It's such an action-reaction type of game that when you have to do everything the same way, I think you lose something."

There is another kind of basketball that has grown up in America. It is not played on asphalt playgrounds with a crowd of kids competing for the court; it is played on macadam driveways by one boy with a ball and a backboard nailed over the garage; it is played in Midwestern gyms and on southern dirt courts. It is a mechanical, precise development of skills (when Don Nelson was an Iowa farm boy his incentive to make his shots was that an errant rebound would land in the middle of chicken droppings), without frills, without flow, but with effectiveness. It is "white" basketball: jagged, sweaty, stumbling, intense. A "black" player overcomes an obstacle with finesse and body control; a "white" player reacts by outrunning or outpowering the obstacle.

By this definition, the Boston Celtics are a classically "white" team. The Celtics almost never use a player with dazzling moves; that would probably make Red Auerbach swallow his cigar. Instead, the Celtics wear you down with execution, with constant running, with the same play run again and again. The rebound triggers the fast break, with everyone racing downcourt; the ball goes to Larry Bird, who pulls up and takes the jump shot, or who fakes the shot and passes off to the man following, the "trailer," who has the momentum to go inside for a relatively easy shot.

Perhaps the most classically "white" position is that of the quick forward, one without great moves to the basket, without highly developed shots, without the height and mobility for rebounding effectiveness. What does he do? He runs. He runs from the opening jump to the last horn. He runs up and down the court, from base line to base line, back and forth under the basket, looking for the opening, for the pass, for the chance to take a quick step and the high-percentage shot. To watch San Antonio's Mark Olberding, a player without speed or moves, is to wonder what he is doing in the NBA—until you see him swing free and throw up a shot that, without demanding any apparent skill, somehow goes in the basket more frequently than the shots of any of his teammates. To watch Kurt Rambis of the Los Angeles Lakers, an ungainly collection of arms, legs, and elbows, thumping up and down the court at half-speed is to wonder whether the NBA has begun a hire-the-handicapped program—until you see Rambis muscling aside an opponent to grab a rebound, or watch him trail the fast-break to steer an errant shot into the basket. And to have watched Boston Celtic immortal John Havlicek is to have seen "white" ball at its best.

Havlicek stands in dramatic contrast to Julius Erving of the Philadelphia 76ers. Erving has the capacity to make legends come true; leaping from the foul line and slam-dunking the ball on his way down; going up for a lay-up, pulling the ball to his body and throwing under and up the other side of the rim, defying gravity and probability with moves and jumps. Havlicek looked like the living embodiment of his small-town Ohio background. He would bring the ball downcourt, weaving left, then right, looking for the path. He would swing the ball to a teammate, cut behind a pick, take the pass and release the shot in a flicker of time. It looked plain, unvarnished. But there are not half a dozen players in the league who can see such possibilities for a free shot, then get that shot off as quickly and efficiently as Havlicek.

To former pro Jim McMillian, a black with "white" attributes, himself a quick forward, "it's a matter of environment. Julius Erving grew up in a different environment from Havlicek—John came from a very small town in Ohio. There everything was done the easy way, the shortest distance between two points. It's nothing fancy, very few times will he go one-on-one; he hits the lay-up, hits the jump shot, makes the free throw, and after the game you look up and you say, 'How did he hurt us that much?'"

"White" ball, then, is the basketball of patience and method. "Black" ball is the basketball of electric self-expression. One player has all the time in the world to perfect his skills, the other a need to prove himself. These are slippery categories, because a poor boy who is black can play "white" and a white boy of middle-class parents can play "black." Jamaal Wilkes and Paul Westphal are athletes who seem to defy these categories. And what makes basketball the most intriguing of sports is how these styles do not necessarily clash; how the punishing intensity of "white" players and the dazzling moves of the "blacks" can fit together, a fusion of cultures that seems more and more difficult in the world beyond the out-of-bounds line.

# THE BROTHER FROM ANOTHER PLANET

## Charles P. Pierce

*"Basketball is a black man's game," says Larry Bird. "I just try to fit in."*

This is some pale stuff out there on the wing. All the other basketball players, Celtics and Pacers alike, have cleared the side, and they have left two of their own all alone. This is the isolation play, an offensive maneuver as simple as milk, yet responsible in large part for the wild and unruly success that has overtaken professional basketball in the past decade. It is out of this alignment that Michael Jordan is cleared for takeoff, and it was out of this alignment that Magic Johnson ground up the hapless on his way to the low post, and it is out of this alignment that Charles Barkley is freed to do both, often on the same play. It is a wonderful set piece—a scorer and a defender, alone with each other, the center of all focus. It is a prideful moment for both players—the Ur-matchup of the American game. One-on-one.

Anyway, this is some pale stuff out there. Larry Bird has the ball cocked high and waiting. He is guarded by an Indiana Pacer named Detlef Schrempf, a blond German with a brush cut who makes Larry Bird look like Sam Cooke. Bird has Schrempf on a string now, moving the ball just slightly, faking with his fingertips. Other Celtics heckle the Pacer forward from the bench. More tiny fakes, and Schrempf is hearing imaginary cutters thundering behind him toward the hoop. His eyes cheat a bit over his shoulders. Finally, with Schrempf utterly discombobulated, Bird dips the ball all the way around his opponent's hip. Schrempf half-turns to help defensively on the man to whom he's sure Bird has just passed the ball. Bird pulls the ball back, looking very much like a dip who's just plucked a rube's gold watch from his vest pocket. He throws up that smooth hay-baler of a jump shot from just above his right ear, and it whispers through the net. The play draws cheers and laughter, and even Bird is smiling a little as the two teams head down the court again.

A few days earlier, Connie Hawkins was nominated for the Basketball Hall of Fame, the final vindication of what poet Jim Carroll has written about basketball, "a game where you can correct all your mistakes instantly, and in midair." Hawkins was a glider and a soarer. A legend in Brooklyn long before he was twenty, he fits snugly between Elgin Baylor and Julius Erving on the path of the game that continues upward to (for the moment) Michael Jordan.

Hawkins's best years were wasted in exile on the game's fringes; his innocent involvement in the point-shaving investigations of 1961 truncated his college career and put him on an NBA blacklist until 1969. He will go into the Hall of Fame only because some people saw him do something wondrous and they told the tale. It is a triumph for the game's oral history, for its living tradition. There is a transcendence about Connie Hawkins and about his legend. It resides out of time and place, floating sweetly there in the air above all convention and cavil.

In large part, of course, this living tradition is an African-American tradition. In reaction to it, basketball's overwhelmingly white establishment assailed the skills of legends like Connie Hawkins, deriding their game as "playground basketball," the result of some atavistic superiority that must be controlled by (predominantly white) coaches for the greater good. Black players were innately talented, of course, but they were lacking in the Fundamentals, which virtually always were defined in a way that brought the game back to earth and removed it from the largely black custodians of its living tradition.

Withal, both sides were talking past each other. The game's white establishment was talking about strategy and tactics. Black players were talking about the psychology of defining oneself as a person by what one did on the court. From this emphasis on psyche came the concept of Face—a philosophy of glorious retribution by which you dunk unto others as they have already dunked unto you, only higher and harder. It's this competitive attitude that makes the Fundamentals interesting. And it's this guilty knowledge that made basketball's white establishment so determined to minimize its obvious importance. Soon, these views ossified into the attitudes by which black players are praised for their "athletic ability"—code for the Super Negro not far removed from William Shockley's laboratory—while white players are usually commended for their "intelligence" and their "work ethic." Both sides internalized these notions, and they were irreconcilable.

By the late 1970s, the NBA, having expanded far too quickly and recklessly for its own good, was floundering. Competition had vanished. So had most of the fans. There were some drug busts, common enough in all sports. At the same time, the league was perceived as becoming blacker; by 1979, 70 percent of the players were African American. People made the usual foul connections. There were the nods and the winks in the executive suites. Disillusioned fans drifted away, and pretty soon the NBA found its championship series being broadcast on tape delay.

In 1979, Larry Bird and Magic Johnson began their careers with the Boston Celtics and the Los Angeles Lakers, respectively. There was a frisson of expectation as soon as they went around the league. By season's end, Bird had been named the NBA Rookie of the Year, and Johnson had propelled the Lakers to the title, scoring forty-two points against the Philadelphia 76ers in the seventh game of the final series. Over the next decade, the two of them played so well and drew so many fans that they are now given undisputed credit for saving professional basketball. Neither one ever evinced eye-popping athletic skills; Bird may be the only great player in history more earthbound than Magic. Their importance lies in the fact that the two irreconcilable halves of the game found in them—and, especially, in Bird—a common ground.

The most fundamental of the traditional Fundamentals is that a great player must make his team greater. Thus does a whirling dunk count only the same two points as a simple layup. Both Bird and Magic pass this test easily. However, the game's living tradition demands that this be accomplished in a way that ups the psychic ante, that forces the cycle of payback onto the opposition. Neither man has ever shrunk from this imperative. What Bird did to Schrempf, he did not do merely to score two points for the Celtics but to break his opponent's will, just as once in a championship game, he looked down to see where the three-point line was, took a conspicuous step back behind it, and then sunk a coup de grace through the Houston Rockets.

In short, the NBA has succeeded because it has become the world's premier athletic show. Playground ball has triumphed completely. It's hard to imagine now that college basketball once thought it was a good idea to ban the dunk, or that former UCLA coach John Wooden *still* thinks it's a good idea. Wooden, supreme guru of the Fundamentals, now sounds like a hopeless crank. What Bird and Magic did was difficult, and damned-near revolutionary—they made the Fundamentals part of the show. They did it by infusing the simple act of throwing a pass with the same special arrogance that so vividly illuminated Connie Hawkins midflight.

"What you've got to understand about Larry is that he plays a white game with a black head," says Atlanta's Dominique Wilkins. "If he could do a three-sixty dunk and laugh at you, he'd do it. Instead, he hits that three, and then he laughs at you."

"There's no doubt about it," adds Indiana's Chuck Person, who has enjoyed a spirited rivalry with Bird. "Larry's a street kid."

It comes from his life—a lost, lonely kid whose father was an amiable drunk who one day called Larry's mother on the phone and, with her listening, blew his brains out. There was grinding poverty. There was hopelessness. Compared to this life, Magic Johnson had it easy, as did Michael Jordan. Compared to this life, Spike Lee, who uses Bird as a cartoon foil, was one of the Cleavers. Instinctively, Larry Bird understands the country's most pernicious division as one of class and not of race—a distinction that a decade of public demagoguery has done its damndest to obscure.

"The poorer person," he muses, "the person who don't have much will spend more time playing sports to get rid of the energy he has." And anger and desperation? "Yeah, them too. Why go home when you got nothing to go home to?"

All his life, he has resisted the notion of being anyone's great white hope, because it never seemed logical to him. "I've always thought of basketball as a black man's game," Bird says. "I just tried to do everything I could to fit in."

Long ago, Indiana was a demographic fluke. Unlike the other midwestern states, it was settled from south to north rather than from east to west. It was flooded with refugees from Tennessee and the Carolinas. They brought with them so much of the Old South that, by 1922, the Ku Klux Klan was virtually running the state. An Indiana town called Martinsville is famous for being the home of two institutions—John Wooden and the modern Klan. When Jerry Sichting, a former NBA player and now the Celtics' radio commentator, left Martinsville to go to Purdue, his black teammates shied away from him. "I said I was from Martinsville, and I got that look," Sichting says. "It's still out there, no question." Larry Bird is from French Lick, which is thirty miles down Highway 37 from Martinsville. Thirty miles south.

Bird seems to have grown up remarkably free of prejudice. Throughout his career, he has managed to stay admirably clear of those who would make him a symbol through which to act out their own fears and bigotry. He has called Magic Johnson his role model, and he referred to former teammate Dennis Johnson as "the greatest player I ever saw." He even delighted in bringing NBA pal Quinn Buckner home to French Lick and into the worst redneck joints in town. "Yeah," recalls Buckner. "He took me to some places that I might not have gotten out of in less than three pieces if I went in alone. But Larry truly doesn't look at it that way. He doesn't want any part of that great white hope stuff. He never did."

"Just the other day," Bird says, "a guy come up to me and says, 'Here, sign this. Put on it that you're the greatest white player to ever play the game.' To me, that don't mean nothing. The greatest player ever to play the game. That means a helluva lot more."

Unfortunately, Bird has been a lightning rod. The Celtics, whose historical record on racial matters is positively revolutionary, have been forced to carry the weight of Boston's abysmal history in the matter of race relations. They were criticized for lightening up their roster in the early Eighties, although it's difficult to make the case that it's immoral to draft Bird and Kevin McHale, or to concoct a roster that won the NBA title three times in the decade. However, on a larger scale, the Eighties was generally a decade of reaction in racial matters. Bird's first season coincided with the ascendancy in culture and politics of the shibboleth of the Oppressed White Male. A society that could straight-facedly equate Allan Bakke with Rosa Parks evolved easily to one that could see no metaphorical distance between Clarence Thomas and the Scottsboro Boys.

Those comforted by the prevailing reactionary zeitgeist were looking for a hero, and Larry Bird and the Celtics qualified. Those revolted by it were looking for a villain, and Bird and the Celtics qualified there too. Thus, when it became fashionable to make Larry Bird into the greatest player of all time—certainly an arguable proposition, particularly up until about 1986—few people were objective about it anymore.

In 1987, after losing to the Celtics in a conference playoff series, Isiah Thomas blurted out the problem. Defending statements made by rookie Dennis Rodman, he said, "If Bird were black, he'd be just another good guy." The comment was graceless and ill-timed, but it was also the truth. Had Bird been black, his physical abilities would've been emphasized at the expense of his intelligence and his diligence at practice. Thomas's statement was excoriated for being racist, which it certainly was not. To identify a racial problem is not racist. One might as well call a black man racist who points out that white people are rather heavily involved in redlining his neighborhood.

By downplaying the comments and refusing to respond, Bird got Thomas out of the situation so deftly that Thomas later credited Bird with saving his public career. Bird would not have been able to do that had he not effectively defused the issue among his peers by connecting with the game's psychology. While he passed and rebounded and got praised for his mastery of the Fundamentals, he exhibited such cutthroat competitive flair that the dunkers sensed a kindred spirit.

"I always said that Larry was one of the most creative players I ever saw," says Celtic center Robert Parish. "That same kind of thing that makes people do a dunk makes Larry throw that touch pass over his shoulder."

Neither was Bird blind to what was happening elsewhere. Just last fall, Celtic rookie Dee Brown was thrown to the ground by police in the chichi suburb of Wellesley because some clerk thought Brown "looked like" the man who had recently robbed the bank.

"It's still a scar," Bird says. "You hear that Boston is a tough town for blacks. I don't know. I can't speak for them because I'm not black. I've seen some incidents, though. Dee Brown. Robert Parish got stopped a couple of times. Just for being black, you know."

Joe Bird's son never talked about him. It was part of a past buried so deeply that when a writer from *Sports Illustrated* mentioned Joe's suicide in an article, some of the boys from French Lick were said to have gone looking for him. But the son talked about Joe Bird this year. Talked freely, if not easily. Talked because a black man, a friend in L.A., was threatened by a fatal disease, and suddenly there was a connection between an amiable and self-destructive drunken white man in a hard little town in Indiana and an amiable and doomed black man in the fastest lane of all. The son of the first saw the connection there between his father and his friend, and he saw it clearly, far beyond the cold balm of convenient banality.

"I thought about when my Dad passed away," said Larry Bird on the night after Magic Johnson announced that he had tested positive for HIV. "I thought about how I wandered around for a week, just numb. That's what this is like."

He said it in that light little twang, the one that the people in southern Indiana brought with them from Tennessee, the one that made even Elvis sound modest in conversation. In truth, Bird has grown up remarkably unmarked by the benefits of his celebrity. "Larry doesn't care about being a famous white player," says Dave Gavitt, the Celtics CEO, "because Larry doesn't care about being famous, period." Indeed, as far as commercial endorsements are concerned, he falls well behind both Johnson and Jordan. He has, however, consciously worked to change the racial debate in a way not easily done. He has proven himself in his way on someone else's terms.

It would have been easy for him to grow up hard in the native bigotry of his place. Once grown, he could have easily sensed in his bones that that bigotry is general throughout the land and exploited it shamelessly. If there are people who would make him the best player ever simply because he is white, then that's their problem. If the Celtics became white America's team, then that's white America's fault. Larry Bird, as an individual basketball player, has defined his enormous abilities in an African-American context, and he has triumphed within it.

In his play—and, therefore, in his life, because the two are inextricably bound—he has declined to profit from the advantages that spring from the worst in our common culture. There are politicians, men infinitely more powerful than Larry Bird, who have proven unable to resist this same impulse. One of them plays horseshoes in the White House now.

They say that basketball's greatness is in its ability to bring people together, but that's a lie. Glib and facile people say that about every sport, and yet sports are as riven by class and race as any other major institution of this culture. Those people are closer to being right in basketball, though, than they are in any other sport. Basketball, much more than baseball or football, unites and makes whole two cultures, and it obliterates the artificial divisions created by faceless, fearful men who cling to their own pathetic advantages. Those who would turn Larry Bird into a symbol useful to that vicious endeavor—and those who would use him as a straw man against whom they could fight back—are all blind to his true genius. They are frightened of the best possibilities of America.

On this night, before he talked about his father and Magic, Larry Bird began the game by throwing a floor-length, behind-the-back pass that nobody could recall having seen Bird ever throw. But everyone on the floor knew it for what it was—an homage, extended in high style and in the game's truest and most precious currency. Everyone who ever had dunked on a man, or had defied both aerodynamics and orthopedics to drop a shot full of life and music, identified it immediately. Dominique Wilkins, trailing the play, saw it for what it was—an entertainer's play, but a bounce pass sure enough, with the arm extended right through to the fingertips, following through just the way that Clair Bee and Nat Holman and all those other guys wrote it down years ago, before the game moved into the air for good. The Fundamentals, but Showtime, too, beyond all measure.

"Larry," said one of his coaches, "was just saying goodbye."

■ ■ ■ ■ ■ ■ ■ ■ ■

# A STUDY OF SPORTS CROWD BEHAVIOR
## The Case of the Great Pumpkin Incident

### Linda Levy
Department of Sociology
Rutgers University

*Disagreement on which theory of collective behavior best predicts or explains how crowd processes work prompted this case study. By closely examining, through participant observation, the unfolding of one episode of nonviolent collective behavior at a professional football game, four frequently applied theories of collective behavior are tested for their utility in sports crowd situations. Each theory is assessed for strengths and weaknesses. Findings show contagion theory, convergence theory, emergent norm theory, and value-added theory all valuable in explaining some facets of observed spectator behavior; therefore a synthesis of theories might prove more useful than applying theories separately. A methodological problem emerged during evaluation, concerning difficulty in distinguishing among the indicators for each theory. Several overlapping theoretical concepts confounded attempts to operationalize unique empirical measures and hence, to compare the theories satisfactorily. Further research is needed to provide adequate measures.*

Controversy exists among social scientists about which theory of collective behavior, if any, proves most applicable to sports crowd situations. Researchers debate the utility of different theories as concern centers around how and why collective processes sometime operate to escalate spectator behavior beyond conventional limits. This paper tests four of the most frequently applied theories of collective behavior on an observed nonviolent collective spectator incident. The purpose is to learn more about sports crowd dynamics and to shed light on which perspective(s) might best predict and explain collective behavior in the sports context.

## Theories of Collective Behavior

The foundations of crowd theory were laid at the end of the nineteenth century in Europe by Gustave LeBon who first called attention to the crowd as a social phenomen. Living in a time of revolutionary upheaval, LeBon took a pathological view, in that under given circumstances he found crowd behavior not only different from but intellectually inferior to individual behavior. LeBon asserted that rather than interpreting phenomena rationally, individuals in crowd situations become dominated by their unconscious personalities. Suggestion, imitation, and contagion result in the infectious spread of emotion, whereby crowd members fall under the influence of a collective mind. Individuals have shed responsibility for their actions in the sea of anonymity (LeBon, 1895). This conceptualization formed a framework for what would later be called contagion theory.

In the mid-twentieth century Herbert Blumer refined contagion theory by introducing the notion of a circular reaction, adapting the earlier ideas of Floyd Allport (Brown and Goldin, 1973). During a circular reaction, responses of individuals within a crowd reproduce the responses of others around them, reflecting stimulation back and forth and thereby causing its intensification. Circular reactions signal the existence of a state of social unrest, which according to Blumer (1951), is the initial process of elementary collective behavior. During social unrest people may become engaged by the occurrence of some exciting event, and successively caught up in milling, collective excitement, and finally in social contagion as arousal intensifies. Individuals become sensitized to one another, experiencing rapport which induces the lowering of social resistance and a loss of normal individual control. Blumer maintains that at this point, infected individuals are most likely to engage in impulsive, non-rational behavior (Blumer, 1951).

Contagion theory met wide criticism due to later empirical findings. LeBon's notion of a group mind was rejected by most subsequent scholars, as was the concept of irrationality. Some social scientists also questioned uniformity of behavior, the process of spontaneous social contagion, and how to account for collective behavior's termination (Turner, 1964; Smelser, 1963; Berk, 1974).

A less popular conception of collective behavior, convergence theory, stems from early psychological theories of Sigmund Freud and Floyd Allport, and was further developed by Neal Miller and John Dollard. Convergence theory maintains that crowd behavior develops because individuals with shared predispositions have converged at the same location (Turner, 1964). Social facilitation then ensues when all respond in a similar manner toward a common stimulus (Wright, 1978). Although convergence theory added a new dimension, it received criticism for lacking a structural framework and not explaining certain crowd dynamics such as behavioral shifts, multiple predispositions, or role acquisition (Turner, 1964; Berk, 1974).

Later theorists, Ralph Turner and Lewis Killian, drew from insight scattered throughout the literature upon which they built a new theory of collective behavior (Wright, 1978). Turner and Killian (1957) theorized that instead of crowd behavior being normless, individual crowd members were simply following new norms rather than traditional ones. It was the mood and imagery particular to an immediate situation which caused these new norms to emerge that were then transmitted to others through social interaction. When a unique circumstance arises, people lack guidelines for defining appropriate action to follow; therefore, they look to see what others are doing and model their own behavior accordingly. In this way, individuals communicate the shared definition, pressuring others around them to conform (Turner and Killian, 1957).

Emergent norm theory received praise for contributing insight about normative implications and for its view of collective behavior as interactionally produced (Brown and Goldin, 1973; Wright, 1978). However, Brown and Goldin (1973) characterized emergent norm theory as incomplete and lacking in scope, while Wright (1978) argued that not enough attention was given to nonverbal processes by Turner and Killian.

Recognizing the shortcomings inherent in each of the preceding theories, Neil Smelser (1963) constructed value-added theory to improve analysis by logically patterning determinants of collective behavior from least to most specific. The focus narrows as a new value is added at each stage, redefining social action and ultimately producing only one possible outcome. The first stage is structural conduciveness: social conditions must favor collective action. Second is structural strain: failure of some aspect of the social system to function effectively, with several sources of strain often occurring in combination. Third is the growth and spread of a shared generalized belief: a belief which identifies and attributes characteristics to the source(s) of strain and then determines an appropriate response. Fourth are precipitating factors: factors which confirm and give substance to the beliefs as well as intensifying the previous determinants. The fifth stage is mobilizing the collectivity for action: leaders emerge as a division of labor takes place, and the type of collective behavior is determined. The sixth stage, social control overarches all: either preventive or interventive measures taken by agencies of social control may interfere with the foregoing determinants at any stage. Smelser applied the preceding stages to several forms of collective behavior. His "hostile outburst" category, to be tested here, is described as "action mobilized on the basis of a generalized belief assigning responsibility for an undesirable state of affairs to some agent" (1963, p. 9).

Criticism of Smelser's theory is mixed. Evans (1969) lauded its significance as did Marx (1972) who approved of value-added theory's conventional rather than abnormal behavioral categories. Brown and Goldin (1973) pointed to Smelser's importance in demonstrating collective behavior's multiple determinants and for his emphasis on shifts in crowd organization over time. Difficulties, however, arose over empirically testing the principles of value-added theory. Quarantelli and Hundley's (1969) research findings showed only limited support for Smelser's theory. Currie and Skolnick (1972) challenged the theory's defining characteristics as ambiguous and simplistic, deeming Smelser's own use of supportive evidence often prejudgmental and biased. Furthermore, Turner (1964) claimed that when applying value-added theory the researcher loses richness of data, since conclusions can only be drawn about the success or lack of success in reaching one of the final collective behavior forms.

To summarize, each of the above theories views crowd behavior from a different point of departure. Contagion theory looks at psychological aspects of irrationality and impulsiveness, describing how individuals immersed in a crowd become infected by a mob mentality. Convergence theory emphasizes how like-minded individuals converging to a crowd situation tend to respond to stimuli in a similar manner. Emergent norm theory focuses on how social interaction creates new ways of behaving in unusual circumstances. Value-added theory analyzes those determinants which limit the possible consequences of a crowd situation. Each seems to address only particular elements of crowd behavior. Several scholars agree that explanations remain incomplete (Evans, 1969; Currie and Skolnick, 1972; Berk, 1974).

## Theoretical Applications to Sports Crowds

Applying the preceding theories and others to spectator crowd behavior, sports scholars found differential utility among models. Hocking (1982), when viewing conventional spectator behavior rather than deviant behavior, reached some impressionistic conclusions. He saw value in each theory he examined. In describing an exciting basketball game, Hocking found convergent theory significant in explaining parallel behaviors within a highly partisan crowd, contagion theory best in accounting for the spread of responsive booing to an ambiguous officiating decision, and emergent norm theory important in revealing why spectators rose for the national anthem.

Mann (1979, 1989) also took an eclectic approach. He attributed uninhibited, impulsive, antisocial behavior stemming from the extreme emotional arousal of either a victory or loss at game's end to contagion. Hooliganism, aggression and violence perpetrated by associated young British males attending soccer contests, is consistent with the convergence model. Regulated, normative behavior among spectators assembled in ticket lines supports an emergent norm perspective. Distorted perceptions of a game by losing fans can lead to shared, generalized beliefs, held a necessary determinant for hostile outbursts according to value-added theory.

Kutcher (1983), however, discarded contagion theory as outdated, and depicted emergent norm theory as that most applicable to sports crowd behavior. Likening sports events to carnivals, Kutcher concluded that many sports events produce unique circumstances for spectators. Conventional roles and norms become relaxed, allowing deviant behavior to emerge that would be negatively sanctioned elsewhere. White (1975), on the other hand, found value-added theory useful in explaining spectator riots, as did Smith (1975), who demonstrated violence to be the primary precipitating factor in collective episodes at sporting events. In contrast, Lewis' (1982) case-history studies showed little evidence of the structural strains, central to Smelser's theory, associated with fan violence. Guttman also described value-added theory as disappointing when applied to "dozens of episodes" of spectator collective behavior (1986, p. 167). He further argued that no single theory adequately explains sports-crowd violence, but found some utility in the emergent norm model.

The present approach reinvestigates the strengths and weaknesses of all mentioned theories by applying each to a single sports crowd incident. Are any useful? How do they contribute to our understanding of crowd behavior? What are their shortcomings when empirical application is attempted? Is anything left unexplained? Systematic analysis of a closely observed sports crowd episode may supply insight not only about how collective behavior theories fare in explaining this particular incident, but also about their utility in predicting or explaining sports crowd behavior in general.

## Research Methods

One problem with studying the dynamics of crowd behavior lies in predicting when or where disturbances will erupt. It is easy to collect data about conditions preceding deviant acts and about the results of misbehavior, but little can be gathered on the group processes themselves. Crowd events occur with great speed, are difficult to anticipate, often happen several at one time, sometimes cover a broad geographic area, have processes leaving few traces, are not conducive to the interviewing of members during the process, frequently produce unreliably remembered accounts, and create a risk of injury to the observer (Berk, 1974). Therefore, most data on sports crowd violence are reconstructed from official records and media accounts (Lang, 1981).

As a student of sports crowd behavior, my attending a professional football game during which the spectator crowd became unruly afforded the rare opportunity for witnessing collective processes as they unfolded. I initially participated in the event for social reasons—to attend a tailgate party prior to the game and to watch a sports contest. Although I had no intention of studying crowd behavior, circumstances soon made it clear that my training in field observation should be put to use. Since research was regrettably unplanned, it was therefore unsystematic. Notes hurriedly written during the event recorded my observations (made both with and without the use of binoculars), while a more detailed reconstruction took place in the hours following the game. Informal conversations with other eyewitnesses (my three companions and additional nearby spectators), a videotape of the game (as televised by ABC), and numerous newspaper accounts provided information used to supplement and validate my first-hand observations. Therefore, this research incorporates both participant observation methods and archival techniques.

Surprising perhaps will be the choice of a relatively insignificant incident for study, considering the game's many episodes involving violent behavior. Rationale for the selection lies first, in my singular opportunity for unobstructed observation of this spontaneous crowd process from the incident's inception to its end. In contrast, none of the more extreme behavioral episodes could be as fully observed from my vantage point. Second, the incident chosen captured not only widespread audience attention, but the most protracted and extensive collective participation by the game's sellout crowd. All episodes of violence involved far fewer actual participants.

Selecting indicators presents another problem inherent in the study of collective behavior. Some guidelines are implicit within theories, but the broadness of propositions makes their interpretation arbitrary, so no standard sets of indicators exist. Therefore empirical measures must be based on what other researchers have used and on what is implied theoretically.

Factors identified as contributors to collective behavior constitute the independent variables. Contagion theory postulates increasing levels of excitement; therefore, determinants of heightened arousal were sought. Kutcher (1983, p.39) described the American sport event as "...a celebration, an escape into fantasy and revelry," depicting the aura of an exciting situation. Both Kutcher (1983) and Eitzen (1981) compared the mood and imagery of sports events to festivals or carnivals. Each social scientist used a different inclusive term but conveyed the same meaning. Combining the characteristics separately specified in both Eitzen's and Kutcher's parallels, carnivals or festivals incorporate: masquerading, music, feasting, merrymaking, liberal consumption of alcohol, and relaxation of everyday norms. The preceding elements signal, according to Eitzen, that individuals may be participating in "relatively unstructured and spontaneous behaviors" (p. 401). Not only does the carnival scene evoke a picture of excitement but it signifies that behavior transcends usual limits, consistent with circumstances under which new norms might emerge, and thus carnival elements become representative of two perspectives on crowd behavior.

Certain crowd dimensions have been previously cited as arousal intensifiers as well. Those used here are size and density (Mann, 1979; Roadburg, 1980; Lang, 1981; Hocking, 1982) and noise (Berkowitz, 1972; Mann, 1979; Roadburg, 1980). Dynamic dimensions elevating arousal include pregame activities (Roadburg, 1980; Kutcher, 1983), spectator expectations about the game (Lang, 1981), and observed aggression which has disinhibiting effects (Goldstein and Arms, 1971; Arms, Russell, and Sandilands, 1979; Eitzen, 1981; Harrell, 1981). Alcohol consumption has also been identified as a trigger to uninhibited and aroused behavior (Mark, Bryant, and Lehman, 1983; Vamplew, 1983; Mann, 1979).

The preceding contagion indicators can correspondingly serve as emergent norm independent indicators which establish a unique situational mood. Moreover, two of the above dimensions represent determinants of value-added theory. High crowd density indicates open channels of communication, providing structural conduciveness to the spread of hostile beliefs. And, the presence or absence of strain, interpreted here in its broadest sense as widespread discontent produced by any factor, may depend on the degree to which spectators' expectations are fulfilled by game action. In addition, it is unusual in contemporary everyday life to see physical aggression firsthand, so observed violence (on or off the field) presents both a unique circumstance indicative of emergent norm theory and a precipitating factor for value-added theory.

Convergence theory requires the researchers to seek similarities among spectators. The sports crowd under study showed some degree of homogeneity in sex, partisanship, and a propensity for consuming alcohol, all identified by prior researchers as relevant to collective behavior. When he delved into explanations for spectator deviance, Guttmann (1986) revealed that over 95 percent of the persons involved in sports crowd disturbances (three studies cited) were male. Lewis' (1982) findings show similar proportions. Smith (1975) maintained that a partisan attitude denotes emotional attachment to a team, often intense, and frequently contributing to tension and strain among sports spectators. According to Roadburg (1980), heavier drinking at British soccer matches heightens excitement, contributing to misbehavior at those contests.

Observed individual spectator responses and general crowd responses act as the dependent variables. Responses receive attention in their behavioral context and as each relates to a specific stimulus to determine which mechanism from which theory might be operating. In order to gain a sense of preconditions influencing the episode, the following describes the game event from its outset. Thereby, any factors acting as precursors to collective behavior can be examined.

## The Great Pumpkin Incident

A haze of smoke hung over the parking lots of Giants Stadium, as food on grills sizzled and beer flowed. At 6:30 p.m. on October 17, 1988, two and one-half hours before starting time for the Monday night football game between the New York Jets and the Buffalo Bills, festivities were well under way.

At one tailgate party, for example, fresh flowers arranged in Jets mugs had been placed on three round tables covered with Jets-green tablecloths, while a more elaborate floral centerpiece sat on the nearby buffet table. Also on the serving table rested six to eight large chafing dishes filled with steaming delicacies. Cases of soda and a keg of beer stood nearby. On yet another table waited a huge sheet cake, decorated as a football field with the slogan "Let's go Jets." The hostess of course wore green and white. Even the potholder and dishtowel she used said "Jets." Many of her guests were attired in Jets green and white sweaters, jackets, or jerseys.

A glance around the parking lots showed other groups similarly engaged in pregame feasting. Some tailgates consisted of sandwiches, some of steak. A party atmosphere prevailed as music blared from radios while people ate, drank, and were merry. Expectations ran high with the home-team Jets favored to win. Fans seemed ready for a night of raucous excitement.

Upon entry to the stadium proper when kickoff time neared, each spectator received a promotional green and white Jets painter's cap, which many immediately donned. Loud rock music greeted newcomers to their seats, blaring through the facility's speakers prior to start time and then later during intermissions. A festive aura of excitement prevailed.

In response to national television coverage received by Monday night games, some fans garb themselves in intricate costumes hoping to attract the camera's eye. Amidst a sea of Jets green and white, Batman, Robin, and a "cone-head" could be spotted, as could a group of teenagers with their faces painted half-green and half-white. One conspicuously flamboyant female attired herself in team colors with "Amazing Jets" emblazoned in large white letters across her green sweater. Large numbers of more moderately outfitted spectators appeared in team jerseys, T-shirts, hats, jackets, or other clothing with home-team emblems. By start-time at nine p.m., most seats had filled with the sellout crowd of 70,218. The national anthem signaled commencement of the sports event. Applause, cheers, and whistles interrupted its singing well before the anthem's conclusion, reflecting the crowd's high level of arousal. Fans could barely check their excitement in anticipation of a victorious night.

As the evening progressed, a change in crowd emotions became apparent, when during the second quarter the Bills' offensive repeatedly overpowered the Jets' defense. More heckling than cheering now echoed through the stands as fans voiced frustration with their team's dismal performance. The crowd booed the Jets' defensive unit, and several times they chanted: "Joe (Jets coach Joe Walton) must go, Joe must go." By halftime, spectators started to exit the stadium as the home-team Jets trailed by 31–7. Following the half, a few fistfights broke out among young male spectators, commanding more crowd attention than the one-sided football contest. The score had run up to 34–7 when the pumpkin incident began late in the third quarter.

In an end-zone lower section, the attention of neighboring fans centered on one male spectator blowing into a giant inflatable pumpkin. Bright orange, it appeared to be about four to five feet across and two feet high, sporting a yellow jack-o-lantern face. As the man puffed into the pumpkin, people nearby chanted, "Blow, blow, blow," which quickly drew the attention of others surrounding the area. Spectators in ever-widening circles thus picked up the chant.

By the time the man fully inflated the pumpkin, a large proportion of the stadium's spectators had focused toward that direction, since the pumpkin was clearly visible from most seats. When inflated, its owner tossed the pumpkin into the air. In accordance with the established practice for circulating footballs, beach balls, and other inflatable toys through the stands at Jets games, when the toy bounced to them, people batted it into the air again, hoping to keep it in motion. After having traveled for a few minutes, the pumpkin drifted down to the lowest seats. Spectators there could not propel it upward, so it descended onto the field. An individual on the field (not in uniform) caught the pumpkin as it bounced down, and sent the toy promptly back into the stands (counter to regulations). Cheers rocked the stadium.

The pumpkin again dropped to the field after another few minutes of being batted around, but this time the security person who retrieved it confiscated the toy, carrying it into a tunnel under the stadium. Spectators were outraged. They first yelled: "Asshole, asshole, asshole" in a sing-song manner. Then, the protest content changed, and increasing numbers of spectators chanted "We want the pumpkin! We want the pumpkin! We want the pumpkin!" until it seemed that the entire crowd had joined in. As they chanted, many spectators angrily stood, waving their fists toward the tunnel entrance where the pumpkin had disappeared. Someone near the tunnel (reported to newspapers as a media person) retrieved the pumpkin and returned it again to the stands (*Asbury Park Press*, October 19, 1988; *The Star-Ledger*, October 19, 1988). The pumpkin's rescuer was understandably greeted by deafening cheers—many spectators even accorded him a standing ovation. Fans again chanted: "Pumpkin! Pumpkin! Pumpkin!"

Shortly after starting to recirculate, the pumpkin lost some air; consequently it became easier to control, and therefore, never fell to the field again. At one stop during its continuing journey, some men who appeared drunk began pummelling the toy. The watching crowd responded with loud boos. In response the group desisted, allowing the pumpkin to move on.

Its short life was over several moments later when, after the crowd's interest had waned, another group of apparently drunk men pounded all air out of the toy. This second destructive act received little notice however because spectator fights had erupted in the meantime, shifting the mood and diverting the audience's focus of attention. The giant pumpkin ultimately traveled about one-fifth of the way around the stadium before deflating. Perhaps the entire episode lasted for seven to ten minutes.

Following the pumpkin incident, crowd behavior deteriorated further. Altercations erupted simultaneously in widely separated sections. Painter's caps, beer, toilet paper, and other debris showered down from upper tiers onto spectators below. Fans ignited fires built with painter's caps and cardboard in several areas of the stadium. It almost appeared as though misbehavior had become the norm.

Not surprisingly, rowdy spectator behavior dominated newspaper headlines about the night's contest instead of action on the field. Officials reported 41 separate incidents to which security personnel responded, which may be compared with 7 and 17 incidents reported at previous 1988 Sunday home games (*The New York Times*, October 19, 1988; *Asbury Park Press*, October 19, 1988; *The Star-Ledger*, October 19, 1988) and five incidents at the next Jets home game on October 30 (*The New York Times*, October 31, 1988). Some individual incidents included as many as ten participants who engaged in throwing objects, trespassing, setting fires, creating disturbances, and fighting.

## Analysis

Although descriptive of many sporting events, the carnival elements mentioned previously—masquerading, music, feasting, merrymaking, liberal consumption of alcohol, and relaxation of everyday norms—seem especially applicable to Monday night's football game, during which all of those components could be observed. When meeting with the press following the game under study, Jets president Steve Gutman described Monday night games as having more of a "carnival atmosphere" when he compared them with Sunday afternoon games (*The Star-Ledger*, October 19, 1988).

### The Spectators

To investigate factors creating the special mood and imagery of carnival on Monday nights one must begin with the individuals attending Monday night games, asking whether and how they differ from people who come on Sunday afternoons. Jets president Gutman (*Asbury Park Press*, October 19, 1988; *The Record*, October 19, 1988) signified that fewer women and children come on Monday nights, a factor he thought contributed to crowd disorders. The presence of more males is probably in part attributable to the late Monday night starting time. Confirming such an assumption are reports of a discussion presently underway between team officials and facility managers about the possibility of moving the 9 p.m. start time back to 8 p.m. in the hope of drawing a different kind of audience. Incidents on October 17 led directly to this negotiation (*The News Tribune*, October 27, 1988). According to Gutman: "Many of the (season) tickets owned by business entities are more likely to be given away on Monday night, whereas for a Sunday game, the proprietor would be more inclined to go to the game with his family" (*Asbury Park Press*, October 19, 1988). Gutman infers that adult males, the presumed recipients of giveaway tickets, behave in less desirable ways than women and children. Perhaps then, attendance by higher proportions of men on Monday nights produces differential behavior, supportive of convergence theory.

Along with age and gender differences, or possibly because of them, spectators attending on Monday nights consume more alcohol than those coming on Sunday afternoons. Jets president Gutman contends that alcohol is "woven into the fabric of the Monday night game" (*Asbury Park Press*, October 19, 1988). The warm evening with temperature in the 60s seemed to further exacerbate beer drinking on October 17. In addition to alcohol consumed at tailgates, many spectators inside the stadium held the easily discernible green or brown beer cups. Drunken revelry in the stands could be observed as well.

A lowering of inhibitions due to excessive alcohol consumption undoubtedly led to some of the unusual behavior that took place that night. Following October 17's game, the drinking/spectator deviance relationship received corroboration from stadium managers and team officials, convinced of alcohol's influence. They agreed to curtail the length of time available for beer sales, the volume of beer sold in one cup, and the amount of cups a patron may purchase at one time (*The Star-Ledger*, October 27, 1988). Thus, consistent with convergence theory is this propensity for drinking among Monday night spectators.

A final predisposition of importance, although not particular to Monday night contests, lies in the vast majority of spectators present who supported the home team. "Defeat is an intolerable deprivation" according to Smith (1975, p. 308). When a Jets' loss seemed irreversible, the intensity of partisan involvement became apparent as fans displayed their feelings of frustration and disappointment.

A young man seated directly behind me exemplifies the prevailing mood. He complained to his friends alongside him about the "f—in' team" playing so poorly, about his having spent $40 for tickets, about having to stay up late, about having to drive a long distance home, and finally about having to get up at 4 a.m. the next day for work. He seemed bitterly disappointed with the Jet's level of play, especially because it was costing him so much in time, energy, and money to be there. The young man left the stadium at half time. His anger and disgust could be heard echoed by other fans who had been eager for a home win. Convergence theory's utility is borne out by the similar emotional reactions of other Jets followers, predisposed for a very different game outcome. However, the social unrest observed among fans also supports contagion theory and can represent the kind of unique situation described by emergent norm theory. Moreover, deprivation of expected victory produced the observed strain among a majority of spectators who favored the home team, providing evidence for the fulfillment of value-added theory's second stage.

### The Environment

If spectator predispositions helped set the scene for collective behavior, so did other aspects of the environment. Kutcher (1983) argued that much of what influences sports crowd behavior goes beyond the game itself. A sporting event is a social happening, of which the contest itself is only a part. Hocking (1982) referred to differences between the game event, related to action on the field, and the stadium event, which includes the contest and everything else occurring within the facility's boundaries.

Monday night's sellout audience appeared to play some role in escalating the generally aroused state among spectators. First, immersion in a large rather than small crowd fosters feelings of anonymity, which then give rise to a sense of invulnerability, and hence, individuals become less inhibited about engaging in excited behavior (Mann, 1979; Hocking, 1982). Second, a full stadium results in high density. Opportunities for communication increase as interpersonal space between individuals decreases. In addition, when people are very close to each other, sudden movements are likely to reverberate through the rest of the crowd, sparking arousal among the multitude (Mann, 1979). Third, a large crowd naturally produces another influence, noise. Interstimulating effects build from sounds of many people vocalizing which encourages others to join in (Berkowitz, 1972). Consequences of the preceding environmental dimensions uphold at least part of what is incorporated into contagion theory. Crowd size, density, and noise appeared to facilitate interstimulation, spreading the dominant mood. Value-added theory's first stage received support as well from findings of high crowd density which provided a structurally conducive context for the rapid communication of shared, generalized beliefs. Another source of influence peripheral to the contest itself is tailgating. Pregame activities in the parking lots ranged from elaborate feasts, such as that described at this paper's start, to groups tossing and catching footballs in almost every aisle, to young people gathered round blaring radios while guzzling beer. For many spectators, hours spent in parking lot festivities serve as stimuli, causing them to enter the stadium in a highly aroused state.

This prior sensitization permits sights and sounds within the stadium to heighten excitement. Inside the gates, eyes, ears, and bodies experience the spectacle. Crowding forces people to push and shove as they move through the concourse to their seats before kickoff. Other spectators jockey for position in food and beverage lines. Bright colors appear everywhere. Festive outfits reflect team symbols among the many, but at the same time flashy costumes stand out worn by a few. Vendors hawk programs, pretzels, and beer, as loud rock music blasts from stadium loudspeakers. Surely like a carnival. Perhaps as Gaskell suggests, "The spectator enters a sphere of unreality in which the rules of everyday life are temporarily suspended" (Gaskell and Pearton, 1979; 284).

*The Social Psychology*

Spectators behave in patterns varying with their usual ones; however, special guidelines for watching sports contests take effect. Attached to the sport spectator role are a set of behavioral expectations. These range from shared understandings about standing for national anthems to cheering for one's team, heckling opponents, and booing officials. To some degree behaviors are based on those expected of sports audiences in general; but in addition, norms vary by the nature of the sport being viewed. Some factors enumerated by Lang (1981) as among those stimulating differential responses include: type of event, amounts and kinds of violence permissible within its rules, and spectators' expectations about the game and its outcome.

Researchers have concluded that game aggression intensifies feelings of hostility and aggression among spectators (Goldstein and Arms, 1971; Smith, 1975; Arms et al., 1979; Eitzen, 1981; Harrell, 1981). Violence is inherent in several sports, one of which is football. Since hitting and tackling are integral parts of football games, spectators observed player aggression on the field at Monday night's football game. Moreover, many witnessed the several spectator altercations which occurred prior to the pumpkin incident. Aroused, hostile states seemed to have been stimulated by both types of observed violence. A gentleman behind me, attired in a business suit and necktie, yelled in response to play on the field: "Kill 'em, kill 'em." Few circumstances other than sporting events would likely have caused him to scream those words.

At a different point during the evening, a fight began in one section of the stands, then a few minutes later in another, until brawls erupted in several areas of the stadium at once. When watching fights, some spectators, not even necessarily near the melee, began waving their fists, yelling: "get him, hit him, go to it man, c'mon." Those closest appeared most animated, although a young man sitting next to me stood up with every fight, wildly gesturing with his arms while urging the combatants to fight on. Witnessing the preceding episodes of aggression then, probably contributed to increased hostility, adding to spectator strain, and thus shaped the collective mood.

Another determining behavioral factor, expectations about the game, would undoubtedly go unfulfilled. Jets fans knew the game's disposition early that night when the Bills established full superiority. Play on the field had taken "the crowd out of the game from the outset" (*Asbury Park Press*, October 19, 1988), although demoralization prevailed only due to most fans' partisanship for the Jets. Had the majority of spectators been Bills fans, game interest would have remained high throughout the contest. By the pumpkin incident's start, the inevitability of a dismal outcome spoiled the game's entertainment value for Jets fans, creating the previously discussed strain among home-team partisans. Frustration and boredom prevailed.

### The Dynamics

Perhaps the pumpkin—colorful, oversized, and festive—became a welcome focus for spectators' attention. The toy added comic relief to a depressing situation. It may have also been symbolic of the victory celebration fans had anticipated, giving spectators something to cheer about since the contest was beyond salvage. Indifference to game play appeared to account for many spectators immediately turning their interest toward the man inflating the pumpkin. And, so did the initial chant of "Blow! Blow! Blow!" Communication plays an important role in both contagion and value-added theories, and according to Mann (1979), chanting represents the principal channel of communication in sports audiences.

What followed seemed dependent on the preceding conditions surrounding this event, which in joining, set the scene, making collective behavior possible. The large, dense, noisy crowd, the music, the food, the alcohol, the tailgating, the large preponderance of males, the beer drinking, the partisanship, the spectator fights, and finally, the game producing violence, frustration, disappointment, and boredom.

On stage in these unique circumstances appeared the new diversion, a toy with which spectators could play. Upon its appearance, communication among individuals seemed to increase, as people could be observed interacting with spectators near them while gesturing toward the pumpkin—ostensibly alerting their neighbors to its existence. On its initial fall to the field, the pumpkin's return to the stands brought understandable cheering. However, when the toy was later confiscated by a security guard, the situation became ambiguous. Bringing the pumpkin back was outside stadium rules (because of safety reasons), and therefore, encouraging its return would constitute a deviant act. Here a unique circumstance presented itself, enveloped in a mood and imagery conducive to collective behavior, as described by emergent norm theory. Or, from the value-added perspective, seizure of the pumpkin functioned as a precipitating factor, introducing a new deprivation to an already strained situation.

Mobilization for action began, according to the value-added model, when somewhere in the stadium a leader began yelling "Asshole!," applying an obscene label to the guard who appropriated the audience's communal toy. Others joining the response seemed to legitimate this reaction, setting a norm, but only for a subgroup of spectators. A glance around the stadium uncovered young males as the primary vocalizers. Nonetheless, grumbling among other spectators revealed their displeasure with the pumpkin's absence, showing many agreed that the toy should be returned yet remained unwilling to yell an obscenity.

Turner (1964) contends that contagion theory depicts a spiralling effect which need not take place. Events at October 17's game give support to Turner's view. That the majority did not participate in the initial, obscene protest suggests limits on the norms people will adopt, even in exciting crowd circumstances. Spectators appeared to make individual decisions by defining and interpreting the situation rationally, engaging if they shared the same emotions to the same degree, but only if behavior fit within their personal codes.

Evidence may also point to different effects among individuals who view aggression, probably depending on one's predisposition. The cry of "Asshole!" directed at a security guard, bespoke hostility and aggression toward authority. Young males, the primary engagers in this chant, may be reflecting both their age and their gender's differential socialization regarding aggression. Or perhaps this group is simply less inhibited than females or other age groups. Eitzen (1981) stated that "youth, especially, are accustomed to venting their emotions" (p. 404). The instigative behavior of the young man seated next to me, and the uninhibited cursing by the young man behind me serve to exemplify such conduct. That both attended with age peers suggests behavioral limits relate to one's personal subgroup. A subgroup follows its own norms, mediating the crowd's influence on individuals (Mann, 1979). One might speculate that there would be behavioral differences if each young man had attended in a family group rather than a peer group. On the other hand, inhibited constraint on the part of most females and older males suggests their internalization of different norms, and conceivably, less alcohol consumption.

Shouts of "Asshole!" faded. Not until after a brief period of unintelligible noise did the chant change to "We want the pumpkin! We want the pumpkin!" This time the chant's initiator proved more creative in providing a message which the masses could comfortably adopt. The resultant scene evoked an overpowering impression of unanimity—even as a participant observer, it seemed at first as though every one took part. However, that deafening "We want the pumpkin!" repeated approximately 15–20 times and involving great numbers of spectators, never included at all. A closeup videotape depicting crowd members clearly shows some spectators quietly seated, although most others stood chanting and/or shaking upraised fists. A man diagonally behind me revealed later that he did not participate. Therefore, what at a glance and from a distance appeared to be uniform behavior, when viewed more carefully and closely is revealed as an illusion. Contagion theorists for many years advanced the concept of crowd homogeneity—everyone being swept up irrationally in the formation of a mob mind. Later studies illustrated the shortcomings of this pathological approach as trained observers reported differential behavior within crowds (Turner, 1964). A detailed reexamination on October 17 uncovered the reality that a dominant orientation within the sports crowd did not equate with a collective mind.

One plausible explanation for misconceptions about the uniformity of Monday's behavior is that those people standing, waving fists obscured the others who remained seated. Furthermore, one might speculate that the sound of even half of the more than 70,000 spectators present would have generated sufficient noise to give an impression of unanimity. A third possibility is that observers tend to focus on the presence of behavior rather than its absence.

Another crowd process must be considered—the manner in which members adopt the behavior of others. Turner and Killian (1957) contend that individuals are pressured by the collectivity to conform to new norms rather than initiating behaviors through spontaneous social contagion. During the collective response "Asshole!" a majority of spectators refused to conform. However, the enthusiastic repetition of "We want the pumpkin!" by so many seemed to show how an idea catches on and spreads because of its broad appeal. There was no sense of collective pressure. Individuals appeared to join in with crowd responses because of their desire for diversion, smiling while imitating the behavior of others.

Following the pumpkin's return, a collective response directed at the group of males viciously punching the toy reveals another crowd mechanism. Loud "boos" immediately showering from the crowd on this group forced the aggressors to stop their attack. Turner (1964) states that individuals exceeding limits set on behavior receive some form of crowd sanction. Swift crowd disapproval of the attack on the toy illustrates that type of social control process, and in this instance, also demonstrates conformity to norms. Therefore, conformity seems to account for some behavior in crowds and contagion through imitation for other crowd behavior.

In the final minutes of the pumpkin episode, a competing incident in progress won the crowd's attention. A fight had broken out in another section of the stadium. Value-added theory maintains that commencement of one hostile outburst paves the way for other crowd members, perhaps with different motivations, to express their own hostility since the situation has become more structurally conducive. This notion could account for the multiple outbreaks of aggression that ensued after the pumpkin episode. Many individuals turned in the direction of the latest altercation, giving the impression of stronger crowd interest in this new diversion. A mood shift had taken place; now a fresh emotional emphasis governed the moment, allowing the final destruction of the pumpkin to go virtually unnoticed.

## Discussion

This analysis has both challenged and upheld some notions within classic theories of crowd behavior. Clearly the study falls short since it examines just one rather trivial incident at a single sporting event. Consequently, some inferences here may reach beyond the data at hand and border on speculation. Furthermore, the lack of advance methodological planning undoubtedly limited the researcher's ability to strategically capture all aspects of the incident. However, findings here point to some tentative conclusions about theoretical assumptions and one significant overall problem with attempts to empirically verify theories of collective behavior—that of measurement.

For a theory to be useful it must be testable, having measures indicative of a unique proposition or set of propositions which can then be compared with those of other theories. As demonstrated, indicators of collective behavior are often interchangeable between theories, since boundaries are not clear. For example: do spectators collectively express frustration with game play because they are predisposed toward one team as postulated by convergence theory, because they have become highly aroused as hypothesized by contagion theory, because the situation is unique as speculated by emergent norm theory, or because they are experiencing a social strain as posited by value-added theory? Or do all theories explain some part of this single behavior? Does a carnival mood denote a state of high excitement as described by contagion theory or the unique circumstances characterized by emergent norm theory or both? Consequently, there can be no clear distinction between perspectives.

Perhaps the foregoing kinds of questions suggest that some synthesis of theories might better describe the total picture without redundancy. One might speculate about the induction of a general theory of crowd behavior formed by combining the original theoretical models. Any effort towards synthesis however, depends on ascertaining the strengths and weaknesses of each theory with the intention of joining the former and dispensing with the latter. Some conclusions drawn from the above findings might prove helpful in achieving such a goal.

There seems strong observational evidence it was among drinking, adult, male Jets fans that arousal became most intense and more collective responses occurred, giving substance to convergence theory's tenets that individuals with similar predispositions converging to the same sports event tend to respond similarly to stimuli. It also appears likely that on October 17 a generalized sense of excitement associated with contagion theory, and perhaps lowered inhibitions and feelings of anonymity, stemmed from the large, dense, noisy crowd and the carnival atmosphere. Observed on- and off-field aggression, the disappointing, frustrating game, the disturbed carnival mood, and finally, the pumpkin, appeared to present some unique circumstances in which everyday norms became suspended and new norms emerged. Proponents of value-added theory might conclude that, limited in their means of expressing dissatisfaction with impending defeat, Jets fans experienced a condition of strain, which in turn produced generalized hostile beliefs to the extent that a precipitating factor (pumpkin confiscation) introducing yet a new deprivation led to the scapegoating of a convenient authority figure (security person). Spectator leaders then emerged with chants that mobilized the audience to participation. Social control agencies, busy with outbreaks of spectator altercations elsewhere, did not intervene quickly enough (perhaps by taking possession of the pumpkin before it drew such widespread attention) to curtail the display of collective hostility. The incident thus seems to fit into four theoretical frameworks. Each theory highlights different factors, rendering all models incomplete without consideration of the others.

Findings more specifically show theories shedding light on determinants that escalate or limit collective behavior. Certain intensifiers or limiters are obvious: the proportion of spectators predisposed to collective behavior converging at the sports event: audience size, noise, and density; the amount of pregame merrymaking; the kinds of music and "color" creating an overall mood; as well as aggression witnessed and the frustrating strain of defeat.

A subtler mechanism demonstrated that spectators set limits on adopting the collective behavior of subgroups, as indicated by differential involvement ranging from enthusiastic participation to non-engagement. Refusal to participate by some individuals reconfirms the inaccuracy of LeBon's concept of a collective mind. Refusal further suggests that crowd members rationally interpret the actions of others when considering engagement, contrary to traditional contagion theory but consistent with emergent norm theory. Supporting contagion theory, on the other hand, were the disinhibiting effects of drinking which seemed to produce higher arousal and subsequent participation in collective behavior.

Questioned is the notion that individuals generally conform to pressures from others in crowd situations as hypothesized by emergent norm theorists. Dynamics of the pumpkin episode implied more infectious behavior than pressure to conform when collective participation peaked. Yet, later when the group of pumpkin attackers bent to crowd demands to stop, the concept of conformity to pressure was upheld. Thus, conformity may be differentially determined and needs more examination.

Repeat of almost the same situation two weeks later at the next Jets home game further highlights the unique combination of factors at work on October 17. An identical inflated pumpkin was again introduced to the stands during a Sunday afternoon game on the day before Halloween. The incident's outcome on October 30, however, contrasted with that of the first episode. When this second pumpkin fell to the field and was speedily removed by a security guard, little protest could be heard from the crowd. Furthermore, that Sunday produced only five incidents to which security responded and included only one altercation. Why the difference?

First, the aggregate of people, at least according to the Jets president, presumably possessed different characteristics. Second, the 1 p.m. Sunday kickoff time implies that less pregame drinking probably took place. Third, beer consumption had been limited by the new stadium rules and possibly by colder temperatures. Fourth, the game was closely contested at the time the pumpkin appeared; therefore, spectator attention was riveted on exciting game action so there was no need for further diversion. Fifth, absence of the underlying strain of impending loss precluded the generalization of hostile beliefs, and hence the same precipitating factor produced a different outcome. Each collective behavior theory might be substantiated by focusing on one or more of the above items. Yet the set of differences points to a more complex answer which requires examination through repeated research to uncover underlying patterns.

Multivariate analysis of data collected from observations of sports events could help to identify significant measures. Linking direct observations of spectator sex, age, race, symbols of partisanship, and drinking behavior to the amounts and types of collective responses occurring during sports events could clarify the extent to which individual predispositions contribute to crowd behavior.

Another possibility involves examination of official records describing incidents of misbehavior. Such records provide information on demographics of involved individuals, perhaps including social class (as defined by occupation), and on the types of disturbance caused. These could in turn be tied to event statistics regarding attendance, alcohol consumption, and game violence while controlling for each to identify significant relationships. Some theoretical assumptions should develop, leading to more specific measures.

An additional research avenue might prove more difficult. Close examination of collective processes using field methods provides access to crowd dynamics and offers a richness unsurpassed by other techniques. However, as indicated at the outset, intentional witnessing of collective episodes is not easy. Lastly, there should be utility in making comparisons between prior studies. Research as diverse as observations of collective behavior, interviews with crowd participants, document study, and reviews of video tapes and/or photographs could be compared to generate suitable indicators. Perhaps triangulation, combining findings from several methods, would ultimately prove most fruitful for uncovering collective behavioral patterns at sports events, and thereby for producing measures for future theory testing.

## REFERENCES

Arms, Robert L., Gordon W. Russell, and Mark L. Sandilands. 1979. "Effects of Viewing Aggressive Sports on the Hostility of Spectators." *Social Psychology Quarterly* 42:275–279.

*Asbury Park (N.J.) Press*. October 19, 1988.

Berk, Richard A. 1974. *Collective Behavior*. Dubuque, Iowa: Wm. C. Brown.

Berkowitz, Leonard. 1972. "Frustrations, Comparison, and Other Sources of Emotion Arousal as Contributors to Social Unrest." *Journal of Social Issues* 28:1:77–91.

Blumer, Herbert. 1951. "Collective Behavior." in *New Outline of the Principles of Sociology*, edited by Alfred McClung Lee. New York: Barnes and Noble.

Brown, Michael and Amy Goldin. 1973. *Collective Behavior: A Review and Reinterpretation of the Literature*. Pacific Palisades, CA: Goodyear Publishing.

Currie, Elliott and Jerome H. Skolnick. 1972. "A Critical Note on Conceptions of Collective Behavior." in *Collective Violence*, edited by James Short, Jr. and Marvin Wolfgang. Chicago: Aldine-Atherton.

Eitzen, D. Stanley. 1981. "Sport and Deviance." Pp. 400–414 in *Handbook of Social Science of Sport*, edited by Gunther R.F. Luschen and George H. Sage. Champaign, Illinois: Stipe Publishing.

Evans, Robert R. 1969. *Readings in Collective Behavior*. Chicago: Rand McNally.

Gaskell, George and Robert Pearton. 1979. "Aggression and Sport" in *Sports, Games and Play*, edited by Jeffrey H. Goldstein. Hillside, N.J.: Lawrence Erlbaum.

Goldstein, Jeffrey and Robert L. Arms. 1971. "Effects of Observing Athletic Contests on Hostility." *Sociometry* 34:83–90.

Guttmann, Allen. 1986. *Sports Spectators*. New York: Columbia University Press.

Harrell, W. Andrew. 1981. "Verbal Aggressiveness in Spectators at Professional Hockey Games: The Effects of Tolerance of Violence and Amount of Exposure to Hockey." *Human Relations* 34:8:632–655.

Hocking, John E. 1982. "Sports and Spectators: Intra-Audience Effects." *Journal of Communication* 32:1:99–108.

Kutcher, Louis. 1983. "The American Sport Event as Carnival: An Emergent Norm Approach to Crowd Behavior." *Journal of Popular Culture* 16:4:34-41.

Lang, Gladys Engel. 1981. "Riotous Outbursts at Sports Events." Pp. 415–436 in *Handbook of Social Science of Sport*, edited by Gunther R.F. Luschen and George H. Sage. Champaign, Illinois: Stipe Publishing.

LeBon, Gustave. 1895. *The Crowd*. London: Ernest Benn. (New York: Ballantine, 1969.)

Lewis, Jerry M. 1982. "Fan Violence: An American Social Problem." Pp. 175–206 in *Research in Social Problems and Public Policy*. edited by Michael Lewis. Greenwich, CO: Jai Press.

Mann, Leon. 1979. "Sports Crowds Viewed from the Perspective of Collective Behavior." Pp. 337–368 in *Sports, Games and Play*. edited by Jeffrey H. Goldstein. Hillsdale, NJ: Lawrence Erlbaum.

—————. 1989. "Sports Crowds and the Collective Behavior Perspective." Pp. 299–332 in *Sports, Games, and Play*. edited by Jeffrey H. Goldstein. Hillsdale, NJ: Lawrence Erlbaum.

Mark, Melvin M., Fred B. Bryant, and Darrin R. Lehman. 1983. "Perceived Injustice and Sports Violence" in *Sports Violence*, edited by Jeffrey H. Goldstein. New York: Springer-Verlag.

Marx, Gary. 1972. "Issueless Riots" in *Collective Violence*, edited by James Short, Jr. and Marvin Wolfgang. Chicago: Aldine-Atherton.

*The New York Times*. October 19, 1988.

*The New York Times*. October 31, 1988.

*The (Woodbridge, NJ) News Tribune*. October 27, 1988.

Quarantelli, Enrico L. and James R. Hundley, Jr. 1969. "A Test of Some Propositions About Crowd Formation and Behavior" in *Readings in Collective Behavior*, edited by Robert Evans. Chicago: Rand McNally.

*The (Bergen, NJ) Record*. October 19, 1988.

Roadburg, Alan. 1980. "Factors Precipitating Fan Violence: A Comparison of Professional Soccer in Britain and North America." *British Journal of Sociology*. 31:265–276.

Smelser, Neil J. 1963. *Theory of Collective Behavior*. New York: Free Press.

Smith, Michael. 1975. "Sport and Collective Violence" Pp. 281–330 in *Sport and the Social Order*, edited by Donald W. Ball and John W. Loy. Reading, MA: Addison-Wesley.

*The (Newark, NJ) Star-Ledger*. October 19, 1988.

*The (Newark, NJ) Star-Ledger*. October 27, 1988.

Turner, Ralph H. 1964. "Collective Behavior." in *Handbook of Modern Sociology*, edited by Robert E. Faris. Chicago: Rand McNally.

Turner, Ralph H. and Lewis M. Killian. 1957. *Collective Behavior*. Englewood Cliffs, NJ: Prentice-Hall.

Vamplew, Wray. 1983. "Unsporting Behavior: The Control of Football and Horse-Racing Crowds in England. 1875–1914" in *Sports Violence*, edited by Jeffrey H. Goldstein. New York: Springer-Verlag.

White, G. 1975. "Violence in Spectator Sports." Pp. 189–211 in *Administrative Theory and Practice in Physical Education and Athletics*, edited by Earle Zeigler and Marcia Spaeth. Englewood Cliffs, NJ: Prentice-Hall.

Wright, Sam. 1978. *Crowds and Riots*. Beverly Hills, CA: Sage.

■ ■ ■ ■ ■ ■ ■ ■

# WHAT IF THEY HELD A SPORTING EVENT AND NOBODY CAME?

## Ron Fimrite

Every time I make a telephone call that is answered by a mechanical voice instructing me to "punch one for ticket information" or "punch two for marketing" and so on, I have the eerie sensation of being transported, as if in a science-fiction novel, to some remote time in the future. I know better, of course, for I am inescapably in the here and now, a place I find less congenial with each such scientific advance. Wouldn't it be nice, I ask myself after one of these telephonic encounters with talking robots, if I could dial a number someday and actually talk to a living person? I stress the word "dial" because the two phones in my residence are not only attached anachronistically to cords, but also have what the mechanical voices tell me are "rotary dials," not keypads, which most of these implements that were manufactured after 1925, or so, apparently feature. And as I have lately discovered, it is almost impossible to call anyone on a rotary phone without being subjected to the full robotic litany before a usually irritable human "information operator" takes over.

In fact, my home is beginning more and more to take on the appearance of a museum, stocked as it is with such antiques as tabletop radios, typewriters and typing paper, an actual phonograph that plays 78's, and a television set with only a 19-inch screen. Where, for heaven's sake, are the home computers, the word processors, the cellular push-button phones, the CD players, the fax machines? How can anyone live in such primitive squalor?

"Happily," I reply, cackling like Lionel Barrymore as Dr. Gillespie.

But I am here not to defend my own resolute fuddy-duddyism, but rather to explore the consequences of this technological onslaught on our lives, particularly our sporting lives, in the fast-approaching 21st century. We Americans are, with few exceptions (note the foregoing), passionate believers in the future and the supposedly life-enhancing gadgetry with which it will surely bless us. Naturally, there is always some attendant fear of what all the new stuff will do to our existing institutions. But we've learned from the past that many of these fears are unfounded: Weren't motion pictures, particularly the talkies, supposed to do away with the legitimate theater? Well, all they really did was to kill vaudeville, which stayed dead only long enough for television to revive it. The legitimate theater, if anything, changed for the better, abandoning much of its froth to the movies while exploring more serious themes. Radio was perceived as a triple threat, menacing the stage, newspapers and sports. What it in fact did was give jobs to unemployed vaudevillians and stage actors, while making fortunes for record producers and advertising agencies. And, not incidentally, while helping to introduce a golden age of sport, the era of Babe Ruth, Red Grange, Jack Dempsey and Bill Tilden.

Major league baseball executives were at first terrified of radio, convinced as they were that it was going to keep people out of their ballparks. Games that were broadcast would be poorly attended, or so the argument went. The executives were, as usual, wrong. The more enlightened among them, particularly Larry MacPhail in his years with the Brooklyn Dodgers, realized that radio was a vital public relations tool. It remains so today, even with television.

Ah, yes, television. It was supposed to finish off radio and just about every other form of mass entertainment, especially spectator sports. It was one thing to hear a game on the radio, the owners lamented, quite another to see it "live" on TV. In truth, TV did pretty much KO the small fight clubs in the 1950s, but it also created a much larger audience for boxing, one that such master performers as Muhammad Ali wisely embraced. Television was the making of professional football, exposing it to the masses and turning it into the fastest-growing sports of the '60s and '70s, while transforming it into a media monster.

The smarter baseball owners discovered, as they had with radio, that television would attract new fans, not discourage them. In fact, some major league teams now televise virtually all of their games. And baseball has drawn larger crowds in the past five years than at any time in its history.

So why worry about what the future may bring, particularly since it already seems to be here? The theater remains a fabulous invalid. Movies seem to be surviving the competition of home videos. Radio has its music, news, sports, weather and interminable talk shows. And people are going to sporting events in record numbers. And all this is happening while American houses are being packed to the ceiling with technological marvels.

And yet, as technology marches relentlessly forward, an insidious process may be taking place in the all-but-forgotten realm of human relations. "There is an accretion of little things," says Philip Zimbardo, a professor of psychology at Stanford University who has specialized in "the influence of social situations on behavior."

The electronic home entertainment centers, with their cable television, CD players, video games and computers, are "in a sense bringing the world to you," says Zimbardo. "Why go to the ballpark or the symphony? Why fight the traffic and the crowds? Why deal with all the inconvenience when your wall television set can bring you the game, plus instant replay? These electronic gadgets make other people irrelevant to you. You don't need people for entertainment. All of this technology is in the name of efficiency. Humans, after all, are inefficient compared with machines. These devices—the computers, the voice mail—buy you time away from people. They are all designed so you don't waste time. They work to isolate you from human contact. Video games are taking the place of playing outdoors for children. You never see kids playing in the streets anymore. What I think we're seeing is a minimizing, a short-circuiting of human relations. It takes practice to be comfortable and effective with other people. Our gadgetry is taking that away from us."

Why, Zimbardo asks, do office workers sitting less than 10 feet from each other choose to communicate by computer instead of speaking? Even the robot telephone operators have a voice, though one scarcely recognizable as human. For that matter, the home computer may well eliminate the office altogether. Who needs it? Voice mail has replaced the telephone operator and the secretary. Computers can gather information faster than any human researcher or reference librarian. The middleman in office life is being snuffed out.

And what of office social life? Where now are the bull sessions by the water cooler? The drinks after work? After a day at the old computer, today's worker goes home to check his electronic answering service, watch his television or listen to his CDs, all in privacy. And with the new home fitness equipment, he doesn't even need to leave the house to exercise. Is the health club, another social center, on the way out?

Even our modern stadiums are beginning to look more like home entertainment centers. They, too, have their powerful sound systems and television screens. "Television has come to define reality," Zimbardo says. "You can go to a ball game now and see people watching their little Sonys, as if to validate what is happening on the field before them. That little screen and the one on the scoreboard become more real for the fan than the athletes he is watching." There is isolation even in a crowd.

At clinics he has conducted on shyness, Zimbardo has observed an increased social ineptitude among "young, intelligent, affluent men whose work is in technology. They are very successful in dealing with their machines, but they don't know how to start a conversation, don't know how to make friends, don't know how to entertain a date. They are like travelers in a foreign country who don't know the language."

At its worst, this sort of social isolation can lead to both physical and mental illness, even to suicidal and homicidal acts. Most serial killers, Zimbardo points out, are loners. "It's odd," he says, "but the worst thing you can do to somebody in prison is put him in solitary confinement. Now we seem to have an entire portion of the population willingly committing itself to solitary confinement. The sad thing is that these people seem to be liking it. What they've really done is break the bond with the rest of us. They are saying, 'Look, I'm happy. I have all this stuff. My CDs, my video games. Leave me alone.' "

Some academicians do not share such a bleak look into the electronic future. "The history of television has been one long bum rap," says Neil J. Smelser, chairman of the sociology department at the University of California, "when, in fact, watching television can be a social occasion. In watching a sports event with friends, for example, you create your own crowd." And the home computer may actually enhance family life, Smelser says, because the home itself becomes the workplace. "It will introduce a new kind of family dynamic. We may, in fact, have to invent barriers to protect the workplace from family intrusion." The new technology will allow us much more "flexibility of time" than we had in the old nine-to-five days, says Smelser. And we'll still get out of the house to go to a ball game or the movies.

"In 1941, when I was 11 and living in the little town of Kahoka, Missouri," Smelser recalls, "our summer entertainment was sitting outdoors, listening to the Cardinals on the radio. And yet, we still regarded driving down to St. Louis on a Sunday for a doubleheader as a big event. Even now, I'd go to every Cal game even if they were all televised. No, there is a culture of conviviality that just won't go away."

Zimbardo would agree in part, but he cautions, "as the technological revolution expands and its things become better and cheaper and therefore more accessible to younger and younger people, the purists who say you actually have to be there at a game will become fewer and fewer."

The fact is, as any restaurateur or bartender will tell you, people just aren't going out that much anymore. Why leave the house when everything you need for work and amusement is but a push button away? That "culture of conviviality" seems to me to be in real danger of extinction as we move into the brave new world of high tech. Perhaps, as Zimbardo suggests, we should start counting the hours in a week that we actually spend in the company of other humans—or, in the dreadful vernacular of the computer, "interfacing" with them. Will the day come when the only times people get together in any significant numbers are at group therapy sessions in stress rehabilitation centers?

It is difficult to envision an America without crowds, without noisy fans at the ballpark, cheering throngs at stadiums and arenas, appreciative audiences at the theater and the music hall. Difficult, did I say? No, it's unthinkable.

Still, even now we are witnessing some of the side effects of our self-imposed isolation. Professional boxing no longer draws the tremendous crowds in its Dempsey-Tunney, Louis-Conn heydays. It is now strictly a studio sport, the matches staged before small live audiences and large numbers of pay-per-view cable television viewers. You don't watch fights in teeming arenas anymore; you watch them at home. In a few years, only a few of us fogies will be able to recall the electric tension in a buzzing arena that preceded a heavyweight championship bout. That shared moment of anticipation was often more thrilling than the fight itself. And boxing is merely showing the way into this dehumanized future, since other major sports are busily examining their pay-per-view options.

There is yet another side effect worth examining here. Maybe there never was anything quite so civilized as crowd etiquette, but if there was, we've lost it. It's as if we've completely forgotten how to behave en masse. Too many movie patrons now chatter annoyingly through even the main feature, heedless of those around them, behaving as if they were home in front of their television sets. And, as we've seen during this past baseball season, crowds at the ballpark are no longer content merely to suggest that performing athletes are "a bunch of bums"; they verbally flay them with pointed references to their sex lives and drinking habits. It's small wonder that the thin-skinned plutocrats who now play baseball are responding in kind. It should also come as no surprise that a generation of fans accustomed to watching games on the tube should regard the players as something less vulnerable than flesh and blood. Seen on TV, they are merely part of the entertainment parades. Besides, a person can say anything he wants at home.

Is this then what we can expect of a crowd-free America? Will we, on those rare occasions when we are all together in one place, behave even more abominably than we do now? All the more reason to stay home, we will probably conclude. And by doing that, we will have deprived ourselves of what we once considered the very spice of life—variety.

These are times when you've got to hold back the future before it runs right over you. I know I'm going to eliminate at least some of the irritation in my life by hanging up on every robot I hear at the other end of my phone line. "I have an important message for you...please hold...." Click! "To reach our ticket office, please punch two...." Click! It's a start, anyway.

# ▪ ▪ ▪ ▪ ▪ ACKNOWLEDGMENTS

Assael, Shaun. "Why Big Tobacco Woos Minorities." *Adweek's Marketing Week*, January 29, 1990, 20-25. Reprinted by permission of the publisher.

Chesler, Phyllis. "The Creation Assignment." From *Sacred Bond: The Legacy of Baby M* by Phyllis Chesler. New York: Times Books, 1988, 3–13. Copyright © 1988 by Phyllis Chesler. Reprinted by permission of Random House, Inc.

Crichton, John. "Morals and Ethics in Advertising." Reprinted by permission of Michael Crichton.

"Dewar's Profile: Lounge Lizard." Reprinted by permission of Leo Burnett Company, Inc., on behalf of Schenley Industries, Inc., and by permission of Jay Maeder.

"Dewar's Profile: Paul Binder." Reprinted by permission of Leo Burnett Company, Inc., on behalf of Schenley Industries, Inc., and by permission of Paul Binder.

Evans, Mary. "Patriarchy at Play." Reprinted from *New Society*, October 27, 1988, 147–48.

Fimrite, Ron. "What If They Held a Sporting Event and Nobody Came?" *Sports Illustrated*, July 22, 1991: 49–52. Reprinted courtesy of *Sports Illustrated* from the July 22, 1991 issue. Copyright © 1991, The Time Inc. Magazine Company. ("What If They Held a Sporting Event and Nobody Came?" Ron Fimrite.) All rights reserved.

Gialanella, Mario and Louis Luedtke. "Air Pollution Control and Waste Management." *American City and County* 106 (January 1991): SWRR 17–22. Reprinted by permission of the publisher.

Glenn, Jim and David Riggle. "The State of Garbage in America." *BioCycle* 32 (April 1988): 34–38. Reprinted by permission of the publisher.

Grand Marnier ad, "Love is Grand." Copyright © 1987 by Carillon Importers, Ltd. Reprinted by permission of Carillon Importers, Ltd.

Greenfield, Jeff. "The Black and White Truth About Basketball." Reprinted by permission of Sterling Lord Literistic, Inc. Copyright © 1975 by Jeff Greenfield.

Heyl, Barbara Sherman. "Commercial Contracts and Human Connectedness." Published by permission of Transaction Publishers, from *Society* 25 (March/April 1988): 11–16. Copyright © 1988 by Transaction Publishers.

Jhally, Sut. "Rock Video, MTV, and the 'Commercialisation' of Culture." From *The Codes of Advertising: Fetishism and the Political Economy of Meaning in the Consumer Society* by Sut Jhally. New York: St. Martin's Press, 1987, 93–102. Reprinted by permission of the publisher.

Jones, John P. "Advertising: Strong Force or Weak Force? Two Views an Ocean Apart." *International Journal of Advertising* 9 (Summer 1990): 233–46. Reprinted by permission of the publisher.

Keane, Noel P. and Dennis L. Breo. "If She's Bright, Beautiful, and Talented and Wants $50,000, Why Not?" From *The Surrogate Mother* by Noel P. Keane and Dennis L. Breo. New York: Everest House Publishers, 1981, 157–85. Copyright © 1981 by Noel P. Keane and Dennis L. Breo. Reprinted by permission of the authors.

Key, Wilson Bryan. "Ad-Media SFPs." From *The Age of Manipulation: The Con in Confidence, the Sin in Sincere* by Wilson Bryan Key. New York: Henry Holt, 1989, 220–26. Copyright © 1989 by Wilson Bryan Key. Reprinted by permission of Henry Holt and Company, Inc.

Thornton, Joe. "The Dioxin Deception." *Greenpeace Magazine,* May/June 1991, 16–21. Reprinted by permission of the publisher.

Williams, Raymond. "Advertising: The Magic System." From *Problems in Materialism and Culture.* London: Verso Editions, 1980, pp. 170–91. First published in *New Left Review,* vol. 4, 1960. Reprinted by permission of Verso, the imprint of New Left Books Ltd.

# INDEX